British Social Attitudes Cumulative Sourcebook
the first six surveys

British Social Attitudes Cumulative Sourcebook

the first six surveys

Compiled by

Lindsay Brook

Susan Hedges

Roger Jowell

Jude Lewis

Gillian Prior

Gary Sebastian

Bridget Taylor

Sharon Witherspoon

Gower

SOCIAL & COMMUNITY
SCPR
PLANNING RESEARCH

© Social and Community Planning Research 1992

Published by
Gower Publishing Company Limited
Gower House
Croft Road
Aldershot
Hants GU11 3HR
England

Gower Publishing Company
Old Post Road
Brookfield
Vermont 05036
USA

British Library Cataloguing in Publication Data

is available

ISBN 0 566 05829 4

Printed in Great Britain at Bookcraft (Bath) Ltd, Avon

Contents

Foreword

by Shell UK Ltd

This *Sourcebook* is the first of a proposed series of volumes designed to complement the now well-established British Social Attitudes annual volumes.

The data are of interest to us because they are produced by a highly respected and entirely independent team of researchers. Shell UK is an organisation operating in the real world where changing attitudes, thoroughly and independently assessed, are vital to a full understanding of trends in society. It is for this reason that we decided to sponsor SPCR with a contribution to this *Sourcebook*, in the hope that by doing so the information could be introduced to a wider audience.

Although the British Social Attitudes annual books have filled a large gap in the information available, we at Shell UK - as frequent users - felt that the data needed also to be accessible in a ready reference format of the time-series so that changes in attitudes could be identified with ease. We hope that this *Sourcebook*, the contents of which are entirely the responsibility of SCPR, will fulfil such a role in the years to come and prove invaluable to more and more individuals and businesses alike.

Introduction

The *British Social Attitudes* (BSA) survey series is now in its ninth year. At each annual fieldwork round, a nationwide probability sample of adults is selected and asked to take part in an hour-long interview; most respondents also agree to fill in a self-completion supplement with another twenty (or so) pages of questions[1]. By 1989, with six surveys completed and funding assured for several further annual rounds, it became clear that a volume of this kind - a comprehensive directory of questions and distributions of responses - was becoming a necessity. Some trend data are of course presented in the annual volumes in the series (also published by Gower)[2], each of which contains interpretative commentaries and - in an appendix - the questionnaires with the percentage distributions of answers. But it is nonetheless far from easy to absorb and keep pace with the mass of information emerging each year.

At that time we lacked funding to fill this gap. Fortunately, however, Shell UK Ltd., who had been using the datasets for their own needs, agreed generously to contribute to the funding of a *Sourcebook* containing data from the first six rounds of the series. We intend to update the material at intervals to show patterns of continuity and change in British social values during the 1980s and 1990s and, we hope, beyond. We are grateful to Shell not only for sponsoring this volume but also for providing some of the impetus to turn the initial idea into a reality.

SCPR's first BSA Survey took place in 1983, with 'seed-funding' from the Nuffield Foundation and from the Economic and Social Research Council (ESRC). Both have since continued to contribute towards it. Since 1984, however, core-funding has come from the Sainsbury Family Charitable Trusts: they now provide about 40 per cent of the funds we need each year to design and carry out the survey, to plan and edit the annual volume, and to deal with the ever-increasing number of enquiries from current and potential users of the datasets. Their generous and regular core-funding, boosted in 1986 to enable us substantially to increase the sample size and cover more subjects, has been the critical element in the stability and independence of the series. It is now secure until at least 1996.

---

[1] Full details are provided in the Technical Reports published annually by SCPR (see next section).

[2] Again references and details are given in the next section.

The balance of the funding comes from a variety of sources. During the 1980s, three government departments (Employment, Environment and Trade and Industry) provided regular financial support to enable us to include (or repeat) questions of mutual interest. Since 1990, three further government departments (Health, the Home Office and, most recently, Social Security) have joined in and now provide annual funding in support of relevant modules of questions. Additional funding has been provided over the years by foundations (notably the Nuffield Foundation), universities, the ESRC and quasi-government organisations (such as the Health Education Authority and the Countryside Commission). The involvement of all these bodies helps not only to ensure that the series continues and thrives, but also that at least part of the questionnaire is pertinent to policy debates. The datasets from each round of the survey are used extensively by both government and the academic community. In addition, findings from each annual book are reported widely in the mass media and in the specialist press.

All funding for the survey is provided on the strict contractual condition that it should in no way compromise the independence and impartiality of the series. Decisions on each survey's detailed content, question-wording, data analysis, interpretation, reporting, timing of publication and archiving are all entirely in the hands of the principal investigators at SCPR.

A quick glance through this *Sourcebook* will give some idea of the size, scope and complexity of the datasets. Some questions are repeated annually, some at less frequent intervals and some (in the latter part of each section) have been asked only once so far. But all questions are designed with a view to repetition, since BSA is above all a time-series. Its primary task is to chart stability and change over time. Those few questions that are unlikely to be repeated are of two types: ones that, despite emerging unscathed from pilot studies, did not seem in the event to work very well; and ones which we failed to foresee would soon become outdated (questions about the poll tax are recent examples).

It is not the role of the BSA series to monitor public reactions to ephemeral issues and transitory events. The commercial polling organisations, with their frequent readings and concentration on quick results, are much better geared to track public opinion towards (for example) the fortunes of the political parties and the course of current political debates and events. The concern of this series is to measure longrun changes in values. Inevitably, however, events overtake a time-series such as the BSA and certain topics, or more frequently particular question-wordings, become obsolete or inappropriate rather sooner than we had anticipated. Moreover there are always a number of emergent issues about which we have not yet been able to include sufficient satisfactory questions (instances are Britain's future relationship with the EC and the restructuring of the NHS). Sometimes we have failed to devise adequate questions; sometimes we pilot questions that we think will provide an adequate baseline and are proved wrong because respondents do not grasp what we are alluding to. The questions may get answers - most questions do - but not ones that stand up to scrutiny. So there are gaps in coverage. Nonetheless, as the subject index at the end of this book will show, a very wide variety of topics has been covered in the first six years of the series, and new topics are added at each round.

All this raises the inevitable question of how subjects are determined in any particular year and which questions are selected for annual rather than less frequent repetition. In truth, these decisions are often arbitrary and dictated by events. Many more questions than can be accommodated compete for space each year, so choices have to be made. A major consideration is inevitably the pattern of funding. If the series has guaranteed financial support for a particular annual module of questions on, say, attitudes to housing or social security, then those topics will be included annually, though the content of each module will vary from year to year according to other considerations. Another factor is academic or theoretical interest in a particular topic. Thus attitudes to controversial political or moral issues, for instance, or to the role of government - subjects which would be unlikely to attract official funding but which are of core importance to the purpose of the series - are included regularly as a matter of course. Similarly, an initial round of questions may be introduced without funding, such as on attitudes to AIDS, in the hope that future support would be offered - as it was, in this instance, by the Health Education Authority. Moreover, the section of the questionnaire on demographic and other classificatory variables, taking up around a fifth of annual questionnaire space, is an unfunded but indispensable feature of the survey.

Other considerations also come into play in determining questionnaire content. For instance, attitudes to some issues seem to be so stable (such as the public's near-unanimous approval of the monarchy) that annual repetition would be wasteful of valuable questionnaire space. In addition, some topic areas tend to travel better in convoy. It would, for example, be ill-advised to include the module on attitudes to AIDS without including in the same questionnaire the module on sexual morality. There are many such instances where the inability to cross-analyse responses to questions on one topic by those on another would be debilitating.

In general, the investigators operate a self-imposed rule not to ask *single* questions on any subject, since almost all topics need to be approached from different angles in order to measure attitudes with confidence. Admittedly this rule does get broken on occasions, but scrutiny of the table title pages at the beginning of each section of this *Sourcebook* will testify to the range of perspectives that each subject tends to command. Another rule, also broken on occasions, is that question-wording should not change from one round to the next. But since circumstances change, say as a result of new legislation which alters vocabularies or changes the way in which an issue is perceived, the same wording over time would not necessarily convey a constant meaning to respondents. In such instances we make changes, faithfully documented in the footnotes to the relevant tables. *Sourcebook* users may therefore make up their own minds as to how to interpret the data.

A more vexed question is that of context effects. Even if the questionnaire were carved in stone and repeated unchanged each year we would have little confidence that context effects could be entirely discounted, since the circumstances of each interview may vary. In any event, the questionnaires contain a different set of modules each year. Where possible, of course, modules are kept largely intact and question order is largely maintained, but there is always an uneasy trade-off between continuity and refreshment. It would be too formidable a task to document every change in question order and idle to speculate generally on the likely effects that such changes might have on responses. Still, the data themselves do provide much reassurance. In the main, when attitudes appear to have moved sharply from year to year, or over the years, the movement is explainable and is supported by other internal (and often external) evidence.

Thanks to funding from the Economic and Social Research Council (ESRC) this volume will be complemented within the next year or so by a combined dataset, providing in one computer file the data for all eight surveys carried out between 1983 and 1991[3]. Like all other individual BSA datasets at present available, the combined dataset will be lodged at the ESRC Data Archive at the University of Essex for the benefit of academic researchers and others who wish to carry out secondary analysis or to use it as a teaching resource[4].

The most public face of the BSA series is the annual edited book containing descriptions and interpretations of the findings. These books are widely reported by the mass media and have served to chart change and continuity in British social values since 1983. But they touch only the surface of the datasets. A very large amount of secondary analysis has also been undertaken by academics in Britain and abroad, much of which continues to appear in British and international journals. The series has always been intended as a resource of this kind.

Between 1989 and 1991, the Nuffield Foundation and the Central Community Relations Unit in Belfast have funded an extension of the annual BSA survey within Northern Ireland - the Northern Ireland Social Attitudes survey (NISA). Around 900 people have been interviewed there each spring by the Policy

---

[3] There was a gap in the BSA series in 1988 since - with extra funding from the ESRC and Pergamon Press - the budget was brought forward in order to carry out the 1987 *British General Election* study, which contains many standard BSA questions. There will be a gap in the series in 1992 for the same reason.

[4] The ESRC Data Archive has recently produced a CD-Rom disk containing the seven individual (not combined) datasets from 1983 to 1990. This will be available in autumn 1991, simultaneously with the publication of *British Social Attitudes: the 8th Report*, based on the 1990 results (see next section for full reference).

Planning and Research Unit, using a questionnaire which contains all of the 'core' questions asked each year on BSA, and several of the 'special' modules in that year. In addition, it contains a module dealing with issues of particular concern to the province (for example, community relations and attitudes towards the security forces); some of these questions are also asked in Britain. The two annual datasets are, of course, independent and cannot simply be added together to provide UK data. But they do allow data-users to make comparisons on a range of issues between the attitudes of UK citizens on either side of the Irish sea[5]. These datasets are also made available *via* the ESRC Data Archive, and by the end of 1992 a combined datatape of NISA 1989-91 will be deposited.

Less parochially, the BSA survey series has an international component, launched in 1985. The International Social Survey Programme (ISSP) now has eighteen self-funding members each of whom conducts some sort of regular national survey of social attitudes. As part of their ISSP obligations, they get together each year to agree a module of questions, compiled by a drafting group, which is then translated (from 'British English' - the drafting language) and subsequently 'bolted on' to each country's annual survey, almost always as a self-completion supplement. These modules are designed for repetition at intervals (for example, the 1985 module on the 'Role of government' was repeated in 1990) to allow comparisons both between countries and over time. The national datasets are all lodged first at the German *ZentralArchiv* in Cologne in the year after the fieldwork round, where a comprehensive codebook, giving full documentation, is produced. The full datasets are also made available through national archives - in Britain's case through the ESRC Archive at Essex. The *Note* below contains a list of the ISSP's participating institutions and of the modules fielded to date (and those planned). It also lists by year those BSA questions which have been asked as part of the ISSP, though not necessarily in every country every year. This *Sourcebook* contains only the British data.

Methodological research has always been a prominent feature of the BSA series. In 1989, SCPR and Nuffield College Oxford set up the Joint Unit for the Study of Social Trends (JUSST), which has been awarded the status of an *ESRC Research Centre*. Part of its role is to initiate further methodological research *via* the BSA series. One of JUSST's tasks, for instance, is to refine a number of attitudinal measures which BSA employs to tap values such as egalitarianism or libertarianism or 'environmentalism'. More work is needed than has been done so far to create standardised scales whose properties are known and are capable of being transported to other academic and governmental studies. The BSA series is, of course, an ideal vehicle on which to test and calibrate these scales, and such work is well under way.

The main purpose of producing this *Sourcebook* is to make the BSA datasets more accessible to current and potential users. The series' funders have always strongly supported SCPR's determination to make the data available to the widest possible audience. Hence the annual published volumes, whose commentaries on the latest results are intended to be in a form and a style that attracts readership well beyond the academic community alone. This *Sourcebook* will, we hope, widen the audience further.

Acknowledgements

Two of the eight compilers of the *Sourcebook*, neither of whom are members of SCPR's staff, deserve a special tribute for making this volume appear. Susan Hedges keyed in the great majority of the tables; and Gary Sebastian provided a database to generate the list of table titles, cross-references and the three indexes.

In addition, we owe a special debt of thanks to Lis Box, Anne-Marie Brody, Debbie Hickmott, Jean Robinson and Elisabeth Valdani, who typed, checked or corrected many of the tables.

---

[5] Preliminary findings are reported in a chapter by J. Curtice and T. Gallagher in *British Social Attitudes: the 7th Report* (1990) - see next section - and more detailed results are given in P. Stringer and G. Robinson (eds), *Social Attitudes in Northern Ireland*, The Blackstaff Press, Belfast (1991).

As always, we appreciate the patience and commitment of our other colleagues at SCPR, including especially the interviewers and coders, who have contributed so much to the quality of the data in this *Sourcebook*. And we reserve our most heartfelt thanks for the 14,000 or so anonymous respondents whose attitudes, values and beliefs are charted in this volume.

Note: the International Social Survey Programme (ISSP)

The following modules have been fielded, or are planned to be fielded, in each of the following years (BSA question numbers, for modules included in this Sourcebook, are shown in brackets):

1985   Role of government (Qs 201-230)

1986   Social networks (Qs A201-A215)

1987   Social inequality (Qs B201-B215)

1988   Women and the family (Qs A201-A219, fielded in 1989)

1989   Work orientations (Qs B201-B221)

1990   Role of government (part-replication)

1991   Religion

1992   Social inequality (part-replication)

1993   Environment

1994   National identity

1995   Role of government (second replication)

The following eighteen institutions comprise the current (1991/92) membership of ISSP:

Australia   Research School of Social Sciences
Australian National University
Canberra

Austria   Institute of Sociology
University of Graz

Bulgaria   Institute for Trade Union and Social Studies
Sofia

Canada   School of Journalism
Carleton University
Ottawa

Czechoslovakia   Institute of Sociology
Czechoslovak Academy of Sciences
Prague

Germany   Zentrum für Umfragen, Methoden und Analysen (ZUMA)
Mannheim

Great Britain   Social and Community Planning Research (SCPR)
London

Hungary	Társadalomkutatási Informatikai Egyesülés (TARKI) Budapest
Israel	Department of Sociology and Anthropology Tel Aviv University
Italy	Eurisko Milan
Japan	Broadcasting Culture Research Institute, NHK Tokyo
Netherlands	Sociaal en Cultureel Planbureau Rijswijk
New Zealand	Faculty of Business Studies Massey University Palmerston North
Norway	Norwegian Social Science Data Services Bergen
Philippines	Social Weather Stations Philippine Social Science Center Quezon City
Republic of Ireland	Social Science Research Centre University College Dublin
USA	National Opinion Research Center (NORC) Chicago
USSR	Soviet Public Opinion Research Center Moscow

Since 1989, the ISSP modules have also been fielded in Northern Ireland, on the Northern Ireland Social Attitude survey - a collaborative project between SCPR, Queens University Belfast and the Policy Planning and Research Unit in Belfast (see Introduction)

The ISSP archivists are:

ZentralArchiv
University of Cologne
Germany

Annotated bibliography of related publications

I. Books

British Social Attitudes: the 8th report, eds. R. Jowell, L. Brook and B. Taylor, with G. Prior, 1991 (forthcoming), Dartmouth Press, Aldershot.

Contains ten chapters on: Consensus and dissensus, civil liberties, social welfare, law and order in Northern Ireland, smoking and health, education, economic issues, working mothers and childcare, environment, housing.

British Social Attitudes: the 7th report, eds. R. Jowell, S. Witherspoon and L. Brook, with B. Taylor, 1990, Gower, Aldershot.

Contains nine chapters on: social welfare, the unions, women and the family, nuclear and environmental concerns, AIDS, self-employment, diet and health, individualism, community relations in Northern Ireland.

British Social Attitudes: special international report, eds. R. Jowell, S. Witherspoon and L. Brook, 1989, Gower, Aldershot.

Contains eight chapters on: Measuring national differences, patterns of employment, the role of government, inequality and welfare, kinship and friendship, understanding of science in Britain and the USA, national pride in Britain and Germany, the family.

British Social Attitudes: the 5th report, eds. R. Jowell, S. Witherspoon and L. Brook, 1988, Gower, Aldershot.

Contains ten chapters on: judging right and wrong, education, permissiveness, working class conservatives and middle class socialists, AIDS, health care, trust in institutions, regional and neighbourhood differences, the countryside, women and work.

British Social Attitudes: the 1987 report, eds. R. Jowell, S. Witherspoon, and L. Brook, 1987, Gower, Aldershot.

Contains eight chapters on: social welfare, business and industry, civic culture, nuclear issues, health and diet, the family, the countryside, party politics.

British Social Attitudes: the 1986 report, eds. R. Jowell, S. Witherspoon and L. Brook, 1986, Gower, Aldershot.

Contains nine chapters on: consistency of attitudes, the work ethic, political partisanship, 'green' issues, British and American attitudes, education, public spending and welfare, housing, social and moral issues.

British Social Attitudes: the 1985 report, eds. R. Jowell and S. Witherspoon, 1985, Gower, Aldershot.

Contains seven chapters on: the social bases of attitudes, prices incomes and consumer issues, sex roles and gender issues, defence and international affairs, right and wrong in public and private life, local government and the environment, measuring individual attitude change.

British Social Attitudes: the 1984 report, eds. R. Jowell and C. Airey, 1984, Gower, Aldershot.

Contains six chapters on: measuring attitudes, political culture, economic policy and expectations, social policy and the welfare state, education, social and moral values.

II.   Articles and substantive reports

'Measuring attitudes to social welfare', R. Jowell in **A Strategy for Social Security Research**, 1991, (forthcoming), HMSO, London

British Social Attitudes Survey: a summary report for the Department of Health, L. Brook, 1991, (forthcoming), SCPR, London (Ref: 19/1090H)

British Social Attitudes Survey: a report for the Employment Department, B. Taylor and G. Prior, 1991, SCPR, London (Ref:19/1090E)

British Social Attitudes Survey: a report for the Employment Department, S. Witherspoon and B. Taylor, 1990, SCPR, London (Ref: 19/1005E)

'Recent Trends in Social Attitudes', L. Brook, R. Jowell and S. Witherspoon, in **Social Trends 19**, 1989, HMSO, London

The 1987 Social Attitudes Survey: a report for the Department of Employment, S. Witherspoon, 1989, SCPR, London (Ref: 19/905E)

The 1985 and 1986 Social Attitudes Surveys: a report for the Department of Employment, S. Witherspoon, 1987, SCPR, London (Ref: 19/815E,806E)

'Attrition in a panel study of attitudes', J. Waterton and D. Lievesley, in **Journal of Official Statistics**, 3:3, 1987

'Beliefs and Attitudes', R. Jowell, in **The Doomsday Disk**, 1986, BBC, London

'Advantages and Limitations of a Panel Approach in an Attitude Survey', D. Lievesley and J. Waterton 1985, in **Proceedings from the 1985 Conference of the International Statistical Institute in Amsterdam,** 1986, ISI, Voorburg

'British Social Attitudes', R. Jowell and C. Airey, in **Social Trends 15,** 1985, HMSO, London

III   Technical reports

British Social Attitudes 1991 Survey - Technical Report, L. Brook, B. Taylor, and G. Prior, 1992 (forthcoming), SCPR, London (Ref: 19/1135)

British Social Attitudes 1990 Survey - Technical Report, L. Brook, B. Taylor, and G. Prior, 1991 (forthcoming), SCPR, London (Ref: 19/1090)

British Social Attitudes 1989 Survey - Technical Report, L. Brook, B. Taylor, and G. Prior, 1990, SCPR, London (Ref: 19/1005)

British Social Attitudes 1987 Survey - Technical Report, L. Brook and S. Witherspoon, 1988, SCPR, London (Ref: 19/905)

British Social Attitudes 1986 Survey - Technical Report, L. Brook and S. Witherspoon, 1987, SCPR, London (Ref: 19/860)

British Social Attitudes 1983-1986 Panel Surveys - Technical Report, K. McGrath and J. Waterton, 1986, SCPR, London (Ref: 19/888)

British Social Attitudes 1985 Survey - Technical Report, S. Witherspoon, 1986, SCPR, London (Ref: 19/815)

British Social Attitudes 1984 Survey - Technical Report, S. Witherspoon, 1985, SCPR, London (Ref: 19/770)

British Social Attitudes 1983 Survey - Technical Report, S. Witherspoon, 1985, SCPR, London (Ref: 19/705)

Notes on how to use this book

1. Tables showing year-by-year distributions of findings (percentages and numbers) are arranged in twenty sections according to subject. Four sections are further subdivided. Page numbering is *within* sections or sub-sections. At the beginning of each section or sub-section a contents page gives table titles, cross-references (to other sections or sub-sections) and page numbers.

2. There are two main types of table, distinguished by their layout and typeface:

    (i)   those giving the distribution of answers to questions that have been asked in two or more annual rounds, and therefore containing trend data; these tables appear at the beginning of each section (except for some derived variables in Section P, which appear at this end of the section)

    (ii) those giving the distribution of answers to questions that have been asked only once between 1983 and 1989; these tables appear towards the end of each section.

    The ordering of both types of tables is by question number within year within section, with tables containing the most recent data (from the 1989 survey) appearing first.

3. On all tables the question wording is given in full. Preambles to questions and other contextual matters are shown [in square brackets], while interviewer instructions which appear on the questionnaire are shown (in round brackets). Any variations in question-wording from one annual survey to another are given in a footnote to the table.

4. Each question's SPSS variable name is shown in italics alongside the question. Some variables are 'derived' from two or more questions. Where this is so, it is clearly indicated and, where appropriate, the source variables (or questions) are given, as are the new column numbers. Where no column numbers are shown for derived variables, they were created in the SPSS set-up file. Where changes have been made to variable names (for instance, when it has been discovered that the same name has been assigned to two different questions), such changes are given in a footnote to the table. A list of such changes appears at the end of these Notes[1].

---

[1] Variable names will be consolidated in the forthcoming combined dataset (see Introduction), where all changes will be documented.

5. The questions are reproduced with full details of how they were administered, for instance whether a show card giving answer categories was used, whether the answer categories were read out to respondents, and so on. Any answer categories that were not revealed to respondents (such as 'don't know') are shown in brackets[2]. Pre-coded response categories are shown in bold; codes which have been added subsequently are shown in standard typeface. Any variations in practice from year to year in question administration are given in a footnote to the table.

6. Year-by-year answers (numbers and percentages) are shown, from 1983 to 1989, for each question asked in each year. Percentage distributions of answers are given to one decimal place, but percentages are *not* shown when the base is less than 50. Because of rounding and weighting, columns do not always add to precisely 100 per cent.

7. In all cases, only *weighted* data are shown. (The unweighted figures are, however, very similar since the weighting factors are applied to only a minority of records and are generally small.) On most tables, the figures shown are based on all respondents to the main questionnaire, or to the self-completion questionnaire (as indicated). In some cases, however, the figures relate to only certain stated groups of respondents (such as the self-employed or owner-occupiers). For any question not asked of the whole sample, the sub-group to which it was administered is defined before the question itself. Since raw (weighted) figures are always given, they may be repercentaged to suit particular purposes.

8. Other information routinely provided in the tables includes:

    (i)   answer category codes. Changes in codes or in coding practice from year to year are shown in footnotes;

    (ii) question number. Questions in the 200 range refer to those asked on the self-completion questionnaire; and those in the 900 range in 1987 and 1989 refer to those asked in the classification section at the end of the main questionnaire. In 1986, 1987 and 1989 two versions (A and B) of the questionnaire were fielded, each asked of a random half of respondents; questions asked of only the half-samples are prefixed A and B;

    (iii) column numbers. In the case of derived variables (see note 4 above) the column numbers on which they are now located in the ascii datafile are also given.

9. Some numeric data have been 'banded' (for example 1-2, 3-5, 6-10), so that the information may be presented in an economical form. Footnotes show where banded data have been presented.

10. Three indexes are provided at the end of this *Sourcebook* for ease of reference:

    (i)   an index of question numbers by year to show at a glance the location of each question in this book;

    (ii) an index of SPSS variable names to provide the data user with a quick guide to the location of each variable;

    (iii) a comprehensive subject index to identify topics covered to date in the series and the tables relevant to each topic.

---

2   There are two exceptions to this convention. Answers to questions inviting a simple 'yes'/'no' (or similar) response are not bracketed; neither are those given by respondents to 'open-ended' questions (that is, those to which respondents are invited to reply in their own words).

Changes to SPSS variable names

1989

Old name	New name
AREACHNG	AREAPAST
AREAFUT	AREANEXT
ATTENDCH	CHATTEND
ECOHELP4	ECOHELPC
HJOBEARN	SEXROLE
HRSWORKD	PDWORK10
JOBBEST	FEMJOB
JOBSATIS	PWLWKSAT
NATNL	NATNLSTN
NDSTRGTU	INDUST5B
NOCONCT	NOCONTCT
PRIVED	PRIVED2
SMALLJOB	HWORK10
SNUMPARS	SANYEMPS
SPUDBAD	CHIPBAD
SPUDEVER	CHIPEVER
SPUDFREQ	CHIPFREQ
SPUDSAME	CHIPSAME
SPUDWHY1-8	CHIPWHY1-8
WORKHARD	PWLWKHRD
WPUNION	WPUNIONS
WRKIPLAN	PWLWKPLN
WUNEMP	WGUNEMP
WUNEMPT	WGUNEMPT

LGOVRUN	LOCALGOV
MANUFRUN	MANUIND
NATNLRUN	NATIND
NHSRUN	NHS
POLICRUN	POLICE
POOR50	POORUB40
POOR62	POORSPNO
PRESSRUN	PRESS
PRIVED	PRIVED2
SMALLJOB	HWORK10
UNIONRUN	TRUNION
WUNEMP	WGUNEMP
WUNEMPT	WGUNEMPT

1987

Old name	New name
AREACHNG	AREAPAST
AREAFUT	AREANEXT
GOVDIFFS	INCDIFF
INSUREDO	INSDO100
INSUREUP	INSUR100
PRIVED	PRIVED2
SEMPSFT	SNUMEMPF
SEMPSPT	SNUMEMPP
SMALLJOB	HWORK10
STORCHDO	CHNGDO10
STORCHKP	CHNGKP10
UNEMPLIV	GOVUNEMP
WOMNWANT	WANTHOME
WOMWKHAP	WWHAPPIR
WORKHARD	PAYDIFF
WUNEMP	WGUNEMP
WUNEMPT	WGUNEMPT

1986

Old name	New name
BANKRUN	BANKS
BBCRUN	BBC
CSRUN	CIVILSER
DIVORCE	DIVORCE2
ECODIF1-10	ECDIF1-10
EDBADJB	EDBADJOB
IBARUN	ITV

1985

Old name	New name
GOVROLE3	GOVROLE8
PRIVED	PRIVED2
REDISTRB	REDWORKG
SMALLJOB	HWORK10
WUNEMP	WGUNEMP
WUNEMPT	WGUNEMPT

1984

Old name	New name
ABORT1-7	ABORT841-847
HNOJOB1-3	NOJOB1-3
MANGIFT	MANGFT50
NEWTECH	TECHRICH
PCHELP	PCFORGET
STORCHDO	CHNGDO10
STORCHKP	CHNGKP10
WUNEMP	WGUNEMP
WUNEMPT	WGUNEMPT

1983

Old name	New name
LEGALRES	LEGLRESP
REVMEET	REVOMEET
REVPUB	REVOPUB
REVTEASC	REVOTEAC
SHCHORE1-7	SHCHR831-837
TAXLO	TAXLOW
WUNEMP	WSUNEMP
WUNEMPT	WSUNEMPT

A Citizenship, role of government and the constitution

Table titles and cross references

SATISFACTION WITH VARIOUS ORGANISATIONS AND SERVICES
Also see Satisfaction with the police, B-15
General satisfaction with the NHS, K-1
Satisfaction with particular aspects of the NHS, K-2
Tenants: satisfaction with landlord, R-28

PERSONAL QUALITIES IMPORTANT FOR MPs AND COUNCILLORS
Also see Accountability of MPs, C-16
Gender stereotyping of jobs, N.2-17

FUTURE OF THE HOUSE OF LORDS

IMPORTANCE OF THE MONARCHY

CENTRAL GOVERNMENT CONTROL OF LOCAL COUNCILS

{CNTLCNCL}

Question: Do you think that *local councils* ought to be controlled by *central government* more, less or about the same amount as now?

	Code	1983 %	No	1984 %	No	1985 %	No	1986 %	No	1987 %	No	1989 %	No
Question No		9a		5a		3a		3a		3a		3a	
Column No		207		160		214		216		217		224	
More	1	13.0	224	13.7	225	14.3	252	14.9	458	18.8	519	15.5	453
Less	2	33.8	580	36.4	598	34.3	607	36.1	1108	34.1	943	37.2	1090
About the same	3	45.2	776	42.0	692	39.0	689	37.2	1140	36.8	1018	37.5	1099
(DK)	8	7.7	133	6.5	107	12.3	218	11.6	355	10.1	280	9.7	285
(NA)	9	0.3	6	1.4	23	0.2	3	0.2	6	0.2	5	0.1	3
Base: All			1719		1645		1769		3066		2766		2930

1983 - (DK), code 4

LOCAL *VERSUS* CENTRAL GOVERNMENT: LEVEL OF RATES/POLL TAX

{RATES}

Question: [And] do you think the *level of local community charges* - that is, *the poll tax or rates* - should be up to the local council to decide, or should central government have the final say?

	Code	1983 %	No	1984 %	No	1985 %	No	1986 %	No	1987 %	No	1989 %	No
Question No				5b		3b		3b		3b		3b	
Column No				161		215		217		218		225	
Local council	1	-	-	74.1	1219	71.7	1269	70.6	2164	67.7	1872	70.0	2051
Central government	2	-	-	18.7	308	19.5	346	19.3	591	23.5	651	20.6	605
(DK)	8	-	-	6.7	111	8.1	142	9.1	280	8.2	227	8.8	258
(NA)	9	-	-	0.5	8	0.7	12	1.0	31	0.6	16	0.6	17
Base: All					1645		1769		3066		2766		2930

1984-1987 inclusive · Q reads: 'And do you think the <u>level of rates</u> should be ...'

LOCAL *VERSUS* CENTRAL GOVERNMENT: LEVEL OF COUNCIL RENTS

{RENTS}

Question: How about the level of *council rents*? Should that be up to the local council to decide or should central government have the final say?

		1983		1984		1985		1986		1987		1989	
		%	No	%	No	%	No	%	No	%	No	%	No
Question No				5c		3c		3c		3c		3c	
Column No				162		216		218		219		226	
	Code												
Local council	1	-	-	76.3	1255	75.7	1339	75.7	2321	73.3	2028	79.0	2314
Central government	2	-	-	16.7	274	15.6	275	14.7	450	18.0	496	12.7	372
(DK)	8	-	-	6.5	107	8.3	146	9.2	282	8.3	229	7.9	232
(NA)	9	-	-	0.6	10	0.5	9	0.4	13	0.4	12	0.4	12
Base: All					1645		1769		3066		2766		2930

PROPOSED UNJUST LAW: WAYS OF PROTESTING

{DOMP} {DOSPK} {DOGOV} {DOTV} {DOSIGN} {DORAIS} {DOPROT} {DOGRP} {DONONE} {DOACT}

Question: (Show card) Suppose a law was being considered by Parliament, which you thought was really unjust and harmful. Which, if any, of the things on this card do you think you would do? Any others?

		1983		1984		1985		1986		1987		1989	
		%	No	%	No	%	No	%	No	%	No	%	No
Question No		10c		6a				B86a				B97a	
Column No		220		163				671				1109	
(i) *{DOMP}*	Code												
Contact my MP													
Wouldn't do	0	52.9	910	44.1	726	-	-	48.3	748	-	-	45.2	661
Would do	1	45.9	789	55.2	908	-	-	51.7	801	-	-	54.2	792
(DK)	8	-	.	0.1	2	-	-	-	-	-	-	0.1	2
(NA)	9	1.2	20	0.6	10	-	-	-	-	-	-	0.4	6
Base: All			1719		1645				1548				1461

PROPOSED UNJUST LAW: WAYS OF PROTESTING (Continued)

			1983		1984		1985		1986		1987		1989	
			%	No	%	No	%	No	%	No	%	No	%	No
	Question No		10c		6a				B86a				B97a	
	Column No		221		164				672				1110	
(ii) {DOSPK}		Code												
Speak to an influential person														
	Wouldn't do	0	88.9	1528	84.7	1394	-	-	85.5	1323	-	-	84.6	1236
	Would do	2	9.9	171	14.6	240	-	-	14.5	225	-	-	14.9	217
	(DK)	8	-	-	0.1	2	-	-	-	-	-	-	0.1	2
	(NA)	9	1.2	20	0.6	10	-	-	-	-	-	-	0.4	6
Base: All				1719		1645				1548				1461

			1983		1984		1985		1986		1987		1989	
	Question No		10c		6a				B86a				B97a	
	Column No		222		165				673				1111	
(iii) {DOGOV}														
Contact a government department														
	Wouldn't do	0	91.8	1578	90.8	1494	-	-	88.5	1370	-	-	87.1	1273
	Would do	3	7.0	121	8.6	141	-	-	11.5	178	-	-	12.3	180
	(DK)	8	-	-	0.1	2	-	-	-	-	-	-	0.1	2
	(NA)	9	1.2	20	0.6	10	-	-	-	-	-	-	0.4	6
Base: All				1719		1645				1548				1461

			1983		1984		1985		1986		1987		1989	
	Question No		10c		6a				B86a				B97a	
	Column No		223		166				674				1112	
(iv) {DOTV}														
Contact radio, TV or a newspaper														
	Wouldn't do	0	85.1	1463	81.7	1344	-	-	85.0	1316	-	-	85.1	1244
	Would do	4	13.7	236	17.6	290	-	-	15.0	232	-	-	14.4	210
	(DK)	8	-	-	0.1	2	-	-	-	-	-	-	0.1	2
	(NA)	9	1.2	20	0.6	10	-	-	-	-	-	-	0.4	6
Base: All				1719		1645				1548				1461

PROPOSED UNJUST LAW: WAYS OF PROTESTING (Continued)

			1983		1984		1985		1986		1987		1989	
			%	No	%	No	%	No	%	No	%	No	%	No
	Question No		10c		6a				B86a				B97a	
	Column No	Code	224		167				675				1113	
(v) {DOSIGN}														
Sign a petition														
	Wouldn't do	0	44.5	765	42.1	693	-		35.4	549	-		28.9	423
	Would do	5	54.3	934	57.2	942	-		64.6	1000	-		70.5	1030
	(DK)	8	-		0.1	2	-		-		-		0.1	2
	(NA)	9	1.2	20	0.6	10	-		-		-		0.4	6
Base: All				1719		1645				1548				1461

			1983		1984		1985		1986		1987		1989	
	Question No		10c		6a				B86a				B97a	
	Column No		225		168				676				1114	
(vi) {DORAIS}														
Raise the issue in an organisation														
I already belong to	Wouldn't do	0	89.6	1539	91.4	1504	-		89.9	1391	-		88.6	1294
	Would do	6	9.3	159	7.9	130	-		10.1	157	-		10.9	159
	(DK)	8	-		0.1	2	-		-		-		0.1	2
	(NA)	9	1.2	20	0.6	10	-		-		-		0.4	6
Base: All				1719		1645				1548				1461

			1983		1984		1985		1986		1987		1989	
	Question No		10c		6a				B86a				B97a	
	Column No		226		169				677				1115	
(vii) {DOPROT}														
Go on a protest or demonstration														
	Wouldn't do	0	91.2	1568	90.4	1487	-		89.5	1386	-		85.5	1249
	Would do	7	7.6	131	8.9	147	-		10.5	163	-		14.0	204
	(DK)	8	-		0.1	2	-		-		-		0.1	2
	(NA)	9	1.2	20	0.6	10	-		-		-		0.4	6
Base: All				1719		1645				1548				1461

PROPOSED UNJUST LAW: WAYS OF PROTESTING (Continued)

		1983		1984		1985		1986		1987		1989	
		%	No	%	No	%	No	%	No	%	No	%	No
Question No		10c		6a				B86a				B97a	
Column No		227		170				678				1116	
(viii) {DOGRP}	Code												
Form a group of like-minded people													
Wouldn't do	0	92.7	1593	91.5	1506	-	-	91.8	1422	-	-	89.8	1313
Would do	1	6.1	105	7.8	129	-	-	8.2	127	-	-	9.6	141
(DK)	8	-	.	0.1	2	-	-	-	-	-	-	0.1	2
(NA)	9	1.2	20	0.6	10	-	-	-	-	-	-	0.4	6
Base: All			1719		1645				1548				1461

		1983		1984		1985		1986		1987		1989	
Question No		10c		6a				B86a				B97a	
Column No		228		171				679				1117	
(ix) {DONONE}													
(None of these)													
Would do one or more	0	86.4	1485	91.1	1498	-	-	89.5	1386	-	-	91.6	1339
Would do none	2	12.4	213	8.3	136	-	-	10.0	155	-	-	7.8	114
(DK)	8	-	.	0.1	2	-	-	0.2	3	-	-	0.1	2
(NA)	9	1.2	20	0.6	10	-	-	0.3	5	-	-	0.4	6
Base: All			1719		1645				1548				1461

		1983		1984		1985		1986		1987		1989	
Question No		10c		6a									
(x) {DOACT}													
Number of protest actions might take: variable derived from {DOMP} -{DONONE}													
None	0	12.4	213	8.3	136	-	.	-	-	-	-	-	-
1 or 2 actions	1	72.1	1239	70.8	1165	-	-	-	-	-	-	-	-
3 or 4 actions	2	12.7	218	18.7	308	-	-	-	-	-	-	-	-
5 or more actions	3	1.7	29	1.6	26	-	-	-	-	-	-	-	-
(DK)	8	-	.	0.1	2	-	-	-	-	-	-	-	-
(NA)	9	1.2	20	0.6	10	-	-	-	-	-	-	-	-
Base: All			1719		1645								

1989 - Derived variable {DODKNA} on column number 1118; (DK) code 8 (n = 2); (NA) code 9 (n = 6)

UNJUST GOVERNMENT ACTION: PROTESTS MADE

{DONEMP} {DONESPK} {DONEGOV} {DONETV} {DONESIGN} {DONERAIS} {DONEPROT} {DONEGRP}
{DONENONE}

Question: (Show card) [And] have you ever done any of the things on this card about a government action which you thought was unjust or harmful? Which ones? Any others?

			1983		1984		1985		1986		1987		1989	
			%	No	%	No	%	No	%	No	%	No	%	No
	Question No		10b						B86b				B97b	
	Column No		211						708				1120	
(i) {DONEMP}		Code												
Contact my MP														
	Never done	0	96.8	1664	-	-	-	-	89.1	1380	-	-	84.4	1233
	Ever done	1	3.1	52	-	-	-	-	10.9	168	-	-	14.6	213
	(DK)	8	-	-	-	-	-	-	-	-	-	-	0.1	1
	(NA)	9	0.1	2	-	-	-	-	-	-	-	-	1.0	14
Base: All				1719						1548				1461

			1983		1984		1985		1986		1987		1989	
	Question No		10b						B86b				B97b	
	Column No		212						709				1121	
(ii) {DONESPK}														
Speak to an influential person														
	Never done	0	98.6	1695	-	-	-	-	96.8	1499	-	-	95.6	1397
	Ever done	2	1.3	22	-	-	-	-	3.2	49	-	-	3.4	49
	(DK)	8	-	-	-	-	-	-	-	-	-	-	0.1	1
	(NA)	9	0.1	2	-	-	-	-	-	-	-	-	1.0	14
Base: All				1719						1548				1461

			1983		1984		1985		1986		1987		1989	
	Question No		10b						B86b				B97b	
	Column No		213						710				1122	
(iii) {DONEGOV}														
Contact a government department														
	Never done	0	99.1	1704	-	-	-	-	97.3	1507	-	-	95.6	1396
	Ever done	3	0.8	13	-	-	-	-	2.7	41	-	-	3.4	50
	(DK)	8	-	-	-	-	-	-	-	-	-	-	0.1	1
	(NA)	9	0.1	2	-	-	-	-	-	-	-	-	1.0	14
Base: All				1719						1548				1461

1983 - Preliminary question: 'Has there ever been an occasion when a law was being considered by Parliament which you thought was really unjust and harmful?' (see p. B-11); followed by: 'Did you do any of the things on this card? Any others?'; no (DK)

UNJUST GOVERNMENT ACTION: PROTESTS MADE (Continued)

			1983		1984		1985		1986		1987		1989	
			%	No	%	No	%	No	%	No	%	No	%	No
	Question No		10b						B86b				B97b	
	Column No		214						711				1123	
(iv) {DONETV}		Code												
Contact radio, TV or a newspaper														
Never done		0	99.2	1705	-	-	-	-	97.2	1505	-	-	94.8	1386
Ever done		4	0.7	11	-	-	-	-	2.8	44	-	-	4.1	60
(DK)		8	-	.	-	-	-	-	-	-	-	-	0.1	1
(NA)		9	0.1	2	-	-	-	-	-	-	-	-	1.0	14
Base: All				1719						1548				1461

			1983		1984		1985		1986		1987		1989	
	Question No		10b						B86b				B97b	
	Column No		215						712				1124	
(v) {DONESIGN}														
Sign a petition														
Never done		0	90.8	1561	-	-	-	-	65.7	1017	-	-	57.8	844
Ever done		5	9.0	155	-	-	-	-	34.3	531	-	-	41.2	602
(DK)		8	-	.	-	-	-	-	-	-	-	-	0.1	1
(NA)		9	0.1	2	-	-	-	-	-	-	-	-	1.0	14
Base: All				1719						1548				1461

			1983		1984		1985		1986		1987		1989	
	Question No		10b						B86b				B97a	
	Column No		216						713				1125	
(vi) {DONERAIS}														
Raise the issue in an organisation														
I already belong to														
Never done		0	97.8	1681	-	-	-	-	95.2	1473	-	-	94.9	1386
Ever done		6	2.1	35	-	-	-	-	4.8	75	-	-	4.1	60
(DK)		8	-	.	-	-	-	-	-	-	-	-	0.1	1
(NA)		9	0.1	2	-	-	-	-	-	-	-	-	1.0	14
Base: All				1719						1548				1461

1983 - No (DK)

UNJUST GOVERNMENT ACTION: PROTESTS MADE (Continued)

		1983		1984		1985		1986		1987		1989	
		%	No	%	No	%	No	%	No	%	No	%	No
Question No		10b						B86b				B97b	
Column No		217						714				1126	

(vii) {DONEPROT}
Go on a protest or demonstration

	Code	%	No	%	No	%	No	%	No	%	No	%	No
Never done	0	98.0	1684	-	-	-	-	94.3	1460	-	-	90.5	1323
Ever done	7	1.9	33	-	-	-	-	5.7	89	-	-	8.4	123
(DK)	8	-		-	-	-	-	-		-	-	0.1	1
(NA)	9	0.1	2	-	-	-	-	-		-	-	1.0	14
Base: All			1719						1548				1461

Question No		10b						B86b				B97b	
Column No		218						715				1127	

(viii) {DONEGRP}
Form a group of like-minded people

	Code	%	No	%	No	%	No	%	No	%	No	%	No
Never done	0	99.3	1707	-	-	-	-	98.5	1525	-	-	96.2	1405
Ever done	1	0.6	10	-	-	-	-	1.5	23	-	-	2.8	41
(DK)	8	-		-	-	-	-	-		-	-	0.1	1
(NA)	9	0.1	2	-	-	-	-	-		-	-	1.0	14
Base: All			1719						1548				1461

Question No		10b						B86b				B97b	
Column No		219						716				1128	

(ix) {DONENONE}
(No - none of these)

	Code	%	No	%	No	%	No	%	No	%	No	%	No
Done one or more	0	80.6	1385	-	-	-	-	43.0	665	-	-	50.8	743
Done none	2	19.3	332	-	-	-	-	55.5	859	-	-	48.1	704
(DK)	8	-		-	-	-	-	0.1	2	-	-	0.1	1
(NA)	9	0.1	2	-	-	-	-	1.4	22	-	-	1.0	14
Base: All			1719						1548				1461

1983 - No (DK). Derived variable {DONEACT} on SPSS file: none of these actions ever taken; code 0, 88.3% (n = 1518); 1-2 actions taken, code 1, 9.6% (n = 165); 3-4 actions taken, code 2, 1.6% (n = 27); 5 or more actions taken, code 3, 0.4%, (n = 7); (NA), code 9, 0.1% (n = 2)

1989 - Derived variable {DONEDKNA} on column number 1129; (DK) code 8 (n = 1); (NA) code 9 (n = 14)

PROPENSITY TO BREAK UNPALATABLE LAW

{BREAKLAW}

Question: Are there any circumstances in which *you* might break a law to which you were very strongly opposed?

			1983		1984		1985		1986		1987		1989	
			%	No	%	No	%	No	%	No	%	No	%	No
Question No			11b		8b				B88b				B98b	
Column No			232		219				726				1131	
		Code												
Yes	1		30.4	522	28.8	474	-	-	31.0	480	-	-	32.8	480
No	2		61.4	1056	62.6	1029	-	-	60.7	940	-	-	57.8	845
(DK)	8		7.9	136	6.7	110	-	-	7.1	110	-	-	8.8	129
(NA)	9		0.3	5	1.9	32	-	-	1.2	18	-	-	0.5	8
Base: All				1719		1645				1548				1461

1983 - (DK), code 3

AREAS OF GOVERNMENT RESPONSIBILITY

{GOVRESP1} {GOVRESP2} {GOVRESP3} {GOVRESP4} {GOVRESP5} {GOVRESP6} {GOVRESP7}

Question: On the whole, do you think it should be or should not be the government's responsibility to ... (read out):

			1983		1984		1985		1986		1987		1989	
			%	No	%	No	%	No	%	No	%	No	%	No
Question No							230a		B226a				B209a	
Column No							2134		2136				1953	

(i) {GOVRESP1}
Provide a job for everyone who wants one

	Code	1983 %	No	1984 %	No	1985 %	No	1986 %	No	1987 %	No	1989 %	No
Definitely should be	1	-	-	-	-	36.1	542	29.7	390	-	-	36.8	462
Probably should be	2	-	-	-	-	31.8	478	32.5	428	-	-	31.1	390
Probably should not be	3	-	-	-	-	15.8	237	16.5	218	-	-	15.4	193
Definitely should not be	4	-	-	-	-	10.6	159	13.4	176	-	-	10.6	133
Can't choose	8	-	-	-	-	4.0	60	6.4	85	-	-	3.8	48
(NA)	9	-	-	-	-	1.7	25	1.4	19	-	-	2.2	28
Base: Self-completion questionnaire respondents							1502		1315				1255

AREAS OF GOVERNMENT RESPONSIBILITY (Continued)

			1983		1984		1985		1986		1987		1989	
			%	No	%	No	%	No	%	No	%	No	%	No
Question No								230b		B226b					
Column No								2135		2137					
(ii) {GOVRESP2}		Code												
Keep prices under control														
Definitely should be	1		-		-		59.4	892	52.1	685	-		-	
Probably should be	2		-		-		31.2	468	37.3	491	-		-	
Probably should not be	3		-		-		5.0	75	5.8	77	-		-	
Definitely should not be	4		-		-		1.8	27	2.6	34	-		-	
Can't choose	8		-		-		1.5	22	1.2	16	-		-	
(NA)	9		-		-		1.1	17	0.9	12	-		-	
								1502		1315				

Base: Self-completion
questionnaire respondents

			1983		1984		1985		1986		1987		1989	
Question No								230c		B226c					
Column No								2136		2138					
(iii) {GOVRESP3}														
Provide health care for the sick														
Definitely should be	1		-		-		84.7	1271	84.1	1106	-		-	
Probably should be	2		-		-		13.0	196	13.8	181	-		-	
Probably should not be	3		-		-		0.6	9	0.7	10	-		-	
Definitely should not be	4		-		-		0.3	5	0.3	5	-		-	
Can't choose	8		-		-		0.2	4	0.3	4	-		-	
(NA)	9		-		-		1.1	17	0.8	11	-		-	
								1502		1315				

Base: Self-completion
questionnaire respondents

			1983		1984		1985		1986		1987		1989	
Question No								230d		B226d					
Column No								2137		2139					
(iv) {GOVRESP4}														
Provide a decent standard of living for the old														
Definitely should be	1		-		-		77.2	1160	80.0	1053	-		-	
Probably should be	2		-		-		19.4	291	17.9	235	-		-	
Probably should not be	3		-		-		1.1	16	0.9	11	-		-	
Definitely should not be	4		-		-		0.5	7	0.4	5	-		-	
Can't choose	8		-		-		0.6	9	0.2	3	-		-	
(NA)	9		-		-		1.3	19	0.6	8	-		-	
								1502		1315				

Base: Self-completion
questionnaire respondents

AREAS OF GOVERNMENT RESPONSIBILITY (Continued)

		1983		1984		1985		1986		1987		1989	
		%	No	%	No	%	No	%	No	%	No	%	No
Question No						230e		B226e					
Column No						2138		2140					

(v) {GOVRESP5}
Provide industry with the help it needs to grow

	Code	1983 %	No	1984 %	No	1985 %	No	1986 %	No	1987 %	No	1989 %	No
Definitely should be	1	-	-	-	-	52.2	784	39.5	519	-	-	-	-
Probably should be	2	-	-	-	-	39.5	593	47.9	630	-	-	-	-
Probably should not be	3	-	-	-	-	3.5	52	7.2	94	-	-	-	-
Definitely should not be	4	-	-	-	-	0.9	13	1.6	21	-	-	-	-
Can't choose	8	-	-	-	-	2.5	37	2.4	32	-	-	-	-
(NA)	9	-	-	-	-	1.5	22	1.5	20	-	-	-	-

Base: Self-completion questionnaire respondents

| | | | | | | | 1502 | | 1315 | | | | |

| Question No | | | | | | 230f | | B226f | | | | B209b | |
| Column No | | | | | | 2139 | | 2141 | | | | 1954 | |

(vi) {GOVRESP6}
Provide a decent standard of living for the unemployed

	Code	1983 %	No	1984 %	No	1985 %	No	1986 %	No	1987 %	No	1989 %	No
Definitely should be	1	-	-	-	-	42.3	635	38.8	510	-	-	43.4	545
Probably should be	2	-	-	-	-	38.5	578	44.3	583	-	-	38.0	476
Probably should not be	3	-	-	-	-	10.1	152	10.2	134	-	-	8.6	108
Definitely should not be	4	-	-	-	-	3.7	55	3.1	40	-	-	4.3	54
Can't choose	8	-	-	-	-	4.1	62	2.6	34	-	-	3.7	47
(NA)	9	-	-	-	-	1.3	20	1.1	14	-	-	1.9	24

Base: Self-completion questionnaire respondents

| | | | | | | | 1502 | | 1315 | | | | 1255 |

| Question No | | | | | | 230g | | B226g | | | | | |
| Column No | | | | | | 2140 | | 2142 | | | | | |

(vii) {GOVRESP7}
Reduce income differences between the rich and poor

	Code	1983 %	No	1984 %	No	1985 %	No	1986 %	No	1987 %	No	1989 %	No
Definitely should be	1	-	-	-	-	45.0	676	45.6	600	-	-	-	-
Probably should be	2	-	-	-	-	24.4	366	26.7	351	-	-	-	-
Probably should not be	3	-	-	-	-	13.6	204	14.6	192	-	-	-	-
Definitely should not be	4	-	-	-	-	10.0	151	8.2	108	-	-	-	-
Can't choose	8	-	-	-	-	5.9	89	3.9	51	-	-	-	-
(NA)	9	-	-	-	-	1.0							

Base: Self-completion questionnaire respondents

POWER OF GOVERNMENT

{GOVPOWER}

Question: And what about the government, does it have too much power or too little power?

		1983		1984		1985		1986		1987		1989	
		%	No	%	No	%	No	%	No	%	No	%	No
Question No						228		B211		A213		B229	
Column No						2128		2034		1564		2114	
	Code												
Far too much power	1	-	-	-	-	16.6	250	19.1	251	16.9	210	23.8	299
Too much power	2	-	-	-	-	31.1	466	31.0	408	26.7	332	29.9	375
About the right amount of power	3	-	-	-	-	40.9	614	40.6	533	43.9	546	37.1	466
Too little power	4	-	-	-	-	3.5	53	4.3	57	4.7	59	2.9	36
Far too little power	5	-	-	-	-	0.5	8	0.3	4	0.8	10	0.1	1
Can't choose	8	-	-	-	-	6.7	101	4.5	59	6.2	77	5.6	70
(NA)	9	-	-	-	-	0.6	10	0.3	4	0.7	9	0.5	7
							1502		1315		1243		1255

Base: Self-completion
questionnaire respondents

1985-1987, 1989 - This question was preceded by two parallel ones, asking about the power of 'trade unions' and of 'business and industry'.

PERCEIVED POLITICAL EFFICACY

{GOVNOSAY} {LOSETCH} {VOTEINTR}

Question: (Show card) Please choose a phrase from this card to say how much you agree or disagree with the following statements.

			1983		1984		1985		1986		1987		1989	
			%	No	%	No	%	No	%	No	%	No	%	No
Question No														
Column No									B92a		B87a			
									741		930			
(i) {GOVNOSAY}	Code													
People like me have no say in what the government does														
Agree strongly	1		-	.	-	.	-	.	22.7	351	19.5	268	-	.
Agree	2		-	.	-	.	-	.	48.4	750	49.8	684	-	.
Neither agree nor disagree	3		-	.	-	.	-	.	8.6	133	9.5	130	-	.
Disagree	4		-	.	-	.	-	.	17.4	270	18.1	249	-	.
Disagree strongly	5		-	.	-	.	-	.	1.3	20	1.4	20	-	.
(DK)	8		-	.	-	.	-	.	0.9	14	1.2	17	-	.
(NA)	9		-	.	-	.	-	.	0.7	11	0.5	7	-	.

Base: All

1548   1375

			1983		1984		1985		1986		1987		1989	
Question No														
Column No									B92c		B87b			
									743		931			
(iii) {LOSETCH}														
Generally speaking, those we elect as MPs lose touch with people pretty quickly														
Agree strongly	1		-	.	-	.	-	.	16.4	254	16.1	222	-	.
Agree	2		-	.	-	.	-	.	53.4	826	54.6	751	-	.
Neither agree nor disagree	3		-	.	-	.	-	.	10.7	166	9.3	128	-	.
Disagree	4		-	.	-	.	-	.	15.4	238	16.0	220	-	.
Disagree strongly	5		-	.	-	.	-	.	0.4	6	0.7	10	-	.
(DK)	8		-	.	-	.	-	.	3.0	47	2.7	38	-	.
(NA)	9		-	.	-	.	-	.	0.7	11	0.5	7	-	.

Base: All

1548   1375

PERCEIVED POLITICAL EFFICACY (Continued)

		1983		1984		1985		1986		1987		1989	
		%	No	%	No	%	No	%	No	%	No	%	No
Question No								B92d		B87c			
Column No								744		932			
(iv) {VOTEINTR}	Code												
Parties are only interested in people's votes, not in their opinions													
Agree strongly	1	-	-	-	-	-	-	18.6	289	15.1	208	-	-
Agree	2	-	-	-	-	-	-	47.5	735	49.3	677	-	-
Neither agree nor disagree	3	-	-	-	-	-	-	12.4	193	9.7	134	-	-
Disagree	4	-	-	-	-	-	-	17.4	270	22.8	314	-	-
Disagree strongly	5	-	-	-	-	-	-	1.2	19	0.6	8	-	-
(DK)	8	-	-	-	-	-	-	2.0	31	1.9	27	-	-
(NA)	9	-	-	-	-	-	-	0.8	13	0.5	7	-	-
									1548		1375		

Base: All

TRUST IN GOVERNMENT

{GOVTRUST}

Question: (Show card) How much do you trust British governments of *any* party to place the needs of the nation above the interests of their own political party? Please choose a phrase from this card.

		1983		1984		1985		1986		1987		1989	
		%	No	%	No	%	No	%	No	%	No	%	No
Question No								B93		B88a			
Column No								745		933			
	Code												
Just about always	1	-	-	-	-	-	-	4.5	70	4.8	66	-	-
Most of the time	2	-	-	-	-	-	-	33.5	519	32.0	440	-	-
Only some of the time	3	-	-	-	-	-	-	45.7	708	49.0	674	-	-
Almost never	4	-	-	-	-	-	-	11.2	173	10.8	148	-	-
(DK/can't say)	8	-	-	-	-	-	-	4.2	65	2.8	39	-	-
(NA)	9	-	-	-	-	-	-	0.8	13	0.6	8	-	-
									1548		1375		

Base: All

1986 -   Q reads: 'How much do you trust a British government of <u>any</u> party...?'

GOVERNMENT RESPONSIBILITY FOR REDUCING INCOME DISPARITIES

{INCDIFF}

Question: Please (tick one box to) show how much you agree or disagree with each statement.

It is the responsibility of the government to reduce the differences in income between people with high incomes and those with low incomes.

	Code	1983 %	No	1984 %	No	1985 %	No	1986 %	No	1987 %	No	1989 %	No
Question No						209		B205		B207b			
Column No						2033		2026		1915			
Agree strongly	1	-	.	-	.	21.9	330	24.3	319	20.5	242	-	.
Agree	2	-	.	-	.	29.3	440	34.8	458	42.0	496	-	.
Neither agree nor disagree	3	-	.	-	.	24.4	366	19.6	258	12.3	145	-	.
Disagree	4	-	.	-	.	17.4	261	16.9	223	19.1	225	-	.
Disagree strongly	5	-	.	-	.	5.9	89	4.1	54	3.0	36	-	.
Can't choose	8	-	.	-	.	0.1	2	-	.	2.5	29	-	.
(NA)	9	-	.	-	.	1.0	15	0.2	3	0.7	8	-	.

Base: Self-completion
questionnaire respondents

	1985	1986	1987
	1502	1315	1181

1985, 1986 - Q reads: 'What is your opinion of the following statement: It is the responsibility of the government...'; (DK), code 8

1987 - SPSS file lists variable as {GOVDIFFS}. Now changed to {INCDIFF}, as in 1985 and 1986

EFFICIENCY OF VARIOUS BRITISH INSTITUTIONS - 1

{NHS} {PRESS} {LOCALGOV} {CIVILSER} {MANUIND} {NATIND} {BANKS} {TRUNION} {BBC} {ITV} {POLICE}

Question: Listed below are some of Britain's institutions. From what you know or have heard about each one, can you say whether, on the whole, you think it is well run or not well run? (Please tick one box for each)

			1983		1984		1985		1986		1987		1989	
			%	No	%	No	%	No	%	No	%	No	%	No
	Question No		207						B217					
	Column No		1037						2068					
(i) {NHS}		Code												
The National Health Service														
	Well run	1	52.4	844	-	-	-	-	36.3	478	-	-	-	-
	Not well run	2	45.2	728	-	-	-	-	62.5	822	-	-	-	-
	(DK)	8	0.1	1	-	-	-	-	0.1	1	-	-	-	-
	(NA)	9	2.3	37	-	-	-	-	1.1	14	-	-	-	-
				1610						1315				

Base: Self-completion questionnaire respondents

			1983		1984		1985		1986		1987		1989	
	Question No		207						B217					
	Column No		1038						2069					
(ii) {PRESS}														
The press														
	Well run	1	52.7	849	-	-	-	-	48.0	632	-	-	-	-
	Not well run	2	42.3	680	-	-	-	-	48.9	643	-	-	-	-
	(DK)	8	0.3	5	-	-	-	-	1.0	14	-	-	-	-
	(NA)	9	4.7	76	-	-	-	-	2.1	27	-	-	-	-
				1610						1315				

Base: Self-completion questionnaire respondents

			1983		1984		1985		1986		1987		1989	
	Question No		207						B217					
	Column No		1039						2070					
(iii) {LOCALGOV}														
Local government														
	Well run	1	34.9	562	-	-	-	-	34.5	454	-	-	-	-
	Not well run	2	59.8	963	-	-	-	-	63.0	828	-	-	-	-
	(DK)	8	0.2	3	-	-	-	-	0.6	7	-	-	-	-
	(NA)	9	5.1	82	-	-	-	-	2.0	26	-	-	-	-
				1610						1315				

Base: Self-completion questionnaire respondents

1986 - SPSS file lists variables as {NHSRUN}, {PRESSRUN}, {LGOVRUN}, now changed as above to variable names used in 1983

1987 - In this year, a similar question was asked about most of these institutions, but a four-point scale ('Very well run' to 'not at all well run') was used. See {NHSRUN} etc. p.A - 27 below

EFFICIENCY OF VARIOUS BRITISH INSTITUTIONS - 1 (Continued)

			1983 %	1983 No	1984 %	1984 No	1985 %	1985 No	1986 %	1986 No	1987 %	1987 No	1989 %	1989 No
	Question No		207						B217					
	Column No		1040						2071					
(iv) {CIVILSER}		Code												
The civil service														
Well run		1	42.5	684	-	-	-		47.2	621	-	-	-	-
Not well run		2	51.5	829	-	-	-		50.0	658	-	-	-	-
(DK)		8	0.6	10	-	-	-		0.6	8	-	-	-	-
(NA)		9	5.4	87	-	-	-		2.2	29	-	-	-	-
Base: Self-completion questionnaire respondents				1610						1315				

			1983 %	1983 No	1984 %	1984 No	1985 %	1985 No	1986 %	1986 No	1987 %	1987 No	1989 %	1989 No
	Question No		207						B217					
	Column No		1041						2072					
(v) {MANUIND}														
Manufacturing industry														
Well run		1	42.7	687	-	-	-		41.1	540	-	-	-	-
Not well run		2	50.0	805	-	-	-		54.8	721	-	-	-	-
(DK)		8	0.7	12	-	-	-		1.0	13	-	-	-	-
(NA)		9	6.5	105	-	-	-		3.1	41	-	-	-	-
Base: Self-completion questionnaire respondents				1610						1315				

			1983 %	1983 No	1984 %	1984 No	1985 %	1985 No	1986 %	1986 No	1987 %	1987 No	1989 %	1989 No
	Question No		207						B217					
	Column No		1042						2073					
(vi) {NATIND}														
Nationalised industries														
Well run		1	21.4	345	-	-	-		30.6	402	-	-	-	-
Not well run		2	73.2	1178	-	-	-		66.0	868	-	-	-	-
(DK)		8	0.3	6	-	-	-		0.9	12	-	-	-	-
(NA)		9	5.0	81	-	-	-		2.5	33	-	-	-	-
Base: Self-completion questionnaire respondents				1610						1315				

1986 - SPSS file lists variables as {CSRUN}, {MANUFRUN}, {NATNLRUN}, now changed as above to variable names used in 1983

1987 - In this year, a similar question was asked about most of these institutions, but a four-point scale ('Very well run' to 'not at all well run') was used. See p. A-27 below

EFFICIENCY OF VARIOUS BRITISH INSTITUTIONS - 1 (Continued)

		1983		1984		1985		1986		1987		1989	
		%	No	%	No	%	No	%	No	%	No	%	No
	Question No	207						B217					
	Column No	1043						2074					
(vii) {BANKS}	Code												
Banks													
Well run	1	90.5	1457	-	-	-	-	91.8	1208	-	-	-	-
Not well run	2	5.4	87	-	-	-	-	6.5	86	-	-	-	-
(DK)	8	0.2	4	-	-	-	-	0.6	8	-	-	-	-
(NA)	9	3.9	62	-	-	-	-	1.1	14	-	-	-	-
			1610						1315				

Base: Self-completion
questionnaire respondents

		1983		1984		1985		1986		1987		1989	
	Question No	207						B217					
	Column No	1044						2075					
(viii) {TRUNION}													
The trade unions													
Well run	1	28.6	460	-	-	-	-	27.3	358	-	-	-	-
Not well run	2	65.9	1061	-	-	-	-	69.8	918	-	-	-	-
(DK)	8	0.2	3	-	-	-	-	0.8	10	-	-	-	-
(NA)	9	5.4	86	-	-	-	-	2.2	29	-	-	-	-
			1610						1315				

Base: Self-completion
questionnaire respondents

		1983		1984		1985		1986		1987		1989	
	Question No	207						B217					
	Column No	1045						2076					
(ix) {BBC}													
The BBC													
Well run	1	72.0	1160	-	-	-	-	69.7	917	-	-	-	-
Not well run	2	23.1	372	-	-	-	-	28.4	374	-	-	-	-
(DK)	8	0.4	6	-	-	-	-	0.4	5	-	-	-	-
(NA)	9	4.4	72	-	-	-	-	1.5	20	-	-	-	-
			1610						1315		1181		

Base: Self-completion
questionnaire respondents

1986 - SPSS file lists variables as {BANKRUN}, {UNIONRUN}, {BBCRUN}, now changed as above to variable names used in 1983

1987 - In this year, a similar question was asked about most of these institutions, but a four-point scale ('Very well run' to 'not at all well run') was used. See p. A-27 below

EFFICIENCY OF VARIOUS BRITISH INSTITUTIONS - 1 (Continued)

			1983		1984		1985		1986		1987		1989	
			%	No	%	No	%	No	%	No	%	No	%	No
	Question No		207						B217					
	Column No		1046						2077					
(x) *{ITV}*		Code												
Independent TV and radio														
Well run		1	74.1	1193	-	-	-	-	83.6	1100	-	-	-	-
Not well run		2	20.8	335	-	-	-	-	14.4	189	-	-	-	-
(DK)		8	0.4	6	-	-	-	-	0.4	5	-	-	-	-
(NA)		9	4.7	75	-	-	-	-	1.6	21	-	-	-	-
Base: Self-completion questionnaire respondents				1610						1315				

			1983		1984		1985		1986		1987		1989	
	Question No		207						B217					
	Column No		1047						2078					
(xi) *{POLICE}*														
The police														
Well run		1	77.0	1240	-	-	-	-	73.6	969	-	-	-	-
Not well run		2	19.4	313	-	-	-	-	24.9	328	-	-	-	-
(DK)		8	0.2	3	-	-	-	-	0.3	4	-	-	-	-
(NA)		9	3.3	54	-	-	-	-	1.1	15	-	-	-	-
Base: Self-completion questionnaire respondents				1610						1315				

1986 -   SPSS file lists variables as {IBARUN}, {POLICRUN}, now changed as above to variable names used in 1983

1987 -   In this year, a similar question was asked about most of these institutions, but a four-point scale ('Very well run' to 'not at all well run') was used. See p. A-27 below

ADMISSIBLE FORMS OF POLITICAL PROTEST

{PROTEST1} {PROTEST2} {PROTEST3} {PROTEST4} {PROTEST5} {PROTEST6}

Question: There are many ways people or organisations can protest against a government action they strongly oppose. Please show which you think should be allowed and which should not be allowed by ticking a box on each line.

			1983		1984		1985		1986		1987		1989	
			%	No	%	No	%	No	%	No	%	No	%	No
Question No							203a		B202a					
Column No							2010		2018					
(i) {PROTEST1}		Code												
Organising public meetings to protest against the government														
Definitely	1		-	.	-	.	59.3	890	54.8	720	-	.	-	.
Probably	2		-	.	-	.	25.3	380	28.0	368	-	.	-	.
Probably not	3		-	.	-	.	4.6	70	6.4	84	-	.	-	.
Definitely not	4		-	.	-	.	6.0	90	5.6	74	-	.	-	.
Can't choose	8		-	.	-	.	3.8	57	4.3	57	-	.	-	.
(NA)	9		-	.	-	.	1.0	15	1.0	13	-	.	-	.
Base: Self-completion questionnaire respondents								1502		1315				

			1983		1984		1985		1986		1987		1989	
Question No							203b		B202b					
Column No							2011		2019					
(ii) {PROTEST2}														
Publishing pamphlets to protest against the government														
Definitely	1		-	.	-	.	54.8	823	42.7	562	-	.	-	.
Probably	2		-	.	-	.	26.2	394	35.5	467	-	.	-	.
Probably not	3		-	.	-	.	6.7	101	9.9	130	-	.	-	.
Definitely not	4		-	.	-	.	6.9	103	7.1	94	-	.	-	.
Can't choose	8		-	.	-	.	3.2	48	3.3	43	-	.	-	.
(NA)	9		-	.	-	.	2.1	32	1.5	20	-	.	-	.
Base: Self-completion questionnaire respondents								1502		1315				

ADMISSIBLE FORMS OF POLITICAL PROTEST (Continued)

			1983		1984		1985		1986		1987		1989	
			%	No	%	No	%	No	%	No	%	No	%	No
Question No							203c		B202c					
Column No							2012		2020					
(iii) {PROTEST3}	Code													
Organising protest marches and demonstrations														
Definitely	1		-	.	-	.	36.0	540	30.2	398	-	.	-	.
Probably	2		-	.	-	.	30.4	457	27.4	360	-	.	-	.
Probably not	3		-	.	-	.	11.4	171	17.9	235	-	.	-	.
Definitely not	4		-	.	-	.	17.3	260	20.7	273	-	.	-	.
Can't choose	8		-	.	-	.	3.0	45	2.7	36	-	.	-	.
(NA)	9		-	.	-	.	1.9	29	1.1	14	-	.	-	.
Base: Self-completion questionnaire respondents								1502		1315				

			1983		1984		1985		1986		1987		1989	
Question No							203d		B202d					
Column No							2013		2021					
(iv) {PROTEST4}	Code													
Occupying a government office and stopping work there for several days														
Definitely	1		-	.	-	.	4.3	65	3.7	49	-	.	-	.
Probably	2		-	.	-	.	6.8	102	6.4	84	-	.	-	.
Probably not	3		-	.	-	.	22.2	333	24.6	324	-	.	-	.
Definitely not	4		-	.	-	.	61.2	919	61.4	807	-	.	-	.
Can't choose	8		-	.	-	.	3.5	53	2.9	38	-	.	-	.
(NA)	9		-	.	-	.	2.0	30	1.1	14	-	.	-	.
Base: Self-completion questionnaire respondents								1502		1315				

ADMISSIBLE FORMS OF POLITICAL PROTEST (Continued)

		1983		1984		1985		1986		1987		1989	
		%	No	%	No	%	No	%	No	%	No	%	No
Question No						203e		B202e					
Column No						2014		2022					

(v) {PROTEST5}
Seriously damaging government buildings

	Code	1983		1984		1985		1986		1987		1989	
Definitely	1	-	.	-	.	0.8	13	1.4	18	-	.	-	.
Probably	2	-	.	-	.	0.4	6	0.7	10	-	.	-	.
Probably not	3	-	.	-	.	3.9	58	3.8	50	-	.	-	.
Definitely not	4	-	.	-	.	90.9	1365	91.3	1201	-	.	-	.
Can't choose	8	-	.	-	.	2.2	33	1.8	23	-	.	-	.
(NA)	9	-	.	-	.	1.8	28	1.0	13	-	.	-	.

Base: Self-completion
          questionnaire respondents   1502   1315

Question No						203f		B202f					
Column No						2015		2023					

(vi) {PROTEST6}
Organising a nationwide strike of all workers against the government

	Code	1983		1984		1985		1986		1987		1989	
Definitely	1	-	.	-	.	12.7	191	12.5	164	-	.	-	.
Probably	2	-	.	-	.	15.2	229	15.2	200	-	.	-	.
Probably not	3	-	.	-	.	13.9	208	14.3	187	-	.	-	.
Definitely not	4	-	.	-	.	51.9	779	53.5	704	-	.	-	.
Can't choose	8	-	.	-	.	4.4	66	3.8	49	-	.	-	.
(NA)	9	-	.	-	.	1.9	28	0.8	10	-	.	-	.

Base: Self-completion
          questionnaire respondents   1502   1315

ABILITY OF GOVERNMENT TO CHANGE THINGS

{GOVTDOPR} {GOVTDOUN} {GOVTDOSL} {GOVTDOSS}

Question: Some people say that British governments nowadays - of whichever party - can actually do very little to change things. Others say they can do quite a bit. Please say whether you think that British governments nowadays can do very little or quite a bit:

			1983		1984		1985		1986		1987		1989	
			%	No	%	No	%	No	%	No	%	No	%	No
	Question No				215				B228					
	Column No				1609				2146					
(i) {GOVTDOPR}		Code												
To keep prices down														
Very little	1		-	-	37.8	575	-	-	29.1	383	-	-	-	-
Quite a bit	2		-	-	58.8	895	-	-	70.0	921	-	-	-	-
(DK)	8		-	-	0.4	6	-	-	0.1	2	-	-	-	-
(NA)	9		-	-	3.1	47	-	-	0.8	10	-	-	-	-
Base: Self-completion questionnaire respondents					1522				1315					
	Question No				215				B228					
	Column No				1610				2147					
(ii) {GOVTDOUN}														
To reduce unemployment														
Very little	1		-	-	45.8	697	-	-	40.2	529	-	-	-	-
Quite a bit	2		-	-	51.2	779	-	-	58.9	774	-	-	-	-
(DK)	8		-	-	0.6	9	-	-	0.1	2	-	-	-	-
(NA)	9		-	-	2.4	37	-	-	0.8	11	-	-	-	-
Base: Self-completion questionnaire respondents					1522				1315					
	Question No				215				B228					
	Column No				1611				2148					
(iii) {GOVTDOSL}														
To improve the general standard of living														
Very little	1		-	-	29.9	455	-	-	30.1	396	-	-	-	-
Quite a bit	2		-	-	65.8	1001	-	-	68.9	906	-	-	-	-
(DK)	8		-	-	0.4	7	-	-	0.1	2	-	-	-	-
(NA)	9		-	-	3.9	59	-	-	0.9	12	-	-	-	-
Base: Self-completion questionnaire respondents					1522				1315					

ABILITY OF GOVERNMENT TO CHANGE THINGS (Continued)

		1983		1984		1985		1986		1987		1989	
		%	No	%	No	%	No	%	No	%	No	%	No
Question No				215				B228					
Column No				1612				2149					
(iv) {GOVTDOSS}	Code												
To improve the health and social services													
Very little	1	-	.	18.9	288	-	.	15.4	203	-	.	-	.
Quite a bit	2	-	.	76.8	1170	-	.	83.8	1102	-	.	-	.
(DK)	8	-	.	0.4	6	-	.	0.1	2	-	.	-	.
(NA)	9	-	.	3.9	59	-	.	0.7	9	-	.	-	.
Base: Self-completion questionnaire respondents					1522				1315				

UNJUST GOVERNMENT ACTION: MOST EFFECTIVE WAY OF PROTESTING

{MOSTEFF}

Question: (Show card) Which *one* of the things on the card do you think would be the most effective in influencing a government to change its mind?

		1983		1984		1985		1986		1987		1989	
		%	No	%	No	%	No	%	No	%	No	%	No
Question No		10d		6b									
Column No		229-30		172-73									
	Code												
Contact my MP	1	33.8	582	42.7	703	-	-	-	-	-	-	-	-
Speak to an influential person	2	4.1	71	3.8	63	-	-	-	-	-	-	-	-
Contact a government department	3	5.2	89	3.9	65	-	-	-	-	-	-	-	-
Contact radio, TV or a newspaper	4	23.1	397	15.8	260	-	-	-	-	-	-	-	-
Sign a petition	5	10.8	186	12.0	197	-	-	-	-	-	-	-	-
Raise the issue in an organisation I already belong to	6	1.8	31	1.5	25	-	-	-	-	-	-	-	-
Go on a protest or demonstration	7	5.0	86	5.7	93	-	-	-	-	-	-	-	-
Form a group of like-minded people	8	4.1	71	3.4	56	-	-	-	-	-	-	-	-
(None of these)	9	9.0	155	7.4	122	-	-	-	-	-	-	-	-
(DK)	98	1.3	23	1.4	23	-	-	-	-	-	-	-	-
(NA)	99	1.7	30	2.4	40	-	-	-	-	-	-	-	-
Base: All			1719		1645								

TRUST IN LOCAL COUNCILLORS

1987   Q.B88b   *{CLRTRUST}*   Column No 934
(Show card) [And] how much do you trust local councillors of *any* party to place the needs of their area above the interests of their own political party? Choose a phrase from the card.

	Code	%	No
Just about always	1	3.9	54
Most of the time	2	26.7	368
Only some of the time	3	51.9	713
Almost never	4	13.4	184
(DK/can't say)	8	3.5	48
(NA)	9	0.6	9
Base : All			1375

TRUST IN JOURNALISTS

1987   Q.B88c   *{PAPTRUST}*   Column No 935
(Continue showing card) And how much do you trust British journalists on national newspapers to pursue the truth above getting a good story?

	Code	%	No
Just about always	1	2.3	32
Most of the time	2	12.8	177
Only some of the time	3	42.4	583
Almost never	4	38.8	534
(DK/can't say)	8	3.1	42
(NA)	9	0.6	8
Base : All			1375

TRUST IN THE POLICE

1987   Q.B88d   *{POLTRUST}*   Column No 936
(Continue showing card) And how much do you trust British police not to bend the rules in trying to get a conviction?

	Code	%	No
Just about always	1	10.8	148
Most of the time	2	40.7	560
Only some of the time	3	33.0	453
Almost never	4	11.4	157
(DK/can't say)	8	3.5	49
(NA)	9	0.6	8
Base : All			1375

RESPONSIBILITY OF THE GOVERNMENT FOR THE UNEMPLOYED

1987   Q.B207f   {*GOVUNEMP*}   Column No 1939
Please [tick one box to] show how much you agree or disagree that the government should provide
a decent standard of living for the unemployed.

	Code	%	No
Agree strongly	1	17.2	203
Agree	2	46.8	553
Neither agree nor disagree	3	17.4	206
Disagree	4	12.5	148
Disagree strongly	5	3.3	38
Can't choose	8	1.7	20
(NA)	9	1.2	14
Base : Self-completion respondents			1181

NB In the SPSS file, this question has the variable name {UNEMPLIV} - the same as that for Q.57b asked in 1987 and Q.61b
asked in 1989, which are different questions (see p. G.5-12). So the variable name for the above question has been changed

EFFICIENCY OF VARIOUS BRITISH INSTITUTIONS - 2

1987 Q.B220a-o {NHSRUN}{PRESSRUN}{LGOVRUN}{CSRUN}{MANUFRUN}{NATNLRUN}{BANKRUN}{UNIONRUN}
{BBCRUN}{IBARUN}{POLICRUN}{STOCKRUN}{CITYRUN}{UNIVRUN}{SCHLRUN} Column Nos 2022-36
Listed below are some of Britain's institutions. From what you know or have heard about each one, can you
say whether, on the whole, you think it is well run or not well run? (Please tick one box for each)

		Very well run 1		Well run 2		Not very well run 3		Not at all well run 4		(DK) 8		(NA) 9	
	Code	%	No	%	No	%	No	%	No	%	No	%	No
a) {NHSRUN} Column No 2022 The National Health Service		3.3	39	32.0	378	49.3	583	14.2	167	0.1	2	1.1	13
b) {PRESSRUN} Column No 2023 The press		1.8	22	37.3	441	41.9	495	15.1	179	0.4	5	3.4	40
c) {LGOVRUN} Column No 2024 Local government		1.0	12	28.2	333	52.3	618	14.4	171	0.4	5	3.6	43
d) {CSRUN} Column No 2025 The civil service		3.0	35	42.7	504	40.4	477	9.5	113	0.6	7	3.8	45
e) {MANUFRUN} Column No 2026 Manufacturing industry		2.3	28	45.2	534	42.7	504	4.7	56	1.0	12	4.1	49
f) {NATNLRUN} Column No 2027 Nationalised industries		3.3	39	29.5	348	47.5	561	14.0	165	1.2	15	4.5	53
g) {BANKRUN} Column No 2028 Banks		29.4	348	61.5	727	4.4	52	1.1	13	0.5	6	3.0	36
h) {UNIONRUN} Column No 2029 The trade unions		3.6	42	23.6	278	48.5	573	20.0	236	0.7	8	3.7	44
i) {BBCRUN} Column No 2030 The BBC		12.1	142	54.9	648	23.1	273	7.1	84	0.3	4	2.5	29
j) {IBARUN} Column No 2031 Independent TV and radio		18.3	216	64.4	761	11.6	137	2.5	29	0.4	5	2.8	34
k) {POLICRUN} Column No 2032 The police		13.1	155	53.1	627	24.8	292	6.3	74	0.2	2	2.5	30
l) {STOCKRUN} Column No 2033 The 'City of London' Stock Exchange		17.5	207	57.7	682	13.8	164	3.9	46	1.9	23	5.1	60
m) {CITYRUN} Column No 2034 The 'City of London' generally		9.8	115	52.0	614	25.2	298	5.9	69	1.9	23	5.3	62
n) {UNIVRUN} Column No 2035 Universities		5.2	62	59.5	703	26.4	311	4.4	52	1.1	14	3.4	40
o) {SCHLRUN} Column No 2036 State schools		1.4	17	28.6	337	49.8	588	17.0	201	0.5	6	2.7	32

Base : Self-completion respondents (n = 1181)

NB A similar question was asked about the first eleven of these institutions in 1983 and 1986 but with different answer categories (see {NHS} etc, pp. A-16 to
A-19) above

TRUST IN INSTITUTIONS TO MAKE THE 'RIGHT' DECISION

1987 Qs. B221a,b, B222a,b, B223a,b {*COPAYPRF*}{*RPAYPRF*}{*TUPAYSUR*}{*RPAYSUR*}{*HOPATDOC*}{*RPATDOC*}
Column Nos 2037-38, 2039-40, 2041-42

Large companies

Q.B221a,b   {*COPAYPRF*}{*RPAYPRF*} Column Nos 2037-38
Suppose a large company *had* to choose between doing something that improves pay and conditions for
its staff, *or* doing something that increases profits.

	Code	Improve pay and conditions for staff 1		Increase profits 2		(DK) 8		(NA) 9	
		%	No	%	No	%	No	%	No
a) {*COPAYPRF*} Column No 2037 Please *tick one box* to show which choice you think most companies would generally make		17.9	212	79.8	943	0.2	2	2.1	24
b) {*RPAYPRF*} Column No 2038 Now please *tick one box* to show which choice *you* would make if it was up to you to decide		68.7	812	27.6	326	0.6	7	3.1	37

Base : Self-completion respondents (n = 1181)

Large trade unions

Q.B222a,b   {*TUPAYSUR*}{*RPAYSUR*} Column Nos 2039-40
Now suppose a large trade union *had* to choose between doing something that improves and industry's long-term
chances of survival *or* doing something that improves the present pay and conditions of the union's members.

	Code	Improve long-term chances of survival 1		Improve present pay and conditions 2		(DK) 8		(NA) 9	
		%	No	%	No	%	No	%	No
a) {*TUPAYSUR*} Column No 2039 Please *tick one box* to show which choice you think most large trade unions would generally make		40.8	482	56.7	669	0.4	5	2.2	25
b) {*RPAYSUR*} Column No 2040 Now please *tick one box* to show which choice *you* would make if it was up to you		78.7	930	18.1	214	0.4	5	2.8	33

Base : Self-completion respondents (n = 1181)

TRUST IN INSTITUTIONS TO MAKE THE 'RIGHT' DECISION (continued)

Large hospitals

Q.B223a,b   {HOPATDOC}{RPATDOC} Column Nos 2041-42
And suppose a large hospital *had* to choose between doing something that makes life a bit easier for patients *or* doing something that makes life a bit easier for doctors.

	Code	Make life easier for patients 1		Make life easier for doctors 2		(DK) 8		(NA) 9	
		%	No	%	No	%	No	%	No
a) {HOPATDOC} Column No 2041 Please *tick one box* to show which choice you think most large hospitals would generally make		63.9	755	33.8	399	0.6	7	1.8	21
b) {RPATDOC} Column No 2042 Now please *tick one box* to show which choice *you* would make if it was up to you		80.2	947	16.7	197	0.8	9	2.3	27

Base : Self-completion respondents (n = 1181)

INFLUENCE OF INSTITUTIONS ON GOVERNMENTS

1987   Qs.B224a-f, B225a-f, B226a-f   {INFLCON1 - INFLCON6}{INFLLAB1 - INFLLAB6}{INFLALL1 - INFLALL6}
Column Nos 2043-48, 2050-55, 2056-61

Q.B224a-f   {INFLCON1} - {INFLCON6} Column Nos 2043-48
Different institutions or groups have a lot of influence over governments, others have less. From what you know or have heard, how much *say* do you think each of these groups would have in what a *Conservative* government does? (Please tick one box on each line)

	Code	A lot of say 1		Quite a bit of say 2		Very little say 3		No say at all 4		(DK) 8		(NA) 9	
		%	No	%	No	%	No	%	No	%	No	%	No
a) {INFLCON1} Column No 2043 Manufacturing industry		12.9	152	41.4	488	36.8	435	5.0	59	0.9	10	3.1	37
b) {INFLCON2} Column No 2044 The 'City of London'		34.1	402	43.8	517	14.8	175	2.7	32	1.3	16	3.3	39
c) {INFLCON3} Column No 2045 The trade unions		5.3	63	14.9	176	47.7	563	27.8	328	0.9	11	3.3	39
d) {INFLCON4} Column No 2046 The police		11.4	135	39.1	462	38.2	451	7.5	88	0.9	10	3.0	35
e) {INFLCON5} Column No 2047 School teachers		3.5	41	13.6	160	55.6	657	23.5	277	0.8	10	3.0	36
f) {INFLCON6} Column No 2048 Farmers		6.4	76	25.4	300	43.9	518	20.5	242	0.8	10	3.0	36

Base : Self-completion respondents (n = 1181)

INFLUENCE OF INSTITUTIONS ON GOVERNMENTS (continued)

Q.B225a-f   *{INFLLAB1} - {INFLLAB6}* Column Nos 2050-55
And how much *say* do you think each of these groups generally has in what a *Labour* government does?
(Please tick one box on each line)

		A lot of say		Quite a bit of say		Very little say		No say at all		(DK)		(NA)	
	Code	1		2		3		4		8		9	
		%	No	%	No	%	No	%	No	%	No	%	No
a) *{INFLLAB1}* Column No 2050 Manufacturing industry		13.6	160	47.3	558	30.4	360	4.4	52	1.2	14	3.1	36
b) *{INFLLAB2}* Column No 2051 The 'City of London'		10.3	122	42.1	497	36.1	426	6.4	76	1.8	21	3.3	39
c) *{INFLLAB3}* Column No 2052 The trade unions		50.5	597	36.1	427	7.2	85	2.1	25	1.0	12	3.0	36
d) *{INFLLAB4}* Column No 2053 The police		5.7	67	29.7	351	50.3	594	9.9	117	1.3	15	3.2	38
e) *{INFLLAB5}* Column No 2054 School teachers		10.2	120	37.7	446	39.0	461	8.8	104	1.1	13	3.1	37
f) *{INFLLAB6}* Column No 2055 Farmers		4.3	50	26.1	308	50.8	599	14.6	172	1.3	15	3.0	36

Base : Self-completion respondents (n = 1181)

Q.B226a-f   *{INFLALL1} - {INFLALL6}* Column Nos 2056-61
And suppose the *Alliance* parties were in government. How much say do you think each of these groups would have in what the government might do? (Please tick one box on each line)

		A lot of say		Quite a bit of say		Very little say		No say at all		(DK)		(NA)	
	Code	1		2		3		4		8		9	
		%	No	%	No	%	No	%	No	%	No	%	No
a) *{INFLALL1}* Column No 2056 Manufacturing industry		10.2	121	53.5	632	27.5	324	3.1	36	2.0	24	3.7	44
b) *{INFLALL2}* Column No 2057 The 'City of London'		14.0	165	50.4	595	25.6	303	4.0	47	2.3	27	3.7	44
c) *{INFLALL3}* Column No 2058 The trade unions		5.7	68	33.9	400	48.1	568	6.8	80	2.0	23	3.5	41
d) *{INFLALL4}* Column No 2059 The police		6.8	81	43.6	515	37.6	444	6.3	74	1.9	22	3.7	44
e) *{INFLALL5}* Column No 2060 School teachers		5.5	65	40.7	481	40.2	475	8.3	98	1.8	21	3.5	41
f) *{INFLALL6}* Column No 2061 Farmers		4.5	53	34.1	403	45.1	532	10.7	127	2.0	24	3.6	43

Base : Self-completion respondents (n = 1181)

ACTIONS LIKELY TO INFLUENCE GOVERNMENT DECISIONS

1986   Q.B87a-h   {MPEFF}{SPKEFF}{GOVEFF}{TVEFF}{SIGNEFF}{RAISEFF}{PROTEFF}{GRPEFF}
Column Nos 717-24

(Show card) Please use a phrase from this card to say *how effective* you think each of the following would be in influencing a government to change its mind? How effective would it be to ... (read out each item in turn):

	Code	Very effective 1		Quite effective 2		Not very effective 3		Not at all effective 4		(DK) 8		(NA) 9	
		%	No	%	No	%	No	%	No	%	No	%	No
a) {MPEFF} Column No 717 Contact your MP		6.9	107	43.0	666	38.0	589	6.7	104	4.6	71	0.7	11
b) {SPKEFF} Column No 718 Speak to an influential person		4.5	70	33.4	517	44.8	694	10.6	164	6.0	92	0.7	11
c) {GOVEFF} Column No 719 Contact a government department		3.3	52	23.0	356	48.2	747	18.9	292	5.9	91	0.7	11
d) {TVEFF} Column No 720 Contact radio, TV or newspaper		10.2	157	48.2	746	27.2	421	9.3	144	4.3	66	0.9	14
e) {SIGNEFF} Column No 721 Sign a petition		4.3	66	40.7	630	40.0	620	11.2	173	3.1	48	0.7	11
f) {RAISEFF} Column No 722 Raise the issue in an organisation you already belong to		2.5	38	29.8	462	41.4	641	13.1	203	12.3	191	0.8	13
g) {PROTEFF} Column No 723 Go on a protest or demonstration		2.2	35	18.4	284	45.5	705	28.6	443	4.6	70	0.8	12
h) {GRPEFF} Column No 724 Form a group of like-minded people		1.7	27	24.4	378	44.2	685	21.3	330	7.6	117	0.7	11

Base : All (n = 1548)

ABILITY OF GOVERNMENT TO REDUCE POVERTY

1986   Q.B228e   {GOVTDOPV} Column Nos 2150
Some people say that British governments nowadays - of whichever party - can actually do very little to change things. Others say they can do quite a bit. Please [tick one box to] say whether you think that British governments nowadays can do very little or quite a bit to reduce poverty.

	Code	%	No
Very little	1	26.9	353
Quite a bit	2	72.0	948
(DK)	8	0.1	2
(NA)	9	1.0	13
			1315

Base : Self-completion respondents

NB   This was added to a list of four items asked about in 1984 (see pp. A-23 to A-24 above)

GOVERNMENT POLICY OPTIONS

1986   Q.B233a-f   {DEFENCE}{PRIVEDUC}{RIDPOVTY}{HLPPRMED}TULAWS}{WORKRSAY} Column Nos 2219-24
Finally please tick one box for each statement below to show whether or not you think the government should:

		Definitely should		Probably should		Probably should not		Definitely should not		(DK)		(NA)	
	Code	1		2		3		4		8		9	
		%	No	%	No	%	No	%	No	%	No	%	No
a) {DEFENCE} Column No 2219 Spend less on defence		28.0	369	33.6	442	23.6	310	13.2	173	0.3	4	1.4	18
b) {PRIVEDUC} Column No 2220 Get rid of private education in Britain		10.1	133	17.0	223	39.7	522	31.7	418	0.2	3	1.3	17
c) {RIDPOVTY} Column No 2221 Spend more money to get rid of poverty		47.3	623	39.7	522	9.1	120	2.4	31	0.1	2	1.3	18
d) {HLPPRMED} Column No 2222 Encourage the growth of private medicine		11.0	144	35.1	462	35.2	463	16.8	221	0.4	5	1.6	21
e) {TULAWS} Column No 2223 Introduce stricter laws to regulate the activities of trade unions		18.7	246	36.0	474	30.0	395	14.0	184	0.3	5	1.0	13
f) {WORKRSAY} Column No 2224 Give workers more say in running the places where they work		28.4	374	51.9	683	15.7	207	2.7	36	0.2	3	1.0	13

Base : Self-completion respondents (n = 1315)

POLITICAL ACTIVISM AND POLITICAL EFFICACY

1985   Q.220a-h,j,k   {POLITIC1} - {POLITIC0}   Column Nos 2067-76

Please show whether you agree or disagree with each of the following statements. (Please tick one box for each)

		Agree 1		Disagree 2		Can't choose 8		(NA) 9	
	Code	%	No	%	No	%	No	%	No
a) {POLITIC1} Column No 2067 The public has little control over what politicians do in office		79.1	1187	12.9	194	6.5	98	1.5	23
b) {POLITIC2} Column No 2068 The average person can get nowhere by talking to public officials		55.7	836	31.0	465	11.3	170	2.0	31
c) {POLITIC3} Column No 2069 The average citizen has considerable influence on politics		15.3	230	74.1	1113	7.9	119	2.7	41
d) {POLITIC4} Column No 2070 The average person has much to say about running local government		24.5	368	64.3	965	9.0	136	2.2	33
e) {POLITIC5} Column No 2071 People like me have much to say about government		35.1	528	49.1	737	12.9	194	2.9	44
f) {POLITIC6} Column No 2072 The average person has a great deal of influence on government decisions		7.3	110	83.0	1247	7.0	105	2.6	40
g) {POLITIC7} Column No 2073 The government is generally responsive to public opinion		25.6	384	61.0	916	10.8	162	2.6	40
h) {POLITIC8} Column No 2074 I am usually interested in local elections		58.0	871	33.5	503	6.1	92	2.4	36
j) {POLITIC9} Column No 2075 By taking an active part in political and social affairs the people can control world affairs		24.4	366	59.1	888	14.5	217	2.0	30
k) {POLITIC0} Column No 2076 Taking everything into account, the world is getting better		19.2	288	64.6	970	14.8	222	1.5	23

Base : Self-completion respondents (n = 1502)

POLITICAL ACTIVISM AGAINST LOCAL COUNCIL

1984   Q.7a,b   {LACNCLLR}{LASPK}{LAOFFCL}{LAMEDIA}{LASIGN}{LARAIS}{LAPROT}{LAGRP}
{LANONE}{LACCT}{LAMSTEFF} Column Nos 207-17

1984   Q.7a   Column Nos 207-15
(Show card) Now suppose your *local council* was proposing a scheme which you thought was really unjust
and harmful. Which, if any, of the things on this card do you think you would do?   (Interviewer : more
than one code may be ringed.)

		Code	%	No
{LACNCLLR}	Column No 207			
Contact my councillor				
	Would do	1	61.0	1003
	Wouldn't do	0	38.1	627
	(DK)	8	0.3	6
	(NA)	9	0.5	9
Base : All				1645
{LASPK}	Column No 208			
Speak to an influential person				
	Would do	2	14.2	233
	Wouldn't do	0	84.9	1398
	(DK)	8	0.3	6
	(NA)	9	0.5	9
Base : All				1645
{LAOFFCL}	Column No 209			
Contact a council official				
	Would do	3	26.0	427
	Wouldn't do	0	73.1	1204
	(DK)	8	0.3	6
	(NA)	9	0.5	9
Base : All				1645
{LAMEDIA}	Column No 210			
Contact local newspaper or radio				
	Would do	4	17.8	292
	Wouldn't do	0	81.3	1338
	(DK)	8	0.3	6
	(NA)	9	0.5	9
Base : All				1645
{LASIGN}	Column No 211			
Sign a petition				
	Would do	5	49.6	817
	Wouldn't do	0	49.5	814
	(DK)	8	0.3	6
	(NA)	9	0.5	9
Base : All				1645
{LARAIS}	Column No 212			
Raise the issue in an organisation I already belong to				
	Would do	6	6.4	105
	Wouldn't do	0	92.8	1526
	(DK)	8	0.3	6
	(NA)	9	0.5	9
Base : All				1645

POLITICAL ACTIVISM AGAINST LOCAL COUNCIL (continued)

		Code	%	No
{LAPROT}	Column No 213			
Go on a protest or demonstration				
	Would do	7	8.1	133
	Wouldn't do	0	91.1	1498
	(DK)	8	0.3	6
	(NA)	9	0.5	9
Base : All				1645
{LAGRP}	Column No 214			
Form a group of like-minded people				
	Would do	1	10.1	166
	Wouldn't do	0	89.0	1465
	(DK)	8	0.3	6
	(NA)	9	0.5	9
Base : All				1645
{LANONE}	Column No 215			
None of these				
	Would do	2	5.4	89
	Wouldn't do	0	93.7	1542
	(DK)	8	0.3	6
	(NA)	9	0.5	9
Base : All				1645
{LAACT}				
(Derived variable) Number of actions respondents would take				
	None	0	8.3	136
	1-2 actions	1	70.8	1165
	3-4 actions	2	18.7	308
	5 or more actions	3	1.6	26
	(DK)	8	0.1	2
	(NA)	9	0.6	10

1984   Q.7b   {LAMSTEFF} Column Nos 216-17

And which *one* of the things on the card do you think would be the most effective in influencing your local council to change its mind?

	Code	%	No
Contact my councillor	1	37.8	622
Speak to influential person	2	5.0	82
Contact a council official	3	7.6	125
Contact local newspaper or radio	4	16.3	268
Sign a petition	5	14.5	239
Raise the issue in an organisation I already belong to	6	1.7	28
Go on a protest or demonstration	7	4.1	68
Form a group of like-minded people	8	4.7	77
None of these	9	4.9	81
(DK)	98	1.0	16
(NA)	99	2.4	39
Base : All			1645

SATISFACTION WITH VARIOUS ORGANISATIONS AND SERVICES

1984   Q. 207a-k   {PRESSSAT}{LGOVSAT}{CSSAT}{BANKSAT}{BBCSAT}{IBASAT}{POLICSAT}{DOCSAT}
{POSTSAT}{BRSAT}{PHONESAT} Column Nos 1549-59
Listed below are a number of organisations or services. From what you know or have heard about each one,
can you say whether you are generally satisfied or not satisfied with the service that each one provides?
(Please tick one box on each line)

	Code	Satisfied 1		Not satisfied 2		(DK) 8		(NA) 9	
		%	No	%	No	%	No	%	No
a) {PRESSSAT} Column No 1549 **The press**		61.8	941	34.4	524	0.9	14	2.8	43
b) {LGOVSAT} Column No 1550 **Local government**		48.8	743	47.5	723	0.8	12	3.0	45
c) {CSSAT} Column No 1551 **The civil service**		53.1	809	41.5	632	1.7	26	3.7	56
d) {BANKSAT} Column No 1552 **Banks**		82.2	1251	13.1	199	1.2	19	3.5	54
e) {BBCSAT} Column No 1553 **The BBC**		65.9	1003	30.2	460	0.6	9	3.3	51
f) {IBASAT} Column No 1554 **Independent TV and radio**		75.6	1150	20.8	317	0.4	7	3.2	48
g) {POLICSAT} Column No 1555 **The police**		79.0	1202	17.4	265	0.4	7	3.2	49
h) {DOCSAT} Column No 1556 **Local doctor**		83.5	1272	13.5	205	0.4	7	2.5	39
i) {POSTSAT} Column No 1557 **The postal service**		75.0	1141	22.0	334	0.4	7	2.7	40
j) {BRSAT} Column No 1558 **British Rail**		51.6	786	41.9	638	2.0	30	4.5	68
k) {PHONESAT} Column No 1559 **The telephone service**		79.9	1217	16.1	245	1.3	21	2.7	41

Base : Self-completion respondents (n = 1522)

NB   Questions on the <u>efficiency</u> of many of these institutions were asked in 1983, 1986 and 1987 (see pp. A-16 to A-19 and p. A-27 above)

PERSONAL QUALITIES IMPORTANT FOR MPS AND COUNCILLORS

1983   Q.8a,b   {MPED}{MPPOOR}{MPBUS}{MPUNION}{MPLOCAL}{MPLOYAL}{MPIND}{MPNONE}{MPOTH1}
{MPNA};{CLRED}{CLRPOOR}{CLRBUS}{CLRUNION}{CLRLOCAL}{CLRLOYAL}{CLRIND}{CLRNONE}{CLROTH2}
{CLROTH1}{CLRNA} Column Nos 152-59, 160-68, 170, 174-76

a) (Show card) [Still thinking of MPs,] which of the personal qualities on this card would you say are
important for an MP to have? You may choose more than one, or none, or suggest others.

b) And which would you say are important for a local councillor to have?

		Personal qualities of										
		(a) an MP						(b) a local councillor					
	Code	Not important 0		Important 1		(NA) 9		Not important 0		Important 1		(NA) 9	
		%	No	%	No	%	No	%	No	%	No	%	No
{MPED}{CLRED} Column Nos 152,160 i) To be well educated		49.0	843	50.4	866	0.6	10	68.6	1179	30.5	525	0.9	15
{MPPOOR}{CLRPOOR} Column Nos 153,161 ii) To know what being poor means		72.7	1249	26.7	460	0.6	10	82.2	1413	16.9	291	0.9	15
{MPBUS}{CLRBUS} Column Nos 154,162 iii) To have business experience		77.8	1337	21.6	372	0.6	10	80.1	1378	19.0	326	0.9	15
{MPUNION}{CLRUNION} Column Nos 155,163 iv) To have trade union experience		85.3	1466	14.1	243	0.6	10	91.1	1566	8.0	138	0.9	15
{MPLOCAL}{CLRLOCAL} Column Nos 156,164 v) To have been brought up in the area he or she represents		51.6	888	47.8	822	0.6	10	23.3	401	75.8	1303	0.9	15
{MPLOYAL}{CLRLOYAL} Column Nos 157,165 vi) To be loyal to the Party he or she represents		57.0	980	42.4	729	0.6	10	77.7	1336	21.4	368	0.9	15
{MPIND}{CLRIND} Column Nos 158,166 vii) To be independent minded		62.0	1066	37.4	643	0.6	10	70.1	1205	29.0	499	0.9	15
{MPNONE}{CLRNONE} Column Nos 159,167 viii) None of these qualities		98.8	1699	0.6	10	0.6	10	98.4	1691	0.7	13	0.9	15
{CLROTH2} Column No 175 ix) (To have a knowledge of local matters)								98.6	1695	0.5	9	0.9	15
{MPOTH1}{CLROTH1} Column Nos 168,174 x) Other important qualities (specified)		96.2	1653	3.3	56	0.6	10	96.3	1655	2.8	48	0.9	15
{MPNA}{CLRNA} Column Nos 170,176 (NA)		99.4	1709	-	-	0.6	10	99.1	1704	-	-	0.9	15

Base : All (n = 1719)

FUTURE OF THE HOUSE OF LORDS

1983   Q.12a   {LORDS} Column No 233

Do you think the House of Lords should remain as it is or is some change needed?

	Code	%	No
Remain as is	1	57.4	987
Change needed	2	33.5	577
(DK)	8	8.3	143
(NA)	9	0.7	12
Base : All			1719

1983   Q.12b   {LORDSHOW} Column No 234

[If change thought necessary] Do you think the House of Lords should be ... (read out) ...

	Code	%	No
[Not asked : no change thought necessary]	0	66.5	1142
... replaced by a different body,	1	9.5	164
abolished and replaced by nothing,	2	7.7	133
or should there be some other kind of change?	3	16.0	274
(NA)	9	0.3	5
Base : All			1719

1983   Q.12c

[If other kind of change] Do you have a particular change in mind? (Interviewer : record, but do not probe).

Responses not coded, but instead listed in British Social Attitudes 1983 Survey : Technical Report, SCPR (1984)

IMPORTANCE OF THE MONARCHY

1983   Q.13   {MONARCHY} Column No 241

How about the monarchy or the Royal Family in Britain. How important or unimportant do you think it is for Britain to continue to have a monarchy ... (read out) ...

	Code	%	No
... very important,	1	64.6	1110
quite important,	2	21.5	369
not very important,	3	7.9	136
not at all important,	4	2.6	44
or do you think the monarchy should be abolished?	5	3.1	53
(NA)	9	0.4	7
Base : All			1719

B Crime, law enforcement and civil liberties

Table titles and cross references

OBEYING THE LAW *VERSUS* FOLLOWING ONE'S CONSCIENCE

{*OBEYLAW*}

Question: In general would you say that people should obey the law without exception, or are there exceptional occasions on which people should follow their consciences even if it means breaking the law?

	Code	1983 %	1983 No	1984 %	1984 No	1985 %	1985 No	1986 %	1986 No	1987 %	1987 No	1989 %	1989 No
Question No		11a		8a				B88a				B98a	
Column No		231		218				725				1130	
Obey law without exception	1	53.1	912	56.6	932	-	-	54.9	850	-	-	50.0	731
Follow conscience on occasions	2	46.0	791	42.2	694	-	-	43.0	666	-	-	48.0	702
(DK)	8	0.4	7	0.8	13	-	-	1.5	23	-	-	1.5	21
(NA)	9	0.6	10	0.4	6	-	-	0.6	10	-	-	0.5	8
Base: All			1719		1645				1548				1461

1985 - This question was asked on the self-completion supplement (Q.202, Column No. 2009) and the variable subsequently renamed {SCOBEYLW}. The distributions were:

	Code	%	No
Obey law without exception	1	37.2	558
Follow conscience on occasions	2	58.2	874
Can't choose	8	4.2	63
(NA)	9	0.4	6
Base: Self-completion respondents			1502

SUPPORT FOR CAPITAL PUNISHMENT

{CAPPUN1} {CAPPUN2} {CAPPUN3}

Question: Are you in favour of or against the death penalty for ... (please tick one box for each):

			1983		1984		1985		1986		1987		1989	
			%	No	%	No	%	No	%	No	%	No	%	No
		Question No	206		206		232						A224	
		Column No	1034		1546		2142						2036	
(i) {CAPPUN1}		Code												
Murder in the course of a terrorist act														
In favour	1		74.2	1195	77.7	1183	76.5	1149	-		-		76.3	972
Against	2		21.0	338	19.6	299	19.1	287	-		-		19.2	244
(DK)	8		0.3	5	0.5	7	0.2	3	-		-		0.4	4
(NA)	9		4.4	71	2.2	33	4.2	63	-		-		4.1	53
Base: Self-completion questionnaire respondents				1610		1522		1502						1274
		Question No	206		206		232						A224	
		Column No	1035		1547		2143						2037	
(ii) {CAPPUN2}														
Murder of a police officer														
In favour	1		70.5	1135	72.5	1104	71.4	1072	-		-		71.4	909
Against	2		23.1	372	23.8	362	23.3	350	-		-		23.4	298
(DK)	8		0.4	6	0.6	10	0.3	5	-		-		0.4	5
(NA)	9		6.0	96	3.0	46	5.0	75	-		-		4.8	61
Base: Self-completion questionnaire respondents				1610		1522		1502						1274
		Question No	206		206		232						A224	
		Column No	1036		1548		2144						2038	
(iii) {CAPPUN3}														
Other murders														
In favour	1		63.1	1015	66.2	1008	65.7	987	-		-		70.3	896
Against	2		32.9	530	30.8	469	30.7	461	-		-		25.8	329
(DK)	8		0.4	7	0.6	10	0.4	6	-		-		0.5	6
(NA)	9		3.6	58	2.3	36	3.2	48	-		-		3.3	42
Base: Self-completion questionnaire respondents				1610		1522		1502						1274

1983, 1984, 1985   -   {CAPPUN2} 'Murder of a policeman'

PREDICTIONS OF FUTURE UPHEAVALS AND CATASTROPHES

{PREDICT1} {PREDICT2} {PREDICT3} {PREDICT4} {PREDICT5} {PREDICT6} {PREDICT7}

Question: Here is a list of predictions. For each one, please say how likely or unlikely you think it is to come true *within the next ten years?*

		1983		1984		1985		1986		1987		1989	
		%	No	%	No	%	No	%	No	%	No	%	No
Question No		210		211				B225		B235		B239	
Column No		1057		1569				2129		2125		2315	

(i) {PREDICT1}
Acts of political terrorism in Britain will be common events — Code

	Code	1983 %	No	1984 %	No	1985 %	No	1986 %	No	1987 %	No	1989 %	No
Very likely	1	15.7	252	19.8	302	-	-	25.1	330	14.8	175	11.9	149
Quite likely	2	40.7	655	42.5	647	-	-	48.6	640	44.9	530	45.4	569
Not very likely	3	35.4	570	29.5	450	-	-	23.9	314	33.2	392	37.3	468
Not at all likely	4	6.3	101	5.2	79	-	-	1.5	19	4.0	47	2.8	35
(DK)	8	-	-	0.8	13	-	-	0.2	2	0.6	7	0.7	9
(NA)	9	1.9	31	2.2	33	-	-	0.8	11	2.5	30	1.9	24

Base: Self-completion questionnaire respondents — 1610, 1522, 1315, 1181, 1255

Question No		210		211				B225		B235		B239	
Column No		1058		1570				2130		2126		2316	

(ii) {PREDICT2}
Riots and civil disturbance in our cities will be common events

	Code	1983 %	No	1984 %	No	1985 %	No	1986 %	No	1987 %	No	1989 %	No
Very likely	1	16.2	261	15.9	242	-	-	19.8	261	15.8	186	9.2	115
Quite likely	2	43.7	703	40.3	613	-	-	44.4	585	50.2	592	37.5	471
Not very likely	3	32.6	525	34.0	518	-	-	31.8	419	27.7	327	46.0	578
Not at all likely	4	5.6	89	6.4	98	-	-	2.5	33	3.3	39	4.5	57
(DK)	8	-	-	0.9	14	-	-	0.3	4	0.6	8	0.6	8
(NA)	9	1.9	31	2.4	37	-	-	1.1	14	2.5	29	2.1	26

Base: Self-completion questionnaire respondents — 1610, 1522, 1315, 1181, 1255

1983 - Q reads: 'Here is a list of predictions about problems that Britain might face. For each one, please say how likely or unlikely you think it is to come true <u>in Britain within the next ten years</u>'; No (DK)

1983, 1984, 1986 - Very likely, code 4, Quite likely, code 3, Not very likely, code 2, Not at all likely, code 1

PREDICTIONS OF FUTURE UPHEAVALS AND CATASTROPHES (Continued)

			1983		1984		1985		1986		1987		1989	
			%	No	%	No	%	No	%	No	%	No	%	No
Question No			210		211				B225		B235		B239	
Column No			1059		1571				2131		2127		2317	

(iii) {PREDICT3}

There will be a world war involving Britain and Europe

	Code	1983 %	No	1984 %	No	1985 %	No	1986 %	No	1987 %	No	1989 %	No
Very likely	1	6.2	100	3.4	52	-	-	5.1	66	2.3	28	1.4	18
Quite likely	2	17.9	288	17.8	272	-	-	17.6	232	8.5	100	7.3	92
Not very likely	3	48.0	773	50.0	762	-	-	51.7	681	56.0	661	54.6	685
Not at all likely	4	25.0	403	24.6	374	-	-	23.8	313	29.4	348	33.9	425
(DK)	8	-	-	1.6	24	-	-	0.6	9	0.9	10	0.6	7
(NA)	9	2.8	45	2.6	39	-	-	1.2	15	2.9	34	2.3	28
Base: Self-completion questionnaire respondents			1610		1522				1315		1181		1255

		1983	1984	1985	1986	1987	1989
Question No		210d	211d		B225d	B235d	B239d
Column No		1060	1572		2132	2128	2318

(iv) {PREDICT4}

There will be a serious accident at a British nuclear power station

	Code	1983 %	No	1984 %	No	1985 %	No	1986 %	No	1987 %	No	1989 %	No
Very likely	1	10.3	165	13.0	199	-	-	16.5	217	12.2	144	11.6	146
Quite likely	2	34.7	558	39.8	606	-	-	42.0	552	39.9	471	45.8	575
Not very likely	3	43.1	694	35.7	544	-	-	34.4	452	36.8	435	34.0	427
Not at all likely	4	9.3	150	8.0	121	-	-	5.8	76	7.9	93	5.7	71
(DK)	8	-	-	1.7	26	-	-	0.3	5	0.7	9	0.6	8
(NA)	9	2.6	42	1.8	27	-	-	1.0	13	2.5	30	2.3	29
Base: Self-completion questionnaire respondents			1610		1522				1315		1181		1255

PREDICTIONS OF FUTURE UPHEAVALS AND CATASTROPHES (Continued)

		1983		1984		1985		1986		1987		1989	
		%	No	%	No	%	No	%	No	%	No	%	No
Question No		210		211				B225		B235		B239	
Column No	Code	1061		1573				2133		2129		2319	

(v) {PREDICT5}

The police in our cities will find it impossible to protect our personal safety on the streets

	Code	%	No	%	No	%	No	%	No	%	No	%	No
Very likely	1	18.1	291	17.8	272	-	-	19.3	254	20.6	243	15.9	199
Quite likely	2	34.9	562	33.9	516	-	-	39.3	517	43.1	509	47.2	592
Not very likely	3	36.9	594	35.0	532	-	-	34.8	458	29.4	347	31.2	391
Not at all likely	4	8.5	136	11.0	167	-	-	5.6	74	3.6	42	3.3	42
(DK)	8	-	.	0.8	12	-	-	0.2	2	0.6	7	0.5	6
(NA)	9	1.7	27	1.6	25	-	-	0.8	11	2.8	33	2.0	24

Base: Self-completion questionnaire respondents

	1610	1522		1315	1181	1255

Question No		210		211				B225		B235		B239	
Column No		1062		1574				2134		2130		2320	

(vi) {PREDICT6}

The government in Britain will be overthrown by revolution

	Code	%	No	%	No	%	No	%	No	%	No	%	No
Very likely	1	2.2	35	2.3	35	-	-	2.0	26	2.2	26	1.6	20
Quite likely	2	5.5	89	8.2	125	-	-	7.5	98	5.9	70	5.3	67
Not very likely	3	32.8	528	32.6	497	-	-	40.7	535	42.3	499	42.3	530
Not at all likely	4	57.3	923	53.8	819	-	-	48.7	641	46.6	550	48.1	604
(DK)	8	-	.	1.0	15	-	-	0.3	4	0.6	7	0.8	10
(NA)	9	2.2	35	2.1	33	-	-	0.9	12	2.4	29	1.9	23

Base: Self-completion questionnaire respondents

	1610	1522		1315	1181	1255

PREDICTIONS OF FUTURE UPHEAVALS AND CATASTROPHES (Continued)

		1983		1984		1985		1986		1987		1989	
		%	No	%	No	%	No	%	No	%	No	%	No
Question No				211				B225		B235		B239	
Column No				1575				2135		2131		2321	
	Code												
(vii) *{PREDICT7}*													
A nuclear bomb will be dropped somewhere in the world													
Very likely	1	-	-	9.4	143	-	-	7.9	104	6.0	71	3.6	46
Quite likely	2	-	-	26.1	397	-	-	26.8	353	22.2	262	20.0	250
Not very likely	3	-	-	38.5	586	-	-	38.8	510	39.3	464	45.4	570
Not at all likely	4	-	-	23.6	359	-	-	25.1	331	29.3	346	28.1	353
(DK)	8	-	-	0.6	10	-	-	0.3	4	0.7	9	0.8	10
(NA)	9	-	-	1.9	29	-	-	1.1	14	2.5	30	2.1	26
					—				—		—		—
Base: Self-completion questionnaire respondents					1522				1325		1181		1255

CONVICTING THE INNOCENT *VERSUS* FREEING THE GUILTY

{JUSTICE}

Question: All systems of justice make mistakes, but which do you think is worse ...

		1983		1984		1985		1986		1987		1989	
		%	No	%	No	%	No	%	No	%	No	%	No
Question No						206		B203					
Column No						2030		2024					
	Code												
... to convict an innocent person,	1	-	-	-	-	67.2	1010	57.8	761	-	-	-	-
... or to let a guilty person go free?	2	-	-	-	-	20.1	303	26.0	342	-	-	-	-
Can't choose	8	-	-	-	-	11.9	179	15.9	209	-	-	-	-
(NA)	9	-	-	-	-	0.7	10	0.3	4	-	-	-	-
							—		—				
Base: Self-completion questionnaire respondents							1502		1315				

FREEDOM OF THE PRESS TO PUBLISH CONFIDENTIAL GOVERNMENT PAPERS

1985   Q.201a,b   *{GOVPAPRI}{GOVPAPR2}* Column Nos 2007-08

a) Suppose a newspaper got hold of confidential government papers about defence plans and wanted to publish them... (please tick one box)...

b) Now suppose the confidential government papers were about economic plans... (please tick one box)...

	Code	a) Defence plans {GOVPAPRI}		b) Economic plans {GOVPAPR2}	
		%	No	%	No
... should the newspaper be allowed to publish the papers,	1	24.3	366	57.9	870
or - should the government have the power to prevent publication?	2	69.0	1037	33.5	503
Can't choose	8	6.0	91	7.7	116
(NA)	9	0.6	9	0.9	13
Base : Self-completion respondents			1502		1502

RIGHTS OF REVOLUTIONARIES AND RACISTS - 1

1985 Q.204a,b {REVMEET}{REVTEASC}{REVPUB}{PRJMEET}{PRJTEASC}{PRJPUB} Column Nos 2016-2021

There are some people whose views are considered extreme by the majority.

a) First, consider people who want to overthrow the government by revolution. Do you think such people should be allowed to ... (please tick one box on each line):

		Definitely 1		Probably 2		Probably not 3		Definitely not 4		Can't choose 8		(NA) 9	
	Code	%	No	%	No	%	No	%	No	%	No	%	No
i) {REVMEET} Column No 2016 Hold public meetings to express their views		27.0	405	24.8	373	10.8	162	33.8	507	2.6	39	1.1	16
ii) {REVTEASC} Column No 2017 Teach 15 year olds in schools		4.4	66	7.2	109	18.4	276	64.6	970	3.5	53	1.8	28
iii) {REVPUB} Column No 2018 Publish books expressing their views		27.0	405	36.9	554	11.0	165	19.9	298	3.4	51	1.9	29

Base : Self-completion respondents (n = 1502)

NB These questions were asked in 1983 (Q.5a) on the interview questionnaire, and the same variable names were used. The change in mode of administration, and the addition of a 'Can't choose' answer category in 1985, severely compromise comparability. Consequently the 1983 variable names have been changed to {REVOMEET}, {REVOTEAC} and {REVOPUB}. (See p. B-12 below)

b) Second, consider people who believe that whites are racially superior to all other races. Do you think such people should be allowed to ... (please tick one box on each line):

		Definitely 1		Probably 2		Probably not 3		Definitely not 4		Can't choose 8		(NA) 9	
	Code	%	No	%	No	%	No	%	No	%	No	%	No
i) {PRJMEET} Column No 2019 Hold public meetings to express their views		19.1	287	18.9	283	18.0	270	40.2	604	2.7	41	1.0	16
ii) {PRJTEASC} Column No 2020 Teach 15 year olds in schools		4.3	64	7.7	116	18.2	273	65.0	975	3.0	46	1.9	28
iii) {PRJPUB} Column No 2021 Publish books expressing their views		20.6	310	29.4	441	14.4	217	30.1	452	3.9	58	1.6	23

Base : Self-completion respondents (n = 1502)

POLICE POWERS

1985   Q.205a,b   {CRIMIN1}-{CRIMIN4} {NONCRIM1}-{NONCRIM4} Column Nos 2022-29

a) Suppose the police get an anonymous tip that a man with a long criminal record is planning to break into a warehouse. Do you think the police should be allowed, without a Court Order ... (please tick one box for each):

	Code	Definitely 1		Probably 2		Probably not 3		Definitely not 4		Can't choose 8		(NA) 9	
		%	No	%	No	%	No	%	No	%	No	%	No
i) {CRIMIN1} Column No 2022 To keep the man under surveillance		68.4	1028	21.3	320	3.3	50	4.7	71	0.9	14	1.3	20
ii) {CRIMIN2} Column No 2023 To tap his telephone		16.5	247	22.0	330	18.9	284	39.1	588	1.8	27	1.7	26
iii) {CRIMIN3} Column No 2024 To open his mail		11.9	178	12.6	189	20.6	310	50.8	763	1.6	24	2.5	38
iv) {CRIMIN4} Column No 2025 To detain the man overnight for questioning		33.6	504	29.5	444	13.0	196	20.2	303	2.3	34	1.3	20

Base : Self-completion respondents (n = 1502)

b) Now, suppose the tip is about a man *without* a criminal record. Do you think the police should be allowed, without a Court Order ... (please tick one box for each):

	Code	Definitely 1		Probably 2		Probably not 3		Definitely not 4		Can't choose 8		(NA) 9	
		%	No	%	No	%	No	%	No	%	No	%	No
i) {NONCRIM1} Column No 2026 To keep the man under surveillance		42.9	644	29.2	438	9.7	146	16.0	241	0.8	12	1.4	21
ii) {NONCRIM2} Column No 2027 To tap his telephone		5.0	75	9.3	139	18.0	270	64.1	963	1.5	22	2.1	32
iii) {NONCRIM3} Column No 2028 To open his mail		3.4	50	5.0	75	16.0	240	72.3	1086	1.4	22	1.9	29
iv) {NONCRIM4} Column No 2029 To detain the man overnight for questioning		13.2	198	19.9	299	19.9	298	43.2	649	2.3	34	1.5	23

Base : Self-completion respondents (n = 1502)

THREAT TO PRIVACY POSED BY COMPUTERS

1985   Q.207   {GOVINFO} Column No 2031

The government has a lot of different pieces of information about people which computers can bring together very quickly. Is this ... (please tick one box) ...

	Code	%	No
... a very serious threat to individual privacy,	1	32.3	486
a fairly serious threat,	2	32.3	486
not a serious threat,	3	23.3	349
or - not a threat at all to individual privacy?	4	5.8	87
Can't choose	8	5.4	81
(NA)	9	0.9	13
Base : Self-completion respondents			1502

LEGAL PROHIBITION *VERSUS* RIGHTS OF INDIVIDUALS

1985   Q.219a-c   {SEATBELT}{BANSMOKE}{SETRETIR} Column Nos 2064-66

Do you think that ... (please tick one box for each):

	Agree strongly 1		Agree 2		Neither agree nor disagree 3		Disagree 4		Disagree strongly 5		(NA) 9	
Code	%	No	%	No	%	No	%	No	%	No	%	No
a) {SEATBELT} Column No 2064 The wearing of seat belts in cars should be required by law	48.8	733	30.2	453	8.8	131	9.0	135	2.2	32	1.1	16
b) {BANSMOKE} Column No 2065 Smoking in public places should be prohibited by law	24.1	361	25.9	389	20.7	310	20.9	314	7.3	109	1.2	19
c) {SETRETIR} Column No 2066 All employees should be required by law to retire at an age set by law	19.5	293	34.7	521	17.5	263	23.1	346	4.1	62	1.0	15

Base : Self-completion respondents (n = 1502)

CIRCUMSTANCES IN WHICH RESPONDENTS MIGHT BREAK THE LAW

1984   Q.8c   {BRKWHEN1}+{BRKWHEN2}+{BRKWHEN3} Column Nos 220-21, 222-23, 224-25
[If might break law] Can you say what those circumstances might be? (Interviewer: probe fully and record verbatim)

	Code	%	No
[Not asked : would not break law]	0	62.6	1029
To protect self or family	1	5.0	83
To intervene in injustice/ill-treatment of others	2	2.3	38
To protect property	3	2.1	35
To protect trade-union rights	4	2.5	41
To protest about defence issues	5	1.2	20
To protest about/protect local authority rights	6	0.6	9
To protect rights to demonstrate/civil liberties/democratic rights	7	1.6	26
Where laws are seen as petty or harassing	8	5.2	86
Where crime is seen as necessary to feed/clothe oneself	9	0.5	8
To protect rights/follow my conscience	95	3.0	49
Depends on the circumstances	96	5.2	85
(Other answers) - no other responses	97	2.9	47
(NA) - exclusive code	98	10.0	165
Base : All			1645

NB Up to 3 responses were coded for each respondent, so that percentages will add up to more than 100%. This question was preceded by Q.8b: 'Are there any circumstances in which **you** might break a law to which you were very strongly opposed?', and only those answering 'yes' were asked Q.8c. See {BREAKLAW} (p. A-9 above)

WHETHER EVER BELIEVED A PARLIAMENTARY MEASURE TO BE UNJUST

1983   Q.10a   {BADLAW} Column No 210
Has there ever been an occasion when a law was being considered by Parliament which you thought was really unjust and harmful?

	Code	%	No
Yes	1	31.0	533
No	2	67.9	1166
(NA)	9	1.1	20
Base : All			1719

RIGHTS OF REVOLUTIONARIES AND RACISTS - 2

1983   Q.5a,b
There are some people whose views are considered extreme by the majority.

1983   Q.5a   {REVOMEET}{REVOTEAC}{REVTEACL}{REVOPUB} Column Nos 142-45
Consider people who wish to overthrow the system of government in Britain by revolution. Do you think
such people should be allowed to ... (read out):

	Code	Yes 1		No 2		(DK) 8		(NA) 9	
		%	No	%	No	%	No	%	No
i) {REVOMEET} Column No 142 Hold public meetings to express their views		57.1	981	41.5	714	1.3	22	0.1	2
ii) {REVOTEAC} Column No 143 Teach in schools		25.3	434	72.2	1241	2.2	38	0.4	7
iii) {REVTEACL} Column No 144 Teach in colleges or universities		36.8	633	60.3	1036	2.5	43	0.4	7
iv) {REVOPUB} Column No 145 Publish books expressing their views		74.2	1276	24.1	414	1.4	24	0.3	5

Base : All (n = 1719)

NB Parts i), ii) and iv) of this question were repeated in 1985 on the self-completion supplement, as part of the ISSP role of government module
(see p. B-8 above). The original variable names, {REVMEET}, {REVTEASC} and {REVPUB}, were used. However, data users should take
note that, since the question was administered in a different way in 1985, responses should not be regarded as comparable. In consequence, the
1983 variable names have been changed as above

1983   Q.5b   {RACMEET}{RACTEASC}{RACTEACL}{RACPUB} Column Nos 146-49
Now consider people who say that all blacks and Asians should be forced to leave Britain. Do you think
such people should be allowed to ... (read out):

	Code	Yes 1		No 2		(DK) 8		(NA) 9	
		%	No	%	No	%	No	%	No
i) {RACMEET} Column No 146 Hold public meetings to express their views		56.3	968	40.9	704	2.1	37	0.6	10
ii) {RACTEASC} Column No 147 Teach in schools		31.2	537	65.6	1127	2.3	39	0.9	16
iii) {RACTEACL} Column No 148 Teach in colleges or universities		40.7	700	56.4	969	1.9	33	1.0	17
iv) {RACPUB} Column No 149 Publish books expressing their views		70.8	1218	26.8	461	1.5	26	0.8	14

Base : All (n = 1719)

FEAR ABOUT CRIME AND PERSONAL SAFETY

1983   Q.72a-c   {VICTIM}{VMWORRY}{SAFEDARK}   Column Nos 553-55

1983   Q.72a   {VICTIM} Column No 553
Do you ever worry about the possibility that you or anyone else who lives with you might be the victim of crime?

		Code	%	No
	Yes	1	69.3	1191
	No	2	30.5	525
	(NA)	9	0.2	3
Base : All				1719

1983   Q.72b   {VMWORRY} Column No 554
[If ever worried] **Is this ... (read out) ...**

	Code	%	No
[Not asked : never worried]	0	30.5	525
... a big worry,	1	18.6	320
a bit of a worry,	2	28.4	489
or an occasional doubt?	3	22.0	378
(NA)	9	0.4	7
Base : All			1719

1983   Q.72c   {SAFEDARK} Column No 555
How safe do you feel walking alone in this area after dark ... (read out) ...

	Code	%	No
... very safe,	1	25.2	434
fairly safe,	2	38.3	659
a bit unsafe,	3	22.0	378
or very unsafe?	4	14.0	241
(NA)	9	0.5	8
Base : All			1719

PREVALENCE OF LOCAL CRIME

1983   Q.73a   {BURGLARY} Column No 556
How common is it for people's homes to be burgled in this area ... (read out) ...

1983   Q.73b   {VANDAL}   Column No 557
How common is deliberate damage done by vandals in this area ... (read out) ...

1983   Q.73c   {MUGGING} Column No 558
How common in this area is it for people to be attacked and to have things stolen from them in the street ... (read out) ...

	Code	a) Burglary {BURGLARY} Column No 556		b) Vandalism {VANDAL} Column No 557		c) Mugging {MUGGING} Column No 558	
		%	No	%	No	%	No
... very common,	1	16.0	275	16.7	287	4.2	72
... fairly common,	2	28.5	490	24.7	424	10.3	178
[or] - not very common?	3	53.2	914	57.8	993	84.1	1446
(DK)	8	0.7	12	0.4	7	0.5	9
(NA)	9	1.6	28	0.4	7	0.8	14
Base : All			1719		1719		1719

RECENT CONTACTS WITH THE POLICE

1983   Q.74a-d   {GOPOLICE}{PCHELP}{PCSTOP}{PCPOLITE}   Column Nos 559-62

1983   Q.74a   {GOPOLICE} Column No 559
During the past two years have you ever reported a crime or accident to the police or gone to them for help or advice?

	Code	%	No
Yes	1	34.7	596
No	2	65.1	1118
(NA)	9	0.2	4
Base : All			1719

1983   Q.74b   {PCHELP} Column No 560
On these occasions how helpful have you found them in the way they dealt with you ... (read out) ...

	Code	%	No
[Not asked : not been to police]	0	65.1	1118
... very helpful,	1	17.3	298
fairly helpful,	2	9.6	165
fairly unhelpful,	3	3.4	59
or very unhelpful?	4	3.0	52
(Varied)	5	1.3	22
(NA)	9	0.3	5
Base : All			1719

1983   Q.74c   {PCSTOP} Column No 561
During the past two years have you ever been stopped or asked questions by the police about an offence which they thought had been committed?

	Code	%	No
Yes	1	16.7	286
No	2	83.1	1428
(NA)	9	0.3	5
Base : All			1719

1983   Q.74d   {PCPOLITE} Column No 562
[If stopped by police in past two years] **On these occasions how polite have you found them when they approached you ... (read out) ....**

	Code	%	No
[Not asked : not stopped by police]	0	83.1	1428
... very polite,	1	8.6	148
fairly polite,	2	4.4	76
fairly impolite,	3	1.6	28
or very impolite?	4	1.9	32
(Varied)	5	0.2	3
(NA)	9	0.3	5
Base : All			1719

NB {PCHELP} was the variable name given to Q.90 (xv) asked in 1984. This has been changed to {PCFORGET} (see p. M.2-9)

SATISFACTION WITH THE POLICE

1983   Q.75a-c   {PCANNOY}{PCPLEASE}{PCSAT} Column Nos 563-65

1983   Q.75a   {PCANNOY} Column No 563
During the past *two years* have you ever been *really annoyed* about the way a police officer behaved towards you, or someone you know, or about the way the police handled a matter in which you were involved?

	Code	%	No
Yes	1	17.8	307
No	2	82.0	1409
(NA)	9	0.2	3
Base: All			1719

1983   Q.75b   {PCPLEASE} Column No 564
During the last *two years* have you ever been *really pleased* about the way a police officer behaved towards you, or someone you know, or about the way the police handled a matter in which you were involved?

	Code	%	No
Yes	1	29.1	500
No	2	70.4	1209
(NA)	9	0.6	10
Base : All			1719

1983   Q.75c   {PCSAT} Column No 565
(Show card) In general, how satisfied or dissatisfied are you with the way the police in Britain do their job? Choose a phrase from this card.

	Code	%	No
Very dissatisfied	1	1.8	31
Quite dissatisfied	2	10.2	176
Neither satisfied nor dissatisfied	3	8.9	153
Quite satisfied	4	48.9	840
Very satisfied	5	29.6	509
(NA)	9	0.5	9
Base : All			1719

EFFICIENCY OF PRISON MANAGEMENT

1983   Q.207l   {PRISON} Column No 1048
From what you know or have heard ..., can you say whether, on the whole, [prisons are] well run or not well run? (Please tick one box)

	Code	%	No
Well run	1	49.4	795
Not well run	2	44.1	709
(DK)	8	0.7	11
(NA)	9	5.9	95
Base : Self-completion respondents			1610

NB 'Prisons' was the last in a list of 12 institutions asked about, and the only one <u>not</u> asked about again in 1986 (see pp. A-16 to A-19).
Since this was not the only item on the list, the question was prefaced by 'Listed below are some of Britain's institutions', and respondents were invited to answer 'about each one'

C Party politics

Table titles and cross references

POLITICAL PARTISANSHIP

{SUPPARTY}

Question: Generally speaking, do you think of yourself as a supporter of any one political party?

	Code	1983 %	No	1984 %	No	1985 %	No	1986 %	No	1987 %	No	1989 %	No
Question No		2a		3a		2a		2a		2a		2a	
Column No		135		153		210		212		212		219	
Yes	1	47.7	821	48.2	792	46.6	825	46.8	1435	48.8	1351	50.9	1491
No	2	52.3	898	51.8	852	53.1	940	53.1	1629	51.1	1413	49.0	1435
(DK)	8	-	-	-	-	-	-	-	-			-	
(NA)	9	-	-	0.1	1	0.2	4	0.1	2	0.1	2	0.1	4
Base: All			1719		1645		1769		3066		2766		2930

1983 - No (DK)

POLITICAL SYMPATHY

{CLOSEPTY}

Question: [If does not support any party] Do you think of yourself as a little closer to one political party than to the others?

	Code	1983 %	No	1984 %	No	1985 %	No	1986 %	No	1987 %	No	1989 %	No
Question No		2c		3c		2c		2c		2c		2b	
Column No		136		154		211		213		213		220	
[Not asked: supports a political party]	0	47.7	821	48.2	793	46.9	829	46.9	1437	48.9	1352	50.9	1491
Yes	1	26.2	450	25.5	420	24.2	428	26.6	815	25.5	707	23.6	690
No	2	25.1	431	25.1	413	28.0	495	25.3	776	24.8	686	24.9	731
(DK)	8	0.1	1	0.1	2	0.1	2	0.0	1	-	-	0.1	2
(NA)	9	1.0	17	1.0	17	0.9	15	1.2	37	0.7	21	0.5	16
Base: All			1719		1645		1769		3066		2766		2930

PARTY POLITICAL IDENTIFICATION

{PARTYID1}

Derived variable combining all levels of political partisanship.

	Code	1983 %	1983 No	1984 %	1984 No	1985 %	1985 No	1986 %	1986 No	1987 %	1987 No	1989 %	1989 No
Question No		2bde		3bde		2bde		2bde		2bde		2cd	
Column No		137-38		155-56		212-13		214-15		214-15		221-22	
Conservative	1	38.6	664	38.6	635	30.8	545	33.7	1035	38.0	1051	39.5	1157
Labour	2	32.9	565	34.9	575	36.5	645	35.0	1072	29.1	804	33.5	982
Social and Liberal Democrat/Liberal/ SLD	3	7.7	133	7.1	116	9.1	161	7.1	219	7.0	194	7.5	221
SDP/Social Democrat	4	6.0	104	4.9	81	6.0	107	7.0	214	6.8	187	3.6	105
Alliance (after probe)	5	0.9	16	1.3	22	2.5	44	3.3	103	4.9	136	0.1	4
Scottish Nationalist	6	0.6	10	0.6	10	0.8	14	0.9	29	0.6	17	2.1	63
Plaid Cymru	7	0.4	7	0.5	9	0.1	2	0.2	6	0.4	11	0.3	8
Other party	8	0.3	4	0.6	9	0.3	6	0.5	14	0.3	10	0.2	5
Other answer	9	-	-	1.9	31	1.1	19	0.9	26	0.8	21	0.3	10
None	10	8.0	137	6.2	102	8.7	154	7.5	231	7.5	208	7.1	208
(Green Party/the Greens/Greenpeace)	95	-		-		-		-		-		0.8	24
Refused/unwilling to say	97	-		-		-		-		-		2.9	86
(DK/undecided)	98	2.2	39	2.3	38	2.9	51	2.5	77	3.6	99	1.5	44
(NA)	99	2.3	40	1.0	17	1.2	22	1.3	40	1.0	28	0.5	13
Base: All			1719		1645		1769		3066		2766		2930

1983 - No Other answer; Other party, code 8, None, code 9, (DK), code 98, (NA), code 99

1983-1987 inclusive -

2b [If supporter of any one political party] 'Which one?'

2c [If not supporter but think of self as a little closer to one political party] 'Which one?'

2d [If not supporter or think of self as little closer to one political party] 'If there was a general election tomorrow, which political party do you think you would be most likely to support?'
No probe on Alliance.

1989 -

2c [If not supporter of one political party or think of self as closer to one party] 'If there were a general election tomorrow, which political party do you think you would be most likely to support?'

2d [If supporter of one political party or think of self as closer to one party] 'Which one?'
[If Alliance at 2c or 2d] 'Social and Liberal Democrats or SDP (Owen)?'
Green Party precoded on questionnaire

PARTY POLITICAL ALLEGIANCE

{PTYALLEG}

Variable derived from responses to questions on party identification

	Code	1983 %	1983 No	1984 %	1984 No	1985 %	1985 No	1986 %	1986 No	1987 %	1987 No	1989 %	1989 No
Column No				1656-57		1059-60		2332-33		2230-31		2346-47	
Conservative:													
partisans	1	24.4	420	23.3	384	19.2	340	20.7	634	25.2	696	24.7	723
sympathisers	2	9.1	157	10.1	167	7.7	137	9.6	293	9.2	256	10.2	298
residual identifiers	3	5.0	87	5.1	85	3.8	68	3.5	107	3.6	100	4.6	136
Labour:													
partisans	4	16.8	289	19.3	317	20.1	355	19.3	592	16.5	456	20.3	596
sympathisers	5	11.1	190	9.7	160	10.6	187	10.4	318	8.8	244	7.8	228
residual identifiers	6	5.0	86	5.9	98	5.8	103	5.3	163	3.7	104	5.4	159
Alliance:													
partisans	7	4.7	81	4.4	72	6.5	115	5.6	171	5.8	162	3.7	107
sympathisers	8	5.4	92	4.8	80	5.3	93	5.8	177	6.8	187	4.1	120
residual identifiers	9	4.6	79	4.1	67	5.8	103	6.1	187	6.1	169	3.5	102
Other party	10	1.2	21	1.7	28	1.2	22	1.6	49	1.3	37	2.6	75
None	11	8.0	137	6.2	102	8.7	154	7.5	231	7.5	208	7.1	208
Other answer, DK, NA	98	4.6	78	5.2	86	5.2	92	4.7	144	5.4	148	5.3	155
Base: All			1719		1645		1769		3066		2766		2930

1989 - SDP/SLD/'Alliance' partisans, sympathisers and residual identifiers.

Green Party added in 1989: - partisans (code 12) 0.3% (n = 8); sympathisers (code 13) 0.3% (n = 9); residual identifiers (code 14) 0.2% (n = 7).

STRENGTH OF PARTY POLITICAL IDENTIFICATION

{IDSTRNG}

Question: [If identifies with any party] **Would you call yourself very strong** ... (quote party named) ... **fairly strong, or not very strong?**

		1983		1984		1985		1986		1987		1989	
		%	No	%	No	%	No	%	No	%	No	%	No
Question No													
Column No											216		223
	Code									2f		2e	
[Not asked: no party identification]	0	-	-	-	-	-	-	-	-	7.5	208	10.0	294
Very strong	1	-	-	-	-	-	-	-	-	11.2	308	11.2	329
Fairly strong	2	-	-	-	-	-	-	-	-	34.9	964	32.9	963
Not very strong	3	-	-	-	-	-	-	-	-	40.1	1108	42.0	1230
(DK)	8	-	-	-	-	-	-	-	-	0.3	8	0.5	15
(NA)	9	-	-	-	-	-	-	-	-	6.1	169	3.4	99
Base: All											2766		2930

INTEREST IN POLITICS

{POLITICS}

Question: **How much interest do you generally have in what is going on in politics** ... (read out) ...

		1983		1984		1985		1986		1987		1989	
		%	No	%	No	%	No	%	No	%	No	%	No
Question No								B82				B96	
Column No								666				1108	
	Code												
... a great deal,	1	-	-	-	-	-	-	7.2	112	-	-	7.3	107
... quite a lot,	2	-	-	-	-	-	-	21.8	338	-	-	20.2	295
... some,	3	-	-	-	-	-	-	31.1	481	-	-	30.4	444
... not very much,	4	-	-	-	-	-	-	26.7	413	-	-	27.9	407
... or not at all?	5	-	-	-	-	-	-	12.8	198	-	-	13.7	201
(DK)	8	-	-	-	-	-	-	0.3	4	-	-	0.2	3
(NA)	9	-	-	-	-	-	-	0.2	3	-	-	0.3	5
Base: All									1548				1461

1986, 1989 - As first question in this section, introduced by: 'Now I'd like to ask some questions about politics.'

STRENGTH OF FEELING ABOUT POLITICAL PARTIES

{CONFEEL} {LABFEEL} {SDPFEEL} {LIBFEEL} {SNPFEEL} {PCFEEL}

Question: (Show card) **Please choose a phrase from this card to say how you feel about ... (read out):**

		1983		1984		1985		1986		1987		1989	
		%	No	%	No	%	No	%	No	%	No	%	No
Question No								B89a		B84a		B99a	
Column No								727		914		1133	
(i) {CONFEEL}	Code												
The Conservative Party													
Very strongly in favour	1	-	.	-	.	-	.	3.6	56	7.2	99	4.3	63
Strongly in favour	2	-	.	-	.	-	.	6.3	98	9.9	137	7.3	107
In favour	3	-	.	-	.	-	.	22.1	343	22.4	308	28.0	409
Neither in favour nor against	4	-	.	-	.	-	.	20.2	312	21.1	290	20.7	302
Against	5	-	.	-	.	-	.	17.0	263	15.1	208	14.2	207
Strongly against	6	-	.	-	.	-	.	10.5	162	8.8	121	9.0	132
Very strongly against	7	-	.	-	.	-	.	16.6	257	13.0	179	14.4	211
(DK/can't say)	8	-	.	-	.	-	.	3.1	48	1.7	23	1.6	23
(NA)	9	-	.	-	.	-	.	0.6	10	0.7	10	0.6	8
Base: All									1548		1375		1461

		1983		1984		1985		1986		1987		1989	
Question No								B89b		B84b		B99b	
Column No								728		915		1134	
(ii) {LABFEEL}													
The Labour Party													
Very strongly in favour	1	-	.	-	.	-	.	5.6	87	6.1	84	5.0	73
Strongly in favour	2	-	.	-	.	-	.	7.7	120	7.3	100	5.6	82
In favour	3	-	.	-	.	-	.	23.8	368	18.0	247	20.5	300
Neither in favour nor against	4	-	.	-	.	-	.	23.4	363	20.6	284	26.1	381
Against	5	-	.	-	.	-	.	22.0	341	23.2	319	26.4	386
Strongly against	6	-	.	-	.	-	.	7.6	118	12.2	168	8.1	118
Very strongly against	7	-	.	-	.	-	.	6.3	98	9.9	136	5.7	83
(DK/can't say)	8	-	.	-	.	-	.	2.9	44	1.9	26	1.8	26
(NA)	9	-	.	-	.	-	.	0.6	10	0.8	11	0.8	12
Base: All									1548		1375		1461

STRENGTH OF FEELING ABOUT POLITICAL PARTIES (Continued)

		1983		1984		1985		1986		1987		1989	
		%	No	%	No	%	No	%	No	%	No	%	No
Question No								B89c		B84c		B99d	
Column No								729		916		1136	
(iii) {SDPFEEL}	Code												
The Social Democrat Party													
Very strongly in favour	1	-	-	-	-	-	-	1.2	18	1.2	17	0.5	7
Strongly in favour	2	-	-	-	-	-	-	2.5	39	3.2	44	1.3	19
In favour	3	-	-	-	-	-	-	20.0	309	21.8	300	11.0	160
Neither in favour nor against	4	-	-	-	-	-	-	43.6	676	42.9	590	51.6	755
Against	5	-	-	-	-	-	-	18.5	287	17.9	246	21.0	307
Strongly against	6	-	-	-	-	-	-	4.5	69	4.7	65	5.0	73
Very strongly against	7	-	-	-	-	-	-	2.9	45	2.8	39	3.3	48
(DK/can't say)	8	-	-	-	-	-	-	6.2	96	4.6	63	5.9	86
(NA)	9	-	-	-	-	-	-	0.6	10	0.8	11	0.4	7
Base: All									1548		1375		1461

		1983		1984		1985		1986		1987		1989	
Question No								B89d		B84d			
Column No								730		917			
(iv) {LIBFEEL}													
The Liberal Party													
Very strongly in favour	1	-	-	-	-	-	-	1.6	24	1.9	26	-	
Strongly in favour	2	-	-	-	-	-	-	3.8	59	3.7	51	-	
In favour	3	-	-	-	-	-	-	22.7	352	24.0	330	-	
Neither in favour nor against	4	-	-	-	-	-	-	46.0	713	44.0	605	-	
Against	5	-	-	-	-	-	-	14.4	223	16.3	224	-	
Strongly against	6	-	-	-	-	-	-	3.6	55	4.0	55	-	
Very strongly against	7	-	-	-	-	-	-	2.4	38	1.7	23	-	
(DK/can't say)	8	-	-	-	-	-	-	4.9	75	3.5	48	-	
(NA)	9	-	-	-	-	-	-	0.6	10	1.0	13	-	
Base: All									1548		1375		

1989 - {SDPFEEL} Optional probe added: 'SDP (Owen)'; {LIBFEEL} Q asked about 'the Social and Liberal Democrat Party' (see {SLDFEEL} p. C-14 below)

STRENGTH OF FEELING ABOUT POLITICAL PARTIES (Continued)

		1983		1984		1985		1986		1987		1989	
		%	No	%	No	%	No	%	No	%	No	%	No
Question No								B89e		B84e		B99e	
Column No								731		918		1137	
(v) {SNPFEEL}	Code												
[In Scotland] **The Scottish Nationalist Party**													
[Not asked: not Scotland]	0	-	.	-	.	-	.	89.5	1385	91.1	1253	90.1	1316
Very strongly in favour	1	-	.	-	.	-	.	0.4	6	-	.	0.3	4
Strongly in favour	2	-	.	-	.	-	.	0.5	7	0.5	7	0.9	13
In favour	3	-	.	-	.	-	.	2.5	38	2.0	28	3.0	43
Neither in favour nor against	4	-	.	-	.	-	.	3.4	53	2.8	38	3.4	50
Against	5	-	.	-	.	-	.	2.5	39	1.9	27	1.2	17
Strongly against	6	-	.	-	.	-	.	0.4	7	0.8	11	0.5	7
Very strongly against	7	-	.	-	.	-	.	0.4	6	0.6	8	0.2	3
(DK/can't say)	8	-	.	-	.	-	.	0.4	7	0.2	2	0.5	8
(NA)	9	-	.	-	.	-	.	-	.	-	.	0.1	1
Base: All									1548		1375		1461

		1983		1984		1985		1986		1987		1989	
Question No								B89f		B84f		B99f	
Column No								732		919		1138	
(vi) {PCFEEL}	Code												
[In Wales] **Plaid Cymru**													
[Not asked: not Wales]	0	-	.	-	.	-	.	94.7	1466	93.8	1290	94.6	1383
Very strongly in favour	1	-	.	-	.	-	.	0.1	1	0.2	3	0.1	1
Strongly in favour	2	-	.	-	.	-	.	0.1	1	0.1	2	0.1	2
In favour	3	-	.	-	.	-	.	1.3	20	1.1	15	0.8	11
Neither in favour or against	4	-	.	-	.	-	.	1.6	25	2.4	33	2.0	29
Against	5	-	.	-	.	-	.	0.9	15	1.5	20	1.3	19
Strongly against	6	-	.	-	.	-	.	0.2	3	0.3	5	0.3	5
Very strongly against	7	-	.	-	.	-	.	0.9	13	0.4	6	0.5	7
(DK/can't say)	8	-	.	-	.	-	.	0.2	3	-	.	0.3	4
(NA)	9	-	.	-	.	-	.	0.1	1	0.1	2	0.1	1
Base: All									1548		1375		1461

VOTING BEHAVIOUR: PARTY *VERSUS* CANDIDATE

{*VOTERESN*}

Question:　(Show card)　**Which of the four statements on this card comes closest to the way you vote in a general election?**

	Code	1983 %	1983 No	1984 %	1984 No	1985 %	1985 No	1986 %	1986 No	1987 %	1987 No	1989 %	1989 No
Question No		3						B83		B80			
Column No		139						667		908			
I vote for a party, regardless of the candidate	1	57.6	990	-	-	-	-	53.6	829	58.7	807	-	-
I vote for a party, only if I approve of the candidate	2	23.6	407	-	-	-	-	23.1	358	23.2	319	-	-
I vote for a candidate, regardless of of his or her party	3	5.5	94	-	-	-	-	4.4	68	5.1	69	-	-
I do not generally vote at all	4	11.8	203	-	-	-	-	17.0	263	11.7	161	-	-
(Too young/haven't voted yet/ not eligible)	5	0.2	4	-	-	-	-	0.9	13	0.6	9	-	-
(Other answer)	6	0.9	15	-	-	-	-	0.4	6	0.3	4	-	-
(DK)	8	0.2	4	-	-	-	-	0.3	5	0.4	6	-	-
(NA)	9	0.2	3	-	-	-	-	0.3	5	0.1	1	-	-
Base:　All			1719						1548		1375		

1983 - Other answer, code 5; Too young/haven't voted yet/not eligible, code 6

LIKELIHOOD OF VOTING IN NEXT GENERAL ELECTION

{VOTEPROB}

Question: How likely do you think you are to vote in the next general election ... (read out) ...

		1983		1984		1985		1986		1987		1989	
		%	No	%	No	%	No	%	No	%	No	%	No
Question No		4a								B81a			
Column No		140								909			
	Code												
... very likely,	1	69.8	1199	-	-	-	-	-	-	72.3	994	-	-
... quite likely,	2	14.7	252	-	-	-	-	-	-	15.5	213	-	-
... not very likely,	3	6.7	116	-	-	-	-	-	-	4.0	55	-	-
... or not at all likely?	4	8.7	149	-	-	-	-	-	-	7.8	107	-	-
(DK)	8	-	-	-	-	-	-	-	-	0.2	3	-	-
(NA)	9	0.2	3	-	-	-	-	-	-	0.2	3	-	-
Base: All			1719								1375		

_____

1983 - No (DK)

LIKELY VOTING BEHAVIOUR IF PREFERRED PARTY HAS NO CHANCE OF WINNING

{VOTENOCH}

Question: [If likely or quite likely to vote] **Suppose in the next general election the party or candidate you prefer has *no chance* of winning in your constituency, do you think you would ... (read out) ...**

		1983		1984		1985		1986		1987		1989	
		%	No	%	No	%	No	%	No	%	No	%	No
Question No		4b								B81b			
Column No		141								910			
	Code												
[Not asked: not very or not at all likely to vote]	0	15.4	265	-		-		-		11.8	162	-	
... still vote for that party or candidate,	1	73.6	1266	-		-		-		74.1	1019	-	
... vote for another party or candidate,	2	5.4	92	-		-		-		8.9	122	-	
... or not bother to vote at all?	3	3.2	55	-		-		-		3.5	48	-	
(DK)	8	1.9	33	-		-		-		1.0	13	-	
(NA)	9	0.5	9	-				-		0.7	10	-	
Base: All			1719								1375		

1983 - (DK), code 4

COALITION GOVERNMENT

{COALITIN}

Question: **Which do you think is generally better for Britain ... (read out) ...**

		1983		1984		1985		1986		1987		1989	
		%	No	%	No	%	No	%	No	%	No	%	No
Question No		6						B84a		B82a			
Column No		150						668		911			
	Code												
... to have a government formed by one political party,	1	47.1	809	-		-		52.4	812	58.2	801	-	
... or for two or more parties to get together to form a government?	2	48.9	840	-		-		43.0	665	37.3	513	-	
(DK)	8	3.6	62	-		-		3.9	60	3.2	44	-	
(NA)	9	0.5	8	-		-		0.7	11	1.2	17	-	
Base: All			1719						1548		1375		

PARTY GROUPINGS THOUGHT TO PROVIDE BEST GOVERNMENT

{TWOPARTY}

Question: [If thinks government of two or more parties better for Britain] **Which of these party groupings do you think would provide the best government for Britain** ... (read out) ...

		1983		1984		1985		1986		1987		1989	
		%	No	%	No	%	No	%	No	%	No	%	No
Question No								B84b		B82b			
Column No								669		912			
	Code												
[Not asked: thinks it better for Britain to have government formed by one political party]	0	-		-		-		52.4	812	58.2	801	-	-
... Conservative and Alliance,	1	-		-		-		13.3	206	12.3	169	-	-
... Labour and Alliance,	2	-		-		-		13.0	202	13.3	183	-	-
... Conservative and Labour,	3	-		-		-		7.6	118	4.9	67	-	-
... or some other grouping?	4	-		-		-		6.1	94	4.3	58	-	-
(DK)	8	-		-		-		2.9	45	2.5	34	-	-
(NA)	9	-		-		-		4.6	71	4.6	64	-	-
Base: All								1548		1375			

PROPORTIONAL REPRESENTATION

{VOTESYST}

Question: **Some people say that we should change the voting system to allow smaller political parties to get a fairer share of MPs. Others say that we should keep the voting system as it is, to produce more effective government. Which view comes closest to your own** ... (read out) ...

		1983		1984		1985		1986		1987		1989	
		%	No	%	No	%	No	%	No	%	No	%	No
Question No								B85		B83			
Column No								670		913			
	Code												
... that we should change the voting system,	1	-		-		-		32.3	500	30.2	415	-	-
... or keep it as it is?	2	-		-		-		59.7	924	64.1	882	-	-
(DK)	8	-		-		-		7.7	119	5.3	73	-	-
(NA)	9	-		-		-		0.3	5	0.4	5	-	-
Base: All								1548		1375			

POLITICAL PARTIES: EXTREME OR MODERATE

{CONXTRME} {LABXTRME} {ALLXTRME}

Question: On the whole, would you describe ...

			1983		1984		1985		1986		1987		1989	
			%	No	%	No	%	No	%	No	%	No	%	No
Question No					4a				B90a		B85a			
Column No					157				733		920			
(i) {CONXTRME}		Code												
... the *Conservative Party* nowadays as extreme or moderate?														
Extreme	1		-	-	**48.1**	791	-	-	**54.1**	838	**44.1**	607	-	-
Moderate	2		-	-	**36.7**	604	-	-	**35.1**	544	**44.5**	611	-	-
(Neither or both)	3		-	-	**5.5**	90	-	-	**2.8**	43	**2.7**	37	-	-
(DK)	8		-	-	**9.6**	157	-	-	**7.2**	111	**8.2**	112	-	-
(NA)	9		-	-	**0.2**	3	-	-	**0.8**	13	**0.5**	8	-	-
Base: All						1645				1548		1375		

			1983		1984		1985		1986		1987		1989	
Question No					4b				B90b		B85b			
Column No					158				734		921			
(ii) {LABXTRME}														
And the *Labour Party* nowadays, is it extreme or moderate?														
Extreme	1		-	-	**41.1**	677	-	-	**39.5**	611	**51.0**	701	-	-
Moderate	2		-	-	**40.9**	673	-	-	**46.0**	712	**36.9**	507	-	-
(Neither or both)	3		-	-	**6.9**	113	-	-	**5.1**	79	**3.2**	44	-	-
(DK)	8		-	-	**10.9**	180	-	-	**8.5**	132	**8.2**	113	-	-
(NA)	9		-	-	**0.2**	3	-	-	**0.9**	14	**0.8**	11	-	-
Base: All						1645				1548		1375		

			1983		1984		1985		1986		1987		1989	
Question No					4c				B90c		B85c			
Column No					159				735		922			
(iii) {ALLXTRME}														
And the *SDP/Liberal Alliance* nowadays, is it extreme or moderate?														
Extreme	1		-	-	**5.7**	94	-	-	**5.1**	79	**5.4**	74	-	-
Moderate	2		-	-	**55.3**	909	-	-	**72.0**	1115	**75.2**	1034	-	-
(Neither or both)	3		-	-	**8.7**	143	-	-	**4.8**	75	**5.5**	75	-	-
(DK)	8		-	-	**29.9**	492	-	-	**17.0**	264	**13.2**	182	-	-
(NA)	9		-	-	**0.4**	7	-	-	**1.0**	16	**0.7**	10	-	-
Base: All						1645				1548		1375		

POLITICAL PARTIES: GOOD FOR ONE CLASS OR GOOD FOR ALL

{CONCLASS} {LABCLASS} {ALLCLASS}

Question: On the whole, would you describe ...

			1983		1984		1985		1986		1987		1989	
			%	No	%	No	%	No	%	No	%	No	%	No
Question No														
Column No								B90d		B85d			
									736		923			
(i) {CONCLASS}		Code												
... the *Conservative Party* as good for one class, or good for all classes?														
Good for one class	1		-	.	-	.	-	.	64.4	996	57.0	783	-	.
Good for all classes	2		-	.	-	.	-	.	28.4	440	35.7	491	-	.
Neither or both	3		-	.	-	.	-	.	2.6	40	2.0	27	-	.
(DK)	8		-	.	-	.	-	.	3.8	59	4.6	63	-	.
(NA)	9		-	.	-	.	-	.	0.8	12	0.7	10	-	.
Base: All									1548		1375			

			1983		1984		1985		1986		1987		1989	
Question No														
Column No								B90e		B85e			
									737		924			
(ii) {LABCLASS}														
And the *Labour Party,* is it good for one class, or good for all classes?														
Good for one class	1		-	.	-	.	-	.	48.8	756	52.6	723	-	.
Good for all classes	2		-	.	-	.	-	.	39.4	610	31.9	439	-	.
Neither or both	3		-	.	-	.	-	.	6.1	94	7.9	109	-	.
(DK)	8		-	.	-	.	-	.	4.9	76	6.7	93	-	.
(NA)	9		-	.	-	.	-	.	0.8	13	0.8	11	-	.
Base: All									1548		1375			

			1983		1984		1985		1986		1987		1989	
Question No														
Column No								B90f		B85f			
									738		925			
(iii) {ALLCLASS}														
And the *Alliance,* is it good for one class, or good for all classes?														
Good for one class	1		-	.	-	.	-	.	9.9	154	11.0	151	-	.
Good for all classes	2		-	.	-	.	-	.	60.1	930	61.1	841	-	.
Neither or both	3		-	.	-	.	-	.	8.8	137	8.3	114	-	.
(DK)	8		-	.	-	.	-	.	20.4	315	18.9	260	-	.
(NA)	9		-	.	-	.	-	.	0.8	12	0.7	9	-	.
Base: All									1548		1375			

STRENGTH OF FEELING ABOUT THE SOCIAL AND LIBERAL DEMOCRATS

1989   Q.B99c   {SLDFEEL} Column No 1135

(Show card) **Please choose a phrase from this card to say how you feel about the Social and Liberal Democrat Party (Liberal/Democrats)?**

	Code	%	No
Very strongly in favour	1	1.3	19
Strongly in favour	2	2.2	32
In favour	3	14.1	206
Neither in favour nor against	4	49.2	719
Against	5	20.3	297
Strongly against	6	4.3	63
Very strongly against	7	2.7	40
(DK/can't say)	8	5.4	79
(NA)	9	0.4	7
Base : All			1461

NB A similar question was asked about all the other main political parties in 1989 (as it had been in 1986 and 1987, when it was asked about the Social Democrat Party and the Liberal Party separately). See p. C-6 above

VOTING IN THE 1983 GENERAL ELECTION

1987   Q.911a,b   {VOTED83}{PARTY83} Column Nos 1434, 1435-36

{VOTED83} Column No 1434

a) **Talking to people, we have found that a lot of people don't manage to vote. How about you? Did you manage to vote in the last general election in _June 1983_?**

	Code	%	No
Yes, voted	1	75.7	2093
No	2	23.8	659
Refused to say	5	0.0	1
(DK)	8	0.3	7
(NA)	9	0.2	4
Base : All			2766

{PARTY83} Column Nos 1435-36

b) **[If voted] Can you remember, which party did you vote for in the 1983 general election?**
(Interviewer : do not prompt - record exact answer given)

	Code	%	No
[Not asked : did not vote]	0	23.8	659
Conservative	1	32.8	908
Labour	2	25.9	716
(SDP/Liberal) Alliance	3	4.6	127
Liberal	4	6.7	184
SDP/Social Democrat	5	1.0	27
Scottish Nationalist	6	0.5	14
Plaid Cymru	7	0.4	11
Refused to say how voted	95	1.6	44
Refused to say if voted	96	0.0	1
Other party	97	0.3	8
Don't know/can't remember	98	1.8	51
(NA)	99	0.5	14
Base : All			2766

MAIN POLITICAL PARTIES : UNITED OR DIVIDED

1987   Q.B85g-i   {CONDIVD}{LABDIVD}{ALLDIVD}   Column Nos 926-28

		United		Divided		Neither or both		(DK)		(NA)	
	Code	1		2		3		8		9	
		%	No	%	No	%	No	%	No	%	No
g) {CONDIVD} Column No 926 [And] would you describe the *Conservative Party* nowadays as united or divided		61.7	848	28.8	395	0.9	13	7.9	109	0.7	9
h) {LABDIVD} Column No 927 And the *Labour Party*, is it united or divided		15.7	216	76.0	1045	0.9	13	6.6	91	0.7	10
i) {ALLDIVD} Column No 928 And the *Alliance*, is it united or divided		50.0	688	31.1	428	2.8	38	15.3	211	0.7	10

Base : All (n = 1375)

PARENTS' VOTING HABITS

1986   Q.A115a,b/B123a,b   {FVOTED}{MVOTED}   Column Nos 1734-37

{FVOTED} Column Nos 1734-35
a) Do you remember which political party your *father* usually voted for when you were growing up?

{MVOTED} Column Nos 1736-37
b) And your *mother*?

		a) Father {FVOTED}		b) Mother {MVOTED}	
	Code	%	No	%	No
Did not vote	0	1.9	58	3.8	117
Conservative	1	23.1	709	23.8	731
Labour	2	45.1	1382	41.3	1265
Liberal	3	5.1	156	6.2	191
Scottish Nationalist	6	0.2	6	0.2	5
Plaid Cymru	7	0.0	2	0.1	3
Not applicable/not brought up in Britain	94	3.5	107	3.2	98
Refused to disclose	95	0.3	9	0.3	8
Varied	96	0.6	19	0.7	23
Other party	97	0.2	5	0.1	3
Can't remember/DK	98	19.6	600	19.8	606
(NA)	99	0.4	13	0.5	15
Base : All			3066		3066

UNDERSTANDING OF POLITICS AND GOVERNMENT

1986   Q.B92b   *{GOVCOMP}* Column No 742

(Show card) Please choose a phrase from this card to say how much you agree or disagree with the following statement. Sometimes politics and government seem so complicated that a person like me cannot really understand what is going on.

	Code	%	No
Agree strongly	1	17.2	266
Agree	2	51.5	797
Neither agree nor disagree	3	7.1	110
Disagree	4	20.1	311
Disagree strongly	5	2.6	41
(DK)	8	0.8	13
(NA)	9	0.7	11
Base : All			1548

ACCOUNTABILITY OF MPS

1983   Q.7   *{MPVIEWS}* Column No 151

(Show card) When an MP is considering a national issue, whose views do you think he or she should *most* take into account? Choose a phrase from the card.

	Code	%	No
The views of the Party as expressed by the Conferences	1	15.7	270
The views of the local Party	2	8.5	146
The views of his or her constituents	3	57.1	982
The views of fellow MPs in the same Party	4	8.3	142
His or her own views	5	7.3	125
(Other answer)	6	0.9	15
(DK)	8	2.0	34
(NA)	9	0.3	6
Base : All			1719

D Defence and international relations

Table titles and cross references

MEMBERSHIP OF EUROPEAN COMMUNITY AND NATO

{*EEC*} {*NATO*}

Question: Do you think Britain should continue to be a member of the EEC - the Common Market - or should it withdraw?

		1983		1984		1985		1986		1987		1989	
		%	No	%	No	%	No	%	No	%	No	%	No
Question No		14a		9a		4a		4a		4a		4a	
Column No		242		226		217		219		220		229	
(i) {*EEC*}	Code												
Continue	1	52.7	906	47.9	788	55.6	983	61.0	1870	62.6	1733	67.9	1990
Withdraw	2	42.4	729	45.3	746	38.3	678	33.1	1015	31.5	871	26.0	761
(DK)	8	4.8	83	5.9	97	5.8	102	5.6	173	5.7	157	5.8	170
(NA)	9	0.1	1	0.9	14	0.3	6	0.3	8	0.2	5	0.3	10
Base: All			1719		1645		1769		3066		2766		2930

		1983		1984		1985		1986		1987		1989	
Question No		14b		9b		4b		4b		4b		4b	
Column No		243		227		218		220		221		230	

(ii) {*NATO*}

And do you think that Britain should
continue to be a member of NATO - the
North Atlantic Treaty Organisation -
or should it withdraw?

		1983		1984		1985		1986		1987		1989	
Continue	1	79.1	1359	79.2	1304	73.5	1301	75.7	2320	78.9	2181	78.6	2302
Withdraw	2	12.7	218	11.0	181	15.0	266	13.0	398	10.7	297	10.9	318
(DK)	8	8.1	139	8.9	147	10.7	190	11.0	336	10.2	281	10.0	293
(NA)	9	0.1	2	0.9	14	0.7	12	0.4	12	0.3	7	0.6	17
Base: All			1719		1645		1769		3066		2766		2930

1983-1989 inclusive · This series of questions was introduced by: 'Now a few questions about Britain's relationships with other countries.'

BRITAIN'S LINKS WITH WESTERN EUROPE AND USA

{NATION}

Question: On the whole, do you think that Britain's interests are better served by ... (read out) ...

		1983		1984		1985		1986		1987		1989	
		%	No	%	No	%	No	%	No	%	No	%	No
Question No				10		5		5		5		5	
Column No				228		219		221		222		231	
	Code												
... closer links with Western Europe,	1	-	-	52.9	870	47.6	842	55.4	1699	57.1	1580	50.3	1474
... or closer links with America?	2	-	-	21.0	346	18.1	320	18.0	553	18.4	510	17.5	512
(Both equally)	3	-	-	15.6	257	20.1	356	16.5	507	13.7	379	19.6	574
(Neither)	4	-	-	3.2	52	3.5	63	2.6	80	2.5	70	2.9	85
(DK)	8	-	-	7.0	115	10.6	187	7.3	225	8.2	226	9.7	284
(NA)	9	-	-	0.3	5	0.1	2	0.0	2	0.0	1	0.0	1
Base: All					1645		1769		3066		2766		2930

US AND INDEPENDENT NUCLEAR MISSILES IN BRITAIN

{USANUKE} {OWNNUKE}

Question: Do you think that the siting of *American* nuclear missiles in Britain makes Britain a safer or a less safe place to live?

		1983		1984		1985		1986		1987		1989	
		%	No	%	No	%	No	%	No	%	No	%	No
Question No		17a		11a		6a		6a		6a		6a	
Column No		253		229		220		222		223		232	
(i) {USANUKE}	Code												
Safer	1	38.5	661	35.9	590	35.8	633	28.5	874	38.6	1067	35.6	1042
Less safe	2	47.6	818	51.1	841	52.8	934	59.8	1834	49.6	1372	51.5	1510
(No difference)	4	11.7	202	3.0	49	1.6	29	3.0	91	1.9	53	1.6	46
(DK)	8	0.5	8	9.5	156	9.7	171	8.5	261	9.6	267	11.2	329
(NA)	9	1.8	30	0.6	10	0.1	2	0.2	5	0.3	7	0.1	3
Base: All			1719		1645		1769		3066		2766		2930

US AND INDEPENDENT NUCLEAR MISSILES IN BRITAIN (Continued)

		1983		1984		1985		1986		1987		1989	
		%	No	%	No	%	No	%	No	%	No	%	No
Question No		17b		11b		6b		6b		6b		6b	
Column No		254		230		221		223		224		233	

(ii) {OWNNUKE}

And do you think that having our *own* nuclear missiles makes Britain a safer or a less safe place to live in?

	Code	%	No	%	No	%	No	%	No	%	No	%	No
Safer	1	60.5	1039	56.1	923	53.5	947	51.7	1584	58.1	1606	54.7	1604
Less safe	2	28.5	490	32.5	534	34.3	607	37.2	1141	30.9	854	33.8	989
(No difference)	4	9.3	160	1.9	31	1.6	28	2.1	64	1.7	48	1.2	34
(DK)	8	0.3	5	8.8	144	10.2	181	8.8	268	9.0	250	10.2	298
(NA)	9	1.4	24	0.7	12	0.3	6	0.3	8	0.3	8	0.2	5
Base: All			1719		1645		1769		3066		2766		2930

1983 - DK (3)

UNILATERAL *VERSUS* MULTILATERAL NUCLEAR DISARMAMENT

{UKNUCPOL}

Question: (Show card) **Which, if either, of these two statements comes closest to your own opinion on British nuclear policy?**

		1983		1984		1985		1986		1987		1989	
		%	No	%	No	%	No	%	No	%	No	%	No
Question No		17c		12		7		7		7		7	
Column No		255		231		222		224		225		234	

	Code	%	No	%	No	%	No	%	No	%	No	%	No
Britain should *rid* itself of nuclear weapons while persuading others to do the same	1	19.3	331	22.7	373	27.2	481	28.1	860	24.6	681	26.1	764
Britain should *keep* its nuclear weapons until we persuade others to reduce theirs	2	77.5	1332	73.4	1207	67.8	1200	68.7	2106	72.4	2003	71.5	2095
(Neither of these)	3	2.8	48	2.9	48	4.1	72	2.3	71	2.1	57	1.9	56
(DK)	8	0.3	5	0.6	10	0.8	14	0.8	26	0.8	23	0.4	12
(NA)	9	0.2	4	0.4	7	0.2	3	0.1	3	0.1	2	0.1	4
Base: All			1719		1645		1769		3066		2766		2930

ENDORSEMENT OF PARTY DEFENCE POLICIES

{DEFPARTY}

Question: Which political party's views on defence would you say comes *closest* to your own views?

	Code	1983 %	1983 No	1984 %	1984 No	1985 %	1985 No	1986 %	1986 No	1987 %	1987 No	1989 %	1989 No
Question No				13		8		8		8		8	
Column No				232		223		225		226		235	
None	0	-	-	3.2	52	3.9	69	2.8	85	2.4	66	4.3	126
Conservative	1	-	-	40.8	671	32.6	576	34.7	1063	42.6	1178	44.0	1289
Labour	2	-	-	24.2	399	23.7	419	24.0	737	20.1	557	22.9	672
Liberal	3	-	-	4.1	68	4.7	83	4.5	137	4.1	113	3.5	101
SDP/Social Democrat	4	-	-	3.7	60	4.4	77	4.5	138	5.5	152	2.2	65
Alliance (after probe)	5	-	-	1.8	30	1.9	34	1.7	52	3.1	86	-	-
Other party	7	-	-	0.8	14	1.1	20	0.9	28	0.6	18	1.1	32
(DK)	8	-	-	20.7	340	27.2	481	26.7	820	21.3	589	21.7	635
(NA)	9	-	-	0.7	11	0.6	10	0.2	6	0.3	8	0.3	10
Base: All					1645		1769		3066		2766		2930

1989 -   Code 3: Social and Liberal Democrat/Liberal/SLD.   Instruction added: Only code Alliance after probe 'Social and Liberal Democrats or SDP (Owen)?'

USA AND RUSSIA AS THREATS TO WORLD PEACE

{PEACE}

Question: (Show card) Which of the phrases on this card is closest to your opinion about threats to world peace?

	Code	1983 %	No	1984 %	No	1985 %	No	1986 %	No	1987 %	No	1989 %	No
Question No				14		9		9		9		9	
Column No				233		224		226		227		236	
America is a greater threat to world peace than Russia	1	-	-	11.1	183	12.8	226	16.6	508	18.3	507	13.9	407
Russia is a greater threat to world peace than America	2	-	-	25.9	426	23.5	415	18.2	557	17.3	479	16.2	473
Russia and America are equally great threats to world peace	3	-	-	54.0	889	54.8	970	53.9	1653	53.6	1482	46.9	1373
Neither is a threat to world peace	4	-	-	5.1	84	5.9	104	8.6	262	7.9	219	19.5	572
(DK)	8	-	-	3.3	54	2.8	49	2.5	78	2.8	76	3.5	102
(NA)	9	-	-	0.6	10	0.2	4	0.2	7	0.1	4	0.1	3
Base: All					1645		1769		3066		2766		2930

LIKELIHOOD OF NUCLEAR WAR BETWEEN RUSSIA AND THE WEST

{NUCWARI}

Question: How likely do you think it is that there will be a nuclear war between Russia and the West before the end of the century. Is it ...

	Code	1983 %	No	1984 %	No	1985 %	No	1986 %	No	1987 %	No	1989 %	No
Question No						249a						B240a	
Column No						2230						2322	
... very likely,	1	-	-	-	-	5.3	80	-	-	-	-	1.7	21
... quite likely,	2	-	-	-	-	17.7	266	-	-	-	-	5.4	68
... not very likely,	3	-	-	-	-	46.8	704	-	-	-	-	44.8	563
Base: Self-completion questionnaire respondents							1502						1255

1985, 1989 - As the first question in this group of questions, it was introduced by 'Finally some questions about nuclear defence.'
1989 - Q reads: '...end of the century - that is, within the next fifteen years?'

LIKELY CONSEQUENCES FOR BRITAIN OF NUCLEAR WAR

{NUCWAR2}

Question: If there *was* a nuclear war between Russia and the West, which of these statements best describes what you think would happen to Britain? (Please tick one box)

		1983		1984		1985		1986		1987		1989	
		%	No	%	No	%	No	%	No	%	No	%	No
Question No						249b						B240b	
Column No						2231						2323	
	Code												
Battlefield nuclear weapons would be used, but there would be few civilian deaths	1	-	-	-	-	1.8	27	-	-	-	-	3.0	38
Some British cities would be destroyed, but much of the country would pull through	2	-	-	-	-	11.7	176	-	-	-	-	17.3	217
Much or all of Britain would be destroyed	3	-	-	-	-	72.1	1083	-	-	-	-	62.1	779
Can't choose	8	-	-	-	-	13.0	195	-	-	-	-	16.2	204
(NA)	9	-	-	-	-	1.4	21	-	-	-	-	1.4	17
Base: Self-completion questionnaire respondents							1502						1255

CIVIL DEFENCE MEASURES IN THE EVENT OF NUCLEAR WAR

{NUCDEFEN}

Question: At the moment, the British government publishes advice on how people should prepare for survival in the event of a nuclear war. Which of the following statements comes closest to your view on what the government *should* do? (Please tick one box)

		1983		1984		1985		1986		1987		1989	
		%	No	%	No	%	No	%	No	%	No	%	No
Question No						250a						B241a	
Column No						2232						2324	
	Code												
It is pointless for the government to do anything, because so few people would survive	1	-	-	-	-	31.0	466	-	-	-	-	29.3	368
The government should continue only to provide advice on how people can protect themselves	2	-	-	-	-	15.9	239	-	-	-	-	19.4	244
The government should also provide nuclear shelters to increase people's chances of survival	3	-	-	-	-	43.5	653	-	-	-	-	39.7	498
Can't choose	8	-	-	-	-	8.3	125	-	-	-	-	9.8	124
(NA)	9	-	-	-	-	1.2	18	-	-	-	-	1.7	21
Base: Self-completion questionnaire respondents							1502						1255

LIKELIHOOD OF A 'NUCLEAR WINTER'

{NUCWINTR}

Question: Please tick one box to show which is the *closest* to your views about the following statement.

If there was a major nuclear war, it would result in a worldwide 'nuclear winter' with hardly any sunlight and little chance of human survival.

		1983		1984		1985		1986		1987		1989	
		%	No	%	No	%	No	%	No	%	No	%	No
Question No						250b						B241b	
Column No						2233						2325	
	Code												
It is highly exaggerated	1	-	-	-	-	6.4	96	-	-	-	-	5.3	66
It is slightly exaggerated	2	-	-	-	-	12.2	184	-	-	-	-	13.9	175
It is more or less true	3	-	-	-	-	67.1	1007	-	-	-	-	63.3	795
Can't choose	8	-	-	-	-	13.3	200	-	-	-	-	16.1	202
(NA)	9	-	-	-	-	1.0	15	-	-	-	-	1.4	17
Base: Self-completion questionnaire respondents							1502						1255

BRITAIN'S COMPARATIVE INFLUENCE ON WORLD EVENTS

1984   Q.202a-h   *{FRANCINF}{CHINAINF}{EGERMINF}{WGERMINF}{CANADINF}{AUSTINF}{ISRLINF}*
{INDIAINF} Column Nos 1513-20
Now thinking of *influence on world events.* Please tick one box for each country below to show whether it
generally has more influence, about the same amount of influence, or less influence than Britain has nowadays.

	Code	More influence than Britain 1		About the same influence as Britain 2		Less influence than Britain 3		(DK) 8		(NA) 9	
		%	No	%	No	%	No	%	No	%	No
a) *{FRANCINF}* Column No 1513 France		16.0	244	57.5	876	19.0	289	3.4	52	4.1	63
b) *{CHINAINF}* Column No 1514 China		27.0	411	21.8	333	41.9	637	4.0	61	5.3	81
c) *{EGERMINF}* Column No 1515 East Germany		14.3	217	25.1	382	50.3	766	4.3	65	6.1	92
d) *{WGERMINF}* Column No 1516 West Germany		26.7	407	55.7	848	9.8	148	3.7	56	4.1	63
e) *{CANADINF}* Column No 1517 Canada		10.3	157	50.2	764	30.9	471	3.6	54	5.0	76
f) *{AUSTINF}* Column No 1518 Australia		7.1	108	46.6	709	37.4	569	3.7	57	5.2	79
g) *{ISRLINF}* Column No 1519 Israel		19.7	299	20.6	313	50.0	762	4.2	64	5.6	85
h) *{INDIAINF}* Column No 1520 India		4.2	64	14.4	220	73.2	1114	4.0	61	4.2	64

Base : Self-completion respondents (n = 1522)

BRITAIN'S IMPORTANCE AS A WORLD POWER

1984   Q.220(vii)   {BRITPOWR} Column No 1647
[Finally,] please tick one box ... to show how much you agree or disagree with [this statement].

The days when Britain was an important world power are over.

	Code	%	No
Disagree strongly	1	8.6	131
Just disagree	2	17.0	258
Neither agree nor disagree	3	16.6	253
Just agree	4	34.1	520
Agree strongly	5	22.3	340
(DK)	8	0.3	4
(NA)	9	1.1	17
Base : Self-completion respondents			1522

NB This item was part of a battery of eleven questions, all of which except this one, {NEWTECH} (renamed {TECHRICH}) and {EQUALPAY} were repeated between 1985 and 1989. The original question wording invited respondents to 'tick one box for each statement below'.

IMPORTANCE OF CLOSE LINKS WITH OTHER COUNTRIES

1983   Q.15a-g   {CHINALNK}{SAFRLNK}{RUSIALNK}{BRAZLLNK}{USALNK}{NGERALNK}{SAUDILNK}
Column Nos 244-50
(Show card) For each of these countries, please use the card to show how important or unimportant you think it is for Britain to have close links with that country. First, how important is it for Britain to have close links with ... (read out):

		Not at all important		Not very important		Quite important		Very important		(NA)		(DK)	
	Code	1		2		3		4		9		0	
		%	No	%	No	%	No	%	No	%	No	%	No
a) {CHINALNK} Column No 244 China		5.6	97	24.5	421	42.7	733	21.9	377	0.1	1	5.2	90
b) {SAFRLNK} Column No 245 South Africa		13.1	226	35.9	617	32.4	557	12.8	221	0.1	2	5.6	97
c) {RUSIALNK} Column No 246 Russia		15.7	270	17.1	293	35.1	604	29.2	502	0.1	1	2.8	48
d) {BRAZLLNK} Column No 247 Brazil		13.0	224	42.4	730	28.8	494	6.9	119	0.3	5	8.6	147
e) {USALNK} Column No 248 USA		1.3	23	3.1	54	28.3	486	65.7	1130	0.1	2	1.4	24
f) {NGERALNK} Column No 249 Nigeria		12.2	210	38.7	665	31.2	536	8.6	148	0.1	2	9.2	158
g) {SAUDILNK} Column No 250 Saudi Arabia		5.2	90	13.9	239	44.4	763	31.7	544	0.1	2	4.8	82

Base : All (n = 1719)

ADMIRATION FOR OTHER COUNTRIES

1983   Q.201a-1   *{USSRAD}{FRANCEAD}{USAAD}{ISRAELAD}{HOLANDAD}{NIGERIAD}{WGERMAD}{BRITAD}*
{SAFRAD}, {BRAZILAD}{SAUDIAAD}{CHINAAD}   Column Nos 1007-18
Please tick one box for each country below to show how much or how little, in general, you admire that country.

	Code	Don't admire at all 1 % No	Don't admire much 2 % No	Quite admire 3 % No	Admire very much 4 % No	(DK) 8 % No	(NA) 9 % No
a) *{USSRAD}* Column No 1007 **Russia**		49.5 797	33.8 543	11.4 183	1.2 19	0.1 1	4.1 66
b) *{FRANCEAD}* Column No 1008 **France**		15.8 254	41.2 663	33.7 543	4.3 69	0.1 1	5.0 80
c) *{USAAD}* Column No 1009 **USA**		5.0 81	21.4 345	49.2 793	20.6 332	0.1 1	3.6 59
d) *{ISRAELAD}* Column No 1010 **Israel**		21.8 351	38.6 621	25.4 409	8.7 139	0.1 2	5.4 88
e) *{HOLANDAD}* Column No 1011 **Holland**		4.5 73	17.6 284	56.6 912	15.3 247	0.3 5	5.6 90
f) *{NIGERIAD}* Column No 1012 **Nigeria**		29.1 468	49.1 791	12.8 206	1.3 20	0.2 4	7.5 121
g) *{WGERMAD}* Column No 1013 **West Germany**		8.6 138	17.9 288	51.3 825	17.5 282	0.1 2	4.6 74
h) *{BRITAD}* Column No 1014 **Britain**		1.3 21	6.4 103	31.3 504	58.4 940	0.1 1	2.5 40
i) *{SAFRAD}* Column No 1015 **South Africa**		37.6 605	37.6 606	16.4 264	3.2 51	0.2 4	5.0 80
j) *{BRAZILAD}* Column No 1016 **Brazil**		26.9 433	48.1 775	16.6 267	1.9 31	0.4 7	6.0 96
k) *{SAUDIAAD}* Column No 1017 **Saudi Arabia**		23.8 384	39.0 628	26.4 425	4.9 78	0.3 6	5.6 89
l) *{CHINAAD}* Column No 1018 **China**		18.3 294	32.8 527	36.1 581	8.2 133	0.2 3	4.4 72

Base : Self-completion respondents (n = 1610)

E Northern Ireland and the troubles

Table titles and cross references

LONG-TERM POLICY FOR NORTHERN IRELAND

{NIRELAND}

Question: Do you think the long term policy for Northern Ireland should be for it ... (read out) ...

	Code	1983 %	1983 No	1984 %	1984 No	1985 %	1985 No	1986 %	1986 No	1987 %	1987 No	1989 %	1989 No
Question No		16a		15a				10a		10a		10a	
Column No		251		234				227		228		237	
... to remain part of the United Kingdom,	1	28.5	489	26.7	440	-	-	26.5	813	26.8	741	30.1	882
... or to reunify with the rest of Ireland?	2	57.9	994	57.7	950	-	-	56.7	1738	57.0	1576	54.8	1605
(Northern Ireland should be an independent state)	3	1.1	19	1.2	20	-	-	1.3	39	0.7	21	0.3	9
(Northern Ireland should be split into two)	4	0.1	1	-	-	-	-	0.1	3	0.0	1	0.1	2
(It is up to the Irish to decide)	5	-		-		-	-	4.7	145	4.1	114	4.2	123
(Other answer)	7	6.5	111	6.2	101	-	-	1.9	59	1.4	39	1.1	33
(DK)	8	5.8	99	7.3	120	-	-	8.3	255	9.5	263	8.7	255
(NA)	9	0.3	4	0.9	14	-	-	0.5	15	0.4	11	0.8	22
Base: All			1719		1645				3066		2766		2930

1983 - Other answer (3); Independent state (4); Split in two (5)

1983, 1984 - 'It is up to the Irish to decide' was not coded as a separate other answer

BRITISH ARMY IN NORTHERN IRELAND

{TROOPOUT}

Question: Some people think that government policy towards Northern Ireland should include a complete withdrawal of British troops. Would you personally *support* or *oppose* such a policy? Strongly or a little?

	Code	1983 %	1983 No	1984 %	1984 No	1985 %	1985 No	1986 %	1986 No	1987 %	1987 No	1989 %	1989 No
Question No		16b		15b				10b		10b		10b	
Column No		252		235				228		229		238	
Support strongly	1	37.7	648	37.1	611	-	-	36.9	1131	38.1	1055	38.0	1115
Support a little	2	20.6	355	22.2	365	-	-	22.7	696	23.2	643	21.1	617
Oppose strongly	3	21.5	370	16.5	271	-	-	17.4	533	15.6	432	18.6	544
Oppose a little	4	13.5	231	15.7	259	-	-	14.6	448	15.1	417	15.6	456
(Withdrawal of troops in the long term/not immediately)	5	0.7	12	1.2	20	-	-	1.2	37	0.8	23	0.4	12
(It is up to the Irish to decide)	6	-	-	-	-	-	-	-	-	0.4	10	0.4	13
(Other answer)	7	2.0	35	2.6	43	-	-	1.9	58	0.7	18	0.9	26
(DK)	8	3.8	66	3.9	65	-	-	4.8	146	5.7	157	4.4	130
(NA)	9	0.1	2	0.7	12	-	-	0.6	17	0.4	11	0.6	17
Base: All			1719		1645				3066		2766		2930

1983 - Other answer (5); Withdrawal of troops in long term (6)

1983, 1984 - 'It is up to the Irish to decide' was not coded as a separate other answer

PERCEIVED EXTENT OF RELIGIOUS PREJUDICE IN NORTHERN IRELAND

1989   Qs.B101,B102   *{PREJRC}{PREJPROT}* Column No 1208,1211

Q.B101   *{PREJRC}* Column No 1208
Thinking of *Catholics* - do you think there is a lot of prejudice against them in Northern Ireland nowadays,
a little, or hardly any?

Q.B102   *{PREJPROT}* Column No 1211
And now, thinking of *Protestants* - do you think there is a lot of prejudice against them in Northern Ireland
nowadays, a little, or hardly any?

	Code	Q.B101 *{PREJRC}*		Q.B102 *{PREJPROT}*	
		%	No	%	No
A lot	1	58.3	852	51.8	757
A little	2	22.3	325	24.8	363
Hardly any	3	5.7	83	9.3	136
(DK)	8	13.2	193	13.5	198
(NA)	9	0.6	9	0.6	9
Base : All			1461		1461

NB   As the first in this module, the question was preceded by: 'Now I would like to ask some questions about religion and religious prejudice'

COMMUNITY RELATIONS IN NORTHERN IRELAND

1989   Q.B104a-c   *{RLRELAGO}{RLRELFUT}{RELGALWY}* Column Nos 1215-17

1989   Q.B104a   *{RLRELAGO}* Column No 1215
What about *relations* between Protestants and Catholics in Northern Ireland? Would you say they are *better* than they
were 5 years ago, *worse*, or about the *same* now as then? (Interviewer : if 'it depends', probe before coding)

	Code	%	No
Better [than they were]	1	13.7	201
Worse [than they were]	2	26.3	384
About the same	3	51.0	745
Other answer	7	0.1	2
(DK)	8	8.1	119
(NA)	9	0.7	11
Base : All			1461

1989   Q.B104b   *{RLRELFUT}* Column No 1216
And what about in 5 years time? Do you think relations between Protestants and Catholics will be *better* than now,
worse than now, or about the *same* as now? (Interviewer: if 'it depends', probe before coding)

	Code	%	No
Better than now	1	13.7	200
Worse than now	2	19.4	283
About the same	3	55.2	806
Other answer	7	0.3	5
(DK)	8	10.7	156
(NA)	9	0.8	12
Base : All			1461

COMMUNITY RELATIONS IN NORTHERN IRELAND (continued)

1989   Q.B104c   *{RELGALWY}*   Column No 1217

Do you think that religion will *always* make a difference to the way people feel about each other in Northern Ireland?

	Code	%	No
Yes	1	86.2	1260
No	2	7.3	106
Other answer	3	1.3	19
(DK)	8	4.5	66
(NA)	9	0.8	11
Base : All			1461

BRITAIN AND THE IRISH REPUBLIC : TAKING SIDES

1989   Q.B107   *{BRTIRSDE}*   Column No 1270

When there is an argument between the British and the Republic of Ireland, do you generally find yourself on the side of the British or of the Irish government?   (Interviewer : probe before coding 'it depends')

	Code	%	No
Generally British government	1	59.2	866
Generally Irish government	2	5.2	76
It depends (after probe)	3	11.2	164
(Neither)	4	12.9	189
(DK)	8	10.7	156
(NA)	9	0.7	11
Base : All			1461

LIKELIHOOD OF A UNITED IRELAND

1989   Q.B108   *{UNTDIREL}*   Column No 1271

At any time in the next 20 years, do you think it is likely or unlikely that there will be a united Ireland? (Interviewer : probe: 'very *likely/unlikely*' or 'quite *likely/unlikely*'?)

	Code	%	No
Very likely	1	3.4	49
Quite likely	2	14.9	217
Quite unlikely	3	26.9	393
Very unlikely	4	41.9	612
(Even chance)	5	1.9	28
(DK)	8	10.3	151
(NA)	9	0.7	11
Base : All			1461

CONFIDENCE IN CONSTITUTIONAL ARRANGEMENTS FOR NORTHERN IRELAND

1989   Q.B109a-c   {GOVINTNI}{STRINTNI}{IREINTNI} Column Nos 1272-74

	Code	Just about always 1		Most of the time 2		Only some of the time 3		Rarely 4		Never 5		(DK) 8		(NA) 9	
		%	No	%	No	%	No	%	No	%	No	%	No	%	No
a) {GOVINTNI} Column No 1272 Under direct rule from Britain, as now, how much do you generally trust *British governments* of *any* party to act in the best interests of Northern Ireland?		5.9	86	33.9	496	35.9	524	9.4	138	3.0	44	11.2	163	0.7	11
b) {STRINTNI} Column No 1273 If there was self-rule, how much do you think you would generally trust a *Stormont government* in Belfast to act in the best interests of Northern Ireland?		4.8	71	30.1	440	29.3	429	10.9	159	4.5	65	19.6	286	0.7	11
c) {IREINTNI} Column No 1274 And if there was a united Ireland, how much do you think you would generally trust an *Irish government* to act in the best interests of Northern Ireland?		5.6	82	29.8	436	30.0	438	9.8	143	5.2	76	18.8	274	0.8	12

Base : All (n = 1461)

IMPROVING COMMUNITY RELATIONS IN NORTHERN IRELAND

1989   Q.B232   {PROTRCMX} Column No 2245

Some people think that better relations between Protestants and Catholics in Northern Ireland will only come about through more *mixing* of the two communities. Others think that better relations will only come about through more *separation.* Which comes closest to your views ... (please tick one box) ...

	Code	%	No
... better relations will come about through more *mixing,*	1	88.3	1108
[or,] better relations will come about through more *separation?*	2	7.5	94
(DK)	8	1.6	20
(NA)	9	2.6	33
Base: Self-completion respondents			1255

EXPERIENCE OF LIVING IN IRELAND

1989   Q.B915a,b   *{EVRLIVNI}{EVRLIVER}* Column Nos 1708-09

1989   Q.B915a   *{EVRLIVNI}* Column No 1708
Have you *ever* lived in Northern Ireland for more than one year?

	Code	%	No
Yes	1	2.8	41
No	2	97.1	1419
(NA)	9	0.1	1
Base : All			1461

1989   Q.B915b   *{EVRLIVER}* Column No 1709
And have you *ever* lived in the Republic of Ireland for more than one year?

	Code	%	No
Yes	1	2.5	36
No	2	96.1	1404
(NA)	9	1.5	21
Base : All			1461

EXPERIENCE OF VISITING IRELAND

1989   Q.B916a,b   *{EVRVISNI}{EVRVISER}* Column Nos 1710-11

1989   Q.B916a   *{EVRVISNI}* Column No 1710
(Show card) In the last 5 years, have you visited Northern Ireland? (If yes) Please tell me from this card how often?

	Code	%	No
No, never visited	1	94.2	1377
Yes, once only	2	3.2	47
Yes, a few times	3	1.8	26
Yes, many times	4	0.5	8
Lived there	5	0.1	1
(NA)	9	0.2	2
Base : All			1461

1989   Q.B916b   *{EVRVISER}* Column No 1711
(Show card) And in the last 5 years, have you visited the Republic of Ireland? (If yes) Please tell me from this card how often?

	Code	%	No
No, never visited	1	92.7	1355
Yes, once only	2	3.5	51
Yes, a few times	3	2.6	38
Yes, many times	4	0.9	14
Lived there	5	-	-
(NA)	9	0.2	4
Base : All			1461

F Economic issues: income inequality, taxes and public spending

Table titles and cross references

Page

Page

Page

EXPECTATIONS FOR INFLATION AND UNEMPLOYMENT IN YEAR AHEAD

{PRICES} {UNEMP}

Question: Now I would like to ask you about two of Britain's economic problems - *inflation* and *unemployment*.

First, inflation: in a year from now, do you expect prices generally to have gone up, to have stayed the same, or to have gone down?

[If gone up or gone down] By **a lot** or **a little**?

		1983 %	1983 No	1984 %	1984 No	1985 %	1985 No	1986 %	1986 No	1987 %	1987 No	1989 %	1989 No
Question No		18		16a		10		11		11		11	
Column No		256		237		225		231		231		241	
(i) *{PRICES}*	Code												
To have gone up by a lot	1	24.3	419	31.2	513	40.0	708	25.8	791	26.2	726	44.6	1306
To have gone up by a little	2	55.8	959	51.7	851	47.9	847	49.0	1501	52.4	1450	43.4	1273
To have stayed the same	3	12.3	211	12.8	211	8.2	145	17.3	532	16.5	456	7.6	224
To have gone down by a little	4	4.7	81	2.6	42	2.3	40	5.8	179	2.8	78	3.1	92
To have gone down by a lot	5	0.6	10	0.2	3	0.5	10	0.6	18	0.2	6	0.4	11
(DK)	8	2.1	37	1.5	24	0.9	16	1.4	43	1.8	49	0.8	24
(NA)	9	0.1	2	0.1	1	0.2	3	0.1	2	0.1	2	0.1	2
Base: All			1719		1645		1769		3066		2766		2930

		1983		1984		1985		1986		1987		1989	
Question No		19		17		11		12		12		12	
Column No		257		241		226		232		232		242	
(ii) *{UNEMP}*													

Second, unemployment: in a year from now, do you expect unemployment to have gone up, to have stayed the same, or to have gone down? [If gone up or gone down] By **a lot** or **a little**?

		1983 %	1983 No	1984 %	1984 No	1985 %	1985 No	1986 %	1986 No	1987 %	1987 No	1989 %	1989 No
To have gone up by a lot	1	31.2	536	24.7	406	33.3	590	28.8	884	16.8	466	9.5	279
To have gone up by a little	2	36.6	630	30.5	503	33.7	595	36.5	1118	23.4	647	15.9	467
To have stayed the same	3	17.3	297	30.8	506	22.6	399	25.0	766	31.8	879	37.3	1092
To have gone down by a little	4	12.5	214	11.3	186	7.8	138	6.7	205	22.6	625	30.0	880
To have gone down by a lot	5	0.9	15	1.1	19	1.2	21	1.1	34	2.2	61	4.8	139
(DK)	8	1.5	27	1.5	25	1.5	26	1.8	54	3.1	86	2.4	71
(NA)	9	0.1	1	0.1	1	-	-	0.1	4	0.1	2	0.0	1
Base: All			1719		1645		1769		3066		2766		2930

1983 - (DK), code 6

HIGHEST PRIORITY FOR GOVERNMENT: INFLATION OR UNEMPLOYMENT

{UNEMPINF}

Question: If the government *had* to choose between keeping down inflation or keeping down unemployment, to which do you think it should give highest priority?

			1983		1984		1985		1986		1987		1989	
			%	No	%	No	%	No	%	No	%	No	%	No
Question No			20		18a		12a		13a		13a		13a	
Column No			258		242		227		233		233		243	
		Code												
Keeping down inflation	1		27.0	464	26.2	430	21.5	381	20.1	615	23.2	642	38.5	1130
Keeping down unemployment	2		69.3	1191	68.9	1134	72.9	1289	74.8	2294	72.6	2008	56.7	1661
(Both equally/can't separate)	3		1.5	25	1.7	27	3.0	53	2.9	88	2.2	62	2.4	70
(Other answer)	7		0.7	11	0.5	9	0.3	6	0.2	6	0.1	2	0.2	5
(DK)	8		1.6	27	2.0	33	1.5	27	1.6	49	1.4	37	1.5	43
(NA)	9		-	-	0.7	12	0.8	14	0.4	14	0.5	15	0.8	22
Base: All				1719		1645		1769		3066		2766		2930

1983 - (Other answer), code 3; (Both equally/can't separate), code 4

PROBLEM OF MOST CONCERN: INFLATION OR UNEMPLOYMENT

{CONCERN}

Question: Which do you think is of most concern to *you and your family* ... (read out) ...

			1983		1984		1985		1986		1987		1989	
			%	No	%	No	%	No	%	No	%	No	%	No
Question No					18b		12b		13b		13b		13b	
Column No					243		228		234		234		245	
		Code												
... inflation,	1		-	-	51.6	849	50.5	893	50.5	1548	54.5	1508	66.5	1947
... or unemployment?	2		-	-	44.4	731	44.2	782	44.5	1364	41.4	1145	29.8	874
(Both equally/can't separate)	3		-	-	1.9	31	3.1	54	2.0	62	2.0	55	1.5	44
(Neither a threat)	4		-	-	0.6	10	0.4	7	0.7	21	0.5	14	0.2	6
(Other answer)	7		-	-	0.1	2	0.1	2	0.0	2	0.1	2	0.1	3
(DK)	8		-	-	1.2	20	1.3	23	1.3	39	1.3	36	1.2	34
(NA)	9		-	-	0.2	3	0.4	7	1.0	31	0.2	7	0.8	23
Base: All						1645		1769		3066		2766		2930

EXPECTATIONS FOR BRITAIN'S INDUSTRIAL PERFORMANCE

{INDUSTRY}

Question: Looking ahead over the next year, do you think Britain's general industrial performance will improve, stay much the same, or decline?

[If improve or decline] By a lot or a little?

			1983		1984		1985		1986		1987		1989	
			%	No	%	No	%	No	%	No	%	No	%	No
	Question No		21		19		13		14		14		14	
	Column No		259		244		229		235		235		245	
		Code												
Improve a lot		1	4.8	82	4.1	68	3.4	60	3.0	92	6.8	188	4.9	144
Improve a little		2	39.4	678	33.8	555	24.5	434	21.9	671	28.7	795	24.7	725
Stay much the same		3	33.6	578	40.6	668	44.3	784	46.6	1430	40.6	1124	47.0	1377
Decline a little		4	12.7	219	11.2	184	15.3	271	15.9	487	11.5	319	12.4	363
Decline a lot		5	4.0	69	4.4	73	5.9	104	7.0	214	5.6	155	4.3	127
DK		8	5.5	94	5.7	94	6.5	115	5.5	169	6.5	180	6.5	192
(NA)		9	-	-	0.1	2	0.1	1	0.1	2	0.2	5	0.1	3
Base: All				1719		1645		1769		3066		2766		2930

1983 - (DK), code 6

POLICIES TO HELP BRITAIN'S ECONOMIC PROBLEMS - 1

{ECOHELP1} {ECOHELP2} {ECOHELP3} {ECOHELP4} {ECOHELPC} {ECOHELP5} {ECOHELP6} {ECOHELP7} {ECOHELP8} {ECOHELP9}

Question: Here are a number of policies which might help Britain's economic problems. As I read them out, will you tell me whether you would support such a policy or oppose it?

			1983		1984		1985		1986		1987		1989	
			%	No	%	No	%	No	%	No	%	No	%	No
	Question No		23(i)		20(i)		14(i)		15(i)		15(i)		15(i)	
	Column No		270		245		230		236		236		246	
		Code												

(i) {ECOHELP1}

Control of *wages* by law

			1983		1984		1985		1986		1987		1989	
Support		1	47.7	819	41.8	688	38.6	682	39.5	1212	34.2	946	27.7	811
Oppose		2	48.5	833	53.4	879	55.7	985	55.6	1704	60.1	1661	68.5	2009
(DK)		8	3.4	59	4.1	68	5.4	95	4.6	142	5.5	153	3.3	98
(NA)		9	0.4	8	0.7	11	0.4	7	0.2	8	0.2	5	0.4	13
Base: All				1719		1645		1769		3066		2766		2930

POLICIES TO HELP BRITAIN'S ECONOMIC PROBLEMS - 1 (Continued)

		1983		1984		1985		1986		1987		1989	
		%	No	%	No	%	No	%	No	%	No	%	No
Question No		23(ii)		20(ii)		14(ii)		15(ii)		15(ii)		15(ii)	
Column No	Code	271		246		231		237		237		247	

(ii) {ECOHELP2}
Control of *prices* by law

	Code	%	No	%	No	%	No	%	No	%	No	%	No
Support	1	70.3	1208	66.1	1088	63.8	1128	60.5	1855	57.9	1600	55.5	1626
Oppose	2	27.2	467	30.0	493	31.9	564	35.4	1085	37.6	1039	42.0	1231
(DK)	8	2.3	40	3.5	57	4.0	72	3.8	115	4.4	122	2.2	65
(NA)	9	0.2	3	0.4	7	0.3	5	0.3	11	0.1	4	0.3	8
Base: All			1719		1645		1769		3066		2766		2930

		1983		1984		1985		1986		1987		1989	
Question No		23(iii)		20(iii)		14(iii)		15(iii)		15(iii)		15(iii)	
Column No		272		247		232		238		238		248	

(iii) {ECOHELP3}
Reducing the level of government
spending on health and education

	Code	%	No	%	No	%	No	%	No	%	No	%	No
Support	1	13.3	229	11.3	185	9.7	172	8.6	263	7.1	196	6.8	198
Oppose	2	85.2	1464	86.9	1430	88.8	1571	89.8	2753	91.5	2531	92.1	2699
(DK)	8	1.0	17	1.2	19	1.2	21	1.4	42	1.0	28	0.8	23
(NA)	9	0.4	8	0.7	12	0.3	6	0.3	8	0.4	11	0.4	11
Base: All			1719		1645		1769		3066		2766		2930

		1983		1984		1985		1986		1987		1989	
Question No		23(iv)		20(iv)		14(iv)		15(iv)		15(iv)		15(iv)	
Column No		273		248		233		239		239		249	

(iv) {ECOHELP4} {ECOHELPC}
Introducing import controls

	Code	%	No	%	No	%	No	%	No	%	No	%	No
Support	1	71.8	1235	67.1	1105	67.2	1190	67.1	2057	68.3	1890	67.2	1969
Oppose	2	23.6	405	26.5	436	25.0	442	25.1	769	23.1	638	28.3	828
(DK)	8	4.4	76	5.7	93	7.5	132	7.4	226	8.2	227	4.0	119
(NA)	9	0.2	3	0.7	11	0.3	6	0.5	15	0.4	10	0.5	14
Base: All			1719		1645		1769		3066		2766		2930

1983-1987 inclusive - {ECOHELP1} Control of wages by legislation; {ECOHELP2} Control of prices by legislation

1989 - {ECOHELP4}: question changed to 'Government controls to cut down goods from abroad'. Variable name is {ECOHELPC} for 1989. Since the responses seem broadly comparable over time, the 1989 data are shown here alongside those from earlier years

POLICIES TO HELP BRITAIN'S ECONOMIC PROBLEMS - 1 (Continued)

		1983		1984		1985		1986		1987		1989	
		%	No	%	No	%	No	%	No	%	No	%	No
Question No		23(v)		20(v)		14(v)		15(v)		15(v)		15(v)	
Column No		274		249		234		240		240		250	

(v) {ECOHELP5}
Increasing government subsidies
for private industry

	Code	1983 %	No	1984 %	No	1985 %	No	1986 %	No	1987 %	No	1989 %	No
Support	1	63.8	1097	60.0	988	61.3	1085	61.0	1871	59.7	1652	52.8	1547
Oppose	2	30.7	527	32.6	536	31.3	554	31.2	957	31.0	859	39.6	1159
(DK)	8	5.0	86	6.5	107	7.0	123	7.2	222	8.9	246	7.1	209
(NA)	9	0.5	9	0.9	14	0.4	7	0.5	16	0.3	8	0.5	15
Base: All			1719		1645		1769		3066		2766		2930

		1983	1984	1985	1986	1987
Question No		23(vi)	20(vi)	14(vi)	15(vi)	15(vi)
Column No		275	250	235	241	241

(vi) {ECOHELP6}
Devaluation of the pound

	Code	1983 %	No	1984 %	No	1985 %	No	1986 %	No	1987 %	No	1989 %	No
Support	1	16.3	281	12.6	207	10.9	193	11.8	362	10.3	284	-	-
Oppose	2	71.0	1221	73.7	1212	74.1	1311	71.9	2203	71.7	1982	-	-
(DK)	8	12.3	211	12.7	209	14.3	252	15.3	468	17.1	474	-	-
(NA)	9	0.4	7	1.1	18	0.7	13	1.0	32	0.9	26	-	-
Base: All			1719		1645		1769		3066		2766		

		1983	1984	1985	1986	1987	1989
Question No		23(vii)	20(vii)	14(vii)	15(vii)	15(vii)	15(vi)
Column No		276	251	236	242	242	251

(vii) {ECOHELP7}
Reducing government spending
on defence

	Code	1983 %	No	1984 %	No	1985 %	No	1986 %	No	1987 %	No	1989 %	No
Support	1	43.8	754	51.4	845	53.8	951	54.9	1685	51.5	1425	55.6	1630
Oppose	2	53.0	910	44.8	737	41.9	741	41.0	1257	44.3	1225	40.4	1183
(DK)	8	3.1	53	3.2	52	3.9	69	3.6	111	3.8	105	3.8	111
(NA)	9	0.1	2	0.7	11	0.4	8	0.5	14	0.4	11	0.2	7
Base: All			1719		1645		1769		3066		2766		2930

POLICIES TO HELP BRITAIN'S ECONOMIC PROBLEMS - 1 (Continued)

			1983		1984		1985		1986		1987		1989	
			%	No	%	No	%	No	%	No	%	No	%	No
	Question No		23(viii)		20(viii)		14(viii)		15(viii)		15(viii)		15(vii)	
	Column No		277		252		237		243		243		252	
(viii) {ECOHELP8}		Code												
Government schemes to encourage job sharing														
	Support	1	61.4	1056	60.4	994	60.4	1069	64.1	1964	61.9	1711	67.3	1972
	Oppose	2	34.5	594	34.5	567	34.1	602	30.1	922	32.0	884	26.9	789
	(DK)	8	3.7	63	4.5	74	5.2	92	5.5	169	6.0	167	5.2	153
	(NA)	9	0.4	7	0.6	11	0.3	6	0.4	11	0.1	4	0.6	16
				1719		1645		1769		3066		2766		2930
Base: All														

			1983		1984		1985		1986		1987		1989	
	Question No		23(ix)		20(ix)		14(ix)		15(ix)		15(ix)		15(viii)	
	Column No		278		253		238		244		244		253	
(ix) {ECOHELP9}														
Government to set up construction projects to create more jobs														
	Support	1	89.3	1535	89.0	1464	90.4	1600	90.6	2778	90.1	2492	86.8	2544
	Oppose	2	8.5	146	8.4	138	7.2	127	7.0	215	7.8	215	11.1	325
	(DK)	8	2.0	34	2.1	34	2.1	37	2.1	66	1.8	50	1.9	54
	(NA)	9	0.2	4	0.6	10	0.3	5	0.2	7	0.3	9	0.2	6
				1719		1645		1769		3066		2766		2930
Base: All														

1983-1987 inclusive - {ECOHELP8} Government incentives to encourage job sharing or splitting

INCOME DISPARITIES

{INCOMGAP}

Question: Thinking of income levels generally in Britain today, would you say that the *gap* between those with high incomes and those with low incomes is ... (read out) ...

		1983		1984		1985		1986		1987		1989	
		%	No	%	No	%	No	%	No	%	No	%	No
Question No		25		22		16		17		18		18	
Column No		307		255		240		246		248		259	
	Code												
... too large,	1	72.3	1243	75.2	1237	77.3	1367	77.8	2385	78.7	2176	79.6	2333
... about right,	2	21.7	373	18.6	307	16.5	292	16.3	500	16.6	460	15.4	450
... or too small?	3	3.1	54	3.6	59	3.9	69	3.4	105	2.1	59	2.6	75
(DK)	8	2.4	41	2.2	35	1.8	32	2.2	68	2.3	63	2.3	68
(NA)	9	0.4	8	0.4	7	0.5	9	0.2	8	0.3	8	0.2	5
Base: All			1719		1645		1769		3066		2766		2930

TAXATION LEVELS FOR DIFFERENT INCOME GROUPS

{TAXHI} {TAXMID} {TAXLOW}

Question: (Show card) Generally, how would you describe *levels of taxation* in Britain today?

		1983		1984		1985		1986		1987		1989	
		%	No	%	No	%	No	%	No	%	No	%	No
Question No		26a						18a		19a		19a	
Column No		308						247		249		260	
(i) {TAXHI}	Code												

Firstly, for those with *high* incomes? Please choose a phrase from this card.

Taxes are:													
Much too low	1	5.1	88	-	-	-	-	5.4	165	6.5	180	10.0	293
Too low	2	27.0	465	-	-	-	-	32.0	981	32.2	891	41.7	1223
About right	3	36.3	624	-	-	-	-	35.5	1088	37.3	1033	33.4	979
Too high	4	19.6	337	-	-	-	-	18.0	551	15.9	439	9.2	271
Much too high	5	9.1	157	-	-	-	-	5.2	160	4.8	132	2.4	71
(DK)	8	2.5	43	-	-	-	-	3.9	119	3.2	89	2.9	86
(NA)	9	0.3	5	-	-	-	-	0.1	2	0.1	2	0.3	7
Base: All			1719						3066		2766		2930

TAXATION LEVELS FOR DIFFERENT INCOME GROUPS (Continued)

			1983		1984		1985		1986		1987		1989	
			%	No	%	No	%	No	%	No	%	No	%	No
	Question No		26b						18b		19b		19b	
	Column No	Code	309						248		250		261	

(ii) {TAXMID}

Next, for those with *middle* incomes? Please choose a phrase from this card.

Taxes are:		Code	1983 %	No	1984 %	No	1985 %	No	1986 %	No	1987 %	No	1989 %	No
	Much too low	1	0.4	7	-	-	-	-	0.3	8	0.1	3	0.4	11
	Too low	2	3.9	67	-	-	-	-	4.4	135	4.7	129	6.0	175
	About right	3	49.9	858	-	-	-	-	51.8	1588	56.1	1551	63.8	1870
	Too high	4	35.8	615	-	-	-	-	36.4	1115	32.5	898	25.3	740
	Much too high	5	7.8	134	-	-	-	-	3.8	115	3.7	102	2.1	61
	(DK)	8	2.1	36	-	-	-	-	3.3	102	2.9	80	2.3	68
	(NA)	9	0.1	1	-	-	-	-	0.1	4	0.1	3	0.2	5
Base: All				1719						3066		2766		2930

			1983						1986		1987		1989	
	Question No		26c						18c		19c		19c	
	Column No		310						249		251		262	

(iii) {TAXLOW}

And lastly, for those with *low* incomes? Please choose a phrase from this card.

Taxes are:		Code	1983 %	No	1984 %	No	1985 %	No	1986 %	No	1987 %	No	1989 %	No
	Much too low	1	0.8	13	-	-	-	-	0.6	18	0.5	14	0.8	23
	Too low	2	2.2	39	-	-	-	-	1.7	51	1.4	39	1.7	49
	About right	3	16.2	279	-	-	-	-	14.6	447	14.1	389	15.3	449
	Too high	4	43.6	750	-	-	-	-	52.9	1622	51.3	1420	50.4	1476
	Much too high	5	35.5	610	-	-	-	-	27.7	848	30.2	835	29.4	862
	(DK)	8	1.5	25	-	-	-	-	2.5	78	2.3	63	2.2	65
	(NA)	9	0.2	3	-	-	-	-	0.1	2	0.2	6	0.3	7
Base: All				1719						3066		2766		2930

1983 - {TAXLOW}: SPSS file lists variable name as {TAXLO}

1983-1989 inclusive - Codes 1-5 appear on the questionnaire and show card in the opposite order from that shown above (which corresponds to that in the SPSS file).

1983 - 'Taxes are:' was not printed on the show card

SELF-ASSESSED INCOME GROUP

{SRINC}

Question: Among which group would you place yourself ... (read out) ...

		1983		1984		1985		1986		1987		1989	
		%	No	%	No	%	No	%	No	%	No	%	No
Question No		27a		23a		17a		19a		20a		20a	
Column No		311		256		241		250		252		263	
	Code												
... high income,	1	2.9	49	1.7	28	2.0	35	2.3	69	3.0	82	2.6	75
... middle income,	2	47.1	809	47.8	786	49.2	870	50.7	1555	50.0	1382	52.1	1526
... or low income?	3	49.5	851	49.9	822	48.3	855	46.4	1422	46.4	1283	44.6	1307
(DK)	8	0.3	5	0.3	5	0.1	2	0.3	9	0.2	6	0.3	10
(NA)	9	0.2	4	0.3	4	0.4	8	0.4	12	0.5	13	0.4	13
Base: All			1719		1645		1769		3066		2766		2930

ADEQUACY OF HOUSEHOLD INCOME

{HINCDIFF}

Question: (Show card) Which of the phrases on this card would you say comes closest to your feelings about your household's income these days?

		1983		1984		1985		1986		1987		1989	
		%	No	%	No	%	No	%	No	%	No	%	No
Question No				23b		17b		19b		20b		20b	
Column No				257		242		251		253		264	
	Code												
Living comfortably on present income	1	-	-	23.5	387	21.1	373	24.4	748	25.3	701	27.1	795
Coping on present income	2	-	-	49.9	822	49.8	880	49.4	1514	50.2	1389	49.4	1447
Finding it difficult on present income	3	-	-	17.8	293	19.5	344	18.0	552	18.2	502	17.1	500
Finding it very difficult on present income	4	-	-	7.9	130	9.1	161	7.9	242	6.0	167	6.1	179
(Other answer)	7	-	-	0.2	3	0.2	4	0.1	2	0.1	2	0.1	4
(DK)	8	-	-	0.2	3	0.1	2	0.1	3	0.1	4	0.0	1
(NA)	9	-	-	0.4	7	0.2	4	0.2	6	0.0	1	0.1	3
Base: All					1645		1769		3066		2766		2930

HOUSEHOLD SPENDING POWER IN PAST YEAR

{HINCPAST}

Question: Looking back over the *last year* or so, would you say your household's income has ... (read out) ...

		1983		1984		1985		1986		1987		1989	
		%	No	%	No	%	No	%	No	%	No	%	No
Question No				24a		18a		20a		21a		21a	
Column No				258		243		252		254		265	
	Code												
... fallen behind prices,	1	-	-	46.4	763	55.2	976	47.4	1454	44.5	1232	48.6	1423
... kept up with prices,	2	-	-	43.7	719	36.6	648	41.3	1267	44.2	1223	39.5	1158
... or gone up by more than prices?	3	-	-	7.8	128	6.5	116	9.0	277	9.4	261	10.2	300
(DK)	8	-	-	1.9	31	1.5	26	2.1	64	1.7	48	1.6	47
(NA)	9	-	-	0.2	4	0.2	3	0.1	4	0.1	2	0.1	2
					1645		1769		3066		2766		2930

Base: All

EXPECTATIONS FOR HOUSEHOLD SPENDING POWER IN YEAR AHEAD

{HINCXPCT}

Question: And looking forward to the *year ahead*, do you expect your household's income will ... (read out) ...

		1983		1984		1985		1986		1987		1989	
		%	No	%	No	%	No	%	No	%	No	%	No
Question No				24b		18b		20b		21b		21b	
Column No				259		244		253		255		266	
	Code												
... fall behind prices,	1	-	-	43.2	711	48.8	863	43.5	1333	39.2	1085	44.8	1313
... keep up with prices,	2	-	-	45.1	743	38.9	688	42.8	1312	46.3	1280	41.0	1202
... or go up by more than prices?	3	-	-	7.6	124	8.1	143	8.9	273	9.8	271	9.7	283
(DK)	8	-	-	3.9	64	4.0	71	4.4	135	4.5	125	4.1	121
(NA)	9	-	-	0.2	3	0.3	5	0.4	14	0.2	5	0.4	11
					1645		1769		3066		2766		2930

Base: All

PRIORITIES FOR EXTRA GOVERNMENT SPENDING

{SPEND1} {SPEND2}

Question: (Show card) Here are some items of government spending. Which of them, if any, would be your highest priority for *extra* spending? And which next? Please read through the whole list before deciding.

	Code	1983 %	1983 No	1984 %	1984 No	1985 %	1985 No	1986 %	1986 No	1987 %	1987 No	1989 %	1989 No
Question No		50		57		69		53		57		67	
Column No		471-72		507-08		639-40		531-32		622-23		741-42	

(i) {SPEND1}
First priority

	Code	1983 %	1983 No	1984 %	1984 No	1985 %	1985 No	1986 %	1986 No	1987 %	1987 No	1989 %	1989 No
Education	1	24.3	418	20.0	329	23.4	413	27.0	828	24.1	665	19.1	561
Defence	2	3.5	60	2.5	41	1.9	34	1.1	33	1.2	34	0.8	25
Health	3	36.7	631	50.9	838	46.6	825	47.2	1448	51.6	1426	60.7	1778
Housing	4	7.3	126	5.8	96	8.1	144	7.0	213	8.2	225	6.5	192
Public transport	5	0.9	16	0.4	7	0.7	13	0.4	12	0.4	11	1.0	29
Roads	6	1.8	30	1.1	18	1.5	26	1.2	38	1.1	30	1.8	52
Police and prisons	7	2.5	44	1.4	23	1.9	33	2.6	78	3.6	100	2.2	64
Social security benefits	8	5.6	96	6.7	110	4.8	85	4.5	138	4.4	120	5.0	147
Help for industry	9	15.9	273	9.5	156	9.2	163	8.0	244	4.6	128	2.2	63
Overseas aid	10	0.2	4	0.3	5	1.1	20	0.5	15	0.2	7	0.2	5
(None of these)	11	0.4	6	0.4	6	0.3	6	0.2	7	0.2	7	0.1	3
(DK)	98	0.7	13	0.8	13	0.5	8	0.3	10	0.4	11	0.4	11
(NA)	99	0.1	2	0.3	4	0.0	1	0.1	2	0.0	1	0.0	1
Base: All			1719		1645		1769		3066		2766		2930

1983 - (DK), code 12

PRIORITIES FOR EXTRA GOVERNMENT SPENDING (Continued)

		1983		1984		1985		1986		1987		1989	
		%	No	%	No	%	No	%	No	%	No	%	No
Question No		50		57		69		53		57		67	
Column No		473-74		509-10		641-42		533-34		624-25		743-44	
(ii) *{SPEND2}*	Code												
Second priority													
Education	1	25.9	444	29.0	478	27.4	485	29.9	916	31.4	868	35.5	1041
Defence	2	4.0	70	3.4	57	2.8	50	2.6	79	2.3	63	2.3	66
Health	3	25.9	446	24.8	408	26.7	472	27.5	843	26.9	744	22.6	663
Housing	4	13.1	225	12.1	200	14.7	260	13.8	422	16.0	443	14.8	434
Public transport	5	1.6	28	1.4	24	2.0	36	1.7	52	0.7	20	1.9	56
Roads	6	2.8	49	2.5	41	2.6	46	2.1	63	2.1	57	3.1	90
Police and prisons	7	5.0	86	4.9	81	3.1	54	5.0	153	4.7	130	5.0	146
Social security benefits	8	6.3	109	8.2	135	7.3	130	6.9	212	7.2	200	8.9	262
Help for industry	9	13.0	224	10.4	172	11.0	195	8.4	258	6.8	189	4.7	139
Overseas aid	10	0.6	10	0.7	12	1.0	18	0.9	26	0.7	19	0.4	11
(None of these)	11	0.6	11	0.7	11	0.3	6	0.4	13	0.3	10	0.1	4
(DK)	98	0.9	16	1.6	26	0.9	16	0.8	24	0.7	20	0.6	17
(NA)	99	0.1	2	0.2	3	0.1	2	0.1	4	0.1	2	0.1	2
Base: All			1719		1645		1769		3066		2766		2930

1983 - (DK), code 12

TAXATION *VERSUS* SOCIAL SPENDING

{*TAXSPEND*}

Question: (Show card) **Suppose the government had to choose between the three options on this card. Which do you think it should choose?**

	Code	1983 %	No	1984 %	No	1985 %	No	1986 %	No	1987 %	No	1989 %	No
Question No		54		61		73		57		61		71	
Column No		480		516		648		540		631		750	
Reduce taxes and spend *less* on health, education and social benefits	1	8.6	147	5.5	90	5.6	100	4.8	146	3.4	93	2.7	79
Keep taxes and spending on these services at the *same* level as now	2	54.3	933	49.5	815	43.0	760	43.6	1336	42.2	1166	36.8	1078
Increase taxes and spend *more* on health, education and social benefits	3	32.2	553	39.1	644	45.3	802	46.0	1410	50.1	1385	56.2	1648
(None)	4	1.7	29	1.9	31	3.3	58	3.4	105	2.6	71	2.4	71
(DK)	8	3.1	54	3.7	61	2.7	47	2.1	65	1.7	47	1.8	51
(NA)	9	0.2	3	0.2	3	0.1	2	0.1	4	0.1	4	0.1	2
Base: All			1719		1645		1769		3066		2766		2930

1983 - (DK), code 5

TAXATION OF HIGH AND LOW INCOME GROUPS

{HIGHINC}

Question: Some people think those with high incomes should pay a larger proportion (percentage) of their earnings in taxes than those who earn low incomes. Other people think that those with high incomes and those with low incomes should pay the same proportion (percentage) of their earnings in taxes.
Do you think those with high incomes should ... (please tick one box):

		1983		1984		1985		1986		1987		1989	
		%	No	%	No	%	No	%	No	%	No	%	No
Question No						208		B204					
Column No						2032		2025					
	Code												
... pay a much larger proportion,	1	-	-	-	-	23.6	354	21.1	278	-	-	-	-
... pay a larger proportion,	2	-	-	-	-	50.4	757	55.5	730	-	-	-	-
... pay the same proportion as those who earn low incomes,	3	-	-	-	-	21.9	329	18.7	246	-	-	-	-
... pay a smaller proportion,	4	-	-	-	-	0.8	12	0.6	8	-	-	-	-
... or pay a much smaller proportion?	5	-	-	-	-	0.0	1	0.4	5	-	-	-	-
Can't choose	8	-	-	-	-	2.6	39	2.6	35	-	-	-	-
(NA)	9	-	-	-	-	0.7	10	1.1	14	-	-	-	-
Base: Self-completion questionnaire respondents							1502		1315				

1987 - A similar but shorter question was asked in 1987 (see p.F - 25 below)

FACTORS INFLUENCING CHANCES OF GETTING AHEAD

{RICHFAM} {PROFFAM} {FAMBACK}

Question: Please (tick one box to) **show whether you agree or disagree with each of the following statements.**

		1983		1984		1985		1986		1987		1989	
		%	No	%	No	%	No	%	No	%	No	%	No
Question No						210a		B206a					
Column No						2034		2027					

(i) {RICHFAM}

A person whose parents are rich has a better chance of earning a lot of money than a person whose parents are poor

	Code	1983 %	No	1984 %	No	1985 %	No	1986 %	No	1987 %	No	1989 %	No
Agree strongly	1	-	.	-	.	28.4	426	29.7	391	-	.	-	.
Agree	2	-	.	-	.	42.7	641	39.6	521	-	.	-	.
Neither agree nor disagree	3	-	.	-	.	12.6	189	12.1	159	-	.	-	.
Disagree	4	-	.	-	.	13.0	196	15.1	199	-	.	-	.
Disagree strongly	5	-	.	-	.	1.9	28	2.3	30	-	.	-	.
(DK)	8	-	.	-	.	0.1	1	0.1	1	-	.	-	.
(NA)	9	-	.	-	.	1.4	22	1.1	15	-	.	-	.

Base: Self-completion
       questionnaire respondents

						1985		1986					
							1502		1315				

Question No						210b		B206b					
Column No						2035		2028					

(ii) {PROFFAM}

A person whose father is a professional person has a better chance of earning a lot of money than a person whose parents are poor

	Code	1983 %	No	1984 %	No	1985 %	No	1986 %	No	1987 %	No	1989 %	No
Agree strongly	1	-	.	-	.	21.9	329	23.6	310	-	.	-	.
Agree	2	-	.	-	.	45.1	678	43.0	566	-	.	-	.
Neither agree nor disagree	3	-	.	-	.	16.0	240	14.0	184	-	.	-	.
Disagree	4	-	.	-	.	13.3	199	16.4	216	-	.	-	.
Disagree strongly	5	-	.	-	.	1.8	27	1.9	25	-	.	-	.
(DK)	8	-	.	-	.	0.1	1	0.1	1	-	.	-	.
(NA)	9	-	.	-	.	1.9	28	1.1	14	-	.	-	.

Base: Self-completion
       questionnaire respondents

						1985		1986					
							1502		1315				

FACTORS INFLUENCING CHANCES OF GETTING AHEAD (Continued)

		1983		1984		1985		1986		1987		1989	
		%	No	%	No	%	No	%	No	%	No	%	No
Question No						210c		B206c					
Column No						2036		2029					
(iii) *{FAMBACK}*	Code												

In Britain what you achieve in life depends largely on your family background

	Code	1983 %	No	1984 %	No	1985 %	No	1986 %	No	1987 %	No	1989 %	No
Agree strongly	1	-	-	-	-	16.2	243	13.9	182	-	-	-	-
Agree	2	-	-	-	-	34.9	524	35.3	465	-	-	-	-
Neither agree nor disagree	3	-	-	-	-	17.2	258	19.4	255	-	-	-	-
Disagree	4	-	-	-	-	25.7	386	26.3	346	-	-	-	-
Disagree strongly	5	-	-	-	-	4.1	61	4.0	52	-	-	-	-
(DK)	8	-	-	-	-	0.1	2	0.2	2	-	-	-	-
(NA)	9	-	-	-	-	1.8	28	1.0	14	-	-	-	-
							1502		1315				

Base: Self-completion questionnaire respondents

LEVEL OF HOUSEHOLD TAXATION

{HHTAX}

Question: Do you consider the amount of income tax that your household has to pay is ... (please tick one box)

	Code	1983 %	No	1984 %	No	1985 %	No	1986 %	No	1987 %	No	1989 %	No
Question No						223		B207					
Column No						2123		2030					
... much too high,	1	-	-	-	-	20.4	306	20.3	267	-	-	-	-
... too high,	2	-	-	-	-	34.7	521	41.1	541	-	-	-	-
... about right,	3	-	-	-	-	25.1	377	23.7	312	-	-	-	-
... too low,	4	-	-	-	-	0.5	8	0.2	3	-	-	-	-
... or much too low?	5	-	-	-	-	0.2	3	-		-	-	-	-
Can't choose	8	-	-	-	-	2.8	43	2.0	26	-	-	-	-
Does not apply	6	-	-	-	-	15.1	227	12.4	163	-	-	-	-
(NA)	9	-	-	-	-	1.2	18	0.2	3	-	-	-	-
							1502		1315				

Base: Self-completion questionnaire respondents

LEVEL OF TAXATION OF BUSINESS AND INDUSTRY

{INDTAX}

Question: Do you consider the amount of tax that business and industry have to pay is too high or too low?
(Please tick one box)

		1983		1984		1985		1986		1987		1989	
		%	No	%	No	%	No	%	No	%	No	%	No
Question No						224		B208					
Column No						2124		2031					
	Code												
Much too high	1	-	-	-	-	9.2	138	10.0	131	-	-	-	-
Too high	2	-	-	-	-	30.2	453	37.6	495	-	-	-	-
About right	3	-	-	-	-	30.5	458	28.9	380	-	-	-	-
Too low	4	-	-	-	-	5.6	84	5.3	70	-	-	-	-
Much too low	5	-	-	-	-	1.3	20	0.6	9	-	-	-	-
Can't choose	8	-	-	-	-	22.4	336	17.2	226	-	-	-	-
(NA)	9	-	-	-	-	0.9	14	0.4	5	-	-	-	-
							—		—				
							1502		1315				

Base: Self-completion
questionnaire respondents

POLICIES TO HELP BRITAIN'S ECONOMIC PROBLEMS - 2

1989   Q.15 (ix) (x)   {*ECOHELPA*} {*ECOHELPB*}   Column Nos 254-55
Here are a number of policies which might help Britain's economic problems. As I read them
out, will you tell me whether you would support such a policy or oppose it?

	Code	Support 1		Oppose 2		(DK) 8		(NA) 9	
		%	No	%	No	%	No	%	No
ix) {*ECOHELPA*} Column No 254 Government action to cut interest rates		83.6	2449	11.6	341	4.4	130	0.4	11
x) {*ECOHELPB*} Column No 255 Government controls on hire purchase and credit		79.3	2324	17.2	504	3.3	95	0.3	7

Base : All (n = 2930)

NB These two items were added in 1989 to a list of policies asked about since 1983 (see pp. F-3 to F-6 above)

NORTH/SOUTH DIFFERENCES IN BRITAIN

1987   Q.A210a-e   {*NORSTH1*}-{*NORSTH5*} Column Nos 1557-61
People in Britain often talk about the differences between the North and the South.

1987   Q.A210a   {*NORSTH1*} Column No 1557
How about employment prospects generally - are they ... (please tick one box) ...

	Code	%	No
... better in the North,	1	0.8	10
better in the South,	2	84.1	1046
or - is there no real difference?	3	13.7	170
(DK)	8	0.8	10
(NA)	9	0.7	8
Base : Self-completion respondents			1243

1987   Q.A210b   {*NORSTH2*} Column No 1558
How about people wanting to start up their own businesses - are there ... (please tick one box) ...

	Code	%	No
... more opportunities in the North,	1	5.2	65
more opportunities in the South,	2	53.8	669
or - is there no real difference?	3	38.8	482
(DK)	8	1.3	16
(NA)	9	1.0	12
Base : Self-completion respondents			1243

NORTH/SOUTH DIFFERENCES IN BRITAIN (continued)

1987   Q.A210c   *{NORSTH3}* Column No 1559
How about young people buying their first home - do they have ... (please tick one box) ...

	Code	%	No
... a better chance in the North,	1	50.9	633
a better chance in the South,	2	20.3	252
or - is there no real difference?	3	26.8	333
(DK)	8	1.2	15
(NA)	9	0.8	10
Base : Self-completion respondents			1243

1987   Q.A210d   *{NORSTH4}* Column No 1560
How about standards of education - are they ... (please tick one box) ...

	Code	%	No
... better in the North,	1	6.7	83
better in the South,	2	20.7	257
or - is there no real difference?	3	69.7	867
(DK)	8	1.8	22
(NA)	9	1.1	14
Base : Self-completion respondents			1243

1987   Q.A210e   *{NORSTH5}* Column No 1561
And how about the National Health Service - is it ... (please tick one box) ...

	Code	%	No
... better in the North,	1	5.1	64
better in the South,	2	16.6	206
or - is there no real difference?	3	74.9	931
(DK)	8	2.3	29
(NA)	9	1.0	13
Base : Self-completion respondents			1243

LOCAL GOVERNMENT RATES *VERSUS* SPENDING ON SERVICES

1987   Q.B86   *{RATESERV}* Column No 329
(Show card) Suppose your local council had to choose between the three options on this card.
Which do you think it should choose?

	Code	%	No
Reduce rates and spend *less* on local services	1	12.5	172
Keep rates and spending on these local services at the *same* level as now	2	68.5	942
Increase rates and spend *more* on local services	3	14.5	199
(None)	4	1.7	24
(DK)	8	2.3	31
(NA)	9	0.4	6
Base : All			1375

CHANCES OF IMPROVING STANDARD OF LIVING

1987   Q.B202   {IMPRLIV}   Column No 1722
Please tick a box to show how much you agree or disagree with the following statement. The way things are in Britain, people like me and my family have a good chance of improving our standard of living.

	Code	%	No
Strongly agree	1	4.4	51
Agree	2	31.4	371
Neither agree nor disagree	3	29.1	343
Disagree	4	26.6	314
Strongly disagree	5	5.0	59
Can't choose	8	3.2	38
(NA)	9	0.4	5
Base : Self-completion respondents			1181

INCOME INEQUALITY AS AN INCENTIVE TO WORK

1987   Q.B203   {PAYDIFF}   Column No 1723
Some people earn a lot of money while others do not earn much at all. In order to get people to work hard, do *you* think large differences in pay are ...(please tick one box) ...

	Code	%	No
... absolutely necessary,	1	13.5	159
probably necessary,	2	47.6	563
probably not necessary,	3	21.8	257
[or,] definitely not necessary,	4	12.4	146
Can't choose	8	4.3	50
(NA)	9	0.5	6
Base : Self-completion respondents			1181

NB   {WORKHARD} above and {WORKHARD} at Q.B213 in 1989 relate to different questions. Consequently {WORKHARD} at Q.B213 (1989) has been changed to {PWLWKHRD} (see p. G.2-2 below); and this variable has been changed to {PAYDIFF}

INCENTIVES AND INEQUALITY

1987   Q.B204a-g   {PAYRESP}{PAYQUALS}{INEQRICH}{PAYSTUDY}{DIFFSNEC}{GOODPROF}{INEQJOIN}
Column Nos 1726-32

Do you agree or disagree with each of these statements?   (Please tick one box on each line)

	Code	Strongly Agree 1		Agree 2		Neither agree nor disagree 3		Disagree 4		Strongly disagree 5		Can't choose 8		(NA) 9	
		%	No	%	No	%	No	%	No	%	No	%	No	%	No
a) {PAYRESP} Column No 1726 People would not want to take extra responsibility at work unless they were paid extra for it		22.9	270	58.3	689	8.6	102	8.7	103	0.5	6	0.4	4	0.6	7
b) {PAYQUALS} Column No 1727 Workers would not bother to get skills and qualifications unless they were paid extra for having them		18.6	220	50.4	595	10.7	127	17.7	209	1.8	21	0.3	4	0.5	6
c) {INEQRICH} Column No 1728 Inequality continues because it benefits the rich and powerful		22.6	267	36.0	425	15.9	187	16.5	195	2.5	29	5.3	63	1.2	15
d) {PAYSTUDY} Column No 1729 No-one would study for years to become a lawyer or doctor unless they expected to earn a lot more than ordinary workers		24.3	287	44.5	526	9.4	111	18.5	218	2.1	25	0.6	8	0.5	6
e) {DIFFSNEC} Column No 1730 Large differences in income are necessary for Britain's prosperity		4.3	50	21.6	255	24.0	283	37.7	446	8.5	100	3.4	40	0.5	6
f) {GOODPROF} Column No 1731 Allowing business to make good profits is the best way to improve everyone's standard of living		10.2	121	42.7	505	19.2	226	21.2	250	3.0	36	2.8	33	0.8	9
g) {INEQJOIN} Column No 1732 Inequality continues to exist because ordinary people don't join together to get rid of it		7.8	93	31.3	370	20.7	245	28.2	333	5.4	64	5.6	66	0.9	11

Base : Self-completion respondents (n = 1181)

PERCEPTIONS OF HOW MUCH PEOPLE IN VARIOUS JOBS EARN

1987   Q.B205a-k   {JOBPAY1} - {JOBPAY11} Column Nos 1733-75, 1809-33
We would like to know what *you* think people in these jobs actually earn.
Please write in how much you think they *usually* earn *each year before taxes.*
(Many people are not exactly sure about this, but your best guess will be close enough. This
may be difficult, but it is important, so please try.)

	Median	(DK) %	(DK) No	(NA) %	(NA) No
a) {JOBPAY1} Column Nos 1733-38 First, *about* how much do *you* think a bricklayer earns	£9,000	6.5	76	6.6	78
b) {JOBPAY2} Column Nos 1739-44 A doctor in general practice	£20,000	6.6	78	6.5	77
c) {JOBPAY3} Column Nos 1745-50 A bank clerk	£8,000	6.7	79	6.7	80
d) {JOBPAY4} Column Nos 1751-56 The owner of a small shop	£10,000	7.2	85	7.5	89
e) {JOBPAY5} Column Nos 1757-63 The chairman of a large national company	£60,000	7.1	84	6.9	81
f) {JOBPAY6} Column Nos 1764-69 A skilled worker in a factory	£10,000	6.6	77	6.6	78
g) {JOBPAY7} Column Nos 1770-75 A farm worker	£6,000	6.6	77	6.7	79
h) {JOBPAY8} Column Nos 1809-14 A secretary	£7,000	6.6	78	7.1	84
i) {JOBPAY9} Column Nos 1815-20 A city bus driver	£8,000	6.6	78	6.9	82
j) {JOBPAY10} Column Nos 1821-26 An unskilled worker in a factory	£6,000	6.6	78	6.7	79
k) {JOBPAY11} Column Nos 1827-33 A cabinet minister in the national government	£30,000	6.9	81	7.2	85

Base : Self-completion respondents (n = 1181)

NB (DK), code 999998; (NA), code 999999. At the following question, respondents were asked how much they thought
people in each of these jobs **should** be paid. See {SHDPAY1} - {SHDPAY11} on p. F-23

HOW MUCH PEOPLE IN VARIOUS JOBS OUGHT TO BE PAID

1987   Q.B206a-k   {SHDPAY1} - {SHDPAY11}   Column Nos 1834-76, 1909-33

Next, *what do you think people in these jobs ought to be paid* - how much do you think they *should* earn *each* year *before* taxes, regardless of what they actually get?   (Please write in how much they *should* earn each year before tax)

		Median	(DK)		(NA)	
			%	No	%	No
a) {SHDPAY1} Column Nos 1834-39 First, *about* how much do *you* think a bricklayer *should* earn		£10,000	6.8	80	8.8	104
b) {SHDPAY2} Column Nos 1840-45 A doctor in general practice		£20,000	6.8	80	8.9	105
c) {SHDPAY3} Column Nos 1846-51 A bank clerk, how much *should (he)/ (she)* earn		£8,500	7.0	82	8.9	105
d) {SHDPAY4} Column Nos 1852-57 The owner of a small shop		£11,000	7.4	88	10.0	118
e) {SHDPAY5} Column Nos 1858-64 The chairman of a large national company		£35,000	7.4	87	9.4	110
f) {SHDPAY6} Column Nos 1865-70 A skilled worker in a factory		£10,000	6.9	81	8.9	105
g) {SHDPAY7} Column Nos 1871-76 A farm worker		£8,000	6.8	80	9.1	108
h) {SHDPAY8} Column Nos 1909-14 A secretary		£8,000	7.0	82	9.1	109
i) {SHDPAY9} Column Nos 1915-20 A city bus driver		£8,500	6.9	81	8.9	105
j) {SHDPAY10} Column Nos 1921-26 An unskilled worker in a factory		£7,000	6.9	81	9.0	106
k) {SHDPAY11} Column Nos 1927-33 A cabinet minister in the national government		£25,000	7.1	83	9.8	116

Base : Self-completion respondents (n = 1181)

NB   (DK), code 999998;   (NA), code 999999

EQUAL OPPORTUNITIES AND REDISTRIBUTION OF WEALTH

1987   Q.B207a,c-e,g   {INCDIFFS}{POORUNIV}{JOBFRALL}{LESSBENF}{BASICINC}
Column Nos 1934,1936-38,1940
Please show how much you agree or disagree with each statement. (Please tick one box on each line)

	Agree Strongly		Agree		Neither agree nor disagree		Disagree		Disagree Strongly		Can't choose		(NA)	
Code	1		2		3		4		5		8		9	
	%	No	%	No	%	No	%	No	%	No	%	No	%	No
a) {INCDIFFS} Column No 1934 Differences in income in Britain are too large	25.4	300	48.8	576	12.3	145	9.5	112	1.4	16	2.0	23	0.6	7
c) {POORUNIV} Column No 1936 The government should provide more chances for children from poor families to go to university	31.0	366	51.0	602	10.8	128	5.3	62	0.5	6	0.7	8	0.8	9
d) {JOBFRALL} Column No 1937 The government should provide a job for everyone who wants one	23.1	273	34.2	404	16.7	197	19.3	228	3.2	38	2.5	30	1.0	11
e) {LESSBENF} Column No 1938 The government should spend *less* on benefits for the poor	0.7	9	3.6	43	12.1	143	52.6	621	28.9	342	0.9	11	1.0	12
g) {BASICINC} Column No 1940 The government should provide everyone with a guaranteed basic income	19.7	232	39.3	464	13.0	153	21.7	256	3.7	44	1.9	23	0.7	9

Base : Self-completion respondents (n = 1181)

PERCEPTIONS OF TAX BURDEN ON VARIOUS INCOME GROUPS

1987   Q.B208a-c   {TAXHISC}{TAXMIDSC}{TAXLOWSC} Column Nos 1941-43
Generally, how would you describe taxes in Britain today? (We mean *all* taxes together, including national insurance, income tax, VAT and all the rest) (Please tick one box for each)

	Much too high		Too high		About right		Too low		Much too low		Can't choose		(NA)	
Code	1		2		3		4		5		8		9	
	%	No	%	No	%	No	%	No	%	No	%	No	%	No
a) {TAXHISC} Column No 1941 First, for those with *high* incomes	7.1	84	16.9	199	32.7	386	30.9	365	9.0	107	2.6	31	0.8	10
b) {TAXMIDSC} Column No 1942 Next, for those with *middle* incomes	8.3	98	31.3	369	52.3	618	4.8	57	0.4	5	2.0	24	0.8	10
c) {TAXLOWSC} Column No 1943 Lastly, for those with *low* incomes	37.4	442	46.8	552	12.3	145	0.6	7	0.2	3	1.9	22	0.8	10

Base : Self-completion respondents (n = 1181)

TAXATION OF PEOPLE WITH HIGH INCOMES

1987   Q.B209   {*HILOWTAX*} Column No 1944

Do you think that people with high incomes should pay a *larger share* of their income in taxes than those with low incomes, the *same share*, or a *smaller share*? (Please tick one box)

	Code	%	No
Much larger share	1	19.2	227
Larger	2	54.9	649
The same share	3	20.7	244
Smaller	4	1.3	16
Much smaller	5	0.0	1
Can't choose	8	2.9	35
(NA)	9	0.9	10
Base : Self-completion respondents			1181

NB A similar version of this question was asked in 1985 and 1986 (see p. F-14 above)

MINIMUM HOUSEHOLD INCOME NEEDED

1986   Q.B78b   {*DERIVED VARIABLE - MININCAT*}

What would you say is the minimum income - after tax - that households like yours would need just to make ends meet? (Interviewer: probe for best estimate of minimum household income needed)

	Code	%	No
Less than £2,000 pa	1	1.3	20
£2,000 - £2,999 pa	2	4.7	72
£2,000 - £3,999 pa	3	8.3	129
£4,000 - £4,999 pa	4	11.3	175
£5,000 - £5,999 pa	5	18.0	278
£6,000 - £6,999 pa	6	10.5	162
£7,000 - £7,999 pa	7	12.2	189
£8,000 - £9,999 pa	8	6.2	97
£10,000 - £11,999 pa	9	7.2	111
£12,000 - £14,999 pa	10	2.9	45
£15,000 - £17,999 pa	11	1.3	20
£18,000 - £19,999 pa	12	0.3	5
£20,000 + pa	13	1.0	15
(DK)	98	14.7	228
(NA)	99	0.2	4
Base : All			1548

NB This variable was derived from {MININC} on Columns 634-52 where best estimate was written in (in terms of the minimum weekly, monthly or annual income needed)

POSSIBLE CAUSES OF BRITAIN'S ECONOMIC DIFFICULTIES - 1

1986   Q.B201a-j   *{ECDIF1}* - *{ECDIF10}*   Column Nos 2008-17

Please tick one box on each line to show how important or unimportant each of these has been as a cause of Britain's economic difficulties.

		Code	%	No
{ECDIF1}	Column No 2008			
a) People are not working hard enough				
	Not at all important	1	4.9	64
	Not very important	2	14.4	190
	Quite important	3	45.6	600
	Very important	4	33.2	437
	(DK)	8	0.1	1
	(NA)	9	1.8	24
Base : Self-completion respondents				1315

		Code	%	No
{ECDIF2}	Column No 2009			
b) Employers are not investing enough				
	Not at all important	1	1.3	17
	Not very important	2	6.6	87
	Quite important	3	42.6	561
	Very important	4	47.7	627
	(DK)	8	0.2	3
	(NA)	9	1.6	21
Base : Self-completion respondents				1315

		Code	%	No
{ECDIF3}	Column No 2010			
c) There has been a decline in world trade				
	Not at all important	1	2.3	31
	Not very important	2	10.7	141
	Quite important	3	41.4	545
	Very important	4	43.5	572
	(DK)	8	0.2	3
	(NA)	9	1.9	25
Base : Self-completion respondents				1315

		Code	%	No
{ECDIF4}	Column No 2011			
d) Wages are too high				
	Not at all important	1	12.2	160
	Not very important	2	31.6	416
	Quite important	3	40.4	531
	Very important	4	13.1	173
	(DK)	8	0.2	3
	(NA)	9	2.5	33
Base : Self-completion respondents				1315

		Code	%	No
{ECDIF5}	Column No 2012			
e) Energy costs are too high for industry				
	Not at all important	1	1.2	15
	Not very important	2	12.4	163
	Quite important	3	43.7	575
	Very important	4	39.9	525
	(DK)	8	0.2	3
	(NA)	9	2.6	34
Base : Self-completion respondents				1315

POSSIBLE CAUSES OF BRITAIN'S ECONOMIC DIFFICULTIES - 1 (continued)

	Code	%	No
{ECDIF6} Column No 2013			
f) Government spending has been too high			
Not at all important	1	8.7	114
Not very important	2	23.5	309
Quite important	3	34.8	458
Very important	4	29.6	389
(DK)	8	0.2	3
(NA)	9	3.3	43
Base : Self-completion respondents			1315

	Code	%	No
{ECDIF7} Column No 2014			
g) British industry is badly managed			
Not at all important	1	1.2	16
Not very important	2	7.8	102
Quite important	3	41.0	539
Very important	4	47.5	625
(DK)	8	0.4	5
(NA)	9	2.1	28
Base : Self-completion respondents			1315

	Code	%	No
{ECDIF8} Column No 2015			
h) British workers are reluctant to accept new ways of working			
Not at all important	1	3.0	39
Not very important	2	14.2	186
Quite important	3	41.9	551
Very important	4	38.6	508
(DK)	8	0.3	4
(NA)	9	2.1	28
Base : Self-completion respondents			1315

	Code	%	No
{ECDIF9} Column No 2016			
i) The government has not done enough to create jobs			
Not at all important	1	2.4	32
Not very important	2	8.9	117
Quite important	3	27.6	363
Very important	4	58.7	773
(DK)	8	0.1	2
(NA)	9	2.3	30
Base : Self-completion respondents			1315

	Code	%	No
{ECDIF10} Column No 2017			
j) The best school and college leavers don't seek jobs in manufacturing industry			
Not at all important	1	5.5	73
Not very important	2	19.8	260
Quite important	3	37.2	489
Very important	4	35.7	469
(DK)	8	0.3	4
(NA)	9	1.6	21
Base : Self-completion respondents			1315

NB A similar question was asked in 1983 on the main questionnaire - see {ECODIF1} - {ECODIF10} on pp. F-34 to F-36 below. Because of differences in both question wording and mode of administration, the two sets of figures are not comparable. Both series of questions were however given the same variable names, so the 1986 names have been changed as shown

GOVERNMENT INTERVENTION IN THE ECONOMY

1985   Q.221a-h   {GOVECON1} - {GOVECON8} Column Nos 2107-14

Here are some things the government might do for the economy. Please show which actions you are in favour
of and which you are against. (Please tick one box for each)

	Code	Strongly in favour 1		In favour 2		Neither in favour nor against 3		Against 4		Strongly against 5		(DK) 8		(NA) 9	
		%	No	%	No	%	No	%	No	%	No	%	No	%	No
a) {GOVECON1} Column No 2107 Control of wages by legislation		10.0	151	21.6	325	20.7	310	35.0	526	10.0	150	0.2	3	2.5	37
b) {GOVECON2} Column No 2108 Control of prices by legislation		19.9	299	38.7	581	15.4	231	19.4	292	3.9	59	0.2	3	2.5	37
c) {GOVECON3} Column No 2109 Cuts in government spending		10.8	162	26.2	394	23.8	357	28.1	422	8.4	126	0.3	4	2.5	37
d) {GOVECON4} Column No 2110 Government financing of projects to create new jobs		36.8	553	49.4	741	7.7	116	3.6	55	0.8	12	-	-	1.7	25
e) {GOVECON5} Column No 2111 Less government regulation of business		12.6	189	40.0	601	32.8	493	9.1	137	1.8	28	0.4	6	3.3	50
f) {GOVECON6} Column No 2112 Support for industry to develop new products and technology		36.7	551	52.2	785	7.3	109	1.6	24	0.2	4	0.1	2	1.8	27
g) {GOVECON7} Column No 2113 Supporting declining industries to protect jobs		18.4	276	30.2	454	20.7	311	24.8	372	3.7	56	0.1	2	2.1	31
h) {GOVECON8} Column No 2114 Reducing the working week to create more jobs		15.4	232	33.5	503	22.4	337	23.2	349	3.7	56	0.2	3	1.5	22

Base : Self-completion respondents (n = 1502)

GOVERNMENT SPENDING PRIORITIES

1985   Q.222a-h   *{GVSPEND1}-{GVSPEND8}* Column Nos 2115-22

Listed below are various areas of government spending. Please show whether you would like to see more or less government spending in each area.

Remember that if you say 'much more', it might require a tax increase to pay for it. (Please tick one box for each)

	Code	Spend much more 1		Spend more 2		Spend the same as now 3		Spend less 4		Spend much less 5		Can't choose 8		(NA) 9	
		%	No	%	No	%	No	%	No	%	No	%	No	%	No
a) *{GVSPEND1}* Column No 2115 **The environment**		6.1	91	27.8	417	51.7	777	4.3	65	0.5	8	5.1	77	4.5	67
b) *{GVSPEND2}* Column No 2116 **Health**		35.1	527	51.5	773	10.6	160	0.5	7	0.3	4	0.7	10	1.4	21
c) *{GVSPEND3}* Column No 2117 **The police and law enforcement**		8.2	123	29.7	445	51.9	779	4.2	63	1.8	26	1.7	26	2.6	39
d) *{GVSPEND4}* Column No 2118 **Education**		21.8	327	50.5	759	22.4	337	1.7	26	0.2	3	1.3	19	2.0	31
e) *{GVSPEND5}* Column No 2119 **The military and defence**		4.9	73	11.8	177	42.7	641	23.9	359	12.2	183	2.0	30	2.6	39
f) *{GVSPEND6}* Column No 2120 **Old age pensions**		24.8	372	48.4	726	22.9	344	0.9	14	0.1	2	1.0	15	1.8	28
g) *{GVSPEND7}* Column No 2121 **Unemployment benefits**		11.8	177	27.7	416	38.0	570	14.3	214	4.1	61	2.3	35	1.8	27
h) *{GVSPEND8}* Column No 2122 **Culture and the arts**		1.1	17	7.9	118	34.7	521	30.2	454	19.8	298	4.4	67	1.8	27

Base : Self-completion respondents (n = 1502)

INFLATION *VERSUS* UNEMPLOYMENT

1985   Q.225   *{UNEMINF2}* Column No 2125

If the government *had* to choose between keeping down inflation or keeping down unemployment, to which do you think it should give highest priority ... (please tick one box) ...

	Code	%	No
... keeping down inflation,	1	27.9	420
[or,] keeping down unemployment?	2	62.8	943
Can't choose	8	8.2	122
(NA)	9	1.1	17
Base : Self-completion respondents			1502

TAXATION *VERSUS* SPENDING ON SOCIAL SERVICES

1985   Q.231   {*TAXSOCSV*}   Column No 2141

If the government had a choice between reducing taxes and spending more on social services, which should it do ... (please tick one box) ...

	Code	%	No
... reduce taxes and spend less on social services	1	30.9	464
... [or,] increase taxes and spend more on social services?	2	39.8	598
Can't choose	8	28.0	421
(NA)	9	1.2	18
Base : Self-completion respondents			1502

REDISTRIBUTION OF INCOMES AND WEALTH

1985   Q.233   {*REDWORKG*}   Column No 2145

Please show whether you agree or disagree with the following statement: income and wealth should be redistributed towards ordinary working people.   (Please tick one box)

	Code	%	No
Agree strongly	1	13.6	204
Agree	2	27.5	413
Neither agree nor disagree	3	29.4	442
Disagree	4	21.2	319
Disagree strongly	5	7.0	105
(DK)	8	0.1	1
(NA)	9	1.2	18
Base : Self-completion respondents			1502

NB This variable is {REDISTRB} on the SPSS file. {REDISTRB} at Q.231i in 1986 (repeated in 1987 and 1989) relates to a different question (see p. T.1-1). Consequently this variable has been renamed

EXPECTATIONS FOR INCREASE IN RPI IN YEAR AHEAD

1984   Q.16b   {PRICESIN}{{PRICESUP}} Column Nos 238-40

[If expect prices to go up] You say that you expect prices generally to go up in the next 12 months. If we look back over the *last* 12 months, prices went up by about 5p in the £, that is by 5%. (Interviewer: enter nearest whole number, if 100 or over, enter 99.) By about what figure would you expect prices to go up in the *next* 12 months?

{PRICESIN}   Column No 238

How answers were given:

	Code	%	No
[Not asked : does not expect prices to go up]	0	15.6	256
Given as pence in the pound	1	26.6	438
Given as percentage	2	51.3	844
(DK)	3	5.0	82
(NA)	4	1.6	26
Base : All			1645

{PRICESUP}   Column Nos 239-240

Expected percentage rise:

	Code	%	No
[Not asked : does not expect prices to go up]	0	15.6	256
One	1	0.0	1
Two	2	1.1	18
Three	3	3.0	49
Four	4	2.7	45
Five	5	39.9	657
Six	6	4.8	79
Seven	7	7.8	129
Eight	8	4.7	78
Nine	9	0.7	11
Ten	10	11.2	184
Eleven	11	0.1	1
Twelve	12	0.5	8
Fifteen	15	0.9	15
Twenty	20	0.6	11
Thirty	30	0.1	2
Fifty	50	0.1	1
(Other)	97	0.1	1
(DK)	98	4.6	76
(NA)	99	1.6	26
Base : All			1645

NB   Prices given as pence in the pound were converted at the coding stage to percentage rises

BRITAIN'S STANDARD OF LIVING COMPARED WITH THAT OF OTHER COUNTRIES

1984   Q.201a-f   {FRANCLIV}{EGERMLIV}{WGERMLIV}{JAPANLIV}{CANADLIV}{AUSTLIV} Column Nos 1507-12
Please tick one box for each country below to show whether you think its *standard of living* is higher, about the same, or lower than Britain's.

	Code	Higher standard of living than Britain's 1		About the same standard of living as Britain's 2		Lower standard of living than Britain's 3		(DK) 8		(NA) 9	
		%	No	%	No	%	No	%	No	%	No
a) {FRANCLIV} Column No 1507 **France**		26.3	400	53.4	812	13.6	208	3.4	51	3.4	51
b) {EGERMLIV} Column No 1508 **East Germany**		12.4	189	17.7	269	60.9	928	4.7	72	4.3	65
c) {WGERMLIV} Column No 1509 **West Germany**		66.3	1009	23.4	356	2.9	44	3.5	53	4.0	62
d) {JAPANLIV} Column No 1510 **Japan**		38.3	584	20.8	317	31.8	484	4.1	63	4.9	75
e) {CANADLIV} Column No 1511 **Canada**		64.9	989	25.8	393	1.8	28	3.5	53	4.0	61
f) {AUSTLIV} Column No 1512 **Australia**		51.6	786	37.1	565	3.5	53	3.2	49	4.5	69

Base : Self-completion respondents (n = 1522)

PERCEIVED RISE IN PRICE OF VARIOUS ITEMS OF EXPENDITURE

1984   Q.216a-l   {FRUITPR}{RAILPR}{ELPRODPR}{ELECTRPR}{HOUSEPR}{RENTSPR}{TVLICPR}{CLOTHSPR}
{BUSPR}{PETROLPR}{POSTALPR}{RATESPR} Column Nos 1613-24
Although the cost of living has been going up for several years now, the prices of some things have been rising
faster than others. For each of the items below, please say whether you think it has gone up more, the same,
or less than the average rise in prices over the past few years. (Please tick one box for each)

	Code	Has gone up more than average 1		Same 2		Has gone up less than average 3		(DK) 8		(NA) 9	
		%	No	%	No	%	No	%	No	%	No
a) {FRUITPR} Column No 1613 Fresh fruit and vegetables		39.6	603	50.2	765	7.2	110	0.8	11	2.2	33
b) {RAILPR} Column No 1614 British Rail fares		67.4	1027	23.2	353	2.1	33	2.9	44	4.3	66
c) {ELPRODPR} Column No 1615 Electrical products for the home		38.3	583	43.4	661	14.1	214	1.3	19	2.9	45
d) {ELECTRPR} Column No 1616 Electricity		77.8	1185	17.7	270	1.6	25	0.7	11	2.2	33
e) {HOUSEPR} Column No 1617 House prices		65.2	993	27.2	413	3.9	60	1.3	19	2.5	37
f) {RENTSPR} Column No 1618 Rents		59.7	910	31.5	480	2.5	39	2.2	33	4.0	61
g) {TVLICPR} Column No 1619 The television licence		58.1	885	33.7	514	4.2	65	1.0	15	2.9	44
h) {CLOTHSPR} Column No 1620 Clothes		44.4	676	46.7	710	5.6	85	0.7	10	2.7	41
i) {BUSPR} Column No 1621 Bus fares		57.9	881	31.3	476	5.8	89	1.5	23	3.5	53
j) {PETROLPR} Column No 1622 Petrol		80.1	1220	14.2	216	2.4	37	1.2	18	2.1	32
k) {POSTALPR} Column No 1623 Postal charges		55.8	850	36.7	559	4.0	61	0.8	12	2.7	42
l) {RATESPR} Column No 1624 Your local rates		63.3	964	30.3	461	2.4	37	1.1	17	2.9	44

Base : Self-completion respondents (n = 1522)

POSSIBLE CAUSES OF BRITAIN'S ECONOMIC DIFFICULTIES - 2

1983   Q.22ab   {ECODIFI} - {ECODIF10}   Column Nos 260-69

a) I am going to read out a number of statements about the possible causes of Britain's economic difficulties. For each one that I read out, can you tell me first whether you think it is true or false?

b) (For each statement coded 'true', show card and ask) How important a factor do you think it has been in causing Britain's economic difficulties?

	Code	%	No
{ECODIF1} Column No 260			
i) People are not working hard enough			
False: not a cause	0	36.7	630
True, not at all important	1	0.1	1
True, not very important	2	1.7	29
True, quite important	3	23.6	406
True, very important	4	36.5	627
(DK)	7	0.6	10
True, but NA how important	8	0.3	6
(NA)	9	0.6	10
Base : All			1719

	Code	%	No
{ECODIF2} Column No 261			
ii) Employers are not investing enough			
False: not a cause	0	26.9	462
True, not at all important	1	0.0	1
True, not very important	2	2.0	34
True, quite important	3	29.1	500
True, very important	4	33.8	581
(DK)	7	6.8	118
True, but NA how important	8	0.2	4
(NA)	9	1.1	19
Base : All			1719

	Code	%	No
{ECODIF3} Column No 262			
iii) There has been a decline in world trade			
False: not a cause	0	9.9	170
True, not at all important	1	0.2	3
True, not very important	2	3.4	58
True, quite important	3	31.3	537
True, very important	4	50.4	866
(DK)	7	3.7	63
True, but NA how important	8	0.6	10
(NA)	9	0.7	13
Base : All			1719

	Code	%	No
{ECODIF4} Column No 263			
iv) Wages are too high			
False: not a cause	0	63.9	1099
True, not at all important	1	0.2	4
True, not very important	2	2.0	34
True, quite important	3	16.1	277
True, very important	4	14.4	247
(DK)	7	2.4	41
True, but NA how important	8	0.3	5
(NA)	9	0.7	13
Base : All			1719

POSSIBLE CAUSES OF BRITAIN'S ECONOMIC DIFFICULTIES - 2 (continued)

	Code	%	No
{ECODIF5} Column No 264			
v) Energy costs are too high for industry			
False: not a cause	0	11.1	190
True, not at all important	1	0.3	5
True, not very important	2	2.8	47
True, quite important	3	31.7	545
True, very important	4	47.8	822
(DK)	7	5.1	88
True, but NA how important	8	0.7	12
(NA)	9	0.6	10
Base : All			1719

	Code	%	No
{ECODIF6} Column No 265			
vi) Government spending has been too high			
False: not a cause	0	45.2	778
True, not at all important	1	0.5	9
True, not very important	2	3.1	53
True, quite important	3	21.3	367
True, very important	4	23.5	403
(DK)	7	4.9	84
True, but NA how important	8	0.4	7
(NA)	9	1.1	19
Base : All			1719

	Code	%	No
{ECODIF7} Column No 266			
vii) British industry is badly managed			
False: not a cause	0	26.5	456
True, not at all important	1	0.1	1
True, not very important	2	2.8	49
True, quite important	3	25.1	431
True, very important	4	39.1	672
(DK)	7	4.9	85
True, but NA how important	8	0.5	9
(NA)	9	1.0	17
Base : All			1719

	Code	%	No
{ECODIF8} Column No 267			
viii) British workers are reluctant to accept new ways of working			
False: not a cause	0	21.6	371
True, not at all important	1	0.3	5
True, not very important	2	5.4	92
True, quite important	3	32.6	561
True, very important	4	36.8	633
(DK)	7	2.3	39
True, but NA how important	8	0.5	9
(NA)	9	0.5	9
Base : All			1719

POSSIBLE CAUSES OF BRITAIN'S ECONOMIC DIFFICULTIES - 2 (continued)

	Code	%	No
{ECODIF9} Column No 268			
ix) The government has not done enough to create jobs			
False: not a cause	0	25.9	445
True, not at all important	1	0.1	3
True, not very important	2	3.4	59
True, quite important	3	22.3	384
True, very important	4	44.6	767
(DK)	7	2.5	44
True, but NA how important	8	0.2	4
(NA)	9	0.8	14
Base : All			1719

	Code	%	No
{ECODIF10} Column No 269			
x) The best school and college leavers don't seek jobs in manufacturing industry			
False: not a cause	0	34.3	589
True, not at all important	1	1.4	24
True, not very important	2	8.9	153
True, quite important	3	26.5	455
True, very important	4	19.0	326
(DK)	7	7.9	136
True, but NA how important	8	0.8	14
(NA)	9	1.2	21
Base : All			1719

NB A similar question was asked in 1986 on the self-completion questionnaire - see {ECDIF1} - {ECDIF10} on pp. F-26 to F-27 above. However, because of differences in both question wording and mode of administration, the two sets of figures are not comparable

ABILITY TO MANAGE ON PRESENT INCOME

1983   Q.27b   {INCMANGE} Column No 312
How well would you say you are managing on your income these days ... (read out) ...

	Code	%	No
...very well,	1	9.2	157
quite well,	2	58.3	1002
not very well,	3	23.2	399
or not at all well?	4	8.8	151
(DK)	8	0.2	3
(NA)	9	0.4	6
Base : All			1719

FINANCIAL POSITION COMPARED WITH FIVE YEARS AGO

1983   Q.27c   {VYEARAGO} Column No 313
[If aged 23 or over] Compared with five years ago would you say you were ... (read out) ...

	Code	%	No
[Not asked: aged 18-22]	0	9.1	157
... better off financially,	1	29.4	506
about the same,	2	24.8	427
or worse off financially?	3	36.4	626
(DK)	8	0.1	2
(NA)	9	0.1	1
Base : All			1719

G Labour market and employment

G1 All respondents

Table titles and cross references

IMPORTANT FACTORS IN CHOICE OF FIRST JOB

{FRSTJOB1} {FRSTJOB2}

Question: Now I'd like to ask a few questions about industry and jobs. Suppose you were advising a young person who was looking for his or her first job.
(Show card) Which *one* of these would you say is the *most* important, and which *next*?

		1983		1984		1985		1986		1987		1989	
		%	No	%	No	%	No	%	No	%	No	%	No
Question No Column No								B94a 751		B89a 941		A92a 1051	
(i) {FRSTJOB1} **Most important**	Code												
Good starting pay	1	-	.	-	.	-	.	3.1	48	2.4	33	4.9	71
A secure job for the future	2	-	.	-	.	-	.	56.5	875	50.6	696	46.0	675
Opportunities for promotion	3	-	.	-	.	-	.	9.3	144	12.0	165	8.9	131
Interesting work	4	-	.	-	.	-	.	26.4	408	29.9	412	35.0	515
Good working conditions	5	-	.	-	.	-	.	3.9	60	4.1	57	4.2	62
(DK)	8	-	.	-	.	-	.	0.5	8	0.6	8	0.7	11
(NA)	9	-	.	-	.	-	.	0.3	5	0.3	4	0.3	5
Base: All									1548		1375		1469

Question No Column No								B94b 752		B89b 942		A92b 1052	
(ii) {FRSTJOB2} **Next most important**													
Good starting pay	1	-	.	-	.	-	.	8.9	138	7.0	96	12.6	185
A secure job for the future	2	-	.	-	.	-	.	17.8	275	20.0	275	20.4	300
Opportunities for promotion	3	-	.	-	.	-	.	29.1	451	31.0	426	27.9	409
Interesting work	4	-	.	-	.	-	.	28.0	433	24.7	339	21.6	318
Good working conditions	5	-	.	-	.	-	.	15.1	234	16.4	225	16.2	237
(DK)	8	-	.	-	.	-	.	0.7	11	0.7	10	0.9	14
(NA)	9	-	.	-	.	-	:	0.4	6	0.3	4	0.4	6
Base: All									1548		1375		1469

PERCEIVED ADVANTAGES OF JOBS IN VARIOUS SECTORS

{STARTPAY} {SECURITY} {PROMOTN} {INTEREST} {CONDITNS}

Question: (Show card) **Suppose this young person** [who was looking for his or her first job] **could choose between different kinds of jobs anywhere in Britain. From what you know or have heard, which** *one* **of these kinds of jobs is most likely to offer him or her ... (read out):**

		1983		1984		1985		1986		1987		1989	
		%	No	%	No	%	No	%	No	%	No	%	No
Question No								B95a		B90a		A93a	
Column No								753		943		1053	
(i) {STARTPAY}	Code												
Good starting pay													
A building society	1	-	-	-	-	-	-	9.2	143	8.7	119	10.0	147
A large firm of accountants	2	-	-	-	-	-	-	12.9	200	14.6	201	16.4	240
A large engineering factory	3	-	-	-	-	-	-	13.4	208	11.0	151	13.2	195
A department store	4	-	-	-	-	-	-	1.8	27	1.1	15	1.4	24
The civil service	5	-	-	-	-	-	-	24.2	375	22.4	309	19.2	283
A large firm making computers	6	-	-	-	-	-	-	29.9	462	33.2	456	31.2	458
(None of these)	0	-	-	-	-	-	-	0.5	8	0.4	6	1.1	16
(DK)	8	-	-	-	-	-	-	7.7	120	8.2	113	7.1	104
(NA)	9	-	-	-	-	-	-	0.4	6	0.4	5	0.4	6
Base: All									1548		1375		1469

								1986		1987		1989	
Question No								B95b		B90b		A93b	
Column No								754		944		1054	
(ii) {SECURITY}													
A secure job for the future. You may choose the same one again or a different one.													
A building society	1	-	-	-	-	-	-	13.4	207	13.1	181	18.2	267
A large firm of accountants	2	-	-	-	-	-	-	13.4	208	13.0	179	12.8	187
A large engineering factory	3	-	-	-	-	-	-	4.7	73	3.9	53	4.6	68
A department store	4	-	-	-	-	-	-	1.3	20	1.2	17	1.1	17
The civil service	5	-	-	-	-	-	-	49.2	762	49.9	686	46.4	681
A large firm making computers	6	-	-	-	-	-	-	14.1	218	15.1	207	14.3	210
(None of these)	0	-	-	-	-	-	-	0.7	10	0.1	2	0.2	4
(DK)	8	-	-	-	-	-	-	2.8	44	3.3	46	2.1	31
(NA)	9	-	-	-	-	-	-	0.4	6	0.4	5	0.3	5
Base: All									1548		1375		1469

PERCEIVED ADVANTAGES OF JOBS IN VARIOUS SECTORS (Continued)

		1983		1984		1985		1986		1987		1989	
		%	No	%	No	%	No	%	No	%	No	%	No
Question No								B95c		B90c		A93c	
Column No								755		945		1055	
(iii) {PROMOTN}	Code												
Opportunities for promotion													
A building society	1	-	.	-	.	-	.	8.5	131	8.5	116	12.2	179
A large firm of accountants	2	-	.	-	.	-	.	16.6	257	16.6	228	17.5	256
A large engineering factory	3	-	.	-	.	-	.	8.9	138	7.2	98	8.3	122
A department store	4	-	.	-	.	-	.	5.3	81	4.6	63	5.0	74
The civil service	5	-	.	-	.	-	.	34.2	530	34.5	475	31.7	466
A large firm making computers	6	-	.	-	.	-	.	17.9	277	21.0	289	16.9	248
(None of these)	0	-	.	-	.	-	.	0.3	5	0.1	2	0.2	3
(DK)	8	-	.	-	.	-	.	7.9	122	7.1	98	7.6	112
(NA)	9	-	.	-	.	-	.	0.4	6	0.4	5	0.6	9
Base: All									1548		1375		1469

								B95d		B90d		A93d	
Question No								756		946		1056	
Column No													
(iv) {INTEREST}													
Interesting work													
A building society	1	-	.	-	.	-	.	6.2	96	4.4	60	8.0	118
A large firm of accountants	2	-	.	-	.	-	.	9.9	154	9.9	136	9.3	136
A large engineering factory	3	-	.	-	.	-	.	16.3	253	17.6	243	18.9	278
A department store	4	-	.	-	.	-	.	8.7	134	8.7	120	8.6	126
The civil service	5	-	.	-	.	-	.	15.8	244	15.8	218	15.0	220
A large firm making computers	6	-	.	-	.	-	.	30.1	467	30.6	421	27.6	406
(None of these)	0	-	.	-	.	-	.	2.7	42	2.6	36	3.7	54
(DK)	8	-	.	-	.	-	.	9.8	151	9.9	136	8.6	126
(NA)	9	-	.	-	.	-	.	0.5	7	0.4	6	0.5	8
Base: All									1548		1375		1469

PERCEIVED ADVANTAGES OF JOBS IN VARIOUS SECTORS (Continued)

		1983		1984		1985		1986		1987		1989	
		%	No	%	No	%	No	%	No	%	No	%	No
Question No								B95e		B90e		A93e	
Column No								757		947		1057	
(v) {CONDITNS}	Code												
Good working conditions													
A building society	1	-	.	-	.	-	.	24.0	371	22.8	313	27.7	406
A large firm of accountants	2	-	.	-	.	-	.	11.9	184	13.0	179	13.7	201
A large engineering factory	3	-	.	-	.	-	.	3.6	56	4.4	61	3.3	49
A department store	4	-	.	-	.	-	.	6.2	96	4.1	56	5.0	74
The civil service	5	-	.	-	.	-	.	31.6	489	29.6	407	29.0	427
A large firm making computers	6	-	.	-	.	-	.	13.5	209	16.0	220	13.5	198
(None of these)	0	-	.	-	.	-	.	0.3	4	0.2	3	0.3	4
(DK)	8	-	.	-	.	-	.	8.3	128	9.2	127	6.9	102
(NA)	9	-	.	-	.	-	.	0.7	10	0.7	9	0.6	9
Base: All									1548		1375		1469

ADVICE GIVEN ON CHOICE OF FIRST JOB

{JBADVIS1} {JBADVIS2} {JBADVIS3}

Question: (Show card) Now taking everything together, which job would you be *most* likely to advise this young person to choose? And which *next*? And which would you be *least likely* to advise him or her to choose?

		1983		1984		1985		1986		1987		1989	
		%	No	%	No	%	No	%	No	%	No	%	No
Question No								B96a		B91a		A94a	
Column No								758		948		1058	
(i) {JBADVIS1}	Code												
Most likely													
A building society	1	-	.	-	.	-	.	11.0	171	10.0	138	12.7	187
A large firm of accountants	2	-	.	-	.	-	.	17.9	277	17.4	240	17.6	258
A large engineering factory	3	-	.	-	.	-	.	7.0	108	8.0	110	9.5	139
A department store	4	-	.	-	.	-	.	1.4	22	1.7	23	1.5	22
The civil service	5	-	.	-	.	-	.	31.5	488	30.9	425	27.2	400
A large firm making computers	6	-	.	-	.	-	.	24.1	373	24.6	338	23.7	348
(None of these)	0	-	.	-	.	-	.	1.2	19	1.1	16	1.9	27
(DK)	8	-	.	-	.	-	.	4.8	75	5.5	76	5.2	77
(NA)	9	-	.	-	.	-	.	1.0	16	0.7	10	0.8	11
Base: All									1548		1375		1469

ADVICE GIVEN ON CHOICE OF FIRST JOB (Continued)

		1983		1984		1985		1986		1987		1989	
		%	No	%	No	%	No	%	No	%	No	%	No
Question No Column No								B96b 759		B91b 949		A94b 1059	
(ii) {JBADVIS2} Next most likely	Code												
A building society	1	-	.	-	.	-	.	19.5	302	16.2	222	21.6	318
A large firm of accountants	2	-	.	-	.	-	.	20.6	318	23.7	326	21.1	310
A large engineering factory	3	-	.	-	.	-	.	10.5	163	11.0	152	8.9	131
A department store	4	-	.	-	.	-	.	4.0	62	2.8	39	2.3	34
The civil service	5	-	.	-	.	-	.	19.8	307	19.4	267	17.6	259
A large firm making computers	6	-	.	-	.	-	.	15.8	245	17.6	242	19.8	291
(None of these)	0	-	.	-	.	-	.	1.6	24	1.3	18	1.5	22
(DK)	8	-	.	-	.	-	.	6.8	106	6.8	93	6.1	89
(NA)	9	-	.	-	.	-	.	1.3	21	1.1	15	1.0	15
Base: All									1548		1375		1469

		1983		1984		1985		1986		1987		1989	
		%	No	%	No	%	No	%	No	%	No	%	No
Question No Column No								B96c 760		B91c 950		A94c 1060	
(iii) {JBADVIS3} Least likely													
A building society	1	-	.	-	.	-	.	4.7	73	3.8	52	4.5	66
A large firm of accountants	2	-	.	-	.	-	.	3.3	51	2.7	37	3.9	57
A large engineering factory	3	-	.	-	.	-	.	20.1	311	20.1	276	19.8	291
A department store	4	-	.	-	.	-	.	50.2	777	52.7	724	49.9	734
The civil service	5	-	.	-	.	-	.	5.6	87	7.3	100	8.9	131
A large firm making computers	6	-	.	-	.	-	.	7.2	111	4.3	60	4.9	72
(None of these)	0	-	.	-	.	-	.	0.8	13	0.8	12	1.0	15
(DK)	8	-	.	-	.	-	.	7.0	108	7.4	102	6.0	88
(NA)	9	-	.	-	.	-	.	1.1	18	0.9	13	1.0	15
Base: All									1548		1375		1469

MEASURES TO HELP REDUCE UNEMPLOYMENT

{UNEMP1} {UNEMP2} {UNEMP3} {UNEMP4}

Question: Here are a number of things which might help to reduce unemployment in Britain. Please tick a box to show for each whether you would suppose or oppose it.

		1983		1984		1985		1986		1987		1989	
		%	No	%	No	%	No	%	No	%	No	%	No
Question No						242a				A230a			
Column No						2171				2163			
(i) {UNEMP1}	Code												
Lower the retirement age to create more jobs for younger people													
Support strongly	1	-	-	-	-	36.9	554	-	-	29.9	372	-	-
Support	2	-	-	-	-	46.4	697	-	-	52.1	648	-	-
Oppose	3	-	-	-	-	12.9	194	-	-	14.8	184	-	-
Oppose strongly	4	-	-	-	-	1.4	21	-	-	2.1	27	-	-
(DK)	8	-	-	-	-	0.2	4	-	-	0.1	2	-	-
(NA)	9	-	-	-	-	2.2	33	-	-	0.9	12	-	-
							1502				1243		

Base: Self-completion
        questionnaire respondents

		1983		1984		1985		1986		1987		1989	
Question No						242b				A230b			
Column No						2172				2164			
(ii) {UNEMP2}													
Shorten the working week and reduce the earnings of those in paid work													
Support strongly	1	-	-	-	-	5.6	84	-	-	2.7	33	-	-
Support	2	-	-	-	-	19.1	287	-	-	4.7	183	-	-
Oppose	3	-	-	-	-	56.2	843	-	-	63.8	793	-	-
Oppose strongly	4	-	-	-	-	15.1	227	-	-	16.8	210	-	-
(DK)	8	-	-	-	-	0.3	5	-	-	0.2	3	-	-
(NA)	9	-	-	-	-	3.7	55	-	-	1.8	22	-	-
							1502				1243		

Base: Self-completion
        questionnaire respondents

MEASURES TO HELP REDUCE UNEMPLOYMENT (Continued)

		1983		1984		1985		1986		1987		1989	
		%	No	%	No	%	No	%	No	%	No	%	No
Question No						242c				A230c			
Column No						2173				2165			

(iii) {UNEMP3}

Introduce job sharing schemes so that two part-timers share one full-time job

	Code	1983 %	No	1984 %	No	1985 %	No	1986 %	No	1987 %	No	1989 %	No
Support strongly	1	-	-	-	-	9.9	149	-	-	6.0	74	-	-
Support	2	-	-	-	-	35.1	527	-	-	35.6	443	-	-
Oppose	3	-	-	-	-	39.6	595	-	-	43.4	540	-	-
Oppose strongly	4	-	-	-	-	12.0	180	-	-	12.5	156	-	-
(DK)	8	-	-	-	-	0.3	5	-	-	0.6	8	-	-
(NA)	9	-	-	-	-	3.1	46	-	-	1.9	23	-	-

Base: Self-completion questionnaire respondents

1985: 1502
1987: 1243

		1983		1984		1985		1986		1987		1989	
Question No						242d				A230d			
Column No						2174				2166			

(iv) {UNEMP4}

Restrict overtime working

	Code	1983 %	No	1984 %	No	1985 %	No	1986 %	No	1987 %	No	1989 %	No
Support strongly	1	-	-	-	-	19.3	289	-	-	12.7	158	-	-
Support	2	-	-	-	-	44.9	674	-	-	41.0	510	-	-
Oppose	3	-	-	-	-	26.3	394	-	-	35.9	446	-	-
Oppose strongly	4	-	-	-	-	6.7	100	-	-	8.1	100	-	-
(DK)	8	-	-	-	-	0.3	4	-	-	0.4	6	-	-
(NA)	9	-	-	-	-	2.7	40	-	-	1.9	23	-	-

Base: Self-completion questionnaire respondents

1985: 1502
1987: 1243

IMPORTANT FACTORS IN DECIDING EMPLOYEES' PAY
{PAYIMP1} {PAYIMP2}

Question: Employers have to consider many things before deciding what to pay employees. Please tick *one box* to show which *should be most important*, and *one box* to show which *should be next most important*, in deciding the level of pay of an employee.

		1983		1984		1985		1986		1987		1989	
		%	No	%	No	%	No	%	No	%	No	%	No
Question No						244a				A231a			
Column No						2212				2167			
(i) {PAYIMP1}	Code												
Should be most important													
The age of the employee	1	-	.	-	.	1.4	21	-	.	2.3	28	-	.
The performance of the individual employee	2	-	.	-	.	31.4	472	-	.	48.9	608	-	.
How long the employee has been with the firm	3	-	.	-	.	1.6	24	-	.	2.1	27	-	.
The employee's family commitments	4	-	.	-	.	1.3	19	-	.	1.6	20	-	.
The going rate for the job	5	-	.	-	.	10.1	151	-	.	18.5	230	-	.
What the firm says it can afford	6	-	.	-	.	2.1	31	-	.	3.2	40	-	.
(Respondent incorrectly coded)	7	-	.	-	.	50.0	750	-	.	-		-	.
(DK)	8	-	.	-	.	0.2	4	-	.	0.2	2	-	.
(NA)	9	-	.	-	.	1.9	29	-	.	23.2	289	-	.

Base: Self-completion questionnaire respondents — 1502 — 1243

		1983		1984		1985		1986		1987		1989	
Question No						244b				A231b			
Column No						2213				2168			
(ii) {PAYIMP2}													
Should be next most important													
The age of the employee	1	-	.	-	.	2.6	38	-	.	4.9	61	-	.
The performance of the individual employee	2	-	.	-	.	9.3	140	-	.	17.5	217	-	.
How long the employee has been with the firm	3	-	.	-	.	7.7	115	-	.	17.4	217	-	.
The employee's family commitments	4	-	.	-	.	3.6	53	-	.	2.9	36	-	.
The going rate for the job	5	-	.	-	.	16.3	245	-	.	23.9	297	-	.
What the firm says it can afford	6	-	.	-	.	7.6	114	-	.	7.5	93	-	.
(Respondent incorrectly coded)	7	-	.	-	.	47.6	715	-	.	-		-	.
(DK)	8	-	.	-	.	0.3	5	-	.	0.2	2	-	.
(NA)	9	-	.	-	.	5.1	77	-	.	25.7	320	-	.

Base: Self-completion questionnaire respondents — 1502 — 1243

1985 - Data users should note that half the respondents failed to answer the question correctly. Even in 1987, when the question layout was changed, around a quarter of respondents did not give an answer. Clearly then, this question was inappropriate for self-completion

EFFECT OF 'NEW TECHNOLOGY' AT THE WORKPLACE

{TECH5YR}

Question: New kinds of technology are being introduced more and more in Britain: computers and word processors, robots in factories and so on. Please tick one box to show what effect you think this technology will have over the *next five years*?

		1983		1984		1985		1986		1987		1989	
		%	No	%	No	%	No	%	No	%	No	%	No
Question No						245				A232			
Column No						2214				2169			
	Code												
It will increase the number of jobs available	1	-	-	-	-	6.3	94	-	-	7.8	98	-	-
It will reduce the number of jobs available	2	-	-	-	-	77.1	1158	-	-	71.3	886	-	-
It will make no difference to the number of jobs available	3	-	-	-	-	14.8	223	-	-	19.3	240	-	-
(DK)	8	-	-	-	-	0.3	4	-	-	0.6	7	-	-
(NA)	9	-	-	-	-	1.5	23	-	-	1.0	13	-	-
Base: Self-completion questionnaire respondents							1502				1243		

1984 - A similar question (Q214a) was asked '...Please tick a box ... to show what effect you think this technology will have over the next three years or so?'; see p. G.1-23 below

IMPACT OF 'NEW TECHNOLOGY'

{TECHBORE} {TECHEASE}

Question: a) Do you think that the introduction of new technology in Britain over the *next five years* will ... (please tick one box) ...

		1983		1984		1985		1986		1987		1989	
		%	No	%	No	%	No	%	No	%	No	%	No
Question No						246a				A233a			
Column No						2215				2170			
(a) {TECHBORE}	Code												
... make work more interesting,	1	-	-	-	-	34.6	520	-	-	40.8	508	-	-
... make work more boring,	2	-	-	-	-	38.3	576	-	-	33.4	416	-	-
... or will it make no difference to work?	3	-	-	-	-	24.1	362	-	-	24.0	299	-	-
(DK)	8	-	-	-	-	0.4	7	-	-	0.6	7	-	-
(NA)	9	-	-	-	-	2.5	38	-	-	1.1	14	-	-
Base: Self-completion questionnaire respondents							1502				1243		

IMPACT OF 'NEW TECHNOLOGY' (Continued)

		1983		1984		1985		1986		1987		1989	
		%	No	%	No	%	No	%	No	%	No	%	No
Question No						246b				A233b			
Column No	Code					2216				2171			

(b) {TECHEASE}

And will it ... (please tick one box) ...

	Code	1983 %	No	1984 %	No	1985 %	No	1986 %	No	1987 %	No	1989 %	No
... make life more difficult	1	-	-	-	-	15.3	229	-	-	13.6	169	-	-
... make life easier,	2	-	-	-	-	58.8	883	-	-	60.6	754	-	-
... or will it make no difference?	3	-	-	-	-	22.8	342	-	-	23.6	294	-	-
(DK)	8	-	-	-	-	0.3	5	-	-	0.7	8	-	-
(NA)	9	-	-	-	-	2.8	42	-	-	1.5	19	-	-
Base: Self-completion questionnaire respondents						1502				1243			

GOVERNMENT ENCOURAGEMENT FOR 'NEW TECHNOLOGY'

{NEWTECH}

Question: Please tick one box to show whether you agree or disagree with the following statement: the government should do more to encourage the spread of new technology in Britain.

		1983		1984		1985		1986		1987		1989	
		%	No	%	No	%	No	%	No	%	No	%	No
Question No						246c				A233c			
Column No						2217				2172			
	Code												
Agree strongly	1	-	-	-	-	20.6	309	-	-	21.4	266	-	-
Agree	2	-	-	-	-	44.4	667	-	-	45.6	568	-	-
Neither agree nor disagree	3	-	-	-	-	26.3	395	-	-	24.7	307	-	-
Disagree	4	-	-	-	-	6.0	90	-	-	5.9	73	-	-
Disagree strongly	5	-	-	-	-	0.8	11	-	-	0.8	10	-	-
(DK)	8	-	-	-	-	0.2	3	-	-	0.4	5	-	-
(NA)	9	-	-	-	-	1.8	26	-	-	1.2	15	-	-
Base: Self-completion questionnaire respondents						1502				1243			

1984 - The SPSS file lists a variable {NEWTECH} which relates to a different question (Q.220c). Consequently the 1984 variable has been renamed {TECHRICH}

ATTITUDES TOWARDS MANAGEMENT AND INDUSTRY

{INDUST1} {INDUST2} {INDUST3} {INDUST4} {INDUST5} {INDUST5B}

Question: Please say whether you agree or disagree with each of these statements about industry today. (Please tick one box for each)

		1983		1984		1985		1986		1987		1989	
		%	No	%	No	%	No	%	No	%	No	%	No
Question No						243a		B230a					
Column No						2207		2156					

(i) *{INDUST1}*
Industry should share more of its profits with its employees

	Code	1983 %	No	1984 %	No	1985 %	No	1986 %	No	1987 %	No	1989 %	No
Agree strongly	1	-	.	-	.	22.7	340	25.3	333	-	.	-	.
Agree	2	-	.	-	.	54.9	824	54.8	721	-	.	-	.
Neither agree nor disagree	3	-	.	-	.	15.0	225	15.0	198	-	.	-	.
Disagree	4	-	.	-	.	4.8	72	3.3	43	-	.	-	.
Disagree strongly	5	-	.	-	.	0.5	8	0.3	4	-	.	-	.
(DK)	8	-	.	-	.	0.1	1	0.2	2	-	.	-	.
(NA)	9	-	.	-	.	2.1	31	1.1	14	-	.	-	.
							1502		1315				

Base: Self-completion
questionnaire respondents

Question No						243b		B230b					
Column No						2208		2157					

(ii) *{INDUST2}*
Full cooperation in firms is impossible because workers and management are really on opposite sides

	Code	1983 %	No	1984 %	No	1985 %	No	1986 %	No	1987 %	No	1989 %	No
Agree strongly	1	-	.	-	.	9.6	145	13.9	183	-	.	-	.
Agree	2	-	.	-	.	40.9	614	43.0	566	-	.	-	.
Neither agree nor disagree	3	-	.	-	.	21.5	323	18.7	246	-	.	-	.
Disagree	4	-	.	-	.	23.2	349	21.0	276	-	.	-	.
Disagree strongly	5	-	.	-	.	1.9	29	2.2	29	-	.	-	.
(DK)	8	-	.	-	.	0.2	4	0.1	1	-	.	-	.
(NA)	9	-	.	-	.	2.6	39	1.1	15	-	.	-	.
							1502		1315				

Base: Self-completion
questionnaire respondents

1989 -   {INDUST2} A similar question was asked in 1989 (see p.G.1 - 16 below)

ATTITUDES TOWARDS MANAGEMENT AND INDUSTRY (Continued)

		1983		1984		1985		1986		1987		1989	
		%	No	%	No	%	No	%	No	%	No	%	No
Question No						243c		B230c					
Column No						2209		2158					
(iii) {INDUST3}	Code												
Managers generally know what's best for a firm and employees ought to go along with it													
Agree strongly	1	-	.	-	.	3.8	58	5.0	65	-	-	-	-
Agree	2	-	.	-	.	30.8	462	27.1	356	-	-	-	-
Neither agree nor disagree	3	-	.	-	.	24.3	364	24.1	317	-	-	-	-
Disagree	4	-	.	-	.	33.7	506	36.5	480	-	-	-	-
Disagree strongly	5	-	.	-	.	4.9	73	6.3	82	-	-	-	-
(DK)	8	-	.	-	.	0.1	2	0.1	1	-	-	-	-
(NA)	9	-	.	-	.	2.4	36	1.0	13	-	-	-	-
Base: Self-completion questionnaire respondents							1502		1315				

		1983		1984		1985		1986		1987		1989	
Question No						243d		B230d		A227e/B238e		A231e/B231e	
Column No						2210		2159		1658		2165	
(iv) {INDUST4}													
Management will always try to get the better of employees if it gets the chance													
Agree strongly	1	-	.	-	.	10.9	164	12.9	170	18.7	454	18.4	464
Agree	2	-	.	-	.	40.6	610	38.7	508	42.2	1022	39.7	1003
Neither agree nor disagree	3	-	.	-	.	21.2	318	19.8	261	17.8	431	21.4	541
Disagree	4	-	.	-	.	22.9	344	24.1	318	17.6	428	17.5	443
Disagree strongly	5	-	.	-	.	1.7	26	3.2	42	2.2	53	1.9	49
(DK)	8	-	.	-	.	0.1	2	0.1	1	0.1	2	-	-
(NA)	9	-	.	-	.	2.5	37	1.1	15	1.4	35	1.1	27
Base: Self-completion questionnaire respondents							1502		1315		2424		2529

1986, 1987, 1989 - {INDUST4} This item forms part of the 'left-right' scale and, as such, also appears on p.T.1 - 3 below

ATTITUDES TOWARDS MANAGEMENT AND INDUSTRY (Continued)

		1983		1984		1985		1986		1987		1989	
		%	No	%	No	%	No	%	No	%	No	%	No
Question No						243e		B230e				B205b	
Column No						2211		2160				1928	
(v) *{INDUST5} {INDUST5B}*	Code												
Employees need strong trade unions to protect their interests													
Agree strongly	1	-	.	-	.	12.5	187	13.9	182	-	.	12.0	150
Agree	2	-	.	-	.	32.5	489	30.4	399	-	.	29.1	365
Neither agree nor disagree	3	-	.	-	.	25.7	386	25.4	334	-	.	21.6	271
Disagree	4	-	.	-	.	21.9	329	23.5	309	-	.	26.4	332
Disagree strongly	5	-	.	-	.	5.0	76	5.7	75	-	.	5.9	75
(DK)	8	-	.	-	.	0.2	4	0.2	2	-	.	3.1	39
(NA)	9	-	.	-	.	2.1	31	1.0	13	-	.	1.8	23
Base: Self-completion questionnaire respondents						1502		1315				1255	

1985, 1986 - Variable name is {INDUST5}

1989 - Q reads 'Workers need stong trade unions ...'; 'Can't choose', code 8, was offered as an answer category on the questionnaire, which appears to have reduced slightly the number of respondents choosing the neutral option 'neither agree nor disagree'. The 1989 variable is {NDSTRGTU} in the SPSS file. This has been changed to {INDUST5B}. Since the responses seem broadly comparable over time, the 1989 data are shown here alongside those from earlier years

CHANGING THE WAY ONE SPENDS ONE'S TIME

1989   Q.B201a-f   *{TMPDJOB}{TMHLDWRK}{TMFAMILY}{TMFRIEND}{TMLEISRE}{TMRELAX}* Column Nos 1908-13
Suppose you could change the way you spend your time, spending more time on some things and less time on others.
Which of the things on the following list would you like to spend *more* time on, which would you like to spend
less time on and which would you like to spend the *same* amount of time on as now? (Please tick one box for each)

		Much more time		A bit more time		Same time as now		A bit less time		Much less time		Can't choose/ doesn't apply		(NA)	
	Code	1		2		3		4		5		8		9	
		%	No	%	No	%	No	%	No	%	No	%	No	%	No
a) *{TMPDJOB}* Column No 1908 Time in a paid job		4.6	57	7.2	91	24.3	305	24.7	310	5.6	70	29.3	368	4.3	54
b) *{TMHLDWRK}* Column No 1909 Time doing household work		2.2	28	11.6	145	37.1	465	19.8	248	13.8	173	10.9	137	4.7	59
c) *{TMFAMILY}* Column No 1910 Time with your family		25.3	318	34.1	428	31.2	391	1.1	14	0.5	6	4.5	56	3.3	42
d) *{TMFRIEND}* Column No 1911 Time with your friends		9.1	115	37.4	469	44.3	556	1.4	18	0.6	8	2.6	33	4.4	56
e) *{TMLEISRE}* Column No 1912 Time in leisure activities		19.0	239	43.4	544	27.7	347	0.9	11	0.8	10	4.7	59	3.6	45
f) *{TMRELAX}* Column No 1913 Time to relax		21.8	274	38.3	480	31.8	399	2.0	25	0.7	8	1.9	24	3.5	44

Base : Self-completion respondents (n = 1255)

IMPORTANCE OF WORK

1989   Q.B202a-c   *{JBERNMNY}{JBENJOY}{WORKIMPA}* Column Nos 1914-16
Please tick one box for each statement below to show how much you agree or disagree with it, *thinking of work in general*.

		Strongly agree		Agree		Neither agree nor disagree		Disagree		Strongly disagree		Can't Choose		(NA)	
	Code	1		2		3		4		5		8		9	
		%	No	%	No	%	No	%	No	%	No	%	No	%	No
a) *{JBERNMNY}* Column No 1914 A job is just a way of earning money - no more		7.0	88	21.6	271	12.8	161	38.9	488	13.1	164	2.1	26	4.5	57
b) *{JBENJOY}* Column No 1915 I would enjoy having a paid job even if I did not need the money		6.6	83	47.0	589	14.2	178	18.7	234	3.9	49	5.2	65	4.5	57
c) *{WORKIMPA}* Column No 1916 Work is a person's most important activity		10.6	133	25.9	325	18.5	232	31.9	401	8.4	106	1.7	22	2.9	37

Base : Self-completion respondents (n = 1255)

FACTORS THAT SHOULD DECIDE EMPLOYEES' RATES OF PAY

1989   Q.B204   {PYSHLONG}{PYSHWELL}{PYSHEXP}{PYSHRATE}{PYSHAGE}{PYSHSEX}{PYSHFAM}
{PYSHQUAL}{PYSHDK}   Column Nos 1918-26

Think of two people doing *the same kind of work*. What do you personally think *should* be important in deciding
how much to pay them?
Looking at the things below, please write '1' in the box next to the thing you think *should be most important*.
Then write '2' next to the thing you think *should be next most important*. And '3' next to the thing you think
should be third most important. Leave the other boxes blank.

	Code	Most important 1		2nd most important 2		3rd most important 3		(Ticked box) 6		(Blank) 10	
		%	No	%	No	%	No	%	No	%	No

In deciding on pay for two people
doing *the same kind of work*, how
important *should be* :

	Code	%	No	%	No	%	No	%	No	%	No
{PYSHLONG} Column No 1918 How long the employee has been with the firm		6.6	82	9.5	119	24.9	313	0.7	9	58.3	732
{PYSHWELL} Column No 1919 How well the employee does the job		51.6	648	19.6	246	7.6	96	0.9	12	20.2	254
{PYSHEXP} Column No 1920 The experience of the employee in doing the work		14.6	184	40.5	508	18.4	231	1.1	14	25.3	317
{PYSHRATE} Column No 1921 The standard rate - giving both employees the same pay		12.7	159	5.6	70	10.1	126	0.5	7	71.1	893
{PYSHAGE} Column No 1922 The age of the employee		0.5	7	2.7	34	4.1	52	0.2	3	92.4	1160
{PYSHSEX} Column No 1923 The sex of the employee		0.2	2	0.5	6	0.6	8	0.1	1	98.6	1238
{PYSHFAM} Column No 1924 The employee's family responsiblities		0.4	5	2.3	29	3.8	48	-	-	93.4	1173
{PYSHQUAL} Column No 1925 The employee's education and formal qualifications		3.0	38	7.7	97	18.0	226	0.6	7	70.7	887

Base : Self-completion respondents (n = 1255)

NB   A variable was derived from {PYSHLONG} - {PYSHQUAL}:

	Code	%	No
{PYSHDK} Column No 1926			
(Three reasons not given)	6	2.0	25
(Misunderstood question)	7	1.9	24
Can't choose	8	3.9	49
(NA)	9	3.2	40
(Blank)	10	89.0	1118
Base : Self-completion respondents			1255

MANAGEMENT-EMPLOYEE RELATIONS

1989   Q.B205a   {ALWYSCON} Column No 1927
How much do you agree or disagree with this statement? There will always be conflict between
management and workers because they are really on opposite sides.
(Please tick one box)

	Code	%	No
Strongly agree	1	7.7	96
Agree	2	30.2	380
Neither agree nor disagree	3	18.7	234
Disagree	4	33.2	416
Strongly disagree	5	5.8	73
Can't choose	8	3.0	38
(NA)	9	1.4	18
Base : Self-completion respondents			1255

IMPORTANT FEATURES OF A JOB

1989   Q.B206a-i   {JBIMSECR}{JBIMHINC}{JBIMADVC}{JBIMTIME}{JBIMINTR}{JBIMINDP}{JBIMHELP}{JBIMUSE}
{JBIMFLEX}   Column Nos 1929-37
From the following list, please tick one box for each item to show how important *you personally* think it is in a job.

	Very important 1		Important 2		Neither important nor unimportant 3		Not important 4		Not important at all 5		Can't choose 8		(NA) 9	
Code	%	No	%	No	%	No	%	No	%	No	%	No	%	No
a) {JBIMSECR} Column No 1929 Job security	57.8	725	37.1	465	2.8	35	0.6	8	0.1	2	0.6	8	1.0	13
b) {JBIMHINC} Column No 1930 High income	17.7	222	61.0	765	13.4	168	4.3	54	0.3	4	0.6	7	2.8	35
c) {JBIMADVC} Column No 1931 Good opportunities for advancement	29.6	371	53.5	671	9.7	121	3.5	44	0.1	1	1.1	14	2.7	33
d) {JBIMTIME} Column No 1932 A job that leaves a lot of leisure time	7.3	92	34.7	435	33.8	424	17.9	225	1.4	17	1.5	19	3.5	43
e) {JBIMINTR} Column No 1933 An interesting job	48.7	611	45.6	572	2.8	35	0.4	5	0.1	1	0.3	4	2.2	28
f) {JBIMINDP} Column No 1934 A job that allows someone to work independently	20.2	254	44.1	553	23.9	300	7.5	94	0.3	4	1.7	21	2.2	28
g) {JBIMHELP} Column No 1935 A job that allows someone to help other people	17.8	223	47.3	594	24.5	308	6.1	76	0.6	8	1.1	14	2.6	33
h) {JBIMUSE} Column No 1936 A job that is useful to society	20.2	254	42.6	534	25.2	316	6.7	84	1.0	12	1.7	21	2.6	33
i) {JBIMFLEX} Column No 1937 A job with flexible working hours	14.0	176	31.3	392	32.1	403	16.1	202	2.9	36	1.6	20	2.0	25

Base : Self-completion respondents (n = 1255)

BAD THINGS ABOUT BEING UNEMPLOYED

1989   Q.B207   {NOCONTCT}{NOMONEY}{NOSLFCON}{LSRESPCT}{FAMTENSN}{LSJBEXPR}{TOOMCHTM} {DKUNEMP} Column Nos 1941-48

Suppose you were unemployed and couldn't find a job. Which of the following problems do you think would be the worst? Please write '1' in the box next to the *worst* thing. Then write '2' beside the *next worst* thing. And '3' beside the *third worst* thing. Leave the other boxes blank.

	Code	Worst thing 1		2nd worst thing 2		3rd worst thing 3		(Ticked box) 6		(Blank) 10	
		%	No	%	No	%	No	%	No	%	No
{NOCONTCT} Column No 1941 Lack of contact with people at work		5.7	71	9.0	113	12.4	156	0.5	6	72.4	909
{NOMONEY} Column No 1942 Not enough money		54.3	682	18.1	227	8.5	107	1.6	19	17.4	219
{NOSLFCON} Column No 1943 Loss of self-confidence		17.1	215	23.4	294	19.8	248	0.8	10	38.9	488
{LSRESPCT} Column No 1944 Loss of respect from friends and acquaintances		1.0	13	3.9	49	5.0	63	0.6	8	89.5	1123
{FAMTENSN} Column No 1945 Family tensions		8.4	105	25.2	316	19.6	247	0.5	7	46.3	581
{LSJBEXPR} Column No 1946 Loss of job experience		2.5	31	6.6	83	12.5	157	0.5	7	77.9	978
{TOOMCHTM} Column No 1947 Not knowing how to fill one's time		1.4	18	3.5	44	10.2	129	0.5	6	84.3	1058

Base : Self-completion respondents (n = 1255)

NB A variable was derived from {NOCONTCT} - {TOOMCHTM}

	Code	%	No
{DKUNEMP} Column No 1948			
(Three reasons not given)	6	2.3	29
(Misunderstood question)	7	1.4	18
Can't choose	8	4.0	50
(NA)	9	2.5	31
(Blank)	10	89.8	1127
Base : Self-completion respondents			1255

NB {NOCONTCT}: SPSS file lists variable name as {NOCONCT}

JOB PREFERENCES: EMPLOYMENT STATUS AND FIRM SIZE

1989   Q.B208a,b   {CHEMPSTA}{CHFRMSIZ} Column Nos 1949-50
Suppose you were working and could choose between different kinds of jobs.

1989   Q.B208a   {CHEMPSTA} Column No 1949
Which of the following would *you personally* choose? I would choose ...
(please tick one box only) ...

	Code	%	No
... being an employee,	1	47.9	602
[or,] being self-employed?	2	43.8	550
Can't choose	8	7.2	90
(NA)	9	1.0	13
Base : Self-completion respondents			1255

1989   Q.B208b   {CHFRMSIZ} Column No 1950
[Which of the following would *you personally* choose?] I would choose ...
(please tick one box only) ...

	Code	%	No
... working in a small firm,	1	61.1	767
[or,] working in a large firm?	2	24.2	304
Can't choose	8	13.3	167
(NA)	9	1.4	17
Base : Self-completion respondents			1255

JOB PREFERENCES: SECTOR

1989   Q.B208c,d   {CHINDSEC} {CHPRVPUB} Column Nos 1951-52

[Suppose you were working and could choose between different kinds of jobs]

1989   Q.B208c   {CHINDSEC} Column No 1951
[And] which of the following would *you personally* choose? I would choose ...
(please tick one box only) ...

	Code	%	No
... working in a manufacturing industry,	1	29.0	364
[or,] working in an office, in sales or in service?	2	51.9	652
Can't choose	8	17.6	221
(NA)	9	1.4	18
Base : Self-completion respondents			1255

1989   Q.B208d   {CHPRVPUB} Column No 1952
[Which of the following would *you personally* choose?] I would choose ...
(please tick one box only) ...

	Code	%	No
... working in a private business,	1	58.4	732
[or,] working for the government or civil service?	2	22.5	283
Can't choose	8	17.4	218
(NA)	9	1.7	22
Base : Self-completion respondents			1255

HOURS WORKED A WEEK

1989   Q.B210   {PDWORK10} Column No 1955
Do you usually work 10 hours or more a week for pay in your (main) job? (Please tick one box only)

	Code	%	No
Yes, I usually work 10 hours or more a week in my (main) job	1	56.6	711
No, I usually work less than 10 hours a week in my (main) job	2	2.4	31
No, I don't work for pay at the moment	3	40.2	505
(NA)	9	0.7	9
Base : Self-completion respondents			1255

NB This variable appears on the SPSS file as {HRSWORKD}

ATTITUDES TO TRAINING AT WORK

1987   Q.A228a-f / B236a-f   {TRAINNG1} - {TRAINNG6} Column Nos 2150-55
Please tick one box to show how much you feel about training for people in work.

	Code	Agree strongly 1		Agree 2		Neither agree nor disagree 3		Disagree 4		Disagree strongly 5		(DK) 8		(NA) 9	
		%	No	%	No	%	No	%	No	%	No	%	No	%	No
a) {TRAINNG1} Column No 2150 Most employers are unwilling to pay for better training for their staff		8.4	203	43.2	1047	24.7	600	20.2	491	1.3	31	0.2	5	2.0	49
b) {TRAINNG2} Column No 2151 People who get training at work find their jobs more interesting		14.0	339	70.8	1718	10.1	246	3.1	76	0.1	3	0.1	3	1.6	40
c) {TRAINNG3} Column No 2152 Having well-trained staff benefits employers more than workers		10.9	263	38.0	922	26.4	641	21.7	525	1.0	23	0.2	5	1.8	45
d) {TRAINNG4} Column No 2153 People who get training at work end up with better pay		6.2	149	50.4	1222	26.0	631	14.2	345	0.8	19	0.2	6	2.1	52
e) {TRAINNG5} Column No 2154 Training at work is really only for young people or people starting new jobs		2.6	62	14.9	361	12.8	310	57.0	1381	10.6	257	0.2	5	2.0	48
f) {TRAINNG6} Column No 2155 The government ought to help employers pay for the training of their staff		8.8	212	42.1	1022	21.6	524	22.8	552	2.7	66	0.2	4	1.8	44

Base : Self-completion respondents (n = 2424)

ATTITUDES TO GOVERNMENT TRAINING AND EMPLOYMENT SCHEMES

1987 Q.A229a-g/B237a-g *{LSCHEME1}-{LSCHEME4} {OSCHEME1}-{OSCHEME3}* Column Nos 2156-59, 2160-62
The government these days pays for a number of schemes for unemployed people.

First, please *tick one box* to show how much you agree or disagree with *each* of these statements about *government training schemes for school-leavers.*

	Agree strongly 1		Agree 2		Neither agree nor disagree 3		Disagree 4		Disagree strongly 5		(DK) 8		(NA) 9	
Code	%	No	%	No	%	No	%	No	%	No	%	No	%	No

Government training schemes for school leavers:

a) {LSCHEME1} Column No 2156
Are a good way of giving young people better job prospects?

9.8	239	50.5	1224	14.7	357	18.9	459	3.9	95	0.2	6	1.9	45

b) {LSCHEME2} Column No 2157
Benefit employers more than the young people taking part?

17.2	416	38.9	943	21.7	526	19.2	465	0.7	17	0.5	12	1.9	46

c) {LSCHEME3} Column No 2158
Are a bad substitute for proper job experience?

15.4	373	36.5	885	20.7	501	23.6	573	1.3	32	0.4	9	2.1	51

d) {LSCHEME4} Column No 2159
Are a good way for young people to get training after they leave school?

6.5	158	54.9	1331	16.5	400	17.0	412	2.9	71	0.3	7	1.8	45

Base : Self-completion respondents (n = 2424)

And now *tick one box* to show how much you agree or disagree with *each* of these statements about *government employment schemes for people other than school leavers:*

	Agree strongly 1		Agree 2		Neither agree nor disagree 3		Disagree 4		Disagree strongly 5		(DK) 8		(NA) 9	
Code	%	No	%	No	%	No	%	No	%	No	%	No	%	No

Government employment schemes for people other than school leavers:

e) {OSCHEME1} Column No 2160
Government employment schemes are a waste of taxpayers' money

6.6	161	15.0	363	26.2	635	45.7	1107	3.7	91	0.4	9	2.4	58

f) {OSCHEME2} Column No 2161
The government should provide more schemes for unemployed people to do work that is useful to society

16.3	395	62.8	1522	11.4	278	6.4	156	0.9	22	0.2	5	1.9	47

g) {OSCHEME3} Column No 2162
The government should do more to encourage unemployed people to set up their own businesses

11.7	283	53.4	1294	23.3	566	8.1	197	0.9	22	0.3	8	2.2	54

Base : Self-completion respondents (n = 2424)

CAREER ADVICE TO GIRL SCHOOL LEAVER

1984   Q.203a   {GIRLADV1} - {GIRLADV8} Column Nos 1521,1523,1525,1527,1529,1531,1533,1535
Suppose you were advising a 16 year old *girl* school leaver on the *two* most important things she should look for in a job. Please put a '1' in the box next to the most important thing in the list, and a '2' next to the *second most* important.

		Most Important 1		Second most important 2		(Not mentioned) 3		(DK) 8		(NA) 9	
	Code	%	No	%	No	%	No	%	No	%	No
i) {GIRLADV1} Column No 1521 High starting wage or salary		4.1	62	4.6	69	84.1	1280	0.3	4	7.0	107
ii) {GIRLADV2} Column No 1523 Secure job for the future		41.7	634	12.7	194	38.4	584	0.2	3	7.1	108
iii) {GIRLADV3} Column No 1525 Opportunities for career development		23.8	363	27.4	417	41.5	632	0.3	5	6.9	106
iv) {GIRLADV4} Column No 1527 Satisfying work		19.4	296	23.3	355	50.0	761	0.3	5	6.9	106
v) {GIRLADV5} Column No 1529 Good working conditions		2.6	39	16.1	245	74.1	1128	0.3	4	7.0	107
vi) {GIRLADV6} Column No 1531 Pleasant people to work with		1.0	15	6.7	102	85.0	1295	0.3	4	7.0	107
vii) {GIRLADV7} Column No 1533 Short working hours		0.1	1	0.9	14	91.7	1397	0.3	4	7.0	107
viii) {GIRLADV8} Column No 1535 A lot of responsibility		0.1	2	1.1	16	91.5	1394	0.3	4	7.0	107

Base : Self-completion respondents (n = 1522)

NB See p. G.1-23 below for a condensed presentation of these data

CAREER ADVICE TO BOY SCHOOL LEAVER

1984   Q.203b   {BOYADV1} - {BOYADV8} Column Nos 1522,1524,1526,1528,1530,1532,1534,1536
And if you were advising a 16 year old *boy* school leaver, which would be the *first* and which the *second* most important? Please place a '1' and '2' in the [appropriate] boxes.

			Most important 1		Second most important 2		(Not mentioned) 3		(DK) 8		(NA) 9	
		Code	%	No	%	No	%	No	%	No	%	No
i)	{BOYADV1} High starting wage or salary	Column No 1522	3.5	53	5.2	79	83.6	1273	0.3	4	7.5	114
ii)	{BOYADV2} Secure job for the future	Column No 1524	52.5	800	17.3	264	22.4	341	0.3	4	7.5	114
iii)	{BOYADV3} Opportunities for career development	Column No 1526	25.2	384	40.3	613	26.8	408	0.3	5	7.4	113
iv)	{BOYADV4} Satisfying work	Column No 1528	9.9	151	17.1	260	65.3	994	0.3	4	7.5	114
v)	{BOYADV5} Good working conditions	Column No 1530	0.7	10	8.8	133	82.9	1261	0.3	4	7.5	114
vi)	{BOYADV6} Pleasant people to work with	Column No 1532	0.1	2	1.4	22	90.7	1381	0.3	4	7.5	114
vii)	{BOYADV7} Short working hours	Column No 1534	-	-	0.4	7	91.8	1398	0.3	4	7.5	114
viii)	{BOYADV8} A lot of responsibility	Column No 1536	0.3	5	1.8	27	90.2	1373	0.3	4	7.5	114

Base : Self-completion respondents (n = 1522)

NB See p. G.1-23 below for a condensed presentation of these data

CAREER ADVICE TO SCHOOL LEAVERS

1984   Q.203a,b   {GIRL1ST}{GIRL2ND};{BOY1ST}{BOY2ND} (Variables derived from Column Nos 1521-36)
a) Suppose you were advising a 16 year old *girl* school leaver on the *two* most important things she should
look for in a job. Please put a '1' in the box next to the *most* important thing in the list, and a '2' next
to the *second most* important [in Column a)]

b) And if you were advising a 16 year old *boy* school leaver, which would be the *first* and which the *second*
most important. Please place a '1' and '2' in the boxes [in Column b)]

| | | a) Girl school leaver | | | | b) Boy school leaver | | | |
| | | Most Important {GIRL1ST} | | Second most important {GIRL2ND} | | Most Important {BOY1ST} | | Second most important {BOY2ND} | |
	Code	%	No	%	No	%	No	%	No
High starting wage or salary	1	4.1	62	4.6	69	3.5	53	5.2	79
Secure job for the future	2	41.7	634	12.7	194	52.5	800	17.3	264
Opportunities for career development	3	23.8	363	27.4	417	25.2	384	40.3	613
Satisfying work	4	19.4	296	23.3	355	9.9	151	17.1	260
Good working conditions	5	2.6	39	16.1	245	0.7	10	8.8	133
Pleasant people to work with	6	1.0	15	6.7	102	0.1	2	1.4	22
Short working hours	7	0.1	1	0.9	14	-	-	0.4	7
A lot of responsibility	8	0.1	2	1.1	16	0.3	5	1.8	27
(DK)	98	0.3	4	0.3	4	0.3	4	0.3	4
(NA)	99	7.0	107	7.0	107	7.0	114	7.5	114
Base : Self-completion respondents			1522		1522		1522		1522

NB These variables were derived from {BOYADV1}-{BOYADV8} and {GIRLADV1}-{GIRLADV8} (see pp. G.1-21 and 22 above):
'most important', code 1; 'second most important', code 2; not mentioned, code 3; (DK), code 8; (NA), code 9

FUTURE EFFECT OF 'NEW TECHNOLOGY' ON NUMBER OF JOBS

1984   Q.214a,b   {TECHEFF1}{TECHEFF2} Column Nos 1607-08
New kinds of technology are being introduced more and more in Britain: computers and word processors,
robots in factories and so on.

a) Please tick a box to show what effect you think this technology will have over the next *three years or so*?

b) Now tick one box to say what effect you think this technology will have over the next *ten years or so*?

| | a) Over next three years {TECHEFF1} | | b) Over next ten years {TECHEFF2} | |
	%	No	%	No
It will increase the number of jobs available	13.2	201	17.5	267
It will reduce the number of jobs available	63.1	961	65.6	998
It will make no difference to the number of jobs available	19.1	291	11.7	177
(DK)	0.8	12	0.9	14
(NA)	3.8	58	4.3	66
Base : Self-completion respondents		1522		1522

NB A similar question was asked in 1985 and 1987 (see p. G.1-9 above)

CAREER ADVICE TO SCHOOL LEAVERS AND GRADUATES

1983   Q.202a,b   *{JOBAD16}{JOBAD21}* Column Nos 1019-20

a) Suppose you were advising a 16 year old school leaver on the most important thing he should look for in a job. Which one of the items on this list would be the most important? (Please tick one box)

b) And if you were advising a 21 year old university or college graduate, which one would be the most important? (Please tick one box)

	a) 16 year old school leaver *{JOBAD16}*		b) 21 year old graduate *{JOBAD21}*	
	%	No	%	No
High starting wage or salary	1.0	15	1.8	28
Secure job for the future	41.0	661	30.9	497
Opportunities for career development	29.4	473	44.2	712
Satisfying work	23.2	373	16.3	263
Good working conditions	1.4	23	1.2	20
Pleasant people to work with	1.3	21	0.8	13
Short working hours	-	-	0.1	2
A lot of responsibility	0.4	6	2.2	36
(NA)	2.4	38	2.4	39
Base : Self-completion respondents		1610		1610

RESPONDENT: ECONOMIC POSITION IN PAST WEEK - 1

{RECONACT}; {RFTEDUC} {RTRAING} {RPAIDWRK} {RWAITWRK} {RREGISTD} {RSEEKWRK} {RNTLOOK} {RSICK} {RRETIRED} {RATHOME} {RELSE}

Question: (Show card) **Which of these descriptions applies to what you were doing last week, that is, in the seven days ending last Sunday? Any others?** (Interviewer: code all that apply)

		1983		1984		1985		1986		1987		1989	
		%	No	%	No	%	No	%	No	%	No	%	No
Question No		28		25		19		21		22		22	
Column No		314-15		272-73		245-46		256-57		256-57		267-68	
(i) {RECONACT}	Code												
In full-time education (at school or college) not paid for by employer (including on vacation)	1	1.9	32	1.6	27	1.4	25	2.1	65	1.9	53	2.2	64
On government training/employment scheme (eg Employment Training, Youth Training programme etc)	2	-	-	0.3	4	0.7	13	0.6	18	0.4	11	0.7	21
In paid work (or away temporarily) for at least 10 hours in the week	3	52.8	907	51.6	848	53.4	945	55.5	1702	55.3	1531	56.4	1652
Waiting to take up paid work already accepted	4	0.5	8	0.2	4	0.5	9	0.3	8	0.5	13	0.2	7
Unemployed *and* registered at a benefit office	5	6.9	118	4.9	80	6.4	114	5.3	163	5.1	142	2.8	82
Unemployed, *not* registered, but actively looking for a job	6	-	-	0.9	15	1.1	20	1.1	35	0.8	23	0.7	21
Unemployed, wanting a job (of at least 10 hours a week), but not actively looking for a job	7	-	-	0.5	8	0.7	12	0.9	29	0.9	24	0.5	16
Permanently sick or disabled	8	2.2	38	3.8	63	2.2	39	2.3	70	2.8	78	3.2	95
Wholly retired from work	9	15.3	263	17.3	284	14.1	249	14.6	448	15.5	428	17.5	512
Looking after the home	10	20.1	346	18.6	307	19.3	341	17.1	524	16.5	457	15.5	454
(Doing something else)	11	0.4	7	0.2	4	0.2	4	0.1	5	0.2	5	0.2	7
(NA)	99	-	-	0.1	1	-	-	-	-	0.0	1	-	-
Base: All			1719		1645		1769		3066		2766		2930

1983-1987, 1989 -   Responses were recorded in two columns, the instructions to the interviewer being: 'If only one code at [column] I, transfer it to column II; if more than one at [column] I, transfer highest on list to [column] II. {RFTEDUC}-{RELSE} were recorded on the column numbers shown on pp.G.1 - 6 to G.1 - 8 below

1984-1987 -   Code 2 '...(eg Community Programme, Youth Training Scheme etc)

1983 -   In full-time education at school or college, not paid for by employer, code 1; In paid work of any sort for at least 10 hours in the week, code 2; 49.8% (n = 856), Away from a paid job because of holiday, temporary illness, etc, code 3; 3.0% (n = 51), Waiting to take up a job already accepted, code 4; Seeking work, code 5; 6.4% (n = 110), Prevented by temporary sickness or injury from seeking work, code 6; 0.5% (n = 8), Permanently sick or disabled, code 7; Wholly retired from work, code 8; Looking after the home, code 9; (Doing something else), code 0; These differences mean that comparisons with subsequent years must be made with some caution

RESPONDENT: ECONOMIC POSITION IN PAST WEEK - 1 (Continued)

			1983		1984		1985		1986		1987		1989	
			%	No	%	No	%	No	%	No	%	No	%	No
Question No					25		19		21		22			
Column No					260		247		258		258			
(ii) {RFTEDUC}		Code												
In full-time education														
Description does not apply	0		-	-	99.8	1642	99.9	1767	99.6	3054	99.7	2758	-	-
Description applies	1		-	-	0.2	3	0.1	2	0.4	12	0.3	8	-	-
Base: All					1645		1769		3066		2766			
Question No					25		19		21		22			
Column No					261		248		259		259			
(iii) {RTRAING}														
On government training/employment scheme														
Description does not apply	0		-	-	99.9	1644	99.7	1763	99.9	3062	100.0	2765	-	-
Description applies	2		-	-	0.1	1	0.3	6	0.1	4	0.0	1	-	-
Base: All					1645		1769		3066		2766			
Question No					25		19		21		22			
Column No					262		249		260		260			
(iv) {RPAIDWRK}														
In paid work for at least 10 hours in the week														
Description does not apply	0		-	-	93.0	1531	87.7	1552	84.9	2604	85.6	2367	-	-
Description applies	3		-	-	7.0	114	12.3	217	15.1	462	14.4	399	-	-
Base: All					1645		1769		3066		2766			
Question No					25		19		21		22			
Column No					263		250		261		261			
(v) {RWAITWRK}														
Waiting to take up paid work already accepted														
Description does not apply	0		-	-	99.9	1643	99.8	1765	99.7	3056	99.5	2753	-	-
Description applies	4		-	-	0.1	2	0.2	4	0.3	10	0.5	13	-	-
Base: All					1645		1769		3066		2766			

1983, 1989 - {RFTEDUC} - {RELSE} not on SPSS file

RESPONDENT: ECONOMIC POSITION IN PAST WEEK - 1 (Continued)

			1983		1984		1985		1986		1987		1989	
			%	No	%	No	%	No	%	No	%	No	%	No
	Question No				25		19		21		22			
	Column No				264		251		262		262			
(vi) *{RREGISTD}*		Code												
Unemployed *and* registered at a benefit office														
Description does not apply		0	-	-	**99.2**	1632	**98.5**	1743	**98.6**	3023	**98.5**	2725	-	-
Description applies		5	-	-	**0.8**	13	**1.5**	26	**1.4**	43	**1.5**	40	-	-
Base: All						1645		1769		3066		2766		
	Question No				25		19		21		22			
	Column No				265		252		263		263			
(vii) *{RSEEKWRK}*														
Unemployed, *not* registered, but actively looking for a job														
Description does not apply		0	-	-	**99.6**	1640	**99.7**	1763	**99.3**	3043	**99.6**	2754	-	-
Description applies		6	-	-	**0.4**	6	**0.3**	6	**0.7**	23	**0.4**	12	-	-
Base: All						1645		1769		3066		2766		
	Question No				25		19		21		22			
	Column No				266		253		264		264			
(viii) *{RNTLOOK}*														
Unemployed, wanting a job, but not actively looking for a job														
Description does not apply		0	-	-	**99.6**	1639	**99.4**	1759	**99.3**	3045	**99.3**	2747	-	-
Description applies		7	-	-	**0.4**	7	**0.6**	10	**0.7**	21	**0.7**	18	-	-
Base: All						1645		1769		3066		2766		
	Question No				25		19		21		22			
	Column No				267		254		265		265			
(ix) *{RSICK}*														
Permanently sick or disabled														
Description does not apply		0	-	-	**98.9**	1627	**99.2**	1755	**99.2**	3042	**98.5**	2725	-	-
Description applies		8	-	-	**1.1**	18	**0.8**	14	**0.8**	24	**1.5**	41	-	-
Base: All						1645		1769		3066		2766		

1983, 1989 - {RFTEDUC} - {RELSE} not on SPSS file

RESPONDENT: ECONOMIC POSITION IN PAST WEEK - 1 (Continued)

		1983		1984		1985		1986		1987		1989	
		%	No	%	No	%	No	%	No	%	No	%	No
Question No				25		19		21		22			
Column No				268		255		266		266			
(x) *{RRETIRED}*	Code												
Wholly retired from work													
Description does not apply	0	-	-	93.7	1541	94.1	1664	93.7	2871	91.7	2536	-	-
Description applies	9	-	-	6.3	104	5.9	105	6.3	194	8.3	230	-	-
Base: All					1645		1769		3066		2766		
Question No				25		19		21		22			
Column No				269		256		267		267			
(xi) *{RATHOME}*													
Looking after the home													
Description does not apply	0	-	-	79.8	1314	79.2	1401	76.2	2336	74.5	2061	-	-
Description applies	1	-	-	20.2	322	20.8	368	23.8	730	25.5	705	-	-
Base: All					1645		1769		3066		2766		
Question No				25		19		21		22			
Column No				270		257		268		268			
(xii) *{RELSE}*													
Doing something else													
Description does not apply	0	-	-	98.7	1625	99.3	1756	99.0	3035	99.1	2740	-	-
Description applies	2	-	-	1.3	21	0.7	13	1.0	31	0.9	26	-	-
Base: All					1645		1769		3066		2766		

1983, 1989 - {RFTEDUC} - {RELSE} not on SPSS file

RESPONDENT: ECONOMIC POSITION IN PAST WEEK - 2

{RECONPOS}

Variable derived from *{RECONACT}*, *{REMPLOYE}* and *{EJBHRCAT}*

		1983		1984		1985		1986		1987		1989	
		%	No	%	No	%	No	%	No	%	No	%	No
Column No				1658-59		970-71		2337-38		2235-36		2357-58	
	Code												
In paid work:													
employee, works full time	1	38.3	659	38.8	638	39.3	695	40.2	1233	39.5	1092	39.5	1159
employee, works part time	2	8.4	144	7.5	123	7.7	135	9.4	287	8.5	236	9.3	272
self-employed, works full time	3	5.5	95	4.7	77	5.4	95	5.2	159	6.1	167	6.3	184
self-employed, works part time	4	0.5	9	0.5	8	0.9	16	0.7	22	0.8	21	1.2	35
status not known	5	-	.	0.1	2	0.2	3	0.0	1	0.5	14	0.1	3
Waiting to take up paid work already accepted	6	0.5	8	0.2	4	0.5	9	0.3	8	0.5	13	0.2	7
Unemployed	7	6.9	119	6.2	102	8.2	146	7.4	227	6.8	189	4.1	119
Looking after the home	8	20.1	346	18.6	307	19.3	341	17.1	524	16.5	457	15.5	454
Retired	9	15.3	263	17.3	284	14.1	249	14.6	448	15.5	428	17.5	512
In full-time education	10	1.9	32	1.6	27	1.4	25	2.1	65	1.9	53	2.2	64
Other	11	2.6	44	4.3	71	3.1	55	3.0	92	3.4	95	4.2	122
(DK/NA)	12	-	.	0.1	1	-		-		0.0	1	-	-
Base: All			1719		1645		1769		3066		2766		2930

1983-1987, 1989 - Full time is '30 or more hours a week'

RESPONDENT: EMPLOYMENT STATUS

{REMPSTAT}

Variable derived from *{RSUPER}*, *{REMPLYEE}* and *{REMPWORK}* (occupational details collected)

	Code	1983 %	1983 No	1984 %	1984 No	1985 %	1985 No	1986 %	1986 No	1987 %	1987 No	1989 %	1989 No
Column No		826-27		859-60		930-31		1637-38		1337-38		1571-72	
[Not coded: never had a job]	0	4.5	77	9.4	154	7.4	131	7.8	238	4.8	132	4.1	122
Self-employed, 25 or more employees	1	0.5	8	0.1	2	0.1	2	0.4	13	0.2	7	0.3	9
Self-employed, 1-24 employees	2	3.4	59	3.7	61	3.5	61	4.1	125	3.5	97	3.5	103
Self-employed, no employees	3	3.5	60	2.8	46	4.9	86	3.5	109	5.0	138	5.7	167
Self-employed, no information about employees	4	0.1	2	0.1	2	0.1	1	0.1	2	0.1	2	0.1	3
Manager, 25 or more employees at workplace	5	3.8	65	3.0	50	4.9	87	5.4	166	5.6	156	5.5	160
Manager, 1-24 employees at workplace	6	3.5	60	4.2	69	3.4	60	3.1	95	3.4	95	3.3	98
Manager, no information about size of workplace	7	-	-	-	-	0.1	2	0.0	1	0.1	2	0.0	1
Foreman or supervisor	8	11.8	204	14.8	244	6.0	106	8.3	255	5.2	144	7.3	213
Other employee	9	47.4	815	60.8	1000	67.9	1202	65.9	2021	71.1	1967	69.3	2032
Employee (unclassifiable)	10	0.1	1	0.0	1	-	-	0.0	1	0.1	3	0.1	2
Information insufficient to classify	11	1.4	23	1.0	17	1.8	31	1.3	41	0.8	23	0.7	22
[Skipped: looks after home]	12	20.1	346	-	-	-	-	-	-	-	-	-	-
Base: All			1719		1645		1769		3066		2766		2930

1983-1987, 1989 - Employment status refers to either current or last job held

1983 - Respondents looking after the home were not asked for any occupational details about their last job. Data users should therefore take note that the 1983 figures are not comparable with those for subsequent years

RESPONDENT: OCCUPATIONAL SECTOR - 1

{RSECTOR}

Question: [If ever an employee] (Show card) **Which of the types of organisation on this card do / (did) you work for?**
(Interviewer: code first to apply)

	Code	1983 %	No	1984 %	No	1985 %	No	1986 %	No	1987 %	No	1989 %	No
Question No				99f		107f		A111f/B119f		907f		908f	
Column No				872-73		945-46		1654-55		1354-55		1617-18	
[Not asked: never an employee]	0	-	-	17.5	288	17.8	314	17.4	532	14.8	409	14.9	437
Private firm or company	1	-	-	52.1	858	53.1	939	52.6	1614	54.1	1496	54.2	1587
Nationalised industry/public corporation	2	-	-	7.2	118	7.5	132	7.0	216	6.2	172	6.0	176
Local Authority/Local Education Authority	3	-	-	11.2	184	10.3	181	11.2	343	11.8	326	11.3	332
Health Authority/NHS hospital	4	-	-	5.5	90	4.6	82	4.9	149	5.4	150	5.3	155
Central government/civil service	5	-	-	4.5	75	2.9	51	3.8	117	4.4	122	4.8	142
Charity or trust	6	-	-	0.9	15	0.9	16	0.9	28	0.9	24	1.0	30
Other	7	-	-	1.0	17	3.0	54	2.0	62	2.3	63	2.3	66
(DK)	98	-	-	-		-		-		0.0	1	0.0	1
(NA)	99	-	-	-		-		0.2	6	0.1	3	0.1	4
Base: All					1645		1769		3066		2766		2930

1984-1987, 1989 - Based on current or last job held
1984-1987 - code 4 = Health Authority/hospital

RESPONDENT: OCCUPATIONAL SECTOR - 2

{RINDSECT}

Variable derived from occupational details collected

	Code	1983 %	1983 No	1984 %	1984 No	1985 %	1985 No	1986 %	1986 No	1987 %	1987 No	1989 %	1989 No
Column No				1661		1062		2355		2253		2367	
Never had a job	0	-	-	9.4	154	7.4	131	7.8	238	4.8	132	4.1	122
Private sector - manufacturing	1	-	-	26.6	438	24.9	441	23.4	718	24.6	680	23.9	702
Private sector - non-manufacturing	2	-	-	32.7	537	38.1	673	37.1	1136	37.6	1040	30.7	899
Public sector - service	3	-	-	23.5	387	20.4	361	22.6	694	24.2	670	22.7	665
Public sector - manufacturing and transport	4	-	-	5.6	91	5.8	103	5.8	177	5.1	140	4.6	135
Insufficient information to classify	9	-	-	2.3	37	3.3	59	3.3	102	3.8	104	13.9	408
Base: All					1645		1769		3066		2766		2930

1984-1987, 1989 - Occupational sector refers to current or last job held

RESPONDENT: SIZE OF WORKPLACE

{REMPWORK}

Question: [If ever had a job] Including yourself, how many people *(are)/(were)* employed at the place you usually *(work)/(worked)* (from)?

[If self-employed] *(Do)/(did)* you have any employees? [If yes] How many?

		1983		1984		1985		1986		1987		1989	
		%	No	%	No	%	No	%	No	%	No	%	No
Question No				99h		107h		A111h/B119h		907h		908h	
Column No				874		947		1656		1356		1619	
	Code												
[Not asked: never had a job]	-1	-	-	9.4	154	7.4	131	7.8	238	4.8	132	4.1	122
No employees	0	-	-	-	-	4.9	87	4.0	124	5.2	143	6.0	175
Under 10	1	-	-	21.2	349	18.2	322	19.2	588	17.8	492	17.1	500
10 - 24	2	-	-	12.7	208	13.4	237	13.5	413	12.9	357	13.2	386
25 - 99	3	-	-	19.7	324	18.0	318	18.9	580	19.4	538	20.5	600
100 - 499	4	-	-	20.3	334	20.6	365	20.2	621	21.3	590	20.6	604
500 or more	5	-	-	14.4	236	14.7	260	14.1	431	15.7	434	16.2	475
(DK)	8	-	-	1.0	16	0.8	14	0.8	24	1.1	31	1.0	30
(NA)	9	-	-	1.4	23	2.0	35	1.6	48	1.8	49	1.3	39
Base: All					1645		1769		3066		2766		2930

1984 - Precode 'no employees' not on questionnaire

RESPONDENT: STANDARD INDUSTRIAL CLASSIFICATION (SIC) - GROUPED

{RINDDIV}

Variable derived from occupational details collected

		1983		1984		1985		1986		1987		1989	
		%	No	%	No	%	No	%	No	%	No	%	No
Column No				1665-66		1063-64		2359-60		2257-58		2369-70	
	Code												
Agriculture	0	1.2	21	2.0	33	1.6	29	1.2	36	1.7	46	1.2	35
Energy and water	1	2.1	36	2.2	36	2.8	50	2.2	68	2.4	65	2.8	83
Metals and mineral extraction	2	2.3	39	2.9	47	2.8	49	3.8	117	3.1	87	4.2	123
Metal goods engineering	3	9.6	166	11.3	185	10.1	179	10.5	323	9.6	264	9.5	277
Other manufacturing	4	9.1	156	12.0	197	11.7	207	9.6	295	10.8	299	10.3	302
Construction	5	4.9	84	5.5	91	5.9	105	4.5	139	6.2	172	5.9	171
Distribution	6	12.6	217	15.0	247	17.8	314	17.9	548	18.4	510	16.9	494
Transport and communications	7	5.1	88	4.8	78	4.8	84	5.9	182	5.5	152	5.0	146
Financial services	8	4.7	81	6.5	107	7.5	132	7.2	219	7.3	201	8.0	236
Other services	9	20.8	357	26.8	440	25.2	445	26.8	821	27.4	757	29.2	855
[Not coded: never had a job]	98	20.1	346	9.4	154	7.4	131	7.8	238	4.8	132	4.1	122
Not classifiable	99	7.4	127	1.7	28	2.4	42	2.6	80	2.9	80	3.0	87
Base: All			1719		1645		1769		3066		2766		2930

1983 - Respondents coded as 'looking after the home' were not asked for their occupational details (and are coded as 98); so data are not comparable with those for subsequent years

1983 - 1987, 1989 - Based on currrent or last job held

RESPONDENT: NON-MANUAL OR MANUAL OCCUPATION

{RMANUAL}

Variable derived from *{RSEG}* (occupational details collected)

	Code	1983 %	1983 No	1984 %	1984 No	1985 %	1985 No	1986 %	1986 No	1987 %	1987 No	1989 %	1989 No
Column No			831		864		935		1542		1342		1576
[Not coded: never had a job]	0	4.5	77	9.4	154	7.4	131	7.8	238	4.8	132	4.1	122
Non-manual occupation	1	35.3	606	44.1	726	45.5	805	47.2	1448	49.6	1371	49.3	1444
Manual occupation	2	38.8	666	45.2	743	44.9	795	43.0	1318	43.6	1207	44.8	1312
[Not asked: looks after home]	7	20.1	346	-	-	-	-	-	-	-	-	-	-
In armed forces	8	0.2	3	0.1	2	0.3	5	0.3	9	0.6	16	0.5	14
Insufficient information to classify	9	1.2	21	1.2	20	1.9	33	1.7	53	1.4	39	1.4	40
Base: All			1719		1645		1769		3066		2766		2930

1983-1987, 1989 - Occupation refers to either current or last job held

1983 - Respondents coded as 'looking after the home' were not asked for their occupational details; so data are not comparable with those for subsequent years

WHETHER CURRENTLY A TRADE UNION MEMBER

{UNION}

Question: Can I just check, are you *now* a member of a trade union or staff association? (Interviewer: probe for union or staff association)

	Code	1983 %	1983 No	1984 %	1984 No	1985 %	1985 No	1986 %	1986 No	1987 %	1987 No	1989 %	1989 No
Question No		96a		100a		108a		A112a/B120a		908a		909a	
Column No		839		875		948		1657		1357		1620	
Yes: trade union	1	}26.9	463	}26.2	430	23.5	417	23.9	733	23.6	654	22.7	666
Yes: staff association	2					2.2	40	2.9	89	3.5	97	3.0	87
No	3	68.3	1174	73.2	1204	74.0	1309	73.0	2238	72.6	2009	74.1	2172
(DK)	8	-	-	-	-	-	-	-	-	-	-	-	-
(NA)	9	4.8	82	0.7	11	0.2	4	0.2	6	0.2	6	0.2	5
Base: All			1719		1645		1769		3066		2766		2930

1983 - No (DK)

1983, 1984 - Yes, code 1; No, code 2; - Trade union and staff association not coded separately

WHETHER EVER A TRADE UNION MEMBER

{UNIONEVR}

Question: [If not currently member of trade union or staff association] **Have you *ever* been a member of a trade union or staff assocation?**

	Code	1983 %	1983 No	1984 %	1984 No	1985 %	1985 No	1986 %	1986 No	1987 %	1987 No	1989 %	1989 No
Question No		96b		100b		108b		A112b/B120b		908b		909b	
Column No		840		876		949		1658		1358		1621	
[Not asked: currently member of trade union or staff association]	0	-	-	26.2	430	25.8	456	26.8	821	27.2	751	25.7	754
Yes: trade union	1	} 55.1	} 947	} 29.8	} 490	25.8	457	27.3	838	27.1	749	28.4	834
Yes: staff association	2					2.5	44	3.0	92	3.1	85	2.8	81
No	3	40.1	689	43.4	714	45.5	804	42.6	1305	42.4	1172	42.5	1246
(DK)	8	-	-	-	-	0.1	1	0.0	1	-	-	-	-
(NA)	9	4.8	83	0.7	11	0.4	7	0.3	9	0.3	10	0.6	17
Base: All			1719		1645		1769		3066		2766		2930

1983 - No (DK); all respondents were asked this question, so data users should note that the 1983 figures are not comparable with those for subsequent years
1983, 1984 - Yes code 1; No, code 2; Trade union and and staff association not coded separately

TRADE UNION ACTIVITIES

{UNION1} {UNION2} {UNION3} {UNION4} {UNION5} {UNION6}

Question: [If ever been member of trade union or staff association] **Have you ever** ... (read out):

	Code	1983 %	1983 No	1984 %	1984 No	1985 %	1985 No	1986 %	1986 No	1987 %	1987 No	1989 %	1989 No
Question No		96c		100c		108c		A112c/B120c		908c		909c	
Column No		841		907		950		1659		1359		1622	
(i) {UNION1} **Attended a union or staff association meeting**													
[Not asked: never been member of trade union or staff association]	0	40.1	689	43.4	714	45.5	805	42.6	1306	42.4	1172	42.5	1246
Yes	1	37.9	651	37.4	615	36.4	645	37.9	1162	38.2	1055	38.2	1119
No	2	16.9	291	18.5	304	17.6	312	19.0	584	18.8	519	18.7	548
(DK)	8	-	-	-	-	-	-	-	-	-	-	0.0	1
(NA)	9	5.1	88	0.8	13	0.4	8	0.5	14	0.7	19	0.6	17
Base: All			1719		1645		1769		3066		2766		2930

TRADE UNION ACTIVITIES (Continued)

	Code	1983 %	1983 No	1984 %	1984 No	1985 %	1985 No	1986 %	1986 No	1987 %	1987 No	1989 %	1989 No
Question No		96c		100c		108c		A112c/B120c		908c		909c	
Column No		842		908		951		1660		1360		1623	

(ii) {UNION2}

Voted in a union or staff association election or meeting

	Code	1983 %	1983 No	1984 %	1984 No	1985 %	1985 No	1986 %	1986 No	1987 %	1987 No	1989 %	1989 No
[Not asked: never been member of trade union or staff association]	0	40.1	689	43.4	714	45.5	805	42.6	1306	42.4	1172	42.5	1246
Yes	1	34.3	590	33.8	556	33.1	586	35.0	1074	34.9	966	36.4	1067
No	2	20.1	345	21.9	361	21.0	371	21.9	672	21.9	606	20.3	596
(DK)	8	-	-	0.1	1	-	-	-	-	0.0	1	0.2	4
(NA)	9	5.5	94	0.8	14	0.4	8	0.5	14	0.8	21	0.6	17
Base: All			1719		1645		1769		3066		2766		2930

		1983		1984		1985		1986		1987		1989	
Question No		96c		100c		108c		A112c/B120c		908c		909c	
Column No		843		909		952		1661		1361		1624	

(iii) {UNION3}

Put forward a proposal or motion at a union or staff association meeting

	Code	1983 %	1983 No	1984 %	1984 No	1985 %	1985 No	1986 %	1986 No	1987 %	1987 No	1989 %	1989 No
[Not asked: never been member of trade union or staff association]	0	40.1	689	43.4	714	45.5	805	42.6	1306	42.4	1172	42.5	1246
Yes	1	13.0	223	11.4	187	11.3	201	14.0	430	12.9	358	12.5	365
No	2	41.0	705	44.3	729	42.7	756	42.9	1315	43.9	1214	44.4	1302
(DK)	8	-	-	-	-	-	-	0.0	1	0.1	2	0.0	1
(NA)	9	5.9	101	0.9	16	0.4	8	0.5	14	0.7	20	0.6	17
Base: All			1719		1645		1769		3066		2766		2930

1983 - No (DK)

TRADE UNION ACTIVITIES (Continued)

		1983		1984		1985		1986		1987		1989	
		%	No	%	No	%	No	%	No	%	No	%	No
Question No		96c		100c		108c		A221c/B120c		908c		909c	
Column No		844		910		953		1662		1362		1625	
(iv) *{UNION4}*	Code												
Gone on strike													
[Not asked: never been member of trade union or staff association]	0	40.1	689	43.4	714	45.5	805	42.6	1306	42.4	1172	42.5	1246
Yes	1	18.6	319	20.0	330	19.8	351	19.0	582	19.7	545	18.8	549
No	2	35.8	615	35.8	589	34.1	604	38.0	1165	37.2	1028	38.2	1118
(DK)	8	-	-	-	-	0.0	1	-	-	0.0	1	-	-
(NA)	9	5.5	95	0.8	13	0.5	9	0.5	13	0.7	20	0.6	17
Base: All			1719		1645		1769		3066		2766		2930

		1983		1984		1985		1986		1987		1989	
Question No		96c		100c		108c		A112c/B120c		908c		909c	
Column No		845		911		954		1663		1363		1626	
(v) *{UNION5}*													
Stood in a picket line													
[Not asked: never been member of trade union or staff association]	0	40.1	689	43.4	714	45.5	805	42.6	1306	42.4	1172	42.5	1246
Yes	1	6.7	116	6.0	99	7.0	125	7.9	243	8.3	228	9.4	275
No	2	47.6	818	49.8	819	46.9	831	49.0	1502	48.6	1345	47.5	1391
(DK)	8	-	-	-	-	-	-	-	-	-	-	-	-
(NA)	9	5.6	96	0.8	13	0.5	9	0.5	15	0.8	21	0.6	18
Base: All			1719		1645		1769		3066		2766		2930

1983 - No (DK)

TRADE UNION ACTIVITIES (Continued)

		1983		1984		1985		1986		1987		1989	
		%	No	%	No	%	No	%	No	%	No	%	No
Question No		96c		100c		108c		A112c/B120c		908c		909c	
Column No		846		912		955		1664		1364		1627	

(vi) *{UNION6}*

Served as a lay representative such as a shop steward or branch committee member

		1983		1984		1985		1986		1987		1989	
[Not asked: never been member of trade union or staff association]	0	40.1	689	43.4	714	45.5	805	42.6	1306	42.4	1172	42.5	1246
Yes	1	6.9	119	9.0	148	7.0	123	8.8	269	7.4	206	7.7	225
No	2	47.4	814	46.8	770	47.0	832	48.0	1473	49.4	1366	49.2	1441
(DK)	8	-	-	-	-	-	-	-	-	-	-	-	-
(NA)	9	5.6	96	0.8	14	0.5	9	0.6	19	0.8	22	0.6	19
Base: All			1719		1645		1769		3066		2766		2930

1983 - '... served as a local official or shop steward'; No (DK)

SPOUSE/PARTNER: ECONOMIC POSITION IN PAST WEEK

{SECONACT}

Question: [If married/living as married] (Show card) **Which of these descriptions applied to what your** *(husband/wife/partner)* **was doing last week, that is the seven days ending last Sunday?** (Interviewer: probe) **Any others?**

		1983		1984		1985		1986		1987		1989	
		%	No	%	No	%	No	%	No	%	No	%	No
Question No				101		109a		A113b/B121a		909a		910a	
Column No				925-26		967-78		1676-77		1376-77		1628-29	
	Code												
[Not asked: not married/living as married]	0	-	-	31.5	519	32.5	575	30.3	930	29.8	825	30.1	883
In full-time education (at school or college) not paid for by employer, (including on vacation)	1	-	-	0.1	2	0.1	2	0.1	3	0.4	11	0.2	6
On government training/employment scheme (eg Employment Training, Youth Training programme etc)	2	-	-	0.1	1	0.4	7	0.1	4	0.1	3	0.2	7
In paid work (or away temporarily) for at least 10 hours in the week	3	-	-	39.1	643	39.9	707	42.8	1313	42.1	1163	42.6	1247
Waiting to take up paid work already accepted	4	-	-	0.1	1	0.1	1	0.2	6	0.1	4	0.1	4
Unemployed *and* registered at a benefit office	5	-	-	2.7	45	3.5	61	2.4	74	2.5	68	1.7	50
Unemployed, *not* registered, but actively looking for a job	6	-	-	0.5	8	0.4	6	0.1	4	0.2	4	0.3	8
Unemployed, wanting a job (of at least 10 hours a week), but not actively looking for a job	7	-	-	0.5	9	0.2	4	0.4	12	0.4	10	0.5	16
Permanently sick or disabled	8	-	-	1.8	29	1.7	30	1.8	54	1.9	51	1.7	49
Wholly retired from work	9	-	-	8.5	140	8.2	144	7.6	234	8.7	240	10.5	309
Looking after the home	10	-	-	14.6	241	13.0	230	14.0	429	13.8	380	12.0	352
(Doing something else)	11	-	-	0.2	3	-	1	0.1	2	0.1	2	0.1	2
(DK)	98	-	-	-	-	-		-	1	-	-	-	-
(NA)	99	-	-	0.2	4	-		-	2	0.1	2	-	-
Base: All					1645		1769		3066		2766		2930

1984-1987 · Code 2 '...(eg Community Programme, Youth Training Scheme etc)'

SPOUSE/PARTNER: EMPLOYMENT STATUS

{SEMPSTAT}

Variable derived from from {SSUPER}, {SEMPLOYE} and {SEMPWORK} (occupational details collected)

	Code	1983 %	1983 No	1984 %	1984 No	1985 %	1985 No	1986 %	1986 No	1987 %	1987 No	1989 %	1989 No
Column No				932-33		1012-13		1713-14		1413-14		1640-41	
[Not coded: not married/living as married; spouse/partner never had a job]	0	-	-	36.4	598	39.9	706	35.9	1100	35.5	981	31.4	921
Self-employed, 25 or more employees	1	-	-	0.2	3	0.2	4	0.2	7	0.3	7	0.3	7
Self-employed, 1-24 employees	2	-	-	2.8	46	1.8	32	2.9	90	3.7	103	3.1	90
Self-employed, no employees	3	-	-	2.8	46	3.0	52	3.7	112	4.1	112	4.2	124
Self-employed, no information about employees	4	-	-	0.2	4	-	-	0.2	5	0.2	5	0.1	3
Manager, 25 or more employees at workplace	5	-	-	2.9	47	3.5	63	3.9	119	4.1	113	4.3	127
Manager, 1-24 employees at workplace	6	-	-	2.9	47	2.3	41	1.8	54	2.4	65	2.5	73
Manager, no information about size of workplace	7	-	-	0.3	5	2.3	41	0.4	11	0.2	5	0.3	8
Foreman or supervisor	8	-	-	7.8	129	5.2	92	5.9	180	3.8	106	4.1	120
Other employee	9	-	-	42.7	703	43.3	767	44.9	1376	45.6	1262	48.8	1430
Employee (unclassifiable)	10	-	-	0.1	1	0.1	1	-	-	0.1	2	0.0	1
Information insufficient to classify	11	-	-	0.9	15	0.5	9	0.4	11	0.1	4	0.8	25
Base: All					1645		1769		3066		2766		2930

1984-1987, 1989 - Occupation refers to either current or last job held

SPOUSE/PARTNER: WHEN LAST HAD A PAID JOB

{SLASTJOB}

Question: [If married/living as married and spouse/partner not in paid job] **How long ago did your** *(husband/wife/partner)* **last have a paid job (other than the government scheme you mentioned) of at least 10 hours a week?**

		1983		1984		1985		1986		1987		1989	
		%	No	%	No	%	No	%	No	%	No	%	No
Question No						109b		A113b/B121b		909b		910b	
Column No						969		1678		1378		1630	
	Code												
[Not asked: not married/living as married; spouse/partner not in paid job]	0	-	-	-	-	76.6	1355	76.3	2340	75.1	2078	75.3	2207
Within past 12 months	1	-	-	-	-	2.3	40	2.4	73	1.9	53	2.0	58
Over 1 to 5 years ago	2	-	-	-	-	6.9	122	6.4	197	7.0	193	6.6	194
Over 5 to 10 years ago	3	-	-	-	-	4.2	75	5.1	155	5.9	164	6.7	195
Over 10 to 20 years ago	4	-	-	-	-	4.5	79	4.3	132	4.5	124	4.7	137
Over 20 years ago	5	-	-	-	-	4.1	72	3.8	116	4.6	126	3.1	92
Never had a paid job of at least ten hours a week	6	-	-	-	-	1.3	22	1.3	40	1.0	27	1.3	38
(DK)	8	-	-	-	-	0.1	1	0.1	2	-	-	-	1
(NA)	9	-	-	-	-	0.2	3	0.3	11	-	-	0.3	9
Base: All							1769		3066		2766		2930

SPOUSE/PARTNER: WHETHER EMPLOYEE OR SELF-EMPLOYED

{SEMPLOYE}

Question: [If married or living as married and spouse/partner ever had a job] *(Is)* **he/she** ... (read out) ...

		1983		1984		1985		1986		1987		1989	
		%	No	%	No	%	No	%	No	%	No	%	No
Question No				102e		110e		A114e/B122e		910e		911e	
Column No				944		1026		1729		1429		1658	
	Code												
[Not asked: not married/living as married; spouse/partner never had a job]	0	-	-	36.4	598	39.9	706	35.9	1100	35.5	981	31.4	921
... an employee,	1	-	-	56.8	934	54.7	967	56.6	1737	55.9	1546	60.0	1757
... or self-employed?	2	-	-	6.3	103	5.0	89	7.3	223	8.5	234	7.9	232
(DK)	8	-	-	0.1	1	0.1	1	-	-	-	-	-	-
(NA)	9	-	-	0.5	9	0.3	6	0.2	6	0.1	4	0.7	21
Base: All					1645		1769		3066		2766		2930

SPOUSE/PARTNER: OCCUPATIONAL SECTOR - 1

{SSECTOR}

Question: [If married/living as married and spouse/partner ever an employee] (Show card) **Which of the types or organisation on this card** *does/did he/she* **work for?** (Interviewer: code first to apply)

		1983		1984		1985		1986		1987		1989	
		%	No	%	No	%	No	%	No	%	No	%	No
Question No				102f		110f		A114f/B122f		910f		911f	
Column No				945-46		1027-28		1730-31		1430-31		1659-60	
	Code												
[Not asked: not married/living as married or spouse/partner never an employee]	0	-	-	43.2	711	45.3	802	43.4	1329	44.1	1219	40.0	1173
Private firm or company	1	-	-	35.5	584	35.7	631	35.2	1078	35.4	980	39.2	1149
Nationalised industry/public corporation	2	-	-	6.1	101	5.3	93	6.0	184	4.3	120	4.7	136
Local Authority/Local Education Authority	3	-	-	7.2	119	6.5	115	8.2	250	8.1	225	7.6	222
Health Authority/NHS hospital	4	-	-	3.9	64	3.4	60	3.0	92	3.5	97	3.2	95
Central government/civil service	5	-	-	2.4	39	2.2	39	2.7	84	2.6	73	3.4	100
Charity or trust	6	-	-	0.8	14	0.2	4	0.6	19	0.9	26	0.5	15
Other	7	-	-	0.7	12	1.4	25	0.8	23	0.8	22	1.3	37
(DK)	98	-	-	0.1	1	0.1	1	0.1	2	-	-	-	-
(NA)	99	-	-	0.1	1	-	-	0.1	4	0.1	4	0.1	4
Base: All					1645		1769		3066		2766		2930

1984-1987, 1989 - Based on current or last job held
1984-1987 - Code 4 = Health Authority/hospital

SPOUSE/PARTNER: OCCUPATIONAL SECTOR - 2

{SINDSECT}

Variable derived from occupational details collected

		1983		1984		1985		1986		1987		1989	
		%	No	%	No	%	No	%	No	%	No	%	No
Column No							1065		2357		2255		2368
	Code												
[Not coded: not married/living as married or spouse/partner not in paid work/never had a job]	0	-	.	-	.	39.9	706	35.9	1100	35.5	981	31.4	921
Private sector - manufacturing	1	-	.	-	.	17.4	308	16.3	499	17.2	476	15.9	466
Private sector - non-manufacturing	2	-	.	-	.	22.5	399	25.6	785	25.8	714	22.6	663
Public sector - service	3	-	.	-	.	13.8	245	15.8	483	15.8	438	15.1	443
Public sector - manufacturing and transport	4	-	.	-	.	4.5	80	4.5	139	3.7	102	3.5	103
Insufficient information to classify	9	-	.	-	.	1.8	31	1.9	59	2.0	54	11.4	335
Base: All							1769		3066		2766		2930

1985-1987, 1989 - Based on current or last job held

SPOUSE/PARTNER: SIZE OF WORKPLACE

{SEMPWORK}

Question: [If married or living as married and spouse/partner ever had a job] Including *(him-)/(herself)*, roughly how many people *(are)/(were)* employed at the place where *(he)/(she)* usually *works/(worked)* (from)?
[If self-employed] *(Does)/(did) (he)/(she)* have any employees? [If yes] How many?

		1983		1984		1985		1986		1987		1989	
		%	No	%	No	%	No	%	No	%	No	%	No
Question No				102h		110h		A114/B122h		910h		911h	
Column No				947		1029		1732		1432		1661	
	Code												
[Not asked: not married/living as married; spouse/partner never had a job]	-1	-	-	36.4	598	39.9	706	35.9	1100	35.5	981	31.4	921
No employees	0	-	-	-	-	3.0	52	3.9	119	4.3	118	4.2	123
Under 10	1	-	-	16.2	266	10.3	183	11.5	352	13.1	362	12.5	367
10-24	2	-	-	8.4	138	7.3	129	8.7	265	7.5	209	8.9	260
25-99	3	-	-	13.1	215	12.1	215	11.9	364	12.4	342	14.0	411
100-499	4	-	-	13.8	227	12.7	225	14.5	445	12.8	353	13.5	396
500 or more	5	-	-	9.8	161	11.4	202	10.6	326	11.0	304	11.9	349
(DK)	8	-	-	1.2	20	2.2	39	2.4	74	2.8	78	2.4	69
(NA)	9	-	-	1.2	20	1.1	19	0.6	18	0.7	20	1.2	34
Base: All					1645		1769		3066		2766		2930

1984 - Precode 'no employees' not on questionnaire

SPOUSE/PARTNER: IN FULL- OR PART-TIME JOB

{SPARTFUL}

Question: [If married/living as married and spouse/partner in paid work] **Is/was the job** ... (read out) ...

		1983		1984		1985		1986		1987		1989	
		%	No	%	No	%	No	%	No	%	No	%	No
Question No				102i		110i		A114i/B122i		910i		911i	
Column No				948		1030		1733		1433		1662	
	Code												
[Not asked: not married/living as married or spouse/partner not in paid work/never had a job]	0	-	-	36.4	598	39.9	706	35.9	1100	35.5	981	31.4	921
... full-time (30 hours +),	1	-	-	48.6	799	49.6	877	49.3	1513	50.4	1393	50.9	1491
... or part-time (10-29 hours)?	2	-	-	12.0	198	9.1	162	13.3	406	12.7	352	13.0	381
(DK)	8	-	-	0.1	1	-	-	-	-	0.0	1	0.0	1
(NA)	9	-	-	3.0	49	1.4	24	1.5	46	1.4	39	4.7	137
Base: All				1645		1769		3066		2766		2930	

1984-1987, 1989 - Based on current or last job held

SPOUSE/PARTNER: NON-MANUAL OR MANUAL OCCUPATION

{SMANUAL}

Variable derived from *{RSEG}* (occupational details collected)

		1983		1984		1985		1986		1987		1989	
		%	No	%	No	%	No	%	No	%	No	%	No
Column No				937		1017		1618		1418		1645	
	Code												
[Not coded: not married/living as married; spouse/partner never had a job]	0	-	-	36.4	598	39.9	706	35.9	1100	35.5	981	31.4	921
Non-manual occupation	1	-	-	31.8	523	30.2	535	32.8	1007	33.8	935	36.0	1056
Manual occupation	2	-	-	30.4	501	29.1	515	30.0	919	29.9	827	30.6	898
In armed forces	8	-	-	0.3	5	0.2	4	0.4	11	0.2	6	0.4	13
Insufficient information to classify	9	-	-	1.1	19	0.5	9	0.9	27	0.6	16	1.5	43
Base: All				1645		1769		3066		2766		2930	

1984-1987, 1989 - Occupation refers to either current or last job held

G Labour market and employment

G2 All in paid work

Table titles and cross references

IN PAID WORK: WHETHER EMPLOYEE OR SELF-EMPLOYED

{REMPLOYE}

Question: [If in paid work or away temporarily] **In your (main) job are you ... (read out) ...**

	Code	1983 %	1983 No	1984 %	1984 No	1985 %	1985 No	1986 %	1986 No	1987 %	1987 No	1989 %	1989 No
Question No		29		26		20		22		23		23	
Column No		316		274		258		269		269		271	
... an employee,	1	88.5	803	89.8	762	87.9	830	89.4	1521	87.7	1342	86.7	1432
... or self-employed?	2	11.5	104	10.2	86	12.1	115	10.6	181	12.3	188	13.3	220
(NA)	9	-	.	-	.	-	.	-	.	-	.	-	.
Base: All in paid work or away temporarily			907		848		945		1702		1531		1652

IN PAID WORK : FEELINGS ABOUT THEIR JOB

1989   Q.B213   {*PWLWKHRD*} Column No 1958
[If in paid job of 10 or more hours a week] Which of the following statements *best* describes your feelings about your job? (Please tick one box only) In my job ...

	Code	%	No
...I only work as hard as I have to	1	5.5	39
I work hard, but not so that it interferes with the rest of my life	2	36.4	262
[or,] I make a point of doing the best work I can, even if it sometimes does interfere with the rest of my life	3	55.8	402
Can't choose	8	0.4	3
(NA)	9	1.8	13
Base : Self-completion respondents in paid work			720

NB   This variable is {WORKHARD} on the SPSS file but has been changed as shown. {WORKHARD} at Q.B203 asked in 1987 relates to a different question (see p. F-20 above), and has now been renamed {PAYDIFF}

IN PAID WORK : WORKING HOURS PREFERENCES

1989   Q.B214   {*WORKEARN*} Column No 1959
[If in paid job of 10 or more hours a week] Think of the number of hours you work, and the money you earn in your main job, including any regular overtime. If you had only *one of these three choices* which of the following would you prefer? (Please tick one box only)

	Code	%	No
Work *longer* hours and earn *more money*	1	22.1	159
Work the *same* number of hours and earn the same money	2	61.8	445
Work *fewer* hours and earn *less money*	3	7.1	51
Can't choose	8	6.1	44
(NA)	9	2.8	20
Base : Self-completion respondents in paid work			720

IN PAID WORK : FACTORS BELIEVED TO DECIDE COLLEAGUES' RATES OF PAY

1989   Q.B215   *{PYISLONG}{PYISWELL}{PYISEXP}{PYISRATE}{PYISAGE}{PYISSEX}{PYISFAM}{PYISQUAL}* *{PYISDK}* Column Nos 1960-68

[If in paid job of 10 or more hours a week] Think of two people doing *the same kind of work* in your place of work. What do you personally think *is important* in deciding how much to pay them?
Looking at the things below, please write '1' in the box next to the thing you think *is most important* at your place of work. Then write '2' next to the thing you think *is next most important*. And '3' next to the thing you think *is third most important*. Leave the other boxes blank.

	Most important		2nd most important		3rd most important		(Ticked box)		(NA)		(Blank)	
Code	1		2		3		6		9		10	
	%	No	%	No	%	No	%	No	%	No	%	No

At your workplace, in deciding on pay for two people doing *the same kind of work*, how important *is*:

{PYISLONG}   Column No 1960
How long the employee has been with the firm

	%	No	%	No	%	No	%	No	%	No	%	No
How long the employee has been with the firm	6.5	47	10.0	72	25.3	182	0.2	2	1.3	9	56.7	408

{PYISWELL}   Column No 1961
How well the employee does the job

	%	No	%	No	%	No	%	No	%	No	%	No
How well the employee does the job	50.8	366	19.4	139	10.1	73	0.6	5	1.3	9	17.8	128

{PYISEXP}   Column No 1962
The experience of the employee in doing the work

	%	No	%	No	%	No	%	No	%	No	%	No
The experience of the employee in doing the work	12.8	92	43.8	315	17.9	129	0.5	3	1.3	9	23.7	171

{PYISRATE}   Column No 1963
The standard rate - giving both employees the same pay

	%	No	%	No	%	No	%	No	%	No	%	No
The standard rate - giving both employees the same pay	15.3	110	5.8	42	11.5	82	0.2	1	1.3	9	66.0	475

{PYISAGE}   Column No 1964
The age of the employee

	%	No	%	No	%	No	%	No	%	No	%	No
The age of the employee	1.1	8	2.4	17	4.0	29	0.1	1	1.3	9	91.2	656

{PYISSEX}   Column No 1965
The sex of the employee

	%	No	%	No	%	No	%	No	%	No	%	No
The sex of the employee	-	-	0.3	2	0.4	3	-	-	1.3	9	98.1	706

{PYISFAM}   Column No 1966
The employee's family responsibilities

	%	No	%	No	%	No	%	No	%	No	%	No
The employee's family responsibilities	0.3	2	1.7	12	2.1	15	0.2	2	1.3	9	94.4	679

{PYISQUAL}   Column No 1967
The employee's education and formal qualifications

	%	No	%	No	%	No	%	No	%	No	%	No
The employee's education and formal qualifications	2.8	20	5.9	42	16.8	121	0.2	2	1.3	9	73.1	526

Base: Self-completion respondents in paid work (n = 720)

NB A variable was derived from {PYISLONG}-{PYISQUAL}:

{PYISDK} Column No 1968	Code	%	No
(Three reasons not given)	6	1.7	12
(Misunderstood question)	7	1.2	9
Can't choose	8	3.4	24
(NA)	9	5.0	36
(Blank)	10	88.8	639
Base : Self-completion respondents in paid work			720

IN PAID WORK : ATTITUDES TOWARDS THEIR JOB

1989   Q.B216a-i   {JBISSECR}{JBISHINC}{JBISADVC}{JBISTIME}{JBISINTR}{JBISINDP}{JBISHELP}
{JBISUSE}{JBISFLEX} Column Nos 1971-79
[If in paid job of 10 or more hours a week] For each of these statements about your (main) job, please
tick one box to show how much you agree or disagree that it applies *to your job*.

		Strongly agree 1		Agree 2		Neither agree nor disagree 3		Disagree 4		Strongly disagree 5		Can't Choose 8		(NA) 9	
	Code	%	No	%	No	%	No	%	No	%	No	%	No	%	No
a) {JBISSECR} Column No 1971 **My job is secure**		16.2	117	38.8	279	20.5	147	14.4	104	4.7	34	1.3	9	4.2	30
b) {JBISHINC} Column No 1972 **My income is high**		2.1	15	14.5	104	31.4	226	36.6	263	10.5	76	0.9	7	3.9	28
c) {JBISADVC} Column No 1973 **My opportunities for advancement are high**		3.6	26	18.3	132	27.5	198	35.4	254	9.8	70	1.3	9	4.2	30
d) {JBISTIME} Column No 1974 **My job leaves a lot of leisure time**		3.2	23	21.9	158	24.6	177	37.0	266	8.5	61	0.5	4	4.2	30
e) {JBISINTR} Column No 1975 **My job is interesting**		19.8	142	55.0	396	13.6	98	6.2	44	1.7	13	0.1	1	3.6	26
f) {JBISINDP} Column No 1976 **I can work independently**		18.2	131	58.8	423	9.2	66	7.9	57	1.5	10	0.4	3	4.2	30
g) {JBISHELP} Column No 1977 **In my job I can help other people**		17.6	126	45.0	324	19.4	140	11.7	84	1.5	11	0.8	5	4.1	29
h) {JBISUSE} Column No 1978 **My job is useful to society**		16.2	116	37.1	267	25.2	182	14.0	101	1.8	13	1.2	9	4.5	32
i) {JBISFLEX} Column No 1979 **My job has flexible working hours**		8.5	62	26.2	188	13.2	95	34.9	251	11.9	85	1.4	10	3.9	28

Base : Self-completion respondents in paid work (n = 720)

IN PAID WORK : CHARACTERISTICS OF THEIR JOB

1989   Q.B217a-g   {WRKEXHST}{WRKPHYSC}{WRKSTRES}{WRKBORED}{WRKDANGR}{WRKUNHEL}{WRKUNPLS}

Column Nos 2008-14

[If in paid job of 10 or more hours a week] Please tick one box for *each* item below to show *how often* it applies to your work.

	Code	Always 1		Often 2		Sometimes 3		Hardly ever 4		Never 5		Can't choose 8		(NA) 9	
		%	No	%	No	%	No	%	No	%	No	%	No	%	No
a) {WRKEXHST} Column No 2008 How often do you come home from work exhausted		6.3	45	36.2	261	45.6	328	7.4	53	1.5	11	0.0	-	3.1	22
b) {WRKPHYSC} Column No 2009 How often do you have to do hard physical work		7.7	55	14.6	105	26.7	192	19.6	141	28.0	201	0.0	-	3.5	25
c) {WRKSTRES} Column No 2010 How often do you find your work stressful		6.3	45	22.2	160	47.8	344	13.6	98	5.9	42	0.3	2	3.9	28
d) {WRKBORED} Column No 2011 How often are you bored at work		1.8	13	3.8	27	31.0	223	33.5	241	26.3	189	0.1	1	3.5	25
e) {WRKDANGR} Column No 2012 How often do you work in dangerous conditions		3.3	24	5.5	39	20.2	145	18.5	133	48.0	345	1.2	8	3.3	24
f) {WRKUNHEL} Column No 2013 How often do you work in unhealthy conditions		2.9	21	5.3	38	22.6	163	18.8	135	45.8	330	1.1	8	3.6	26
g) {WRKUNPLS} Column No 2014 How often do you work in physically unpleasant conditions		2.3	16	5.2	38	18.5	133	18.6	134	51.1	367	0.9	7	3.4	25

Base : Self-completion respondents in paid work (n = 720)

IN PAID WORK : AUTONOMY AT WORK

1989   Q.B218   {PWLWKPLN} Column No 2015

[If in paid job of 10 or more hours a week] [And] which of the following statements about your work is *most* true? (Please tick one box only)

	Code	%	No
My job allows me to design or plan *most* of my daily work	1	37.9	273
My job allows me to design or plan *parts* of my daily work	2	37.4	269
My job *does not really* allow me to design or plan my daily work	3	22.0	158
(NA)	9	2.8	20
			720

Base : Self-completion respondents in paid work

NB This variable appears as {WRKIPLAN} in the SPSS file

IN PAID WORK : EASE OF FINDING AN 'ACCEPTABLE' JOB

1989   Q.B219   *{FNDJBEZ}* Column No 2016
[If in paid job of 10 or more hours a week] If you lost your job for any reason, and were looking actively for
another one, how easy or difficult do you think it would be for you to find an acceptable job? (Please tick one
box only)

	Code	%	No
Very easy	1	9.1	66
Fairly easy	2	35.9	258
Neither easy nor difficult	3	18.9	136
Fairly difficult	4	21.9	157
Very difficult	5	9.8	70
Can't choose	8	1.5	11
(NA)	9	2.9	21
Base : Self-completion respondents in paid work			720

IN PAID WORK : MANAGEMENT-EMPLOYEE RELATIONS AT THE WORKPLACE

1989   Q.B220a,b   *{WKINDREL}{WKMATREL}* Column Nos 2017-18
[If in paid job of 10 or more hours a week] In general, how would you describe relations at your workplace ...
(please tick one box for each):

	Very good		Quite good		Neither good nor bad		Quite bad		Very bad		Can't choose		(NA)	
Code	1		2		3		4		5		8		9	
	%	No	%	No	%	No	%	No	%	No	%	No	%	No
a) *{WKINDREL}* Column No 2017														
Between management and employees	21.0	151	43.9	316	19.6	141	7.1	51	2.2	16	2.8	20	3.5	25
b) *{WKMATREL}* Column No 2018														
Between workmates/colleagues	39.8	286	43.1	310	9.4	68	1.2	9	0.1	1	2.0	15	4.4	32

Base : Self-completion respondents in paid work (n = 720)

IN PAID WORK : JOB SATISFACTION

1989   Q.B221   *{PWLWKSAT}* Column No 2019
[If in paid job of 10 or more hours a week] How satisfied are you in your (main) job? (Please tick one box only)

	Code	%	No
Completely satisfied	1	11.0	79
Very satisfied	2	26.6	192
Fairly satisfied	3	44.5	320
Neither satisfied nor dissatisfied	4	7.8	56
Fairly dissatisfied	5	5.2	37
Very dissatisfied	6	1.9	14
Completely dissatisfied	7	0.7	5
Can't choose	8	0.1	-
(NA)	9	2.2	16
Base : Self-completion respondents in paid work			720

NB This variable appears as {JOBSATIS} in the SPSS file

G Labour market and employment

G3 Employees

Table titles and cross references

EMPLOYEES: LENGTH OF WORKING WEEK

{EJBHOURS - Banded} {EJBHRCAT}

Question: [If employee] **How many hours a week do you *normally* work in your *(main)* job?** (Interviewer: if respondent cannot answer, ask about last week. Write in [number of hours] and code)

		1983		1984		1985		1986		1987		1989	
		%	No	%	No	%	No	%	No	%	No	%	No
Question No						21		23		24		24	
Column No						259-60		270-71		270-71		273-74	
(i) *{EJBHOURS - Banded}*	Code												
10-15 hours a week		-	-	-	-	5.4	45	6.5	99	6.5	87	5.9	84
16-23 hours a week		-	-	-	-	7.3	61	8.6	131	7.3	97	7.7	111
24-29 hours a week		-	-	-	-	3.1	26	3.6	54	3.9	52	5.0	71
30-34 hours a week		-	-	-	-	4.5	37	3.8	58	4.6	62	3.8	54
35-39 hours a week		-	-	-	-	37.3	309	36.5	556	34.4	462	32.2	461
40-44 hours a week		-	-	-	-	19.8	164	20.3	309	20.3	272	18.9	270
45-49 hours a week		-	-	-	-	8.9	74	7.4	112	9.2	124	8.9	127
50-59 hours a week		-	-	-	-	8.1	67	7.7	117	8.8	118	9.9	142
60 or more hours a week		-	-	-	-	3.8	31	4.9	75	4.0	54	6.0	87
(DK)	98	-	-	-	-	0.3	2	0.1	1	0.1	1	0.2	3
(NA)	99	-	-	-	-	1.6	14	0.6	10	1.0	13	1.5	22
Base: All employees							830		1521		1342		1432
Question No				27		21		23		24		24	
Column No				275		261		272		272		275	
(ii) *{EJBHRCAT}*													
10-15 hours a week	1	-	-	7.2	55	5.5	46	6.5	99	6.5	87	6.0	86
16-23 hours a week	2	-	-	5.7	43	7.7	64	8.6	131	7.3	97	7.9	113
24-29 hours a week	3	-	-	3.2	25	3.1	26	3.8	57	3.9	52	5.2	74
30 or more hours a week	4	-	-	83.7	638	83.7	695	81.0	1233	81.4	1092	80.9	1159
(DK)	8	-	-	0.1	1	-	-	-	-	0.1	1	-	-
(NA)	9	-	-	-	-	-	-	0.1	1	1.0	13	0.1	1
Base: All employees					762		830		1521		1342		1432

1983 - Employees were asked (Q.30) only if they normally worked full-time (30 + hours a week) or part-time (10-29 hours a week). The distributions for this variable {EFPTTIME} were: full-time (code 1), 82.1% (n = 659); part-time (code 2), 8.4% (n = 144) based on all employees (n = 803)

1984 - Q reads: 'In this (main) job do you normally work ... (read out) ...'

1985-1987, 1989 - A few respondents in each year were coded under {EJBHRCAT} but not under {EJBHOURS}, hence the slight discrepancy between the two sets of figures. In 1987, however, the responses of those answering the second but not the first part of the question were removed from the data file

EMPLOYEES: ADEQUACY OF THEIR PAY

{WAGENOW}

Question: [If employee] How would you describe the wages or salary you are paid for the job you do - on the low side, reasonable, or on the high side? [If low] Very low or a bit low?

			1983		1984		1985		1986		1987		1989	
			%	No	%	No	%	No	%	No	%	No	%	No
Question No			31a		28a		22a		24a		25a		25a	
Column No			318		276		262		273		273		276	
	Code													
Very low	1		13.1	105	10.3	79	12.7	105	11.3	171	11.6	156	11.3	162
A bit low	2		28.1	225	30.5	232	26.9	223	28.9	440	30.1	404	28.4	406
Reasonable	3		54.0	434	54.7	417	56.2	467	55.1	838	53.6	720	55.7	797
On the high side	4		4.6	37	3.7	28	3.8	32	4.2	64	4.5	60	4.5	64
(Other answer)	7		0.2	2	0.5	4	0.4	3	0.2	3	-	-	-	-
(DK)	8		-	-	-	-	-	-	0.1	1	0.1	1	0.1	1
(NA)	9		-	-	0.3	3	-	-	0.3	4	0.1	1	0.1	2
Base: All employees				803		762		830		1521		1342		1432

1983 -   Other answer, code 5; No (DK)

EMPLOYEES: GAP BETWEEN PAY LEVELS AT THEIR WORKPLACE

{PAYGAP}

Question: [If employee] (Show card) Thinking of the *highest* and the *lowest* paid people at your place of work, how would you describe the *gap* between their pay, as far as you know? Please choose a phrase from this card.

		1983		1984		1985		1986		1987		1989	
		%	No	%	No	%	No	%	No	%	No	%	No
Question No		31b		28b		22b		24b		25b		25b	
Column No		319		277		263		274		274		277	
	Code												
Much too big a gap	1	18.3	147	15.2	116	14.6	121	14.2	216	15.2	204	14.1	202
Too big	2	21.7	174	22.7	173	24.0	199	24.6	375	25.4	342	30.6	438
About right	3	44.8	360	49.0	373	48.2	400	47.9	728	45.6	612	43.0	615
Too small	4	3.9	31	2.7	20	3.4	29	3.3	51	3.3	45	2.4	34
Much too small a gap	5	1.3	10	1.0	8	0.4	3	0.6	10	0.5	6	0.4	6
(Other answer)	7	-	.	-	.	0.5	4	0.3	5	0.2	3	0.1	1
(DK)	8	9.7	78	8.6	66	9.0	74	8.4	127	9.2	123	9.3	134
(NA)	9	0.3	3	0.8	6	-	.	0.6	10	0.6	8	0.1	2
Base: All employees			803		762		830		1521		1342		1432

1983 - No (Other answer); (DK), code 6
1984 - No (Other answer)

EMPLOYEES: EXPECTATIONS ABOUT THEIR PAY OVER NEXT YEAR

{WAGEXPCT}

Question: [If employee] If you stay in this job, would you expect your wages or salary over the coming year to ...
(read out) ...

	Code	1983 %	1983 No	1984 %	1984 No	1985 %	1985 No	1986 %	1986 No	1987 %	1987 No	1989 %	1989 No
Question No		32a		29a		23a		25a		26a		26a	
Column No		320		278		264		275		275		278	
... rise by *more* than the cost of living,	1	14.6	117	12.9	98	14.8	123	20.1	306	18.4	247	15.3	218
... rise by the *same* as the cost of living,	2	45.8	368	47.2	360	44.2	367	44.7	679	51.8	695	43.7	626
... rise by *less* than the cost of living,	3	26.9	216	26.3	200	29.7	247	21.9	333	19.0	255	29.6	424
... or *not* to rise at all?	4	9.0	72	9.9	75	7.5	62	9.6	146	7.8	105	8.1	115
(Will not stay in job)	5	2.2	18	0.9	7	1.2	10	0.9	14	1.3	17	0.9	13
(DK)	8	1.5	12	2.6	19	2.6	22	2.8	42	1.6	22	2.2	32
(NA)	9	-	-	0.3	3	-	-	0.1	1	0.1	1	0.2	3
Base: All employees			803		762		830		1521		1342		1432

1983 - (DK), code 6

EMPLOYEES: EXPECTATIONS ABOUT EMPLOYMENT AT THEIR WORKPLACE OVER NEXT YEAR

{NUMEMP}

Question:　[If employee]　**Over the coming year do you expect your workplace will be ... (read out) ...**

			1983		1984		1985		1986		1987		1989	
			%	No	%	No	%	No	%	No	%	No	%	No
	Question No		32b		29b		23b		25b		26b		26b	
	Column No		321		279		265		276		276		279	
		Code												
... increasing its number of employees,		1	15.6	125	18.1	138	21.7	181	20.5	311	23.4	314	25.5	365
... reducing its number of employees,		2	28.7	231	28.7	218	23.9	198	23.3	355	21.9	294	19.6	280
... or will the number of employees stay about the same?		3	53.7	431	51.1	389	51.7	429	53.7	817	52.0	698	52.7	755
(Other answer)		7	0.8	7	0.8	6	1.0	8	0.1	1	0.4	6	0.2	3
(DK)		8	0.8	6	0.7	5	1.5	12	2.1	32	1.2	16	2.0	28
(NA)		9	0.4	3	0.7	5	0.2	2	0.3	5	1.0	14	0.1	1
Base:　All employees				803		762		830		1521		1342		1432

1983　-　(Other answer), code 4; No (DK)

EMPLOYEES: LIKELIHOOD OF LEAVING PRESENT JOB OVER NEXT YEAR

{LEAVEJOB}

Question: [If employee] Thinking now about your own job. How likely or unlikely is it that you will leave this employer over the next year for any reason? Is it ... (read out) ...

			1983		1984		1985		1986		1987		1989	
			%	No	%	No	%	No	%	No	%	No	%	No
Question No			32c		29c		24a		26a				27a	
Column No			322		280		266		308				308	
		Code												
... very likely,		1	8.5	69	12.9	98	11.4	95	10.8	165	-	-	11.1	158
... quite likely,		2	9.8	79	12.9	98	12.0	100	11.4	173	-	-	12.1	174
... not very likely,		3	26.3	211	26.4	201	30.8	256	29.8	453	-	-	27.7	397
... or not at all likely?		4	54.7	439	47.5	362	45.7	379	47.7	725	-	-	48.7	698
(DK)		8	-	.	0.2	2	0.1	1	0.2	2	-	-	0.2	3
(NA)		9	0.7	6	0.2	2	-	.	0.1	2	-	-	0.1	2
Base: All employees				803		762		830		1521				1432

1983 - No (DK)

EMPLOYEES: REASONS FOR LEAVING PRESENT JOB

{WHYGO1} {WHYGO2} {WHYGO3} {WHYGO4} {WHYGO5} {WHYGO6} {WHYGO7} {WHYGO8} {WHYGO9} {WHYGO10}

Question: [If employee and if very or quite likely to leave present job over the next year] (Show card) **Why do you think you will leave? Please choose a phrase from this card or tell me what other reason there is.** (Interviewer: more than one code may be ringed)

			1983		1984		1985		1986		1987		1989	
			%	No	%	No	%	No	%	No	%	No	%	No
Question No			32d		29d		24b		26b				27b	
Column No			323		307		267		309				309	
(i) {WHYGO1}		Code												
Firm will close down														
[Not asked: not likely to leave]		-1	81.7	656	74.3	566	76.5	635	77.8	1183	-	-	76.5	1095
Not a reason		0	16.8	135	24.2	185	22.0	182	20.7	314	-	-	22.0	314
Yes		1	1.5	12	1.5	12	1.4	12	1.5	23	-	-	1.1	16
(DK)		8	-	-	-	-	-	-	-	-	-	-	0.2	3
(NA)		9	-	.	-	.	0.1	1	0.1	1	-	-	0.3	4
Base: All employees				803		762		830		1521				1432

EMPLOYEES: REASONS FOR LEAVING PRESENT JOB (Continued)

		1983		1984		1985		1986		1987		1989	
		%	No	%	No	%	No	%	No	%	No	%	No
Question No		32d		29d		24b		26b				27b	
Column No		324		308		268		310				310	

(ii) {WHYGO2}
I will be declared redundant

	Code	1983 %	No	1984 %	No	1985 %	No	1986 %	No	1987 %	No	1989 %	No
[Not asked: not likely to leave]	-1	81.7	656	74.3	566	76.5	635	77.8	1183	-	-	76.5	1095
Not a reason	0	14.2	114	20.7	158	19.2	159	17.9	273	-		20.0	286
Yes	2	4.2	33	5.0	38	4.2	35	4.2	65	-		3.0	44
(DK)	8	-	.	-	.	-	.	-	.	-		0.2	3
(NA)	9	-	.	-	.	0.1	1	0.1	1	-		0.3	4
Base: All employees			803		762		830		1521				1432

		1983		1984		1985		1986		1987		1989	
Question No		32d		29d		24b		26b				27b	
Column No		325		309		269		311				311	

(iii) {WHYGO3}
I will reach normal retirement age

	Code	1983 %	No	1984 %	No	1985 %	No	1986 %	No	1987 %	No	1989 %	No
[Not asked: not likely to leave]	-1	81.7	656	74.3	566	76.5	635	77.8	1183	-		76.5	095
Not a reason	0	16.4	132	24.3	185	22.1	183	20.9	318	-		22.1	317
Yes	3	1.9	15	1.5	11	1.3	11	1.3	19	-		0.9	13
(DK)	8	-	.	-	.	-	.	-	.	-		0.2	3
(NA)	9	-	.	-	.	0.1	1	0.1	1	-		0.3	4
Base: All employees			803		762		830		1521				1432

		1983		1984		1985		1986		1987		1989	
Question No		32d		29d		24b		26b				27b	
Column No		326		310		270		312				312	

(iv) {WHYGO4}
My contract of employment will expire

	Code	1983 %	No	1984 %	No	1985 %	No	1986 %	No	1987 %	No	1989 %	No
[Not asked: not likely to leave]	-1	81.7	656	74.3	566	76.5	635	77.8	1183	-	-	76.5	1095
Not a reason	0	17.8	143	24.4	186	21.9	182	21.2	323	-	-	21.9	313
Yes	4	0.5	4	1.3	10	1.4	12	0.9	14	-	-	1.2	3
(DK)	8	-	.	-	.	-	.	-	.	-	-	0.2	3
(NA)	9	-	.	-	.	0.1	1	0.1	1	-	-	0.3	4
Base: All employees			803		762		830		1521				1432

1983 - No (DK)

EMPLOYEES: REASONS FOR LEAVING PRESENT JOB (Continued)

		1983		1984		1985		1986		1987		1989	
		%	No	%	No	%	No	%	No	%	No	%	No
Question No		32d		29d		24b		26b				27b	
Column No		327		311		271		313				313	
(v) {WHYGO5}	Code												
I will take early retirement													
[Not asked: not likely to leave]	-1	81.7	656	74.3	566	76.5	635	77.8	1183	-		76.5	1095
Not a reason	0	17.7	142	24.2	184	22.4	186	1.1	321	-		22.2	318
Yes	5	0.6	5	1.5	12	1.0	8	1.0	16	-		0.8	12
(DK)	8	-		-		-		-		-		0.2	3
(NA)	9	-		-		0.1	1	0.1	1	-		0.3	4
Base: All employees			803		762		830		1521				1432
Question No		32d		29d		24b		26b				27b	
Column No		328		312		272		314				314	
(vi) {WHYGO6}													
I will decide to leave and work for another employer													
[Not asked: not likely to leave]	-1	81.7	656	74.3	566	76.5	635	77.8	1183	-		76.5	1095
Not a reason	0	11.0	88	13.9	106	12.0	100	12.4	189	-		9.4	134
Yes	6	7.3	59	11.8	90	11.3	94	9.8	149	-		13.7	196
(DK)	8	-		-		-		-		-		0.2	3
(NA)	9	-		-		0.1	1	0.1	1	-		0.3	4
Base: All employees			803		762		830		1521				1432
Question No		32d		29d		24b		26b				27b	
Column No		329		313		273		315				315	
(vii) {WHYGO7}													
I will decide to leave and work for myself, as self-employed													
[Not asked: not likely to leave]	-1	81.7	656	74.3	566	76.5	635	77.8	1183	-		76.5	1095
Not a reason	0	17.1	138	23.6	180	22.2	184	19.9	303	-		20.9	299
Yes	1	1.2	10	2.1	16	1.2	10	2.2	34	-		2.1	31
(DK)	8	-		-		-		-		-		0.2	3
(NA)	9	-		-		0.1	1	0.1	1	-		0.3	4
Base: All employees			803		762		830		1521				1432

1983 - No (DK); {WHYGO7} Yes, code 7

EMPLOYEES: REASONS FOR LEAVING PRESENT JOB (Continued)

	Code	1983 %	1983 No	1984 %	1984 No	1985 %	1985 No	1986 %	1986 No	1987 %	1987 No	1989 %	1989 No
Question No				29d		24b		26b				27b	
Column No				314		274		316				316	
(viii) {WHYGO10}													
I will leave to look after home/ children/relative													
[Not asked: not likely to leave]	-1	-	-	74.3	566	76.5	635	77.8	1183	-	-	76.5	1095
Not a reason	0	-	-	23.9	182	21.8	181	20.3	309	-	-	21.3	305
Yes	2	-	-	1.8	14	1.6	13	1.8	28	-	-	1.8	25
(DK)	8	-	-	-	-	-	-	-	-	-	-	0.2	3
(NA)	9	-	-	-	-	0.1	1	0.1	1	-	-	0.3	4
Base: All employees					762		830		1521				1432
Question No		32d		29d		24b		26b				27b	
Column No		330		315		275		317				317	
(ix) {WHYGO8}													
(Other answer)													
[Not asked: not likely to leave]	-1	81.7	656	74.3	566	76.5	635	77.8	1183	-	-	76.5	1095
Not given	0	15.7	126	23.2	176	20.9	173	20.5	312	-	-	22.2	317
Given	7	2.6	21	2.6	20	2.5	21	1.7	26	-	-	0.9	13
(DK)	8	-	-	-	-	-	-	-	-	-	-	0.2	3
(NA)	9	-	-	-	-	0.1	1	0.1	1	-	-	0.3	4
Base: All employees			803		762		830		1521				1432

1983 -   No (DK); {WHYGO8} Yes, code 1; {WHYGO10} not on the show card in 1983 so that comparisons between 1983 data and those for later years should be made with great caution

1983,1984 -   additional variable {WHYGO9} for 'Question answered', code 0 (1983: n = 147; 1984: n = 197)

EMPLOYEES: IF LOST JOB, COURSE OF ACTION

{ELOOKJOB}

Question: [If employee] **Suppose you lost your job for one reason or another - would you start looking for another job, would you wait for several months or longer before you started looking, or would you decide *not* to look for another job?**

		1983		1984		1985		1986		1987		1989	
		%	No	%	No	%	No	%	No	%	No	%	No
Question No		33a		33a		25a		28a				28a	
Column No		336		332		307		321				323	
	Code												
Start looking	1	83.9	674	87.5	667	88.1	732	87.2	1327	-	-	87.4	1252
Wait several months or longer	2	5.7	46	4.3	32	3.5	29	4.7	72	-	-	5.1	73
Decide not to look	3	8.7	69	7.7	59	7.6	63	7.2	110	-	-	6.8	98
(DK)	8	1.2	9	0.3	3	0.4	4	0.7	10	-	-	0.6	9
(NA)	9	0.6	5	0.2	2	0.4	3	0.1	2	-	-	0.1	1
Base: All employees			803		762		830		1521				1432

1983 - Q reads: 'Suppose you were made redundant or your firm closed down, would you ...'; (DK), code 4

EMPLOYEES: IF LOST JOB, ESTIMATED LENGTH OF JOBSEARCH

{EFINDJOB - Banded}

Question: [If employee and if lost job would start looking for another] **How long do you think it would take you to find an acceptable replacement job?**

	Code	1983 %	1983 No	1984 %	1984 No	1985 %	1985 No	1986 %	1986 No	1987 %	1987 No	1989 %	1989 No
Question No		33b		33b		25b		28b				28b	
Column No		338-41		334-36		309-12		323-26				325-28	
[Not asked: would delay looking for another job, or decide not to look]	-1	15.5	124	12.0	91	11.1	92	12.0	182	-	-	11.9	171
1-2 months		33.9	272	37.2	284	38.7	320	38.2	580	-	-	52.6	753
3-6 months		26.3	211	21.4	163	19.6	163	20.8	316	-	-	16.5	236
7-12 months		10.3	83	7.1	54	6.8	57	6.1	93	-	-	3.0	43
More than 1 year		2.9	25	2.1	17	1.8	15	1.7	28	-	-	0.8	12
Never	96	-	-	-	-	-	-	3.9	59	-	-	2.3	32
(Other answer)	97	-	-	-	-	1.0	9	-	-	-	-	-	-
(DK)	98	8.1	65	18.9	144	20.1	167	16.4	250	-	-	12.3	176
(NA)	99	2.8	23	1.2	9	0.9	8	0.1	1	-	-	0.7	10
[Not asked: DK if would start looking for another job, or NA]	999	-	-	-	-	-	-	0.8	12	-	-	-	-
Base: All employees			803		762		830		1521				1432

1983 - No Never, No (DK), No (Other answer), No (Not asked: DK if would start looking ...); (DK), code 9998 on questionnaire, code 998 on SPSS file; (NA), code 9999 questionnaire, code 999 on SPSS file

1984 - No Never, No (Other answer), No (Not asked: DK if would start looking ...); (DK), code 998, (NA), code 999

1985 - No Never; No (Not asked: DK if would start looking ...)

1986 - No (Other answer)

1989 Never, code 996; (DK) code 998; (NA), code 999

EMPLOYEES: IF LOST JOB, WILLINGNESS TO RETRAIN FOR A DIFFERENT ONE

{ERETRAIN}

Question: [If employee; and if lost job would start looking for replacement but would not expect to find one in less than three months] **How willing do you think you would be in these circumstances to retrain for a different job ...** (read out) ...

	Code	1983 %	1983 No	1984 %	1984 No	1985 %	1985 No	1986 %	1986 No	1987 %	1987 No	1989 %	1989 No
Question No		33c		33c		25c		28c				28c	
Column No		342		337		313		327				329	
... very willing,	1	23.4	188	15.8	120	15.1	126	26.7	376	-	-	14.4	206
... quite willing,	2	11.0	89	10.2	77	9.1	75	15.8	223	-	-	12.4	177
... or not very willing?	3	4.8	38	4.6	35	4.8	40	8.2	115	-	-	6.1	88
[Not asked: would not start looking for replacement job]	6	15.5	124	12.0	91	11.1	92	5.1	72	-	-	11.9	171
[Not asked: expects to find job in less than three months]	7	33.9	272	37.2	284	38.6	321	41.2	580	-	-	52.6	753
(DK)	8	0.2	2	-		0.1	1	0.6	9	-	-	0.7	10
(NA/not asked - *see footnote*)	9	11.2	90	20.2	154	21.2	176	2.5	35	-	-	1.9	28
Base: All employees			803		762		830		1521				1432

1983 - (DK), code 4

1983, 1984, 1985 - Respondents answering 'never' or 'don't know' to the preceding question {EFINDJOB} were not asked this question, so data are not comparable with those for 1986 and 1989

EMPLOYEES: IF LOST JOB, WILLINGNESS TO MOVE TO FIND 'ACCEPTABLE' JOB

{EJOBMOVE}

Question: [If employee; and if lost job would start looking for replacement but would not expect to find one in less than three months] **And how willing do you think you would be to move to a different area to find an acceptable job ... (read out) ...**

	Code	1983 %	1983 No	1984 %	1984 No	1985 %	1985 No	1986 %	1986 No	1987 %	1987 No	1989 %	1989 No
Question No		33d		33d		25d		28d				28d	
Column No		343		338		314		328				330	
... very willing,	1	6.4	52	5.9	45	5.2	43	7.1	100	-	-	3.4	49
... quite willing,	2	10.3	83	7.0	54	5.5	46	9.3	131	-	-	6.5	93
... or not very willing?	3	22.6	182	17.3	132	18.1	151	34.0	479	-	-	22.9	328
[Not asked: would not start looking for replacement job]	6	15.5	124	12.0	91	11.1	92	5.1	72	-	-	11.9	171
[Not asked: expects to find job in less than three months]	7	33.9	272	37.2	284	38.6	321	41.2	580	-	-	52.6	753
(DK)	8	-	.	0.3	2	0.3	2	1.0	14	-	-	0.7	10
(NA/not asked - *see footnote*)	9	11.2	90	20.2	154	21.2	176	2.3	33	-	-	2.0	28
Base: All employees			803		762		830		1521				1432

1983 - (DK), code 4

1983, 1984, 1985 - Respondents answering 'never' or 'don't know' to a preceding question {EFINDJOB} were not asked this question, so data are not comparable with those for 1986 and 1989

EMPLOYEES: IF LOST JOB, WILLINGNESS TO TAKE 'UNACCEPTABLE' JOB

{EBADJOB}

Question: [If employee; and if lost job would start looking for replacement but would not expect to find one in less than three months] **And how willing do you think you would be in these circumstances to take what you now consider to be an *un*acceptable job ... (read out) ...**

		1983		1984		1985		1986		1987		1989	
		%	No	%	No	%	No	%	No	%	No	%	No
Question No		33e		33e				28e				28e	
Column No		344		339				329				331	
	Code												
... very willing,	1	6.5	52	4.5	34	-	-	6.7	95	-	-	3.2	46
... quite willing,	2	15.1	122	11.3	86	-	-	18.6	262	-	-	10.6	151
... or not very willing?	3	16.7	134	14.7	112	-	-	24.2	342	-	-	18.6	266
[Not asked: would not start looking for replacement job]	6	15.5	124	12.0	91	-	-	5.1	72	-	-	11.9	171
[Not asked: expects to find job in less than three months]	7	33.9	272	37.2	284	-	-	41.2	580	-	-	52.6	753
(DK)	8	1.0	8	0.1	1	-	-	1.8	26	-	-	1.2	17
(NA/not asked - *see footnote*)	9	11.2	90	20.2	154	-	-	2.3	33	-	-	2.0	28
Base: All employees			803		762				1521				1432

1983 - (DK), code 4

1983, 1984 - Respondents answering 'never' or 'don't know' to a preceding question {EFINDJOB} were not asked this question, so data are not comparable with those for 1986 and 1989

EMPLOYEES: WHETHER WOULD HAVE PAID JOB IF ONE NOT NEEDED

{EPREFJOB}

Question: [If employee] If without having to work, you had what you would regard as a reasonable living income, do you think you would still prefer to have a paid job or wouldn't you bother?

		1983		1984		1985		1986		1987		1989	
		%	No	%	No	%	No	%	No	%	No	%	No
Question No				34		26		29				29	
Column No				340		315		330				332	
	Code												
Still prefer paid job	1	-	.	68.8	524	71.9	597	72.1	1097	-	.	73.7	1056
Wouldn't bother	2	-	.	28.6	218	26.5	220	25.9	394	-	.	25.1	360
(Prefer voluntary work)	4	-	.	1.0	8	-	.	-	.	-	.	-	.
(Other answer)	7	-	.	1.2	9	1.3	11	1.1	17	-	.	0.7	10
(DK)	8	-	.	0.3	2	0.2	2	0.7	11	-	.	0.3	5
(NA)	9	-	.	0.1	1	-	.	0.1	2	-	.	0.1	1
Base: All employees					762		830		1521				1432

1984 - Extra code 4; 'Prefer voluntary work' not used in subsequent years

1985, 1986 - Derived variable {PREFJOB} combines the responses to this question of employees, self-employed, unemployed, those in full-time education, and those on a government scheme or waiting to take up paid work

EMPLOYEES: RECENT EXPERIENCE OF UNEMPLOYMENT

{EUNEMP}

Question: [If employee] During the last five years - that is since March 1984 - have you been unemployed and seeking work for any period?

		1983		1984		1985		1986		1987		1989	
		%	No	%	No	%	No	%	No	%	No	%	No
Question No		35a		36a		27a		30a		31a		30a	
Column No		346		342		316		331		328		333	
	Code												
Yes	1	18.1	146	22.7	173	22.0	183	20.0	304	21.5	288	20.1	288
No	2	81.9	657	77.2	588	78.0	648	79.8	1214	78.5	1054	79.8	1143
(DK)	8	-	.	-	.	-	.	-	.	-	.	-	.
(NA)	9	-	.	0.1	1	-	.	0.2	3	-	.	0.1	1
Base: All employees			803		762		830		1521		1342		1432

1983 - Q reads: '...(that is since March 1978)...'; No (DK)
1984 - (that is since March 1979)
1985 - (that is since March 1980)
1986 - (that is since March 1981)
1987 - (that is since March 1982)

EMPLOYEES: LENGTH OF ANY RECENT PERIOD OF UNEMPLOYMENT

{EUNEMPT - Banded}

Question: [If employee, and unemployed and seeking work within past five years] **For how many months in total during the last five years** (have you been unemployed?)

	Code	1983 %	No	1984 %	No	1985 %	No	1986 %	No	1987 %	No	1989 %	No
Question No		35b		36b		27b		30b		31b		30b	
Column No		347-50		343-44		317-20		332-35		329-32		334-37	
[Not asked: not been unemployed within past five years]	-1	81.9	657	77.2	588	78.0	648	79.8	1214	78.5	1054	79.8	1143
1 month	1	2.0	16	4.3	33	3.6	30	3.3	50	3.4	45	3.5	51
2-3 months		5.1	41	4.9	37	4.2	35	4.3	65	4.1	55	4.4	63
4-6 months		4.6	37	3.0	23	4.7	39	4.3	65	4.2	57	4.4	62
7 months-1 year		3.6	29	4.6	35	5.5	46	4.2	64	4.2	56	3.9	56
More than 1 year - up to 2 years		2.3	18	4.5	34	2.4	20	2.7	41	3.8	51	2.0	29
More than 2 years - up to 5 years		0.6	5	0.8	6	1.6	14	1.1	16	1.6	22	1.8	26
(DK)	98	-	.	0.3	2	-	.	0.1	1	0.1	2	0.1	2
(NA)	99	-	.	0.5	4	-	.	0.3	4	-	.	0.1	1
Base: All employees			803		762		830		1521		1342		1432

EMPLOYEES: RECENT EXPERIENCE OF WORKING AS SELF-EMPLOYED

{ESELFEM}

Question: [If employee] **For any period during the last five years have you worked as a *self-employed* person as your main job?**

	Code	1983 %	No	1984 %	No	1985 %	No	1986 %	No	1987 %	No	1989 %	No
Question No		36a		37a				31a		32a		31a	
Column No		351		345				336		333		338	
Yes	1	2.5	20	4.5	35	-	.	3.2	49	4.4	59	4.4	64
No	2	97.5	782	95.4	727	-	.	96.7	1471	95.4	1281	95.5	1367
(DK)	8	-	.	-	.	-	.	-	.	-	.	-	.
(NA)	9	-	.	0.1	1	-	.	0.1	2	0.1	2	0.1	1
Base: All employees			803		762				1521		1342		1432

1983 - No (DK)

EMPLOYEES: LENGTH OF ANY RECENT PERIOD OF SELF-EMPLOYMENT

{ESELFEMT - Banded}

Question: [If employee and worked as self-employed during last five years] **In total, for how many months during the last five years have you been self-employed?**

	Code	1983 %	1983 No	1984 %	1984 No	1985 %	1985 No	1986 %	1986 No	1987 %	1987 No	1989 %	1989 No
Question No		36b		37b				31b		32b		31b	
Column No		352-55		346-47				337-40		334-37		339-42	
[Not asked: not been self-employed during last five years]	-1	97.5	782	95.4	727	-	-	96.7	1471	95.4	1281	95.5	1367
1 month	1	0.1	1	-	.	-	-	-	.	-	.	-	.
2-3 months		0.1	1	0.9	7	-	.	0.4	6	0.5	7	0.5	7
4-6 months		0.3	2	1.2	9	-	.	0.2	2	0.1	2	0.5	7
7 months - up to 1 year		0.4	4	0.7	6	-	.	0.8	13	1.3	17	0.8	11
More than 1 - up to 2 years		1.1	9	0.7	6	-	.	0.8	12	1.3	18	0.8	12
More than 2 - up to 5 years		0.5	4	0.7	5	-	.	1.0	15	1.0	14	1.9	27
(DK)	98	-	.	-	.	-	.	-	.	-	.	-	.
(NA)	99	-	.	0.4	3	-	.	0.2	3	0.3	4	0.1	1
Base: All employees			803		762				1521		1342		1432

1983 -   (DK/can't remember), code 9988; (NA), code 9999 on questionnaire but not on SPSS file

EMPLOYEES: HOW SERIOUSLY CONSIDERED WORKING AS SELF-EMPLOYED

{*ESELFSER*}

Question: [If employee and has not been self-employed during last five years] **How seriously in the last five years have you considered working as a self-employed person** ... (read out) ...

		1983		1984		1985		1986		1987		1989	
		%	No	%	No	%	No	%	No	%	No	%	No
Question No		36c		37c				31c		32c		31c	
Column No		356		348				341		338		343	
	Code												
... very seriously,	1	5.1	41	6.2	47	-	-	6.0	91	4.7	63	5.1	74
... quite seriously,	2	11.6	93	9.9	75	-	-	9.2	139	9.1	123	9.2	132
... not very seriously,	3	12.3	98	11.7	89	-	-	13.7	209	13.3	178	11.3	161
... or not at all seriously?	4	68.5	550	67.4	514	-	-	67.5	1027	67.9	911	69.6	997
[Not asked: has been self-employed]	7	2.5	20	4.5	35	-	-	3.2	49	4.4	59	4.4	64
(DK)	8	-	.	-		-	-	-		-		-	
(NA)	9	-	.	0.2	2	-	-	0.4	6	0.6	8	0.3	4
Base: All employees			803		762				1521		1342		1432

1983 - No (DK)

EMPLOYEES: COMMITMENT TO WORK - 1

{EMPEARN}

Question: [If employee] Now for some more general questions about your work.

For some people their job is simply something they do in order to earn a living. For others it means much more than that. On balance, is your present job ... (read out) ...

		1983		1984		1985		1986		1987		1989	
		%	No	%	No	%	No	%	No	%	No	%	No
Question No						28a						32a	
Column No						321						344	
	Code												
... just a means of earning a living,	1	-	-	-	-	29.9	248	-	-	-	-	30.8	441
... or does it mean much more to you than that?	2	-	-	-	-	70.1	582	-	-	-	-	69.1	989
(DK)	8	-	-	-	-	-		-	-	-	-	-	
(NA)	9	-	-	-	-	0.1	1	-	-	-	-	0.2	3
Base: All employees							830						1432

EMPLOYEES: COMMITMENT TO WORK - 2

{EMPLIV}

Question: [If employee and if present job is just a means of earning a living] **Is that because** ... (read out) ...

		1983		1984		1985		1986		1987		1989	
		%	No	%	No	%	No	%	No	%	No	%	No
Question No						28b						32b	
Column No						322						345	
	Code												
... there are no better jobs around here,	1	-	-	-	-	9.5	79	-	-	-	-	7.7	111
... you don't have the right skills to get a better job,	2	-	-	-	-	6.7	56	-	-	-	-	7.5	109
... or because you would feel the same about *any* job you had?	3	-	-	-	-	12.1	101	-	-	-	-	12.9	185
[Not asked: job means more than just earning a living]	7	-	-	-	-	70.1	582	-	-	-	-	69.1	989
(DK)	8	-	-	-	-	0.4	3	-	-	-	-	0.4	6
(NA)	9	-	-	-	-	1.2	10	-	-	-	-	2.4	34
Base: All employees							830						1432

EMPLOYEES: IMPORTANT FACTORS IN CHOICE OF A NEW JOB

{NEWJOB1} {NEWJOB2} {NEWJOB3}

Question: [If employee] (Show card)

a) Suppose you were looking for another job - which of the things on this card would be *most* important to you in choosing a new job? Please read through the whole list before deciding.

b) And which would be *next* most important?

c) And which would be *third* most important?

		1983		1984		1985		1986		1987		1989	
		%	No	%	No	%	No	%	No	%	No	%	No
Question No						30a						33a	
Column No						324-25						346-47	
(i) *{NEWJOB1}*	Code												
Most important in choosing job													
Convenient working hours	1	-	.	-	.	13.8	114	-	.	-	.	15.2	218
Possibility of promotion	2	-	.	-	.	6.3	52	-	.	-	.	6.0	86
Clean/pleasant working conditions	3	-	.	-	.	1.8	15	-	.	-	.	1.6	23
Strong trade union	4	-	.	-	.	0.3	3	-	.	-	.	0.3	4
Interesting work that makes use of your skills	5	-	.	-	.	30.4	253	-	.	-	.	29.5	422
Work that helps others	6	-	.	-	.	3.4	29	-	.	-	.	4.3	62
Opportunity to get on with your work in your own way	7	-	.	-	.	5.2	43	-	.	-	.	3.8	54
Job security	8	-	.	-	.	18.3	152	-	.	-	.	18.1	259
Outdoor work	9	-	.	-	.	1.8	15	-	.	-	.	1.4	21
Good pay	10	-	.	-	.	12.3	102	-	.	-	.	13.9	199
Friendliness of people you work with	11	-	.	-	.	5.0	41	-	.	-	.	4.0	57
Good fringe benefits (pension, sick pay)	12	-	.	-	.	0.6	5	-	.	-	.	0.9	13
Short working hours	13	-	.	-	.	0.7	6	-	.	-	.	0.4	6
(None of these)	97	-	.	-	.	-	.	-	.	-	.	0.4	6
(DK)	98	-	.	-	.	0.2	2	-	.	-	.	0.1	1
(NA)	99	-	.	-	.	-	.	-	.	-	.	0.1	2

Base: All employees

830

1432

EMPLOYEES: IMPORTANT FACTORS IN CHOICE OF A NEW JOB (Continued)

		1983		1984		1985		1986		1987		1989	
		%	No	%	No	%	No	%	No	%	No	%	No
Question No						30b						33b	
Column No						326-27						348-49	
(ii) {NEWJOB2} Next most important	Code												
Convenient working hours	1	-	.	-	.	5.0	42	-	.	-	.	8.1	116
Possibility of promotion	2	-	.	-	.	7.9	66	-	.	-	.	6.2	89
Clean/pleasant working conditions	3	-	.	-	.	3.6	30	-	.	-	.	3.7	52
Strong trade union	4	-	.	-	.	0.7	6	-	.	-	.	0.7	10
Interesting work that makes use of your skills	5	-	.	-	.	14.3	119	-	.	-	.	14.9	214
Work that helps others	6	-	.	-	.	5.4	44	-	.	-	.	5.1	73
Opportunity to get on with your work in your own way	7	-	.	-	.	10.9	90	-	.	-	.	8.8	125
Job security	8	-	.	-	.	15.2	126	-	.	-	.	11.7	167
Outdoor work	9	-	.	-	.	2.1	18	-	.	-	.	1.3	19
Good pay	10	-	.	-	.	19.0	158	-	.	-	.	22.0	315
Friendliness of people you work with	11	-	.	-	.	9.2	76	-	.	-	.	10.8	155
Good fringe benefits (pension, sick pay)	12	-	.	-	.	5.0	42	-	.	-	.	4.8	69
Short working hours	13	-	.	-	.	1.2	10	-	.	-	.	1.5	22
(None of these)	97	-	.	-	.	-	.	-	.	-	.	0.3	4
(DK)	98	-	.	-	.	0.3	3	-	.	-	.	0.1	1
(NA)	99	-	.	-	.	-	.	-	.	-	.	0.1	2
Base: All employees							830						1432

EMPLOYEES: IMPORTANT FACTORS IN CHOICE OF A NEW JOB (Continued)

		1983		1984		1985		1986		1987		1989	
		%	No	%	No	%	No	%	No	%	No	%	No
Question No						30c						33c	
Column No						328-29						350-51	
(iii) *{NEWJOB3}*	Code												
Third most important													
Convenient working hours	1	-	.	-	.	5.3	44	-	.	-	.	7.3	104
Possibility of promotion	2	-	.	-	.	9.7	80	-	.	-	.	8.1	116
Clean/pleasant working conditions	3	-	.	-	.	3.8	32	-	.	-	.	5.8	83
Strong trade union	4	-	.	-	.	1.4	12	-	.	-	.	1.2	17
Interesting work that makes use of your skills	5	-	.	-	.	8.8	73	-	.	-	.	9.1	130
Work that helps others	6	-	.	-	.	3.8	31	-	.	-	.	3.6	52
Opportunity to get on with your work in your own way	7	-	.	-	.	8.9	74	-	.	-	.	10.1	144
Job security	8	-	.	-	.	12.9	107	-	.	-	.	10.9	156
Outdoor work	9	-	.	-	.	1.2	10	-	.	-	.	1.3	19
Good pay	10	-	.	-	.	13.7	114	-	.	-	.	16.6	237
Friendliness of people you work with	11	-	.	-	.	17.1	142	-	.	-	.	14.2	204
Good fringe benefits (pension, sick pay)	12	-	.	-	.	8.4	70	-	.	-	.	8.4	120
Short working hours	13	-	.	-	.	4.3	36	-	.	-	.	2.7	39
(None of these)	97	-	.	-	.	0.2	2	-	.	-	.	0.3	5
(DK)	98	-	.	-	.	0.4	4	-	.	-	.	0.2	3
(NA)	99	-	.	-	.	0.1	1	-	.	-	.	0.1	2
Base: All employees							830						1432

EMPLOYEES: METHOD OF PAYMENT

{PAYMENT}

Question: [If employee] **Apart from overtime are you paid ... (read out) ...** (Interviewer: payment for unsociable hours counts as 'by the hour')

		1983		1984		1985		1986		1987		1989	
		%	No	%	No	%	No	%	No	%	No	%	No
Question No						31a						34a	
Column No						332						352	
	Code												
... the same amount per week or month	1	-	.	-	.	67.1	557	-	.	-	.	68.5	981
...by the hour, so if your hours vary your pay varies,	2	-	.	-	.	22.7	188	-	.	-	.	23.9	342
...or does your pay include some sort of piecework, payment by performance or commission?	3	-	.	-	.	9.9	82	-	.	-	.	7.4	105
(DK)	8	-	.	-	.	-	.	-	.	-	.	-	.
(NA)	9	-	.	-	.	0.4	3	-	.	-	.	0.2	4
Base: All employees							830						1432

EMPLOYEES: REGULAR OVERTIME WORKING

{OVERTIME}

Question: [If employee] **Do you regularly do** *paid* **overtime at work - by regularly, I mean most weeks?**

		1983		1984		1985		1986		1987		1989	
		%	No	%	No	%	No	%	No	%	No	%	No
Question No						31b						34b	
Column No						333						353	
	Code												
Yes	1	-	.	-	.	24.9	207	-	.	-	.	28.6	409
No	2	-	.	-	.	72.8	604	-	.	-	.	68.7	984
(DK)	8	-	.	-	.	-	.	-	.	-	.	0.1	1
(NA)	9	-	.	-	.	2.3	19	-	.	-	.	2.6	38
Base: All employees							830						1432

EMPLOYEES: SATISFACTION WITH LENGTH OF WORKING WEEK

{PREFHOUR}

Question: [If employee] **Thinking about the number of hours you work each week, including regular overtime, would you prefer a job where you worked ... (read out) ...**

		1983		1984		1985		1986		1987		1989	
		%	No	%	No	%	No	%	No	%	No	%	No
Question No						32a						35a	
Column No						334						354	
	Code												
... more hours per week,	1	-	-	-	-	4.3	36	-	-	-	-	4.5	64
... fewer hours per week,	2	-	-	-	-	22.9	190	-	-	-	-	30.0	429
... or are you happy with the number of hours you work at present?	3	-	-	-	-	72.5	602	-	-	-	-	65.2	934
(DK)	8	-	-	-	-	0.2	2	-	-	-	-	0.1	2
(NA)	9	-	-	-	-	0.1	1	-	-	-	-	0.2	3
Base: All employees							830						1432

EMPLOYEES: REASONS FOR NOT WORKING MORE HOURS A WEEK

{MOREHOUR}

Question: [If employee and would prefer to work more hours per week] **Is the reason why you don't work more hours because ... (read out) ...**

		1983		1984		1985		1986		1987		1989	
		%	No	%	No	%	No	%	No	%	No	%	No
Question No						32b						35b	
Column No						335						355	
	Code												
... your employer can't offer you more hours,	1	-	-	-	-	3.4	28	-	-	-	-	3.8	54
... or your personal circumstances don't allow it?	2	-	-	-	-	0.9	8	-	-	-	-	0.5	7
(Both)	3	-	-	-	-	-	-	-	-	-	-	0.2	3
[Not asked: would not prefer to work more hours per week]	4	-	-	-	-	95.4	792	-	-	-	-	95.2	1363
(Other reason)	7	-	-	-	-	-	-	-	-	-	-	-	-
(DK)	8	-	-	-	-	-	-	-	-	-	-	-	-
(NA)	9	-	-	-	-	0.3	3	-	-	-	-	0.3	5
Base: All employees							830						1432

EMPLOYEES: PREFERRED WAY OF SHORTENING WORKING WEEK

{FEWHOUR}

Question: [If employee and would prefer to work fewer hours per week] **In which of these ways would you like your working hours to be shortened ... (read out) ...**

		1983		1984		1985		1986		1987		1989	
		%	No	%	No	%	No	%	No	%	No	%	No
Question No						32c						35c	
Column No						336						356	
	Code												
...shorter hours each day	1	-	-	-	-	9.1	76	-	-	-	-	10.8	155
...or fewer days each week?	2	-	-	-	-	13.0	108	-	-	-	-	18.4	263
[Not asked: would not prefer to work fewer hours per week]	4	-	-	-	-	76.7	637	-	-	-	-	69.7	998
(Other answer)	7	-	-	-	-	0.5	4	-	-	-	-	0.4	6
(DK)	8	-	-	-	-	0.1	1	-	-	-	-	0.1	2
(NA)	9	-	-	-	-	0.5	4	-	-	-	-	0.6	9
Base: All employees							830						1432

EMPLOYEES: WORKING FEWER HOURS *VERSUS* EARNING LESS MONEY

{EARNHOUR}

Question: [If employee and would prefer to work fewer hours per week] **Would you still like to work fewer hours if it meant earning less money as a result?**

		1983		1984		1985		1986		1987		1989	
		%	No	%	No	%	No	%	No	%	No	%	No
Question No						32d						35d	
Column No						337						357	
	Code												
Yes	1	-	-	-	-	5.6	46	-	-	-	-	6.8	98
No	2	-	-	-	-	16.0	133	-	-	-	-	20.6	295
It depends	3	-	-	-	-	1.2	10	-	-	-	-	1.5	21
[Not asked: would not prefer to work fewer hours per week]	4	-	-	-	-	76.7	637	-	-	-	-	69.7	998
(DK)	8	-	-	-	-	-	-	-	-	-	-	0.5	8
(NA)	9	-	-	-	-	0.5	4	-	-	-	-	0.9	13
Base: All employees							830						1432

EMPLOYEES: SAY IN WORKPLACE DECISIONS

{SAYJOB}

Question: [If employee] Suppose there was going to be some decision made at your place of work that changed the way you do your job. Do you think that *you personally* would have any say in the decision about the change, or not?

		1983		1984		1985		1986		1987		1989	
		%	No	%	No	%	No	%	No	%	No	%	No
Question No						35a				33a		36a	
Column No						340				339		358	
	Code												
Yes	1	-	-	-	-	61.9	514	-	-	50.5	678	49.7	712
No	2	-	-	-	-	33.6	279	-	-	45.1	605	46.8	670
(It depends/DK)	8	-	-	-	-	4.5	37	-	-	4.3	58	3.3	47
(NA)	9	-	-	-	-	-		-	-	0.1	1	0.2	3
Base: All employees							830				1342		1432

EMPLOYEES: EXTENT OF INFLUENCE OVER WORKPLACE DECISIONS

{MUCHSAY}

Question: [If employee and would have any say in decision about change in way his or her job done] **How much say or chance to influence the decision do you think you would have ... (read out) ...**

		1983		1984		1985		1986		1987		1989	
		%	No	%	No	%	No	%	No	%	No	%	No
Question No						35b				33b		36b	
Column No						341				340		359	
	Code												
... a great deal,	1	-	-	-	-	12.4	103	-	-	10.6	142	9.6	138
... quite a lot,	2	-	-	-	-	24.9	207	-	-	18.8	253	20.5	294
... or just a little?	3	-	-	-	-	22.5	187	-	-	19.9	267	17.9	257
[Not asked: would have no say decision, or it depends/DK]	7	-	-	-	-	38.1	316	-	-	49.4	663	50.1	717
(It depends/DK)	8	-	-	-	-	2.1	18	-	-	1.1	14	1.4	20
(NA)	9	-	-	-	-	-		-	-	0.1	2	0.4	6
Base: All employees							830				1342		1432

EMPLOYEES: SATISFACTION WITH AMOUNT OF SAY IN WORKPLACE DECISIONS

{MORESAY}

Question: [If employee] Do you think you should have *more* say in decisions affecting your work, or are you satisfied with the way things are?

		1983		1984		1985		1986		1987		1989	
		%	No	%	No	%	No	%	No	%	No	%	No
Question No						35c				33c		36c	
Column No						342				341		360	
	Code												
Should have more say	1	-	.	-	.	36.2	301	-	.	46.1	619	44.3	634
Satisfied with the way things are	2	-	.	-	.	62.9	523	-	.	52.5	705	53.8	770
(DK)	8	-	.	-	.	0.5	4	-	.	0.8	11	1.0	15
(NA)	9	-	.	-	.	0.4	3	-	.	0.6	8	0.9	13
Base: All employees							830				1342		1432

EMPLOYEES: UNION RECOGNITION AT THEIR WORKPLACE

{WPUNIONS}

Question: [If employee] At your place of work are there unions, staff associations, or groups of unions recognised by the management for negotiating pay and conditions of employment? (Interviewer: if yes, probe for whether union or staff association)

		1983		1984		1985		1986		1987		1989	
		%	No	%	No	%	No	%	No	%	No	%	No
Question No		37a		38a		39a		32a		40a		37a	
Column No		364		356		420		349		431		361	
	Code												
Yes: trade union(s)	1	66.4	533	62.9	479	62.5	519	61.6	937	62.5	839	49.2	705
Yes: staff association	2	-	.	-	.	-	.	-	.	-	.	4.5	64
No, none	3	33.2	267	36.7	280	37.1	308	37.3	568	36.8	495	41.7	598
(Both)	4	-	.	-	.	-	.	-	.	-	.	3.9	56
(DK)	8	-	.	0.3	3	0.4	3	0.9	14	0.7	9	-	.
(NA)	9	0.3	3	0.1	1	-	.	0.2	3	-	.	0.6	9
Base: All employees			803		762		830		1521		1342		1432

1983 - No (DK)
1983-1987 - Yes, code 1, No, code 2; No (Both). Since the interviewer was instructed to probe 'union or staff association' for the first time in 1989 the data for 1989 are not exactly comparable with those for earlier years
1989 - SPSS file lists variable as {WPUNION}; this has been changed to {WPUNIONS}

EMPLOYEES: EFFECTIVENESS OF WORKPLACE UNIONS
{WPUNIONW}

Question: [If employee and recognised union(s) or staff association at place of work] **On the whole, do you think these unions or staff associations do their job well or not?**

		1983		1984		1985		1986		1987		1989	
		%	No	%	No	%	No	%	No	%	No	%	No
Question No		37b		38b		39b		32b		40b		37b	
Column No		365		357		421		350		432		362	
	Code												
Yes	1	38.8	312	39.2	299	35.7	297	37.3	567	38.9	522	32.8	469
No	2	26.2	210	21.0	160	23.3	194	22.3	340	20.5	276	21.4	307
[Not asked: no recognised union(s) or staff association at workplace]	3	33.2	267	36.7	280	37.1	308	37.3	568	36.8	495	41.7	598
(DK)	8	-	.	2.2	17	3.1	26	1.7	26	3.0	40	3.1	44
(NA)	9	1.8	14	1.0	7	0.7	6	1.4	21	0.8	11	1.0	15
Base: All employees			803		762		830		1521		1342		1432

1983 - No (DK)

EMPLOYEES: MANAGEMENT-EMPLOYEE RELATIONS AT THEIR WORKPLACE
{INDREL}

Question: [If employee] **In general how would you describe relations between management and other employees at your workplace ... (read out) ...**

		1983		1984		1985		1986		1987		1989	
		%	No	%	No	%	No	%	No	%	No	%	No
Question No		38a		39a		40a		33a		41a		38a	
Column No		366		358		422		351		433		364	
	Code												
... very good,	1	37.3	300	35.7	272	37.9	314	33.5	510	34.3	460	32.0	458
... quite good,	2	46.8	376	47.1	359	45.0	374	46.7	710	47.5	638	48.6	695
... not very good,	3	10.5	84	13.1	100	12.2	102	13.7	209	14.0	188	14.2	203
... or not at all good?	4	4.5	36	3.3	25	4.3	35	4.9	75	3.6	48	4.3	62
(DK)	8	-	.	0.3	2	0.2	2	0.4	6	0.4	5	0.3	4
(NA)	9	0.9	7	0.5	4	0.4	4	0.8	12	0.3	4	0.7	11
Base: All employees			803		762		830		1521		1342		1432

1983 - No (DK)

EMPLOYEES: PERCEPTIONS OF MANAGEMENT AT THEIR WORKPLACE

{WORKRUN}

Question: [If employee] **And in general, would you say your workplace was ... (read out) ...**

			1983		1984		1985		1986		1987		1989	
			%	No	%	No	%	No	%	No	%	No	%	No
Question No			38b		39b		40b		33b		41b		38b	
Column No			367		359		423		352		434		365	
	Code													
... very well managed,	1		30.0	241	28.1	214	27.9	232	26.8	408	26.0	349	25.6	367
... quite well managed,	2		50.0	402	51.3	391	53.3	443	51.5	784	53.7	721	54.4	779
... or not well managed?	3		19.7	158	19.3	147	18.4	153	20.4	311	19.6	263	18.3	262
(DK)	8		-	-	0.7	6	0.4	3	0.4	7	0.1	2	0.3	4
(NA)	9		0.3	2	0.6	5	0.1	1	0.8	12	0.5	7	1.4	20
Base: All employees				803		762		830		1521		1342		1432

1983 - No (DK)

EMPLOYEES (MEN): JOB SEGREGATION

{EMSMEWRK}

Question: [If male employee] **Where you work, are there any *women* doing the same sort of work as you?**

			1983		1984		1985		1986		1987		1989	
			%	No	%	No	%	No	%	No	%	No	%	No
Question No					30						27			
Column No					317						277			
	Code													
[Not asked: female employee]	0		-	-	42.7	325	-	-	-	-	46.5	624	-	-
Yes	1		-	-	15.6	119	-	-	-	-	17.4	233	-	-
No	2		-	-	41.3	315	-	-	-	-	35.1	471	-	-
Works alone	3		-	-	-	-	-	-	-	-	0.1	1	-	-
No-one else doing same job	4		-	-	0.1	1	-	-	-	-	0.7	10	-	-
(DK)	8		-	-	-	-	-	-	-	-	-	-	-	-
(NA)	9		-	-	0.3	2	-	-	-	-	0.3	4	-	-
Base: All employees						762						1342		

1984 - SPSS file lists variable as {SAMEWORK}. Only one question was asked: 'Where you work are there any (women)/(men) doing the same sort of work as you?' and the interviewer was instructed to vary the wording according to whether the respondent was male or female. To obtain a comparison between 1984 and 1987 data, the former are shown separately for male employees. No code 4, No-one else doing same job, on the questionnaire

EMPLOYEES (MEN): JOB STEREOTYPING

{EMSEXWRK}

Question: [If male employee] **Do you think of your work as ... (read out) ...**

		1983		1984		1985		1986		1987		1989	
		%	No	%	No	%	No	%	No	%	No	%	No
Question No				31						28a			
Column No				318						278			
	Code												
[Not asked: female employee]	0	-	-	42.7	325	-	-	-	-	46.5	624	-	-
... mainly men's work	1	-	-	28.1	214	-	-	-	-	24.9	334	-	-
... mainly women's work,	2	-	-	0.1	1	-	-	-	-	0.3	4	-	-
... or work that either men or women do?	3	-	-	28.9	220	-	-	-	-	28.4	381	-	-
(Other answer)	7	-	-	0.1	1	-	-	-	-	-	-	-	-
(DK)	8	-	-	-	-	-	-	-	-	-	-	-	-
(NA)	9	-	-	0.1	1	-	-	-	-	-	-	-	-
Base: All employees					762						1343		

1984 -   SPSS variable name is {SEXWORK}. Again only one question was asked: 'Where you work are there any <u>(women)</u>/<u>(men)</u> doing the same sort of work as you?' and the interviewer was instructed to vary the wording according to whether the respondent was male or female. To obtain a comparison between 1984 and 1987 data, the former are shown separately for <u>male</u> employees

EMPLOYEES (WOMEN): JOB SEGREGATION

{*EWSMEWRK*}

Question: [If female employee] **Where you work, are there any *men* doing the same sort of work as you?**

		1983		1984		1985		1986		1987		1989	
		%	No	%	No	%	No	%	No	%	No	%	No
Question No				30						29			
Column No				317						316			
	Code												
[Not asked: male employee]	0	-	-	57.3	437	-	-	-	-	53.5	718	-	-
Yes	2	-	-	20.1	153	-	-	-	-	22.6	303	-	-
No	3	-	-	21.9	167	-	-	-	-	22.8	306	-	-
Works alone	4	-	-	0.7	5	-	-	-	-	0.2	3	-	-
No-one else doing same job	5	-	-	-	-	-	-	-	-	0.3	4	-	-
(DK)	8	-	-	-	-	-	-	-	-	0.1	2	-	-
(NA)	9	-	-	-	-	-	-	-	-	0.4	6	-	-
Base: All employees				762						1342			

1984 -   SPSS variable name is {SAMEWORK}. Only one question was asked: 'Where you work are there any _(women)/(men)_ doing the same sort of work as you?' and the interviewer was instructed to vary the wording according to whether the respondent was male or female. To obtain a comparison between 1984 and 1987 data, the former are shown separately for _female_ employees. No code 4, No-one else doing same job, on the questionnaire

EMPLOYEES (WOMEN): JOB STEREOTYPING

{EWSEXWRK}

Question: [If female employee] Do you think of your work as ... (read out) ...

		1983		1984		1985		1986		1987		1989	
		%	No	%	No	%	No	%	No	%	No	%	No
Question No				31						30a			
Column No				318						317			
	Code												
[Not asked: male employee]	0	-	-	57.3	437	-	-	-	-	53.5	718	-	-
... mainly women's work	1	-	-	15.5	118	-	-	-	-	13.3	178	-	-
... mainly men's work,	2	-	-	0.3	3	-	-	-	-	0.7	10	-	-
... or work that either men or women do?	3	-	-	26.8	204	-	-	-	-	32.3	434	-	-
(Other answer)	7	-	-	-	-	-	-	-	-	-	-	-	-
(DK)	8	-	-	-	-	-	-	-	-	-	-	-	-
(NA)	9	-	-	-	-	-	-	-	-	0.1	2	-	-
Base: All employees					762						1342		

1984 - SPSS variable name is {SEXWORK}. Again only one question was asked: 'Where you work are there any (women)/(men) doing the same sort of work as you?' and the interviewer was instructed to vary the wording according to whether the respondent was male or female. To obtain a comparison between 1984 and 1987 data, the former are shown separately for female employees

EMPLOYEES: BENEFITS AND BONUSES AT WORK

{PAYBEN1} {PAYBEN2} {PAYBEN3} {PAYBEN4} {PAYBEN5} {PAYBEN6}

Question: [If employee] (Show card)

    a) Some organisations have schemes which link pay or employee benefits to the financial performance of the organisation. As far as you know, does your organisation have any of the schemes on this card?

    b) (For each mentioned at a) Have you personally received any payments or benefits under the ... (item mentioned at a) ... in the last twelve months?

	Code	1983 %	1983 No	1984 %	1984 No	1985 %	1985 No	1986 %	1986 No	1987 %	1987 No	1989 %	1989 No
Question No						36ab				34ab			
Column No						343,349				342,348			
(i) {PAYBEN1}													
Productivity-linked bonus scheme													
Organisation has scheme and respondent has received payment or benefit	1	-	-	-	-	13.7	114	-	-	13.2	177	-	-
Organisation has scheme but respondent has not received payment or benefit	2	-	-	-	-	6.4	53	-	-	5.7	76	-	-
Organisation does not have scheme	3	-	-	-	-	77.5	643	-	-	78.4	1052	-	-
Organisation has scheme but respondent does not state if has received payment or benefit	7	-	-	-	-	0.1	1	-	-	0.1	1	-	-
(DK)	8	-	-	-	-	1.7	14	-	-	1.8	24	-	-
(NA)	9	-	-	-	-	0.6	5	-	-	0.9	12	-	-
Base: All employees							830				1342		

	Code	1983 %	1983 No	1984 %	1984 No	1985 %	1985 No	1986 %	1986 No	1987 %	1987 No	1989 %	1989 No
Question No						36ab				34ab			
Column No						344,350				343,349			
(ii) {PAYBEN2}													
Annual bonus (at organisation's discretion)													
Organisation has scheme and respondent has received payment or benefit	1	-	-	-	-	11.1	92	-	-	13.0	174	-	-
Organisation has scheme but respondent has not received payment or benefit	2	-	-	-	-	4.4	37	-	-	3.5	47	-	-
Organisation does not have scheme	3	-	-	-	-	82.2	683	-	-	80.9	1085	-	-
Organisation has scheme but respondent does not state if has received payment or benefit	7	-	-	-	-	-	-	-	-	-	-	-	-
(DK)	8	-	-	-	-	1.7	14	-	-	1.8	24	-	-
(NA)	9	-	-	-	-	0.6	5	-	-	0.9	12	-	-
Base: All employees							830				1342		

EMPLOYEES: BENEFITS AND BONUSES AT WORK (Continued)

		1983		1984		1985		1986		1987		1989	
		%	No	%	No	%	No	%	No	%	No	%	No
Question No						36ab				34ab			
Column No						345,351				344,350			
(iii) {PAYBEN3}	Code												
Share ownership or share option scheme													
Organisation has scheme and respondent has received payment or benefit	1	-	-	-	-	4.0	33	-	-	5.2	70	-	-
Organisation has scheme but respondent has not received payment or benefit	2	-	-	-	-	6.5	54	-	-	6.9	92	-	-
Organisation does not have scheme	3	-	-	-	-	87.2	724	-	-	85.0	1141	-	-
Organisation has scheme but respondent does not state if has received payment or benefit	7	-	-	-	-	-	-	-	-	0.2	3	-	-
(DK)	8	-	-	-	-	1.7	14	-	-	1.8	24	-	-
(NA)	9	-	-	-	-	0.6	5	-	-	0.9	12	-	-
Base: All employees							830				1342		

		1983		1984		1985		1986		1987		1989	
Question No						36ab				34ab			
Column No						346,352				345,351			
(iv) {PAYBEN4}													
Profit-sharing scheme													
Organisation has scheme and respondent has received payment or benefit	1	-	-	-	-	5.1	43	-	-	6.3	84	-	-
Organisation has scheme but respondent has not received payment or benefit	2	-	-	-	-	3.1	26	-	-	2.7	37	-	-
Organisation does not have scheme	3	-	-	-	-	89.3	742	-	-	88.3	1186	-	-
Organisation has scheme but respondent does not state if has received payment or benefit	7	-	-	-	-	0.1	1	-	-	-	-	-	-
(DK)	8	-	-	-	-	1.7	14	-	-	1.8	24	-	-
(NA)	9	-	-	-	-	0.6	5	-	-	0.9	12	-	-
Base: All employees							830				1342		

EMPLOYEES: BENEFITS AND BONUSES AT WORK (Continued)

		1983		1984		1985		1986		1987		1989	
		%	No	%	No	%	No	%	No	%	No	%	No
Question No						36a				34a			
Column No						347				346			
(v) {PAYBEN5}	Code												
(None of these)													
Organisation has one or more	1	-	-	-	-	43.3	359	-	-	41.5	557	-	-
Organisation has none	6	-	-	-	-	54.4	452	-	-	55.8	750	-	-
(DK)	8	-	-	-	-	1.7	14	-	-	1.8	24	-	-
(NA)	9	-	-	-	-	0.6	5	-	-	0.9	12	-	-
Base: All employees							830				1342		

1985, 1987 - Additional variable {PAYBEN6} for 'Question answered' (1985, column no 348: n = 811; 1987, column no 347: n = 1306)

EMPLOYEES: 'NEW TECHNOLOGY' AT THEIR WORKPLACE

{ETECWRK1} {ETECWRK2} {ETECWRK3} {ETECWRK4} {ETECWRK5} {ETECWRK6} {ETECWRK7} {ETECWRK8} {ETECWRK9} {ETECWRK0}

Question: [If employee] Now I'd like to ask you about new technology at your workplace. (Show card)

     a)   Which, if any, of these kinds of new technology are installed at your place of work? It doesn't matter whether you work with them or not, just tell me all that you know of at your workplace.

     b)   (For each mentioned at a) Do you yourself use, or does your own work involve the use of ... (item mentioned at a)?

		1983		1984		1985		1986		1987		1989	
		%	No	%	No	%	No	%	No	%	No	%	No
Question No						37ab				38ab			
Column No						353-54,407				370-71,418			
(i) {ETECWRK1}	Code												
Main Frame computer													
At work and respondent uses	1	-	-	-	-	11.0	92	-	-	13.3	179	-	-
At work, respondent does not use	2	-	-	-	-	20.3	169	-	-	18.2	244	-	-
Not at work	3	-	-	-	-	62.2	516	-	-	62.5	839	-	-
At work, respondent did not state whether uses	7	-	-	-	-	1.1	9	-	-	1.3	18	-	-
(DK)	8	-	-	-	-	5.2	44	-	-	4.5	61	-	-
(NA)	9	-	-	-	-	0.1	1	-	-	0.1	2	-	-
Base: All employees							830				1342		

EMPLOYEES: 'NEW TECHNOLOGY' AT THEIR WORKPLACE (Continued)

		1983		1984		1985		1986		1987		1989	
		%	No	%	No	%	No	%	No	%	No	%	No
Question No						37ab				38ab			
Column No						355-56,408				372-73,419			
(ii) {ETECWRK2}	Code												
Telephone link to computer at another place													
At work and respondent uses	1	-	-	-	-	7.9	66	-	-	9.7	130	-	-
At work, respondent does not use	2	-	-	-	-	15.1	125	-	-	16.9	227	-	-
Not at work	3	-	-	-	-	70.4	584	-	-	67.5	906	-	-
At work, respondent did not state whether uses	7	-	-	-	-	1.3	10	-	-	1.3	17	-	-
(DK)	8	-	-	-	-	5.2	44	-	-	4.5	61	-	-
(NA)	9	-	-	-	-	0.1	1	-	-	0.1	2	-	-
Base: All employees							830				1342		

		1983		1984		1985		1986		1987		1989	
Question No						37ab				38ab			
Column No						357-58,409				374-75,420			
(iii) {ETECWRK3}													
Micro/mini computer													
At work and respondent uses	1	-	-	-	-	15.7	131	-	-	15.6	210	-	-
At work, respondent does not use	2	-	-	-	-	13.9	115	-	-	14.3	192	-	-
Not at work	3	-	-	-	-	64.3	534	-	-	64.7	868	-	-
At work, respondent did not state whether uses	7	-	-	-	-	0.8	6	-	-	0.8	11	-	-
(DK)	8	-	-	-	-	5.2	44	-	-	4.5	61	-	-
(NA)	9	-	-	-	-	0.1	1	-	-	0.1	2	-	-
Base: All employees							830				1342		

EMPLOYEES: 'NEW TECHNOLOGY' AT THEIR WORKPLACE (Continued)

		1983		1984		1985		1986		1987		1989	
		%	No	%	No	%	No	%	No	%	No	%	No
Question No						37ab				38ab			
Column No						359-60,410				376-77,421			
(iv) {ETECWRK4}	Code												
Computer – type unknown													
At work and respondent uses	1	-	-	-	-	3.3	28	-	-	3.7	50	-	-
At work, respondent does not use	2	-	-	-	-	12.5	104	-	-	17.5	235	-	-
Not at work	3	-	-	-	-	78.1	649	-	-	73.4	985	-	-
At work, respondent did not state whether uses	7	-	-	-	-	0.7	6	-	-	0.7	9	-	-
(DK)	8	-	-	-	-	5.2	44	-	-	4.5	61	-	-
(NA)	9	-	-	-	-	0.1	1	-	-	0.1	2	-	-
Base: All employees							830				1342		

		1983		1984		1985		1986		1987		1989	
Question No						37ab				38ab			
Column No						361-62,411				378-79,422			
(v) {ETECWRK5}													
Word processor													
At work and respondent uses	1	-	-	-	-	8.1	67	-	-	12.1	162	-	-
At work, respondent does not use	2	-	-	-	-	23.3	193	-	-	27.9	374	-	-
Not at work	3	-	-	-	-	61.6	511	-	-	53.5	718	-	-
At work, respondent did not state whether uses	7	-	-	-	-	1.8	5	-	-	1.9	26	-	-
(DK)	8	-	-	-	-	5.2	44	-	-	4.5	61	-	-
(NA)	9	-	-	-	-	0.1	1	-	-	0.1	2	-	-
Base: All employees							830				1342		

EMPLOYEES: 'NEW TECHNOLOGY' AT THEIR WORKPLACE (Continued)

		1983		1984		1985		1986		1987		1989	
		%	No	%	No	%	No	%	No	%	No	%	No
Question No						37ab				38ab			
Column No						363-64,412				408-09,423			
(vi) {ETECWRK6}	Code												
Electronic memory typewriter													
At work and respondent uses	1	-	.	-	.	5.5	45	-	.	7.1	95	-	.
At work, respondent does not use	2	-	.	-	.	21.0	174	-	.	24.4	328	-	.
Not at work	3	-	.	-	.	66.4	551	-	.	62.1	833	-	.
At work, respondent did not state whether uses	7	-	.	-	.	1.8	15	-	.	1.8	24	-	.
(DK)	8	-	.	-	.	5.2	44	-	.	4.5	61	-	.
(NA)	9	-	.	-	.	0.1	1	-	.	0.1	2	-	.
Base: All employees							830				1342		

		1983		1984		1985		1986		1987		1989	
Question No						37ab				38ab			
Column No						365-66,413				410-11,424			
(vii) {ETECWRK7}													
Computer controlled plant, machinery or equipment (including robots) used for design, assembly, handling, production													
At work and respondent uses	1	-	.	-	.	7.3	60	-	.	6.6	88	-	.
At work, respondent does not use	2	-	.	-	.	10.4	86	-	.	11.3	151	-	.
Not at work	3	-	.	-	.	76.1	632	-	.	76.2	1022	-	.
At work, respondent did not state whether uses	7	-	.	-	.	0.9	7	-	.	1.3	18	-	.
(DK)	8	-	.	-	.	5.2	44	-	.	4.5	61	-	.
(NA)	9	-	.	-	.	0.1	1	-	.	0.1	2	-	.
Base: All employees							830				1342		

1985 - {ETECWRK7}: the word 'production' does not appear on questionnaire or show card

EMPLOYEES: 'NEW TECHNOLOGY' AT THEIR WORKPLACE (Continued)

			1983		1984		1985		1986		1987		1989	
			%	No	%	No	%	No	%	No	%	No	%	No
	Question No						37ab				38ab			
	Column No						367-68,414				412-13,425			
(viii) {ETECWRK8}	Code													
Other new technology														
At work and respondent uses	1		-	-	-	-	3.3	28	-	-	4.6	62	-	-
At work, respondent does not use	2		-	-	-	-	2.0	16	-	-	2.9	39	-	-
Not at work	3		-	-	-	-	89.2	741	-	-	87.6	1176	-	-
At work, respondent did not state whether uses	7		-	-	-	-	0.1	1	-	-	0.2	3	-	-
(DK)	8		-	-	-	-	5.2	44	-	-	4.5	61	-	-
(NA)	9		-	-	-	-	0.1	1	-	-	0.1	2	-	-
Base: All								830				1342		

			1983		1984		1985		1986		1987		1989	
	Question No						37a				38a			
	Column No						371-72				414-15			
(ix) {ETECWRK9}														
(None of these)														
One or more at work	01		-	-	-	-	68.2	567	-	-	73.4	986	-	-
(DK)	08		-	-	-	-	5.2	44	-	-	4.5	61	-	-
(NA)	09		-	-	-	-	0.1	1	-	-	0.1	2	-	-
None at work	96		-	-	-	-	26.4	219	-	-	21.9	294	-	-
Base: All								830				1342		

1985, 1987 - Additional variable {ETECWRKO} on Column Nos 416-17 listed on the SPSS file for 'Question answered' = code 1 (1985 : n = 786; 1987 : n = 128 for DK = code 98 (1985 : n = 44; 1987 : n = 61); and for NA = code 99 (1985 : n = 1; 1987 : n = 2).

EMPLOYEES: EFFECT OF 'NEW TECHNOLOGY' ON THEIR JOB

{ETECAFCT}

Question: [If employee and any new technology at workplace] Would you say that the use of new technology at your place of work has affected *your own* job ... (read out) ...

		1983		1984		1985		1986		1987		1989	
		%	No	%	No	%	No	%	No	%	No	%	No
Question No						38a				39a			
Column No						415				426			
	Code												
... for the better,	1	-	.	-	.	30.5	253	-	.	32.7	439	-	.
... for the worse,	2	-	.	-	.	3.8	32	-	.	4.1	55	-	.
... or has it made no difference?	3	-	.	-	.	33.0	274	-	.	35.5	477	-	.
[Not asked: no new technology at workplace]	6	-	.	-	.	26.4	219	-	.	21.9	294	-	.
(DK)	8	-	.	-	.	0.5	4	-	.	-	.	-	.
(NA)	9	-	.	-	.	5.9	49	-	.	5.8	78	-	.
Base: All employees							830				1342		

1987 - No (DK)

EMPLOYEES: EFFECTS OF 'NEW TECHNOLOGY' ON FELLOW EMPLOYEES

{TECHSKIL} {TECHRESP} {TECHPAY}

Question: [If employee and any new technology at workplace] **Now thinking about all employees affected by new technology. Has new technology at your workplace *generally* meant ... (read out):**

		1983		1984		1985		1986		1987		1989	
		%	No	%	No	%	No	%	No	%	No	%	No
Question No						38b				39b			
Column No						416				427			

(i) *{TECHSKIL}*

That those affected by it have to work at a *more* or *less* skilled level, or has it made no difference

	Code	1983 %	No	1984 %	No	1985 %	No	1986 %	No	1987 %	No	1989 %	No
More	1	-	-	-	-	24.6	204	-	-	29.1	391	-	-
Less	2	-	-	-	-	6.3	52	-	-	4.5	60	-	-
No difference	3	-	-	-	-	29.8	248	-	-	33.4	449	-	-
[Not asked: no new technology at workplace]	6	-	-	-	-	26.4	219	-	-	21.9	294	-	-
(Other answers)	7	-	-	-	-	0.1	1	-	-	-	-	-	-
(DK)	8	-	-	-	-	6.8	57	-	-	5.7	76	-	-
(NA)	9	-	-	-	-	5.9	49	-	-	5.4	72	-	-
Base: All employees							830				1342		

Question No						38b				39b			
Column No						417				428			

(ii) *{TECHRESP}*

That those affected by it have *more* or *less* responsibility in their work, or has it made no difference

	Code	1983 %	No	1984 %	No	1985 %	No	1986 %	No	1987 %	No	1989 %	No
More	1	-	-	-	-	21.5	179	-	-	25.1	337	-	-
Less	2	-	-	-	-	4.8	40	-	-	3.6	49	-	-
No difference	3	-	-	-	-	32.9	273	-	-	38.4	516	-	-
[Not asked: no new technology at workplace]	6	-	-	-	-	26.4	219	-	-	21.9	294	-	-
(Other answers)	7	-	-	-	-	0.1	1	-	-	-	-	-	-
(DK)	8	-	-	-	-	8.2	68	-	-	5.6	75	-	-
(NA)	9	-	-	-	-	6.0	50	-	-	5.3	71	-	-
Base: All employees							830				1342		

1987 - No (Other answers)

EMPLOYEES: EFFECTS OF 'NEW TECHNOLOGY' ON FELLOW EMPLOYEES (Cont.)

	Code	1983 %	1983 No	1984 %	1984 No	1985 %	1985 No	1986 %	1986 No	1987 %	1987 No	1989 %	1989 No
Question No						38b				39b			
Column No						418				429			

(iii) {TECHPAY}
That those affected by it are
paid *more* or *less*, or has it made
no difference

	Code	1983 %	1983 No	1984 %	1984 No	1985 %	1985 No	1986 %	1986 No	1987 %	1987 No	1989 %	1989 No
More	1	-	-	-	-	8.6	71	-	-	9.7	130	-	-
Less	2	-	-	-	-	1.1	9	-	-	0.6	9	-	-
No difference	3	-	-	-	-	45.9	382	-	-	51.5	691	-	-
[Not asked: no new technology at workplace]	6	-	-	-	-	26.4	219	-	-	21.9	294	-	-
(Other answers)	7	-	-	-	-	-		-	-	-		-	-
(DK)	8	-	-	-	-	12.2	102	-	-	11.0	147	-	-
(NA)	9	-	-	-	-	5.8	48	-	-	5.3	71	-	-
Base: All employees							830				1342		

1987 - No (Other answers)

EMPLOYEES: EFFECT OF 'NEW TECHNOLOGY' ON WORKFORCE SIZE
{TECHJOBS}

Question: [If employee and any new technology at workplace] **[And] has the use of new technology at your workplace meant that ... (read out) ...**

	Code	1983 %	1983 No	1984 %	1984 No	1985 %	1985 No	1986 %	1986 No	1987 %	1987 No	1989 %	1989 No
Question No						38c				39c			
Column No						419				430			
.....the organisation has increased the number of employees,	1	-	-	-	-	8.9	74	-	-	11.2	151	-	-
...reduced the number of employees,	2	-	-	-	-	14.8	123	-	-	16.3	219	-	-
...or has it made no difference?	3	-	-	-	-	40.0	332	-	-	41.0	550	-	-
[Not asked: no new technology at workplace]	6	-	-	-	-	26.4	219	-	-	21.9	294	-	-
(DK)	8	-	-	-	-	4.2	35	-	-	4.3	58	-	-
(NA)	9	-	-	-	-	5.7	48	-	-	5.2	70	-	-
Base: All employees							830				1342		

EMPLOYEES: REASONS FOR NOT BECOMING SELF-EMPLOYED

{WHYNSEM1} + {WHYNSEM2} + {WHYNSEM3}

Question: [If employee and if in last five years has very or quite seriously considered becoming self-employed]
     What were the main reasons you did not become self-employed? (Interviewer: probe fully and record verbatim)

			1983		1984		1985		1986		1987		1989	
			%	No	%	No	%	No	%	No	%	No	%	No
Question No			36d		37d				31d					
Column No			357-62		349-54				342-47					
	Code													
Cost/lack of capital/lack of money	1		10.1	81	9.1	69	-	-	7.3	111	-	-	-	-
Risk involved	2		3.0	24	3.8	29	-	-	4.9	74	-	-	-	-
Recession/economic climate	3		0.6	5	1.3	10	-	-	0.3	4	-	-	-	-
[Not asked: has been self-employed]	90		2.5	20	4.6	35	-	-	3.2	49	-	-	-	-
[Not asked: has not seriously considered working as self-employed]	91		80.7	648	79.1	603	-	-	81.3	1236	-	-	-	-
Other answer	97		6.7	54	7.0	53	-	-	4.7	71	-	-	-	-
(DK)	98		-	-	-	-	-	-	0.1	1	-	-	-	-
(NA)	99		0.1	1	0.4	3	-	-	0.6	9	-	-	-	-
Base: All employees				803		762				1521				

1983, 1984, 1986 - {WHYNSEM2}, {WHYNSEM3}: No further reason given, code 96

EMPLOYEES: LIKELIHOOD OF SELF-EMPLOYMENT IN NEAR FUTURE

{ESELFLKY}

Question: [If employee and if in last five years has very or quite seriously considered working as self-employed] How likely or unlikely is it that you will work as a self-employed person as your main job in the next five years ... (read out) ...

		1983		1984		1985		1986		1987		1989	
		%	No	%	No	%	No	%	No	%	No	%	No
Question No		36e		37e				31e					
Column No		363		355				348					
	Code												
... very likely,	1	2.1	17	3.2	24	-	-	1.5	23	-		-	
... quite likely,	2	6.4	51	5.0	38	-	-	4.6	70	-		-	
... not very likely,	3	5.2	42	3.9	30	-	-	5.3	81	-		-	
... or not at all likely?	4	2.3	18	3.9	30	-	-	3.3	49	-		-	
[Not asked: has not seriously considered working as self-employed]	6	80.7	648	79.1	603	-	-	81.3	1236	-		-	
[Not asked: has been self-employed]	7	2.5	20	4.6	35	-	-	3.2	49	-		-	
(DK)	8	0.7	5	0.1	1	-	-	0.5	7	-		-	
(NA)	9	-	-	0.2	2	-	-	0.4	6	-		-	
Base: All employees			803		762				1521				

1983 - (DK), code 5

EMPLOYEES: SECOND JOBS IN PAST YEAR

{EOTHJOB}

Question: [If employee] Have you in the past *year* done any regular paid work *outside* your main job?

		1983		1984		1985		1986		1987		1989	
		%	No	%	No	%	No	%	No	%	No	%	No
Question No		34		35									
Column No		345		341									
	Code												
Yes	1	5.6	45	6.9	53	-	-	-	-	-	-	-	-
No	2	94.2	757	92.6	705	-	-	-	-	-	-	-	-
(DK)	8	-	-	-	-	-	-	-	-	-	-	-	-
(NA)	9	0.1	1	0.5	4	-	-	-	-	-	-	-	-
Base: All employees			803		762								

EMPLOYEES : NUMBER OF UNIONS RECOGNISED AT THEIR WORKPLACE

1989   Q.37c   {ONEUNION} Column No 361
[If employee] Is there *only one* union or staff association [at your place of work] recognised by the management
or *more than one*?

	Code	%	No
Only one	1	22.9	328
More than one	2	33.0	473
[Not asked : no workplace union(s)]	3	41.7	598
(DK)	8	1.5	21
(NA)	9	0.8	12
Base : All employees			1432

EMPLOYEES : MANAGEMENT'S ATTITUDE TO UNIONS AT THEIR WORKPLACE

1989   Q.39   {MANATTTU} Column No 366
[If employee] How would you describe the management's attitude to trade unions at the place where you work?
Would you say management ... (read out) ...

	Code	%	No
... *encourages* trade union membership,	1	10.3	148
accepts it or would accept it,	2	32.0	458
discourages trade union membership,	3	10.4	149
or - isn't it really an issue at your workplace?	4	45.0	644
(DK)	8	1.8	25
(NA)	9	0.5	8
Base : All employees			1432

EMPLOYEES: COMPULSORY UNION MEMBERSHIP

1989   Q.40   {UNIONREQ} Column No 367
[If employee] (Show card) Suppose you left your present job. Which *one* of these statements
would apply to a person who replaced you?

	Code	%	No
They would:			
... have to be a union member *before being considered* for the job,	1	1.9	27
... have to join a union *before starting* the job,	2	3.1	45
... have to join a union *after starting* the job,	3	10.1	145
... [or] *not* be required to join a union	4	82.5	1182
(DK)	8	2.2	31
(NA)	9	0.2	3
Base : All employees			1432

EMPLOYEES WITH RECOGNISED UNION AT THEIR WORKPLACE : WHAT UNIONS SHOULD TRY TO DO

1989   Q.41b-d   {TUSHOUD1}-{TUSHOUD3} Column Nos 369-74
[If employee with recognised union(s) or staff association at workplace] (Show card) **Listed on the card are a number of things trade unions or staff associations can do. Which, if any, do you think are the *three most important* things they should try to do *at your workplace*?**

{TUSHOUD1} Column Nos 369-70
b) First, tell me the *most* important.

{TUSHOUD2} Column Nos 371-72
c) Then, tell me the *second* most important.

{TUSHOUD3} Column Nos 373-74
d) And then, the *third* most important.

	Code	b) Most important {TUSHOUD1}		c) Second most important {TUSHOUD2}		d) Third most important {TUSHOUD3}	
		%	No	%	No	%	No
Improve working conditions	1	20.8	174	22.1	185	17.0	142
Improve pay	2	28.3	236	23.2	193	17.0	142
Protect existing jobs	3	27.9	233	19.4	162	16.6	139
Have more say over how work is done day-to-day	4	3.4	28	6.3	52	8.7	73
Have more say over management's long-term plans	5	6.4	53	9.5	79	12.1	101
Work for equal opportunities for women	6	2.8	23	6.2	52	7.7	65
Work for equal opportunities for ethnic minorities	7	0.2	2	2.0	17	2.7	23
Reduce pay differences at the workplace	8	5.8	48	5.4	45	8.5	71
None of these	90	2.0	17	2.9	24	5.1	43
(DK)	98	1.0	9	1.2	10	2.4	20
(NA)	99	1.4	12	1.8	15	2.0	17
			834		834		834

Base : All employees with recognised trade union(s)
or staff association at workplace

EMPLOYEES WITH RECOGNISED UNION AT THEIR WORKPLACE: UNION POWER

1989   Q.42   {WTUPOWER} Column No 375
[If employee with recognised union(s) or staff association at workplace] (Show card) **Do you think that the union(s) or staff association *at your workplace* has too much or too little power? Please use a phrase from the card.**

	Code	%	No
Far too much power	1	0.1	1
Too much power	2	3.6	30
About the right amount of power	3	51.3	428
Too little power	4	31.4	262
Far too little power	5	5.8	49
(DK/can't say)	8	6.2	52
(NA)	9	1.4	12
			834

Base : All employees with recognised trade
union(s) or staff association at workplace

EMPLOYEES : WHETHER UNION MEMBER AND REASONS FOR BELONGING

1989   Q.43a,b   *{EUNION}{WHYTUM1}-{WHYTUM8}*   Column Nos 413, 414-21

{EUNION} Column No 413
a) [If employee] Are you now a member of a trade union or staff association, either at your workplace or somewhere else?
(Interviewer : probe for union or staff association)

	Code	%	No
Yes - trade union member	1	**38.8**	556
Yes - staff association member	2	**4.8**	68
No - not member	3	**56.4**	808
Base : All employees			1432

{WHYTUM1}-{WHYTUM8} Column Nos 414-21
b) [If employee and union or staff association member] (Show card) I am going to read some reasons people may have for belonging to a trade union or staff association. For each one, please use the card to say how important it is *to you personally.*

		Very important		Fairly important		Not very important		Not at all important		Does not apply to me		(DK)		(NA)	
	Code	1		2		3		4		5		8		9	
		%	No	%	No	%	No	%	No	%	No	%	No	%	No
i) *{WHYTUM1}* Column No 414 It's a condition of having my job		21.7	135	15.9	100	10.2	64	13.8	86	38.3	239	-	-	-	-
ii) *{WHYTUM2}* Column No 415 To get higher pay and better working conditions		39.8	248	40.1	250	9.7	61	4.0	25	6.4	40	-	-	0.2	1
iii) *{WHYTUM3}* Column No 416 To get members' benefits, like financial or health schemes		33.9	212	36.4	228	15.0	94	7.7	48	6.4	40	0.2	1	0.4	3
iv) *{WHYTUM4}* Column No 417 I believe in them in principle		27.4	171	39.6	247	19.9	124	9.3	58	3.7	23	-	-	0.2	1
v) *{WHYTUM5}* Column No 418 Most of my workmates and colleagues are members		26.1	163	29.0	181	21.0	131	17.6	110	6.0	37	0.2	1	0.2	1
vi) *{WHYTUM6}* Column No 419 To protect me if problems come up		63.4	396	29.4	183	3.7	23	2.2	13	0.4	3	0.2	1	0.7	5
vii) *{WHYTUM7}* Column No 420 It's a tradition in my family		7.0	44	8.2	51	16.3	102	34.9	218	33.2	207	0.2	1	0.2	1
viii) *{WHYTUM8}* Column No 421 To help other people I work with		34.0	212	42.3	264	9.6	60	7.9	49	5.4	34	0.2	1	0.6	4

Base : All employees in union or staff association (n = 624)

EMPLOYEES NOT UNION MEMBERS : REASONS FOR NOT BELONGING TO A UNION

1989   Q.44   {NOTTUM1}-{NOTTUM10} Column Nos 422-31
[If employee and not union or staff association member] (Show card) I am going to read some reasons people may have for *not* belonging to a trade union or staff association. For each one, please say how important it is *to you personally.*

| | Very important 1 | | Fairly important 2 | | Not very important 3 | | Not at all important 4 | | Does not apply to me 5 | | (DK) 8 | | (NA) 9 | |
Code	%	No	%	No	%	No	%	No	%	No	%	No	%	No
i) {NOTTUM1} Column No 4221 There is no union at my workplace	9.0	73	8.0	64	16.2	130	27.6	223	37.7	305	0.7	6	0.8	7
ii) {NOTTUM2} Column No 423 No-one has ever asked me to join	5.3	43	5.5	45	16.8	135	28.7	232	42.3	342	0.2	2	1.1	9
iii) {NOTTUM3} Column No 424 I don't approve of the one I could join at my workplace	1.6	13	3.5	28	6.6	53	11.8	95	74.9	605	0.5	4	1.1	9
iv) {NOTTUM4} Column No 425 It costs too much	1.4	11	4.7	38	8.9	72	23.7	192	59.4	479	0.6	5	1.4	11
v) {NOTTUM5} Column No 426 I disagree with them in principle	11.3	91	11.6	93	15.4	124	26.3	212	33.5	270	0.7	5	1.3	11
vi) {NOTTUM6} Column No 427 It is not really appropriate for my kind of work	10.9	88	15.5	125	13.1	106	19.3	156	38.2	309	0.9	7	2.0	16
vii) {NOTTUM7} Column No 428 I can't see any advantage in joining	13.2	106	15.1	122	13.4	108	15.8	127	40.8	329	0.4	3	1.5	12
viii) {NOTTUM8} Column No 429 I feel it would damage my job prospects	6.3	51	4.9	40	9.2	74	23.6	190	53.9	435	0.8	7	1.3	11
ix) {NOTTUM9} Column No 430 Management disapproves of them at my workplace	6.9	56	6.6	53	8.8	71	21.5	174	53.0	428	1.9	15	1.3	11
x) {NOTTUM10} Column No 431 They would only cause trouble at my workplace	9.1	74	7.8	63	8.5	69	22.5	182	49.4	399	1.4	11	1.3	11

Base : All employees not in union or staff association (n = 808)

EMPLOYEES : OTHER PAID WORK

1989　　Q.45a,b　　　　*{OTHERJOB}{OTHERJBT}*　Column Nos 432-34

1989　　Q.45a　　　　*{OTHERJOB}*　Column No 432

[If employee] Aside from your main job, do you have any *other* paid jobs, like a second job or other paid work?
(Interviewer : if 'yes', ask) Is that regular work or do you only do it sometimes?

	Code	%	No
Yes - regularly	1	**5.1**	74
Yes - sometimes	2	**3.0**	43
No, no other paid work	3	**91.7**	1313
(NA)	9	**0.2**	3
Base : All employees			1432

1989　　Q.45b　　　　*{OTHERJBT - Banded}*　Column Nos 433-34

[If employee and has other paid work] How many hours a week do you *normally* work in these *other* jobs,
not including time spent travelling to work?

	Code	%	No
[Not asked : no other paid work]	-2	**91.7**	1313
One hour	1	0.5	7
Two hours	2	0.5	7
Three hours	3	0.6	9
Four hours	4	0.6	8
Five hours	5	0.7	10
Six hours	6	0.5	7
Seven hours	7	0.3	5
Eight hours	8	0.5	7
Nine hours	9	0.1	1
Ten hours	10	1.3	19
Eleven to fifteen hours		1.0	15
Sixteen to twenty hours		0.7	10
Twenty-one hours or more		0.3	5
(DK)	98	0.4	6
(NA)	99	0.4	6
Base : All employees			1432

NB   Banded from eleven hours upwards

EMPLOYEES (MEN): GENDER STEREOTYPING AT WORK

1987   Q.28b-d   *{EMWOMCLD}{EMWOMWLD}{EMWHYM1}-{EMWHYM3}*   Column Nos 279-80, 308-13

{EMWOMCLD} Column No 279
b) [If male employee and thinks his work is mainly men's work] **Do you think that women *could* do the same sort of work as you?**

	Code	%	No
[Not asked : female employee]	0	46.5	624
Yes	1	14.3	192
No	2	10.1	136
[Not asked : work not mainly men's work]	6	28.7	385
(DK)	8	0.4	5
Base : All employees			1342

{EMWOMWLD} Column No 280
c)   [If male employee and thinks his work is mainly men's work] **Do you think that women *would be willing* to do the same sort of work as you?**

	Code	%	No
[Not asked : female employee]	0	46.5	624
Yes	1	7.4	99
No	2	6.5	87
[Not asked : work not mainly men's work]	6	28.7	385
[Not asked : women could not do same work]	7	10.1	136
(DK)	8	0.6	8
(NA)	9	0.1	2
Base : All employees			1342

{EMWHYM1}+{EMWHYM2}+{EMWHYM3} Column Nos 308-09, 310-11, 312-13
d) [If male employee and thinks his work is mainly men's work] **Why do you think your sort of work is mainly done by men?** (Interviewer : probe fully and record verbatim)

	Code	%	No
[Not asked : female employee]	0	46.5	624
Work is too heavy for women/women do not have physical strength	1	16.8	226
Physical conditions would be too unpleasant /dangerous/dirty for women	2	7.2	96
Women (or other men) would be uncomfortable or embarrassed/men prefer to deal with other men	3	1.0	14
Women haven't got mechanical aptitude/technical skills/technical training/ Women wouldn't be interested in it for technical reasons	4	1.6	21
Women wouldn't do the job for family reasons	5	0.1	1
Women just don't do the job/never have done job /just traditional for women not to do it	6	5.0	67
Women don't or can't work night shift/too much travelling involved/long hours, etc	7	2.4	32
[Not asked : work not mainly men's work]	90	28.7	385
Other answers	97	0.8	11
(DK/no other response)	98	0.2	3
(NA/no other response)	99	0.4	6
Base : All employees			1342

NB Up to 3 responses were coded for each respondent, so percentages add up to more than 100%

EMPLOYEES (WOMEN): GENDER STEREOTYPING AT WORK

1987   Q.30b-d   *{EWMENCLL}{EWMENWLD}{EWWHYW1}-{EWWHYW3}*   Column Nos 318-25

{EWMENCLD} Column No 318

b) [If female employee and thinks of her work as mainly women's work] **Do you think that men**
could **do the same sort of work as you?**

	Code	%	No
[Not asked : male employee]	0	53.5	718
Yes	1	11.8	159
No	2	1.1	15
[Not asked : work not mainly women's work]	6	33.1	444
(DK)	8	0.1	2
(NA)	9	0.4	5
Base : All employees			1342

{EWMENWLD} Column No 319

c) [If female employee and thinks of her work as mainly women's work] **Do you think that men** *would*
be willing **to do the same sort of work as you?**

	Code	%	No
[Not asked : male employee]	0	53.5	718
Yes	1	4.8	64
No	2	6.8	91
[Not asked : work not mainly women's work]	6	33.1	444
[Not asked : men could not do same work]	7	1.1	15
(DK)	8	0.4	5
(NA)	9	0.4	5
Base : All employees			1342

d) *{EWWHYW1}*+*{EWWHYW2}*+*{EWWHYW3}* Column Nos 320-21, 322-23, 324-25
[If female employee and thinks of her work as mainly women's work] **Why do you think your sort of work**
is mainly done by women? (Interviewer : probe fully and record verbatim)

	Code	%	No
[Not asked : male employee]	0	53.5	718
Men don't have the right personal skills/ temperament/women are better at dealing with people	1	2.1	28
Men don't have the right technical skills/ work requires manual dexterity/men are clumsy/ men just aren't trained *technically* to do work	2	0.7	9
Women's pay is too low/is part-time work	3	3.0	40
Work is boring/tedious/frustrating	4	1.3	18
It would be embarrassing for men/men would be considered effeminate	5	0.7	10
Type of work is/has been/should be 'women's work' (in respondent's or other people's opinion)	6	7.2	97
Men just don't/have never done this sort of work	7	1.1	15
[Not asked : work not mainly women's work]	90	33.1	444
Other answers	97	0.1	2
(DK/no other response)	98	0.1	1
(NA/no other response)	99	0.4	5
Base : All employees			1342

NB Up to 3 responses were coded for each respondent, so percentages add up to more than 100%.

EMPLOYEES : RECENT TRAINING RECEIVED

1987   Q.35a,b   *{ECOURSE}{ECOURSET - Banded}* Column Nos 352-55

{ECOURSE} Colomn No 352

a) [If employee] In the last *two* years, have you been on any courses or had other formal training, which was part of your work or helpful to your work? (Interviewer: any training which is related to respondent's past, present, or future work may be counted, but do not include leisure courses or hobbies which are not job-related.)

	Code	%	No
Yes, had training related to work	1	39.8	535
No, had none	2	60.1	807
(DK)	8	-	-
(NA)	9	0.1	1
Base : All employees			1342

{ECOURSET - Banded} Column No 353-55

b) [If employee and had any recent training] *In all,* about how many full days have you spent in this kind of training over the last two years? (Interviewer: probe for total time spent in job-related training in past or present job; write in as appropriate. If less than half a day, write in '000').

	Code	%	No
[Not asked : had no recent training]	-1	60.1	807
Less than half a day	0	0.2	3
1 day	1	1.8	24
2 days	2	2.3	31
3 days	3	2.6	35
4 days	4	2.4	32
5 days	5	5.5	74
6 days	6	1.3	18
7 days	7	1.6	21
8 days	8	0.5	6
9 days	9	0.1	2
10 days	10	3.8	51
11-15 days		3.7	50
16-20 days		1.8	25
21-30 days		3.8	52
31-60 days		3.5	47
61-90 days		0.9	12
Over 90 days		3.0	41
(DK)	98	0.6	9
(NA)	99	0.4	5
Base : All employees			1342

NB   Eleven days and over are banded

EMPLOYEES : DESIRE FOR TRAINING

1987   Q.36a   {ELKCOURS} Column No 361
[If employee] Over the *next* two years, would you *like* to have any *(more)* courses or formal training for your work, or are you not that bothered?

	Code	%	No
Yes, would like to	1	48.6	653
No, not that bothered	2	48.3	649
(DK/depends)	8	2.6	35
(NA)	9	0.4	6
Base : All employees			1342

EMPLOYEES : EXPECTATIONS FOR TRAINING

1987   Q.36b   {EXPCOURS} Column No 362
[If employee] And apart from what you would like, do you *expect* to have any (more) courses or training for your work in the next two years?

	Code	%	No
Yes, expect to	1	39.1	525
No, don't expect to	2	55.2	741
(DK/depends)	8	4.9	66
(NA)	9	0.7	10
Base : All employees			1342

EMPLOYEES : KINDS OF TRAINING RECEIVED

1987   Q.37a-g   {ELEARN1} - {ELEARN7} {ELEARN0}   Column Nos 363-69
[If employee] In the last two years, have you done any of the following things in connection with your work? Please just answer yes or no. (Read out) :

{ELEARN1} Column No 363
a) Have you been asked to do anything just for *practice* in order to learn the work?

	Code	%	No
Yes	1	29.6	397
No	2	70.3	944
(DK)	8	0.0	1
(NA)	9	0.1	1
Base : All employees			1342

{ELEARN2} Column No 364
b) Have you been given any special talks or lectures about the work?

	Code	%	No
Yes	1	41.2	553
No	2	58.7	788
(DK)	8	-	-
(NA)	9	0.1	2
Base : All employees			1342

EMPLOYEES : KINDS OF TRAINING RECEIVED (continued)

{ELEARN3} Column No 365
c) Have you been placed with more experienced people to see how the work should be done?

	Code	%	No
Yes	1	30.7	412
No	2	69.2	929
(DK)	8	0.1	1
(NA)	9	0.0	1
Base : All employees			1342

{ELEARN4} Column No 366
d) Have you been sent round to different parts of the organisation to see what sort of work is done?

	Code	%	No
Yes	1	22.9	307
No	2	77.1	1035
(DK)	8	0.1	1
(NA)	9	-	-
Base : All employees			1342

{ELEARN5} Column No 367
e) Have you been asked to read things to help you learn about the work?

	Code	%	No
Yes	1	44.0	591
No	2	56.0	751
(DK)	8	-	-
(NA)	9	-	-
Base : All employees			1342

{ELEARN6} Column No 368
f) Have you been taught or trained by anybody while you were actually doing the work?

	Code	%	No
Yes	1	35.7	480
No	2	64.3	863
(DK)	8	-	-
(NA)	9	-	-
Base : All employees			1342

{ELEARN7} Column No 369
g) Have you been sent on any courses to introduce you to new methods of working?

	Code	%	No
Yes	1	23.5	315
No	2	76.5	1027
(DK)	8	-	-
(NA)	9	-	-
Base : All employees			1342

{ELEARN0} Variable derived from {ELEARN1} - {ELEARN7} Column No. 426
Whether employee has done any of a) - g) in connection with his or her work:

	Code	%	No
Yes	1	71.2	955
No	2	28.8	387
Base : All employees			1342

EMPLOYEES : PERCEIVED COMPARATIVE PAY RATES

1986   Q.27a-c   *{EPAYEDU}{EGOTAHD}{EPAYJOB}*   Column Nos 318-20

{EPAYEDU} Column No 318

a) [If employee] Comparing yourself with people with the *same* level of education and training, would you say that *your pay* is ... (read out) ...

	Code	%	No
... very high,	1	1.8	27
a little high,	2	10.6	162
about average,	3	52.7	802
a little low,	4	23.6	358
or - very low?	5	9.4	144
(DK)	8	1.7	26
(NA)	9	0.2	3
Base : All employees			1521

{EGOTAHD} Column No 319

b) [If employee] And still comparing yourself with people with the same level of education and training, what would you say about the *level* of your job, that is, how quickly do you think you've got ahead ... (read out) ...

	Code	%	No
... very quickly,	1	7.6	115
quite quickly,	2	20.7	314
about average,	3	48.8	743
not very quickly,	4	10.9	165
or - not at all quickly?	5	7.0	106
(DK)	8	4.0	61
(NA)	9	1.1	17
Base : All employees			1521

{EPAYJOB} Column No 320

c) [If employee] And now thinking of people in similarly demanding jobs to yours, would you say that *your pay* is ... (read out) ...

	Code	%	No
... very high,	1	0.7	11
a little high,	2	8.1	124
about average,	3	52.7	802
a little low,	4	27.1	412
or - very low?	5	9.5	145
(DK)	8	1.6	24
(NA)	9	0.3	4
Base : All employees			1521

EMPLOYEES : FEELINGS ABOUT WORK

1985   Q.29   *{EMPFEEL}* Column No 323
[If employee] (Show card) **Which of the statements on this card *best* describes your feelings about your work?**

	Code	%	No
Work is only a business transaction. The more I get paid the more I do; the less I get paid the less I do	1	7.2	59
I make a point of doing the best work I can, regardless of pay	2	60.5	502
I want to work hard, but not so that it interferes with the rest of my life	3	30.0	249
(None of these)	4	2.3	19
(NA)	9	0.1	1
Base : All employees			830

EMPLOYEES: JOB MOBILITY AS A ROUTE TO ADVANCEMENT

1985   Q.33   *{JOBMOBIL}*   Column No 338
[If employee] **From your experience, when it comes to getting a better job, do you think people like yourself are better off ... (read out) ...**

	Code	%	No
... staying with the same employer a long time,	1	62.2	517
or, moving around between employers?	2	28.2	234
(People like me can't get better jobs)	3	1.1	9
(It depends/DK)	8	8.4	70
(NA)	9	0.1	1
Base : All employees			830

EMPLOYEES : AUTONOMY AT WORK

1985   Q.34   *{JOBTASKS}* Column No 339
[If employee] **Do you decide the *specific* tasks or jobs you carry out each day, or does someone else?**
(Interviewer : if both respondent and someone else, ask : Who *mainly* decides the *specific* tasks you do each day?)

	Code	%	No
Respondent decides	1	50.4	418
Someone else	2	46.2	383
(Can't choose/DK)	8	3.5	29
Base : All employees			830

EMPLOYEES : REASONS FOR WORKING

1984   Q.32a   {EWORK1}-{EWORK10} Column Nos 319-27
[If employee] (Show card) Now I'd like you to look at the statements on the card and tell me which
ones best describe your own reasons for working at present. (Interviewer : code all that apply)

	Code	%	No
{EWORK1} Column No 319			
Working is the normal thing to do			
Given as a reason	1	35.3	269
Not given as a reason	0	64.7	493
Base : All employees			762
{EWORK2} Column No 320			
Need money for basic essentials such as food, rent or mortgage			
Given as reason	2	71.1	542
Not given as reason	0	28.9	220
Base : All employees			762
{EWORK3} Column No 321			
To earn money to buy extras			
Given as reason	3	37.0	282
Not given as reason	0	63.0	480
Base : All employees			762
{EWORK4} Column No 322			
To earn money of my own			
Given as reason	4	28.4	217
Not given as reason	0	71.6	545
Base : All employees			762
{EWORK5} Column No 323			
For the company of other people			
Given as reason	5	24.7	188
Not given as reason	0	75.3	574
Base : All employees			762
{EWORK6} Column No 324			
Enjoy working			
Given as reason	6	50.8	387
Not given as reason	0	49.2	375
Base : All employees			762
{EWORK7} Column No 325			
To follow my career			
Given as reason	1	27.9	212
Not given as reason	0	72.1	550
Base : All employees			762

EMPLOYEES : REASONS FOR WORKING (continued)

		Code	%	No
{EWORK8}	Column No 326			
For a change from my children or housework				
Given as reason		2	5.5	42
Not given as reason		0	94.5	720
Base : All employees				762
{EWORK9}	Column No 327			
Other reason				
Given as reason		7	1.3	752
Not given as reason		0	98.7	10
Base : All employees				762

NB   A further variable {EWORK10} was derived - 'more than one reason given - code 0 (n = 762). Therefore all employees gave more than one reason for working

EMPLOYEES : MAIN REASON FOR WORKING

1984   Q.32b   **{EWRKMAIN}** Column Nos 329-30
[If employee and gave more than one reason] (Continue showing card) **And which one of these would you say is your *main* reason for working?**

	Code	%	No
Working is the normal thing to do	1	5.9	45
Need money for basic essentials such as food, rent or mortgage	2	61.7	470
To earn money to buy extras	3	7.6	58
To earn money of my own	4	6.1	46
For the company of other people	5	1.0	8
Enjoy working	6	9.4	72
To follow my career	7	6.3	48
For a change from my children or housework	8	0.5	4
Other reasons	97	0.8	6
(DK)	98	0.2	2
(NA)	99	0.5	4
Base : All employees			762

G Labour market and employment

G4 Self-employed

Table titles and cross references

SELF-EMPLOYED: LENGTH OF WORKING WEEK - 1

{SJBHOURS - Banded}

Question: [If self-employed] How many hours a week do you *normally* work in your (main) job? (Interviewer: if respondent cannot answer, ask about last week)

		1983		1984		1985		1986		1987		1989	
		%	No	%	No	%	No	%	No	%	No	%	No
Question No						41a		34a		42a		46a	
Column No						425-26		356-57		436-37		461-62	
	Code												
10-15 hours a week		-	-	-	-	6.3	7	5.0	9	4.3	8	4.6	10
16-23 hours a week		-	-	-	-	6.3	7	3.6	7	5.1	10	8.8	19
24-29 hours a week		-	-	-	-	0.9	1	3.1	6	1.6	3	2.0	5
30-34 hours a week		-	-	-	-	0.9	1	4.9	9	3.7	7	4.5	10
35-39 hours a week		-	-	-	-	10.2	12	6.1	11	0.8	2	4.3	9
40-44 hours a week		-	-	-	-	18.7	21	13.5	24	16.4	31	16.6	37
45-49 hours a week		-	-	-	-	8.7	10	9.8	18	11.8	22	11.2	25
50-59 hours a week		-	-	-	-	11.4	13	18.4	33	22.9	43	16.3	36
60 or more hours a week		-	-	-	-	31.4	36	34.2	62	33.3	63	27.8	61
(DK)	98	-	-	-	-	1.7	2	1.1	2	-	-	0.2	1
(NA)	99	-	-	-	-	3.5	4	0.3	1	-	-	3.8	8
Base: All self-employed							115		181		188		220

SELF-EMPLOYED: LENGTH OF WORKING WEEK - 2

{SJBHRCAT}

Question: [If self-employed] **How many hours a week do you normally work in your (main) job?** (Interviewer: if respondent cannot answer, ask about 'last week'. Write in number of hours and code)

		1983		1984		1985		1986		1987		1989	
		%	No	%	No	%	No	%	No	%	No	%	No
Question No				40a		41a		34a		42a		46a	
Column No				360		427		358		438		463	
	Code												
10-15 hours a week	1	-	.	5.3	5	6.3	7	5.3	10	4.3	8	5.1	11
16-23 hours a week	2	-	.	-	.	7.1	8	3.6	7	5.1	10	8.8	19
24-29 hours a week	3	-	.	4.3	4	0.9	1	3.1	6	1.6	3	2.0	5
30 or more hours a week	4	-	.	89.2	77	83.1	95	88.0	159	89.0	167	83.3	184
(NA)	9	-	.	1.2	1	2.6	3	-	.	-	.	0.8	2
Base: All self-employed					86		115		181		188		220

1984 - Interviewer instructed to read out each response category; exact number of hours not recorded
1985-1987, 1989 - see {SJBHOURS - Banded} above.

SELF-EMPLOYED: LENGTH OF TIME DOING SAME WORK

{SHOWLONG - Banded}

Question: [If self-employed] **For about how many years have you been self-employed and doing the same sort of work as now?** (Interviewer: probe for best estimate)

		1983		1984		1985		1986		1987		1989	
		%	No	%	No	%	No	%	No	%	No	%	No
Question No										42b		46b	
Column No										439-40		464-65	
	Code												
1 year or less	1	-	.	-	.	-	.	-	.	19.3	36	22.7	50
More than 1 - up to 5 years		-	.	-	.	-	.	-	.	26.9	51	31.4	69
More than 5 - up to 10 years		-	.	-	.	-	.	-	.	21.3	40	19.2	42
More than 10 - up to 20 years		-	.	-	.	-	.	-	.	19.0	36	17.8	39
Over 20 years		-	.	-	.	-	.	-	.	13.0	25	7.7	17
(NA)	99	-	.	-	.	-	.	-	.	0.5	1	1.2	3
Base: All self-employed											188		220

SELF-EMPLOYED: RECENT EXPERIENCE OF UNEMPLOYMENT

{SUNEMP}

Question: [If self-employed] During the last 5 years - that is since March 1984 - have you been *unemployed* and seeking work for any period?

		1983		1984		1985		1986		1987		1989	
		%	No	%	No	%	No	%	No	%	No	%	No
Question No		39b		40b		41b		34b		42c		46c	
Column No		369		361		428		359		441		466	
	Code												
Yes	1	20.9	22	14.1	12	12.3	14	15.2	27	17.9	34	24.9	55
No	2	79.1	82	85.9	74	84.4	97	84.5	153	81.6	154	71.1	157
(DK)	8	-		-		-		-		-		-	
(NA)	9	-		-		3.3	4	0.3	1	0.5	1	4.0	9
Base: All self-employed			104		86		115		181		188		220

1987 - (that is since March 1982)
1986 - (that is since March 1981)
1985 - (that is since March 1980)
1984 - (that is since March 1979)
1983 - (that is since March 1978)

SELF-EMPLOYED: WHETHER WOULD HAVE PAID JOB IF ONE NOT NEEDED

{SPREFJOB}

Question: [If self-employed] If without having to work, you had what you would regard as a reasonable living income, do you think you would still prefer to do paid work, or wouldn't you bother?

		1983		1984		1985		1986		1987		1989	
		%	No	%	No	%	No	%	No	%	No	%	No
Question No				41		42		35				47	
Column No				364		433		364				467	
	Code												
Still prefer paid job	1	-		77.1	67	66.0	76	75.2	136	-		77.6	171
Wouldn't bother	2	-		17.7	15	28.3	33	22.6	41	-		19.9	44
Other answer	7	-		3.0	3	3.1	4	0.6	1	-		2.0	5
(DK)	8	-		2.3	2	-		1.1	2	-		-	
(NA)	9	-		-		2.6	3	0.6	1	-		0.5	1
Base: All self-employed					86		115		181				220

1984,1985,1986 - Derived variable {PREFJOB} combines the responses to this question of employees, self-employed, unemployed, those in full-time education, and those on a government scheme or waiting to take up paid work

SELF EMPLOYED: RECENT EXPERIENCE OF WORKING AS EMPLOYEE

{SEMPLEE}

Question: [If self-employed] Have you, for any period in the last five years, worked as an *employee* as your main job rather than as self-employed?

		1983		1984		1985		1986		1987		1989	
		%	No	%	No	%	No	%	No	%	No	%	No
Question No		40a		43a		43a		36a		43a		48a	
Column No		374		378		434		365		446		468	
	Code												
Yes	1	31.0	32	36.6	32	29.8	34	31.9	58	31.8	60	41.9	92
No	2	69.0	72	63.4	55	68.5	79	68.1	123	67.7	127	57.8	127
(DK)	8	-	.	-	.	-	.	-	.	-	.	-	.
(NA)	9	-	.	-	.	1.7	2	-	.	0.5	1	0.3	1
Base: All self-employed			104		86		115		181		188		220

1983 - No (DK)

SELF-EMPLOYED: LENGTH OF ANY RECENT PERIOD AS EMPLOYEE

{SEMPLEET - Banded}

Question: [If self-employed and if worked as an employee during last five years] **In total for how many months during the last five years have you been an employee?**

		1983		1984		1985		1986		1987		1989	
		%	No	%	No	%	No	%	No	%	No	%	No
Question No		40b		43b		43b		36b		43b		48b	
Column No		375-78		379-80		435-38		366-69		447-50		469-72	
	Code												
[Not asked: not been an employee during last five years]	-1	69.0	72	63.4	55	68.5	79	68.1	123	67.7	127	57.8	127
1-6 months		1.9	2	-	.	1.3	2	1.9	4	3.1	6	3.6	8
7-12 months		2.4	3	9.8	8	0.9	1	4.1	7	4.8	9	5.2	11
13-24 months		11.0	11	6.6	6	6.7	8	10.5	19	7.6	14	12.3	27
More than 2 years		14.7	15	20.3	18	20.9	24	15.0	27	16.3	31	20.3	45
(DK)	98	-	.	-	.	-	.	0.4	1	-	.	0.5	1
(NA)	99	1.0	1	-	.	1.7	2	-	.	0.5	1	0.3	1
Base: All self-employed			104		86		115		181		188		220

SELF-EMPLOYED: HOW SERIOUSLY CONSIDERED WORKING AS EMPLOYEE

{SEMPLSER}

Question: [If self-employed and not worked as employee during last five years] **How seriously in the last five years have you considered getting a job as an *employee* ... (read out) ...**

	Code	1983 %	No	1984 %	No	1985 %	No	1986 %	No	1987 %	No	1989 %	No
Question No		40c		43c		43c		36c		43c		48c	
Column No		407		407		439		370		451		473	
... very seriously,	1	2.6	3	1.2	1	4.9	6	3.9	7	4.8	9	1.5	3
... quite seriously,	2	5.4	6	3.5	3	9.4	11	7.2	13	5.8	11	5.7	13
... not very seriously,	3	3.8	4	4.6	4	6.5	8	5.8	11	6.4	12	7.4	16
... or not at all seriously?	4	57.2	59	54.1	47	47.6	55	51.3	93	50.6	95	42.2	93
[Not asked: has worked as employee]	7	31.0	32	36.6	32	29.8	34	31.9	58	31.8	60	41.9	92
(DK)	8	-	-	-	-	-	-	-	-	-	-	-	-
(NA)	9	-	-	-	-	1.7	2	-	-	0.5	1	1.2	3
Base: All self-employed			104		86		115		181		188		220

1983 - No (DK)

SELF-EMPLOYED: CURRENT PROSPERITY OF THEIR BUSINESS

{BUS1OK}

Question: [If self-employed] Compared with *a year ago*, would you say your business is doing ... (read out) ...

		1983		1984		1985		1986		1987		1989	
		%	No	%	No	%	No	%	No	%	No	%	No
Question No		41a		44a		44a		37a		44a		49a	
Column No		417		415		440		371		452		474	
	Code												
... very well,	1	11.0	12	16.7	14	11.6	13	11.1	20	12.2	23	14.3	32
... quite well,	2	24.7	26	18.8	16	24.0	27	27.3	49	21.0	40	20.9	46
... about the same,	3	48.2	50	47.3	41	40.0	46	41.8	76	42.3	80	40.1	88
... not very well,	4	7.4	8	7.5	6	5.6	6	9.6	17	10.7	20	8.9	20
... or not at all well?	5	5.2	5	1.2	1	11.3	13	3.8	7	1.4	3	0.7	2
(Business not in existence then)	6	1.6	2	8.5	7	5.8	7	6.4	12	11.9	22	13.3	29
(DK)	8	-	.	-	.	-	.	-	.	-	.	-	.
(NA)	9	1.9	2	-	.	1.7	2	-	.	0.5	1	1.8	4
Base: All self-employed			104		86		115		181		188		220

1983 - Self-employed respondents were also asked how their business was doing compared with five years ago: see {BUS5OK}, p.G.4 - 24 below

1987 - Q reads: '...would you say (your work or) your business is doing ...'

SELF-EMPLOYED: FUTURE PROSPECTS FOR THEIR BUSINESS

{BUS1FUT}

Question: [If self-employed] [And] over *the coming year*, do you think your business will do ... (read out) ...

	Code	1983 %	No	1984 %	No	1985 %	No	1986 %	No	1987 %	No	1989 %	No
Question No				44b		44b		37b		44b		49b	
Column No				416		441		372		453		475	
... better,	1	-	-	40.4	35	33.2	38	36.1	65	39.3	74	41.5	92
... about the same,	2	-	-	45.6	39	47.5	54	49.8	90	48.1	91	42.9	95
... or worse than this year?	3	-	-	3.3	3	14.4	17	5.4	10	6.9	13	5.9	13
(Other answer)	7	-	-	1.5	1	0.9	1	2.0	4	0.5	1	2.3	5
(DK)	8	-	-	9.3	8	1.7	2	5.9	11	4.7	9	5.5	12
(NA)	9	-	-	-	-	2.3	3	0.8	2	0.5	1	1.8	4
Base: All self-employed					86		115		181		188		220

1987 ·   Q reads: '...do you think (your work or) your business will do...'

SELF-EMPLOYED: WHETHER HAS PARTNERS

{SPARTNRS}

Question: [If self-employed] In your work or business, do you have any partners or other self-employed colleagues?
(Interviewer: do not include employees)

	Code	1983 %	No	1984 %	No	1985 %	No	1986 %	No	1987 %	No	1989 %	No
Question No										45a		50a	
Column No										454		476	
Yes, have partner(s)	1	-	-	-	-	-	-	-	-	47.0	88	40.1	88
No	2	-	-	-	-	-	-	-	-	52.5	99	59.0	130
(DK)	8	-	-	-	-	-	-	-	-	-	-	-	-
(NA)	9	-	-	-	-	-	-	-	-	0.5	1	0.9	2
Base: All self-employed											188		220

SELF-EMPLOYED: WHETHER HAS EMPLOYEES

{SANYEMPS}

Question: [If self-employed] [And] in your work or business, do you have any employees or not? (Interviewer: family members may be employees only if they receive a regular wage or salary)

		1983		1984		1985		1986		1987		1989	
		%	No	%	No	%	No	%	No	%	No	%	No
Question No										46a		50b	
Column No										458		477	
	Code												
Yes, has employees	1	-	.	-	.	-	.	-	.	34.2	64	29.9	66
No	2	-	.	-	.	-	.	-	.	65.2	123	65.7	145
(NA)	9	-	.	-	.	-	.	-	.	0.5	1	4.4	10
											—		—
Base: All self-employed											188		220

1989 - SPSS file lists the variable name as {SNUMPARS}, although the question was exactly the same; consequently the 1989 variable name has been changed to {SANYEMPS}

SELF-EMPLOYED: COMMITMENT TO WORK - 1

{SEMPEARN}

Question: [If self-employed] Now for some more general questions about your work.

For some people their job is simply something they do in order to earn a living. For others it means much more than that. On balance, is your present job ... (read out) ...

		1983		1984		1985		1986		1987		1989	
		%	No	%	No	%	No	%	No	%	No	%	No
Question No						45a						51a	
Column No						442						478	
	Code												
... just a means of earning a living,	1	-	-	-	-	34.4	39	-	-	-	-	28.4	63
... or does it mean much more to you than that?	2	-	-	-	-	63.8	73	-	-	-	-	71.6	158
(DK)	8	-	-	-	-	-		-	-	-	-	-	
(NA)	9	-	-	-	-	1.7	2	-	-	-	-		

Base: All self-employed   115   220

SELF-EMPLOYED: COMMITMENT TO WORK - 2

{SEMPLIV}

Question: [If self-employed and present job is just a means of earning a living] Is that because ... (read out) ...

		1983		1984		1985		1986		1987		1989	
		%	No	%	No	%	No	%	No	%	No	%	No
Question No						45b						51b	
Column No						443						479	
	Code												
... there are no better jobs around here,	1	-	-	-	-	12.7	15	-	-	-	-	5.7	13
... you don't have the right skills to get a better job,	2	-	-	-	-	5.4	6	-	-	-	-	7.2	16
... or because you would feel the same about *any* job you had?	3	-	-	-	-	12.0	14	-	-	-	-	12.3	27
[Not asked: job means more than just earning a living]	7	-	-	-	-	63.8	73	-	-	-	-	71.6	158
(DK)	8	-	-	-	-	-		-	-	-	-	0.3	1
(NA)	9	-	-	-	-	6.1	7	-	-	-	-	2.9	6

Base: All self-employed   115   220

SELF-EMPLOYED: LENGTH OF ANY RECENT PERIOD OF UNEMPLOYMENT

{SUNEMPT - Banded}

Question: If self-employed and had been unemployed and seeking work during last 5 years] **For how many months in total during last 5 years** [have you been unemployed and seeking work]?

		1983		1984		1985		1986		1987		1989	
		%	No	%	No	%	No	%	No	%	No	%	No
Question No		39c		40c		41c		34c		42d			
Column No		370-73		362-63		429-32		360-63		442-45			
	Code												
[Not asked: not been unemployed and seeking work during last 5 years]	-1	79.1	82	85.9	74	84.4	97	84.5	153	81.6	154	-	
1 month	1	2.6	3	3.5	3	3.5	4	1.1	2	1.2	2	-	
2-3 months		2.6	3	3.5	3	-	-	3.3	6	2.3	4	-	
4-6 months		6.7	7	3.1	3	1.3	2	3.6	7	2.1	4	-	
7-12 months		1.8	2	1.7	1	2.2	3	3.3	6	7.5	14	-	
13-24 months		4.3	5	2.3	2	2.8	3	1.7	3	3.5	7	-	
Over 24 months		1.9	2	-	-	2.5	3	2.2	4	1.1	2	-	
(DK)	8	-	-	-	-	-	-	-	-	0.3	1	-	
(NA)	9	1.0	1	-	-	3.3	4	0.3	1	0.5	1	-	
Base: All self-employed			104		86		115		181		188		

1983 - (NA), code 999

SELF-EMPLOYED: 'NEW TECHNOLOGY' IN THEIR WORK

{STECWRK1} {STECWRK2} {STECWRK3} {STECWRK4} {STECWRK5} {STECWRK6} {STECWRK7} {STECWRK8} {STECWRK9}

Question: [If self-employed] (Show card) **Which, if any, of these kinds of new technology do you have or use in your work?**

		1983		1984		1985		1986		1987		1989	
		%	No	%	No	%	No	%	No	%	No	%	No
Question No						48a				47a			
Column No						455-56				471-72			
(i) {STECWRK1}	Code												
Main frame computer													
Respondent has or uses in work	1	-	.	-	.	3.5	4	-	.	0.9	2	-	.
Respondent does not have or use	96	-	.	-	.	94.8	109	-	.	99.1	186	-	.
(DK)	98	-	.	-	.	-	.	-	.	-	.	-	.
(NA)	99	-	.	-	.	1.7	2	-	.	-	.	-	.
Base: All self-employed							115				188		

		1983		1984		1985		1986		1987		1989	
Question No						48a				47a			
Column No						457-58				473-74			
(ii) {STECWRK2}													
Telephone link to computer at another place													
Respondent has or uses in work	2	-	.	-	.	5.2	6	-	.	1.1	2	-	.
Respondent does not have or use	96	-	.	-	.	93.0	107	-	.	98.9	186	-	.
(DK)	98	-	.	-	.	-	.	-	.	-	.	-	.
(NA)	99	-	.	-	.	1.7	2	-	.	-	.	-	.
Base: All self-employed							115				188		

		1983		1984		1985		1986		1987		1989	
Question No						48a				47a			
Column No						459-60				475-76			
(iii) {STECWRK3}													
Micro/mini computer													
Respondent has or uses in work	3	-	.	-	.	11.9	14	-	.	8.2	16	-	.
Respondent does not have or use	96	-	.	-	.	86.3	99	-	.	91.8	173	-	.
(DK)	98	-	.	-	.	-	.	-	.	-	.	-	.
(NA)	99	-	.	-	.	1.7	2	-	.	-	.	-	.
Base: All self-employed							115				188		

SELF-EMPLOYED: 'NEW TECHNOLOGY' IN THEIR WORK (Continued)

		1983		1984		1985		1986		1987		1989	
		%	No	%	No	%	No	%	No	%	No	%	No
Question No						48a				47a			
Column No						461-62				477-78			
(iv) *{STECWRK4}*	Code												
Computer - type unknown													
Respondent has or uses in work	4	-	.	-	.	0.9	1	-	.	1.9	4	-	.
Respondent does not have or use	96	-	.	-	.	97.4	112	-	.	98.1	185	-	.
(DK)	98	-	.	-	.	-	.	-	.	-	.	-	.
(NA)	99	-	.	-	.	1.7	2	-	.	-	.	-	.
Base: All self-employed							115				188		

		1983		1984		1985		1986		1987		1989	
Question No						48a				47a			
Column No						463-64				479-80			
(v) *{STECWRK5}*													
Word processor													
Respondent has or uses in work	5	-	.	-	.	7.9	9	-	.	10.0	19	-	.
Respondent does not have or use	96	-	.	-	.	90.4	104	-	.	90.0	169	-	.
(DK)	98	-	.	-	.	-	.	-	.	-	.	-	.
(NA)	99	-	.	-	.	1.7	2	-	.	-	.	-	.
Base: All self-employed							115				188		

		1983		1984		1985		1986		1987		1989	
Question No						48a				47a			
Column No						465-66				508-09			
(vi) *{STECWRK6}*													
Electronic memory typewriter													
Respondent has or uses in work	6	-	.	-	.	7.0	8	-	.	4.2	8	-	.
Respondent does not have or use	96	-	.	-	.	91.3	105	-	.	95.8	180	-	.
(DK)	98	-	.	-	.	-	.	-	.	-	.	-	.
(NA)	99	-	.	-	.	1.7	2	-	.	-	.	-	.
Base: All self-employed							115				188		

SELF-EMPLOYED: 'NEW TECHNOLOGY' IN THEIR WORK (Continued)

		1983		1984		1985		1986		1987		1989	
		%	No	%	No	%	No	%	No	%	No	%	No
Question No						48a				47a			
Column No						467-68				510-11			
(vii) {STECWRK7}	Code												

Computer controlled plant, machinery or equipment, including robots, [used for design, assembly, handling, production]

	Code	1983 %	No	1984 %	No	1985 %	No	1986 %	No	1987 %	No	1989 %	No
Respondent has or uses in work	7	-	-	-	-	3.5	4	-	-	0.5	1	-	-
Respondent does not have or use	96	-	-	-	-	94.8	109	-	-	99.5	187	-	-
(DK)	98	-	-	-	-	-	-	-	-	-	-	-	-
(NA)	99	-	-	-	-	1.7	2	-	-	-	-	-	-

Base: All self-employed — 115 — 188

| Question No | | | | | | 48a | | | | 47a | | | |
| Column No | | | | | | 469-70 | | | | 512-13 | | | |

(viii) {STECWRK8}

Other new technology

	Code	1983 %	No	1984 %	No	1985 %	No	1986 %	No	1987 %	No	1989 %	No
Respondent has or uses in work	95	-	-	-	-	4.4	5	-	-	2.5	5	-	-
Respondent does not have or use	96	-	-	-	-	93.9	108	-	-	97.5	184	-	-
(DK)	98	-	-	-	-	-	-	-	-	-	-	-	-
(NA)	99	-	-	-	-	1.7	2	-	-	-	-	-	-

Base: All self-employed — 115 — 188

| Question No | | | | | | 48a | | | | 47a | | | |
| Column No | | | | | | 471-72 | | | | 514-15 | | | |

(ix) {STECWRK9}

(None of these)

	Code	1983 %	No	1984 %	No	1985 %	No	1986 %	No	1987 %	No	1989 %	No
Respondent has or uses one or more in work	1	-	-	-	-	18.0	21	-	-	17.6	33	-	-
Respondent does not have or use any	96	-	-	-	-	80.2	92	-	-	82.4	155	-	-
(DK)	98	-	-	-	-	-	-	-	-	-	-	-	-
(NA)	99	-	-	-	-	1.7	2	-	-	-	-	-	-

Base: All self-employed — 115 — 188

1985 - {STECWRK7} The work 'production' does not appear on the show card
1985, 1987 - {STECWRK7} [ ] = printed on show card but not on questionnaire

SELF-EMPLOYED: EFFECT OF 'NEW TECHNOLOGY' ON THEIR WORK

{STECAFCT}

Question: [If self-employed and has or uses any new technology in work] **Would you say that the use of new technology has affected your work ... (read out) ...**

	Code	1983 %	No	1984 %	No	1985 %	No	1986 %	No	1987 %	No	1989 %	No
Question No						48b				47b			
Column No						473				516			
... for the better,	1	-	-	-	-	12.8	15	-	-	13.3	25	-	-
... for the worse,	2	-	-	-	-	-	-	-	-	0.3	1	-	-
... or has it made no difference?	3	-	-	-	-	4.4	5	-	-	4.0	7	-	-
[Not asked: does not have or use new technology in work]	6	-	-	-	-	80.2	92	-	-	82.4	155	-	-
(DK)	8	-	-	-	-	-	-	-	-	-	-	-	-
(NA)	9	-	-	-	-	2.6	3	-	-	-	-	-	-
Base: All self-employed							115				188		

SELF-EMPLOYED: LIKELIHOOD OF WORKING AS EMPLOYEE IN NEAR FUTURE

{SEMPLKY}

Question: [If self-employed and if in last five years has very or quite seriously considered working as employee] **How likely or unlikely is it that you will work as an employee, in your main job, in the next five years ... (read out) ...**

		1983		1984		1985		1986		1987		1989	
		%	No	%	No	%	No	%	No	%	No	%	No
Question No		40e		43e									
Column No		414		414									
	Code												
... very likely,	1	1.1	1	-	-	-	-	-	-	-	-	-	-
... quite likely,	2	1.0	1	-	-	-	-	-	-	-	-	-	-
... not very likely,	3	1.9	2	1.2	1	-	-	-	-	-	-	-	-
... or not at all likely?	4	3.0	3	3.5	3	-	-	-	-	-	-	-	-
[Not asked: has not seriously considered working as employee]	6	61.0	63	58.7	51	-	-	-	-	-	-	-	-
[Not asked: has worked as employee]	7	31.0	32	36.6	32	-	-	-	-	-	-	-	-
(DK)	8	1.0	1	-	-	-	-	-	-	-	-	-	-
(NA)	9	-	-	-	-	-	-	-	-	-	-	-	-
Base: All self-employed		104		86									

1983 - (DK), code 5

SELF-EMPLOYED : IMPORTANT FEATURES OF A NEW JOB

1989   Q.52a-c   {SNEWJOB1}-{SNEWJOB3}   Column Nos 508-13

{SNEWJOB1}   Column Nos 508-09
a) [If self-employed] (Show card) Suppose you were looking for another job - which of the things on this card would be *most* important to you in choosing a new job? Please read through the whole list before deciding.

{SNEWJOB2}   Column Nos 510-11
b) [If self-employed] (Continue showing card) And which would be the *next* most important?

{SNEWJOB3}   Column Nos 512-13
c) [If self-employed] (Continue showing card) And which would be the *third* most important?

	Code	a) Most important {SNEWJOB1} %	No	b) Next most important {SNEWJOB2} %	No	c) Third most important {SNEWJOB} %	No
Convenient working hours	1	14.2	31	4.6	10	4.9	11
Possibility of promotion	2	3.2	7	4.7	10	4.8	11
Clean/pleasant working conditions	3	0.5	1	2.7	6	5.3	12
Strong trade union	4	0.9	2	-	-	0.9	2
Interesting work that makes use of your skills	5	36.5	80	19.4	43	9.9	22
Work that helps others	6	4.0	9	7.3	16	5.3	12
Opportunity to get one with your work in your own way	7	8.7	19	14.7	32	13.1	29
Job security	8	11.9	26	9.9	22	7.4	16
Outdoor work	9	2.0	4	2.8	6	2.3	5
Good pay	10	13.7	30	20.3	45	18.2	40
Friendliness of people you work with	11	2.6	6	9.0	20	17.2	38
Good fringe benefits (pension, sick pay)	12	0.5	1	1.4	3	6.1	13
Short working hours	13	0.8	2	2.3	5	2.9	7
(None of these)	97	0.3	1	-	-	0.5	1
(DK)	98	0.4	1	0.4	1	0.8	2
(NA)	99	-	-	0.5	1	0.5	1
Base : All self-employed			220		220		220

SELF-EMPLOYED: NUMBER OF PARTNERS

1987   Q.45b   *{SNUMPARS - Banded}*   Column Nos 455-57
[If self-employed and has partner(s)] **How many partners or self-employed colleagues do you work with?**

	Code	%	No
[Not asked: no partners]	0	52.5	99
One	1	32.2	61
Two	2	5.9	11
Three	3	2.0	4
Four	4	2.4	5
Five	5	1.1	2
Six or more		2.7	5
(DK)	998	0.5	1
(NA)	999	1.1	2
Base : All self-employed			188

NB Six and upwards have been banded

SELF-EMPLOYED: NUMBERS OF FULL- AND PART-TIME EMPLOYEES

1987   Q.46b,c   *{SNUMEMPF - Banded}{SNUMEMPP - Banded}*   Column Nos 459-66

{SNUMEMPF - Banded} Column Nos 459-62
b) [If self-employed and has employees] **How many *full-time* employees do you have now?** (Interviewer : prompt if necessary: 'full-time is 30+ hours per week')

{SNUMEMPP - Banded} Column Nos 463-66
c) [If self-employed and has employees] **And how many *part-time* employees?**

	Code	b) Full-time {SNUMEMPF}		c) Part-time {SNUMEMPP}	
		%	No	%	No
[Not asked : no employees]	-1	65.2	123	65.2	123
None working *full-/part-*time	0	12.6	24	7.5	14
One	1	5.3	10	9.6	18
Two	2	3.7	7	5.6	11
Three	3	2.5	5	5.6	11
Four	4	0.8	2	0.6	1
Five	5	1.9	4	1.6	3
Six to ten		3.2	6	2.7	5
Eleven or more		1.6	3	0.5	1
(DK: fewer than twenty-five)	9995	-	-	0.5	1
(DK: twenty-five or more)	9996	-	-	-	-
(NA)	9999	2.7	5	0.5	1
Base : All self-employed			188		188

NB Six and upwards have been banded
{SNUMEMPF} and {SNUMEMPP} appear on the SPSS file as {SEMPSFT} and {SEMPSPT}, respectively

SELF-EMPLOYED : EXPECTATIONS FOR TAKING ON EMPLOYEES

1987   Q.46d   {SMOREFT} Column No 467
[If self-employed and has employees] **Over the coming year, do you expect to ... (read out) ...**

	Code	%	No
[Not asked : no employees]	-1	65.2	123
... take on (additional) *full*-time employees,	1	7.8	15
reduce the number of full-time employees,	2	-	-
or - keep about the same number as now?	3	21.6	41
(DK)	8	2.9	5
(NA)	9	2.4	5
Base : All self-employed			188

1987   Q.46e   {SMOREPT} Column No 468
[If self-employed and has employees] **And over the coming year, do you expect to ... (read out) ...**

	Code	%	No
[Not asked : no employees]	-1	65.2	123
... take on (additional) *part*-time employees,	1	5.2	10
reduce the number of part-time employees	2	1.9	4
or - keep about the same number as now?	3	23.5	44
(DK)	8	2.4	4
(NA)	9	1.9	4
Base : All self-employed			188

1987   Q.46f   {STAKEEMP} Column No 469
[If self-employed with no employees] **Over the coming year, do you expect to take on any employees, or do you think this is unlikely?**

	Code	%	No
[Not asked : has employees]	-1	34.2	64
Expect to take on employees	1	7.7	14
Unlikely	2	57.0	107
(DK)	8	0.5	1
(NA)	9	0.5	1
Base : All self-employed			188

SELF-EMPLOYED : JOB STEREOTYPING

1987   Q.47c   {SSEXWRK} Column No 517
[If self-employed] **Do you think of your work as ... (read out) ...**

	Code	%	No
... mainly men's work,	1	36.3	68
mainly women's work,	2	3.0	6
or - work that either men or women do?	3	60.7	114
Base : All self-employed			188

SELF-EMPLOYED (WOMEN): GENDER STEREOTYPING AT WORK

1987   Q.47d   Derived variables - {SWWHYW1} + {SWWHYW2} + {SWWHYW3}
Original Column Nos 518-19, 520-21, 522-23
[If self-employed, female and thinks her work is mainly women's work] Why do you think your
sort of work is mainly done by women? (Interviewer: probe fully and record verbatim)

	Code	%	No
[Not asked: self-employed and male]		76.1	143
Men don't have the right personal skills/ temperament/women are better at dealing with people	1	1.1	2
Women's pay is too low/is part-time work	3	1.6	3
It would be embarrassing for men/men would be considered effeminate	5	1.1	2
Type of work is/has been/should be women's work	6	1.1	2
[Not asked: work not mainly women's work]	90	20.7	39
Base: All self-employed			188

NB Up to 3 responses were coded for each respondent, so percentages add up to more than 100%

SELF-EMPLOYED (MEN) : GENDER STEREOTYPING AT WORK

1987   Q.47d   Derived variables - {SMWHYM1} + {SMWHYM2} + {SMWHYM3}
Original Column Nos 518-19, 520-21, 522-23
[If self-employed, male and thinks his work is mainly men's work] Why do you think your
sort of work is mainly done by men? (Interviewer: probe fully and record verbatim).

	Code	%	No
[Not asked: self-employed and female]		23.9	45
Work is too heavy for women/women do not have physical strength	1	28.7	54
Physical conditions would be too unpleasant/dirty/dangerous for women	2	9.0	17
Women wouldn't be interested in it for technical reasons	4	3.2	6
Women just don't do the job/never have done job/just traditional for women not to do it	6	6.9	13
Women don't or can't work night shift/ too much travelling involved/ long hours, etc	7	2.7	5
[Not asked: work not mainly men's work]	90	41.0	77
Base : All self-employed			188

NB Up to 3 responses were coded for each respondent, so percentages add up to more than 100%

SELF-EMPLOYED : PERCEIVED COMPARATIVE PAY RATES

1986   Q.38a-c   *{SPAYEDU}{SGOTAHD}{SPAYJOB}* Column Nos 373-75

{SPAYEDU} Column No 373

a) [If self-employed] Comparing yourself with people with the *same* level of education and training, would you say that *your pay* is ... (read out) ...

	Code	%	No
... very high,	1	4.1	8
a little high,	2	18.6	34
about average,	3	49.2	89
a little low,	4	19.7	36
or - very low?	5	5.3	9
(DK)	8	3.0	5
Base : All self-employed			181

{SGOTAHD} Column No 374

b) [If self-employed] And still comparing yourself with people with the same level of education and training, what would you say about the *level* of your job, that is, how quickly do you think you've got ahead ... (read out) ...

	Code	%	No
... very quickly,	1	12.0	22
quite quickly,	2	27.8	50
about average,	3	44.6	81
not very quickly,	4	7.3	13
or - not at all quickly?	5	1.8	3
(DK)	8	6.5	12
Base : All self-employed			181

{SPAYJOB} Column No 375

c) [If self-employed] And now thinking of people in similarly demanding jobs to yours, would you say that *your pay* is ... (read out) ...

	Code	%	No
... very high,	1	1.1	2
a little high,	2	4.1	7
about average,	3	69.9	126
a little low,	4	16.2	29
or - very low?	5	6.0	11
(DK)	8	2.7	5
Base : All self-employed			181

SELF-EMPLOYED: FEELINGS ABOUT WORK

1985   Q.46   {SEMPFEEL}   Column No 444
[If self-employed] (Show card) **Which of the statements on this card best describes your feelings about your work?**

	Code	%	No
Work is only a business transaction. The more I get paid the more I do; the less I get paid the less I do	1	8.0	9
I make a point of doing the best work I can, regardless of pay	2	68.7	79
I want to work hard, but not so that it interferes with the rest of my life	3	19.8	23
(None of those)	4	1.7	2
(NA)	9	1.7	2
Base : All self-employed			115

SELF-EMPLOYED: ADVANTAGES OF SELF-EMPLOYMENT

1985   Q.47   {SEMPADV1} - {SEMPADV4}   Column Nos 445-46, 447-48, 449-50, 451-52
[If self-employed] **What are the advantages to you of being self-employed rather than an employee? Any other advantages?** (Interviewer: probe fully and record verbatim)

	Code	%	No
Freedom to do what you want/flexibility (unspecified)	1	17.4	20
Flexible hours/can work hours to suit oneself	2	43.5	50
Freedom of decision-making/ responsibility	3	4.2	48
Can fit in domestic responsibilities	4	7.0	8
Freedom to do what customers/clients want	5	5.2	6
More money/profitable	6	29.6	34
Wish to work for self (not someone else)/one's family	7	7.8	9
Job security	8	3.5	4
No advantages (no other response)	96	11.3	13
Other answers (no other response)	97	8.5	10
(DK)	98	0.9	1
(NA)	99	1.7	2
Base : All self-employed			115

NB Up to 4 responses were coded for each respondent, so percentages add up to more than 100%.
Variable {SEMPADV5} (for more than 4 responses per respondent) was not used

SELF-EMPLOYED : REASONS FOR WORKING

1984   Q.42a   {SWORK1}-{SWORK10}   Column Nos 365-73
[If self-employed] (Show card) Now I'd like you to look at the statements on the card and tell me which ones best describe *your own* reasons for working at present. (Interviewer : code all that apply)

	Code	%	No
{SWORK1} Column No 365 **Work is the normal thing to do**			
Given as reason	1	48.6	42
Not given as reason	0	51.4	44
Base : All self-employed			86
{SWORK2} Column No 366 **Need money for essentials such as food, rent or mortgage**			
Given as reason	2	72.7	63
Not given as reason	0	27.3	24
Base : All self-employed			86
{SWORK3} Column No 367 **To earn money to buy extras**			
Given as reason	3	33.7	29
Not given as reason	0	66.3	57
Base : All self-employed			86
{SWORK4} Column No 368 **To earn money of my own**			
Given as reason	4	35.0	30
Not given as reason	0	65.0	56
Base : All self-employed			86
{SWORK5} Column No 369 **For the company of other people**			
Given as reason	5	16.4	14
Not given as reason	0	83.6	72
Base : All self-employed			86
{SWORK6} Column No 370 **Enjoy working**			
Given as reason	6	60.1	52
Not given as reason	0	39.9	34
Base : All self-employed			86
{SWORK7} Column No 371 **To follow my career**			
Given as reason	1	23.4	20
Not given as reason	0	76.6	66
Base : All self-employed			86

SELF-EMPLOYED : REASONS FOR WORKING (continued)

		Code	%	No

{SWORK8}   Column No 372
For a change from my children or housework

	Code	%	No
Given as reason	2	7.9	7
Not given as reason	0	92.1	80
Base : All self-employed			86

{SWORK9}   Column No 373
Other reason

	Code	%	No
Given as reason	7	1.2	1
Not given as reason	0	98.8	85
Base : All self-employed			86

NB   A further variable {SWORK10} was derived - 'more than one reason given', code 0 (n = 86). Therefore all self-employed respondents gave more than one reason for working

SELF-EMPLOYED : MAIN REASON FOR WORKING

1984   Q.42b   *{SWRKMAIN}* Column Nos 375-76
[If self-employed and gave more than one reason] (Continue showing card) **And which one of these would you say is your *main* reason for working?**

	Code	%	No
Working is the normal thing to do	1	11.0	10
Need money for basic essentials such as food, rent or mortgage	2	62.1	54
To earn money to buy extras	3	4.6	4
To earn money of my own	4	5.1	4
For the company of other people	5	1.2	1
Enjoy working	6	12.0	10
To follow my career	7	0.7	1
For a change from my children or housework	8	1.2	1
Other reasons	97	2.1	2
Base : All self-employed			86

SELF-EMPLOYED : FULL- OR PART-TIME WORKING

1983   Q.39a   *{SFPTTIME}* Column No 368
[If self-employed] In your (main) job do you normally work ... (read out) ...

	Code	%	No
... full-time (30 hrs+)	1	91.4	95
or part-time (10-29 hrs)?	2	8.6	9
Base : All self-employed			104

SELF-EMPLOYED : PROSPERITY OF BUSINESS COMPARED WITH RECENT PAST

1983   Q.41b   *{BUS5OK}* Column No 418
[If self-employed] Compared with five years ago, would you say your business is doing ... (read out) ...

	Code	%	No
... very well,	1	14.9	16
quite well,	2	20.3	21
about the same,	3	23.5	25
not very well,	4	10.1	11
or not at all well?	5	4.5	5
(Business not in existence then)	6	23.8	25
(NA)	9	2.9	3
Base : All self-employed			104

G Labour market and employment

G5 Unemployed

Table titles and cross references

UNEMPLOYED: LENGTH OF TIME SPENT SEEKING WORK

{UUNEMPT - Banded}

Question: [If unemployed] In total, how many months *in the last five years* (that is, since March 1984) have you been unemployed and seeking work?

		1983		1984		1985		1986		1987		1989	
		%	No	%	No	%	No	%	No	%	No	%	No
Question No						53a				49a		55a	
Column No						515-18				529-32		561-64	
	Code												
1-2 months		-	-	6.8	7	7.9	12	8.4	19	5.7	11	7.9	9
3-6 months		-	-	15.5	16	8.6	13	14.1	32	15.0	28	17.9	21
7-12 months		-	-	15.5	16	17.6	26	15.9	36	16.0	30	12.5	15
13 - 24 months		-	-	24.3	25	16.5	24	18.5	42	24.0	45	21.1	25
25 - 59 months		-	-	27.1	28	35.3	51	28.6	65	25.5	48	23.2	28
5 years		-	-	7.8	8	12.7	18	12.7	29	13.1	25	14.8	18
(DK)	98	-	-	-		-		-		-		0.8	1
(NA)	99	-	-	1.9	2	1.4	2	1.3	3	0.8	2	1.7	2
Base: All unemployed					103		146		227		189		119

1983 - This question was also asked in 1983 as Q.44a (variable name also {UUNEMPT}); but as a third of responses were coded 'Don't know', the data are clearly not comparable with those for subsequent years, and so are not shown here

1984,1986 - This question was asked separately of all unemployed and seeking work, and of all unemployed but not actively looking for a job (variable names {LUNEMPT} and {NUNEMPT} respectively). These have been combined on this table to allow comparison across the years. The relevant question and column numbers for {LUNEMPT} are Q.49a, Column Nos 428-29 in 1984 and Q.43a, Column Nos 426-29 in 1986; and for {NUNEMPT} are Q.51a, Column Nos 443-44 in 1984 and Q.45a, Column Nos 447-50 in 1986

1984 - 'Less than one month' was code 0 (n = 2), and has been added to 1-2 months (code 1) in this table. Q reads : '...(that is, since March 1979)...'

1985 - Q reads: '...(that is since March 1980)...'

1986 - Q reads: '...(that is since March 1981)...'

1987 - Q reads: '...(that is since March 1982)...'

UNEMPLOYED: LENGTH OF PRESENT PERIOD OF UNEMPLOYMENT

{CURUNEMP - Banded}

Question: [If unemployed] How long has this *present* period of unemployment and seeking work lasted so far?

	Code	1983 %	1983 No	1984 %	1984 No	1985 %	1985 No	1986 %	1986 No	1987 %	1987 No	1989 %	1989 No
Question No		44b				53b				49b		55b	
Column No		436-39				520-23				534-37		566-69	
Less than 1 month	1	0.9		2.9	3	-	-	-	-	-	-	-	-
1 - 2 months		16.4	18	10.7	11	11.0	16	16.7	38	15.6	29	17.7	21
3 - 6 months		22.3	25	18.4	19	21.9	32	18.1	41	21.7	41	26.2	31
7 - 12 months		25.1	28	24.3	25	17.1	25	18.1	41	19.2	36	17.0	20
13 - 24 months		17.9	20	13.6	14	13.7	20	15.4	35	14.1	27	12.4	15
25 - 60 months		14.7	16	28.2	25	32.9	48	24.7	56	22.8	43	17.6	21
More than 5 years		1.8	2	1.0	1	2.1	3	5.7	13	5.5	10	7.4	9
(DK)	98	-	-	-	-	-	-	-	-	-	-	-	-
(NA)	99	0.9	1	-	-	1.4	2	0.9	2	1.1	2	1.7	2
Base: All unemployed			110		103		146		227		189		119

1983 -   Base: All unemployed and seeking work

1984, 1986 -   This question was asked separately of all unemployed and seeking work, and of all unemployed but not actively looking for a job (variable names {LCURUNEM} and {NCURUNEM} respectively). These have been combined on this table to allow comparison across the years. The relevant question and column numbers for {CURUNEM} are Q.49b, Column Nos 431-33 in 1984 and Q.43b, Column Nos 431-34 in 1986; and for {NCURUNEM} are Q.51b, Column Nos 446 - 48 in 1984 and Q.45b, Column Nos 452 - 55 in 1986

UNEMPLOYED: CONFIDENCE OF FINDING SUITABLE JOB

{JOBQUAL}

Question: [If unemployed] How confident are you that you will find a job to match your qualifications
... (read out) ...

		1983		1984		1985		1986		1987		1989	
		%	No	%	No	%	No	%	No	%	No	%	No
Question No		44d		49c		53c		43c		49c		55c	
Column No		441		434		524		435		538		570	
	Code												
... very confident,	1	5.0	6	9.6	9	7.4	11	3.9	8	13.5	25	18.4	22
... quite confident,	2	24.5	27	9.3	9	19.6	29	29.3	58	26.9	51	27.6	33
... not very confident,	3	40.2	44	44.0	42	41.7	61	26.8	53	26.5	50	27.3	32
... or not at all confident?	4	30.3	33	37.1	35	29.5	43	38.6	76	31.2	59	25.1	30
(DK)	8	-	-	-	-	-	-	0.5	1	-	-	-	-
(NA)	9	-	-	-	-	1.8	3	0.9	2	1.9	4	1.7	2
Base: All unemployed			110		95		146		198		189		119

1983, 1984, 1986   -   Base: All unemployed and seeking work

UNEMPLOYED: ESTIMATED LENGTH OF JOBSEARCH

{UFINDJOB - Banded}

Question: [If unemployed] **Although it may be difficult to judge, how long *from now* do you think it will be before you find an acceptable job?**

	Code	1983 %	1983 No	1984 %	1984 No	1985 %	1985 No	1986 %	1986 No	1987 %	1987 No	1989 %	1989 No
Question No		44e		49d		53d				49d		55d	
Column No		443-46		436-38		526-29				540-43		572-75	
1-2 months	1	18.9	21	15.8	15	8.0	12	18.5	42	20.8	39	26.0	31
3-6 months	2	20.5	23	19.0	18	14.7	21	16.7	38	17.1	32	20.3	24
7-12 months	3	14.6	16	5.3	5	8.7	13	9.7	22	7.5	14	5.1	6
More than 1 year	4	14.1	16	6.9	7	5.9	9	8.4	19	9.3	8	3.4	4
Never	996	-	.	-	.	2.6	4	20.3	46	5.4	10	13.1	16
(DK)	998	29.6	33	48.6	46	58.9	85	25.6	58	39.1	74	30.5	36
(NA)	999	2.3	3	2.6	3	1.2	2	0.9	2	0.8	2	1.7	2
Base: All unemployed			110		95		146		227		189		119

1983, 1984 - Base: All unemployed and seeking work; No 'Never' on questionnaire or in SPSS file

1984 - SPSS file lists variable name as {LFINDJOB}. 'Other', code 997 (n = 2);

1985 - 'Never' not a precode on the questionnaire

1986 - This question was asked separately of all unemployed and seeking work, and of all unemployed but not actively looking for a job (variable names {LFINDJOB} and {NFINDJOB} respectively) These have been combined on this table to allow comparison across the years. The relevant question and column numbers for {LFINDJOB} are Q.43d, Column Nos 437-40; and for {NFINDJOB} are Q.46a, Column Nos 462-66

UNEMPLOYED: WILLINGNESS TO RETRAIN FOR A DIFFERENT JOB

{URETRAIN}

Question: [If unemployed and does not expect to find job in less than three months] **How willing do you think you would be in these circumstances to retrain for a different job ... (read out) ...**

	Code	1983 %	1983 No	1984 %	1984 No	1985 %	1985 No	1986 %	1986 No	1987 %	1987 No	1989 %	1989 No
Question No		44f		49e		53e						56b	
Column No		447		439		530						577	
... very willing,	1	25.7	28	20.6	19	38.2	55	32.2	73	-	-	21.2	25
... quite willing,	2	15.2	17	4.7	5	22.9	33	26.4	60	-	-	23.9	28
... or not very willing?	3	7.0	8	7.5	7	22.2	32	19.8	45	-	-	19.3	23
[Not asked: expects to find job in less than three months]	7	18.9	21	16.0	15	8.0	12	18.5	42	-	-	26.0	31
(DK)	8	1.4	2	-	-	5.2	8	0.9	2	-	-	2.9	3
(NA)	9	31.9	35	51.2	49	3.5	5	1.8	4	-	-	6.7	8
Base: All unemployed			110		95		146		227				119

1983, 1984 - Base: All unemployed and seeking work; (DK), code 4. The interviewer instructions did not make it sufficiently clear whether those who said that they did not know how long it might take to find an acceptable job should be asked the three follow-up questions (of which this is the first). This served to inflate the (NA) response categories for all three questions in both years, and so data users cannot directly compare figures for 1983 and 1984 with those for subsequent years

1984 - SPSS file lists variable name as {LRETRAIN}

1986 - This question was asked separately of all unemployed and seeking work, and of all unemployed but not actively looking for a job (variable names {LRETRAIN} and {NRETRAIN} respectively). These have been combined on this table to allow comparison with subsequent years. The relevant question and column numbers for {LRETRAIN} are Q.43e, Column No 441; and for {NRETRAIN} are Q.46b, Column No 467

UNEMPLOYED: WILLINGNESS TO MOVE TO FIND 'ACCEPTABLE' JOB

{UJOBMOVE}

Question: [If unemployed and does not expect to find job in less than three months] **How willing would you be to move to a different area to find an acceptable job ... (read out) ...**

	Code	1983 %	No	1984 %	No	1985 %	No	1986 %	No	1987 %	No	1989 %	No
Question No		44g		49f		53f						56c	
Column No		448		440		531						578	
... very willing,	1	14.1	15	7.4	7	19.0	28	12.8	29	-	-	11.2	13
... quite willing,	2	4.8	5	1.6	2	10.3	15	13.2	30	-	-	5.4	6
... or not very willing?	3	29.4	32	23.8	23	55.7	81	52.0	118	-	-	49.0	58
[Not asked: expects to find job in less than three months]	7	18.9	21	16.0	15	8.0	12	18.5	42	-	-	26.0	31
(DK)	8	1.1	1	-	-	4.1	6	1.3	3	-	-	1.7	2
(NA)	9	31.9	35	51.2	49	2.8	4	1.8	4	-	-	6.7	8
Base: All unemployed			110		95		146		227				119

1983, 1984 - Base: All unemployed and seeking work; (DK), code 4. The interviewer instructions did not make it sufficiently clear whether those who said that they did not know how long it might take to find an acceptable job should be asked the three follow-up questions (of which this is the second). This served to inflate the (NA) response categories for all three questions in both years, and so data users cannot directly compare figures for 1983 and 1984 with those for subsequent years

1984 - SPSS file lists variable name as {LJOBMOVE}

1986 - This question was asked separately of all unemployed and seeking work, and of all unemployed but not actively looking for a job (variable names {LJOBMOVE} amd {NJOBMOVE} respectively). These have been combined on this table to allow comparison across the years. The relevant question and column numbers for {LJOBMOVE} are Q.43f, Column No 442; and for {NJOBMOVE} are Q.46c, Column No 468

UNEMPLOYED: WILLINGNESS TO TAKE 'UNACCEPTABLE' JOB

{UBADJOB}

Question: [If unemployed and does not expect to find job in less than three months] [And] how willing do you think you would be in these circumstances to take what you now consider to be an *un*acceptable job ... (read out) ...

		1983		1984		1985		1986		1987		1989	
		%	No	%	No	%	No	%	No	%	No	%	No
Question No		44h		49g		53g						56d	
Column No		449		441		532						579	
	Code												
... very willing,	1	12.2	13	9.9	9	11.7	17	7.9	18	-	-	6.9	8
... quite willing,	2	16.0	18	5.9	6	23.9	35	23.3	53	-	-	18.4	22
... or not very willing?	3	21.1	23	17.0	16	48.1	70	45.8	104	-	-	39.8	47
[Not asked: expects to find job in less than three months]	7	18.9	21	16.0	15	8.0	12	18.5	42	-	-	26.0	31
(DK)	8	-	-	-	-	5.5	8	2.6	6	-	-	1.7	2
(NA)	9	31.9	35	51.2	49	2.8	4	1.8	4	-	-	7.3	9
Base: All unemployed			110		95		146		227				119

1983, 1984 - Base: All unemployed and seeking work; (DK), code 4. The interviewer instructions did not make it sufficiently clear whether those who said that they did not know how long it might take to find an acceptable job should be asked the three follow-up questions (of which this is the third). This served to inflate the NA response categories for all three questions in both years, and so data users cannot directly compare figures for 1983 and 1984 with those for subsequent years

1984 - SPSS file lists variable name as {LBADJOB}

1986 - This question was asked separately of all unemployed and seeking work, and of all unemployed but not actively looking for work (variable names {LBADJOB} and {NBADJOB} respectively). These have been combined on this table to allow comparison across the years. The relevant question and column numbers for {UBADJOB} are Q.43g, Column No 443; and for {NBADJOB} are Q.46d, Column No 469

UNEMPLOYED: WHETHER WOULD HAVE PAID JOB IF ONE NOT NEEDED

{UPREFJOB}

Question: [If unemployed] If without having to work, you had what you would regard as a reasonable living income, do you think you would still prefer to have a paid job or wouldn't you bother?

		1983		1984		1985		1986		1987		1989	
		%	No	%	No	%	No	%	No	%	No	%	No
Question No		45		50		54						57	
Column No		450		442		533						580	
	Code												
Still prefer paid job	1	94.1	104	70.1	66	68.1	99	74.4	169	-	-	75.8	90
Wouldn't bother	2	5.9	7	20.8	20	28.8	42	21.6	49	-	-	20.2	24
(Other answer)	7	-	.	6.7	6	2.3	3	1.3	3	-	-	-	.
(DK)	8	-	.	-	.	-	.	0.9	2	-	-	2.3	3
(NA)	9	-	.	2.5	2	0.7	1	1.8	4	-	-	1.7	2
Base: All unemployed				110		95		146		227		119	

1983 - Base: All unemployed and seeking work; Q reads: 'If you received what you would regard as a reasonable living income while unemployed, do you think you would still prefer to get a job or wouldn't you bother?'; (Other answer), code 4

1984 - Base: All unemployed and seeking work; SPSS file lists variable as {LPREFJOB}; (Other answer), code 3

1985 - (Other answer), code 3

1985, 1986 - Derived variable {PREFJOB} combines the responses to this question of employees, self-employed, unemployed, those in full-time education and those on a government scheme or waiting to take up paid work

1986 - This question was asked separately of all unemployed and seeking work, and of all unemployed but not actively looking for a job (variable names {LPREFJOB} and {NPREFJOB} respectively). These have been combined on this table to allow comparison over the years. The relevant question and column numbers for {LPREFJOB} are Q.44, Column No 444; and for {NPREFJOB} are Q.47, Column No 470

UNEMPLOYED: WHETHER CONSIDERED MOVING TO FIND WORK

{CONMOVE}

Question: [If unemployed] Have you ever *actually* considered moving to a different area - an area other than the one you live in now - to try to find work?

		1983		1984		1985		1986		1987		1989	
		%	No	%	No	%	No	%	No	%	No	%	No
Question No						55a				49e		58a	
Column No						534				544		616	
	Code												
Yes	1	-	.	-	.	33.9	49	-	.	29.9	56	31.5	37
No	2	-	.	-	.	65.4	95	-	.	69.3	131	66.9	79
(DK)	8	-	.	-	.	-	.	-	.	-	.	-	.
(NA)	9	-	.	-	.	0.7	1	-	.	0.8	2	1.7	2
Base: All unemployed						146				189		119	

1987 - Q reads: 'Have you ever considered...?' ('actually' omitted)

UNEMPLOYED: REASONS FOR NOT MOVING TO FIND WORK

{NOTMOVE1} + {NOTMOVE2} + {NOTMOVE3} + {NOTMOVE4}

Question: [If unemployed and considered moving to a different area to find work] **Why did you not move to a different area?**
Any other reasons? (Interviewer: probe fully and record verbatim)

	Code	1983 %	No	1984 %	No	1985 %	No	1986 %	No	1987 %	No	1989 %	No
Question No						55b				49f		58b	
Column No						535-42				545-52		617-24	
Other areas just as bad	1	-	-	-	-	4.1	6	-	-	4.2	8	5.0	6
Legislation limiting benefit for movers	2	-	-	-	-	2.1	3	-	-	-	-	-	-
Hoping/waiting/planning to move	3	-	-	-	-	4.8	7	-	-	5.3	10	5.0	6
Housing shortage/inflexibility of provision	4	-	-	-	-	6.8	10	-	-	7.4	14	10.1	12
Have already moved in the past	5	-	-	-	-	6.2	9	-	-	6.9	13	5.0	6
Moving causes too much upheaval	6	-	-	-	-	6.2	9	-	-	6.9	13	7.6	9
[Not asked: has not considered moving to a different area]	90	-	-	-	-	65.1	95	-	-	69.3	131	75.6	79
Other answer	97	-	-	-	-	8.9	13	-	-	5.8	11	5.9	7
DK	98	-	-	-	-	-	-	-	-	-	-	0.8	1
(NA)	99	-	-	-	-	0.7	1	-	-	1.1	2	1.7	2
Base: All unemployed							146				189		119

1985, 1987, 1989 - {NOTMOVE2} - {NOTMOVE4}: No further reason given (code 96). Up to 4 responses could be coded for each respondent, so percentages add up to more than 100%

UNEMPLOYED: CHANCE OF FINDING JOB IN LOCAL AREA

{UJOBCHNC}

Question: [If unemployed] Do you think that there is a real chance nowadays that you will get a job in this area, or is there *no* real chance nowadays?

		1983		1984		1985		1986		1987		1989	
		%	No	%	No	%	No	%	No	%	No	%	No
Question No										51		59	
Column No										565		625	
	Code												
Real chance	1	-	.	-	.	-	.	-	.	49.8	94	62.3	74
No real chance	2	-	.	-	.	-	.	-	.	49.5	93	35.2	42
(DK)	8	-	.	-	.	-	.	-	.	0.4	1	-	
(NA)	9	-	.	-	.	-	.	-	.	0.3	1	2.5	3
Base: All unemployed											189		119

UNEMPLOYED: PREFERENCE FOR WORKING HOURS

{FPTWORK} {PARTTIME - Banded}

Question: [If unemployed] Would you prefer full- or part-time work, if you had the choice?

			1983		1984		1985		1986		1987		1989	
			%	No	%	No	%	No	%	No	%	No	%	No
	Question No						56a						60a	
	Column No						543						626	
(i) {FPTWORK}		Code												
Full-time	1		-	-	-	-	64.1	93	-	-	-	-	69.7	83
Part-time	2		-	-	-	-	31.6	46	-	-	-	-	25.2	30
Not looking for work	3		-	-	-	-	3.2	5	-	-	-	-	2.1	3
DK/can't say	8		-	-	-	-	-	-	-	-	-	-	1.3	2
(NA)	9		-	-	-	-	1.1	2	-	-	-	-	1.7	2
Base: All unemployed								146						119

			1983		1984		1985		1986		1987		1989	
	Question No						56b						60b	
	Column No						544-45						627-28	

(ii) {PARTTIME - Banded}

[If part-time] How many hours
per week would like to work?

		1983		1984		1985		1986		1987		1989	
[Not asked: prefers full-time work or is not looking for work]	1	-	-	-	-	67.3	98	-	-	-	-	72.9	86
11-20 hours a week	2	-	-	-	-	14.9	22	-	-	-	-	10.6	13
21-30 hours a week	3	-	-	-	-	9.8	15	-	-	-	-	12.1	15
(DK)	8	-	-	-	-	6.9	10	-	-	-	-	1.3	2
(NA)	9	-	-	-	-	1.1	2	-	-	-	-	2.9	4
Base: All unemployed						146						119	

UNEMPLOYED: COMMITMENT TO WORK - 1

{*UNEMEARN*}

Question: [If unemployed] For some people their job is simply something they do in order to earn a living. For others it means much more than that. On balance, do you think of work as ... (read out) ...

		1983		1984		1985		1986		1987		1989	
		%	No	%	No	%	No	%	No	%	No	%	No
Question No						57a						61a	
Column No						546						629	
	Code												
... just a means of earning a living,	1	-	-	-	-	35.6	52	-	-	-	-	35.5	42
... or does it mean much more to you than that?	2	-	-	-	-	63.7	93	-	-	-	-	62.8	75
(DK)	8	-	-	-	-	-	-	-	-	-	-	-	-
(NA)	9	-	-	-	-	0.7	1	-	-	-	-	1.7	2
Base: All unemployed							146						119

UNEMPLOYED: COMMITMENT TO WORK - 2

{*UNEMPLIV*}

Question: [If unemployed and if work is just a means of earning a living] Is that because ... (read out) ...

		1983		1984		1985		1986		1987		1989	
		%	No	%	No	%	No	%	No	%	No	%	No
Question No						57b						61b	
Column No						547						630	
	Code												
... there are no good jobs around here,	1	-	-	-	-	8.7	13	-	-	-	-	10.6	13
... you don't have the right skills to get a good job,	2	-	-	-	-	9.3	14	-	-	-	-	11.5	14
... or because you would feel the same about *any* job you had?	3	-	-	-	-	16.9	25	-	-	-	-	12.7	15
[Not asked: work means much more than just earning a living]	7	-	-	-	-	63.7	93	-	-	-	-	62.8	75
(DK)	8	-	-	-	-	-	-	-	-	-	-	0.6	1
(NA)	9	-	-	-	-	1.4	2	-	-	-	-	1.7	2
Base: All unemployed							146						119

1987 - {UNEMPLIV} is the variable name on the SPSS file for Q.B207f although the latter is a different question; consequently that variable has been renamed {GOVUNEMP} (see p. A-26)

UNEMPLOYED : RECENT JOBSEARCH ACTIVITY

1987   Q.50a-i   *{U4FIND1} - {U4FIND9}* Column Nos 553-561
[If unemployed] Now thinking about the last 4 weeks, have you done any of the following?
Please just answer yes or no. (Read out)

{U4FIND1} Column No 553
a) Have you had your name registered at a Jobcentre or Government Employment or Careers
Office, or with Professional and Executive Recruitment?

	Code	%	No
Yes	1	53.6	101
No	2	45.6	86
(NA)	9	0.8	2
Base : All unemployed			189

{U4FIND2} Column No 554
b) Have you had your name registered at a private employment agency?

	Code	%	No
Yes	1	7.7	14
No	2	92.1	174
(NA)	9	0.3	1
Base : All unemployed			189

{U4FIND3} Column No 555
c) Have you studied situations vacant columns in newspapers and journals?

	Code	%	No
Yes	1	82.2	155
No	2	17.0	32
(NA)	9	0.8	2
Base : All unemployed			189

{U4FIND4} Column No 556
d) Have you advertised for jobs in newspapers and journals?

	Code	%	No
Yes	1	8.3	16
No	2	91.0	172
(NA)	9	0.7	1
Base : All unemployed			189

{U4FIND5} Column No 557
e) And in the last four weeks, have you answered advertisements for jobs in
newspapers or journals?

	Code	%	No
Yes	1	30.8	58
No	2	69.0	130
(NA)	9	0.3	1
Base : All unemployed			189

UNEMPLOYED : RECENT JOBSEARCH ACTIVITY (continued)

{U4FIND6} Column No 558
f) Have you applied directly to employers?

	Code	%	No
Yes	1	38.8	73
No	2	61.0	115
(NA)	9	0.3	1
Base : All unemployed			189

{U4FIND7} Column No 559
g) Have you asked friends, relatives, colleagues or trade unions about jobs?

	Code	%	No
Yes	1	54.9	104
No	2	44.8	85
(NA)	9	0.3	1
Base : All unemployed			189

{U4FIND8} Column No 560
h) And at any time in the last four weeks were you waiting for the results of any job applications?

	Code	%	No
Yes	1	34.1	64
No	2	65.6	124
(NA)	9	0.3	1
Base : All unemployed			189

{U4FIND9} Column No 561
i) And [at any time in the last four weeks] did you do anything else to find work?

	Code	%	No
Yes	1	10.2	19
No	2	89.6	169
(NA)	9	0.3	1
Base : All unemployed			189

UNEMPLOYED : WHETHER REGISTERED WITH A JOBCENTRE

1983   Q.44c   *{JOBCENT}* Column No 440
[If unemployed and seeking work] **Are you registered with a Jobcentre as unemployed?**

	Code	%	No
Yes	1	86.8	96
No	2	13.2	15
Base: All unemployed and seeking work			110

G Labour market and employment

G6 All economically inactive

Table titles and cross references

IN FULL-TIME EDUCATION: JOBSEARCH INTENTIONS

{EDLOOKJB}

Question: [If in full-time education] When you leave full-time education, do you think you will start looking for a job, will you wait several months or longer before you start looking, or will you decide not to look for a job?

		1983		1984		1985		1986		1987		1989	
		%	No	%	No	%	No	%	No	%	No	%	No
Question No		43a		47a		51a		41a					
Column No		424		421		507		414					
	Code												
Start looking	1		23		20		22	68.2	45	-	-	-	-
Wait several months or longer	2		2		4		2	6.6	4	-	-	-	-
Decide not to look	3		.		.		.	-	-	-	-	-	-
(Other answer)	7		6		4		2	18.6	12	-	-	-	-
(DK)	8		1		-		.	4.3	3	-	-	-	-
(NA)	9		.		.		.	2.3	2	-	-	-	-
Base: All in full-time education			32		27		25		65				

1983 - (DK), code 4; Other answer, code 5

IN FULL-TIME EDUCATION: ESTIMATED LENGTH OF JOBSEARCH

{EDFINDJB - Banded}

Question: [If in full-time education and will start looking for job after it ends] **How long do you think it will take you to find an acceptable job?**

		1983		1984		1985		1986		1987		1989	
		%	No	%	No	%	No	%	No	%	No	%	No
Question No		43b		47b		51b		41b					
Column No		426-29		423-25		509-12		416-19					
	Code												
[Not asked: will delay looking for a job, or decide not to look]	-1		9		8		4	25.2	16		-		-
Less than a month	0		-		1		-		-		-		-
1 - 2 months			9		5		9	26.2	17		-		-
3 - 6 months			10		8		6	24.9	16		-		-
7 - 12 months			3		1		-	4.2	3		-		-
More than 1 year			1		-		-	12.9	8		-		-
Never	96		-		-		-		-		-		-
(DK)	98		1		4		6		-		-		-
(NA)	99		-		-		-	6.6	4		-		-
Base: All in full-time education			32		27		25		65				

1983 -   (DK), code 9998; (NA), code 9999
1984 -   (DK), code 998; (NA), code 999
1983-1985   No 'Never'

IN FULL-TIME EDUCATION: WILLINGNESS TO TAKE 'UNACCEPTABLE' JOB

{EDBADJOB}

Question: [If in full-time education and will start looking for job when leaves full-time education but thinks this would take three months or more] How willing do you think you would be in these circumstances to take what you now consider to be an *un*acceptable job ... (read out) ...

	Code	1983 %	1983 No	1984 %	1984 No	1985 %	1985 No	1986 %	1986 No	1987 %	1987 No	1989 %	1989 No
Question No			43c		47c		51c		41c				
Column No			430		426		513		420				
... very willing,	1		5		3		1		-		-		-
... quite willing,	2		7		6		2	19.6	13		-		-
... or not very willing?	3		2		2		3	22.4	15		-		-
[Not asked: will delay looking for a job, or decide not to look]	6		9		8		4	25.2	16		-		-
[Not asked: expects to find job in less than three months]	7		9		6		9	26.2	17		-		-
(DK)	8		.		.		.		-		-		-
(NA)	9		1		4		6	6.6	4		-		-
Base: All in full-time education			32		27		25		65				

1983 - (DK), code 4

1986 - The SPSS file lists the variable name as {EDBADJB}, subsequently changed to {EDBADJOB} as in earlier years.

1986 - Those not answering the preceding question (see p.G.6 - 2) were not asked this question. To maintain comparability with earlier years, these (NA) responses are included on this table.

IN FULL-TIME EDUCATION: WHETHER WOULD HAVE PAID JOB IF ONE NOT NEEDED

{EDPREFJB}

Question: [If in full-time education] If without having to work, you had what you would regard as a reasonable living income, do you think you would still prefer to have a paid job or wouldn't you bother?

		1983		1984		1985		1986		1987		1989	
		%	No	%	No	%	No	%	No	%	No	%	No
Question No				48		52		42					
Column No				427		514		421					
	Code												
Still prefer paid job	1	-	-		20		20	84.3	55	-	-	-	-
Wouldn't bother	2	-	-		7		6	15.7	10	-	-	-	-
(Other answer)	7	-	-		-		-	-		-	-	-	-
(DK)	8	-	-		-		-	-		-	-	-	-
(NA)	9	-	-		-		-	-		-	-	-	-
Base: All in full-time education					27		25		65				

1984,1985,1986 - Derived variable {PREFJOB} combines the responses to this question of employees, self-employed, unemployed, those in full-time education and those on government schemes or waiting to take up paid work

ON GOVERNMENT SCHEME OR WAITING TO TAKE UP PAID WORK: RECENT EXPERIENCE OF UNEMPLOYMENT

{WSUNEMP} {WGUNEMP}

Question: [If on government scheme or waiting to take up paid work] **During the last five years (that is since March 1984) have you been unemployed *and* seeking work for any period?**

		1983		1984		1985		1986		1987		1989	
		%	No	%	No	%	No	%	No	%	No	%	No
Question No		42a		45a		49a		39a		48a		53a	
Column No		419		417		474		408		524		541	
	Code												
Yes	1	10		7		16		21		21		17	
No	2	6		1		6		4		3		9	
(DK)	8	-		-		-		-		-		-	
(NA)	9	-		-		-		1		-		1	
Base: All on government schemes or waiting to take up paid work		16		8		21		26		24		28	

1983 - {WSUNEMP} Base: All waiting to take up job or temporarily prevented from seeking work. When asked about their current economic position, respondents were not given the option of saying that they were on a government training or employment scheme and were not routed to this question. Therefore the 1983 data are not strictly comparable with those for subsequent years. Q reads: '... (that is since March 1978)...'. The variable appears as {WUNEMP} on the the SPSS file, which has now been changed to {WSUNEMP} to reflect the different base

1984, 1985, 1986, 1987, 1989 - {WGUNEMP}: the variable appears as {WUNEMP} on the SPSS file. The name has now been changed to differentiate it from the 1983 variable, which was based on a different group of respondents

1984 - (that is since March 1979)

1985 - (that is since March 1980)

1986 - (that is since March 1981)

1987 - (that is since March 1982)

ON GOVERNMENT SCHEME OR WAITING TO TAKE UP PAID WORK: LENGTH OF ANY RECENT PERIOD OF UNEMPLOYMENT

{WSUNEMPT - Banded} {WGUNEMPT - Banded}

Question: [If on government scheme or waiting to take up paid work; and if unemployed and seeking work during last five years] For how many months in total during last five years?

		1983		1984		1985		1986		1987		1989	
		%	No	%	No	%	No	%	No	%	No	%	No
Question No		42b		45b		49b		39b		48b		53b	
Column No		420-23		418-19		475-78		409-12		525-28		542-45	
	Code												
[Not asked: not been unemployed]	-1		6		1		6		4		3		9
1-6 months			4		1		6		5		6		3
7-12 months			2		2		4		7		5		3
13-24 months			1		4		2		4		7		3
More than 2 years - under 5 years			3		1		4		4		2		6
5 years			1		-		-		1		-		3
(NA)	99		-		-		-		1		1		1
Base: All on government schemes or waiting to take up paid work			16		8		21		26		24		28

1983 - {WSUNEMPT}: Base: All waiting to take up job or temporarily prevented from seeking work. When asked about their current economic position, respondents were not given the option of saying that they were on a government training or employment scheme and were not routed to this question. Therefore the 1983 data are not strictly comparable with those for subsequent years. The variable appears as {WUNEMPT} on the SPSS file, which has now been changed to {WSUNEMPT} to reflect the different base

1984, 1985, 1986, 1987, 1989 - {WGUNEMPT}: the variable appears as {WUNEMPT} on the SPSS file. The name has now been changed to differentiate it from the 1983 variable, which was based on a different group of respondents

ON GOVERNMENT SCHEME OR WAITING TO TAKE UP PAID WORK: WHETHER WOULD HAVE PAID JOB IF ONE NOT NEEDED

{WPREFJOB}

Question: [If on government scheme or waiting to take up paid work] If without having to work, you had what you would regard as a reasonable living income, do you think you would still prefer to have a paid job or wouldn't you bother?

		1983		1984		1985		1986		1987		1989	
		%	No	%	No	%	No	%	No	%	No	%	No
Question No				46		50		40				54	
Column No				420		479		413				546	
	Code												
Still prefer paid job	1		-		6		20		19		-		23
Wouldn't bother	2		-		1		-		6		-		4
(Other answer)	7		-		-		1		-		-		-
(DK)	8		-		-		-		-		-		-
(NA)	9		-		1		-		1		-		1
Base: All on government schemes or waiting to take up paid work					8		21		26				28

1984,1985,1986 - Derived variable {PREFJOB} combines the responses to this question of employees, self-employed, unemployed, those in full-time education an those on government schemes or waiting to take up paid work

WHOLLY RETIRED: WHETHER OCCUPATIONAL PENSION RECEIVED

{EMPLPEN}

Question: [If wholly retired from work] **Do you (does your husband/wife) receive a pension from any past employer?**

		1983		1984		1985		1986		1987		1989	
		%	No	%	No	%	No	%	No	%	No	%	No
Question No		46d		52a		58a		48a		52a		62a	
Column No		454		455		548		473		566		667	
	Code												
Yes	1	49.8	131	51.3	146	52.6	131	58.3	261	58.7	251	56.8	291
No	2	50.0	131	48.7	138	45.0	112	41.4	186	40.8	174	41.9	214
(DK)	8	-	.	-	.	-	.	-	.	-	.	-	.
(NA)	9	0.2	1	-	.	2.4	6	0.2	1	0.5	2	1.3	7
Base: All wholly retired from work			263		284		249		448		428		512

1983 -   Q reads '...receive a pension from a past employer(s)?'; No (DK)

WHOLLY RETIRED: WHETHER OF PENSIONABLE AGE

{RETAGE}

Question: [If wholly retired from work] **(Can I just check) are you over** (for men) **65**/(for women) **60?**

		1983		1984		1985		1986		1987		1989	
		%	No	%	No	%	No	%	No	%	No	%	No
Question No		46a		52b		58b		48b		52b		62b	
Column No		451		456		549		474		567		668	
	Code												
Yes	1	90.0	237	92.1	262	86.2	214	90.7	406	89.0	380	91.8	470
No	2	10.0	26	7.9	23	12.6	31	9.1	41	11.0	47	8.0	41
(DK)	8	-	.	-	.	-	.	-	.	-	.	-	.
(NA)	9	-	.	-	.	1.2	3	0.2	1	-	.	0.2	1
Base: All wholly retired from work			263		284		249		448		428		512

WHOLLY RETIRED: ADEQUACY OF STATE RETIREMENT PENSION

{RPENSION}

Question: [If wholly retired from work and of pensionable age] **On the whole would you say the present *state* pension is on the low side, reasonable, or on the high side?** [If on the low side] **Very low or a bit low?**

		1983		1984		1985		1986		1987		1989	
		%	No	%	No	%	No	%	No	%	No	%	No
Question No		46b		52c		58c		48c		52c		62c	
Column No		452		457		550		475		568		669	
	Code												
Very low	1	22.6	59	32.1	91	32.9	82	35.6	160	43.8	187	46.4	238
A bit low	2	41.1	108	36.0	102	34.1	85	31.0	139	29.2	125	30.8	158
Reasonable	3	25.4	67	22.7	65	17.3	43	22.9	102	14.2	61	13.7	70
On the high side	4	0.4	1	-	.	0.4	1	-	.	-	.	-	.
[Not asked: not of pensionable age]	7	10.0	26	7.9	23	12.4	31	9.1	41	11.0	47	8.0	41
(DK)	8	-	.	0.2	1	0.4	1	0.8	4	0.9	4	0.1	1
(NA)	9	0.6	2	1.1	3	2.0	5	0.7	3	0.8	4	1.1	6
Base: All wholly retired from work			263		284		249		448		428		512

1983 - No (DK)

1985 - No code 7; instead the 31 respondents not of pensionable age were included with the 1520 non-pensioners as a missing value (code 0: n = 1552). To maintain comparability with other years, these 31 respondents have been shown at code 7

WHOLLY RETIRED: EXPECTATIONS FOR FUTURE PURCHASING POWER OF STATE PENSION

{RPENINYR}

Question: [If wholly retired from work and of pensionable age] Do you expect your state pension in a year's time to purchase *more* than it does now, *less*, or about the *same*?

	Code	1983 %	No	1984 %	No	1985 %	No	1986 %	No	1987 %	No	1989 %	No
Question No		46c		52d		58d		48d		52d		62d	
Column No		453		458		551		476		569		670	
More	1	5.0	13	4.0	12	3.6	9	3.5	16	3.7	16	2.6	13
Less	2	45.1	119	51.8	147	54.2	135	52.6	236	50.9	218	62.4	319
About the same	3	35.0	92	31.1	88	26.5	66	31.4	141	29.5	126	23.1	118
[Not asked: not of pensionable age]	7	10.0	26	7.9	23	12.4	31	9.1	41	11.0	47	8.0	41
(DK)	8	4.4	12	3.7	11	0.8	2	2.7	12	3.6	15	2.9	15
(NA)	9	0.6	2	1.4	4	2.0	5	0.7	3	1.3	6	1.1	6
Base: All wholly retired from work			263		284		249		448		428		512

1983 - (DK), code 4
1985 - No code 7; instead the 31 respondents not of pensionable age were included with the 1520 non-pensioners as a missing value (code 0 : n = 1552). To maintain comparability with other years, these 31 respondents have been shown at code 7

WHOLLY RETIRED: RETIREMENT AGE

{RETIRAGE - Banded}

Question: [If wholly retired from work and under pensionable age] At what age did you retire from work?

	Code	1983 %	No	1984 %	No	1985 %	No	1986 %	No	1987 %	No	1989 %	No
Question No				52e		58e		48e		52e		62e	
Column No				459-60		552-53		477-78		570-71		671-72	
Aged under 50		-	-	1.1	3	0.4	1	0.7	3	0.6	3	1.1	6
Aged 50 to 59		-	-	2.8	8	6.3	16	4.6	21	6.5	28	4.5	23
Aged 60 to 64		-	-	3.5	10	5.5	14	3.6	16	3.7	16	2.2	11
[Not asked: of pensionable age]	97	-	-	92.1	262	86.2	214	90.7	406	89.0	380	91.8	470
(NA)	99	-	-	0.5	2	1.6	4	0.4	2	0.2	1	0.4	2
Base: All wholly retired from work					284		249		448		428		512

LOOKING AFTER HOME: WHETHER HAS ANY PAID JOB

{HWORK10}

Question: [If looking after home] **Do you currently have a paid job of less than 10 hours a week?** (Interviewer: include those temporarily away from a paid job of less than 10 hours a week)

	Code	1983 %	1983 No	1984 %	1984 No	1985 %	1985 No	1986 %	1986 No	1987 %	1987 No	1989 %	1989 No
Question No						59		49a		53a		63a	
Column No						554		508		572		708	
Yes	1	-	-	-	-	9.6	33	11.3	59	12.4	57	12.6	57
No	2	-	-	-	-	90.0	307	87.7	459	85.6	391	87.0	395
(DK)	8	-	-	-	-	-		-		-		-	
(NA)	9	-	-	-	-	0.4	2	1.1	6	2.0	9	0.3	2
Base: All looking after home							341		524		457		454

1985, 1986, 1987, 1989   -   This variable appears as {SMALLJOB} on the SPSS file

LOOKING AFTER HOME: REASONS FOR NOT HAVING A PAID JOB

{NOJOB1} + {NOJOB2} + {NOJOB3} + {NOJOB4} + {NOJOB5}

Question: [If looking after home] What are the *main* reasons you do not have a paid job outside the home?
(Interviewer: probe fully for main reasons and record verbatim)

		1983		1984		1985		1986		1987		1989	
		%	No	%	No	%	No	%	No	%	No	%	No
Question No				53				49b		53b		63b	
Column No				469-74				509-18		573-80		709-716	
										608-09			
	Code												
[Not asked: currently has paid job of less than 10 hours a week]	-1	-	-	-	-	-	-	11.3	59	-	-	-	-
Looking after children at home	1	-	-	39.4	121	-	-	31.5	165	34.4	157	35.7	162
Above retirement age/OAP/too old to work	2	-	-	26.7	82	-	-	21.0	110	24.1	110	20.3	92
Prefer to look after home/family	3	-	-	14.0	43	-	-	17.6	92	21.9	100	15.9	72
No jobs available	4	-	-	8.5	26	-	-	3.4	18	4.8	22	3.5	16
Not suitable for available jobs	5	-	-	7.8	24	-	-	1.7	9	1.5	7	2.0	9
Feel married women should not work	6	-	-	1.6	5	-	-	2.9	15	0.7	3	1.1	5
Husband against working	7	-	-	2.0	6	-	-	2.5	15	3.1	14	2.2	10
Do voluntary work	8	-	-	0.7	2	-	-	2.7	14	1.3	6	2.6	12
Pregnancy/ill health of respondent	9	-	-	6.8	21	-	-	12.8	67	11.4	52	11.0	50
Dependent relative	10	-	-	2.9	9	-	-	5.7	30	4.8	22	5.5	25
'Poverty trap' - loss of benefit if started work	11	-	-	1.3	4	-	-	4.6	24	3.1	14	3.3	15
Already has paid job (of less than 10 hours a week)	12	-	-	2.3	7	-	-	-	-	3.3	15	3.5	16
High cost/low availability of childcare	13	-	-	1.0	3	-	-	1.0	5	0.9	4	4.4	20
Works as unpaid help on family farm/in spouse's business	14	-	-	1.6	5	-	-	1.9	10	2.4	11	0.7	3
Other answer (no further response)	97	-	-	6.8	21	-	-	4.6	24	3.9	18	1.1	5
(DK)		-	-	-	-	-	-	-	-	-	-	0.7	3
(NA)	99	-	-	1.0	3	-	-	2.5	13	6.3	29	11.5	52
Base: All looking after home					307				524		457		454

1984 - No (DK). SPSS file lists variable names as {HNOJOB1}, {HNOJOB2}, {HNOJOB3} these have been changed to {NOJOB1} - {NOJOB3}. Up to
3 reasons only coded

1986 - Not asked of those with a paid job of less than 10 hours a week, so data are not exactly comparable with those for 1984, 1987 and 1989

1986, 1987 - {NOJOB2} - {NOJOB5}: No further reason given (code 96)

1989 - {NOJOB5} (up to 4 reasons only coded)

1984, 1986, 1987, 1989 - Up to 5 responses could be coded for each respondent, so percentages add up to more than 100%

LOOKING AFTER HOME: RECENT EXPERIENCE OF A PAID JOB

{EVERJOB}

Question: [If looking after home] Have you, *during the last five years*, ever had a full- or part-time job of 10 hours per week or more?

		1983		1984		1985		1986		1987		1989	
		%	No	%	No	%	No	%	No	%	No	%	No
Question No		47a		54a		60a		50a		54a		64a	
Column No		455		475		555		519		610		717	
	Code												
Yes	1	31.7	110	31.5	97	25.8	88	26.0	136	29.9	137	32.2	146
No	2	67.7	234	68.1	209	72.9	249	73.2	383	68.2	312	67.2	305
(DK)	8	-	.	-	.	-	.	-	.	-	.	-	.
(NA)	9	0.6	2	0.3	1	1.3	5	0.8	4	2.0	9	0.7	3
Base: All looking after home			346		307		341		524		457		454

1983 - No (DK)

LOOKING AFTER HOME: HOW LONG AGO LEFT LAST PAID JOB

{EVERJOBT - Banded}

Question: [If looking after home and had a paid job of 10 hours a week or more within past 5 years] **How long ago was it that you left that job?**

		1983		1984		1985		1986		1987		1989	
		%	No	%	No	%	No	%	No	%	No	%	No
Question No		47b		54b		60b		50b		54b		64b	
Column No		456-59		476-77		556-59		520-23		611-14		718-21	
	Code												
[Not asked: not had a paid job within past 5 years]	-1	67.7	234	68.1	209	72.9	249	73.2	383	68.2	312	67.2	305
1-6 months		4.8	17	6.6	20	4.8	16	4.6	24	7.5	34	7.1	32
7-12 months		5.2	18	4.7	15	3.2	11	4.6	24	3.2	15	6.1	28
More than 1, up to 2 years		10.0	35	7.5	23	7.4	25	6.2	33	5.1	23	8.1	37
More than 2, up to 5 years		11.7	40	12.7	39	9.8	33	10.5	55	13.8	63	10.7	49
(NA)	99	0.6	2	0.3	1	1.9	7	1.0	5	2.2	10	0.9	4
Base: All looking after home			346		307		341		524		457		454

1983 - Q reads: 'How long ago was the last occasion?'

LOOKING AFTER HOME: HOW SERIOUSLY CONSIDERED GETTING A FULL-TIME JOB

{FTJOBSER}

Question: [If looking after home and not had a paid job of 10 hours a week or more within past 5 years] How seriously in the past five years have you considered getting a *full-time* job? ... (read out) ...

(Interviewer: prompt, if necessary: 'full-time is 30 or more hours per week')

			1983		1984		1985		1986		1987		1989	
			%	No	%	No	%	No	%	No	%	No	%	No
Question No			48a		55a				51a		55a		65a	
Column No			461		478				524		615		722	
		Code												
... very seriously,		1	1.9	7	2.8	9	-	-	2.8	15	2.3	11	2.3	10
... quite seriously,		2	4.0	14	2.8	9	-	-	1.3	7	5.0	23	2.3	10
... not very seriously,		3	6.4	22	3.2	10	-	-	4.9	26	5.4	25	4.4	20
... or not at all seriously?		4	54.4	188	59.0	181	-	-	63.4	332	55.5	254	57.5	261
[Not asked: had paid job within past 5 years]		7	31.7	110	31.5	97	-	-	26.0	136	29.9	137	32.2	146
(DK)		8	-	-	-	-	-	-	-	-	-	-	-	-
(NA)		9	1.4	5	0.6	2	-	-	1.6	9	2.0	9	1.3	6
Base: All looking after home				346		307				524		457		454

1983 - No (DK). Those answering 'very' or 'quite seriously' to either Q.48a about a full-time job or Q.48b about a part-time job were asked Q.48c 'What are the main reasons you did not get a job?' {WHYNOJB1} + {WHYNOJB2} on Column Nos 463-64, 465-66 and 467-68. The responses were: 'already had a job of less than 10 hours a week', code 1, 0 = 3% (n = 1); 'had children/dependent relatives', code 2, 6.9% (n = 24); other answer, code 97, 6.1% (n = 21); NA, code 99, 1.7% (n = 6), based on all looking after the home (n = 346)

LOOKING AFTER HOME: HOW SERIOUSLY CONSIDERED GETTING A PART-TIME JOB

{PTJOBSER}

Question: [If looking after home, not had a paid job of 10 hours a week or more within past 5 years and has not seriously considered getting a full-time job] **How seriously in the past five years have you considered getting a *part-time* job? ... (read out) ...**

	Code	1983 %	No	1984 %	No	1985 %	No	1986 %	No	1987 %	No	1989 %	No
Question No		48b		55b				51b		55b		65b	
Column No		462		479				525		616		723	
... very seriously,	1	1.7	6	2.1	6	-	-	1.9	10	2.2	10	0.9	4
... quite seriously,	2	4.6	16	5.0	15	-	-	3.7	19	5.1	23	5.2	24
... not very seriously,	3	7.9	27	6.3	19	-	-	7.3	38	6.4	29	7.4	33
... or not at all seriously?	4	46.4	160	47.9	147	-	-	54.9	288	45.8	209	48.3	219
[Not asked: has seriously considered getting a full-time job]	6	6.0	21	5.6	17	-	-	4.1	21	7.3	33	4.6	21
[Not asked: had paid job within past 5 years]	7	31.7	110	31.5	97	-	-	26.0	136	29.9	137	32.2	146
(DK)	8	-		-		-		-		-		-	
(NA)	9	1.6	6	1.6	5	-	-	2.1	11	3.3	15	1.5	7
Base: All looking after home			346		307				524		457		454

1983 - No (DK). See footnote to previous table {FTJOBSER}

LOOKING AFTER HOME: LIKELIHOOD OF LOOKING FOR A PAID JOB

{HLOOKJOB}

Question: [If looking after home] Do you think you are likely to look for a paid job in the next five years? [If yes]
Full-time or part-time?

		1983		1984		1985		1986		1987		1989	
		%	No	%	No	%	No	%	No	%	No	%	No
Question No				56		61		52		56		66	
Column No				480		560		526		617		724	
	Code												
Yes - full-time	1	-	-	5.9	18	7.9	27	7.2	38	7.7	35	6.3	29
Yes - part-time	2	-	-	31.5	97	25.9	88	26.5	139	27.9	128	31.7	144
No	3	-	-	58.7	180	59.7	204	60.7	318	58.0	265	54.1	246
(Other answer)	7	-	-	1.7	5	1.1	4	0.7	4	1.0	5	0.7	3
(DK)	8	-	-	1.5	5	3.8	13	3.6	19	3.2	15	6.4	29
(NA)	9	-	-	0.7	2	1.6	6	1.3	7	2.2	10	0.9	4
				—		—		—		—		—	
Base: All looking after home				307		341		524		457		454	

NOT IN PAID WORK : WHETHER WOULD LIKE A PAID JOB

1989   Q.B211   {WTPAIDJB}   Column No 1956
[If in paid job of less than 10 hours a week or no paid job at all] **Would you like to have a paid job now?**
(Please tick one box only)

	Code	%	No
Yes, I would like a *full-time* job now (30 hours or more per week)	1	13.7	75
Yes, I would like a *part-time* job now (10-29 hours per week)	2	14.3	78
Yes, I would like a job with *less than 10 hours* a week now	3	11.1	61
No, I *would not like* to have a paid job now	4	56.4	307
(NA)	9	4.5	24
Base : Self-completion respondents in paid job of less than 10 hours a week or no paid job at all			545

NOT IN PAID WORK : EASE OF FINDING AN 'ACCEPTABLE' JOB

1989   Q.B212   {LKJOBEZ}   Column No 1957
[If in paid job of less than 10 hours a week or no paid job at all] **If you were looking actively, how easy or difficult do you think it would be for you to find an acceptable job?** (Please tick one box only)

	Code	%	No
[Not asked : does not want paid job now]	-	59.3	323
Very easy	1	2.0	11
Fairly easy	2	6.4	35
Neither easy or difficult	3	4.6	25
Fairly difficult	4	11.7	64
Very difficult	5	12.3	67
Can't choose	8	1.5	8
(NA)	9	2.2	12
Base : Self-completion respondents in paid job of less than 10 hours a week or no paid job at all			545

NB   [Not asked : does not want paid job now] inserted here as missing value, although it is not coded as such in the SPSS data file

LOOKING AFTER HOME : WHETHER LEFT LAST JOB VOLUNTARILY

1983   Q.47c   {OWNGO} Column No 460
[If looking after the home and had a paid job of 10 hours a week or more within the past 5 years]
On this last occasion [you had a job] did you leave the job of your own accord or not?

	Code	%	No
Yes	1	24.7	85
No	2	7.0	24
[Not asked: not had a paid job within past 5 years]	7	67.7	234
(NA)	9	0.6	2
			346

Base : All looking after home

LOOKING AFTER HOME : LIKELIHOOD OF GETTING A JOB IN NEAR FUTURE

1983   Q.49a   {FTJOBLKY} Column No 469
[If looking after home] **How likely or unlikely is it that you will get a full-time job in the *next* five years?**
Is it ... (read out) ...

1983   Q.49b   {PTJOBLKY} Column No 470
[If looking after home] **How likely or unlikely is it that you will get a part-time job in the *next* five years?**
Is it ... (read out) ...

		a) Full-time job {FTJOBLKY}		b) Part-time job {PTJOBLKY}	
	Code	%	No	%	No
... very likely,	1	3.8	13	10.2	35
quite likely,	2	6.2	22	22.6	78
not very likely,	3	16.7	58	11.0	38
not at all likely?	4	70.6	244	52.2	181
(DK)	5	0.9	3	2.5	9
(NA)	9	1.7	6	1.4	5
			346		346

Base : All looking after home

H Business and industry

Table titles and cross references

STATE OWNERSHIP OF INDUSTRY

{STATEOWN}

Question: On the whole would you like to see *more* or *less* state ownership of industry, or about the *same* amount as now?

		1983		1984		1985		1986		1987		1989	
		%	No	%	No	%	No	%	No	%	No	%	No
Question No		9c		21		15		16		16		16	
Column No		209		254		239		245		245		256	
	Code												
More	1	11.0	189	10.0	165	12.7	224	15.6	477	16.5	456	17.8	521
Less	2	48.9	841	35.9	590	30.7	543	30.4	931	30.2	835	24.0	703
About the same amount	3	33.1	569	50.1	825	51.4	909	49.4	1513	48.4	1340	52.7	1545
(DK)	8	6.6	114	3.7	61	5.2	91	4.7	143	4.9	134	5.3	155
(NA)	9	0.3	6	0.3	5	0.1	2	0.1	2	0.1	2	0.2	7
Base: All			1719		1645		1769		3066		2766		2930

1983 - (DK), code 4

BRITAIN'S COMPARATIVE INDUSTRIAL PERFORMANCE

{SELLGDS} {INVENT} {GDDESIGN} {INVESTMT} {BESTMNGR} {BESTWKRS} {GOODSBUY} {INDRLTNS} {TRAINING}

Question: (Show card) How good do you think Britain is at *selling its goods abroad*, compared with other countries that compete with us? Please choose a phrase from this card. And in inventing new products? (Interviewer: repeat for each statement iii - ix)

		1983		1984		1985		1986		1987		1989	
		%	No	%	No	%	No	%	No	%	No	%	No
Question No								B97a		B92a		A95a	
Column No								761		951		1061	
(i) {SELLGDS} In selling its goods abroad	Code												
Better than most	1	-	-	-	-	-	-	9.5	147	9.4	129	10.0	147
Worse than most	2	-	-	-	-	-	-	46.0	712	48.0	660	52.5	771
About the same	3	-	-	-	-	-	-	38.1	590	37.5	515	31.8	467
(DK/it varies)	8	-	-	-	-	-	-	5.5	86	4.7	65	5.2	77
(NA)	9	-	-	-	-	-	-	0.8	13	0.4	6	0.5	7
Base: All									1548		1375		1469

BRITAIN'S COMPARATIVE INDUSTRIAL PERFORMANCE (Continued)

			1983		1984		1985		1986		1987		1989	
			%	No	%	No	%	No	%	No	%	No	%	No
	Question No								B97b		B92b		A95b	
	Column No	Code							762		952		1062	
(ii) {INVENT}														
In inventing new products														
Better than most	1		-	-	-	-	-	-	52.4	811	48.8	671	43.4	637
Worse than most	2		-	-	-	-	-	-	14.0	216	16.0	220	18.4	270
About the same	3		-	-	-	-	-	-	27.4	424	29.9	412	32.3	474
(DK/varies)	8		-	-	-	-	-	-	5.3	82	4.7	65	5.4	80
(NA)	9		-	-	-	-	-	-	1.0	16	0.5	7	0.5	8
Base: All										1548		1375		1469

		1983		1984		1985		1986		1987		1989	
Question No								B97c		B92c		A95c	
Column No								763		953		1063	
(iii) {GDDESIGN}													
In making well-designed products													
Better than most	1	-	-	-	-	-	-	46.9	726	45.0	619	41.6	611
Worse than most	2	-	-	-	-	-	-	10.1	157	12.6	173	11.7	172
About the same	3	-	-	-	-	-	-	36.1	559	37.3	513	41.1	604
(DK/it varies)	8	-	-	-	-	-	-	5.8	90	4.4	61	4.9	72
(NA)	9	-	-	-	-	-	-	1.1	17	0.6	8	0.7	11
Base: All									1548		1375		1469

		1983		1984		1985		1986		1987		1989	
Question No								B97d		B92d		A95d	
Column No								764		954		1064	
(iv) {INVESTMT}													
In investing in new machinery and technology													
Better than most	1	-	-	-	-	-	-	11.6	180	9.8	135	12.8	188
Worse than most	2	-	-	-	-	-	-	48.7	755	48.2	662	46.3	679
About the same	3	-	-	-	-	-	-	30.7	475	35.5	488	31.9	469
(DK/it varies)	8	-	-	-	-	-	-	7.9	123	5.9	82	8.5	124
(NA)	9	-	-	-	-	-	-	1.1	17	0.6	8	0.5	8
Base: All									1548		1375		1469

BRITAIN'S COMPARATIVE INDUSTRIAL PERFORMANCE (Continued)

		1983		1984		1985		1986		1987		1989	
		%	No	%	No	%	No	%	No	%	No	%	No
Question No								B97e		B92e		A95e	
Column No								765		955		1065	

(v) {BESTMNGR}
In attracting the best people to
manage its industries

	Code	1983 %	No	1984 %	No	1985 %	No	1986 %	No	1987 %	No	1989 %	No
Better than most	1	-	-	-	-	-	-	12.0	186	8.8	121	11.6	171
Worse than most	2	-	-	-	-	-	-	38.5	596	40.3	555	36.8	541
About the same	3	-	-	-	-	-	-	39.0	603	42.5	584	40.1	589
(DK/varies)	8	-	-	-	-	-	-	9.7	150	7.7	105	10.8	159
(NA)	9	-	-	-	-	-	-	0.9	14	0.7	10	0.7	10
Base: All									1548		1375		1469

Question No								B97f		B92f		A95f	
Column No								766		956		1066	

(vi) {BESTWKRS}
In attracting the best people to
work in manufacturing industries

	Code	1983 %	No	1984 %	No	1985 %	No	1986 %	No	1987 %	No	1989 %	No
Better than most	1	-	-	-	-	-	-	10.5	163	8.3	114	9.5	140
Worse than most	2	-	-	-	-	-	-	33.0	511	31.6	435	31.9	469
About the same	3	-	-	-	-	-	-	45.2	701	50.4	693	45.8	673
(DK/varies)	8	-	-	-	-	-	-	10.1	157	9.0	124	12.0	176
(NA)	9	-	-	-	-	-	-	1.1	18	0.6	8	0.7	11
Base: All									1548		1375		1469

Question No								B97g		B92g		A95g	
Column No								767		957		1067	

(vii) {GOODSBUY}
In making goods that people really
want to buy

	Code	1983 %	No	1984 %	No	1985 %	No	1986 %	No	1987 %	No	1989 %	No
Better than most	1	-	-	-	-	-	-	22.8	354	22.1	304	19.2	283
Worse than most	2	-	-	-	-	-	-	22.9	355	22.1	304	25.0	367
About the same	3	-	-	-	-	-	-	47.6	737	51.2	704	50.6	743
(DK/varies)	8	-	-	-	-	-	-	5.6	87	3.9	54	4.5	67
(NA)	9	-	-	-	-	-	-	1.0	16	0.6	9	0.7	10
Base: All									1548		1375		1469

BRITAIN'S COMPARATIVE INDUSTRIAL PERFORMANCE (Continued)

		1983		1984		1985		1986		1987		1989	
		%	No	%	No	%	No	%	No	%	No	%	No
Question No								B97h		B92h		A95h	
Column No								768		958		1068	
(viii) {INDRLTNS}	Code												
In keeping good relations between management and other employees													
Better than most	1	-	.	-	.	-	.	11.0	170	11.3	155	12.0	176
Worse than most	2	-	.	-	.	-	.	42.5	658	35.0	482	35.2	516
About the same	3	-	.	-	.	-	.	39.2	607	45.9	631	44.7	657
(DK/varies)	8	-	.	-	.	-	.	6.4	98	7.1	98	7.5	110
(NA)	9	-	.	-	.	-	.	1.0	16	0.7	10	0.7	10
Base: All								1548		1375		1469	

		1983		1984		1985		1986		1987		1989	
Question No								B97i		B92i		A95i	
Column No								769		959		1069	
(ix) {TRAINING}													
In training employees in new skills													
Better than most	1	-	.	-	.	-	.	17.0	263	15.2	210	18.9	277
Worse than most	2	-	.	-	.	-	.	34.8	539	35.4	486	37.5	551
About the same	3	-	.	-	.	-	.	38.9	602	41.7	574	35.0	514
(DK/varies)	8	-	.	-	.	-	.	8.3	129	7.0	97	7.9	116
(NA)	9	-	.	-	.	-	.	0.9	15	0.6	9	0.7	11
Base: All								1548		1375		1469	

LIKELY USE OF WINDFALL PROFITS

{PROFTDO1} {PROFTDO2}

Question: (Show card) Suppose a big British firm made a large profit in a particular year. Which one of these things do you think it would be *most likely* to do? And which one would it be *next most likely* to do?

		1983		1984		1985		1986		1987		1989	
		%	No	%	No	%	No	%	No	%	No	%	No
Question No								B98a		B93a		A96a	
Column No								770-71		960-61		1070-71	
(i) {PROFTDO1}	Code												
Most likely to do													
Increase dividends to the share-holders	1	-	-	-	-	-	-	36.1	559	34.1	469	32.1	472
Give the employees a pay rise	2	-	-	-	-	-	-	3.4	52	4.2	57	4.6	68
Cut the prices of its products	3	-	-	-	-	-	-	2.1	33	2.5	35	2.2	33
Invest in new machinery or new technology	4	-	-	-	-	-	-	19.5	302	20.4	280	19.9	293
Improve the employees' working conditions	5	-	-	-	-	-	-	1.7	27	1.7	24	1.8	27
Research into new products	6	-	-	-	-	-	-	10.2	157	10.2	141	9.0	133
Invest in training for the employees	7	-	-	-	-	-	-	2.4	38	1.9	26	2.2	33
Give a bonus to top management	8	-	-	-	-	-	-	18.9	292	21.1	290	24.1	354
(None of these)	00	-	-	-	-	-	-	0.1	1	0.3	4	0.2	3
(DK)	98	-	-	-	-	-	-	4.9	75	3.0	41	3.1	45
(NA)	99	-	-	-	-	-	-	0.8	13	0.6	9	0.7	11
Base: All								1548		1375		1469	

LIKELY USE OF WINDFALL PROFITS (Continued)

		1983		1984		1985		1986		1987		1989	
		%	No	%	No	%	No	%	No	%	No	%	No
Question No								B98b		B93b		B96b	
Column No								772-73		962-63		1072-73	
(ii) *{PROFTDO2}*													
Next most likely to do	Code												
Increase dividends to the shareholders	1	-	.	-	.	-	.	17.5	272	17.0	234	18.5	272
Give the employees a pay rise	2	-	.	-	.	-	.	5.2	81	3.6	49	5.1	75
Cut the prices of its products	3	-	.	-	.	-	.	3.8	58	3.3	45	2.4	35
Invest in new machinery or new technology	4	-	.	-	.	-	.	20.3	315	22.1	304	21.0	309
Improve the employees' working conditions	5	-	.	-	.	-	.	3.0	47	3.3	46	4.6	67
Research into new products	6	-	.	-	.	-	.	19.9	308	19.0	261	17.9	264
Invest in training for the employees	7	-	.	-	.	-	.	4.0	62	4.3	59	5.1	75
Give a bonus to top management	8	-	.	-	.	-	.	18.8	292	22.7	312	20.8	306
(None of these)	00	-	.	-	.	-	.	0.1	2	0.2	3	0.3	4
(DK)	98	-	.	-	.	-	.	6.1	94	3.8	53	3.4	50
(NA)	99	-	.	-	.	-	.	1.1	18	0.6	9	0.9	13
Base: All									1548		1375		1469

PREFERRED USE OF WINDFALL PROFITS

{FSTPRIOR} {SECPRIOR}

[Suppose a big British firm made a large profit in a particular year]
Now which one do you think *should* be its first priority? And which *should* be its *next* priority?

		1983		1984		1985		1986		1987		1989	
		%	No	%	No	%	No	%	No	%	No	%	No
Question No								B98c		B93c		A96c	
Column No								774-75		964-65		1074-75	
	Code												
(iii) *{FSTPRIOR}*													
First priority													
Increase dividends to the share-holders	1	-	-	-	-	-	-	4.1	64	3.0	41	3.3	49
Give the employees a pay rise	2	-	-	-	-	-	-	20.7	320	22.5	309	25.3	371
Cut the prices of its products	3	-	-	-	-	-	-	12.6	195	12.5	172	10.7	157
Invest in new machinery or new technology	4	-	-	-	-	-	-	30.9	479	28.9	397	27.0	397
Improve the employees' working conditions	5	-	-	-	-	-	-	6.8	106	8.1	111	9.5	140
Research into new products	6	-	-	-	-	-	-	10.3	159	11.8	162	8.8	129
Invest in training for the employees	7	-	-	-	-	-	-	11.5	178	10.5	145	13.1	193
Give a bonus to top management	8	-	-	-	-	-	-	0.3	4	0.3	5	0.2	3
(None of these)	00	-	-	-	-	-	-	-	-	0.1	1	0.0	1
(DK)	98	-	-	-	-	-	-	2.1	32	1.7	23	1.2	18
(NA)	99	-	-	-	-	-	-	0.8	13	0.7	10	0.9	13
Base: All								1548		1375		1469	

PREFERRED USE OF WINDFALL PROFITS (Continued)

		1983		1984		1985		1986		1987		1989	
		%	No	%	No	%	No	%	No	%	No	%	No
Question No								B98d		B93d		A96d	
Column No								776-77		966-97		1076-77	
(iv) {SECPRIOR} Next priority	Code												
Increase dividends to the share-holders	1	-	.	-	.	-	.	2.1	33	1.8	24	3.1	45
Give the employees a pay rise	2	-	.	-	.	-	.	12.1	187	11.9	163	13.2	194
Cut the prices of its products	3	-	.	-	.	-	.	11.8	182	10.5	144	10.4	152
Invest in new machinery or new technology	4	-	.	-	.	-	.	16.7	258	19.0	261	16.4	241
Improve the employees' working conditions	5	-	.	-	.	-	.	14.7	228	15.4	212	16.9	249
Research into new products	6	-	.	-	.	-	.	18.6	289	20.3	280	17.7	260
Invest in training for the employees	7	-	.	-	.	-	.	19.4	301	17.8	245	19.0	280
Give a bonus to top management	8	-	.	-	.	-	.	0.9	14	0.8	11	0.7	10
(None of these)	00	-	.	-	.	-	.	-	.	0.1	1	0.2	2
(DK)	98	-	.	-	.	-	.	2.6	40	1.7	23	1.4	21
(NA)	99	-	.	-	.	-	.	1.1	17	0.7	10	1.0	15
Base: All									1548		1375		1469

EFFICIENCY OF BRITISH INDUSTRY COMPARED WITH PAST

{EFFPAST}

Question: Do you think that British industry is *more* efficient than it was five years ago, *less* efficient, or about the same?

		1983		1984		1985		1986		1987		1989	
		%	No	%	No	%	No	%	No	%	No	%	No
Question No								B99a		B94a		A97a	
Column No								778		968		1078	
	Code												
More efficient	1	-	-	-	-	-	-	31.7	491	38.8	534	43.9	645
Less efficient	2	-	-	-	-	-	-	24.3	377	18.4	253	13.5	199
About the same	3	-	-	-	-	-	-	36.8	570	37.4	514	36.4	535
(DK)	8	-	-	-	-	-	·	6.3	97	4.9	68	5.7	83
(NA)	9	-	-	-	-	-	-	0.9	14	0.4	6	0.4	7
Base: All									1548		1375		1469

EFFICIENCY OF BRITISH INDUSTRY IN THE FUTURE

{EFFUTURE}

Question: And do you think that, *in five years' time*, British industry will be *more* efficient or *less* efficient compared with now, or about the same?

		1983		1984		1985		1986		1987		1989	
		%	No	%	No	%	No	%	No	%	No	%	No
Question No								B99b		B94b		A97b	
Column No								779		969		1079	
	Code												
More efficient	1	-	-	-	-	-	-	35.7	553	44.7	614	42.8	628
Less efficient	2	-	-	-	-	-	-	13.4	208	8.3	114	7.3	108
About the same	3	-	-	-	-	-	-	41.6	644	39.9	548	40.8	600
(DK)	8	-	-	-	-	-	-	8.3	128	6.7	92	8.5	125
(NA)	9	-	-	-	-	-	-	1.0	16	0.5	6	0.6	8
Base: All									1548		1375		1469

SHARE OWNERSHIP

{OWNSHARE}

Question: Do you (or your husband/wife/partner) own any shares quoted on the Stock Exchange, including unit trusts?

		1983		1984		1985		1986		1987		1989	
		%	No	%	No	%	No	%	No	%	No	%	No
Question No						112		A119/B127		915		919	
Column No						1035		1757		1457		1729	
	Code												
Yes	1	-	.	-	.	14.0	248	16.5	507	25.1	695	26.0	762
No	2	-	.	-	.	85.1	1505	82.7	2535	73.9	2044	73.3	2147
(DK)	8	-	.	-	.	-	.	0.0	2	0.1	4	0.1	2
(NA)	9	-	.	-	.	0.9	16	0.7	23	0.8	23	0.7	19
Base: All							1769		3066		2766		2930

NATIONALISATION *VERSUS* PRIVATISATION

{NATNLSTN}

Question: Are you generally in favour of ... (read out) ... more *nationalisation* of companies by government, more *privatisation* of companies by government, or should things be left as they are now?

[If more nationalisation or privatisation] A lot more *(nationalisation)/(privatisation)* or a little more?

		1983		1984		1985		1986		1987		1989	
		%	No	%	No	%	No	%	No	%	No	%	No
Question No								B91ab				B100ab	
Column No								739-40				1139-40	
	Code												
A lot more nationalisation	1	-	.	-	.	-	.	4.9	75	-	.	8.4	123
A little more nationalisation	2	-	.	-	.	-	.	8.4	130	-	.	10.0	146
Leave things as they are now	3	-	.	-	.	-	.	50.9	788	-	.	59.2	865
A little more privatisation	4	-	.	-	.	-	.	14.3	222	-	.	10.4	152
A lot more privatisation	5	-	.	-	.	-	.	13.8	214	-	.	5.9	86
(Other answer)	7	-	.	-	.	-	.	0.7	11	-	.	0.7	10
(DK)	8	-	.	-	.	-	.	5.4	83	-	.	4.3	63
(NA)	9	-	.	-	.	-	.	1.6	25	-	.	1.2	17
Base: All									1548				1461

1989 -   This variable has the name {NATNL} on the SPSS file, although the question is identical to the one asked in 1986, so the name has been changed to {NATNLSTN}

BIG BUSINESSES *VERSUS* SMALL BUSINESSES

{*BIGBUSN1*} {*BIGBUSN2*} {*BIGBUSN3*} {*BIGBUSN4*} {*BIGBUSN5*} {*BIGBUSN6*} {*BIGBUSN7*} {*BIGBUSN8*}
{*BIGBUSN9*} {*BIGBUSN0*}

Question: Do you think big businesses or small businesses are generally better at each of these things, or is there no difference? (Please tick one box for each)

		1983		1984		1985		1986		1987		1989	
		%	No	%	No	%	No	%	No	%	No	%	No
Question No								B213		B216		A232	
Column No								2041		1968		2208	
(i) {*BIGBUSN1*}	Code												
Inventing new products													
Big businesses are better	1	-	.	-	.	-	.	42.1	554	51.9	612	39.2	500
Small businesses are better	2	-	.	-	.	-	.	26.4	348	20.5	242	22.2	283
There is no difference	3	-	.	-	.	-	.	28.8	379	23.6	279	36.5	464
(DK)	8	-	.	-	.	-	.	0.6	8	0.7	8	0.5	6
(NA)	9	-	.	-	.	-	.	2.1	28	3.3	39	1.6	20
Base: Self-completion questionnaire respondents								1315		1181		1274	

		1983		1984		1985		1986		1987		1989	
Question No								B213		B216		A232	
Column No								2042		1969		2209	
(ii) {*BIGBUSN2*}													
Making well-designed products													
Big businesses are better	1	-	.	-	.	-	.	26.0	341	28.1	332	26.7	341
Small businesses are better	2	-	.	-	.	-	.	39.2	515	38.0	448	32.2	410
There is no difference	3	-	.	-	.	-	.	31.9	420	29.3	346	39.0	496
(DK)	8	-	.	-	.	-	.	0.5	7	0.7	8	0.4	6
(NA)	9	-	.	-	.	-	.	2.4	32	3.9	46	1.6	21
Base: Self-completion questionnaire respondents								1315		1181		1274	

BIG BUSINESSES *VERSUS* SMALL BUSINESSES (Continued)

		1983		1984		1985		1986		1987		1989	
		%	No	%	No	%	No	%	No	%	No	%	No
Question No								B213		B216		A232	
Column No								2043		1970		2210	
(iii) {BIGBUSN3}	Code												
Investing in new machinery and technology													
Big businesses are better	1	-	.	-	.	-	.	77.4	1019	79.4	937	75.9	966
Small businesses are better	2	-	.	-	.	-	.	7.7	102	6.0	71	7.4	95
There is no difference	3	-	.	-	.	-	.	12.7	167	10.0	118	14.4	183
(DK)	8	-	.	-	.	-	.	0.5	7	0.8	10	0.3	4
(NA)	9	-	.	-	.	-	.	1.7	22	3.7	44	2.0	25
Base: Self-completion questionnaire respondents									1315		1181		1274

		1983		1984		1985		1986		1987		1989	
Question No								B213		B216		A232	
Column No								2044		1971		2211	
(iv) {BIGBUSN4}													
Attracting the best people to work in them													
Big businesses are better	1	-	.	-	.	-	.	58.9	774	59.7	705	56.8	724
Small businesses are better	2	-	.	-	.	-	.	17.5	230	15.5	183	16.0	204
There is no difference	3	-	.	-	.	-	.	20.8	274	20.2	238	24.9	317
(DK)	8	-	.	-	.	-	.	0.6	8	1.1	13	0.1	1
(NA)	9	-	.	-	.	-	.	2.2	29	3.6	42	2.2	28
Base: Self-completion questionnaire respondents									1315		1181		1274

		1983		1984		1985		1986		1987		1989	
Question No								B213		B216		A232	
Column No								2045		1972		2212	
(v) {BIGBUSN5}													
Making goods that people really want to buy													
Big businesses are better	1	-	.	-	.	-	.	19.3	254	22.8	269	21.8	278
Small businesses are better	2	-	.	-	.	-	.	40.8	536	35.4	418	29.3	373
There is no difference	3	-	.	-	.	-	.	37.4	492	37.3	440	46.8	596
(DK)	8	-	.	-	.	-	.	0.6	8	0.8	10	0.3	4
(NA)	9	-	.	-	.	-	.	1.9	26	3.7	43	1.8	23
Base: Self-completion questionnaire respondents									1315		1181		1274

BIG BUSINESSES *VERSUS* SMALL BUSINESSES (Continued)

		1983		1984		1985		1986		1987		1989	
		%	No	%	No	%	No	%	No	%	No	%	No
Question No								B213		B216		A232	
Column No								2046		1973		2213	

(vi) {BIGBUSN6}
Keeping good relations between management and other employees

	Code							1986		1987		1989	
Big businesses are better	1	-	.	-	.	-	.	5.3	70	6.3	74	7.2	92
Small businesses are better	2	-	.	-	.	-	.	77.3	1016	74.2	877	70.4	897
There is no difference	3	-	.	-	.	-	.	15.2	200	15.6	184	20.2	257
(DK)	8	-	.	-	.	-	.	0.5	7	0.8	10	0.3	4
(NA)	9	-	.	-	.	-	.	1.7	22	3.1	37	1.9	24
Base: Self-completion questionnaire respondents									1315		1181		1274

Question No								B213		B216		A232	
Column No								2047		1974		2214	

(vii) {BIGBUSN7}
Training employees in new skills

								1986		1987		1989	
Big businesses are better	1	-	.	-	.	-	.	49.2	647	52.4	619	44.8	571
Small businesses are better	2	-	.	-	.	-	.	26.2	344	22.5	266	23.6	301
There is no difference	3	-	.	-	.	-	.	22.4	295	20.3	239	29.1	370
(DK)	8	-	.	-	.	-	.	0.6	9	0.9	11	0.1	1
(NA)	9	-	.	-	.	-	.	1.6	21	3.9	46	2.3	30
Base: Self-completion questionnaire respondents									1315		1181		1274

Question No								B213		B216		A232	
Column No								2048		1975		2215	

(viii) {BIGBUSN8}
Paying their employees a fair wage

								1986		1987		1989	
Big businesses are better	1	-	.	-	.	-	.	36.9	486	39.5	467	34.0	433
Small businesses are better	2	-	.	-	.	-	.	26.6	350	23.1	273	23.2	295
There is no difference	3	-	.	-	.	-	.	34.5	454	32.9	389	40.8	519
(DK)	8	-	.	-	.	-	.	0.6	8	1.0	12	0.2	3
(NA)	9	-	.	-	.	-	.	1.4	18	3.4	41	1.8	23
Base: Self-completion questionnaire respondents									1315		1181		1274

BIG BUSINESSES *VERSUS* SMALL BUSINESSES (Continued)

		1983		1984		1985		1986		1987		1989	
		%	No	%	No	%	No	%	No	%	No	%	No
Question No								B213		B216		A232	
Column No								2049		1976		2216	

(ix) {BIGBUSN9} — Code

Charging fair prices for their products

	Code	1983 %	No	1984 %	No	1985 %	No	1986 %	No	1987 %	No	1989 %	No
Big businesses are better	1	-	.	-	.	-	.	21.7	285	22.0	260	20.1	256
Small businesses are better	2	-	.	-	.	-	.	39.3	517	37.4	442	34.4	438
There is no difference	3	-	.	-	.	-	.	36.7	483	36.3	429	42.9	546
(DK)	8	-	.	-	.	-	.	0.5	7	0.8	9	0.5	6
(NA)	9	-	.	-	.	-	.	1.8	24	3.4	41	2.2	28

Base: Self-completion questionnaire respondents — 1315, 1181, 1274

Question No								B213		B216		A232	
Column No								2050		1977		2217	

(x) {BIGBUSN0}

Caring about their customers

	Code	1983 %	No	1984 %	No	1985 %	No	1986 %	No	1987 %	No	1989 %	No
Big businesses are better	1	-	.	-	.	-	.	4.6	60	4.4	52	4.9	63
Small businesses are better	2	-	.	-	.	-	.	71.3	937	72.2	852	64.2	817
There is no difference	3	-	.	-	.	-	.	22.2	292	19.6	231	28.6	365
(DK)	8	-	.	-	.	-	.	0.5	7	0.7	9	0.2	3
(NA)	9	-	.	-	.	-	.	1.5	20	3.0	36	2.1	26

Base: Self-completion questionnaire respondents — 1315, 1181, 1274

BENEFICIARIES OF PROFITS MADE BY BRITISH FIRMS

{BENPROFT}

Question: Who do you think benefits *most* from the profits made by British firms? (Please tick one box)

		1983		1984		1985		1986		1987		1989	
		%	No	%	No	%	No	%	No	%	No	%	No
Question No								B214		B217		A233	
Column No								2051		1978		2218	
	Code												
Mainly their owners or shareholders	1	-	.	-	.	-	.	71.4	939	68.3	807	63.6	810
Mainly their directors and managers	2	-	.	-	.	-	.	19.8	260	20.8	246	26.7	340
Mainly their employees	3	-	.	-	.	-	.	2.3	30	3.2	38	1.6	21
The public generally	4	-	.	-	.	-	.	4.6	61	6.0	71	5.4	68
(DK)	8	-	.	-	.	-	.	0.3	4	0.2	3	0.3	4
(NA)	9	-	.	-	.	-	.	1.6	21	1.5	17	2.4	30
Base: Self-completion questionnaire respondents									1315		1181		1274

ATTITUDES TO BRITISH INDUSTRY

{CONSUMER} {PRFTABRD} {BIGPROFT} {MANUFIND} {XSPROFIT} {SCHLFAIL} {EMPSHARE} {INDPROFT} {BUYBRIT}

Question: Please tick one box for *each* statement to show how much you agree or disagree with it.

		1983		1984		1985		1986		1987		1989	
		%	No	%	No	%	No	%	No	%	No	%	No
Question No								B215a		B218a		A234a	
Column No								2052		1979		2219	
(i) {CONSUMER} Consumers are given too little protection by the law	Code												
Agree strongly	1	-	.	-	.	-	.	17.2	226	11.7	139	12.5	159
Agree	2	-	.	-	.	-	.	41.7	548	42.3	499	48.1	613
Neither agree nor disagree	3	-	.	-	.	-	.	23.9	314	25.0	295	22.5	287
Disagree	4	-	.	-	.	-	.	15.5	204	18.3	217	15.0	191
Disagree strongly	5	-	.	-	.	-	.	1.0	13	0.6	7	0.5	6
(DK)	8	-	.	-	.	-	.	0.2	2	0.2	3	0.1	1
(NA)	9	-	.	-	.	-	.	0.7	9	1.9	22	1.3	17
Base: Self-completion questionnaire respondents									1315		1181		1274

ATTITUDES TO BRITISH INDUSTRY (Continued)

		1983		1984		1985		1986		1987		1989	
		%	No	%	No	%	No	%	No	%	No	%	No
Question No								B215b		B218b		A234b	
Column No								2053		1980		2220	
(ii) *{PRFTABRD}*	Code												
Too much of industry's profits go abroad													
Agree strongly	1	-	.	-	.	-	.	16.0	211	13.5	159	9.0	114
Agree	2	-	.	-	.	-	.	37.2	489	39.8	470	40.5	516
Neither agree nor disagree	3	-	.	-	.	-	.	33.3	438	31.1	367	37.5	477
Disagree	4	-	.	-	.	-	.	10.9	143	12.1	143	10.7	137
Disagree strongly	5	-	-	-	.	-	.	0.8	10	0.6	7	0.3	4
(DK)	8	-	.	-	.	-	.	0.4	5	0.7	9	0.3	4
(NA)	9	-	.	-	.	-	.	1.5	20	2.2	26	1.6	21
Base: Self-completion questionnaire respondents									1315		1181		1274

		1983		1984		1985		1986		1987		1989	
Question No								B215c		B218c		A234c	
Column No								2054		2008		2221	
(iii) *{BIGPROFT}*													
We would all be better off if British firms made bigger profits													
Agree strongly	1	-	.	-	.	-	.	20.1	264	14.0	165	8.5	108
Agree	2	-	.	-	.	-	.	36.5	481	43.7	516	41.0	522
Neither agree nor disagree	3	-	.	-	.	-	.	22.7	299	22.4	265	25.7	327
Disagree	4	-	.	-	.	-	.	18.3	241	16.3	192	21.0	268
Disagree strongly	5	-	.	-	.	-	.	1.5	19	1.2	15	1.9	24
(DK)	8	-	.	-	.	-	.	0.1	1	0.3	3	0.2	2
(NA)	9	-	.	-	.	-	.	0.8	11	2.1	25	1.8	23
Base: Self-completion questionnaire respondents									1315		1181		1274

ATTITUDES TO BRITISH INDUSTRY (Continued)

		1983		1984		1985		1986		1987		1989	
		%	No	%	No	%	No	%	No	%	No	%	No
Question No								B215d		B218d		A234dd	
Column No	Code							2055		2009		2222	

(iv) {MANUFIND}
Britain's economy can prosper without manufacturing industry

		1983		1984		1985		1986		1987		1989	
Agree strongly	1	-	-	-	-	-	-	1.7	22	1.9	22	1.6	21
Agree	2	-	-	-	-	-	-	5.3	69	3.6	42	4.2	53
Neither agree nor disagree	3	-	-	-	-	-	-	11.5	152	12.6	148	15.8	202
Disagree	4	-	-	-	-	-	-	52.3	688	57.4	678	59.9	763
Disagree strongly	5	-	-	-	-	-	-	27.5	362	21.4	253	16.4	209
(DK)	8	-	-	-	-	-	-	0.3	4	0.4	5	0.3	4
(NA)	9	-	-	-	-	-	-	1.4	18	2.7	32	1.7	22

Base: Self-completion questionnaire respondents — 1315, 1181, 1274

| Question No | | | | | | | | B215e | | B218e | | A234e | |
| Column No | | | | | | | | 2056 | | 2010 | | 2223 | |

(v) {XSPROFIT}
British firms make too much profit

		1983		1984		1985		1986		1987		1989	
Agree strongly	1	-	-	-	-	-	-	4.7	62	3.3	39	3.3	42
Agree	2	-	-	-	-	-	-	13.6	179	13.3	158	15.8	201
Neither agree nor disagree	3	-	-	-	-	-	-	32.5	427	31.0	367	33.0	420
Disagree	4	-	-	-	-	-	-	39.9	524	43.3	512	40.2	512
Disagree strongly	5	-	-	-	-	-	-	7.9	104	5.4	63	5.0	64
(DK)	8	-	-	-	-	-	-	0.2	3	0.5	6	0.3	4
(NA)	9	-	-	-	-	-	-	1.2	16	3.2	38	2.4	30

Base: Self-completion questionnaire respondents — 1315, 1181, 1274

ATTITUDES TO BRITISH INDUSTRY (Continued)

		1983		1984		1985		1986		1987		1989	
		%	No	%	No	%	No	%	No	%	No	%	No
Question No								B215f		B218f		A234f	
Column No								2057		2011		2224	
(vi) *{SCHLFAIL}*	Code												
Britain's schools fail to teach the kind of skills that British industry needs													
Agree strongly	1	-	.	-	.	-	.	25.6	337	20.4	240	13.9	177
Agree	2	-	.	-	.	-	.	46.5	611	49.8	588	51.5	656
Neither agree nor disagree	3	-	.	-	.	-	.	15.1	198	15.9	188	18.3	233
Disagree	4	-	.	-	.	-	.	10.0	131	9.9	117	13.9	177
Disagree strongly	5	-	.	-	.	-	.	1.8	24	1.5	18	0.7	9
(DK)	8	-	.	-	.	-	.	0.1	1	0.5	6	0.2	2
(NA)	9	-	.	-	.	-	.	1.0	13	2.1	24	1.5	19
Base: Self-completion questionnaire respondents								1315		1181		1274	
Question No								B215g		B218g		A234g	
Column No								2058		2012		2225	
(vii) *{EMPSHARE}*													
Employees who have shares in their companies tend to work harder													
Agree strongly	1	-	.	-	.	-	.	23.7	311	13.5	160	13.4	170
Agree	2	-	.	-	.	-	.	51.8	681	57.9	683	57.9	738
Neither agree nor disagree	3	-	.	-	.	-	.	14.2	186	17.4	205	15.6	199
Disagree	4	-	.	-	.	-	.	8.4	110	8.4	100	10.8	138
Disagree strongly	5	-	.	-	.	-	.	0.9	12	0.8	10	0.5	7
(DK)	8	-	.	-	.	-	.	0.2	2	-	.	0.1	1
(NA)	9	-	.	-	.	-	.	0.9	12	2.0	23	1.6	21
Base: Self-completion questionnaire respondents								1315		1181		1274	

ATTITUDES TO BRITISH INDUSTRY (Continued)

		1983		1984		1985		1986		1987		1989	
		%	No	%	No	%	No	%	No	%	No	%	No
Question No								B215h		B218h		A234h	
Column No								2059		2013		2226	

(viii) {INDPROFT}

The less profitable British industry is, the less money there is for governments to spend on things like education and health

	Code												
Agree strongly	1	-		-		-		16.8	221	12.9	153	9.4	120
Agree	2	-		-		-		47.9	630	52.2	616	51.1	651
Neither agree nor disagree	3	-		-		-		19.2	253	19.1	225	23.0	293
Disagree	4	-		-		-		13.5	178	11.6	137	13.0	166
Disagree strongly	5	-		-		-		1.4	18	0.9	11	1.6	21
(DK)	8	-		-		-		0.2	3	0.7	9	0.2	3
(NA)	9	-		-		-		1.0	13	2.6	30	1.6	20

Base: Self-completion questionnaire respondents

| | | | | | | | 1315 | | 1181 | | 1274 | |

		Question No		220iv				B215i		B218i		A234i	
		Column No		1644				2060		2014		2227	

(ix) {BUYBRIT}

British people should try to buy British goods even when they have to pay a bit more for them

	Code												
Agree strongly	1	-		36.3	552	-		20.6	271	16.9	199	13.3	169
Agree	2	-		29.8	454	-		38.5	507	45.2	534	45.7	582
Neither agree nor disagree	3	-		13.8	210	-		17.3	228	17.0	201	18.0	229
Disagree	4	-		12.9	196	-		19.7	259	17.6	208	19.8	252
Disagree strongly	5	-		6.3	96	-		3.3	43	2.0	24	1.9	24
(DK)	8	-		0.1	1	-		0.1	1	-		0.1	1
(NA)	9	-		0.9	14	-		0.5	6	1.2	14	1.2	16

Base: Self-completion questionnaire respondents

| | | | | 1522 | | | | 1315 | | 1181 | | 1274 | |

1984 - {BUYBRIT} Disagree strongly, code 1; just disagree, code 2; just agree, code 4; agree strongly, code 5

GOVERNMENT HELP FOR INDUSTRY

{GOVHELP1} {GOVHELP2} {GOVHELP3} {GOVHELP4} {GOVHELP5} {GOVHELP6} {GOVHELP7}

Question: Please tick one box on [for each statement] to show your views on government help for industry. Remember that if you say 'definitely' or 'probably', it might require an increase in income tax to pay for it.

Do you think the government should (please tick one box for each):

			1983		1984		1985		1986		1987		1989
			%	No	%	No	%	No	%	No	%	No	%	No
Question No									B216		B219		A235	
Column No									2061		2015		2228	
(i) {GOVHELP1}		Code												
Help industry pay for research into new products														
Definitely	1		-	.	-	.	-	.	22.8	299	25.7	304	22.2	282
Probably	2		-	.	-	.	-	.	38.1	502	37.2	440	42.8	546
Probably not	3		-	.	-	.	-	.	28.5	376	26.0	307	25.8	328
Definitely not	4		-	.	-	.	-	.	8.0	105	8.1	95	6.4	82
(DK)	8		-	.	-	.	-	.	0.4	6	0.3	3	0.3	4
(NA)	9		-	.	-	.	-	.	2.1	28	2.7	32	2.5	32
Base: Self-completion questionnaire respondents									1315		1181		1274	
Question No									B216		B219		A235	
Column No									2062		2016		2229	
(ii) {GOVHELP2}														
Help pay for new factories in areas of high unemployment														
Definitely	1		-	.	-	.	-	.	42.6	561	44.6	526	39.7	506
Probably	2		-	.	-	.	-	.	41.1	540	41.5	490	46.9	598
Probably not	3		-	.	-	.	-	.	10.8	143	9.0	106	8.5	109
Definitely not	4		-	.	-	.	-	.	3.6	47	2.4	28	2.5	31
(DK)	8		-	.	-	.	-	.	0.3	4	0.2	2	0.2	2
(NA)	9		-	.	-	.	-	.	1.6	21	2.4	28	2.2	28
Base: Self-completion questionnaire respondents									1315		1181		1274	

GOVERNMENT HELP FOR INDUSTRY (Continued)

		1983		1984		1985		1986		1987		1989	
		%	No	%	No	%	No	%	No	%	No	%	No
Question No								B216		B219		A235	
Column No								2063		2017		2230	

(iii) {GOVHELP3}

Help industry pay for the cost of
replacing out-dated machinery and
equipment

	Code	1983 %	1983 No	1984 %	1984 No	1985 %	1985 No	1986 %	1986 No	1987 %	1987 No	1989 %	1989 No
Definitely	1	-	.	-	.	-	.	18.5	244	19.5	231	20.4	260
Probably	2	-	.	-	.	-	.	35.8	471	32.5	384	37.4	477
Probably not	3	-	.	-	.	-	.	32.1	422	35.0	413	31.1	395
Definitely not	4	-	.	-	.	-	.	11.7	154	10.1	120	8.5	108
(DK)	8	-	.	-	.	-	.	0.3	4	0.3	3	0.2	2
(NA)	9	-	.	-	.	-	.	1.6	21	2.5	30	2.5	32

Base: Self-completion
questionnaire respondents

Base totals: 1315, 1181, 1274

		1986	1987	1989
Question No		B216	B219	A235
Column No		2064	2018	2231

(iv) {GOVHELP4}

Help industry pay the wages of
people working in declining industries

	Code	1983 %	1983 No	1984 %	1984 No	1985 %	1985 No	1986 %	1986 No	1987 %	1987 No	1989 %	1989 No
Definitely	1	-	.	-	.	-	.	11.3	149	14.0	165	13.3	169
Probably	2	-	.	-	.	-	.	26.8	353	24.4	288	26.9	343
Probably not	3	-	.	-	.	-	.	40.3	530	42.7	504	42.9	546
Definitely not	4	-	.	-	.	-	.	19.0	250	16.0	189	13.7	174
(DK)	8	-	.	-	.	-	.	0.5	7	0.4	5	0.3	4
(NA)	9	-	.	-	.	-	.	2.0	26	2.6	31	2.9	37

Base: Self-completion
questionnaire respondents

Base totals: 1315, 1181, 1274

GOVERNMENT HELP FOR INDUSTRY (Continued)

		1983		1984		1985		1986		1987		1989	
		%	No	%	No	%	No	%	No	%	No	%	No
Question No								B216		B219		A235	
Column No								2065		2019		2232	

(v) *{GOVHELP5}*
Code

Give people grants to start their own business

	Code	1983 %	No	1984 %	No	1985 %	No	1986 %	No	1987 %	No	1989 %	No
Definitely	1	-	.	-	.	-	.	37.4	492	38.4	453	39.9	508
Probably	2	-	.	-	.	-	.	46.9	617	46.8	553	48.0	612
Probably not	3	-	.	-	.	-	.	10.8	143	8.8	104	8.0	101
Definitely not	4	-	.	-	.	-	.	2.8	36	3.4	40	1.8	23
(DK)	8	-	.	-	.	-	.	0.3	4	0.2	2	0.2	2
(NA)	9	-	.	-	.	-	.	1.9	24	2.4	29	2.2	28
									1315		1181		1274

Base: Self-completion
questionnaire respondents

		1986		1987		1989	
Question No		B216		B219		A235	
Column No		2066		2020		2233	

(vi) *{GOVHELP6}*

Give firms more help in selling goods abroad

	Code	1983 %	No	1984 %	No	1985 %	No	1986 %	No	1987 %	No	1989 %	No
Definitely	1	-	.	-	.	-	.	38.1	501	34.4	406	35.2	448
Probably	2	-	.	-	.	-	.	36.6	481	42.1	498	43.8	557
Probably not	3	-	.	-	.	-	.	18.5	243	16.2	192	14.8	189
Definitely not	4	-	.	-	.	-	.	5.1	67	4.5	53	3.4	43
(DK)	8	-	.	-	.	-	.	0.3	4	0.4	5	0.2	2
(NA)	9	-	.	-	.	-	.	1.5	20	2.4	28	2.7	34
									1315		1181		1274

Base: Self-completion
questionnaire respondents

GOVERNMENT HELP FOR INDUSTRY (Continued)

		1983		1984		1985		1986		1987		1989	
		%	No	%	No	%	No	%	No	%	No	%	No
Question No								B216		B219		A235	
Column No								2067		2021		2234	

(vii) {GOVHELP7}

Help industry pay for training employees in new skills

	Code	1983 %	1983 No	1984 %	1984 No	1985 %	1985 No	1986 %	1986 No	1987 %	1987 No	1989 %	1989 No
Definitely	1	-	.	-	.	-	.	36.2	476	36.3	429	39.8	507
Probably	2	-	.	-	.	-	.	42.8	563	42.4	500	44.9	571
Probably not	3	-	.	-	.	-	.	16.2	214	15.9	187	10.7	136
Definitely not	4	-	.	-	.	-	.	3.1	41	3.0	35	2.4	31
(DK)	8	-	.	-	.	-	.	0.3	4	0.3	3	0.2	2
(NA)	9	-	.	-	.	-	.	1.4	18	2.2	26	2.1	27

Base: Self-completion questionnaire respondents — 1315 — 1181 — 1274

ATTITUDES TO THE CITY OF LONDON

{THECITY1} {THECITY2} {THECITY3} {THECITY4}

Question: 'The City' of London is often called the financial centre of Britain.

Please *tick one box* to show how much you agree or disagree with each of these statements about 'The City'.

		1983		1984		1985		1986		1987		1989	
		%	No	%	No	%	No	%	No	%	No	%	No
Question No										B227a		A236a	
Column No										2062		2235	

(i) {THECITY1}

The success of 'The City' is essential to the success of Britain's economy

	Code	1983 %	1983 No	1984 %	1984 No	1985 %	1985 No	1986 %	1986 No	1987 %	1987 No	1989 %	1989 No
Agree strongly	1	-	.	-	.	-	.	-	.	22.1	261	12.7	162
Agree	2	-	.	-	.	-	.	-	.	51.3	606	48.1	612
Neither agree nor disagree	3	-	.	-	.	-	.	-	.	16.5	194	24.1	307
Disagree	4	-	.	-	.	-	.	-	.	7.1	84	11.1	141
Disagree strongly	5	-	.	-	.	-	.	-	.	0.5	6	1.4	18
(DK)	8	-	.	-	.	-	.	-	.	0.8	9	0.5	6
(NA)	9	-	.	-	.	-	.	-	.	1.8	21	2.1	27

Base: Self-completion questionnaire respondents — 1181 — 1274

ATTITUDES TO THE CITY OF LONDON (Continued)

		1983		1984		1985		1986		1987		1989	
		%	No	%	No	%	No	%	No	%	No	%	No
Question No										B227b		A236b	
Column No										2063		2236	

(ii) {THECITY2}

'The City' can be relied on to uncover dishonest financial deals without government intervention

	Code												
Agree strongly	1	-	.	-	.	-	.	-	.	4.4	52	2.5	32
Agree	2	-	.	-	.	-	.	-	.	26.4	311	16.7	213
Neither agree nor disagree	3	-	.	-	.	-	.	-	.	31.4	370	34.2	435
Disagree	4	-	.	-	.	-	.	-	.	27.2	322	35.5	452
Disagree strongly	5	-	.	-	.	-	.	-	.	7.5	89	8.4	107
(DK)	8	-	.	-	.	-	.	-	.	1.1	13	0.6	8
(NA)	9	-	.	-	.	-	.	-	.	2.0	24	2.1	27

Base: Self-completion questionnaire respondents — 1181, 1274

										B227c		A236c	
Question No / Column No										2064		2237	

(iii) {THECITY3}

The government should encourage as many ordinary people as possible to buy shares in British firms

	Code												
Agree strongly	1	-	.	-	.	-	.	-	.	14.1	166	8.6	109
Agree	2	-	.	-	.	-	.	-	.	46.9	553	47.8	609
Neither agree nor disagree	3	-	.	-	.	-	.	-	.	24.7	291	28.4	362
Disagree	4	-	.	-	.	-	.	-	.	8.5	100	11.3	144
Disagree strongly	5	-	.	-	.	-	.	-	.	3.2	38	1.6	20
(DK)	8	-	.	-	.	-	.	-	.	0.9	11	0.4	5
(NA)	9	-	.	-	.	-	.	-	.	1.8	21	1.9	24

Base: Self-completion questionnaire respondents — 1181, 1274

ATTITUDES TO THE CITY OF LONDON (Continued)

		1983		1984		1985		1986		1987		1989	
		%	No	%	No	%	No	%	No	%	No	%	No
Question No										B227d		A236d	
Column No										2065		2238	
(iv) {THECITY4}	Code												

Too many 'City' institutions go for quick profits at the expense of long-term investment in British industry

		1983		1984		1985		1986		1987		1989	
Agree strongly	1	-	.	-	.	-	.	-	.	19.1	226	16.6	211
Agree	2	-	.	-	.	-	.	-	.	45.6	538	48.1	613
Neither agree nor disagree	3	-	.	-	.	-	.	-	.	26.3	311	26.7	340
Disagree	4	-	.	-	.	-	.	-	.	5.3	63	4.4	56
Disagree strongly	5	-	.	-	.	-	.	-	.	0.7	9	1.2	15
(DK)	8	-	.	-	.	-	.	-	.	1.2	14	0.6	8
(NA)	9	-	.	-	.	-	.	-	.	1.7	20	2.4	31

Base: Self-completion questionnaire respondents — 1187, 1274

POWER OF TRADE UNIONS

{TUPOWER}

Question: Do you think that trade unions in this country have too much power or too little power? (Please tick one box)

		1983		1984		1985		1986		1987		1989	
		%	No	%	No	%	No	%	No	%	No	%	No
Question No						226		B209		A211		B227	
Column No						2126		2032		1562		2112	
	Code												
Far too much power	1	-	.	-	.	22.7	341	18.6	245	17.4	217	10.8	135
Too much power	2	-	.	-	.	31.0	466	34.6	455	30.2	375	29.0	363
About the right amount of power	3	-	.	-	.	27.7	415	30.0	395	31.9	397	32.7	411
Too little power	4	-	.	-	.	9.1	137	9.3	122	10.6	131	15.6	196
Far too little power	5	-	.	-	.	1.8	26	1.8	23	2.0	25	2.9	37
Can't choose	8	-	.	-	.	6.5	98	5.5	72	7.4	92	8.8	110
(NA)	9	-	.	-	.	1.2	18	0.3	4	0.6	7	0.3	4

Base: Self-completion questionnaire respondents — 1502, 1315, 1243, 1255

POWER OF BUSINESS AND INDUSTRY

{BUSPOWER}

Question: How about business and industry? Do they have too much power or too little power? (Please tick one box)

		1983		1984		1985		1986		1987		1989	
		%	No	%	No	%	No	%	No	%	No	%	No
Question No						227		B210		A212		B228	
Column No						2127		2033		1563		2113	
	Code												
Far too much power	1	-	-	-	-	3.9	59	4.8	64	5.7	71	9.4	118
Too much power	2	-	-	-	-	16.9	254	22.3	293	20.0	248	26.5	333
About the right amount of power	3	-	-	-	-	46.8	703	45.5	598	47.7	593	41.8	525
Too little power	4	-	-	-	-	11.8	177	14.6	193	10.8	135	7.0	88
Far too little power	5	-	-	-	-	1.2	18	0.7	10	1.2	15	0.7	9
Can't choose	8	-	-	-	-	18.7	280	11.6	152	13.6	169	14.0	176
(NA)	9	-	-	-	-	0.6	10	0.5	6	1.0	12	0.6	7
Base: Self-completion questionnaire respondents						1502		1315		1243		1255	

GOVERNMENT OWNERSHIP AND CONTROL OF INDUSTRIES AND SERVICES

{GOVROLE1} {GOVROLE2} {GOVROLE3} {GOVROLE4} {GOVROLE5} {GOVROLE6}

Question: What do you think the government's role in each of these industries and services should be?

		1983		1984		1985		1986		1987		1989	
		%	No	%	No	%	No	%	No	%	No	%	No
Question No						229a		B212a		A214a		B230a	
Column No						2129		2035		1565		2115	
	Code												
(i) {GOVROLE1} **Electricity**													
Own it	1	-	-	-	-	25.0	375	27.7	364	26.3	327	32.1	403
Control prices and profits but not own it	2	-	-	-	-	42.3	635	41.8	550	42.2	525	46.1	579
Neither own it nor control its prices and profits	3	-	-	-	-	25.1	377	24.2	319	22.9	285	14.4	180
Can't choose	8	-	-	-	-	6.4	17	4.9	64	7.4	92	6.5	81
(NA)	9	-	-	-	-	1.1	17	1.4	19	1.1	14	0.9	11
Base: Self-completion questionnaire respondents						1502		1315		1243		1255	

GOVERNMENT OWNERSHIP AND CONTROL OF INDUSTRIES AND SERVICES (Continued)

		1983		1984		1985		1986		1987		1989	
		%	No	%	No	%	No	%	No	%	No	%	No
Question No						229b		B212b		A214b		B230b	
Column No						2130		2036		1566		2116	

(ii) {GOVROLE2}
Local public transport

		1983 %	1983 No	1984 %	1984 No	1985 %	1985 No	1986 %	1986 No	1987 %	1987 No	1989 %	1989 No
Own it	1	-	-	-	-	17.3	260	20.3	267	18.9	235	17.6	221
Control prices and profits but not own it	2	-	-	-	-	35.8	538	34.5	454	36.5	454	42.3	531
Neither own it nor control its prices and profits	3	-	-	-	-	38.5	578	38.3	504	35.4	440	30.2	379
Can't choose	8	-	-	-	-	6.1	92	5.4	71	7.3	91	7.4	92
(NA)	9	-	-	-	-	2.2	33	1.5	19	1.8	22	2.6	32
Base: Self-completion questionnaire respondents							1502		1315		1243		1255

								1986		1987		1989	
Question No								B212c		A214c		B230c	
Column No								2037		1567		2117	

(iii) {GOVROLE3}
Gas

		1983 %	1983 No	1984 %	1984 No	1985 %	1985 No	1986 %	1986 No	1987 %	1987 No	1989 %	1989 No
Own it	1	-	-	-	-	-	-	28.1	370	26.3	327	31.0	389
Control prices and profits but not own it	2	-	-	-	-	-	-	40.2	529	40.0	497	46.3	581
Neither own it nor control its prices and profits	3	-	-	-	-	-	-	25.0	328	24.4	304	15.2	190
Can't choose	8	-	-	-	-	-	-	4.6	61	7.0	87	5.3	66
(NA)	9	-	-	-	-	-	-	2.0	27	2.3	28	2.3	29
Base: Self-completion questionnaire respondents									1315		1243		1255

						1985		1986		1987		1989	
Question No						229d		B212d		A214d		B230d	
Column No						2132		2038		1568		2118	

(iv) {GOVROLE4}
Banking and insurance

		1983 %	1983 No	1984 %	1984 No	1985 %	1985 No	1986 %	1986 No	1987 %	1987 No	1989 %	1989 No
Own it	1	-	-	-	-	8.2	123	6.3	83	6.6	82	4.4	56
Control prices and profits but not own it	2	-	-	-	-	30.7	461	31.8	419	29.2	363	36.7	461
Neither own it nor control its prices and profits	3	-	-	-	-	47.8	717	50.4	662	51.2	637	46.7	586
Can't choose	8	-	-	-	-	10.7	161	9.9	130	10.8	135	10.2	128
(NA)	9	-	-	-	-	2.6	39	1.6	21	2.2	27	1.9	24
Base: Self-completion questionnaire respondents							1502		1315		1243		1255

GOVERNMENT OWNERSHIP AND CONTROL OF INDUSTRIES AND SERVICES (Continued)

		1983		1984		1985		1986		1987		1989	
		%	No	%	No	%	No	%	No	%	No	%	No
Question No						229e		B212e		A214e		B230e	
Column No						2133		2039		1569		2119	
(v) {GOVROLE5}	Code												
The car industry													
Own it	1	-	.	-	.	7.9	118	7.7	101	8.1	101	3.7	46
Control prices and profits but not own it	2	-	.	-	.	28.4	426	27.3	359	25.0	311	31.1	390
Neither own it nor control its prices and profits	3	-	.	-	.	52.0	781	54.9	722	53.7	668	52.4	658
Can't choose	8	-	.	-	.	9.6	144	8.2	108	11.2	140	10.2	127
(NA)	9	-	.	-	.	2.2	33	2.0	26	2.0	24	2.7	33
Base: Self-completion questionnaire respondents						1502		1315		1243		1255	

		1983		1984		1985		1986		1987		1989	
Question No								B212f		A214f		B230f	
Column No								2040		1570		2120	
(vi) {GOVROLE6}													
The telephone system													
Own it	1	-	.	-	.	-	.	22.2	292	23.1	288	23.2	292
Control prices and profits but not own it	2	-	.	-	.	-	.	38.2	503	38.5	478	44.7	560
Neither own it nor control its prices and profits	3	-	.	-	.	-	.	33.0	434	29.2	363	23.9	300
Can't choose	8	-	.	-	.	-	.	5.3	69	7.8	96	6.7	84
(NA)	9	-	.	-	.	-	.	1.3	17	1.5	18	1.6	20
Base: Self-completion questionnaire respondents								1315		1243		1255	

1985 - {GOVROLE3}: 'The steel industry' was asked about instead of 'Gas', but both questions were given the same variable name. Consequently, {GOVROLE3} in 1985 has been changed to {GOVROLE9} (see p. H - 30 below)

1989 - 'The water supply' added (see p. H - 30 below)

INFLUENCE OF TRADE UNIONS ON PEOPLE'S LIVES

{TUINF1} {TUINF2}

Question: How much influence would you say the trade unions have on the lives of people in Britain these days? (Please tick one box)
Do you think they have too much influence, about the right amount, or too little influence?
(Please tick one box)

		1983		1984		1985		1986		1987		1989	
		%	No	%	No	%	No	%	No	%	No	%	No
Question No		212a		212a									
Column No		1576		1064									
(i) {TUINF1}	Code												
A great deal of influence	1	30.6	492	27.7	422	-		-		-		-	
Quite a bit of influence	2	40.7	656	39.5	601	-		-		-		-	
Some influence	3	23.3	375	26.5	85	-		-		-		-	
Not much influence	4	4.3	70	5.6	85	-		-		-		-	
(DK)	8	-		0.2	3	-		-		-		-	
(NA)	9	1.1	17	0.5	8	-		-		-		-	
Base: Self-completion questionnaire respondents		1610		1522									

		1983		1984		1985		1986		1987		1989	
Question No		212b		212b									
Column No		1065		1577									
(ii) {TUINF2}													
Too much influence	1	59.2	953	56.8	864	-		-		-		-	
About the right amount	2	33.7	542	33.5	510	-		-		-		-	
Too little influence	3	5.1	82	8.1	123	-		-		-		-	
(DK)	8	-		0.3	4	-		-		-		-	
(NA)	9	2.0	33	1.4	21	-		-		-		-	
Base: Self-completion questionnaire respondents		1610		1522									

1984 - Two parallel questions were asked about the influence of big business on people's lives - see p.H - 31 below

GOVERNMENT'S ROLE IN THE WATER SUPPLY INDUSTRY

1989   Q.B230g   {GOVROLE7} Column No 2121
What do you think the government's role in the water supply industry should be? (Please tick one box)

	Code	%	No
Own it	1	41.5	520
Control prices and profits but not own it	2	36.9	464
Neither own it nor control its prices and profits	3	14.2	178
Can't choose	8	6.2	78
(NA)	9	1.2	15
Base : Self-completion respondents			1255

NB   This item was part of a series of questions covering a range of industries and services (see pp. H-26 to 28 above)

GOVERNMENT'S ROLE IN THE STEEL INDUSTRY

1985   Q.229c   {GOVROLE8}   Column No 2131
What do you think the government's role in [the steel industry] should be?

	Code	%	No
Own it	1	16.0	240
Control prices and profits but not own it	2	29.6	445
Neither own it nor control its prices and profits	3	40.9	615
Can't choose	8	11.2	167
(NA)	9	2.3	34
Base : Self-completion respondents			1502

NB   This item was part of a series of questions covering a range of industries and services, all of which except this
one were repeated in later years. The original question wording was '... role in each of these industries and services ...'.
The variable {GOVROLE3} listed in the SPSS files for 1986, 1987 and 1989 relates to 'gas', not to 'the steel industry', so
the variable name of this question has been changed to {GOVROLE8}

INFLUENCE OF BIG BUSINESS ON PEOPLE'S LIVES

1984   Q.213a,b   {BIGINF1}{BIGINF2} Column No 1578-79

{BIGINF1}   Column No 1578
a) How much influence would you say big business has on the lives of people in Britain these days?
(Please tick one box)

	Code	%	No
A great deal of influence	1	41.5	632
Quite a bit of influence	2	38.2	581
Some influence	3	15.7	238
Not much influence	4	3.3	50
(DK)	8	0.6	9
(NA)	9	0.8	11
Base : Self-completion respondents			1522

{BIGINF2}   Column No 1579
b) Do you think big business has too much influence, about the right amount, or too little influence?
(Please tick one box)

	Code	%	No
Too much influence	1	45.6	695
About the right amount	2	49.9	760
Too little influence	3	2.2	33
(DK)	8	0.9	14
(NA)	9	1.4	21
Base : Self-completion respondents			1522

GOVERNMENT CONTROL OF INDUSTRY

1983   Q.9b   {CNTLIND} Column No 208
[And] do you think that British industry ought to be controlled by central government more,
less or about the same as now?

	Code	%	No
More	1	11.3	194
Less	2	43.0	740
About the same	3	37.7	647
(DK)	4	7.7	132
(NA)	9	0.3	6
Base : All			1719

NB This question was the second of three, all in the same format. The first and third were repeated in subsequent years -
see {CNTLCNCL} and {STATEOWN} (pp. A-1 and H-1 above)

I Education

Table titles and cross references

SELECTIVE *VERSUS* COMPREHENSIVE EDUCATION

{SELECTED}

Question: Some people think it is best for secondary schoolchildren to be separated into grammar and secondary modern schools according to how well they have done when they leave primary school. Others think it is best for secondary schoolchildren *not* to be separated in this way, and to attend comprehensive schools.

On balance, which system do you think provides the best all-round education for secondary schoolchildren ... (read out) ...

	Code	1983 %	1983 No	1984 %	1984 No	1985 %	1985 No	1986 %	1986 No	1987 %	1987 No	1989 %	1989 No
Question No					70		87				72		79	
Column No					539		722				654		771	
... a system of grammar and secondary modern schools,	1	-	-	49.7	818	46.2	818	-	-	52.3	1447	46.9	1374
... or a system of comprehensive schools?	2	-	-	39.7	653	45.4	803	-	-	41.1	1138	45.7	1338
(Other answer)	7	-	-	2.4	40	1.6	29	-	-	0.9	24	0.8	23
(DK)	8	-	-	7.5	123	6.7	119	-	-	5.5	153	6.4	188
(NA)	9	-	-	0.4	7	-	-	-	-	0.1	4	0.2	7
Base: All					1645		1769				2766		2930

1984 - SPSS file lists code 3 = 'Neither', 0.4% (n = 6)

PRIVILEGED ACCESS TO EDUCATION

{SAMEEDUC}

Question: Should the quality of education be the same for all children, or should parents who can afford it be able to pay for better education?

	Code	1983 %	1983 No	1984 %	1984 No	1985 %	1985 No	1986 %	1986 No	1987 %	1987 No	1989 %	1989 No
Question No								B81b				B95b	
Column No								658				859	
Same for everyone	1	-	-	-	-	-	-	46.6	721	-	-	52.3	765
Able to pay for better	2	-	-	-	-	-	-	51.9	803	-	-	45.8	670
(DK)	8	-	-	-	-	-	-	1.3	20	-	-	1.4	20
(NA)	9	-	-	-	-	-	-	0.3	4	-	-	0.5	7
Base: All									1548				1461

1986, 1989 - This question was part of a series. Similar questions were asked about health (see {SAMEHLTH}, p.K - 15) and pensions (see {SAMEPENS}, p.J - 10)

RESPONDENT: WHETHER EVER ATTENDED PRIVATE SCHOOL

{RPRIVED}

Question: Have you ever attended a *private* primary or secondary school in the United Kingdom? (Interviewer: 'private' includes public and direct grant schools, but excludes nursery schools and voluntary-aided schools)

		1983		1984		1985		1986		1987		1989	
		%	No	%	No	%	No	%	No	%	No	%	No
Question No						99a		A107a/B115a		903a		904a	
Column No						837		1560		1261		1509	
	Code												
Yes	1	-	-	-	-	11.3	200	11.3	345	13.0	359	11.9	348
No	2	-	-	-	-	88.6	1567	88.6	2716	86.6	2396	87.6	2567
(DK/couldn't establish)	8	-	-	-	-	0.1	1	0.1	3	0.1	2	0.1	2
(NA)	9	-	-	-	-	0.1	2	0.1	2	0.3	9	0.5	13
Base: All						1769		3066		2766		2930	

1984 - Variable {RSCHTYPE} on Column No 1162 derived from {RSCH1} - {RSCH7}:

	Code	%	No
Respondent attended state or LA school(s) only	1	73.2	1205
Respondent attended private school(s) only	2	3.5	58
All other cases	0	23.2	382
Base: All			1645

SPOUSE/PARTNER: WHETHER EVER ATTENDED PRIVATE SCHOOL

{SPRIVED}

Question: [If married or living as married] And has your *(husband/wife/partner)* ever attended a *private* primary or secondary school in the United Kingdom?

		1983		1984		1985		1986		1987		1989	
		%	No	%	No	%	No	%	No	%	No	%	No
Question No						99b		A107b/B115b		903b		904b	
Column No						838		1561		1262		1510	
	Code												
[Not asked: not married or living as married]	0	-	-	-	-	30.3	930	30.5	936	29.8	825	30.1	883
Yes	1	-	-	-	-	7.1	126	7.4	226	7.8	215	6.9	202
No	2	-	-	-	-	59.9	1060	61.6	1890	61.7	1705	62.2	1824
(DK/couldn't establish)	8	-	-	-	-	0.3	5	0.4	12	0.3	9	0.3	8
(NA)	9	-	-	-	-	0.1	2	0.1	2	0.4	11	0.5	14
Base: All						1769		3066		2766		2930	

CHILD(REN): WHETHER EVER ATTENDED PRIVATE SCHOOL

{CHPRIVED}

Question: [If has son or daughter over 5 years old] And *(have any of your children/has your child)* ever attended a *private* primary or secondary school in the United Kingdom?

	Code	1983 %	No	1984 %	No	1985 %	No	1986 %	No	1987 %	No	1989 %	No
Question No						99c		A107c/B115c		903c		904c	
Column No						839		1562		1263		1511	
[Not asked: does not have son or daughter over 5 years old]	0	-	-	-	-	60.5	1071	58.5	1795	59.7	1652	59.9	1755
Yes	1	-	-	-	-	2.9	51	4.4	136	4.1	113	4.4	128
No	2	-	-	-	-	36.0	637	36.2	1109	34.7	959	34.2	1003
(DK/couldn't establish)	8	-		-		-		-		-		0.0	1
(NA)	9	-	-	-	-	0.6	10	0.9	26	1.5	42	1.5	44
Base: All							1769		3066		2766		2930

TERMINAL EDUCATION AGE

{TEA}

Question: How old were you when you completed your continuous full-time education? (Interviewer: probe as necessary)

		1983		1984		1985		1986		1987		1989	
		%	No	%	No	%	No	%	No	%	No	%	No
Question No		93		96		100		A108/B116		904		906	
Column No		818-19		843-44		840-41		1563-64		1264-65		1530	
	Code												
15 or under	1	55.7	957	53.2	876	51.0	903	50.3	1541	46.9	1298	46.4	1358
16	2	22.2	381	23.7	390	24.9	440	24.6	754	24.5	679	25.4	743
17	3	6.3	108	7.8	128	7.1	125	7.7	235	8.6	237	7.3	213
18	4	5.2	89	5.7	94	5.5	97	6.1	186	6.7	186	6.6	193
19 or over	5	8.6	148	7.2	119	10.2	181	9.3	284	11.6	320	12.2	358
Still at school	6	0.2	4	0.1	1	0.5	8	0.2	5	0.1	3	0.2	7
Still at college, polytechnic or university	7	1.7	29	1.6	26	0.7	13	1.8	55	1.3	37	2.0	58
Other answer	97	-	.	0.1	1	0.1	2	-	.	0.1	3	-	.
(DK)	98	-	.	-	.	-		-	.	-		-	.
(NA)	99	0.2	3	0.7	11	0.0	1	0.2	6	0.1	4	0.0	1
Base: All			1719		1645		1769		3066		2766		2930

1983 - Other answer, code 8; No (DK)

1983, 1984 - No question: instead the interviewer was instructed to ask for 'Age of completing full-time education'

EXAMINATIONS PASSED/QUALIFICATIONS HELD

{NOEDQUAL} {EDQUAL1} {EDQUAL2} {EDQUAL3} {EDQUAL4} {EDQUAL5} {EDQUAL6} {EDQUAL7} {EDQUAL8} {EDQUAL9} {EDQUAL10} {EDQUAL11} {EDQUAL12} {EDQUAL13} {EDQUAL14} {EDQUAL15} {EDQUAL16}

Question: (Show card) Have you passed any exams or got any of the qualifications on this card?

		1983 %	No	1984 %	No	1985 %	No	1986 %	No	1987 %	No	1989 %	No
	Question No					101a		A109a/B117a		905a		907a	
	Column No					842		1565		1266		1531	
(i) {NOEDQUAL}	Code												
Yes	1	-	.	-	.	55.0	972	55.0	1687	58.0	1605	57.5	1686
No	2	-	.	-	.	45.0	797	44.8	1372	41.8	1156	42.3	1239
(NA)	9	-	.	-	.	-		0.2	7	0.2	6	0.2	6
Base: All							1769		3066		2766		2930

	Question No					101b		A109b/B117b		905b		907b	
	Column No					843-44		1566-67		1267-68		1532-33	

[If passed exams or got qualifications on card] **Which ones? Any others?**

(ii) {EDQUAL1}
CSE Grades 2-5/GCSE Grades D-G

		1983		1984		1985		1986		1987		1989	
Does not have qualification	0	-	.	-	.	87.3	1544	87.9	2694	86.9	2405	86.0	2521
Has qualification	1	-	.	-	.	12.7	225	12.1	372	13.1	361	14.0	409
Base: All							1769		3066		2766		2930

	Question No					101b		A109b/B117b		905b		907b	
	Column No					845-46		1568-69		1269-70		1534-35	

(iii) {EDQUAL2}
CSE Grade1/GCE O' level/GCSE Grade A-C/School certificate/ Scottish (SCE) Ordinary/Scottish School-leaving Certificate lower grade/SUPE Ordinary/Northern Ireland Junior Certificate

		1983		1984		1985		1986		1987		1989	
Does not have qualification	0	-	.	-	.	65.3	1155	65.2	2000	62.2	1721	61.5	1803
Has qualification	2	-	.	-	.	34.7	615	34.8	1066	37.8	1045	38.5	1128
Base: All							1769		3066		2766		2930

1985-1987 · {NOEDQUAL} No, none, code 2. {EDQUAL1} CSE Grades 2-5, code 1; CSE Grade 1/GCE O' level/School certificate/Scottish (SCE) Ordinary, code 2

EXAMINATIONS PASSED/QUALIFICATIONS HELD (Continued)

		1983		1984		1985		1986		1987		1989	
		%	No	%	No	%	No	%	No	%	No	%	No
Question No						101b		A109b/B117b		905b		907b	
Column No						847-48		1570-71		1271-72		1536-37	

(iv) {EDQUAL3}
GCE A' level/S' level/Higher School certificate/Matriculation/Scottish SCE/SLC/SUPE at Higher grade/ Northern Ireland Senior Certificate

	Code	%	No	%	No	%	No	%	No	%	No	%	No
Does not have qualification	0	-	.	-	.	85.2	1507	86.0	2635	83.4	2306	84.4	2474
Has qualification	3	-	.	-	.	14.8	262	14.0	431	16.6	460	15.6	456
Base: All							1769		3066		2766		2930

Question No						101b		A109b/B117b		905b		907b	
Column No						849-50		1572-73		1273-74		1538-39	

(v) {EDQUAL4}
Overseas School Leaving Exam/ Certificate

	Code	%	No	%	No	%	No	%	No	%	No	%	No
Does not have qualification	0	-	.	-	.	99.0	1752	99.2	3040	98.9	2735	98.8	2896
Has qualification	4	-	.	-	.	1.0	17	0.8	26	1.1	31	1.2	34
Base: All							1769		3066		2766		2930

Question No						101b		A109b/B117b		905b		907b	
Column No						851-52		1574-75		1275-76		1540-41	

(vi) {EDQUAL5}
Recognised trade apprenticeship completed

	Code	%	No	%	No	%	No	%	No	%	No	%	No
Does not have qualification	0	-	.	-	.	93.2	1648	93.7	2874	93.9	2598	94.0	2756
Has qualification	5	-	.	-	.	6.8	121	6.3	192	6.1	168	6.0	175
Base: All							1769		3066		2766		2930

1985-1987 - {EDQUAL3} GCE A'level/S' level/Higher certificate/Matriculation/Scottish (SCE) Higher, code 3

EXAMINATIONS PASSED/QUALIFICATIONS HELD (Continued)

		1983		1984		1985		1986		1987		1989	
		%	No	%	No	%	No	%	No	%	No	%	No
Question No						101b		A109b/B117b		905b		907b	
Column No						853-54		1576-77		1277-78		1542-43	

(vii) {EDQUAL6}
RSA/other clerical, commercial qualification

	Code	1983		1984		1985		1986		1987		1989	
Does not have qualification	0	-	.	-	.	92.4	1634	91.9	2818	91.9	2541	91.8	2691
Has qualification	6	-	.	-	.	7.6	135	8.1	248	8.1	225	8.2	240
Base: All							1769		3066		2766		2930

Question No						101b		A109b/B117b		905b		907b	
Column No						855-56		1578-79		1279-80		1544-45	

(viii) {EDQUAL7}
City & Guilds Certificate - Craft/ Intermediate/Ordinary/Part I

	Code	1983		1984		1985		1986		1987		1989	
Does not have qualification	0	-	.	-	.	94.2	1666	93.6	2869	93.5	2586	92.6	2713
Has qualification	7	-	.	-	.	5.8	103	6.4	197	6.5	180	7.4	217
Base: All							1769		3066		2766		2930

Question No						101b		A109b/B117b		905b		907b	
Column No						857-58		1608-09		1308-09		1546-47	

(ix) {EDQUAL8}
City & Guilds Certificate - Advanced/Final/Part II or Part III

	Code	1983		1984		1985		1986		1987		1989	
Does not have qualification	0	-	.	-	.	96.5	1707	96.8	2967	96.2	2662	95.7	2805
Has qualification	8	-	.	-	.	3.5	62	3.2	99	3.8	104	4.3	125
Base: All							1769		3066		2766		2930

Question No						101b		A109b/B117b		905b		907b	
Column No						859-60		1610-11		1310-11		1548-49	

(x) {EDQUAL9}
City & Guilds Certificate - Full technological

	Code	1983		1984		1985		1986		1987		1989	
Does not have qualification	0	-	.	-	.	98.5	1742	96.8	2967	98.3	2720	97.7	2862
Has qualification	9	-	.	-	.	1.5	27	3.2	99	1.7	46	2.3	69
Base: All							1769		3066		2766		2930

EXAMINATIONS PASSED/QUALIFICATIONS HELD (Continued)

		1983		1984		1985		1986		1987		1989	
		%	No	%	No	%	No	%	No	%	No	%	No
Question No						101b		A109b/B117b		905b		907b	
Column No						861-62		1612-13		1312-13		1550-51	

(xi) {EDQUAL10}
BEC/TEC General/Ordinary National Certificate (ONC) or Diploma (OND)

	Code												
Does not have qualification	0	-	.	-	.	96.6	1709	98.4	3017	96.5	2668	95.9	2811
Has qualification	10	-	.	-	.	3.4	60	1.6	49	3.5	98	4.1	119
Base: All							1769		3066		2766		2930

Question No						101b		A109b/B117b		905b		907b	
Column No						863-64		1614-15		1314-15		1552-53	

(xii) {EDQUAL11}
BEC/TEC Higher/Higher National Certificate (HNC) or Diploma (HND)

Does not have qualification	0	-	.	-	.	97.8	1730	97.6	2992	97.3	2690	97.4	2855
Has qualification	11	-	.	-	.	2.2	39	2.4	73	2.7	75	2.6	76
Base: All							1769		3066		2766		2930

Question No						101b		A109b/B117b		905b		907b	
Column No						865-66		1616-17		1316-17		1554-55	

(xiii) {EDQUAL12}
Teacher training qualification

Does not have qualification	0	-	.	-	.	96.4	1706	97.0	2974	96.4	2666	96.1	2816
Has qualification	12	-	.	-	.	3.6	63	3.0	92	3.6	99	3.9	115
Base: All							1769		3066		2766		2930

Question No						101b		A109b/B117b		905b		907b	
Column No						867-68		1618-19		1318-19		1556-57	

(xiv) {EDQUAL13}
Nursing qualification

Does not have qualification	0	-	.	-	.	97.8	1730	96.9	2971	97.1	2685	96.6	2832
Has qualification	13	-	.	-	.	2.2	39	3.1	94	2.9	80	3.4	99
Base: All							1769		3066		2766		2930

EXAMINATIONS PASSED/QUALIFICATIONS HELD (Continued)

		1983		1984		1985		1986		1987		1989	
		%	No	%	No	%	No	%	No	%	No	%	No
Question No						101b		A109b/B117b		905b		907b	
Column No						869-70		1620-21		1320-21		1558-59	
(xv) *{EDQUAL14}*	Code												
Other technical or business qualification/certificate													
Does not have qualification	0	-	-	-	-	94.5	1672	94.1	2885	94.0	2598	93.8	2750
Has qualification	14	-	-	-	-	5.5	97	5.9	181	6.0	167	6.2	180
Base: All							1769		3066		2766		2930
Question No						101b		A109b/B117b		905b		907b	
Column No						871-72		1622-23		1322-23		1560-61	
(xvi) *{EDQUAL15}*													
University or CNAA degree or diploma													
Does not have qualification	0	-	-	-	-	93.0	1646	93.3	2860	92.1	2547	92.8	2719
Has qualification	15	-	-	-	-	7.0	123	6.7	206	7.9	219	7.2	212
Base: All							1769		3066		2766		2930
Question No						101b		A109b/B117b		905b		907b	
Column No						873-74		1624-25		1324-25		1562-63	
(xvii) *{EDQUAL16}*													
Other recognised qualification													
Does not have qualification	0	-	-	-	-	97.2	1720	98.2	3010	99.2	2744	98.9	2899
Has qualification	97	-	-	-	-	2.8	49	1.8	55	0.7	21	1.0	29
(DK)	98	-	-	-	-	-	-	-	-	0.0	1	0.0	1
(NA)	99	-	-	-	-	-	-	-	-	0.0	1	0.0	1
Base: All							1769		3066		2766		2930

HIGHEST EDUCATIONAL QUALIFICATION (COMPRESSED)

{HEDQUAL}

Variable derived from *{EDQUAL1}-{EDQUAL16}*

	Code	1983 %	1983 No	1984 %	1984 No	1985 %	1985 No	1986 %	1986 No	1987 %	1987 No	1989 %	1989 No
Column No							1069		2367		2265		2374
Degree	1	-	.	-	.	7.0	123	6.7	206	7.9	219	7.2	212
Higher education below degree level	2	-	.	-	.	11.3	199	11.9	366	13.1	362	13.9	407
A' level or equivalent	3	-	.	-	.	8.7	154	8.8	268	9.0	248	10.3	302
O' level/GCSE Grade A-C or equivalent	4	-	.	-	.	17.3	306	18.6	571	19.0	526	17.7	520
CSE/GCSE Grade D-G or equivalent	5	-	.	-	.	9.3	165	8.1	249	8.2	227	7.9	233
Foreign and other	6	-	.	-	.	1.4	25	0.9	26	0.8	21	0.4	11
No qualifications	7	-	.	-	.	45.0	797	44.8	1372	41.8	1156	42.3	1239
(DK)/(NA)	8	-	.	-	.	-	.	0.2	7	0.3	7	0.3	8
Base: All							1769		3066		2766		2930

1985-1987 - GCSE not included. Codes were O' level/CSE Grade 1 (or equivalent) - code 4; CSE Grades 2-5 or equivalent - code 5

HOUSEHOLD MEMBERS: WHETHER EVER ATTENDED PRIVATE SCHOOL

{PRIVED} Variable derived from *{RSCH1} - {RSCH7}*
{PRIVED2} Variable derived from *{RPRIVED}, {SPRIVED}* and *{CHPRIVED}*

			1983		1984		1985		1986		1987		1989	
			%	No	%	No	%	No	%	No	%	No	%	No
(i) *{PRIVED}*	Column No		964		1663									
	Code													
No-one in household has attended private school	0		86.8	1491	86.4	1421	-	-	-	-	-	-	-	-
One or more household members has attended private school	1		13.2	228	13.6	224	-	-	-	-	-	-	-	-
Base: All				1719		1645								
(ii) *{PRIVED2}*	Column No						1068		2635		2263		2373	
	Code													
Respondent attended private school	1		-	-	-	-	11.3	200	11.3	345	13.0	359	11.9	348
Respondent has not but spouse/ partner or children attended private school	2		-	-	-	-	5.1	91	6.0	183	5.8	161	5.5	162
No-one in household has attended private school	3		-	-	-	-	82.7	1464	81.6	2502	79.2	2191	80.3	2354
(DK/NA)	8		-	-	-	-	0.9	15	1.2	36	2.0	55	2.2	65
Base: All								1769		3066		2766		2930

1983, 1984 - {PRIVED} The interviewer asked, for each household member: 'Which of these types of school have you (has he/she) <u>ever</u> attended?'; and showed a card on which was listed:

Primary: state or local authority; private; voluntary/maintained.

Secondary: state or local authority; private; voluntary/maintained.

Data for the respondent are on the following column nos:

1983: 656, code 1; 657, code2; 658, code 3; 659, code 4; 660, code 5; 661, code 6

1984: 667, code 1; 668, code 2; 669, code 3; 670, code 4; 671, code 5; 672, code 6; 673, code 7; (this last code for 'No secondary school attended')

The form of the question was subsequently simplified (see {PRIVED2} above)

1985-1987, 1989 - {PRIVED} changed to {PRIVED2} since the question changed in 1985

MULTICULTURAL EDUCATION

{IMCHILD1} {IMCHILD2} {IMCHILD3} {IMCHILD4} {IMCHILD5} {IMCHILD6}

Question: There has been a lot of debate among teachers about how British schools should cater for children whose parents come from other countries and cultures. Do you think in general that schools with many such children should ... (please tick one box on each line):

		1983		1984		1985		1986		1987		1989	
		%	No	%	No	%	No	%	No	%	No	%	No
Question No		216								A206		B223	
Column No		1107								1540		2063	

(i) *{IMCHILD1}*   Code

Provide them with special classes in English if they require them

		1983 %	No	1984		1985		1986		1987 %	No	1989 %	No
Yes		82.7	1331	-		-		-		80.2	997	79.9	1003
No		14.5	233	-		-		-		18.8	234	18.1	227
(DK)		-	.	-		-		-		0.2	3	0.2	3
(NA)		2.6	45	-		-		-		0.8	10	1.8	23

Base: Self-completion
        questionnaire respondents   1610   1243   1255

Question No		216								A206		B223	
Column No		1108								1541		2064	

(ii) *{IMCHILD2}*

Provide them with separate religious instruction if their parents request it

	Code	1983 %	No	1984		1985		1986		1987 %	No	1989 %	No
Yes	1	34.5	555	-		-		-		36.9	458	40.2	505
No	2	60.1	967	-		-		-		62.1	772	57.2	718
(DK)	8	-	.	-		-		-		0.2	2	0.3	4
(NA)	9	5.4	87	-		-		-		0.9	11	2.3	28

Base: Self-completion
        questionnaire respondents   1610   1243   1255

Question No		216								A206		B223	
Column No		1109								1542		2065	

(iii) *{IMCHILD3}*

Allow those for whom it is important to wear their traditional dress at school

	Code	1983 %	No	1984		1985		1986		1987 %	No	1989 %	No
Yes	1	46.1	743	-		-		-		44.9	559	43.2	543
No	2	49.1	791	-		-		-		54.1	673	54.6	686
(DK)	8	-	.	-		-		-		0.2	3	0.3	4
(NA)	9	4.7	76	-		-		-		0.7	9	1.9	23

Base: Self-completion
        questionnaire respondents   1610   1243   1255

1983 - No (DK)

MULTICULTURAL EDUCATION (Continued)

		1983		1984		1985		1986		1987		1989	
		%	No	%	No	%	No	%	No	%	No	%	No
Question No		216								A206		B223	
Column No		1110								1543		2066	

(iv) {IMCHILD4}
Allow them to study their mother tongue in school hours Code

		1983 %	No	1984		1985		1986		1987 %	No	1989 %	No
Yes	1	17.6	283	-	.	-	.	-	.	17.0	212	19.9	250
No	2	77.9	1254	-	.	-	.	-	.	82.2	1022	77.3	970
(DK)	8	-	.	-	.	-	.	-	.	0.2	3	0.5	7
(NA)	9	4.6	73	-	.	-	.	-	.	0.5	7	2.3	29

Base: Self-completion questionnaire respondents   1610   1243   1255

Question No		216								A206		B223	
Column No		1111								1544		2067	

(v) {IMCHILD5}
Teach them about the history of their parents' country of origin and its culture

		%	No							%	No	%	No
Yes	1	43.2	695	-	.	-	.	-	.	40.2	499	41.4	519
No	2	51.0	821	-	.	-	.	-	.	58.3	725	55.8	700
(DK)	8	-	.	-	.	-	.	-	.	0.2	3	0.4	5
(NA)	9	5.9	94	-	.	-	.	-	.	1.3	16	2.5	31

Base: Self-completion questionnaire respondents   1610   1243   1255

Question No		216								A206		B223	
Column No		1112								1545		2068	

(vi) {IMCHILD6}
Teach _all_ children about the history and culture of these countries

		%	No							%	No	%	No
Yes	1	78.7	1267	-	.	-	.	-	.	73.7	917	75.0	941
No	2	17.2	277	-	.	-	.	-	.	25.1	312	22.8	286
(DK)	8	-	.	-	.	-	.	-	.	0.2	3	0.4	5
(NA)	9	4.1	66	-	.	-	.	-	.	0.9	12	1.9	24

Base: Self-completion questionnaire respondents   1610   1243   1255

1983 - No (DK)

PRIORITIES FOR EXTRA SPENDING ON EDUCATION

{EDSPEND1} {EDSPEND2}

Question: (Show card) First, which of the groups on this card, if any, would be your highest priority for *extra* government spending on education, and which next?

		1983 %	1983 No	1984 %	1984 No	1985 %	1985 No	1986 %	1986 No	1987 %	1987 No	1989 %	1989 No
Question No		65				84				69			
Column No		533				715				647			
(i) *{EDSPEND1}* **First priority**	Code												
Nursery/pre-school children	1	10.4	178	-	-	9.8	174	-	-	7.6	210	-	-
Primary school children	2	16.3	280	-	-	12.6	222	-	-	15.0	416	-	-
Secondary school children	3	28.6	492	-	-	30.9	546	-	-	36.9	1021	-	-
Less able children with special needs	4	32.2	553	-	-	33.7	597	-	-	28.5	788	-	-
Students at colleges, universities or polytechnics	5	9.4	162	-	-	9.2	164	-	-	9.2	254	-	-
(None of these)	6	1.0	18	-	-	0.9	15	-	-	0.4	11	-	-
(DK)	8	1.9	32	-	-	2.8	50	-	-	2.2	62	-	-
(NA)	9	0.3	5	-	-	0.1	1	-	-	0.1	4	-	-
Base: All			1719				1769				2766		

		1983 %	1983 No	1984 %	1984 No	1985 %	1985 No	1986 %	1986 No	1987 %	1987 No	1989 %	1989 No
Question No		65				84				69			
Column No		534				716				648			
(ii) *{EDSPEND2}* **Second priority**													
Nursery/pre-school children	1	11.8	203	-	-	10.9	193	-	-	9.1	251	-	-
Primary school children	2	17.2	295	-	-	16.8	297	-	-	17.2	476	-	-
Secondary school children	3	25.2	433	-	-	25.6	453	-	-	25.6	708	-	-
Less able children with special needs	4	26.6	457	-	-	24.0	425	-	-	25.1	694	-	-
Students at colleges, universities or polytechnics	5	14.6	251	-	-	17.8	316	-	-	19.2	532	-	-
(None of these)	6	1.7	29	-	-	1.0	19	-	-	0.7	20	-	-
(DK)	8	2.5	43	-	-	3.7	65	-	-	2.9	80	-	-
(NA)	9	0.5	8	-	-	0.1	3	-	-	0.2	5	-	-
Base: All			1719				1769				2766		

1983, 1985, 1987 - Q introduced by: 'Now a few questions on education.'
1983 - (DK), code 7

IMPROVING PRIMARY AND SECONDARY SCHOOL EDUCATION

{PRIMEED} {SECED}

Question: (Show card) Here are a number of factors that some people think would improve education in our schools.

Which do you think is the *most* important one for children in *primary* schools - aged 5-11 years. Please look at the whole list before deciding.

		1983		1984		1985		1986		1987		1989	
		%	No	%	No	%	No	%	No	%	No	%	No
Question No		66a				85a				70a			
Column No		535-36				717-18				649-50			
(i) {PRIMEED} Primary schools	Code												
More resources for books and equipment	1	15.5	266	-	-	16.8	297	-	-	20.7	572	-	-
Better buildings	2	2.3	39	-	-	1.6	27	-	-	1.9	53	-	-
Better pay for teachers	3	1.4	24	-	-	3.8	66	-	-	3.5	97	-	-
More involvement of parents in governing bodies	4	3.0	52	-	-	2.4	43	-	-	2.5	70	-	-
More discussion between parents and teachers	5	9.5	163	-	-	8.4	148	-	-	7.5	208	-	-
Smaller classes	6	30.6	526	-	-	27.1	480	-	-	28.8	796	-	-
More emphasis on preparation for exams	7	0.9	15	-	-	2.0	36	-	-	1.6	45	-	-
More emphasis on developing the child's skills and interests	8	19.2	330	-	-	20.3	360	-	-	16.3	450	-	-
More training and preparation for jobs	9	1.0	17	-	-	1.7	30	-	-	1.7	47	-	-
More emphasis on arts subjects	10	-	-	-	-	0.2	4	-	-	0.1	2	-	-
More emphasis on mathematics	11	1.1	19	-	-	1.0	17	-	-	1.1	29	-	-
More emphasis on English	12	1.3	23	-	-	1.3	24	-	-	2.0	55	-	-
Stricter discipline	13	11.2	193	-	-	11.3	201	-	-	10.8	298	-	-
(None of these)	96	0.2	4	-	-	0.8	15	-	-	0.7	19	-	-
(Other answer)	97	-	-	-	-	0.2	4	-	-	-	-	-	-
(DK)	98	2.2	37	-	-	1.0	17	-	-	0.8	22	-	-
(NA)	99	0.6	11	-	-	-	-	-	-	0.1	3	-	-
Base: All			1719				1769				2766		

1983 - None of these, code 14; DK, code 15, printed on questionnaire; No (Other answer)

1987 - No (Other answer)

IMPROVING PRIMARY AND SECONDARY SCHOOL EDUCATION (Continued)

	Code	1983 %	1983 No	1984 %	1984 No	1985 %	1985 No	1986 %	1986 No	1987 %	1987 No	1989 %	1989 No
Question No		66b				85b				70b			
Column No		537-38				719-20				651-52			

(ii) *{SECED}*

And which do you think is the *most* important one for children in *secondary* schools - aged 11-18 years?

	Code	1983 %	No	1984 %	No	1985 %	No	1986 %	No	1987 %	No	1989 %	No
More resources for books and equipment	1	9.8	168	-	-	8.6	152	-	-	13.5	374	-	-
Better buildings	2	0.8	14	-	-	0.4	7	-	-	0.7	21	-	-
Better pay for teachers	3	0.8	13	-	-	2.6	47	-	-	4.2	115	-	-
More involvement of parents in governing bodies	4	1.5	25	-	-	1.0	17	-	-	1.0	27	-	-
More discussion between parents and teachers	5	4.6	78	-	-	2.7	48	-	-	2.9	80	-	-
Smaller classes	6	10.5	180	-	-	8.5	151	-	-	9.1	253	-	-
More emphasis on preparation for exams	7	6.8	117	-	-	8.6	152	-	-	8.9	246	-	-
More emphasis on developing the child's skills and interests	8	13.3	229	-	-	14.5	257	-	-	10.3	286	-	-
More training and preparation for jobs	9	27.2	467	-	-	26.8	474	-	-	25.4	703	-	-
More emphasis on arts subjects	10	0.1	2	-	-	0.2	3	-	-	0.1	2	-	-
More emphasis on mathematics	11	2.2	38	-	-	1.7	30	-	-	2.0	56	-	-
More emphasis on English	12	1.0	17	-	-	1.4	24	-	-	1.5	42	-	-
Stricter discipline	13	18.7	321	-	-	20.6	364	-	-	18.8	519	-	-
(None of these)	96	0.2	3	-	-	1.2	22	-	-	0.6	18	-	-
(Other answer)	97	-	-	-	-	-	-	-	-	-	-	-	-
(DK)	98	2.1	35	-	-	1.2	22	-	-	0.7	20	-	-
(NA)	99	0.6	11	-	-	-	-	-	-	0.1	2	-	-
Base: All			1719				1769				2766		

1983 - None of these, code 14; DK, code 15, printed on questionnaire; No (Other answer)
1987 - No (Other answer)

WHO SHOULD DECIDE SCHOOL CURRICULUM

{EDCURRIC}

Question: Do you think that what is taught in schools should be up to ... (read out) ...

		1983		1984		1985		1986		1987		1989	
		%	No	%	No	%	No	%	No	%	No	%	No
Question No				68		86				71			
Column No				528		721				653			
	Code												
... the *local* education authority to decide,	1	-	-	52.6	866	52.4	927	-	-	47.8	1321	-	-
... or should *central* government have the final say?	2	-	-	39.2	644	40.4	715	-	-	46.5	1287	-	-
(Other answer)	7	-	-	-	-	0.3	5	-	-	0.3	10	-	-
(DK)	8	-	-	7.4	121	6.5	116	-	-	4.9	136	-	-
(NA)	9	-	-	0.9	14	0.4	7	-	-	0.4	12	-	-
Base: All					1645		1769				2766		

1984 · Introduced by: 'Now a few questions on education'; No (Other answer)

PRIVATE SCHOOLS: INCREASE, DECREASE OR ABOLISH

{PRIVSCH}

Question: Generally speaking, what is your opinion about private schools in Britain? Should there be ... (read out) ...

		1983		1984		1985		1986		1987		1989	
		%	No	%	No	%	No	%	No	%	No	%	No
Question No		67a		71a		89a		65a		73a			
Column No		539		531		724		556		655			
	Code												
... more private schools,	1	10.9	187	8.9	146	8.5	150	13.4	410	10.6	294	-	-
... about the same number as now,	2	67.4	1159	68.2	1122	59.3	1048	63.8	1955	64.7	1788	-	
... fewer private schools,	3	8.4	144	9.8	162	13.4	237	9.1	280	10.9	302	-	
... or no private schools at all?	4	10.7	184	9.4	154	15.8	279	10.3	315	10.5	291	-	
(Other answer)	7	0.7	12	1.6	27	1.2	21	1.1	34	0.8	22	-	
(DK)	8	1.6	27	1.7	28	1.8	32	2.3	69	2.3	63	-	
(NA)	9	0.4	7	0.5	8	0.1	2	0.1	2	0.2	6	-	-
Base: All			1719		1645		1769		3066		2766		

1983 - Q reads: '... opinion about private or independent schools ...'; Other answer, code 5

PRIVATE SCHOOLS: EFFECT ON STATE SCHOOLS

{PRIVEFCT}

Question: If there were *fewer* private schools in Britain today do you think, on the whole, that state schools would ... (read out) ...

		1983		1984		1985		1986		1987		1989	
		%	No	%	No	%	No	%	No	%	No	%	No
Question No		67b		71b		89b		65b		73b			
Column No		540		532		725		557		656			
	Code												
... benefit,	1	17.8	305	17.1	281	24.1	427	19.2	588	19.6	542	-	-
... suffer,	2	18.4	316	14.4	237	11.6	205	15.7	482	15.7	435	-	-
... or would it make no difference?	3	59.4	1020	63.7	1049	58.2	1030	60.2	1846	59.8	1653	-	
(DK)	8	4.2	72	4.3	70	5.7	102	4.7	145	4.7	130	-	
(NA)	9	0.3	5	0.5	8	0.3	6	0.2	5	0.2	5	-	-
Base: All			1719		1645		1769		3066		2766		

1983 - (DK), code 4

OPPORTUNITIES FOR HIGHER EDUCATION

{HEDOPP}

Question: Do you feel that opportunities for young people in Britain to go on to *higher education* - to a university, college or polytechnic - should be increased or reduced, or are they at about the right level now?

[If increased or reduced] A lot or a little?

		1983		1984		1985		1986		1987		1989	
		%	No	%	No	%	No	%	No	%	No	%	No
Question No		71a				90a				74a			
Column No		551				726				657			
	Code												
Increased a lot	1	21.6	371	-	-	25.3	447	-	-	29.2	806	-	-
Increased a little	2	22.2	382	-	-	23.6	418	-	-	23.5	649	-	-
About right	3	48.8	839	-	-	42.5	751	-	-	42.0	1161	-	-
Reduced a little	4	3.7	64	-	-	3.2	56	-	-	1.9	54	-	-
Reduced a lot	5	1.0	18	-	-	1.3	24	-	-	0.8	22	-	-
(DK)	8	2.4	41	-	-	4.1	72	-	-	2.5	70	-	-
(NA)	9	0.3	5	-	-	0.1	1	-	-	0.1	3	-	-
Base: All			1719				1769				2766		

1983 - (DK), code 6

STUDENT GRANTS *VERSUS* LOANS

{HEGRANT}

Question: When British students go to university or college they generally get grants from the local authority. Do you think they should get *grants* as now, or *loans* which would have to be paid back when they start working?

	Code	1983 %	No	1984 %	No	1985 %	No	1986 %	No	1987 %	No	1989 %	No
Question No		71b				90b				74b			
Column No		552				727				658			
Grants	1	57.0	980	-	.	60.4	1068	-	-	64.7	1788	-	-
Loans	2	37.8	650	-	.	34.0	602	-	-	31.3	865	-	-
(Other answer)	4	0.1	2	-	.	-	.	-	-	0.4	11	-	-
(Both)	7	-	.	-	.	0.8	15	-	-	-	.	-	-
(DK)	8	4.4	75	-	.	4.4	79	-	-	3.3	92	-	-
(NA)	9	0.7	12	-	.	0.3	6	-	-	0.4	10	-	-
Base: All			1719				1769				2766		

1983 - DK, code 3; No (Both)
1985 - No (Other answer)

PUBLICATION OF EXAM RESULTS

{PUBRES}

Question: It is now compulsory for state secondary schools to publish their GCE and CSE exam results. How useful do you think this information is for parents of present or future pupils? Is it ... (read out) ...

	Code	1983 %	No	1984 %	No	1985 %	No	1986 %	No	1987 %	No	1989 %	No
Question No		70a				88							
Column No		543				723							
... very useful,	1	31.5	542	-	.	30.2	534	-	-	-	-	-	-
... quite useful,	2	34.5	593	-	.	36.5	647	-	-	-	-	-	-
... or not really useful?	3	24.1	414	-	.	25.4	449	-	-	-	-	-	-
(DK)	8	9.5	163	-	.	7.9	140	-	-	-	-	-	-
(NA)	9	0.3	6	-	.	-	-	-	-	-	-	-	-
Base: All			1719				1769						

1983 - (DK), code 4

SCHOOL EDUCATION STANDARDS NOW COMPARED WITH PAST

{EDSTD}

Question: In general, how would you compare the overall standards of education in schools today with the standards when you were at school. Would you say that standards today are higher, lower, or about the same?

[If higher or lower] **A lot or a little?**

		Code	1983 %	1983 No	1984 %	1984 No	1985 %	1985 No	1986 %	1986 No	1987 %	1987 No	1989 %	1989 No
Question No			69		69									
Column No			542		529									
A lot higher now		1	22.0	378	20.0	329	-	-	-	-	-	-	-	-
A little higher now		2	17.4	298	16.7	275	-	-	-	-	-	-	-	-
About the same		3	15.1	259	18.4	303	-	-	-	-	-	-	-	-
A little lower now		4	18.7	322	16.9	278	-	-	-	-	-	-	-	-
A lot lower now		5	21.7	372	21.2	348	-	-	-	-	-	-	-	-
Not educated here		6	1.1	20	1.5	25	-	-	-	-	-	-	-	-
(Still at school/not applicable)		7	-	-	0.1	2	-	-	-	-	-	-	-	-
(DK)		8	3.6	62	4.4	73	-	-	-	-	-	-	-	-
(NA)		9	0.5	9	0.7	11	-	-	-	-	-	-	-	-
Base: All				1719		1645								

_____

1983 - (DK), code 7

INCOME GROUP BENEFITING MOST FROM EDUCATION SPENDING

{EDVALUE}

Question: On the whole, which of these three types of family would you say gets best value from their taxes out of government spending on education ... (read out) ...

		1983		1984		1985		1986		1987		1989	
		%	No	%	No	%	No	%	No	%	No	%	No
Question No		68		72									
Column No		541		533									
	Code												
... those with high incomes,	1	34.0	584	31.3	515	-	.	-	.	-	.	-	.
... those with middle incomes,	2	22.5	387	21.2	349	-	.	-	.	-	.	-	.
... or those with low incomes?	3	29.9	514	31.2	513	-	.	-	.	-	.	-	.
(No difference)	4	12.3	211	2.3	38	-	.	-	.	-	.	-	.
(DK)	8	0.2	4	13.6	224	-	.	-	.	-	.	-	.
(NA)	9	1.1	19	0.4	7	-	.	-	.	-	.	-	.
Base: All			1719		1645								

1983 - (DK), code 4; (No difference), code 5

ATTITUDES TOWARDS SECONDARY SCHOOLING

1987   Q.A203a-d   *{SECSCHL1} - {SECSCHL4}*   Column Nos 1526 - 1529
Please tick one box to show how much you agree or disagree with each of these statements about *secondary schooling*.

	Agree strongly		Agree		Neither agree nor disagree		Disagree		Disagree strongly		(DK)		(NA)	
Code	1		2		3		4		5		8		9	
	%	No	%	No	%	No	%	No	%	No	%	No	%	No
a) *{SECSCHL1}* Column No 1526 Formal exams are the best way of judging the ability of pupils	8.6	107	35.9	446	17.0	212	31.2	388	6.5	81	0.1	1	0.7	8
b) *{SECSCHL2}* Column No 1527 On the whole, pupils are too young when they have to decide which subjects to specialise in	11.2	140	51.8	645	15.9	198	18.9	235	1.2	15	0.4	5	0.4	5
c) *{SECSCHL3}* Column No 1528 The present law allows pupils to leave school when they are too young	4.5	55	20.7	258	21.0	262	49.2	612	4.1	51	0.2	2	0.3	4
d) *{SECSCHL4}* Column No 1529 So much attention is given to exam results in Britain that a pupil's everyday classroom work counts for too little	18.6	231	51.6	642	12.4	154	15.4	191	1.3	17	0.2	3	0.4	5

Base : Self-completion respondents (n = 1243)

PERFORMANCE OF SECONDARY SCHOOLS

1987   Q.A204a-c   *{STATSEC1}-{STATSEC3}*   Column Nos 1530-32
From what you know or have heard, please tick one box on each line to show how well you think *state secondary schools nowadays*:

	Very well		Quite well		Not very well		Not at all well		(DK)		(NA)	
Code	1		2		3		4		8		9	
	%	No	%	No	%	No	%	No	%	No	%	No
a) *{STATSEC1}* Column No 1530 Prepare young people for work	1.8	23	27.4	341	54.4	676	14.9	185	0.6	7	0.9	11
b) *{STATSEC2}* Column No 1531 Teach young people basic skills such as reading, writing and maths	10.4	130	46.2	575	31.4	390	11.0	137	0.2	3	0.7	9
c) *{STATSEC3}* Column No 1532 Bring out young people's natural abilities	3.2	40	31.7	394	48.8	606	15.2	189	0.5	6	0.7	9

Base : Self-completion respondents (n = 1243)

PUPILS AND TEACHERS IN SECONDARY SCHOOLS

1987   Q.A205a-g   {SCHLLEAV}{TEACHPAY}{CLASSBEH}{PARTEACH}{PUPTEACH}{TEACHDED}{TEACHDIF}
Column Nos 1533-39

From what you know or have heard, please tick one box for each statement about *state secondary schools* now compared with 10 years ago.

	Much better now than 10 years ago		A little better		About the same		A little worse		Much worse now than 10 years ago		(DK)		(NA)	
Code	1		2		3		4		5		8		9	
	%	No	%	No	%	No	%	No	%	No	%	No	%	No
a) {SCHLLEAV} Column No 1533 On the whole, do you think school-leavers are *better* qualified or *worse* qualified nowadays than they were 10 years ago	11.7	145	24.8	308	25.6	319	21.2	263	15.3	190	0.6	8	0.8	10
b) {TEACHPAY} Column No 1534 Do you think teachers are *better* paid or *worse* paid nowadays than they were 10 years ago	30.5	379	24.9	309	19.4	241	14.3	177	9.4	116	0.8	10	0.8	10
c) {CLASSBEH} Column No 1535 And do you think classroom behaviour is *better* or *worse* nowadays than it was 10 years ago	0.3	4	1.9	24	10.4	129	26.8	334	59.3	738	0.5	6	0.7	9

	Much more now than 10 years ago		A little more		About the same		A little less		Much less now than 10 years ago		(DK)		(NA)	
d) {PARTEACH} Column No 1536 Do you think parents have *more* respect or *less* respect for teachers nowadays than they did 10 years ago	1.3	16	3.9	48	22.8	283	41.4	515	29.9	371	0.2	3	0.5	7
e) {PUPTEACH} Column No 1537 And do you think pupils have *more* respect or *less* respect for teachers nowadays than they did 10 years ago	0.3	4	1.9	24	9.5	118	31.6	393	56.0	696	0.2	2	0.5	7
f) {TEACHDED} Column No 1538 Do you think teachers are *more* dedicated to their jobs or *less* dedicated than they were 10 years ago	1.4	18	4.3	54	33.5	416	35.9	446	24.1	300	0.4	5	0.4	5
g) {TEACHDIF} Column No 1539 And, on the whole, do you think the job of state secondary school teacher is *more* difficult or *less* difficult nowadays than 10 years ago	32.2	400	29.9	372	15.7	196	10.4	129	11.2	139	0.2	2	0.5	6

Base : Self-completion respondents (n = 1243)

WHAT SCHOOLS SHOULD TEACH FIFTEEN YEAR OLDS

1985   Q.215a-h,j   *{TEACHXV1} - {TEACHXV9}* Column Nos 2043-51

[And now a few questions about education.] Here are some things that might be taught in school. How important is it that schools teach each of these to 15 year olds? (Please tick one box for each)

	Essential, must be taught		Very important		Fairly important		Not very important		Not needed, should not be taught		Can't choose		(NA)	
Code	1		2		3		4		5		8		9	
	%	No	%	No	%	No	%	No	%	No	%	No	%	No
a) *{TEACHXV1}* Column No 2043 Reading, writing and mathematics	86.6	1301	10.5	158	1.4	21	0.1	1	0.0	1	0.2	3	1.2	17
b) *{TEACHXV2}* Column No 2044 Sex education	17.4	261	24.2	363	35.3	530	13.2	198	6.6	99	1.9	29	1.4	21
c) *{TEACHXV3}* Column No 2045 Respect for authority	41.2	618	36.0	540	18.0	270	2.1	31	1.1	16	0.6	9	1.1	17
d) *{TEACHXV4}* Column No 2046 History, literature and the arts	14.1	211	21.8	327	40.8	613	19.1	287	0.9	14	1.6	24	1.7	25
e) *{TEACHXV5}* Column No 2047 Ability to make one's own judgements	40.7	612	40.8	613	13.4	202	1.8	28	0.9	13	0.9	13	1.4	21
f) *{TEACHXV6}* Column No 2048 Job training	38.4	576	38.5	578	16.0	240	3.7	55	1.3	19	0.9	14	1.3	19
g) *{TEACHXV7}* Column No 2049 Science and technology	31.9	479	34.6	519	24.2	363	5.3	80	0.5	8	1.4	21	2.1	31
h) *{TEACHXV8}* Column No 2050 Concern for minorities and the poor	23.1	347	31.8	478	30.3	455	9.2	138	2.7	41	1.3	20	1.6	24
j) *{TEACHXV9}* Column No 2051 Discipline and orderliness	49.8	747	32.7	491	13.1	197	1.6	25	0.7	11	0.9	14	1.1	17

Base : Self-completion respondents (n = 1502)

OPPORTUNITIES FOR UNIVERSITY EDUCATION

1985   Q.216   {YNGEDOP} Column No 2052
How do you feel about opportunities for young people to go to university?
Should opportunities be ... (please tick one box) ...

	Code	%	No
... increased a lot,	1	29.2	439
increased a little,	2	25.9	389
kept the same as now,	3	34.5	518
reduced a little,	4	4.1	61
or, reduced a lot?	5	1.0	15
Can't choose	8	4.9	74
(NA)	9	0.3	5
Base: Self-completion respondents			1502

GOVERNMENT FINANCIAL SUPPORT FOR STUDENTS

1985   Q.217a-c   {STUDENT1}-{STUDENT3} Column Nos 2053-55
Some people think the government should provide financial assistance to university students. Others think the government should not provide such aid. In each of the circumstances listed below should the government provide grants that would *not* have to be paid back, provide loans which the student *would* have to pay back, or should the government not provide any financial assistance? (Please tick one box for each)

	Government should give grants		Government should make loans		No government assistance		Can't choose		(NA)	
Code	1		2		3		8		9	
	%	No	%	No	%	No	%	No	%	No
a) {STUDENT1} Column No 2053 For students whose parents have a low income	80.5	1210	16.1	242	0.9	13	1.4	21	1.1	16
b) {STUDENT2} Column No 2054 For students who have outstanding exam results in secondary school	65.1	978	26.8	402	2.4	36	4.4	66	1.3	20
c) {STUDENT3} Column No 2055 For students who have average exam results and middle income parents	41.8	628	44.0	660	7.0	105	5.7	86	1.5	22

Base : Self-completion respondents (n = 1502)

INFORMATION THAT SECONDARY SCHOOLS SHOULD GIVE PARENTS

1983   Q.70b   {EDINFO} Column Nos 544

b) Is there any information you can think of [other than GCE and CSE exam results] that secondary schools should make available to parents of present or future pupils?

	Code	%	No
Yes	1	24.2	416
No	2	72.4	1245
(NA)	9	3.3	57
Base : All			1719

1983   Q.70c   {EDINFO1}+{EDINFO2}+{EDINFO3} Column Nos 545-46, 547-48, 549-50

[If yes] What information is this?

	Code	%	No
[Not asked: no other information need be made available]	0	75.8	1303
Records of children's/pupils' behaviour	1	6.6	114
Teachers' qualifications	2	2.0	35
Curriculum	3	2.7	46
Class size/teacher-pupil ratio	4	2.2	38
Level of contact between parents and teachers	5	4.4	76
Extra-curricular courses available	6	1.2	21
Extent of job training/careers guidance/advice	7	1.7	29
Other answer (no other response)	97	9.9	170
(DK)	98	-	-
(NA)	99	-	-
Base : All			1719

NB Up to 3 responses were coded for each respondent, so percentages will add up to more than 100%

GOVERNMENT SUPPORT FOR THE ARTS

1983   Q.214a,b   *{ARTHELP}{ARTSUP1}{ARTSUP2}* Column Nos 1071-73

1983   Q.214a   *{ARTHELP}* Column No 1071

a) The government helps to support the arts in Britain. On the whole would you like to see ...

	Code	%	No
... more government support for the arts	1	18.6	299
or less government support for the arts	2	13.9	224
or about the same as now	3	59.0	950
or none at all	4	7.3	118
(DK)	8	0.3	6
(NA)	9	0.9	14
Base: Self-completion respondents			1610

1983   Q.214b   *{ARTSUP1}{ARTSUP2}* Column Nos 1072-73

b) Which of the items below do you think should have the highest priority in government support for the arts?   ... and which next?

	Code	Highest priority {ARTSUP1} %	No	Next highest priority {ARTSUP2} %	No
National Institutions, such as the Royal Opera House, Royal Shakespeare Company, National Theatre	1	18.8	303	12.8	207
Arts events in the regions	2	11.2	180	11.4	183
Museums and art galleries	3	23.7	381	17.0	274
Arts events in schools	4	14.6	236	14.2	228
Promising individual writers, artists and composers	5	9.0	145	13.0	209
Rock and pop concerts for young people	6	2.7	44	3.4	55
Arts events for ethnic minorities	7	0.5	7	1.8	29
Non-professional/amateur art events	8	5.9	96	9.7	157
(NA)	9	13.5	218	16.6	268
Base: Self-completion respondents			1610		1610

J Social welfare and poverty

Table titles and cross references

PRIORITIES FOR EXTRA SPENDING ON SOCIAL BENEFITS

{SOCBEN1} {SOCBEN2}

Question: (Show card) Thinking now only of the government's spending on *social benefits* like those on the card. Which, if any, of these would be your highest priority for *extra* spending? And which next?

		1983		1984		1985		1986		1987		1989	
		%	No	%	No	%	No	%	No	%	No	%	No
Question No		51		58		70		54		58		68	
Column No		475		511		643		535		626		745	

(i) {SOCBEN1}
First priority   Code

	Code	%	No	%	No	%	No	%	No	%	No	%	No
Retirement pensions	1	40.8	701	43.2	710	41.2	730	40.4	1239	47.2	1306	43.0	1261
Child benefits	2	7.7	133	9.4	154	9.7	172	10.5	323	9.0	249	13.8	405
Benefits for the unemployed	3	17.6	302	17.9	294	15.7	279	16.0	489	15.5	428	11.1	324
Benefits for disabled people	4	24.4	419	21.2	349	25.7	455	25.0	765	20.6	569	25.8	757
Benefits for single parents	5	8.0	138	6.5	107	5.7	100	6.8	209	6.0	167	5.5	160
(None of these)	6	0.6	11	0.7	11	1.1	20	0.4	11	0.8	21	0.2	6
(DK)	8	0.7	13	1.0	16	0.7	13	0.9	27	0.8	23	0.5	13
(NA)	9	0.1	3	0.2	3	0.1	1	0.1	3	0.0	1	0.1	3

Base: All

	1719		1645		1769		3066		2766		2930

Question No		51		58		70		54		58		68	
Column No		476		512		644		536		627		746	

(ii) {SOCBEN2}
Second priority

	Code	%	No	%	No	%	No	%	No	%	No	%	No
Retirement pensions	1	23.5	404	22.7	374	22.3	395	24.2	743	21.0	581	23.7	695
Child benefits	2	12.6	216	12.5	206	13.1	232	12.5	382	14.5	402	15.7	462
Benefits for the unemployed	3	14.9	255	17.2	283	15.7	278	16.8	515	17.4	481	13.7	401
Benefits for disabled people	4	33.3	572	34.2	563	32.7	578	33.0	1011	33.8	935	33.8	990
Benefits for single parents	5	13.1	226	9.5	156	12.0	212	11.1	340	10.4	286	11.4	334
(None of these)	6	1.2	21	1.7	28	2.0	35	0.7	22	1.5	41	0.8	25
(DK)	8	1.0	17	1.4	23	1.7	30	1.6	49	1.3	37	0.7	20
(NA)	9	0.4	8	0.7	12	0.5	9	0.1	4	0.1	3	0.1	4

Base: All

	1719		1645		1769		3066		2766		2930

1983 - (DK), Code 7

EXTENT OF FALSE CLAIMS AND UNDERCLAIMING FOR BENEFIT

{FALSECLM} {FAILCLM}

Question: I will read two statements. For each one please say whether you agree or disagree. Strongly or slightly?

			1983		1984		1985		1986		1987		1989	
			%	No	%	No	%	No	%	No	%	No	%	No
Question No			52a		59a		71a		55a		59a		69a	
Column No			477		513		645		537		628		747	
(i) {FALSECLM}	Code													
Large numbers of people these days *falsely* claim benefits														
Agree strongly	1		40.1	689	37.2	613	42.5	752	44.8	1374	38.9	1077	38.6	1130
Agree slightly	2		25.1	431	27.2	448	24.3	430	25.4	780	27.6	764	26.9	788
Disagree slightly	3		12.8	220	13.8	227	11.6	206	11.0	336	13.4	372	13.9	407
Disagree strongly	4		12.1	209	11.5	189	10.0	177	10.1	310	11.7	323	12.3	359
(DK)	8		9.7	166	9.8	162	11.4	202	8.6	265	8.1	224	8.4	245
(NA)	9		0.2	4	0.4	7	0.1	2	0.0	1	0.2	5	0.0	1
Base: All				1719		1645		1769		3066		2766		2930

			1983		1984		1985		1986		1987		1989	
Question No			52b		59b		71b		55b		59b		69b	
Column No			478		514		646		538		629		748	
(ii) {FAILCLM}														
Large numbers of people who are eligible for benefits these days *fail* to claim them														
Agree strongly	1		49.1	844	45.8	754	50.2	889	48.7	1493	48.1	1330	50.7	1486
Agree slightly	2		31.9	548	32.6	536	33.6	594	33.6	1030	35.1	970	33.0	967
Disagree slightly	3		8.2	142	8.9	146	6.3	111	8.0	244	7.4	204	6.3	184
Disagree strongly	4		3.3	57	4.1	68	2.3	40	3.2	99	3.4	93	3.3	98
(DK)	8		7.3	125	8.2	135	7.6	135	6.5	199	6.0	166	6.7	196
(NA)	9		0.2	3	0.4	7	0.0	1	0.0	1	0.1	3	0.0	1
Base: All				1719		1645		1769		3066		2766		2930

1983 - (DK), code 5

LEVEL OF UNEMPLOYMENT BENEFIT

{DOLE}

Question: Opinions differ about the level of benefits for the unemployed. Which of these two statements comes *closest* to your own ... (read out) ...

	Code	1983 %	1983 No	1984 %	1984 No	1985 %	1985 No	1986 %	1986 No	1987 %	1987 No	1989 %	1989 No
Question No			53		60		72		56		60		70
Column No			479		515		647		539		630		749
... benefits for the unemployed are *too low* and cause hardship,	1	45.9	790	48.9	805	44.4	785	44.2	1355	50.7	1402	51.8	1518
... or benefits for the unemployed are *too high* and discourage people from finding jobs?	2	34.8	599	28.0	461	34.0	601	33.4	1024	29.4	814	26.8	787
(Neither)	3	12.7	219	7.7	126	6.9	121	6.1	188	6.0	167	7.9	232
(Both: cause hardship but, because wages are low, offer no incentive)	4	-	-	0.8	13	1.0	18	1.1	33	0.8	21	0.5	15
(Both: some people benefit, some people suffer/it depends)	5	-	-	5.5	90	5.2	93	7.5	231	5.5	151	4.5	131
(About right/in between the two)	6	-	-	1.2	20	1.4	25	1.6	50	1.2	32	0.9	26
(Other answer)	7	-	-	1.3	21	1.5	26	1.1	34	1.3	35	0.8	24
(DK)	8	6.2	106	6.3	104	5.7	100	4.8	146	5.1	140	6.7	197
(NA)	9	0.3	6	0.3	4	-	-	0.2	5	0.1	4	0.0	1
Base: All			1719		1645		1769		3066		2766		2930

1983 · (DK), code 4; codes 5, 6, 7 and 8 not provided
1986 · code 5 = 'Both: some people benefit, some people suffer' (no 'it depends')

PERCEIVED EXTENT OF POVERTY

{MUCHPOV}

Question: Some people say there is very little *real* poverty in Britain today. Others say there is quite a lot. Which comes closest to *your* view ... (read out) ...

		1983		1984		1985		1986		1987		1989	
		%	No	%	No	%	No	%	No	%	No	%	No
Question No								B75a				B89a	
Column No								626				846	
	Code												
... that there is very little real poverty in Britain,	1	-		-		-		41.0	635	-		33.6	491
... or that there is quite a lot?	2	-		-		-		55.4	858	-		62.8	918
(DK)	8	-		-		-		3.5	54	-		3.2	47
(NA)	9	-		-		-		0.1	1	-		0.3	5
Base: All								1548				1461	

PERCEPTIONS OF PAST AND FUTURE EXTENT OF POVERTY

{PASTPOV} {FUTURPOV}

Question: Over the last ten years, do you think that poverty in Britain has been increasing, decreasing or staying at about the same level?

		1983		1984		1985		1986		1987		1989	
		%	No	%	No	%	No	%	No	%	No	%	No
Question No								B75b				B89b	
Column No								627				847	
(i) {PASTPOV}	Code												
Increasing	1	-		-		-		51.1	792	-		49.5	724
Decreasing	2	-		-		-		15.2	235	-		16.4	240
Staying at same level	3	-		-		-		29.9	462	-		30.9	452
(DK)	8	-		-		-		3.8	59	-		2.9	42
(NA)	9	-		-		-		0.1	1	-		0.3	4
Base: All								1548				1461	

PERCEPTIONS OF PAST AND FUTURE EXTENT OF POVERTY (Continued)

		1983		1984		1985		1986		1987		1989	
		%	No	%	No	%	No	%	No	%	No	%	No
Question No								B75c				B89c	
Column No								628				848	
(ii) {*FUTURPOV*}	Code												

And over the *next* ten years, do you think that poverty in Britain will ... (read out) ...

	Code	%	No	%	No	%	No	%	No	%	No	%	No
... increase,	1	-	-	-	-	-	-	44.5	689	-	-	43.7	639
... decrease,	2	-	-	-	-	-	-	12.5	193	-	-	15.6	228
... or stay at about the same level?	3	-	-	-	-	-	-	35.8	554	-	-	34.4	503
(DK)	8	-	-	-	-	-	-	7.2	111	-	-	6.0	87
(NA)	9	-	-	-	-	-	-	0.1	1	-	-	0.3	5
Base: All									1548				1461

DEFINITION OF POVERTY - 1

{*POVERTY1*} {*POVERTY2*} {*POVERTY3*}

Question: Would you say someone in Britain *was* or *was not* in poverty if ... (read out):

		1983		1984		1985		1986		1987		1989	
		%	No	%	No	%	No	%	No	%	No	%	No
Question No								B76a				B90a	
Column No								629				849	
(i) {*POVERTY1*}	Code												

They had enough to buy the things they really needed, but not enough to buy the things most people take for granted

	Code	%	No	%	No	%	No	%	No	%	No	%	No
Was	1	-	-	-	-	-	-	24.6	381	-	-	25.3	370
Was not	2	-	-	-	-	-	-	71.6	1109	-	-	71.2	1040
(DK)	8	-	-	-	-	-	-	3.6	56	-	-	3.0	44
(NA)	9	-	-	-	-	-	-	0.1	2	-	-	0.5	7
Base: All									1548				1461

DEFINITION OF POVERTY - 1 (Continued)

			1983		1984		1985		1986		1987		1989	
			%	No	%	No	%	No	%	No	%	No	%	No
	Question No								B76b				B90b	
	Column No								630				850	

(ii) {POVERTY2}

They had enough to eat and live, but not enough to buy other things they needed

		1983		1984		1985		1986		1987		1989	
Was	1	-		-		-		54.6	846	-		60.0	877
Was not	2	-		-		-		42.6	659	-		38.0	555
(DK)	8	-		-		-		2.6	40	-		1.5	23
(NA)	9	-		-		-		0.2	3	-		0.5	7
Base: All									1548				1461

			B76c			B90c	
	Question No		631			851	
	Column No						

(iii) {POVERTY3}

They had not got enough to eat and live without getting into debt

		1983		1984		1985		1986		1987		1989	
Was	1	-		-		-		95.1	1473	-		95.1	1390
Was not	2	-		-		-		3.1	47	-		3.0	44
(DK)	8	-		-		-		1.6	25	-		1.3	19
(NA)	9	-		-		-		0.2	3	-		0.6	9
Base: All									1548				1461

1986 - Code 1 = 'Yes'; code 2 = 'No'

CAUSES OF POVERTY

{WHYNEED}

Question: (Show card) Why do you think there are people who live in need? Of the four views on this card, which *one* comes closest to your own?

		1983		1984		1985		1986		1987		1989	
		%	No	%	No	%	No	%	No	%	No	%	No
Question No								B77				B91	
Column No								632				852	
	Code												
Because they have been unlucky	1	-	-	-	-	-	-	11.1	171	-	-	10.6	155
Because of laziness or lack of willpower	2	-	-	-	-	-	-	18.8	291	-	-	19.4	283
Because of injustice in our society	3	-	-	-	-	-	-	25.0	386	-	-	29.1	425
It's an inevitable part of modern life	4	-	-	-	-	-	-	36.8	570	-	-	34.3	501
(None of these)	5	-	-	-	-	-	-	1.1	18	-	-	2.3	34
(Ignorance)	6	-	-	-	-	-	-	0.8	13	-	-	0.3	5
(Other answer)	7	-	-	-	-	-	-	3.5	55	-	-	1.8	27
(DK)	8	-	-	-	-	-	-	2.8	43	-	-	1.8	27
(NA)	9	-	-	-	-	-	-	0.1	1	-	-	0.4	6
Base: All									1548				1461

HOW OFTEN OWN HOUSEHOLD FEELS POOR

{FEELPOOR}

Question: How often do *you* and your household feel poor nowadays ... (read out) ...

		1983		1984		1985		1986		1987		1989	
		%	No	%	No	%	No	%	No	%	No	%	No
Question No								B78a				B92	
Column No								633				853	
	Code												
... never,	1	-	-	-	-	-	-	40.1	620	-	-	43.1	630
... every now and then,	2	-	-	-	-	-	-	42.1	652	-	-	39.6	578
... often,	3	-	-	-	-	-	-	9.4	145	-	-	9.7	142
... or almost all the time?	4	-	-	-	-	-	-	7.7	119	-	-	6.8	99
(DK)	8	-	-	-	-	-	-	0.6	10	-	-	0.4	6
(NA)	9	-	-	-	-	-	-	0.1	2	-	-	0.4	6
Base: All									1548				1461

LIVING STANDARDS OF UNEMPLOYED COUPLE

{UBPOOR} {POORUB40}

Question: Think of a married couple without children living only on unemployment benefit. Would you say that they are ... (read out) ...

	Code	1983 %	No	1984 %	No	1985 %	No	1986 %	No	1987 %	No	1989 %	No
Question No								B79a				B93a	
Column No								653				854	
(i) {UBPOOR}													
... really poor,	1	-	.	-	.	-	.	12.3	191	-	.	12.4	181
... hard up,	2	-	.	-	.	-	.	46.9	726	-	.	49.4	721
... have enough to live on,	3	-	.	-	.	-	.	28.3	438	-	.	26.8	391
... or have more than enough?	4	-	.	-	.	-	.	0.7	10	-	.	1.6	23
(DK)	8	-	.	-	.	-	.	11.6	180	-	.	9.5	138
(NA)	9	-	.	-	.	-	.	0.3	4	-	.	0.4	6
Base: All									1548				1461

	Code	1983 %	No	1984 %	No	1985 %	No	1986 %	No	1987 %	No	1989 %	No
Question No								B80a				B94a	
Column No								655				856	

(ii) {POORUB40}

Now thinking of a married couple without children living on 53 per week. Would you say they are ... (read out) ...

	Code	1986 %	No	1989 %	No
... really poor,	1	38.5	597	42.3	618
... hard up,	2	50.5	782	48.9	714
... have enough to live on,	3	7.7	119	6.4	94
... or have more than enough?	4	0.5	8	0.1	2
(DK)	8	2.5	38	1.8	26
(NA)	9	0.3	5	0.5	8
Base: All			1548		1461

1986 - SPSS file lists variable as {POOR50}; 'Now thinking of a married couple without children living on £50 per week?' Both amounts were the then current benefits available (without taking into account any housing benefit for which this couple might be eligible), so the 1986 variable name has been changed to {POORUB40}

LIVING STANDARDS OF PENSIONER COUPLE

{PENSPOOR} {POORSPNO}

Question: Now thinking of a married couple living only on the state pension. Would you say they are ... (read out) ...

		1983		1984		1985		1986		1987		1989	
		%	No	%	No	%	No	%	No	%	No	%	No
(i) *{PENSPOOR}*	Question No Column No							B79b 654				B93b 855	
	Code												
... really poor,	1	-	-	-	-	-	-	19.3	300	-	-	22.1	322
... hard up,	2	-	-	-	-	-	-	50.9	788	-	-	55.2	807
... have enough to live on,	3	-	-	-	-	-	-	23.1	358	-	-	18.7	273
... or have more than enough?	4	-	-	-	-	-	-	0.4	6	-	-	0.2	3
(DK)	8	-	-	-	-	-	-	6.2	96	-	-	3.4	49
(NA)	9	-	-	-	-	-	-	0.1	1	-	-	0.4	6
Base: All									1548				1461

		1983		1984		1985		1986		1987		1989	
(ii) *{POORSPNO}*	Question No Column No							B80b 656				B94b 857	
And what about a pensioner couple living on 66 per week. Would you say they are ... (read out) ...													
... really poor,	1	-	-	-	-	-	-	23.1	358	-	-	30.3	442
... hard up,	2	-	-	-	-	-	-	48.7	754	-	-	51.5	753
... have enough to live on,	3	-	-	-	-	-	-	24.5	379	-	-	15.9	233
... or have more than enough?	4	-	-	-	-	-	-	0.5	8	-	-	0.3	5
(DK)	8	-	-	-	-	-	-	2.5	39	-	-	1.5	21
(NA)	9	-	-	-	-	-	-	0.6	10	-	-	0.5	8
Base: All									1548				1461

1986 - SPSS file lists variable as {POOR62}; 'And what about a pensioner couple living on £62 per week?' Both amounts were the then current benefits available (without taking into account any housing benefit for which this couple might be eligible), so the 1986 variable name has been changed to {POORSPNO}

PRIVILEGED ACCESS TO PENSIONS

{SAMEPENS}

Question: And do you think that pensions should be the same for everyone, or should people who can afford it be able to pay for better pensions?

			1983		1984		1985		1986		1987		1989	
			%	No	%	No	%	No	%	No	%	No	%	No
Question No									B81c				B95c	
Column No									659				860	
	Code													
Same for everyone	1		-		-		-		36.2	560	-		33.2	485
Able to pay for better	2		-		-		-		60.6	938	-		63.1	923
(DK)	8		-		-		-		3.1	48	-		3.1	45
(NA)	9		-		-		-		0.1	2	-		0.6	9
Base: All										1548				1461

1986, 1989 - This question was part of a series. Similar questions were asked about health (see {SAMEHLTH}, p.K - 15) and education (see {SAMEEDUC}, p.I - 1)

POWERS OF SOCIAL WORKERS

{SOCWCHLD} {SOCWPOWR}

Question: Please tick one box for each statement to show how much you agree or disagree with it.

			1983		1984		1985		1986		1987		1989	
			%	No	%	No	%	No	%	No	%	No	%	No
Question No			217xvi				234a				A207a		A230a	
Column No			1113				2146				1546		2154	
(i) {SOCWCHLD}		Code												
Social workers should put the child's interests first even if it means taking a child away from its natural parents														
Agree strongly	1		31.9	513	-		38.0	571	-		28.4	354	23.2	295
Agree	2		33.2	534	-		45.4	682	-		50.1	623	45.5	579
Neither agree nor disagree	3		17.6	284	-		11.0	166	-		12.7	158	17.4	222
Disagree	4		10.9	176	-		3.3	49	-		6.5	80	11.5	147
Disagree strongly	5		5.3	85	-		0.8	13	-		1.3	17	1.4	17
(DK)	8		-		-		0.1	1	-		0.2	2	0.2	2
(NA)	9		1.1	8	-		1.4	21	-		0.8	9	0.9	11
Base: Self-completion questionnaire respondents				1610				1502				1243		1274

1983 - No (DK)

1983, 1984 - Agree strongly, code 5; just agree, code 4; just disagree, code 2; disagree strongly, code 1

POWERS OF SOCIAL WORKERS (Continued)

		1983		1984		1985		1986		1987		1989	
		%	No	%	No	%	No	%	No	%	No	%	No
Question No		217xvii				234b				A207b		A230b	
Column No		1114				2147				1547		2155	
(ii) {SOCWPOWR}	Code												

Social workers have too much power to interfere with people's lives

	Code	%	No	%	No	%	No	%	No	%	No	%	No
Agree strongly	1	20.4	329	-	-	7.7	115	-	-	7.8	97	9.0	115
Agree	2	27.0	435	-	-	23.4	351	-	-	23.7	295	27.2	346
Neither agree nor disagree	3	32.2	519	-	-	40.4	607	-	-	39.3	489	34.5	440
Disagree	4	13.6	219	-	-	24.9	374	-	-	25.8	321	25.8	329
Disagree strongly	5	5.5	88	-	-	2.0	31	-	-	2.7	33	2.6	33
(DK)	8	-		-	-	0.1	2	-	-	0.1	1	0.1	1
(NA)	9	1.2	20	-	-	1.5	22	-	-	0.6	8	0.8	10
Base: Self-completion questionnaire respondents			1610				1502				1243		1274

1983 - No (DK)
1983, 1984 - Agree strongly, code 5; just agree, code 4; just disagree, code 2; disagree strongly, code 1

IMAGES OF THE WELFARE STATE

{WELFRESP} {WELFSTIG} {WELFHELP}

Question: Please tick one box for each statement to show how much you agree or disagree with it.

		1983		1984		1985		1986		1987		1989	
		%	No	%	No	%	No	%	No	%	No	%	No
Question No		217xviii		220viii		234c		B232vi		A207c		A230c	
Column No		1115		1648		2148		2213		1548		2156	
(i) {WELFRESP}	Code												

The welfare state makes people nowadays less willing to look after themselves

	Code	%	No	%	No	%	No	%	No	%	No	%	No
Agree strongly	1	23.7	382	23.1	352	11.0	165	11.6	152	12.0	149	8.6	110
Agree	2	28.6	460	28.2	429	32.5	488	38.1	501	40.3	501	30.2	385
Neither agree nor disagree	3	20.9	336	15.9	243	23.3	351	19.6	258	18.6	231	23.2	295
Disagree	4	16.7	269	19.3	293	27.5	413	24.7	326	24.1	300	31.7	404
Disagree strongly	5	9.1	147	12.3	188	4.2	64	5.1	67	4.4	55	5.4	69
(DK)	8	-		0.1	2	0.1	1	0.2	3	-		-	
(NA)	9	1.0	17	1.0	16	1.3	20	0.7	9	0.6	8	0.8	11
Base: Self-completion questionnaire respondents			1610		1522		1502		1315		1243		1274

1983, 1984 - Agree strongly, code 5; just agree, code 4; just disagree, code 2; disagree strongly, code 1.

IMAGES OF THE WELFARE STATE (Continued)

		1983		1984		1985		1986		1987		1989	
		%	No	%	No	%	No	%	No	%	No	%	No
Question No		217xix		220ix		234d		B232vii		A207d		A230d	
Column No	Code	1116		1649		2149		2214		1549		2157	

(ii) {WELFSTIG}
People receiving social security are made to feel like second class citizens

	Code	1983 %	No	1984 %	No	1985 %	No	1986 %	No	1987 %	No	1989 %	No
Agree strongly	1	22.1	356	25.6	389	17.1	257	14.4	189	15.1	188	13.7	175
Agree	2	26.2	422	26.9	409	32.5	487	38.3	504	34.5	428	39.3	500
Neither agree nor disagree	3	20.7	334	19.4	296	23.1	348	21.8	287	20.7	257	22.5	286
Disagree	4	18.6	300	16.8	256	23.5	353	21.8	287	26.0	323	21.7	277
Disagree strongly	5	11.1	178	10.1	153	2.3	35	2.9	38	3.0	37	2.1	27
(DK)	8	-	.	0.3	4	0.1	1	0.2	2	0.2	2	0.0	1
(NA)	9	1.3	21	1.0	15	1.4	21	0.7	9	0.6	8	0.7	9
Base: Self-completion questionnaire respondents			1610		1522		1502		1315		1243		1274

		217xx		220x		234e				A207e		A230e	
Question No													
Column No		1117		1650		2150				1550		2158	

(iii) {WELFHELP}
The welfare state encourages people to stop helping each other

	Code	1983 %	No	1984 %	No	1985 %	No	1986 %	No	1987 %	No	1989 %	No
Agree strongly	1	13.5	217	14.0	213	5.6	84	-	-	7.4	92	4.6	58
Agree	2	23.5	378	23.8	362	26.9	404	-	-	32.5	404	27.1	345
Neither agree nor disagree	3	28.2	454	22.3	339	29.6	444	-	-	22.5	279	26.7	340
Disagree	4	23.2	373	25.5	387	32.4	487	-	-	32.5	404	35.4	451
Disagree strongly	5	10.1	162	13.1	199	3.5	53	-	-	4.1	51	5.3	68
(DK)	8	-	.	0.1	2	0.1	1	-	-	0.2	2	-	-
(NA)	9	1.6	26	1.3	20	1.9	29	-	-	0.9	11	1.0	12
Base: Self-completion questionnaire respondents			1610		1522		1502				1243		1274

1983 - No DK

1983, 1984 - Agree strongly, code 5; just agree, code 4; just disagree, code 2; disagree strongly, code 1

WELFARE BENEFITS RECEIVED WITHIN PAST FIVE YEARS

{BENEFT1} {BENEFT2} {BENEFT3} {BENEFT4} {BENEFT5} {BENEFT6} {BENEFT7} {BENEFT8} {BENEFT9} {BENEFT10} {BENEFT11} {BENEFT12} {BENEFT13} {BENEFT14}

Question: (Show card) **Have you or anyone in this household received any of the benefits on this card during the last** *five years?* [If yes] **Which ones? Any others?**

		1983		1984		1985		1986		1987		1989	
		%	No	%	No	%	No	%	No	%	No	%	No
	Question No							A117/B125		913		914	
	Column No							1739		1439		1665	
(i) {BENEFT1}	Code												
Child benefit (family allowance)													
Not received	0	-		-		-		53.2	1631	55.7	1541	55.6	1630
Received	1	-		-		-		46.8	1435	44.3	1225	44.4	1300
Base: All								3066		2766		2930	
	Question No							A117/B125		913		914	
	Column No							1740		1440		1666	
(ii) {BENEFT2}													
Maternity benefit or allowance													
Not received	0	-		-		-		89.4	2741	90.3	2497	90.1	2640
Received	2	-		-		-		10.6	325	9.7	269	9.9	290
Base: All								3066		2766		2930	
	Question No							A117/B125		913		914	
	Column No							1741		1441		1667	
(iii) {BENEFT3}													
One-parent benefit													
Not received	0	-		-		-		97.1	2976	96.5	2669	96.2	2819
Received	3	-		-		-		2.9	90	3.5	96	3.8	112
Base: All								3066		2766		2930	
	Question No							A117/B125		913		914	
	Column No							1742		1442		1668	
(iv) {BENEFT4}													
Family credit (family income supplement)													
Not received	0	-		-		-		97.8	2999	97.9	2709	97.1	2846
Received	4	-		-		-		2.2	67	2.1	57	2.9	85
Base: All								3066		2766		2930	

1986, 1987 - {BENEFT4} Family Income Supplement

WELFARE BENEFITS RECEIVED WITHIN PAST FIVE YEARS (Continued)

			1983		1984		1985		1986		1987		1989	
			%	No	%	No	%	No	%	No	%	No	%	No
	Question No								A117/B125		913		914	
	Column No								1743		1443		1669	
(v) {BENEFT5}		Code												
State retirement or widow's pension														
Not received	0		-	-	-	-	-	-	76.9	2358	76.1	2106	75.1	2202
Received	5		-	-	-	-	-	-	23.1	708	23.9	660	24.9	729
Base: All										3066		2766		2930

			1983		1984		1985		1986		1987		1989	
	Question No								A117/B125		913		914	
	Column No								1744		1444		1670	
(vi) {BENEFT6}														
State supplementary pension														
Not received	0		-	-	-	-	-	-	96.8	2968	97.1	2686	98.3	2880
Received	6		-	-	-	-	-	-	3.2	98	2.9	79	1.7	50
Base: All										3066		2766		2930

			1983		1984		1985		1986		1987		1989	
	Question No								A117/B125		913		914	
	Column No								1745		1445		1671	
(vii) {BENEFT7}														
Invalidity or disabled pension or benefit														
Not received	0		-	-	-	-	-	-	93.8	2876	93.2	2578	92.7	2716
Received	1		-	-	-	-	-	-	6.2	189	6.8	187	7.3	214
Base: All										3066		2766		2930

			1983		1984		1985		1986		1987		1989	
	Question No								A117/B125		913		914	
	Column No								1746		1446		1672	
(viii) {BENEFT8}														
Attendance/Invalid care/Mobility allowance														
Not received	0		-	-	-	-	-	-	97.0	2973	96.9	2680	96.2	2818
Received	2		-	-	-	-	-	-	3.0	93	3.1	85	3.8	113
Base: All										3066		2766		2930

1986 - {BENEFT6} Supplementary pension

WELFARE BENEFITS RECEIVED WITHIN PAST FIVE YEARS (Continued)

		1983		1984		1985		1986		1987		1989	
		%	No	%	No	%	No	%	No	%	No	%	No
	Question No							A117/B125		913		914	
	Column No							1747		1447		1673	
(ix) {BENEFT9}	Code												
State sickness or injury benefit													
Not received	0	-		-		-		86.5	2651	88.0	2433	90.3	2645
Received	3	-		-		-		13.5	415	12.0	333	9.7	285
Base: All									3066		2766		2930

		1983		1984		1985		1986		1987		1989	
	Question No							A117/B125		913		914	
	Column No							1748		1448		1674	
(x) {BENEFT10}													
Unemployment benefit													
Not received	0	-		-		-		79.4	2434	79.1	2188	83.1	2436
Received	4	-		-		-		20.6	631	20.9	578	16.9	495
Base: All									3066		2766		2930

		1983		1984		1985		1986		1987		1989	
	Question No							A117/B125		913		914	
	Column No							1749		1449		1675	
(xi) {BENEFT11}													
Income support (supplementary benefit)													
Not received	0	-		-		-		85.3	2615	83.7	2314	89.3	2617
Received	5	-		-		-		14.7	451	16.3	452	10.7	314
Base: All									3066		2766		2930

		1983		1984		1985		1986		1987		1989	
	Question No							A117/B125		913		914	
	Column No							1750		1450		1676	
(xii) {BENEFT12}													
Housing benefit/rate or rent rebate or allowance													
Not received	0	-		-		-		81.1	2488	81.9	2265	86.5	2535
Received	6	-		-		-		18.9	578	18.1	501	13.5	395
Base: All									3066		2766		2930

1986, 1987 - {BENEFT9} Sickness or injury benefit; {BENEFT11} Supplementary benefit
1986,1987,1989 - {BENEFT12} 'Housing benefit' not on show card

WELFARE BENEFITS RECEIVED WITHIN PAST FIVE YEARS (Continued)

		1983		1984		1985		1986		1987		1989	
		%	No	%	No	%	No	%	No	%	No	%	No
Question No								A117/B125		913		914	
Column No								1751		1451		1677	
(xiii) {BENEFT13}	Code												
Other state benefit(s) volunteered													
Not received	0	-		-		-		99.6	3053	99.8	2761	99.9	2928
Received	7	-		-		-		0.4	13	0.2	5	0.1	2
Base: All									3066		2766		2930
Question No								A117/B125		913		914	
Column No								1752		1452		1678	
(xiv) {BENEFT14}													
[Summary] During past five years													
One or more benefits received	0	-		-		-		84.6	2594	84.1	2326	82.5	2417
No benefits received	1	-		-		-		15.1	464	15.8	436	17.4	509
(DK)	8	-		-		-		0.1	3	0.0	1	-	
(NA)	9	-		-		-		0.1	4	0.1	3	0.2	5
Base: All									3066		2766		2930

1986 - {BENEFT14} No benefits received, code 0; Superannuation (but not clear whether private or state), code 1 (n = 1), One or more benefits received, code 2. 'Benefits' volunteered that were not state benefits were not coded.

MAINTENANCE PAYMENTS TO FORMER WIVES WITHOUT CHILDREN

{PAYWIFE1} {PAYWIFE2} {PAYWIFE3}

Question: Now I would like to ask you about the obligations that people who have been married have if they divorce.

		1983		1984		1985		1986		1987		1989	
		%	No	%	No	%	No	%	No	%	No	%	No
Question No				79a						A80a			
Column No				561						708			

(i) {PAYWIFE1}

Consider a married couple, both aged about 45, with no children at home. They are both working at the time of the divorce. In your opinion should the man make maintenance payments to support the wife?

	Code	%	No	%	No	%	No	%	No	%	No	%	No
Yes	1	-	-	13.5	222	-	-	-	-	14.3	198	-	-
No	2	-	-	79.4	1307	-	-	-	-	80.7	1123	-	-
(Depends who was guilty party)	3	-	-	1.9	32	-	-	-	-	1.7	24	-	-
(Depends on circumstances)	4	-	-	1.6	26	-	-	-	-	1.1	16	-	-
(Depends on earnings/income/wealth)	5	-	-	1.1	17	-	-	-	-	0.9	12	-	-
(Other answer)	7	-	-	1.0	17	-	-	-	-	0.3	4	-	-
(DK)	8	-	-	1.0	16	-	-	-	-	0.9	12	-	-
(NA)	9	-	-	0.5	9	-	-	-	-	0.1	2	-	-

Base: All

1645   1391

		1983		1984		1985		1986		1987		1989	
Question No				79b						A80b			
Column No				562						709			

(ii) {PAYWIFE2}

Consider a similar couple, also aged about 45, with no children at home. They are both working at the time of the divorce, but the woman's earnings are much lower than the man's. In your opinion should the man make maintenance payments to support the wife?

	Code	%	No	%	No	%	No	%	No	%	No	%	No
Yes	1	-	-	44.2	727	-	-	-	-	48.3	671	-	-
No	2	-	-	44.2	728	-	-	-	-	43.5	604	-	-
(Depends who was guilty party)	3	-	-	3.2	53	-	-	-	-	3.1	42	-	-
(Depends on circumstances)	4	-	-	3.1	51	-	-	-	-	2.1	29	-	-
(Depends on earnings/income/wealth)	5	-	-	1.3	21	-	-	-	-	1.4	19	-	-
(Other answer)	7	-	-	2.2	36	-	-	-	-	0.1	2	-	-
(DK)	8	-	-	1.3	21	-	-	-	-	1.6	22	-	-
(NA)	9	-	-	0.5	9	-	-	-	-	0.0	1	-	-

Base: All

1645   1391

MAINTENANCE PAYMENTS TO FORMER WIVES WITHOUT CHILDREN (Continued)

			1983		1984		1985		1986		1987		1989	
			%	No	%	No	%	No	%	No	%	No	%	No
Question No					79c						A80c			
Column No					563						710			

(iii) *{PAYWIFE3}*

Finally, consider another couple, also aged about 45 with no children at home. The man is working at the time of the divorce, but the woman has never worked in a paid job outside the home. In your opinion should the man make maintenance payments to support the wife?

	Code	1983 %	No	1984 %	No	1985 %	No	1986 %	No	1987 %	No	1989 %	No
Yes	1	-	.	72.1	1187	-	.	-	.	77.1	1072	-	.
No	2	-	.	17.5	287	-	.	-	.	17.4	242	-	.
(Depends on who was guilty party)	3	-	.	3.4	56	-	.	-	.	2.5	35	-	.
(Depends on circumstances)	4	-	.	2.7	45	-	.	-	.	1.5	21	-	.
(Depends on earnings/income/wealth)	5	-	.	0.4	7	-	.	-	.	0.5	7	-	.
(Other answer)	7	-	.	2.6	42	-	.	-	.	-	.	-	.
(DK)	8	-	.	0.7	12	-	.	-	.	1.1	15	-	.
(NA)	9	-	.	0.6	10	-	.	-	.	-	.	-	.

Base: All   1645   1391

LEVEL OF STATE BENEFITS

1986   Q.B227a-c   {BENEFIT1}-{BENEFIT3} Column Nos 2143-45
Please say for each item whether you think its level is too high, too low or about right.
(Please tick one box for each)

		Too high 1		Too low 2		About right 3		(DK) 8		(NA) 9	
	Code	%	No	%	No	%	No	%	No	%	No
a) {BENEFIT1} Column No 2143 **State pensions**		0.5	6	77.7	1022	21.1	278	0.1	1	0.7	9
b) {BENEFIT2} Column No 2144 **Unemployment benefit**		10.0	132	48.7	641	39.4	518	0.4	6	1.5	20
c) {BENEFIT3} Column No 2145 **Child benefit**		13.5	177	38.8	511	46.3	609	0.3	4	1.1	14

Base : Self-completion respondents (n = 1315)

WHO BENEFITS FROM 'NEW TECHNOLOGY'

1984   Q.220(iii)   {TECHRICH} Column No 1643
[Finally,] please tick one box ... to show how much you agree or disagree with [this statement].

New technology will benefit the rich more than the poor in Britain.

	Code	%	No
Disagree strongly	1	7.1	108
Just disagree	2	13.3	202
Neither agree nor disagree	3	26.8	408
Just agree	4	23.5	359
Agree strongly	5	27.8	423
(DK)	8	0.4	7
(NA)	9	1.1	16
Base : Self-completion respondents			1522

NB This item was part of a battery of eleven questions, all of which except this one, {BRITPOWR} and {EQUALPAY} were repeated subsequently. The original question wording invited respondents to 'tick one box for each statement below'. The variable {NEWTECH} listed in the SPSS files for 1985 and 1987 relates to a different question (see p. G.1-10), so the variable name for this question has been changed from {NEWTECH} to {TECHRICH}

PERCEIVED EXISTENCE OF POVERTY

1983   Q.78a   {POVERTY} Column No 572
Do you think there is such a thing as *real poverty* in Britain today?

	Code	%	No
Yes	1	54.7	940
No	2	44.1	758
(NA)	9	1.2	21
Base : All			1719

DEFINITION OF POVERTY - 2

1983   Q.78b   *{POVVIEW}* Column No 573
(Show card) There are different views about what real poverty is nowadays. Please look at this card
and tell me which of the statements, if either, comes closest to your own view?

	Code	%	No
Poverty in Britain today is mainly about the shortage of absolute necessities such as food and clothing	1	26.4	454
People in Britain today have enough to eat and wear; the main hardship is in not being able to keep up with the living standards that most people have	2	67.5	1160
Neither of these	3	4.3	75
(NA)	9	1.8	31
Base : All			1719

MAINTENANCE PAYMENTS TO CHILDREN AND FORMER WIVES

1983   Q.84a-c   *{CHSUP}{CHWSUP}{NCHWSUP}{NMARWSUP}* Column Nos 627-30
Now I would like to ask you about the obligations that people who have been married or have lived together
have towards each other if they separate.

a) Consider a married couple aged about 35, both working at the time of the divorce. They have children at
primary school, who remain with the wife.

i) *{CHSUP}* Column No 627
In your opinion, should the man make maintenance payments to support the children?

	Code	%	No
Yes	1	91.6	1574
No	2	3.7	63
(Depends who was guilty party)	3	0.7	13
(Depends on circumstances)	4	1.8	30
(Depends on earnings/income/wealth)	5	0.5	9
(Other answer)	7	0.7	12
(DK)	8	0.6	10
(NA)	9	0.4	7
Base : All			1719

ii) *{CHWSUP}* Column No 628
In your opinion, should the man make maintenance payments to support the wife?

	Code	%	No
Yes	1	26.1	448
No	2	64.3	1106
(Depends who was guilty party)	3	2.7	46
(Depends on circumstances)	4	2.6	45
Depends on earnings/income/wealth)	5	1.5	26
(Other answer)	7	1.7	30
(DK)	8	0.7	12
(NA)	9	0.3	6
Base : All			1719

MAINTENANCE PAYMENTS TO CHILDREN AND FORMER WIVES (continued)

b) *{NCHWSUP}* Column No 629
Consider another couple also aged 35, both working at the time of the divorce. They have been married for
10 years but have *no children.* In your opinion, should the man make maintenance payments to support the wife?

	Code	%	No
Yes	1	9.5	164
No	2	85.9	1477
(Depends who was guilty party)	3	1.4	24
(Depends on circumstances)	4	1.1	18
(Depends on earnings/income/wealth)	5	0.6	10
(Other answer)	7	0.8	14
(DK)	8	0.4	7
(NA)	9	0.3	5
Base : All			1719

c) *{NMARWSUP}* Column No 630
Finally, consider another couple aged 35, both working. They are *un*married and have no children. They separate
after living together for 10 years. In your opinion, should the man make maintenance payments to support the woman?

	Code	%	No
Yes	1	4.5	77
No	2	93.4	1606
(Depends who was guilty party)	3	0.3	5
(Depends on circumstances)	4	0.3	5
(Depends on earnings/income/wealth)	5	0.3	6
(Other answer)	7	0.5	8
(DK)	8	0.4	7
(NA)	9	0.3	5
Base : All			1719

K Health services

Table titles and cross references

GENERAL SATISFACTION WITH THE NHS

{NHSSAT}

Question: (Show card) All in all, how satisfied or dissatisfied would you say you are with the way in which the National Health Service runs nowadays? Choose a phrase from this card.

		1983		1984		1985		1986		1987		1989	
		%	No	%	No	%	No	%	No	%	No	%	No
Question No		56		63				58		62		72	
Column No		508		518				541		632		751	
	Code												
Very satisfied	1	10.8	187	11.1	183	-	-	6.4	196	6.5	181	6.4	189
Quite satisfied	2	43.7	751	40.0	658	-	-	34.0	1043	33.7	931	30.2	886
Neither satisfied nor dissatisfied	3	19.6	336	18.8	310	-	-	19.3	591	20.1	557	17.6	515
Quite dissatisfied	4	18.3	314	19.1	314	-	-	23.3	715	24.1	665	24.5	719
Very dissatisfied	5	7.3	126	10.8	177	-	-	16.5	505	15.5	428	21.0	616
(DK)	8	-	-	-	-	-	-	0.4	12	0.1	3	0.1	2
(NA)	9	0.3	5	0.3	4	-	-	0.1	4	0.0	1	0.1	3
Base: All			1719		1645				3066		2766		2930

1983 - Very satisfied, code 5; Quite satisfied, code 4; Quite dissatisfied, code 2; Very dissatisfied, code 1
1983, 1984 - No (DK)

SATISFACTION WITH PARTICULAR ASPECTS OF THE NHS

{GPSAT} {DENTSAT} {HVSAT} {DNSAT} {INPATSAT} {OUTPASAT}

Question: (Show card) **From your own experience, or from what you have heard, please say how satisfied or dissatisfied you are with the way in which each of these parts of the National Health Service runs nowadays.**

		1983		1984		1985		1986		1987		1989	
		%	No	%	No	%	No	%	No	%	No	%	No
Question No		57						59i		63i		73i	
Column No		509						542		633		752	

(i) {GPSAT}
First, local doctors/GPs

	Code	1983 %	No	1986 %	No	1987 %	No	1989 %	No
Very satisfied	1	32.7	562	26.7	818	27.2	752	30.0	879
Quite satisfied	2	47.3	813	50.7	1553	52.1	1440	49.9	1462
Neither satisfied nor dissatisfied	3	6.9	118	8.3	253	7.7	212	7.8	227
Quite dissatisfied	4	9.4	161	9.6	294	9.1	251	8.2	240
Very dissatisfied	5	3.5	60	4.4	135	3.5	97	3.8	113
(DK)	8	0.1	1	0.3	9	0.4	11	0.3	7
(NA)	9	0.2	3	0.1	3	0.1	2	0.1	2
Base: All			1719		3066		2766		2930

		1983		1986		1987		1989	
Question No		57		59ii		63ii		73ii	
Column No		510		543		634		753	

(ii) {DENTSAT}
National Health Service dentists

	Code	1983 %	No	1986 %	No	1987 %	No	1989 %	No
Very satisfied	1	23.7	407	19.1	585	19.3	535	19.7	577
Quite satisfied	2	49.3	847	54.9	1684	54.8	1515	50.5	1479
Neither satisfied nor dissatisfied	3	15.3	263	13.7	420	13.8	380	15.7	459
Quite dissatisfied	4	6.7	116	6.5	200	6.4	176	7.9	231
Very dissatisfied	5	2.9	50	3.0	92	2.9	79	3.1	91
(DK)	8	1.7	30	2.7	82	2.8	77	3.0	88
(NA)	9	0.3	6	0.1	4	0.1	3	0.2	6
Base: All			1719		3066		2766		2930

1983 - Very satisfied, code 5; Quite satisfied, code 4; Quite dissatisfied, code 2; Very dissatisfied, code 1

SATISFACTION WITH PARTICULAR ASPECTS OF THE NHS (Continued)

			1983		1984		1985		1986		1987		1989	
			%	No	%	No	%	No	%	No	%	No	%	No
	Question No		57						59iii		63iii		73iii	
	Column No		511						544		635		754	
(iii) {HVSAT}		Code												
Health visitors														
Very satisfied		1	14.1	242	-	.	-	.	12.3	379	11.4	316	12.1	355
Quite satisfied		2	33.5	576	-	.	-	.	36.6	1122	35.0	967	33.4	978
Neither satisfied nor dissatisfied		3	38.6	664	-	.	-	.	28.8	883	29.8	824	27.9	819
Quite dissatisfied		4	4.3	74	-	.	-	.	6.3	193	5.8	161	6.2	180
Very dissatisfied		5	2.0	35	-	.	-	.	2.2	68	2.6	72	2.2	64
(DK)		8	6.4	110	-	.	-	.	13.5	414	15.2	420	17.9	524
(NA)		9	1.1	18	-	.	-	.	0.3	8	0.2	5	0.3	10
Base: All				1719						3066		2766		2930

			1983		1984		1985		1986		1987		1989	
	Question No		57						59iv		63iv		73iv	
	Column No		512						545		636		755	
(iv) {DNSAT}														
District nurses														
Very satisfied		1	22.2	381	-	.	-	.	18.6	571	17.1	473	16.8	492
Quite satisfied		2	37.8	650	-	.	-	.	40.5	1242	38.2	1055	36.6	1074
Neither satisfied nor dissatisfied		3	30.9	532	-	.	-	.	25.3	777	26.9	744	26.2	768
Quite dissatisfied		4	1.3	21	-	.	-	.	2.5	77	2.6	72	3.1	90
Very dissatisfied		5	0.9	16	-	.	-	.	0.6	19	0.7	19	1.1	31
(DK)		8	6.0	102	-	.	-	.	12.3	377	14.3	396	15.8	464
(NA)		9	0.9	16	-	.	-	.	0.1	3	0.2	6	0.4	12
Base: All				1719						3066		2766		2930

1983 - Very satisfied, code 5; Quite satisfied code 4; Quite dissatisfied, code 2; Very dissatisfied, code 1

SATISFACTION WITH PARTICULAR ASPECTS OF THE NHS (Continued)

	Code	1983 %	No	1984 %	No	1985 %	No	1986 %	No	1987 %	No	1989 %	No
Question No		57						59v		63v		73v	
Column No		513						546		637		756	

(v) {INPATSAT}
Being in hospital as an in-patient

	Code	1983 %	No	1984 %	No	1985 %	No	1986 %	No	1987 %	No	1989 %	No
Very satisfied	1	34.0	584	-	-	-	-	24.9	765	24.0	663	23.9	700
Quite satisfied	2	39.7	682	-	-	-	-	42.3	1295	43.2	1196	41.5	1215
Neither satisfied nor dissatisfied	3	17.4	299	-	-	-	-	15.2	466	15.5	428	13.8	405
Quite dissatisfied	4	5.4	94	-	-	-	-	10.1	309	9.7	268	11.1	326
Very dissatisfied	5	1.2	21	-	-	-	-	3.2	99	3.6	98	4.3	127
(DK)	8	1.9	32	-	-	-	-	4.3	130	3.9	107	5.2	152
(NA)	9	0.4	7	-	-	-	-	0.1	2	0.2	5	0.1	4
Base: All			1719						3066		2766		2930

		1983						1986		1987		1989	
Question No		57						59vi		63vi		73vi	
Column No		514						547		638		757	

(vi) {OUTPASAT}
Attending hospital as an out-patient

	Code	1983 %	No	1984 %	No	1985 %	No	1986 %	No	1987 %	No	1989 %	No
Very satisfied	1	21.1	363	-	-	-	-	13.9	426	13.8	381	15.3	448
Quite satisfied	2	39.6	681	-	-	-	-	40.8	1251	39.8	1101	37.2	1089
Neither satisfied nor dissatisfied	3	16.1	276	-	-	-	-	14.0	430	14.6	404	14.1	414
Quite dissatisfied	4	15.3	263	-	-	-	-	18.7	572	18.7	518	18.6	544
Very dissatisfied	5	5.9	102	-	-	-	-	10.0	306	10.0	277	11.0	321
(DK)	8	1.6	28	-	-	-	-	2.6	80	3.0	82	3.8	111
(NA)	9	0.3	6	-	-	-	-	0.1	3	0.1	2	0.1	3
Base: All			1719						3066		2766		2930

1983 - Very satisfied, code 5; Quite satisfied, code 4; Quite dissatisfied, code 2; Very dissatisfied, code 1

PRIVATE HEALTH INSURANCE: WHETHER COVERED AND WHO PAYS

{PRIVMED}

Question: Are you covered by a private health insurance scheme, that is an insurance scheme that allows you to get private medical treatment?

			1983		1984		1985		1986		1987		1989	
			%	No	%	No	%	No	%	No	%	No	%	No
	Question No		58a		64a				60a		64a		74a	
	Column No		515		519				548		639		758	
(i) {PRIVMED}		Code												
	Yes	1	10.8	185	10.9	179	-	-	13.9	425	14.3	394	15.0	438
	No	2	89.1	1532	88.8	1460	-	-	86.0	2638	85.6	2367	84.9	2489
	(DK)	8	-	-	0.1	2	-	-	0.1	2	0.1	2	0.1	2
	(NA)	9	0.1	2	0.3	4	-	-	0.0	1	0.1	3	0.0	1
Base: All				1719		1645				3066		2766		2930

			1983		1984		1985		1986		1987		1989	
	Question No		58b		64b				60b		64b		74b	
	Column No		516		521				549		640		759	

(ii) {PRIVPAID}

[If covered by private health insurance] **Does your employer *(your husband's / wife's employer)* pay the majority of the cost of membership of this scheme?**

			1983		1984		1985		1986		1987		1989	
[Not asked: not covered by private health insurance]		0	89.1	1532	88.8	1460	-	-	86.1	2638	85.6	2367	84.9	2489
	Yes	1	5.7	99	5.5	91	-	-	7.2	222	7.7	214	8.3	243
	No	2	4.4	76	4.9	80	-	-	6.0	184	6.0	165	6.1	178
	(DK)	8	0.4	7	0.4	6	-	-	0.3	11	0.4	10	0.3	10
	(NA)	9	0.3	6	0.5	8	-	-	0.3	11	0.3	10	0.4	11
Base: All				1719		1645				3066		2766		2930

1983 - {PRIVMED} No (DK); {PRIVPAID} (DK), code 3

PRIVATE MEDICAL TREATMENT IN HOSPITALS - 1

{PRMEDNHS}

Question: (i) Do you think that the existence of private medical treatment in National Health Service hospitals is a good or bad thing for the National Health Service, or doesn't it make any difference to the NHS?

		1983		1984		1985		1986		1987		1989	
		%	No	%	No	%	No	%	No	%	No	%	No
Question No				65a				61a		65a		75a	
Column No				522				550		641		760	
	Code												
Good thing	1	-	-	23.1	381	-	-	26.7	817	23.1	640	24.0	704
Bad thing	2	-	-	42.0	691	-	-	39.8	1219	44.0	1216	47.0	1378
No difference	3	-	-	29.5	486	-	-	28.2	866	28.9	800	24.3	712
(DK)	8	-	-	5.0	83	-	-	5.1	156	3.9	109	4.5	132
(NA)	9	-	-	0.3	5	-	-	0.3	8	0.0	1	0.1	4
Base: All					1645				3066		2766		2930

				1984				1986		1987		1989	
Question No				65b				61b		65b		75b	
Column No				523				551		642		761	

(ii) {PRMEDPRV}

And do you think the existence of private medical treatment in *private* hospitals is a good thing or a bad thing for the *National Health Service, or doesn't it make any difference to the NHS?*

		%	No	%	No	%	No	%	No	%	No	%	No
Good thing	1	-	-	35.0	577	-	-	37.1	1136	39.1	1081	38.5	1128
Bad thing	2	-	-	19.2	316	-	-	18.5	567	19.7	543	20.9	614
No difference	3	-	-	41.7	686	-	-	40.0	1225	36.9	1021	36.1	1058
(DK)	8	-	-	3.8	62	-	-	4.3	133	4.0	112	4.2	122
(NA)	9	-	-	0.3	4	-	-	0.1	4	0.3	8	0.3	9
Base: All					1645				3066		2766		2930

1984 - {PRMEDNHS}: Q preceded by: 'Now thinking of private medical treatment in hospitals.'

PRIVATE MEDICAL TREATMENT IN HOSPITALS - 2

{PRMEDABO}

Question: (Show card) **Which of the views on this card comes** *closest* **to your own views about private medical treatment in hospitals?**

		1983		1984		1985		1986		1987		1989	
		%	No	%	No	%	No	%	No	%	No	%	No
Question No				65c				62		66		76	
Column No				524				552		643		762	
	Code												
Private medical treatment in *all* hospitals should be abolished	1	-	-	9.3	153	-	-	10.9	335	10.0	276	11.8	345
Private medical treatment should be allowed in private hospitals, but *not* in National Health Service hospitals	2	-	-	48.2	794	-	-	46.3	1419	51.1	1412	50.2	1472
Private medical treatment should be allowed in *both* private and National Health Service hospitals	3	-	-	39.0	642	-	-	40.8	1251	36.6	1012	35.3	1034
(DK)	8	-	-	3.2	52	-	-	1.8	56	2.3	63	2.5	72
(NA)	9	-	-	0.3	4	-	-	0.2	5	0.1	3	0.3	7
Base: All					1645				3066		2766		2930

1984 - Q wording: '... comes closest to your own about ...'

NHS GPs AND DENTISTS TAKING ON PRIVATE PATIENTS

{NHSGP} {NHSDENT}

Question: **Do you think that National Health Service GPs should or should not be free to take on** *private patients*?

		1983		1984		1985		1986		1987		1989	
		%	No	%	No	%	No	%	No	%	No	%	No
Question No				66a				63a		67a		77a	
Column No				525				553		644		763	
(i) {NHSGP}	Code												
Should	1	-	-	59.4	978	-	-	57.3	1757	54.1	1495	54.3	1591
Should not	2	-	-	35.5	583	-	-	38.3	1176	41.3	1141	41.3	1212
(DK)	8	-	-	4.8	78	-	-	4.0	123	4.4	122	4.0	118
(NA)	9	-	-	0.3	5	-	-	0.3	10	0.3	7	0.3	10
Base: All					1645				3066		2766		2930

NHS GPs AND DENTISTS TAKING ON PRIVATE PATIENTS (Continued)

		1983		1984		1985		1986		1987		1989	
		%	No	%	No	%	No	%	No	%	No	%	No
Question No				66b				63b		67b		77b	
Column No				526				554		645		764	

(ii) {NHSDENT}

And do you think that National Health Service dentists should or should not be free to give *private treatment*?

	Code	1983 %	No	1984 %	No	1985 %	No	1986 %	No	1987 %	No	1989 %	No
Should	1	-	-	64.1	1054	-	-	62.0	1900	60.3	1669	59.1	1732
Should not	2	-	-	31.1	511	-	-	33.1	1016	34.7	960	36.2	1061
(DK)	8	-	-	4.5	75	-	-	4.6	140	4.7	130	4.2	124
(NA)	9	-	-	0.3	5	-	-	0.3	10	0.3	7	0.4	13
Base: All					1645				3066		2766		2930

1984,1986,1987,1989 - Q introduced by : 'Now thinking of GPs and dentists.'

'TWO-TIER' NHS

{NHSLIMIT}

Question: It has been suggested that the National Health Service should be available *only to those with lower incomes*. This would mean that contributions and taxes could be lower and most people would then take out medical insurance or pay for health care. Do you support or oppose this idea?

		1983		1984		1985		1986		1987		1989	
		%	No	%	No	%	No	%	No	%	No	%	No
Question No		60		67				64		68		78	
Column No		535		527				555		646		765	
	Code												
Support	1	29.2	502	22.9	377	-	-	26.9	823	25.7	711	21.6	633
Oppose	2	63.8	1097	69.5	1144	-	-	67.3	2062	68.2	1886	73.9	2164
(DK)	8	6.8	117	7.2	119	-	-	5.8	177	5.2	145	4.3	127
(NA)	9	0.2	3	0.3	5	-	-	0.1	3	0.9	24	0.2	7
Base: All		1719		1645				3066		2766		2930	

1983 - (DK), code 3

GROUPS AT RISK FROM AIDS

{AIDSRSK1} {AIDSRSK2} {AIDSRSK3} {AIDSRSK4} {AIDSRSK5} {AIDSRSK6} {AIDSRSK7} {AIDSRSK8}

Question: Now I'd like to ask you about the disease called AIDS.
I'm going to read out a list of different kinds of people. (Show card) **Please choose a phrase from this card to tell me how much at risk you think each of these groups is from AIDS ... (read out) ...**

		1983		1984		1985		1986		1987		1989	
		%	No	%	No	%	No	%	No	%	No	%	No
Question No										A107a		A103a	
Column No										846		1361	
(i) {AIDSRSK1}	Code												
People who have sex with many different partners of the opposite sex													
Greatly at risk	1	-	.	-	.	-	.	-	.	70.9	986	69.3	1018
Quite a lot at risk	2	-	.	-	.	-	.	-	.	24.4	339	26.7	392
Not very much at risk	3	-	.	-	.	-	.	-	.	3.4	48	2.4	35
Not at all at risk	4	-	.	-	.	-	.	-	.	0.2	3	0.1	2
(DK)	8	-	.	-	.	-	.	-	.	0.8	11	1.1	16
(NA)	9	-	.	-	.	-	.	-	.	0.3	4	0.5	7
Base: All											1391		1469

		1983		1984		1985		1986		1987		1989	
Question No										A107b		A103b	
Column No										847		1362	
(ii) {AIDSRSK2}													
Married couples who have sex only with each other													
Greatly at risk	1	-	.	-	.	-	.	-	.	0.1	1	0.2	3
Quite a lot at risk	2	-	.	-	.	-	.	-	.	0.1	1	0.4	6
Not very much at risk	3	-	.	-	.	-	.	-	.	15.5	216	17.2	252
Not at all at risk	4	-	.	-	.	-	.	-	.	83.3	1159	81.0	1189
(DK)	8	-	.	-	.	-	.	-	.	0.7	10	0.7	11
(NA)	9	-	.	-	.	-	.	-	.	0.3	4	0.5	8
Base: All											1391		1469

1987 - Q reads: 'I'm going to read out a list of different kinds of people in Britain'

GROUPS AT RISK FROM AIDS (Continued)

		1983		1984		1985		1986		1987		1989	
		%	No	%	No	%	No	%	No	%	No	%	No
Question No										A107c		A103c	
Column No										848		1363	
(iii) {AIDSRSK3}	Code												

Married couples who occasionally have sex with someone other than their regular partner

		1983		1984		1985		1986		1987		1989	
Greatly at risk	1	-	.	-	.	-	.	-	.	12.3	171	10.1	149
Quite a lot at risk	2	-	.	-	.	-	.	-	.	52.3	728	50.3	738
Not very much at risk	3	-	.	-	.	-	.	-	.	32.7	455	35.6	523
Not at all at risk	4	-	.	-	.	-	.	-	.	1.2	16	1.5	23
(DK)	8	-	.	-	.	-	.	-	.	1.1	15	1.7	26
(NA)	9	-	.	-	.	-	.	-	.	0.4	6	0.7	11
Base: All											1391		1469

							1987		1989	
Question No							A107d		A103d	
Column No							849		1364	

(iv) {AIDSRSK4}

People who have had a blood transfusion

		1983		1984		1985		1986		1987		1989	
Greatly at risk	1	-	.	-	.	-	.	-	.	11.5	160	10.0	147
Quite a lot at risk	2	-	.	-	.	-	.	-	.	23.8	330	27.1	398
Not very much at risk	3	-	.	-	.	-	.	-	.	48.6	675	47.2	693
Not at all at risk	4	-	.	-	.	-	.	-	.	13.5	188	13.0	190
(DK)	8	-	.	-	.	-	.	-	.	2.3	33	2.3	33
(NA)	9	-	.	-	.	-	.	-	.	.3	5	0.5	8
Base: All											1391		1469

GROUPS AT RISK FROM AIDS (Continued)

		1983		1984		1985		1986		1987		1989	
		%	No	%	No	%	No	%	No	%	No	%	No
Question No										A107e		A103e	
Column No										850		1365	
(v) {AIDSRSK5}	Code												
Doctors and nurses who treat people who have AIDS													
Greatly at risk	1	-		-		-		-		4.8	66	12.7	186
Quite a lot at risk	2	-		-		-		-		17.9	250	29.1	427
Not very much at risk	3	-		-		-		-		44.9	624	43.4	637
Not at all at risk	4	-		-		-		-		29.7	413	11.0	162
(DK)	8	-		-		-		-		2.4	34	3.4	50
(NA)	9	-		-		-		-		0.3	4	0.4	6
Base: All											1391		1469

		1983		1984		1985		1986		1987		1989	
Question No										A107f		A103f	
Column No										851		1366	
(vi) {AIDSRSK6}													
Male homosexuals - that is, gays													
Greatly at risk	1	-		-		-		-		87.0	1210	79.4	1166
Quite a lot at risk	2	-		-		-		-		10.5	147	16.7	246
Not very much at risk	3	-		-		-		-		1.4	19	1.4	21
Not at all at risk	4	-		-		-		-		0.0	1	0.1	2
(DK)	8	-		-		-		-		0.8	11	1.4	21
(NA)	9	-		-		-		-		0.3	4	0.9	13
Base: All											1391		1469

GROUPS AT RISK FROM AIDS (Continued)

		1983		1984		1985		1986		1987		1989	
		%	No	%	No	%	No	%	No	%	No	%	No
Question No										A107g		A103g	
Column No										852		1367	
(vii) {AIDSRSK7}	Code												
Female homosexuals - that is, lesbians													
Greatly at risk	1	-	.	-	.	-	.	-	.	43.2	600	42.7	627
Quite a lot at risk	2	-	.	-	.	-	.	-	.	17.0	237	21.9	322
Not very much at risk	3	-	.	-	.	-	.	-	.	17.4	241	18.7	274
Not at all at risk	4	-	.	-	.	-	.	-	.	14.5	202	9.2	136
(DK)	8	-	.	-	.	-	.	-	.	7.7	107	6.7	99
(NA)	9	-	.	-	.	-	.	-	.	0.3	4	0.7	11
Base: All											1391		1469

		1983		1984		1985		1986		1987		1989	
Question No										A107h		A103h	
Column No										853		1368	
(viii) {AIDSRSK8}													
People who inject themselves with drugs using shared needles													
Greatly at risk	1	-	.	-	.	-	.	-	.	92.7	1289	93.6	1375
Quite a lot at risk	2	-	.	-	.	-	.	-	.	6.4	89	5.2	76
Not very much at risk	3	-	.	-	.	-	.	-	.	0.2	3	0.2	3
Not at all at risk	4	-	.	-	.	-	.	-	.	-	.	0.1	1
(DK)	8	-	.	-	.	-	.	-	.	0.4	6	0.6	9
(NA)	9	-	.	-	.	-	.	-	.	0.2	3	0.4	6
Base: All											1391		1469

DISCRIMINATION AGAINST PEOPLE WITH AIDS

{AIDSSACK} {AIDSDOCS} {AIDSXPEL}

Question: (Show card) **Please look at this card and tell me whether ... (read out):**

		1983		1984		1985		1986		1987		1989	
		%	No	%	No	%	No	%	No	%	No	%	No
Question No										A108a		A104a	
Column No										854		1369	
(i) {AIDSSACK} Employees should or should not have the legal right to dismiss people who have AIDS	Code												
Definitely should	1	-		-		-		-		12.9	180	13.2	194
Probably should	2	-		-		-		-		24.7	343	22.5	331
Probably should not	3	-		-		-		-		29.0	403	30.3	444
Definitely should not	4	-		-		-		-		28.0	389	27.7	407
(DK)	8	-		-		-		-		5.0	69	5.5	81
(NA)	9	-		-		-		-		0.5	7	0.8	12
Base: All											1391		1469

		1983		1984		1985		1986		1987		1989	
Question No										A108b		A104b	
Column No										855		1370	
(ii) {AIDSDOCS} Doctors and nurses should or should not have the legal right to refuse to treat people who have AIDS													
Definitely should	1	-		-		-		-		10.5	147	11.0	161
Probably should	2	-		-		-		-		20.4	283	21.0	309
Probably should not	3	-		-		-		-		26.2	364	27.7	407
Definitely should not	4	-		-		-		-		40.6	564	36.9	541
(DK)	8	-		-		-		-		2.2	30	2.9	42
(NA)	9	-		-		-		-		0.2	3	0.5	8
Base: All											1391		1469

DISCRIMINATION AGAINST PEOPLE WITH AIDS (Continued)

			1983		1984		1985		1986		1987		1989	
			%	No	%	No	%	No	%	No	%	No	%	No
Question No											A108c		A104c	
Column No											856		1371	
(iii) {AIDSXPEL}	Code													
Schools should or should not have the legal right to expel children who have AIDS														
Definitely should	1		-		-		-		-		8.1	113	8.8	130
Probably should	2		-		-		-		-		16.1	224	17.8	262
Probably should not	3		-		-		-		-		30.1	419	28.8	422
Definitely should not	4		-		-		-		-		40.2	559	39.1	574
(DK)	8		-		-		-		-		5.3	74	5.1	74
(NA)	9		-		-		-		-		0.2	3	0.5	7
Base: All												1391		1469

SYMPATHY FOR PEOPLE WITH AIDS

{AIDSSYMP} {AIDSRESR}

Question: I am going to read out two statements. For each one, please say whether you agree or disagree. Strongly or a little?

			1983		1984		1985		1986		1987		1989	
			%	No	%	No	%	No	%	No	%	No	%	No
Question No											A109a		A105a	
Column No											857		1372	
(i) {AIDSSYMP}	Code													
People who have AIDS get much less sympathy from society than they ought to get														
Strongly agree	1		-		-		-		-		24.9	346	27.1	399
Agree a little	2		-		-		-		-		35.3	491	34.5	507
Disagree a little	3		-		-		-		-		21.4	297	21.4	314
Strongly disagree	4		-		-		-		-		12.0	167	11.0	161
(DK)	8		-		-		-		-		5.7	79	5.3	78
(NA)	9		-		-		-		-		0.7	10	0.7	10
Base: All												1391		1469

SYMPATHY FOR PEOPLE WITH AIDS (Continued)

		1983		1984		1985		1986		1987		1989	
		%	No	%	No	%	No	%	No	%	No	%	No
Question No										A109b		A105b	
Column No										858		1373	
(ii) {AIDSRESR}	Code												

More money should be spent trying to
find a cure for AIDS, even if it
means that research into *other*
serious diseases is delayed

		1983		1984		1985		1986		1987		1989	
Strongly agree	1	-	.	-	.	-	.	-	.	31.6	440	20.4	300
Agree a little	2	-	.	-	.	-	.	-	.	25.6	355	22.7	334
Disagree a little	3	-	.	-	.	-	.	-	.	20.4	283	24.5	359
Strongly disagree	4	-	.	-	.	-	.	-	.	17.8	247	26.3	387
(DK)	8	-	.	-	.	-	.	-	.	4.2	58	5.3	78
(NA)	9	-	.	-	.	-	.	-	.	0.5	7	0.8	11
Base: All											1391		1469

PRIVILEGED ACCESS TO HEALTH CARE

{SAMEHLTH}

Question: Do you think that health care should be the same for everyone, or should people who can afford it be able to
pay for better health care?

		1983		1984		1985		1986		1987		1989	
		%	No	%	No	%	No	%	No	%	No	%	No
Question No									B81a				B95a	
Column No									657				858	
	Code													
Same for everyone	1	-	.	-	.	-	.	45.6	705	-	.	49.8	727
Able to pay for better	2	-	.	-	.	-	.	53.1	822	-	.	48.9	715
(DK)	8	-	.	-	.	-	.	1.2	19	-	.	0.8	12
(NA)	9	-	.	-	.	-	.	0.1	2	-	.	0.5	7
Base: All									1548				1461

1986, 1989 - This question was part of a series. Similar questions were asked about education (see {SAMEDUC}, p.I - 1) and pensions
(see {SAMEPENS}, p.J - 10)

ASPECTS OF THE NHS IN NEED OF IMPROVEMENT

{HSAREA1} {HSAREA2} {HSAREA3} {HSAREA4} {HSAREA5} {HSAREA6} {HSAREA7} {HSAREA8} {HSAREA9} {HSAREA10} {HSAREA11} {HSAREA12}

Question: From what you know or have heard, please tick a box for *each* of the items below to show whether you think the National Health Service *in your area* is, on the whole, satisfactory or in need of improvement.

		1983		1984		1985		1986		1987		1989	
		%	No	%	No	%	No	%	No	%	No	%	No
Question No										A201a		A225a	
Column No										1509		2041	
(i) {HSAREA1}	Code												
GPs' appointment systems													
In need of *a lot* of improvement	1	-	.	-	.	-	.	-	.	11.3	140	12.4	158
In need of *some* improvement	2	-	.	-	.	-	.	-	.	35.6	442	33.1	421
Satisfactory	3	-	.	-	.	-	.	-	.	40.2	499	43.0	548
Very good	4	-	.	-	.	-	.	-	.	10.5	131	10.6	136
(DK)	8	-	.	-	.	-	.	-	.	0.9	11	0.0	1
(NA)	9	-	.	-	.	-	.	-	.	1.6	20	0.8	10
										1243		1274	

Base: Self-completion questionnaire respondents

		1983		1984		1985		1986		1987		1989	
Question No										A201b		A225b	
Column No										1510		2042	
(ii) {HSAREA2}													
Amount of time GP gives to each patient													
In need of *a lot* of improvement	1	-	.	-	.	-	.	-	.	6.9	86	8.3	106
In need of *some* improvement	2	-	.	-	.	-	.	-	.	25.8	320	26.1	333
Satisfactory	3	-	.	-	.	-	.	-	.	51.9	646	53.7	684
Very good	4	-	.	-	.	-	.	-	.	13.7	170	11.2	143
(DK)	8	-	.	-	.	-	.	-	.	0.5	7	0.0	1
(NA)	9	-	.	-	.	-	.	-	.	1.2	14	0.6	8
										1243		1274	

Base: Self-completion questionnaire respondents

ASPECTS OF THE NHS IN NEED OF IMPROVEMENT (Continued)

		1983		1984		1985		1986		1987		1989	
		%	No	%	No	%	No	%	No	%	No	%	No
Question No										A201c		A225c	
Column No										1511		2043	
(iii) *{HSAREA3}*	Code												
Being able to choose which GP to see													
In need of *a lot* of improvement	1	-	.	-	.	-	.	-	.	8.0	99	9.1	115
In need of *some* improvement	2	-	.	-	.	-	.	-	.	20.5	255	20.7	264
Satisfactory	3	-	.	-	.	-	.	-	.	50.2	625	55.6	708
Very good	4	-	.	-	.	-	.	-	.	19.6	244	13.5	172
(DK)	8	-	.	-	.	-	.	-	.	0.5	6	0.0	1
(NA)	9	-	.	-	.	-	.	-	.	1.2	15	1.1	14
Base: Self-completion questionnaire respondents											1243		1274

		1983		1984		1985		1986		1987		1989	
Question No										A201d		A225d	
Column No										1512		2044	
(iv) *{HSAREA4}*													
Quality of medical treatment by GPs													
In need of *a lot* of improvement	1	-	.	-	.	-	.	-	.	5.9	74	6.4	82
In need of *some* improvement	2	-	.	-	.	-	.	-	.	20.2	252	20.3	259
Satisfactory	3	-	.	-	.	-	.	-	.	49.5	615	53.8	685
Very good	4	-	.	-	.	-	.	-	.	22.6	281	18.7	239
(DK)	8	-	.	-	.	-	.	-	.	0.5	6	0.1	1
(NA)	9	-	.	-	.	-	.	-	.	1.3	17	0.6	8
Base: Self-completion questionnaire respondents											1243		1274

		1983		1984		1985		1986		1987		1989	
Question No										A201e		A225e	
Column No										1513		2045	
(v) *{HSAREA5}*													
Hospital waiting lists for *non-*emergency operations													
In need of *a lot* of improvement	1	-	.	-	.	-	.	-	.	43.1	536	45.2	575
In need of *some* improvement	2	-	.	-	.	-	.	-	.	43.6	542	39.5	503
Satisfactory	3	-	.	-	.	-	.	-	.	9.3	116	12.9	164
Very good	4	-	.	-	.	-	.	-	.	0.9	11	0.8	11
(DK)	8	-	.	-	.	-	.	-	.	1.4	18	0.6	8
(NA)	9	-	.	-	.	-	.	-	.	1.6	20	1.0	12
Base: Self-completion questionnaire respondents											1243		1274

ASPECTS OF THE NHS IN NEED OF IMPROVEMENT (Continued)

		1983		1984		1985		1986		1987		1989	
		%	No	%	No	%	No	%	No	%	No	%	No
Question No										A201f		A225f	
Column No										1514		2046	
(vi) {HSAREA6}	Code												
Waiting time before getting appointments with hospital consultants													
In need of *a lot* of improvement	1	-	.	-	.	-	.	-	.	45.5	565	49.0	624
In need of *some* improvement	2	-	.	-	.	-	.	-	.	37.9	471	37.1	473
Satisfactory	3	-	.	-	.	-	.	-	.	12.3	153	11.0	140
Very good	4	-	.	-	.	-	.	-	.	1.2	15	1.1	14
(DK)	8	-	.	-	.	-	.	-	.	1.1	14	0.6	7
(NA)	9	-	.	-	.	-	.	-	.	2.0	25	1.2	16
											1243		1274

Base: Self-completion
questionnaire respondents

		1983		1984		1985		1986		1987		1989	
Question No										A201g		A225g	
Column No										1515		2047	
(vii) {HSAREA7}													
General condition of hospital buildings													
In need of *a lot* of improvement	1	-	.	-	.	-	.	-	.	15.0	187	21.2	270
In need of *some* improvement	2	-	.	-	.	-	.	-	.	37.9	472	39.6	504
Satisfactory	3	-	.	-	.	-	.	-	.	34.4	428	31.3	398
Very good	4	-	.	-	.	-	.	-	.	9.7	120	7.0	89
(DK)	8	-	.	-	.	-	.	-	.	0.8	10	0.2	2
(NA)	9	-	.	-	.	-	.	-	.	2.1	26	0.8	11
											1243		1274

Base: Self-completion
questionnaire respondents

		1983		1984		1985		1986		1987		1989	
Question No										A201h		A225h	
Column No										1516		2048	
(viii) {HSAREA8}													
Hospital casualty departments													
In need of *a lot* of improvement	1	-	.	-	.	-	.	-	.	18.1	225	22.4	285
In need of *some* improvement	2	-	.	-	.	-	.	-	.	35.9	446	36.9	471
Satisfactory	3	-	.	-	.	-	.	-	.	33.6	417	31.6	402
Very good	4	-	.	-	.	-	.	-	.	9.1	114	7.8	99
(DK)	8	-	.	-	.	-	.	-	.	1.4	17	0.3	4
(NA)	9	-	.	-	.	-	.	-	.	2.0	25	1.0	13
											1243		1274

Base: Self-completion
questionnaire respondents

ASPECTS OF THE NHS IN NEED OF IMPROVEMENT (Continued)

		1983		1984		1985		1986		1987		1989	
		%	No	%	No	%	No	%	No	%	No	%	No
Question No										A201i		A225i	
Column No										1517		2049	
(ix) *{HSAREA9}*	Code												
Staffing level of nurses in hospitals													
In need of *a lot* of improvement	1	-	.	-	.	-	.	-	.	34.5	430	34.5	439
In need of *some* improvement	2	-	.	-	.	-	.	-	.	40.3	501	40.9	521
Satisfactory	3	-	.	-	.	-	.	-	.	18.6	232	19.5	249
Very good	4	-	.	-	.	-	.	-	.	3.5	43	3.6	46
(DK)	8	-	.	-	.	-	.	-	.	1.3	16	0.6	7
(NA)	9	-	.	-	.	-	.	-	.	1.7	21	0.9	12
										—		—	
Base: Self-completion questionnaire respondents										1243		1274	
Question No										A201j		A225j	
Column No										1518		2050	
(x) *{HSAREA10}*													
Staffing level of doctors in hospitals													
In need of *a lot* of improvement	1	-	.	-	.	-	.	-	.	26.0	323	35.2	449
In need of *some* improvement	2	-	.	-	.	-	.	-	.	44.3	551	39.8	506
Satisfactory	3	-	.	-	.	-	.	-	.	23.4	291	20.0	255
Very good	4	-	.	-	.	-	.	-	.	3.1	39	3.2	41
(DK)	8	-	.	-	.	-	.	-	.	1.2	15	0.6	7
(NA)	9	-	.	-	.	-	.	-	.	1.9	24	1.2	15
										—		—	
Base: Self-completion questionnaire respondents										1243		1274	
Question No										A201k		A225k	
Column No										1519		2051	
(xi) *{HSAREA11}*													
Quality of medical treatment in hospitals													
In need of *a lot* of improvement	1	-	.	-	.	-	.	-	.	5.6	69	9.2	117
In need of *some* improvement	2	-	.	-	.	-	.	-	.	24.4	303	26.9	342
Satisfactory	3	-	.	-	.	-	.	-	.	48.9	608	46.8	597
Very good	4	-	.	-	.	-	.	-	.	18.5	230	15.9	203
(DK)	8	-	.	-	.	-	.	-	.	1.1	13	0.4	5
(NA)	9	-	.	-	.	-	.	-	.	1.6	20	0.7	9
										—		—	
Base: Self-completion questionnaire respondents										1243		1274	

ASPECTS OF THE NHS IN NEED OF IMPROVEMENT (Continued)

			1983		1984		1985		1986		1987		1989	
			%	No	%	No	%	No	%	No	%	No	%	No
	Question No										A2011		A2251	
	Column No										1520		2052	
(xii) *{HSAREA12)*		Code													
Quality of nursing care in hospitals															
In need of *a lot* of improvement		1	-	.	-	.	-	.	-	.	4.2	52	7.9	101
In need of *some* improvement		2	-	.	-	.	-	.	-	.	17.2	214	19.2	245
Satisfactory		3	-	.	-	.	-	.	-	.	41.7	519	41.8	533
Very good		4	-	.	-	.	-	.	-	.	34.5	429	30.0	382
(DK)		8	-	.	-	.	-	.	-	.	0.8	10	0.3	3
(NA)		9	-	.	-	.	-	.	-	.	1.5	19	0.8	10
Base: Self-completion questionnaire respondents												1243		1274

RECENT EXPERIENCE OF THE NHS AND PRIVATE TREATMENT

{NHSDOC} {NHSOUTP} {NHSINP} {NHSVISIT} {PRIVPAT}

Question: In the last *two* years, have you or a close family member .... (please tick one box for each):

			1983		1984		1985		1986		1987		1989	
			%	No	%	No	%	No	%	No	%	No	%	No
	Question No										A202		A226	
	Column No										1521		2053	
(i) *{NHSDOC}*		Code													
Visited an NHS GP															
Yes		1	-	.	-	.	-	.	-	.	95.0	1182	94.2	1200
No		2	-	.	-	.	-	.	-	.	4.3	54	4.5	58
(DK)		8	-	.	-	.	-	.	-	.	-		-	-
(NA)		9	-	.	-	.	-	.	-	.	0.7	8	1.3	16
Base: Self-completion questionnaire respondents												1243		1274

RECENT EXPERIENCE OF THE NHS AND PRIVATE TREATMENT (Continued)

		1983		1984		1985		1986		1987		1989	
		%	No	%	No	%	No	%	No	%	No	%	No
Question No										A202		A226	
Column No										1522		2054	
(ii) {*NHSOUTP*}													
Been an out-patient in an NHS hospital													
Yes	1	-		-		-		-		**66.8**	830	**65.9**	839
No	2	-		-		-		-		**31.4**	390	**31.4**	400
(DK)	8	-		-		-		-		-		-	
(NA)	9	-		-		-		-		**1.9**	23	**2.7**	34
Base: Self-completion questionnaire respondents										1243		1274	

		1983		1984		1985		1986		1987		1989	
Question No										A202		A226	
Column No										1523		2055	
(iii) {*NHSINP*}													
Been an in-patient in an NHS hospital													
Yes	1	-		-		-		-		**47.1**	585	**46.6**	593
No	2	-		-		-		-		**50.6**	629	**49.8**	635
(DK)	8	-		-		-		-		-		-	
(NA)	9	-		-		-		-		**2.4**	29	**3.6**	46
Base: Self-completion questionnaire respondents										1243		1274	

		1983		1984		1985		1986		1987		1989	
Question No										A202		A226	
Column No										1524		2056	
(iv) {*NHSVISIT*}													
Visited a patient in an NHS hospital													
Yes	1	-		-		-		-		**76.3**	949	**73.6**	937
No	2	-		-		-		-		**22.4**	279	**23.8**	304
(DK)	8	-		-		-		-		-		-	
(NA)	9	-		-		-		-		**1.3**	16	**2.6**	33
Base: Self-completion questionnaire respondents										1243		1274	

RECENT EXPERIENCE OF THE NHS AND PRIVATE TREATMENT (Continued)

			1983		1984		1985		1986		1987		1989	
			%	No	%	No	%	No	%	No	%	No	%	No
Question No											A202		A226	
Column No											1525		2057	
(v) {PRIVPAT}	Code													
... had any medical treatment as a *private* patient?														
Yes	1		-	.	-	.	-	.	-	.	13.7	171	11.7	149
No	2		-	.	-	.	-	.	-	.	84.3	1048	85.8	1093
(DK)	8		-	.	-	.	-	.	-	.	-	.	-	.
(NA)	9		-	.	-	.	-	.	-	.	2.0	25	2.4	31
Base: Self completion questionnaire respondents												1243		1274

PREDICTIONS ABOUT THE SPREAD OF AIDS

{AIDSKILL}

Question: Now a few questions about the disease called AIDS.

Please tick one box to show which is closest to your views about the following statement.   **Within five years AIDS will cause more deaths in Britain than any other single disease.**

			1983		1984		1985		1986		1987		1989	
			%	No	%	No	%	No	%	No	%	No	%	No
Question No											A224		A237	
Column No											1643		2258	
	Code													
It is highly exaggerated	1		-	.	-	.	-	.	-	.	10.8	134	14.2	181
It is slightly exaggerated	2		-	.	-	.	-	.	-	.	26.9	335	31.4	399
It is more or less true	3		-	.	-	.	-	.	-	.	60.3	750	52.9	673
(DK)	8		-	.	-	.	-	.	-	.	0.4	5	0.4	5
(NA)	9		-	.	-	.	-	.	-	.	1.6	20	1.2	16
Base: Self-completion questionnaire respondents												1243		1274

ATTITUDES TOWARDS AIDS

{AIDSBLME} {AIDSMONY} {AIDSWRNG} {AIDSVACC} {AIDSPUN}

Question: Please tick one box for each statement to show how much you agree or disagree with it.

		1983		1984		1985		1986		1987		1989	
		%	No	%	No	%	No	%	No	%	No	%	No
Question No										A225a		A238a	
Column No										1644		2259	
(i) {AIDSBLME}	Code												
Most people with AIDS have only themselves to blame													
Agree strongly	1	-	.	-	.	-	.	-	.	23.8	296	15.7	201
Agree	2	-	.	-	.	-	.	-	.	33.4	415	39.4	502
Neither agree nor disagree	3	-	.	-	.	-	.	-	.	14.6	182	16.6	212
Disagree	4	-	.	-	.	-	.	-	.	20.6	256	22.7	290
Disagree strongly	5	-	-	-	-	-	.	-	.	6.8	84	4.4	56
(DK)	8	-	.	-	.	-	.	-	.	0.2	2	-	.
(NA)	9	-	.	-	.	-	.	-	.	0.7	8	1.1	14

Base: Self-completion
        questionnaire respondents

1243   1274

		1983		1984		1985		1986		1987		1989	
Question No										A225b		A238b	
Column No										1645		2260	
(ii) {AIDSMONY}													
The National Health Service should spend more of its resources on giving better care to people dying from AIDS													
Agree strongly	1	-	.	-	.	-	.	-	.	7.9	98	6.2	79
Agree	2	-	.	-	.	-	.	-	.	34.0	423	33.8	431
Neither agree nor disagree	3	-	.	-	.	-	.	-	.	28.7	357	34.4	437
Disagree	4	-	.	-	.	-	.	-	.	22.8	284	20.9	266
Disagree strongly	5	-	.	-	.	-	.	-	.	5.3	66	3.6	45
(DK)	8	-	.	-	.	-	.	-	.	0.2	3	0.1	1
(NA)	9	-	.	-	.	-	.	-	.	1.0	13	1.1	14

Base: Self-completion
        questionnaire respondents

1243   1274

ATTIDUDES TOWARDS AIDS (Continued)

			1983		1984		1985		1986		1987		1989	
			%	No	%	No	%	No	%	No	%	No	%	No
Question No											A225c		A238c	
Column No											1646		2261	

(iii) {AIDSWRNG}
Official warnings about AIDS should
say that some sexual practices are
morally wrong

	Code	1983 %	No	1984 %	No	1985 %	No	1986 %	No	1987 %	No	1989 %	No
Agree strongly	1	-	.	-	.	-	.	-	.	31.2	388	22.7	289
Agree	2	-	.	-	.	-	.	-	.	35.4	440	38.8	494
Neither agree nor disagree	3	-	.	-	.	-	.	-	.	13.1	163	14.7	187
Disagree	4	-	.	-	.	-	.	-	.	14.3	178	18.3	233
Disagree strongly	5	-	.	-	.	-	.	-	.	5.1	64	4.4	56
(DK)	8	-	.	-	.	-	.	-	.	0.1	1	0.1	1
(NA)	9	-	.	-	.	-	.	-	.	0.8	10	1.0	13

Base: Self-completion
       questionnaire respondents

1987: 1243   1989: 1274

		1987		1989	
Question No		A225d		A238d	
Column No		1647		2262	

(iv) {AIDSVACC}
Within the next five years doctors
will discover a vaccine against AIDS

	Code	1983 %	No	1984 %	No	1985 %	No	1986 %	No	1987 %	No	1989 %	No
Agree strongly	1	-	.	-	.	-	.	-	.	4.2	52	2.8	36
Agree	2	-	.	-	.	-	.	-	.	30.5	379	30.5	389
Neither agree nor disagree	3	-	.	-	.	-	.	-	.	44.9	558	44.9	571
Disagree	4	-	.	-	.	-	.	-	.	16.3	202	17.5	223
Disagree strongly	5	-	.	-	.	-	.	-	.	2.7	34	2.4	30
(DK)	8	-	.	-	.	-	.	-	.	0.4	5	0.2	3
(NA)	9	-	.	-	.	-	.	-	.	1.0	12	1.6	21

Base: Self-completion
       questionnaire respondents

1987: 1243   1989: 1274

ATTITUDES TOWARDS AIDS (Continued)

		1983		1984		1985		1986		1987		1989	
		%	No	%	No	%	No	%	No	%	No	%	No
Question No										A225e		A238e	
Column No										1648		2263	
(v) {AIDSPUN}	Code												
AIDS is a way of punishing the world for its decline in moral standards													
Agree strongly	1	-	-	-	-	-	-	-	-	9.6	119	7.1	91
Agree	2	-	-	-	-	-	-	-	-	18.6	231	19.5	248
Neither agree nor disagree	3	-	-	-	-	-	-	-	-	25.1	312	22.4	285
Disagree	4	-	-	-	-	-	-	-	-	24.1	300	29.0	370
Disagree strongly	5	-	-	-	-	-	-	-	-	21.9	272	20.3	258
(DK)	8	-	-	-	-	-	-	-	-	0.1	1	0.2	3
(NA)	9	-	-	-	-	-	-	-	-	0.7	8	1.5	19
Base: Self-completion questionnaire respondents											1243		1274

INCOME GROUP BENEFITING MOST FROM SPENDING ON THE NHS

{NHSVALUE}

Question: On the whole, which of these three types of family would you say gets best value from their taxes out of the National Health Service ... (read out) ...

		1983		1984		1985		1986		1987		1989	
		%	No	%	No	%	No	%	No	%	No	%	No
Question No		55		62									
Column No		507		517									
	Code												
... those with high incomes,	1	24.5	420	28.0	461	-	-	-	-	-	-	-	-
... those with middle incomes,	2	14.4	248	14.6	240	-	-	-	-	-	-	-	-
.... or those with low incomes?	3	43.7	751	41.4	680	-	-	-	-	-	-	-	-
(No difference)	4	15.7	269	13.1	215	-	-	-	-	-	-	-	-
(DK)	8	0.4	7	2.4	40	-	-	-	-	-	-	-	-
(NA)	9	1.4	24	0.5	9	-	-	-	-	-	-	-	-
Base: All			1719		1645								

1983 -   (DK), code 4; (No difference), code 5
1983, 1984   -   Q introduced by: 'Turning now to the National Health Service'

SCREENING FOR THE AIDS VIRUS

1989   Qs.A239,A240   *{AIDSBLOD}{AIDSTELL}* Column Nos 2264-65

Q.A239   *{AIDSBLOD}* Column No 2264
As one way of getting to know how AIDS is spreading, it has been suggested that hospitals should be allowed to test any patient's blood (that has been taken for other reasons) to see whether it contains the virus that causes AIDS. Do you agree or disagree with this suggestion? (Please tick one box)

	Code	%	No
Agree strongly	1	45.6	581
Agree	2	41.3	526
Neither agree nor disagree	3	5.9	75
Disagree	4	5.1	65
Disagree strongly	5	1.1	14
(DK)	8	0.1	1
(NA)	9	0.9	11
Base : Self-completion respondents			1274

Q.A240   *{AIDSTELL}* Column No 2265
Thinking of patients whose blood has been tested for the AIDS virus without their knowledge - should they ... (please tick one box) ...

	Code	%	No
...*not* be told the test has been carried out	1	5.5	70
be told about the test, *but not* be told the result	2	1.1	13
be told about the test, *and* have the choice of knowing or not knowing the result	3	38.0	484
[or,] be told about the test, *and* be told the result	4	54.5	694
(DK)	8	0.1	2
(NA)	9	0.9	11
Base : Self-completion respondents			1274

ACQUAINTANCE WITH PEOPLE WITH HIV

1989   Q.A241   *{AIDSKNOW}* Column No 2266
As far as you know, have you ever met anyone who was confirmed as having the virus that causes AIDS?

	Code	%	No
Yes	1	4.6	59
No	2	94.7	1206
(DK)	8	-	-
(NA)	9	0.7	9
Base : Self-completion respondents			1274

EFFECT OF AIDS ON YOUNG PEOPLE

1987   Q.A225f   {AIDSYONG} Column No 1649
Please tick one box to show how much you agree or disagree [that] AIDS is a tragedy for young people because it surrounds their sex lives with fear.

	Code	%	No
Agree strongly	1	20.7	258
Agree	2	42.6	529
Neither agree nor disagree	3	16.8	208
Disagree	4	15.5	193
Disagree strongly	5	3.7	46
(DK)	8	0.1	1
(NA)	9	0.7	9
Base: Self-completion respondents			1243

NB   This was one of a battery of six questions, only one of which (A.225f) was not repeated in 1989 (see pp. K-23 to K-25 above)

EFFECT ON THE NHS OF PRIVATE HEALTH SCHEMES

1983   Q.58c   {PRINSNHS} Column No 517
Do you consider the existence of private health schemes to be a good thing or a bad thing for the National Health Service, or don't they make any difference to the NHS?

	Code	%	No
Good	1	36.9	634
Bad	2	23.0	396
No difference	3	35.0	601
(DK)	4	4.8	83
(NA)	9	0.3	6
Base : All			1719

EFFECT ON THE NHS OF PRIVATE MEDICAL TREATMENT

1983   Q.59a   {PRTRTNHS} Column No 518
Now thinking of private medical treatment in general. Do you consider the existence of private medical treatment in Britain to be a good thing for the National Health Service, or doesn't it make any difference to the NHS?

	Code	%	No
Good thing	1	35.7	613
Bad thing	2	24.9	428
No difference	3	35.3	607
(DK)	4	3.9	68
(NA)	9	0.2	3
Base : All			1719

PRIVATE MEDICAL TREATMENT : PRESENT AND FUTURE POLICIES

1983   Q.59b   *{HVIEWS1}-{HVIEWS6}* Column Nos 519-24
(Show card) **Which of the views on this card do you support? You may choose more than one, or none.**

i) *{HVIEWS1}* Column No 519
Private medical treatment in Britain should be abolished

	Code	%	No
[Does not support]	0	89.5	1538
Supports	1	9.8	169
(DK)	8	0.5	9
(NA)	9	0.2	3
Base : All			1719

ii) *{HVIEWS2}* Column No 520
Private treatment in National Health Service hospitals should be abolished

	Code	%	No
[Does not support]	0	73.5	1263
Supports	2	25.8	443
(DK)	8	0.5	9
(NA)	9	0.2	3
Base : All			1719

iii) *{HVIEWS3}* Column No 521
The present arrangements for private medical treatment and the National Health Service are about right

	Code	%	No
[Does not support]	0	58.2	1000
Supports	3	41.1	707
(DK)	8	0.5	9
(NA)	9	0.2	3
Base : All			1719

iv) *{HVIEWS4}* Column No 522
Private treatment outside National Health Service hospitals should be encouraged to expand

	Code	%	No
[Does not support]	0	73.6	1265
Supports	4	25.7	441
(DK)	8	0.5	9
(NA)	9	0.2	3
Base : All			1719

PRIVATE MEDICAL TREATMENT : PRESENT AND FUTURE POLICIES (continued)

v) *{HVIEWS5}* Column No 523
Private medical treatment generally should be encouraged to expand

	Code	%	No
[Does not support]	0	79.3	1364
Supports	5	20.0	343
(DK)	8	0.5	9
(NA)	9	0.2	3
Base : All			1719

vi) *{HVIEWS6}* Column No 524
None of these

	Code	%	No
One or more supported	0	95.5	1641
None supported	6	3.8	66
(DK)	8	0.5	9
(NA)	9	0.2	3
Base : All			1719

L Diet, health and lifestyle

Table titles and cross references

HOW OFTEN VARIOUS FOODS EATEN

{HAMFREQ} {MEATFREQ} {EGGSFREQ} {FISHFREQ} {VEGFREQ} {BREDFREQ}

Question: Now some questions on food.
(Show card) **How often do you eat** _____ (food) **nowadays?** (Interviewer: ask about *each* listed food before going to ask about the next)

		1983		1984		1985		1986		1987		1989	
		%	No	%	No	%	No	%	No	%	No	%	No
Question No								A89a(i)				A88a(i)	
Column No								1231				908	
(i) {HAMFREQ} Processed meat like sausages, ham or tinned meat	Code												
Every day	1	-	.	-	.	-	.	4.4	66	-	.	4.6	67
4-6 days a week	2	-	.	-	.	-	.	5.9	90	-	.	4.8	70
2-3 days a week	3	-	.	-	.	-	.	27.3	414	-	.	27.0	397
About once a week	4	-	.	-	.	-	.	38.3	581	-	.	37.6	553
Less often	5	-	.	-	.	-	.	17.1	259	-	.	19.3	284
Never nowadays	6	-	.	-	.	-	.	6.7	101	-	.	6.5	95
(DK)	8	-	.	-	.	-	.	-		-	.	-	
(NA)	9	-	.	-	.	-	.	0.4	6	-	.	0.1	2
Base: All									1518				1469

		1983		1984		1985		1986		1987		1989	
Question No								A89a(ii)				A88a(ii)	
Column No								1234				920	
(ii) {MEATFREQ} Beef, lamb or pork													
Every day	1	-	.	-	.	-	.	3.3	49	-	.	3.5	52
4-6 days a week	2	-	.	-	.	-	.	12.7	192	-	.	12.4	182
2-3 days a week	3	-	.	-	.	-	.	37.4	568	-	.	38.5	565
About once a week	4	-	.	-	.	-	.	35.0	531	-	.	31.8	467
Less often	5	-	.	-	.	-	.	7.8	118	-	.	9.4	138
Never nowadays	6	-	.	-	.	-	.	3.5	54	-	.	4.2	62
(DK)	8	-	.	-	.	-	.	-		-	.	-	
(NA)	9	-	.	-	.	-	.	0.3	5	-	.	0.2	3
Base: All									1518				1469

HOW OFTEN VARIOUS FOODS EATEN (Continued)

		1983		1984		1985		1986		1987		1989	
		%	No	%	No	%	No	%	No	%	No	%	No
Question No								A89a(iii)				A88a(iii)	
Column No								1237				932	
(iii) *{EGGSFREQ}*	Code												
Eggs													
Every day	1	-	.	-	.	-	.	9.8	149	-	.	6.6	97
4-6 days a week	2	-	.	-	.	-	.	9.4	143	-	.	8.3	121
2-3 days a week	3	-	.	-	.	-	.	40.5	615	-	.	32.2	473
About once a week	4	-	.	-	.	-	.	25.7	390	-	.	26.2	385
Less often	5	-	.	-	.	-	.	10.3	156	-	.	15.6	229
Never nowadays	6	-	.	-	.	-	.	3.9	59	-	.	10.8	158
(DK)	8	-	.	-	.	-	.	-	.	-	.	-	.
(NA)	9	-	.	-	.	-	.	0.3	5	-	.	0.3	5
Base: All									1518				1469

		1983		1984		1985		1986		1987		1989	
Question No								A89a(iv)				A88a(iv)	
Column No								1240				944	
(iv) *{FISHFREQ}*													
Fish	Code												
Every day	1	-	.	-	.	-	.	0.2	3	-	.	0.4	7
4-6 days a week	2	-	.	-	.	-	.	1.5	22	-	.	2.0	29
2-3 days a week	3	-	.	-	.	-	.	20.4	309	-	.	25.8	379
About once a week	4	-	.	-	.	-	.	49.2	747	-	.	43.3	636
Less often	5	-	.	-	.	-	.	21.1	319	-	.	21.7	318
Never nowadays	6	-	.	-	.	-	.	7.4	112	-	.	6.6	97
(DK)	8	-	.	-	.	-	.	-	.	-	.	-	.
(NA)	9	-	.	-	.	-	.	0.3	5	-	.	0.2	3
Base: All									1518				1469

HOW OFTEN VARIOUS FOODS EATEN (Continued)

			1983		1984		1985		1986		1987		1989	
			%	No	%	No	%	No	%	No	%	No	%	No
	Question No								A89a(vi)				A88a(vi)	
	Column No								1246				968	
(v) {VEGFREQ}		Code												
Fresh fruit and vegetables														
Every day	1		-	.	-	.	-	.	57.3	869	-	.	56.9	836
4-6 days a week	2		-	.	-	.	-	.	19.8	301	-	.	19.9	293
2-3 days a week	3		-	.	-	.	-	.	15.5	235	-	.	15.7	230
About once a week	4		-	.	-	.	-	.	4.5	68	-	.	4.7	70
Less often	5		-	.	-	.	-	.	1.9	29	-	.	1.8	27
Never nowadays	6		-	.	-	.	-	.	0.7	11	-	.	0.7	10
(DK)	8		-	.	-	.	-	.	-	.	-	.	-	.
(NA)	9		-	.	-	.	-	.	0.3	5	-	.	0.3	4
										—				—
Base: All										1518				1469

			1983		1984		1985		1986		1987		1989	
	Question No								A89a(vii)				A88a(viii)	
	Column No								1249				1020	
(vi) {BREDFREQ}														
Bread														
Every day	1		-	.	-	.	-	.	21.5	326	-	.	18.4	270
4-6 days a week	2		-	.	-	.	-	.	34.0	517	-	.	34.8	512
2-3 days a week	3		-	.	-	.	-	.	33.4	507	-	.	34.7	509
About once a week	4		-	.	-	.	-	.	6.1	92	-	.	6.6	96
Less often	5		-	.	-	.	-	.	3.8	57	-	.	4.2	61
Never nowadays	6		-	.	-	.	-	.	0.9	14	-	.	1.0	15
(DK)	8		-	.	-	.	-	.	-	.	-	.	-	.
(NA)	9		-	.	-	.	-	.	0.3	5	-	.	0.4	6
										—				—
Base: All										1518				1469

WHETHER VARIOUS FOODS NEVER EATEN AT ALL OR CUT OUT

{HAMEVER} {MEATEVER} {EGGSEVER} {FISHEVER} {VEGEVER} {BREDEVER}

Question: [If never eaten nowadays] Have you *never* eaten _____ (food), or have you cut *it/them* out in the last 2 or 3 years or longer ago?

		1983		1984		1985		1986		1987		1989	
		%	No	%	No	%	No	%	No	%	No	%	No
Question No								A89b(i)				A88b(i)	
Column No								1232				909	
(i) {HAMEVER}	Code												
Processed meat like sausages, ham or tinned meat													
[Not asked: eaten nowadays]	0	-	.	-	.	-	.	92.9	1410	-	.	93.4	1372
Never eaten [at all]	1	-	.	-	.	-	.	0.9	13	-	.	2.0	29
Cut out in last 2 or 3 years	2	-	.	-	.	-	.	3.5	53	-	.	2.6	38
Cut out longer ago	3	-	.	-	.	-	.	2.2	34	-	.	1.6	24
(DK)	8	-	.	-	.	-	.	-	.	-	.	-	.
(NA)	9	-	.	-	.	-	.	0.5	7	-	.	0.5	7
Base: All									1518				1469
Question No								A89b(ii)				A88b(ii)	
Column No								1235				921	
(ii) {MEATEVER}													
Beef, lamb or pork													
[Not asked: eaten nowadays]	0	-	.	-	.	-	.	96.1	1459	-	.	95.6	1404
Never eaten [at all]	1	-	.	-	.	-	.	0.5	7	-	.	0.7	11
Cut out in last 2 or 3 years	2	-	.	-	.	-	.	2.0	30	-	.	1.5	22
Cut out longer ago	3	-	.	-	.	-	.	1.1	17	-	.	1.6	23
(DK)	8	-	.	-	.	-	.	-	.	-	.	-	.
(NA)	9	-	.	-	.	-	.	0.3	5	-	.	0.6	9
Base: All									1518				1469

WHETHER VARIOUS FOODS NEVER EATEN AT ALL OR CUT OUT (Continued)

		1983		1984		1985		1986		1987		1989	
		%	No	%	No	%	No	%	No	%	No	%	No
Question No								A89b(iii)				A88b(iii)	
Column No								1238				933	
(iii) {EGGSEVER}	Code												
Eggs													
[Not asked: eaten nowadays]	0	-	-	-	-	-	-	95.7	1453	-	-	88.9	1306
Never eaten [at all]	1	-	-	-	-	-	-	1.0	15	-	-	2.3	34
Cut out in last 2 or 3 years	2	-	-	-	-	-	-	1.4	21	-	-	5.9	87
Cut out longer ago	3	-	-	-	-	-	-	1.6	24	-	-	1.2	18
(DK)	8	-	-	-	-	-	-	-	-	-	-	-	-
(NA)	9	-	-	-	-	-	-	0.3	5	-	-	1.6	24
Base: All									1518				1469

		1983		1984		1985		1986		1987		1989	
Question No								A89b(iv)				A88b(iv)	
Column No								1241				945	
(iv) {FISHEVER}													
Fish													
[Not asked: eaten nowadays]	0	-	-	-	-	-	-	92.3	1401	-	-	93.2	1369
Never eaten [at all]	1	-	-	-	-	-	-	2.1	32	-	-	3.0	44
Cut out in last 2 or 3 years	2	-	-	-	-	-	-	2.4	37	-	-	2.2	33
Cut out longer ago	3	-	-	-	-	-	-	2.8	42	-	-	0.9	13
(DK)	8	-	-	-	-	-	-	-	-	-	-	-	-
(NA)	9	-	-	-	-	-	-	0.4	6	-	-	0.7	10
Base: All									1518				1469

		1983		1984		1985		1986		1987		1989	
Question No								A89b(vi)				A88b(vi)	
Column No								1247				969	
(v) {VEGEVER}													
Fresh fruit and vegetables													
[Not asked: eaten nowadays]	0	-	-	-	-	-	-	98.9	1502	-	-	99.0	1455
Never eaten [at all]	1	-	-	-	-	-	-	-	-	-	-	0.3	5
Cut out in last 2 or 3 years	2	-	-	-	-	-	-	0.4	6	-	-	0.2	3
Cut out longer ago	3	-	-	-	-	-	-	0.3	5	-	-	0.1	1
(DK)	8	-	-	-	-	-	-	-	-	-	-	-	-
(NA)	9	-	-	-	-	-	-	0.3	5	-	-	0.3	5
Base: All									1518				1469

WHETHER VARIOUS FOODS NEVER EATEN AT ALL OR CUT OUT (Continued)

			1983		1984		1985		1986		1987		1989	
			%	No	%	No	%	No	%	No	%	No	%	No
	Question No								A89b(vii)				A88b(viii)	
	Column No								1250				1021	
(vi) {BREDEVER}		Code												
Bread														
[Not asked: eaten nowadays]		0	-	.	-	.	-	.	98.7	1498	-	.	98.6	1448
Never eaten [at all]		1	-	.	-	.	-	.	0.1	2	-	.	0.2	3
Cut out in last 2 or 3 years		2	-	.	-	.	-	.	0.7	10	-	.	0.7	10
Cut out longer ago		3	-	.	-	.	-	.	0.1	2	-	.	0.1	2
(DK)		8	-	.	-	.	-	.	-	.	-	.	-	.
(NA)		9	-	.	-	.	-	.	0.3	5	-	.	0.5	7
Base: All										1518				1469

AMOUNT OF VARIOUS FOODS EATEN COMPARED WITH RECENT PAST

{HAMSAME} {MEATSAME} {EGGSSAME} {FISHSAME} {VEGSAME} {BREDSAME}

Question: [If ever eaten nowadays] **Are you eating about the same amount as you did 2 or 3 years ago, or more _____ (food) or less _____ (food)?**

			1983		1984		1985		1986		1987		1989	
			%	No	%	No	%	No	%	No	%	No	%	No
	Question No								A89c(i)				A88c(i)	
	Column No								1233				910	
(i) {HAMSAME}		Code												
Processed meat like sausages, ham or tinned meat														
[Not asked: never eaten nowadays]		0	-	.	-	.	-	.	6.7	101	-	.	6.5	95
About the same amount		1	-	.	-	.	-	.	54.3	825	-	.	57.5	845
More		2	-	.	-	.	-	.	6.9	105	-	.	5.3	78
Less		3	-	.	-	.	-	.	31.4	476	-	.	29.8	437
(DK)		8	-	.	-	.	-	.	-	.	-	.	-	.
(NA)		9	-	.	-	.	-	.	0.7	10	-	.	0.9	13
Base: All										1518				1469

AMOUNT OF VARIOUS FOODS EATEN COMPARED WITH RECENT PAST
(Continued)

		1983		1984		1985		1986		1987		1989	
		%	No	%	No	%	No	%	No	%	No	%	No
Question No								A89c(ii)				A88c(ii)	
Column No								1236				922	
(ii) {MEATSAME}	Code												
Beef, lamb or pork													
[Not asked: never eaten nowadays]	0	-	.	-	.	-	.	3.6	54	-	.	4.2	62
About the same amount	1	-	.	-	.	-	.	65.2	990	-	.	63.4	931
More	2	-	.	-	.	-	.	7.0	106	-	.	6.7	98
Less	3	-	.	-	.	-	.	23.7	360	-	.	24.8	365
(DK)	8	-	.	-	.	-	.	-	.	-	.	-	.
(NA)	9	-	.	-	.	-	.	0.5	7	-	.	0.9	13
Base: All									1518				1469

		1983		1984		1985		1986		1987		1989	
Question No								A89c(iii)				A88c(iii)	
Column No								1239				934	
(iii) {EGGSAME}													
Eggs													
[Not asked: never eaten nowadays]	0	-	.	-	.	-	.	3.9	59	-	.	10.8	158
About the same amount	1	-	.	-	.	-	.	65.5	994	-	.	57.1	839
More	2	-	.	-	.	-	.	9.7	147	-	.	6.5	95
Less	3	-	.	-	.	-	.	20.4	309	-	.	24.3	357
(DK)	8	-	.	-	.	-	.	-	.	-	.	-	.
(NA)	9	-	.	-	.	-	.	0.6	9	-	.	1.4	20
Base: All									1518				1469

		1983		1984		1985		1986		1987		1989	
Question No								A89c(iv)				A88c(iv)	
Column No								1242				946	
(iv) {FISHSAME}													
Fish													
[Not asked: never eaten nowadays]	0	-	.	-	.	-	.	7.4	112	-	.	6.6	97
About the same amount	1	-	.	-	.	-	.	60.5	918	-	.	67.3	988
More	2	-	.	-	.	-	.	19.4	295	-	.	14.8	218
Less	3	-	.	-	.	-	.	12.3	186	-	.	9.9	146
(DK)	8	-	.	-	.	-	.	-	.	-	.	-	.
(NA)	9	-	.	-	.	-	.	0.4	6	-	.	1.3	19
Base: All									1518				1469

AMOUNT OF VARIOUS FOODS EATEN COMPARED WITH RECENT PAST
(Continued)

		1983		1984		1985		1986		1987		1989	
		%	No	%	No	%	No	%	No	%	No	%	No
Question No								A89c(vi)				A88c(vi)	
Column No								1248				970	
(v) {VEGSAME}	Code												
Fresh fruit and vegetables													
[Not asked: never eaten nowadays]	0	-	.	-	.	-	.	0.7	11	-	.	0.7	10
About the same amount	1	-	.	-	.	-	.	66.4	1008	-	.	65.9	968
More	2	-	.	-	.	-	.	26.4	400	-	.	26.5	390
Less	3	-	.	-	.	-	.	5.9	89	-	.	6.1	89
(DK)	8	-	.	-	.	-	.	-	.	-	.	-	.
(NA)	9	-	.	-	.	-	.	0.7	11	-	.	0.8	12
Base: All									1518				1469
Question No								A89c(vii)				A88c(viii)	
Column No								1251				1022	
(vi) {BREDSAME}													
Bread													
[Not asked: never eaten nowadays]	0	-	.	-	.	-	.	0.9	14	-	.	1.0	15
About the same amount	1	-	.	-	.	-	.	62.6	951	-	.	68.3	1003
More	2	-	.	-	.	-	.	9.2	139	-	.	6.9	101
Less	3	-	.	-	.	-	.	26.4	401	-	.	22.1	324
(DK)	8	-	.	-	.	-	.	-	.	-	.	-	.
(NA)	9	-	.	-	.	-	.	0.9	13	-	.	1.8	26
Base: All									1518				1469
Question No								A89c(vii)				A89b	
Column No								1251				1041	
(vii) {SUGSAME}													
Sugar in hot drinks													
[Not asked: never eaten nowadays]	0	-	.	-	.	-	.	45.8	695	-	.	50.8	746
About the same amount	1	-	.	-	.	-	.	36.6	555	-	.	30.9	454
More	2	-	.	-	.	-	.	2.3	35	-	.	1.7	24
Less	3	-	.	-	.	-	.	14.8	225	-	.	16.3	240
(DK)	8	-	.	-	.	-	.	-	.	-	.	-	.
(NA)	9	-	.	-	.	-	.	0.5	7	-	.	0.3	4
Base: All									1518				1469

PERCEIVED HEALTH PROPERTIES OF VARIOUS FOODS

{HAMBAD} {MEATBAD} {EGGSBAD} {FISHBAD} {VEGBAD} {BREDBAD}

Question: [If eats same amount as 2 or 3 years ago] *Is/Are* _____ (food) **good for people, bad for people or neither?**

		1983		1984		1985		1986		1987		1989	
		%	No	%	No	%	No	%	No	%	No	%	No
Question No								A89d(i)				A88d(i)	
Column No								1255				911	

(i) {HAMBAD}
Processed meat like sausages, ham or tinned meat

	Code	1983 %	No	1984 %	No	1985 %	No	1986 %	No	1987 %	No	1989 %	No
[Not asked: never eats or has recently changed amount eaten]	0	-	-	-	-	-	-	44.9	682	-	-	41.6	611
Good for people	1	-	-	-	-	-	-	12.3	187	-	-	12.5	183
Bad for people	2	-	-	-	-	-	-	7.9	120	-	-	9.7	143
Neither	3	-	-	-	-	-	-	33.1	503	-	-	33.6	493
(DK)	8	-	-	-	-	-	-	0.5	8	-	-	0.4	6
(NA)	9	-	-	-	-	-	-	1.1	17	-	-	2.2	33
Base: All									1518				1469

				1986				1989	
Question No				A89d(ii)				A88d(ii)	
Column No				1264				923	

(ii) {MEATBAD}
Beef, lamb or pork

	Code	1983 %	No	1984 %	No	1985 %	No	1986 %	No	1987 %	No	1989 %	No
[Not asked: never eats or has recently changed amount eaten]	0	-	-	-	-	-	-	34.3	520	-	-	35.7	525
Good for people	1	-	-	-	-	-	-	42.8	650	-	-	36.4	534
Bad for people	2	-	-	-	-	-	-	2.0	31	-	-	3.5	51
Neither	3	-	-	-	-	-	-	19.8	300	-	-	21.9	321
(DK)	8	-	-	-	-	-	-	0.1	1	-	-	0.1	1
(NA)	9	-	-	-	-	-	-	1.0	15	-	-	2.5	37
Base: All									1518				1469

1986 - Q reads: 'Is/are _____ (food) on the whole good for one, bad for one or neither?'; Good for one, code 1; Bad for one, code 2

PERCEIVED HEALTH PROPERTIES OF VARIOUS FOODS (Continued)

			1983		1984		1985		1986		1987		1989	
			%	No	%	No	%	No	%	No	%	No	%	No
Question No									A89d(iii)				A88d(iii)	
Column No									1308				935	
(iii) {EGGSBAD}		Code												
Eggs														
[Not asked: never eats or has recently changed amount eaten]	0		-	.	-	.	-	.	33.9	515	-	.	41.5	610
Good for people	1		-	.	-	.	-	.	47.6	723	-	.	38.2	561
Bad for people	2		-	.	-	.	-	.	2.4	37	-	.	1.8	26
Neither	3		-	.	-	.	-	.	15.0	228	-	.	15.7	231
(DK)	8		-	.	-	.	-	.	-	.	-	.	-	.
(NA)	9		-	.	-	.	-	.	0.9	14	-	.	2.8	41
Base: All										1518				1469

		1983		1984		1985		1986		1987		1989	
Question No								A89d(iv)				A88d(iv)	
Column No								1317				947	
(iv) {FISHBAD}													
Fish													
[Not asked: never eats or has recently changed amount eaten]	0	-	.	-	.	-	.	39.1	593	-	.	31.4	462
Good for people	1	-	.	-	.	-	.	55.0	835	-	.	59.6	875
Bad for people	2	-	.	-	.	-	.	0.1	1	-	.	0.3	5
Neither	3	-	.	-	.	-	.	4.9	74	-	.	5.7	83
(DK)	8	-	.	-	.	-	.	-	.	-	.	0.1	1
(NA)	9	-	.	-	.	-	.	1.0	15	-	.	2.9	43
Base: All									1518				1469

1986 - Q reads: 'Is/are _____ (food) on the whole good for one, bad for one or neither?'; Good for one, code 1; Bad for one, code 2

PERCEIVED HEALTH PROPERTIES OF VARIOUS FOODS (Continued)

		1983		1984		1985		1986		1987		1989	
		%	No	%	No	%	No	%	No	%	No	%	No
Question No								A89d(vi)				A88d(vi)	
Column No								1335				971	
(v) {VEGBAD}	Code												
Fresh fruit and vegetables													
[Not asked: never eats or has recently changed amount eaten]	0	-	-	-	-	-	-	32.9	500	-	-	33.3	489
Good for people	1	-	.	-	.	-	.	63.4	962	-	.	61.7	906
Bad for people	2	-	.	-	.	-	.	0.1	1	-	.	0.3	4
Neither	3	-	.	-	.	-	.	2.2	34	-	.	2.2	32
(DK)	8	-	.	-	.	-	.	-		-	.	-	
(NA)	9	-	.	-	.	-	.	1.3	20	-	.	2.7	39
Base: All									1518				1469

		1983		1984		1985		1986		1987		1989	
Question No								A89d(vii)				A88d(viii)	
Column No								1353				1023	
(vi) {BREDBAD}													
Bread													
[Not asked: never eats or has recently changed amount eaten]	0	-	-	-	-	-	-	36.5	554	-	-	30.0	440
Good for people	1	-	.	-	.	-	.	43.6	662	-	.	47.2	693
Bad for people	2	-	.	-	.	-	.	2.1	32	-	.	1.6	24
Neither	3	-	.	-	.	-	.	16.1	244	-	.	17.5	257
(DK)	8	-	.	-	.	-	.	-		-	.	0.1	1
(NA)	9	-	.	-	.	-	.	1.6	25	-	.	3.7	54
Base: All									1518				1469

1986 - Q reads: 'Is/are ___ (food) on the whole good for one, bad for one or neither?'; Good for one, code 1; Bad for one, code 2

REASONS FOR CHANGING EATING HABITS
Processed meat

{HAMWHY1} {HAMWHY2} {HAMWHY3} {HAMWHY4} {HAMWHY5} {HAMWHY6} {HAMWHY7} {HAMWHY8}

Question: [If recently changed amount eaten] You said that you had changed the amount of processed meat you eat like sausages, ham or tinned meat. Have you changed for any of *these* reasons? Any other of these reasons? (Interviewer: probe until 'No')

		1983		1984		1985		1986		1987		1989	
		%	No	%	No	%	No	%	No	%	No	%	No
Question No								A89e(i)				A88e(i)	
Column No								1256				912	
(i) {HAMWHY1}	Code												
To help control my weight													
[Not asked: not recently changed amount eaten]	-1	-		-		-		55.3	839	-		59.5	874
Not given as reason	0	-		-		-		36.6	555	-		32.3	474
Given as reason	1	-		-		-		5.6	85	-		6.3	92
(DK)	8	-		-		-		0.3	4	-		0.1	1
(NA)	9	-		-		-		2.3	35	-		1.9	28
Base: All									1518				1469
Question No								A89e(ii)				A88e(ii)	
Column No								1257				913	
(ii) {HAMWHY2}													
I was told to for medical reasons													
[Not asked: not recently changed amount eaten]	-1	-		-		-		55.3	839	-		59.5	874
Not given as reason	0	-		-		-		39.2	595	-		34.6	508
Given as reason	2	-		-		-		3.0	46	-		3.9	58
(DK)	8	-		-		-		0.3	4	-		0.1	1
(NA)	9	-		-		-		2.3	35	-		1.9	28
Base: All									1518				1469

1986 - {HAMWHY1} SPSS file does not show a 'not asked' figure, but has an (unlabelled) code 10 instead

REASONS FOR CHANGING EATING HABITS
Processed meat (Continued)

			1983		1984		1985		1986		1987		1989	
			%	No	%	No	%	No	%	No	%	No	%	No
	Question No								A89e(iii)				A88e(iii)	
	Column No								1258				914	
(iii) {HAMWHY3}		Code												
It is good value for money														
[Not asked: not recently changed amount eaten]		-1	-		-		-		55.3	839	-		59.5	874
Not given as reason		0	-		-		-		40.3	612	-		37.1	545
Given as reason		3	-		-		-		1.8	28	-		1.4	21
(DK)		8	-		-		-		0.3	4	-		0.1	1
(NA)		9	-		-		-		2.3	35	-		1.9	28
Base: All										1518				1469

		1983		1984		1985		1986		1987		1989	
	Question No							A89e(iv)				A88e(iv)	
	Column No							1259				915	
(iv) {HAMWHY4}													
It is poor value for money													
[Not asked: not recently changed amount eaten]	-1	-		-		-		55.3	839	-		59.5	874
Not given as reason	0	-		-		-		37.4	568	-		36.9	542
Given as reason	4	-		-		-		4.7	72	-		1.6	24
(DK)	8	-		-		-		0.3	4	-		0.1	1
(NA)	9	-		-		-		2.3	35	-		1.9	28
Base: All									1518				1469

		1983		1984		1985		1986		1987		1989	
	Question No							A89e(v)				A88e(v)	
	Column No							1260				916	
(v) {HAMWHY5}													
I wanted to keep healthy													
[Not asked: not recently changed amount eaten]	-1	-		-		-		55.3	839	-		59.5	874
Not given as reason	0	-		-		-		30.3	460	-		25.5	375
Given as reason	5	-		-		-		11.9	181	-		13.0	191
(DK)	8	-		-		-		0.3	4	-		0.1	1
(NA)	9	-		-		-		2.3	35	-		1.9	28
Base: All									1518				1469

REASONS FOR CHANGING EATING HABITS
Processed meat (Continued)

		1983		1984		1985		1986		1987		1989	
		%	No	%	No	%	No	%	No	%	No	%	No
Question No								A89e(vi)				A88e(vi)	
Column No								1261				917	

(vi) {HAMWHY6}
I just like it more

	Code												
[Not asked: not recently changed amount eaten]	-1	-		-		-		55.3	839	-		59.5	874
Not given as reason	0	-		-		-		39.9	606	-		37.2	547
Given as reason	6	-		-		-		2.3	35	-		1.3	19
(DK)	8	-		-		-		0.3	4	-		0.1	1
(NA)	9	-		-		-		2.3	35	-		1.9	28
Base: All									1518				1469

Question No								A89e(vii)				A88e(vii)	
Column No								1262				918	

(vii) {HAMWHY7}
I just don't like it as much

[Not asked: not recently changed amount eaten]	-1	-		-		-		55.3	839	-		59.5	874
Not given as reason	0	-		-		-		31.0	471	-		30.9	454
Given as reason	7	-		-		-		11.2	170	-		7.6	112
(DK)	8	-		-		-		0.3	4	-		0.1	1
(NA)	9	-		-		-		2.3	35	-		1.9	28
Base: All									1518				1469

Question No								A89e(viii)				A88e(viii)	
Column No								1263				919	

(viii) {HAMWHY8}
One or more reasons given

[Not asked: not recently changed amount eaten]	-1	-		-		-		55.3	839	-		59.5	874
None of these reasons	0	-		-		-		7.2	110	-		11.2	164
One or more reasons given	1	-		-		-		34.9	530	-		27.4	402
(DK)	8	-		-		-		0.3	4	-		0.1	1
(NA)	9	-		-		-		2.3	35	-		1.9	28
Base: All									1518				1469

REASONS FOR CHANGING EATING HABITS
Beef, lamb or pork

{MEATWHY1} {MEATWHY2} {MEATWHY3} {MEATWHY4} {MEATWHY5} {MEATWHY6} {MEATWHY7} {MEATWHY8}

Question: [If recently changed amount eaten] You said that you had changed the amount of beef, lamb or pork you eat.
Have you changed for any of *these* reasons? Any other of these reasons? (Interviewer: probe until 'No')

		1983		1984		1985		1986		1987		1989	
		%	No	%	No	%	No	%	No	%	No	%	No
Question No								A89e(i)				A88e(i)	
Column No								1265				924	
(i) {MEATWHY1}	Code												
To help control my weight													
[Not asked: not recently changed amount eaten]	-1	-	.	-	.	-	.	65.7	997	-	-	64.1	942
Not given as reason	0	-	.	-	.	-	.	30.6	464	-	-	29.8	438
Given as reason	1	-	.	-	.	-	.	1.8	28	-	-	3.7	55
(DK)	8	-	.	-	.	-	.	0.1	1	-	-	0.1	1
(NA)	9	-	.	-	.	-	.	1.8	27	-	-	2.2	32
Base: All									1518				1469

		1983		1984		1985		1986		1987		1989	
Question No								A89e(ii)				A88e(ii)	
Column No								1266				925	
(ii) {MEATWHY2}													
I was told to for medical reasons													
[Not asked: not recently changed amount eaten]	-1	-	.	-	.	-	.	65.7	997	-	-	64.1	942
Not given as reason	0	-	.	-	.	-	.	30.5	463	-	-	30.2	444
Given as reason	2	-	.	-	.	-	.	2.0	30	-	-	3.4	50
(DK)	8	-	.	-	.	-	.	0.1	1	-	-	0.1	1
(NA)	9	-	.	-	.	-	.	1.8	27	-	-	2.2	32
Base: All									1518				1469

1986 - {MEATWHY1} SPSS file does not show a 'not asked' figure, but has an (unlabelled) code 10 instead

REASONS FOR CHANGING EATING HABITS
Beef, lamb or pork (Continued)

			1983		1984		1985		1986		1987		1989	
			%	No	%	No	%	No	%	No	%	No	%	No
	Question No								A89e(iii)				A88e(iii)	
	Column No								1267				926	

(iii) {MEATWHY3}
It is good value for money

	Code	1983 %	1983 No	1984 %	1984 No	1985 %	1985 No	1986 %	1986 No	1987 %	1987 No	1989 %	1989 No
[Not asked: not recently changed amount eaten]	-1	-	-	-	-	-	-	65.7	997	-	-	64.1	942
Not given as reason	0	-	.	-	.	-	.	31.0	470	-	.	33.2	487
Given as reason	3	-	.	-	.	-	.	1.4	22	-	.	0.4	6
(DK)	8	-	.	-	.	-	.	0.1	1	-	.	0.1	1
(NA)	9	-	.	-	.	-	.	1.8	27	-	.	2.2	32
Base: All									1518				1469

	Question No	A89e(iv)	A88e(iv)
	Column No	1268	927

(iv) {MEATWHY4}
It is poor value for money

	Code	1983 %	1983 No	1984 %	1984 No	1985 %	1985 No	1986 %	1986 No	1987 %	1987 No	1989 %	1989 No
[Not asked: not recently changed amount eaten]	-1	-	-	-	-	-	-	65.7	997	-	-	64.1	942
Not given as reason	0	-	.	-	.	-	.	22.9	347	-	.	30.3	445
Given as reason	4	-	.	-	.	-	.	9.6	146	-	.	3.3	48
(DK)	8	-	.	-	.	-	.	0.1	1	-	.	0.1	1
(NA)	9	-	.	-	.	-	.	1.8	27	-	.	2.2	32
Base: All									1518				1469

	Question No	A89e(v)	A88e(v)
	Column No	1269	928

(v) {MEATWHY5}
I wanted to keep healthy

	Code	1983 %	1983 No	1984 %	1984 No	1985 %	1985 No	1986 %	1986 No	1987 %	1987 No	1989 %	1989 No
[Not asked: not recently changed amount eaten]	-1	-	-	-	-	-	-	65.7	997	-	-	64.1	942
Not given as reason	0	-	.	-	.	-	.	25.2	382	-	.	24.4	358
Given as reason	5	-	.	-	.	-	.	7.3	111	-	.	9.3	136
(DK)	8	-	.	-	.	-	.	0.1	1	-	.	0.1	1
(NA)	9	-	.	-	.	-	.	1.8	27	-	.	2.2	32
Base: All									1518				1469

REASONS FOR CHANGING EATING HABITS
Beef, lamb or pork (Continued)

		1983		1984		1985		1986		1987		1989	
		%	No	%	No	%	No	%	No	%	No	%	No

	Code												
Question No Column No								A89e (vi) 1270				A88e (vi) 929	
(vi) {MEATWHY6} I just like it more													
[Not asked: not recently changed amount eaten]	-1	-	-	-	-	-	-	65.7	997	-	-	64.1	942
Not given as reason	0	-	-	-	-	-	-	29.7	451	-	-	31.7	465
Given as reason	6	-	-	-	-	-	-	2.7	41	-	-	1.9	28
(DK)	8	-	-	-	-	-	-	0.1	1	-	-	0.1	1
(NA)	9	-	-	-	-	-	-	1.8	27	-	-	2.2	32
Base: All									1518				1469

	Code												
Question No Column No								A89e (vii) 1271				A88e (vii) 930	
(vii) {MEATWHY7} I just don't like it as much													
[Not asked: not recently changed amount eaten]	-1	-	-	-	-	-	-	65.7	997	-	-	64.1	942
Not given as reason	0	-	-	-	-	-	-	27.6	419	-	-	29.0	426
Given as reason	7	-	-	-	-	-	-	4.9	74	-	-	4.6	67
(DK)	8	-	-	-	-	-	-	0.1	1	-	-	0.1	1
(NA)	9	-	-	-	-	-	-	1.8	27	-	-	2.2	32
Base: All									1518				1469

	Code												
Question No Column No								A89e (viii) 1272				A88e (viii) 931	
(viii) {MEATWHY8} None of these reasons													
[Not asked: not recently changed amount eaten]	-1	-	-	-	-	-	-	65.7	997	-	-	64.1	942
None of these reasons	0	-	-	-	-	-	-	5.7	87	-	-	11.8	173
One or more reasons given	1	-	-	-	-	-	-	26.7	405	-	-	21.8	320
(DK)	8	-	-	-	-	-	-	0.1	1	-	-	0.1	1
(NA)	9	-	-	-	-	-	-	1.8	27	-	-	2.2	32
Base: All									1518				1469

REASONS FOR CHANGING EATING HABITS
Eggs

{EGGSWHY1} {EGGSWHY2} {EGGSWHY3} {EGGSWHY4} {EGGSWHY5} {EGGSWHY6} {EGGSWHY7} {EGGSWHY8}

Question: [If recently changed amount eaten] **You said that you had changed the amount of eggs you eat. Have you changed for any of** *these* **reasons? Any other of these reasons?** (Interviewer: probe until 'No')

		1983		1984		1985		1986		1987		1989	
		%	No	%	No	%	No	%	No	%	No	%	No
Question No								A89e(i)				A88e(i)	
Column No								1309				936	
(i) *{EGGSWHY1}*	Code												
To help control my weight													
[Not asked: not recently changed amount eaten]	-1	-	.	-	.	-	.	66.5	1009	-	.	59.4	873
Not given as reason	0	-	.	-	.	-	.	30.0	455	-	.	35.1	516
Given as reason	1	-	.	-	.	-	.	1.6	25	-	.	1.8	26
(DK)	8	-	.	-	.	-	.	0.1	2	-	.	0.1	1
(NA)	9	-	.	-	.	-	.	1.8	27	-	.	3.7	54
Base: All									1518				1469

		1983		1984		1985		1986		1987		1989	
Question No								A89e(ii)				A88e(ii)	
Column No								1310				937	
(ii) *{EGGSWHY2}*													
I was told to for medical reasons													
[Not asked: not recently changed amount eaten]	-1	-	.	-	.	-	.	66.5	1009	-	.	59.4	873
Not given as reason	0	-	.	-	.	-	.	29.1	441	-	.	32.3	475
Given as reason	2	-	.	-	.	-	.	2.6	39	-	.	4.5	66
(DK)	8	-	.	-	.	-	.	0.1	2	-	.	0.1	1
(NA)	9	-	.	-	.	-	.	1.8	27	-	.	3.7	54
Base: All									1518				1469

1986 · {EGGSWHY1} SPSS file does not show a 'not asked' figure, but has an (unlabelled) code 10 instead

REASONS FOR CHANGING EATING HABITS
Eggs (Continued)

			1983		1984		1985		1986		1987		1989	
			%	No	%	No	%	No	%	No	%	No	%	No
Question No									A89e(iii)				A88e(iii)	
Column No									1311				938	
(iii) {EGGSWHY3}		Code												
It is good value for money														
[Not asked: not recently changed amount eaten]	-1		-		-		-		66.5	1009	-		59.4	873
Not given as reason	0		-		-		-		28.5	433	-		35.3	518
Given as reason	3		-		-		-		3.1	47	-		1.6	24
(DK)	8		-		-		-		0.1	2	-		0.1	1
(NA)	9		-		-		-		1.8	27	-		3.7	54
Base: All										1518				1469

			1983		1984		1985		1986		1987		1989	
Question No									A89e(iv)				A88e(iv)	
Column No									1312				939	
(iv) {EGGSWHY4}														
It is poor value for money														
[Not asked: not recently changed amount eaten]	-1		-		-		-		66.5	1009	-		59.4	873
Not given as reason	0		-		-		-		31.5	478	-		36.8	540
Given as reason	4		-		-		-		0.1	2	-		0.1	1
(DK)	8		-		-		-		0.1	2	-		0.1	1
(NA)	9		-		-		-		1.8	27	-		3.7	54
Base: All										1518				1469

			1983		1984		1985		1986		1987		1989	
Question No									A89e(v)				A88e(v)	
Column No									1313				940	
(v) {EGGSWHY5}														
I wanted to keep healthy														
[Not asked: not recently changed amount eaten]	-1		-		-		-		66.5	1009	-		59.4	873
Not given as reason	0		-		-		-		24.3	369	-		25.3	371
Given as reason	5		-		-		-		7.3	111	-		11.6	171
(DK)	8		-		-		-		0.1	2	-		0.1	1
(NA)	9		-		-		-		1.8	27	-		3.7	54
Base: All										1518				1469

1986 - {HAMWHY1} SPSS file does not show a 'not asked' figure, but has an (unlabelled) code 10 instead

REASONS FOR CHANGING EATING HABITS
Eggs (Continued)

		1983		1984		1985		1986		1987		1989	
		%	No	%	No	%	No	%	No	%	No	%	No
Question No								A89e(vi)				A88e(vi)	
Column No								1314				941	

(vi) {EGGSWHY6}
I just like it more

	Code	1983 %	No	1984 %	No	1985 %	No	1986 %	No	1987 %	No	1989 %	No
[Not asked: not recently changed amount eaten]	-1	-	.	-	.	-	.	66.5	1009	-	-	59.4	873
Not given as reason	0	-	.	-	.	-	.	28.3	429	-	-	34.8	511
Given as reason	6	-	.	-	.	-	.	3.3	50	-	-	2.1	31
(DK)	8	-	.	-	.	-	.	0.1	2	-	-	0.1	1
(NA)	9	-	.	-	.	-	.	1.8	27	-	-	3.7	54
Base: All									1518				1469

								A89e(vii)				A88e(vii)	
Question No													
Column No								1315				942	

(vii) {EGGSWHY7}
I just don't like it as much

	Code	1983 %	No	1984 %	No	1985 %	No	1986 %	No	1987 %	No	1989 %	No
[Not asked: not recently changed amount eaten]	-1	-	.	-	.	-	.	66.5	1009	-	-	59.4	873
Not given as reason	0	-	.	-	.	-	.	22.7	345	-	-	30.8	453
Given as reason	7	-	.	-	.	-	.	8.9	135	-	-	6.1	89
(DK)	8	-	.	-	.	-	.	0.1	2	-	-	0.1	1
(NA)	9	-	.	-	.	-	.	1.8	27	-	-	3.7	54
Base: All									1518				1469

								A89e(viii)				A88e(viii)	
Question No													
Column No								1316				943	

(viii) {EGGSWHY8}
None of these reasons

	Code	1983 %	No	1984 %	No	1985 %	No	1986 %	No	1987 %	No	1989 %	No
[Not asked: not recently changed amount eaten]	-1	-	.	-	.	-	.	66.5	1009	-	-	59.4	873
None of these reasons	0	-	.	-	.	-	.	6.4	97	-	-	11.9	175
One or more reasons given	1	-	.	-	.	-	.	25.2	383	-	-	25.0	367
(DK)	8	-	.	-	.	-	.	0.1	2	-	-	0.1	1
(NA)	9	-	.	-	.	-	.	1.8	27	-	-	3.7	54
Base: All									1518				1469

REASONS FOR CHANGING EATING HABITS
Fish

{FISHWHY1} {FISHWHY2} {FISHWHY3} {FISHWHY4} {FISHWHY5} {FISHWHY6} {FISHWHY7} {FISHWHY8}

Question: [If recently changed amount eaten] You said that you had changed the amount of fish you eat. Have you changed for any of *these* reasons? Any other of these reasons? (Interviewer: probe until 'No')

			1983		1984		1985		1986		1987		1989	
			%	No	%	No	%	No	%	No	%	No	%	No
Question No									A89e(i)				A88e(i)	
Column No									1318				948	
(i) {FISHWHY1}	Code													
To help control my weight														
[Not asked: not recently changed amount eaten]	-1		-	-	-	-	-	-	62.6	950	-	-	70.3	1032
Not given as reason	0		-	-	-	-	-	-	32.5	494	-	-	24.5	360
Given as reason	1		-	-	-	-	-	-	2.2	34	-	-	2.4	35
(DK)	8		-	-	-	-	-	-	0.1	1	-	-	0.1	1
(NA)	9		-	-	-	-	-	-	2.6	39	-	-	2.8	41
Base: All										1518				1469
Question No									A89e(ii)				A88e(ii)	
Column No									1319				949	
(ii) {FISHWHY2}														
I was told to for medical reasons														
[Not asked: not recently changed amount eaten]	-1		-	-	-	-	-	-	62.6	950	-	-	70.3	1032
Not given as reason	0		-	-	-	-	-	-	33.1	502	-	-	25.1	368
Given as reason	2		-	-	-	-	-	-	1.6	25	-	-	1.8	27
(DK)	8		-	-	-	-	-	-	0.1	1	-	-	0.1	1
(NA)	9		-	-	-	-	-	-	2.6	39	-	-	2.8	41
Base: All										1518				1469

1986 - {FISHWHY1} SPSS file does not show a 'not asked' figure, but has an (unlabelled) code 10 instead

REASONS FOR CHANGING EATING HABITS
Fish (Continued)

		1983		1984		1985		1986		1987		1989	
		%	No	%	No	%	No	%	No	%	No	%	No
Question No								A89e(iii)				A88e(iii)	
Column No								1320				950	
(iii) {FISHWHY3}	Code												
It is good value for money													
[Not asked: not recently changed amount eaten]	-1	-	.	-	.	-	.	62.6	950	-	.	70.3	1032
Not given as reason	0	-	.	-	.	-	.	31.1	472	-	.	25.1	369
Given as reason	3	-	.	-	.	-	.	3.6	55	-	.	1.8	26
(DK)	8	-	.	-	.	-	.	0.1	1	-	.	0.1	1
(NA)	9	-	.	-	.	-	.	2.6	39	-	.	2.8	41
Base: All									1518				1469

		1983		1984		1985		1986		1987		1989	
Question No								A89e(iv)				A88e(iv)	
Column No								1321				951	
(iv) {FISHWHY4}													
It is poor value for money													
[Not asked: not recently changed amount eaten]	-1	-	.	-	.	-	.	62.6	950	-	.	70.3	1032
Not given as reason	0	-	.	-	.	-	.	31.3	475	-	.	25.1	368
Given as reason	4	-	.	-	.	-	.	3.5	53	-	.	1.8	27
(DK)	8	-	.	-	.	-	.	0.1	1	-	.	0.1	1
(NA)	9	-	.	-	.	-	.	2.6	39	-	.	2.8	41
Base: All									1518				1469

		1983		1984		1985		1986		1987		1989	
Question No								A89e(v)				A88e(v)	
Column No								1322				952	
(v) {FISHWHY5}													
I wanted to keep healthy													
[Not asked: not recently changed amount eaten]	-1	-	.	-	.	-	.	62.6	950	-	.	70.3	1032
Not given as reason	0	-	.	-	.	-	.	27.0	410	-	.	19.7	289
Given as reason	5	-	.	-	.	-	.	7.8	118	-	.	7.2	106
(DK)	8	-	.	-	.	-	.	0.1	1	-	.	0.1	1
(NA)	9	-	.	-	.	-	.	2.6	39	-	.	2.8	41
Base: All									1518				1469

REASONS FOR CHANGING EATING HABITS
Fish (Continued)

		1983		1984		1985		1986		1987		1989	
		%	No	%	No	%	No	%	No	%	No	%	No

	Question No Column No							A89e(vi) 1323				A88e(vi) 953	
(vi) {FISHWHY6} **I just like it more**	Code												
[Not asked: not recently changed amount eaten]	-1	-		-		-		62.6	950	-		70.3	1032
Not given as reason	0	-		-		-		27.4	416	-		21.9	322
Given as reason	6	-		-		-		7.3	111	-		5.0	73
(DK)	8	-		-		-		0.1	1	-		0.1	1
(NA)	9	-		-		-		2.6	39	-		2.8	41
Base: All									1518				1469

	Question No Column No							A89e(vii) 1324				A88e(vii) 954	
(vii) {FISHWHY7} **I just don't like it as much**													
[Not asked: not recently changed amount eaten]	-1	-		-		-		62.6	950	-		70.3	1032
Not given as reason	0	-		-		-		28.3	429	-		23.6	347
Given as reason	7	-		-		-		6.5	99	-		3.3	49
(DK)	8	-		-		-		0.1	1	-		0.1	1
(NA)	9	-		-		-		2.6	39	-		2.8	41
Base: All									1518				1469

	Question No Column No							A89e(viii) 1325				A88e(viii) 955	
(viii) {FISHWHY8} **None of these reasons**													
[Not asked: not recently changed amount eaten]	-1	-		-		-		62.6	950	-		70.3	1032
None of these reasons	0	-		-		-		7.0	107	-		7.7	113
One or more reasons given	1	-		-		-		27.7	421	-		19.2	282
(DK)	8	-		-		-		0.1	1	-		0.1	1
(NA)	9	-		-		-		2.6	39	-		2.8	41
Base: All									1518				1469

REASONS FOR CHANGING EATING HABITS
Fresh fruit and vegetables

{VEGWHY1} {VEGWHY2} {VEGWHY3} {VEGWHY4} {VEGWHY5} {VEGWHY6} {VEGWHY7} {VEGWHY8}

Question: [If recently changed amount eaten] You said that you had changed the amount of fresh fruit and vegetables you eat. Have you changed for any of *these* reasons? Any other of these reasons? (Interviewer: probe until 'No')

		1983		1984		1985		1986		1987		1989	
		%	No	%	No	%	No	%	No	%	No	%	No
Question No								A89e(i)				A88e(i)	
Column No								1336				972	
(i) {VEGWHY1}	Code												
To help control my weight													
[Not asked: not recently changed amount eaten]	-1	-		-		-		**66.4**	1008	-		**66.2**	973
Not given as reason	0	-		-		-		**27.9**	424	-		**27.2**	400
Given as reason	1	-		-		-		**4.1**	61	-		**4.4**	64
(DK)	8	-		-		-		-		-		**0.1**	1
(NA)	9	-		-		-		**1.6**	25	-		**2.2**	32
Base: All									1518				1469

		1983		1984		1985		1986		1987		1989	
Question No								A89e(ii)				A88e(ii)	
Column No								1337				973	
(ii) {VEGWHY2}													
I was told to for medical reasons													
[Not asked: not recently changed amount eaten]	-1	-		-		-		**66.4**	1008	-		**66.2**	973
Not given as reason	0	-		-		-		**30.7**	466	-		**28.1**	413
Given as reason	2	-		-		-		**1.3**	19	-		**3.5**	51
(DK)	8	-		-		-		-		-		**0.1**	1
(NA)	9	-		-		-		**1.6**	25	-		**2.2**	32
Base: All									1518				1469

1986 -   {VEGWHY1} SPSS file does not show a 'not asked' figure, but has an (unlabelled) code 10 instead

REASONS FOR CHANGING EATING HABITS
Fresh fruit and vegetables (Continued)

		1983		1984		1985		1986		1987		1989	
		%	No	%	No	%	No	%	No	%	No	%	No
Question No Column No								A89e(iii) 1338				A88e(iii) 974	
(iii) {VEGWHY3} **It is good value for money**	Code												
[Not asked: not recently changed amount eaten]	-1	-		-		-		**66.4**	1008	-		**66.2**	973
Not given as reason	0	-		-		-		**29.4**	447	-		**29.7**	436
Given as reason	3	-		-		-		**2.6**	39	-		**1.9**	28
(DK)	8	-		-		-		-		-		**0.1**	1
(NA)	9	-		-		-		**1.6**	25	-		**2.2**	32
Base: All									1518				1469

		1983		1984		1985		1986		1987		1989	
Question No Column No								A89e(iv) 1339				A88e(iv) 975	
(iv) {VEGWHY4} **It is poor value for money**													
[Not asked: not recently changed amount eaten]	-1	-		-		-		**66.4**	1008	-		**66.2**	973
Not given as reason	0	-		-		-		**30.2**	459	-		**30.7**	451
Given as reason	4	-		-		-		**1.7**	26	-		**0.9**	13
(DK)	8	-		-		-		-		-		**0.1**	1
(NA)	9	-		-		-		**1.6**	25	-		**2.2**	32
Base: All									1518				1469

		1983		1984		1985		1986		1987		1989	
Question No Column No								A89e(v) 1340				A88e(v) 976	
(v) {VEGWHY5} **I wanted to keep healthy**													
[Not asked: not recently changed amount eaten]	-1	-		-		-		**66.4**	1008	-		**66.2**	973
Not given as reason	0	-		-		-		**15.2**	231	-		**14.0**	205
Given as reason	5	-		-		-		**16.7**	254	-		**17.6**	259
(DK)	8	-		-		-		-		-		**0.1**	1
(NA)	9	-		-		-		**1.6**	25	-		**2.2**	32
Base: All									1518				1469

REASONS FOR CHANGING EATING HABITS
Fresh fruit and vegetables (Continued)

		1983		1984		1985		1986		1987		1989	
		%	No	%	No	%	No	%	No	%	No	%	No
Question No								A89e(vi)				A88e(vi)	
Column No								1341				977	

(vi) {VEGWHY6}
I just like it more

	Code												
[Not asked: not recently changed amount eaten]	-1	-		-		-		66.4	1008	-		66.2	973
Not given as reason	0	-		-		-		25.0	380	-		25.6	376
Given as reason	6	-		-		-		7.0	106	-		6.0	88
(DK)	8	-		-		-		-		-		0.1	1
(NA)	9	-		-		-		1.6	25	-		2.2	32
Base: All									1518				1469

Question No								A89e(vii)				A88e(vii)	
Column No								1342				978	

(vii) {VEGWHY7}
I just don't like it as much

	Code												
[Not asked: not recently changed amount eaten]	-1	-		-		-		66.4	1008	-		66.2	973
Not given as reason	0	-		-		-		29.7	451	-		30.0	440
Given as reason	7	-		-		-		2.2	34	-		1.6	24
(DK)	8	-		-		-		-		-		0.1	1
(NA)	9	-		-		-		1.6	25	-		2.2	32
Base: All									1518				1469

Question No								A89e(viii)				A88e(viii)	
Column No								1343				979	

(viii) {VEGWHY8}
None of these reasons

	Code												
[Not asked: not recently changed amount eaten]	-1	-		-		-		66.4	1008	-		66.2	973
None of these reasons	0	-		-		-		3.6	54	-		4.7	69
One or more reasons given	1	-		-		-		28.5	432	-		26.8	394
(DK)	8	-		-		-		-		-		0.1	1
(NA)	9	-		-		-		1.6	25	-		2.2	32
Base: All									1518				1469

REASONS FOR CHANGING EATING HABITS
Bread

{BREDWHY1} {BREDWHY2} {BREDWHY3} {BREDWHY4} {BREDWHY5} {BREDWHY6} {BREDWHY7} {BREDWHY8}

Question: [If recently changed amount eaten] **You said that you had changed the amount of bread you eat. Have you changed for any of *these* reasons? Any other of these reasons?** (Interviewer: probe until 'No')

		1983		1984		1985		1986		1987		1989	
		%	No	%	No	%	No	%	No	%	No	%	No
Question No								A89e(i)				A88e(i)	
Column No								1345				1024	
(i) {BREDWHY1}	Code												
To help control my weight													
[Not asked: not recently changed amount eaten]	-1	-	-	-	-	-	-	62.8	954	-	-	68.5	1006
Not given as reason	0	-	-	-	-	-	-	22.7	344	-	-	19.5	286
Given as reason	1	-	-	-	-	-	-	12.0	183	-	-	9.7	142
(DK)	8	-	-	-	-	-	-	-	-	-	-	0.1	1
(NA)	9	-	-	-	-	-	-	2.5	37	-	-	2.3	34
Base: All									1518				1469

		1983		1984		1985		1986		1987		1989	
Question No								A89e(ii)				A88e(ii)	
Column No								1346				1025	
(ii) {BREDWHY2}													
I was told to for medical reasons													
[Not asked: not recently changed amount eaten]	-1	-	-	-	-	-	-	62.8	954	-	-	68.5	1006
Not given as reason	0	-	-	-	-	-	-	32.8	498	-	-	27.2	400
Given as reason	2	-	-	-	-	-	-	1.8	28	-	-	1.9	28
(DK)	8	-	-	-	-	-	-	-	-	-	-	0.1	1
(NA)	9	-	-	-	-	-	-	2.4	37	-	-	2.3	34
Base: All									1518				1469

1986 -   {BREDWHY1} SPSS file does not show a 'not asked' figure, but has an (unlabelled) code 10 instead

REASONS FOR CHANGING EATING HABITS
Bread (Continued)

		1983		1984		1985		1986		1987		1989	
		%	No	%	No	%	No	%	No	%	No	%	No
Question No Column No								A89e (iii) 1347				A88e (iii) 1026	
(iii) {BREDWHY3} **It is good value for money**	Code												
[Not asked: not recently changed amount eaten]	-1	-	-	-	-	-	-	**62.8**	954	-	-	**68.5**	1006
Not given as reason	0	-	-	-	-	-	-	**33.5**	509	-	-	**28.3**	416
Given as reason	3	-	-	-	-	-	-	**1.2**	18	-	-	**0.7**	11
(DK)	8	-	-	-	-	-	-	-	-	-	-	**0.1**	1
(NA)	9	-	-	-	-	-	-	**2.4**	37	-	-	**2.3**	34
Base: All								1518				1469	

		1983		1984		1985		1986		1987		1989	
Question No Column No								A89e (iv) 1348				A88e (iv) 1027	
(iv) {BREDWHY4} **It is poor value for money**													
[Not asked: not recently changed amount eaten]	-1	-	-	-	-	-	-	**62.8**	954	-	-	**68.5**	1006
Not given as reason	0	-	-	-	-	-	-	**34.5**	523	-	-	**29.1**	427
Given as reason	4	-	-	-	-	-	-	**0.3**	4	-	-	**0.1**	1
(DK)	8	-	-	-	-	-	-	-	-	-	-	**0.1**	1
(NA)	9	-	-	-	-	-	-	**2.4**	37	-	-	**2.3**	34
Base: All								1518				1469	

		1983		1984		1985		1986		1987		1989	
Question No Column No								A89e (v) 1349				A88e (v) 1028	
(v) {BREDWHY5} **I wanted to keep healthy**													
[Not asked: not recently changed amount eaten]	-1	-	-	-	-	-	-	**62.8**	954	-	-	**68.5**	1006
Not given as reason	0	-	-	-	-	-	-	**28.7**	435	-	-	**22.5**	331
Given as reason	5	-	-	-	-	-	-	**6.0**	91	-	-	**6.6**	97
(DK)	8	-	-	-	-	-	-	-	-	-	-	**0.1**	1
(NA)	9	-	-	-	-	-	-	**2.4**	37	-	-	**2.3**	34
Base: All								1518				1469	

REASONS FOR CHANGING EATING HABITS
Bread (Continued)

		1983		1984		1985		1986		1987		1989	
		%	No	%	No	%	No	%	No	%	No	%	No
Question No								A89e(vi)				A88e(vi)	
Column No								1350				1029	

(vi) {BREDWHY6}
I just like it more

	Code	1983 %	No	1984 %	No	1985 %	No	1986 %	No	1987 %	No	1989 %	No
[Not asked: not recently changed amount eaten]	-1	-	-	-	-	-	-	62.8	954	-	-	68.5	1006
Not given as reason	0	-	-	-	-	-	-	31.6	480	-	-	27.5	404
Given as reason	6	-	-	-	-	-	-	3.1	47	-	-	1.6	24
(DK)	8	-	-	-	-	-	-	-	-	-	-	0.1	1
(NA)	9	-	-	-	-	-	-	2.4	37	-	-	2.3	34
Base: All									1518				1469

								A89e(vii)				A88e(vii)	
Question No / Column No								1351				1030	

(vii) {BREDWHY7}
I just don't like it as much

	Code	1983 %	No	1984 %	No	1985 %	No	1986 %	No	1987 %	No	1989 %	No
[Not asked: not recently changed amount eaten]	-1	-	-	-	-	-	-	62.8	954	-	-	68.5	1006
Not given as reason	0	-	-	-	-	-	-	29.3	445	-	-	25.5	375
Given as reason	7	-	-	-	-	-	-	5.4	82	-	-	3.6	53
(DK)	8	-	-	-	-	-	-	-	-	-	-	0.1	1
(NA)	9	-	-	-	-	-	-	2.4	37	-	-	2.3	34
Base: All									1518				1469

								A89e(viii)				A88e(viii)	
Question No / Column No								1352				1031	

(viii) {BREDWHY8}
None of these reasons

	Code	1983 %	No	1984 %	No	1985 %	No	1986 %	No	1987 %	No	1989 %	No
[Not asked: not recently changed amount eaten]	-1	-	-	-	-	-	-	62.8	954	-	-	68.5	1006
None of these reasons	0	-	-	-	-	-	-	7.9	120	-	-	9.0	132
One or more reasons given	1	-	-	-	-	-	-	26.7	406	-	-	20.1	296
(DK)	8	-	-	-	-	-	-	-	-	-	-	0.1	1
(NA)	9	-	-	-	-	-	-	2.4	37	-	-	2.3	34
Base: All									1518				1469

RECENT CHANGES TO HEALTHIER EATING - 1

{SPREADS} {GRILFOOD} {FISHPOUL} {SKIMMILK} {BREAD}

Question: Compared with *two or three years ago*, would you say you are now ... (read out each statement in turn):

		1983		1984		1985		1986		1987		1989	
		%	No	%	No	%	No	%	No	%	No	%	No
Question No								A90				A91a	
Column No								1438				1044	

(i) {SPREADS}

Using more low fat spreads or
soft margarine *instead* of butter,
or not

Code

		1983		1984		1985		1986		1987		1989	
Yes	1	-	.	-	.	-	.	54.4	825	-	.	60.0	881
No	2	-	.	-	.	-	.	44.8	679	-	.	39.3	578
(DK)	8	-	.	-	.	-	.	0.2	3	-	.	0.6	9
(NA)	9	-	.	-	.	-	.	0.6	10	-	.	0.1	1

Base: All   1518   1469

Question No								A90				A91b	
Column No								1439				1045	

(ii) {GRILFOOD}

Eating more grilled food *instead*
of fried food, or not

		1983		1984		1985		1986		1987		1989	
Yes	1	-	.	-	.	-	.	56.3	854	-	.	61.0	896
No	2	-	.	-	.	-	.	42.7	647	-	.	38.3	563
(DK)	8	-	.	-	.	-	.	0.5	8	-	.	0.6	9
(NA)	9	-	.	-	.	-	.	0.5	8	-	.	0.1	1

Base: All   1518   1469

Question No								A90				A91c	
Column No								1440				1046	

(iii) {FISHPOUL}

Eating more fish and poultry
instead of red meat, or not

		1983		1984		1985		1986		1987		1989	
Yes	1	-	.	-	.	-	.	43.6	662	-	.	45.5	669
No	2	-	.	-	.	-	.	55.6	844	-	.	53.9	792
(DK)	8	-	.	-	.	-	.	0.3	4	-	.	0.5	8
(NA)	9	-	.	-	.	-	.	0.5	8	-	.	0.1	1

Base: All   1518   1469

RECENT CHANGES TO HEALTHIER EATING - 1 (Continued)

			1983		1984		1985		1986		1987		1989	
			%	No	%	No	%	No	%	No	%	No	%	No
									Question No					
									A90				A91d	
									Column No					
									1441				1047	

(iv) {SKIMMILK}
Drinking or using more semi-skimmed or skimmed milk _instead_ of full cream milk, or not

	Code	1983 %	No	1984 %	No	1985 %	No	1986 %	No	1987 %	No	1989 %	No
Yes	1	-	-	-	-	-	-	32.5	493	-	-	42.8	629
No	2	-	-	-	-	-	-	66.9	1016	-	-	56.8	835
(DK)	8	-	-	-	-	-	-	0.1	1	-	-	0.2	3
(NA)	9	-	-	-	-	-	-	0.5	8	-	-	0.1	2
Base: All									1518				1469

		Question No	A90	A91e
		Column No	1442	1048

(v) {BREAD}
Eating more wholemeal bread _instead_ of white bread, or not

	Code	1983 %	No	1984 %	No	1985 %	No	1986 %	No	1987 %	No	1989 %	No
Yes	1	-	-	-	-	-	-	55.5	843	-	-	55.6	817
No	2	-	-	-	-	-	-	43.9	666	-	-	44.0	647
(DK)	8	-	-	-	-	-	-	0.0	1	-	-	0.2	3
(NA)	9	-	-	-	-	-	-	0.5	8	-	-	0.1	2
Base: All									1518				1469

1989 -   A sixth item was added to this question: see {BAKEDPOT} p.L - 40 below

ATTITUDES TO DIET AND HEALTH

{*FOODEXPV*} {*FOODPREP*} {*EXERCISE*} {*HEARTDIS*} {*FOODEXPT*} {*WEIGHT*} {*HLTHLUCK*} {*MEATVEG*}

Question: Please tick one box for *each* statement, to show how much you agree or disagree with it.

		1983		1984		1985		1986		1987		1989	
		%	No	%	No	%	No	%	No	%	No	%	No
Question No								A222b				A227b	
Column No								1940				2142	
(ii) {*FOODEXPV*}	Code												
Food that is good for you is usually more expensive													
Agree strongly	1	-	-	-	-	-	-	17.9	248	-	-	17.8	227
Just agree	2	-	-	-	-	-	-	30.8	428	-	-	31.0	394
Neither agree nor disagree	3	-	-	-	-	-	-	16.2	225	-	-	14.3	182
Just disagree	4	-	-	-	-	-	-	25.6	355	-	-	24.1	307
Disagree strongly	5	-	-	-	-	-	-	8.4	117	-	-	12.1	154
(DK)	8	-	-	-	-	-	-	0.1	2	-	-	-	
(NA)	9	-	-	-	-	-	-	1.0	14	-	-	0.7	9
Base: Self-completion questionnaire respondents									1387				1274

		1983		1984		1985		1986		1987		1989	
Question No								A222c				A227c	
Column No								1941				2143	
(iii) {*FOODPREP*}													
Food that is good for you generally takes too long to prepare													
Agree strongly	1	-	-	-	-	-	-	3.9	54	-	-	2.8	35
Just agree	2	-	-	-	-	-	-	15.5	215	-	-	12.9	164
Neither agree nor disagree	3	-	-	-	-	-	-	25.2	350	-	-	26.0	331
Just disagree	4	-	-	-	-	-	-	37.8	525	-	-	39.8	507
Disagree strongly	5	-	-	-	-	-	-	16.1	224	-	-	17.9	228
(DK)	8	-	-	-	-	-	-	0.1	2	-	-	-	
(NA)	9	-	-	-	-	-	-	1.2	17	-	-	0.6	8
Base: Self-completion questionnaire respondents									1387				1274

1989 -   The wording of three items in this battery of eleven questions was changed when they were repeated in 1989. See {FOODTST2}, {FOODFND2} and {FOODFAM2}, on p. L - 41 below; and {FOODTAST}, {FOODFIND} and {FOODFAM} on p. L - 45 below

ATTITUDES TO DIET AND HEALTH (Continued)

		1983		1984		1985		1986		1987		1989	
		%	No	%	No	%	No	%	No	%	No	%	No

Question No								A222f				A227f	
Column No								1944				2146	

(vi) {*EXERCISE*}
As long as you take enough exercise you can eat whatever foods you want

	Code	1983 %	No	1984 %	No	1985 %	No	1986 %	No	1987 %	No	1989 %	No
Agree strongly	1	-	.	-	.	-	.	9.9	137	-	.	5.1	65
Just agree	2	-	.	-	.	-	.	20.9	290	-	.	21.6	276
Neither agree nor disagree	3	-	.	-	.	-	.	16.7	232	-	.	17.0	217
Just disagree	4	-	.	-	.	-	.	33.8	468	-	.	36.2	461
Disagree strongly	5	-	.	-	.	-	.	17.1	238	-	.	19.4	247
(DK)	8	-	.	-	.	-	.	0.2	3	-	.	-	.
(NA)	9	-	.	-	.	-	.	1.4	19	-	.	0.6	8

Base: Self-completion
questionnaire respondents

		1986	1989
		1387	1274

Question No								A222g				A227g	
Column No								1945				2147	

(vii) {*HEARTDIS*}
If heart disease is in your family, there is little you can do to reduce your chances of getting it

	Code	1983 %	No	1984 %	No	1985 %	No	1986 %	No	1987 %	No	1989 %	No
Agree strongly	1	-	.	-	.	-	.	4.1	58	-	.	3.3	42
Just agree	2	-	.	-	.	-	.	11.0	152	-	.	8.3	105
Neither agree nor disagree	3	-	.	-	.	-	.	12.7	177	-	.	12.1	154
Just disagree	4	-	.	-	.	-	.	38.6	535	-	.	36.8	469
Disagree strongly	5	-	.	-	.	-	.	31.6	438	-	.	38.6	491
(DK)	8	-	.	-	.	-	.	0.4	6	-	.	-	.
(NA)	9	-	.	-	.	-	.	1.6	22	-	.	0.9	12

Base: Self-completion
questionnaire respondents

		1986	1989
		1387	1274

ATTITUDES TO DIET AND HEALTH (Continued)

		1983		1984		1985		1986		1987		1989	
		%	No	%	No	%	No	%	No	%	No	%	No
Question No								A222h				A227h	
Column No								1946				2148	

(viii) {FOODEXPT}
The experts contradict each other
over what makes a healthy diet

	Code	1983 %	1983 No	1984 %	1984 No	1985 %	1985 No	1986 %	1986 No	1987 %	1987 No	1989 %	1989 No
Agree strongly	1	-	-	-	-	-	-	30.4	422	-	-	26.6	339
Just agree	2	-	-	-	-	-	-	42.1	584	-	-	43.9	559
Neither agree nor disagree	3	-	-	-	-	-	-	14.9	207	-	-	11.0	140
Just disagree	4	-	-	-	-	-	-	7.8	108	-	-	13.3	169
Disagree strongly	5	-	-	-	-	-	-	3.3	46	-	-	3.9	49
(DK)	8	-	-	-	-	-	-	0.2	3	-	-	-	-
(NA)	9	-	-	-	-	-	-	1.3	19	-	-	1.4	18

Base: Self-completion
questionnaire respondents

			1986			1989
			1387			1274

Question No						A222i				A227i	
Column No						1947				2149	

(ix) {WEIGHT}
People worry too much about their
weight

	Code	1983 %	1983 No	1984 %	1984 No	1985 %	1985 No	1986 %	1986 No	1987 %	1987 No	1989 %	1989 No
Agree strongly	1	-	-	-	-	-	-	16.3	226	-	-	15.6	199
Just agree	2	-	-	-	-	-	-	43.7	606	-	-	44.7	569
Neither agree nor disagree	3	-	-	-	-	-	-	16.2	224	-	-	17.1	218
Just disagree	4	-	-	-	-	-	-	17.9	249	-	-	17.7	226
Disagree strongly	5	-	-	-	-	-	-	4.2	58	-	-	3.9	50
(DK)	8	-	-	-	-	-	-	0.1	2	-	-	-	-
(NA)	9	-	-	-	-	-	-	1.5	21	-	-	0.9	11

Base: Self-completion
questionnaire respondents

			1986			1989
			1387			1274

ATTITUDES TO DIET AND HEALTH (Continued)

		1983		1984		1985		1986		1987		1989	
		%	No	%	No	%	No	%	No	%	No	%	No
Question No								A222j				A227j	
Column No								1948				2150	

(x) {HLTHLUCK}

Good health is just a matter of good luck

	Code	1983 %	No	1984 %	No	1985 %	No	1986 %	No	1987 %	No	1989 %	No
Agree strongly	1	-		-		-		4.3	59	-		4.2	54
Just agree	2	-		-		-		12.4	172	-		10.1	128
Neither agree nor disagree	3	-		-		-		13.0	180	-		13.4	171
Just disagree	4	-		-		-		36.4	504	-		35.0	445
Disagree strongly	5	-		-		-		32.1	446	-		36.4	464
(DK)	8	-		-		-		0.1	2	-		-	-
(NA)	9	-		-		-		1.7	24	-		0.9	11

Base: Self-completion
completion respondents

| | | | | | | | | | 1387 | | | | 1274 |

Question No								A222k				A227k	
Column No								1949				2151	

(xi) {MEATVEG}

A proper meal should include meat and vegetables

	Code	1983 %	No	1984 %	No	1985 %	No	1986 %	No	1987 %	No	1989 %	No
Agree strongly	1	-		-		-		30.5	423	-		25.3	323
Just agree	2	-		-		-		31.2	434	-		33.0	420
Neither agree nor disagree	3	-		-		-		14.7	204	-		14.2	181
Just disagree	4	-		-		-		16.5	229	-		19.2	244
Disagree strongly	5	-		-		-		5.8	80	-		7.9	101
(DK)	8	-		-		-		0.1	2	-		-	-
(NA)	9	-		-		-		1.1	16	-		0.4	6

Base: Self-completion
questionnaire respondents

| | | | | | | | | | 1387 | | | | 1274 |

DIETARY PATTERNS : CHIPS/BISCUITS

1989   Q.A88a-e   {CHIPFREQ}{CHIPEVER}{CHIPSAME}{CHIPBAD}{CHIPWHY1}-{CHIPWHY8};{CAKEFREQ}
{CAKEEVER}{CAKESAME}{CAKEBAD}{CAKEWHY1}-{CAKEWHY8}   Column Nos 956-59, 1008-11; 960-67, 1021-28

Eating habits

{CHIPFREQ}{CAKEFREQ}   Column Nos 956,1008
a) [Now, some questions on food] How often do you eat chips or roast potatoes; [then] biscuits, pastries and cakes nowadays?

	Code	Chips or roast potatoes {CHIPFREQ}		Biscuits, pastries and cakes {CAKEFREQ}	
		%	No	%	No
Every day	1	2.9	43	28.6	420
4-6 days a week	2	8.2	120	11.0	162
2-3 days a week	3	36.0	529	23.8	349
About once a week	4	30.7	451	17.2	252
Less often	5	15.6	229	13.9	204
Never nowadays	6	6.4	93	5.3	78
(NA)	9	0.3	4	0.3	4
Base : All			1469		1469

{CHIPEVER}{CAKEEVER}   Column Nos 957,1009
b) [If never eaten nowadays] Have you *never* eaten chips or roast potatoes; [then] biscuits, pastries and cakes, or have you cut them out in the last two or three years, or longer ago?

	Code	Chips or roast potatoes {CHIPEVER}		Biscuits, pastries and cakes {CAKEEVER}	
		%	No	%	No
[Not asked : eaten nowadays]	0	93.3	1371	94.4	1387
Never eaten [at all]	1	0.6	9	1.6	23
Cut out in the last 2 or 3 years	2	3.6	53	2.2	33
Cut out longer ago	3	1.6	23	1.0	14
(NA)	9	0.9	13	0.8	12
Base : All			1469		1469

{CHIPSAME}{CAKESAME}   Column Nos 958,1010
c) [If ever eaten nowadays] Are you eating about the same amount as you did two or three years ago, or more, or less?

	Code	Chips or roast potatoes {CHIPSAME}		Biscuits, pastries and cakes {CAKESAME}	
		%	No	%	No
[Not asked : never eaten nowadays]	0	6.3	93	5.3	78
About the same amount	1	59.8	879	58.1	853
More	2	5.0	73	5.8	85
Less	3	27.8	408	29.8	438
(NA)	9	1.0	15	1.0	14
Base : All			1469		1469

NB {CHIPFREQ}, {CHIPEVER}, {CHIPSAME} have variable names {SPUDFREQ}, {SPUDEVER}, {SPUDSAME} on the SPSS file. Since the latter were used in 1986 for a parallel set of questions about 'potatoes' (not 'chips or roast potatoes'), the names have been changed as shown

DIETARY PATTERNS : CHIPS/BISCUITS (continued)

Perceived health properties

1989   Q.A88d   {CHIPBAD}{CAKEBAD} Column Nos 959,1011
[If eats the same amount as 2 or 3 years ago] Are chips or roast potatoes; [then] biscuits, pastries and cakes on the whole good for people, bad for people or neither?

	Code	Chips or roast potatoes {CHIPBAD} %	No	Biscuits, pastries and cakes {CAKEBAD} %	No
[Not asked : never eats or has recently changed amount eaten]	0	39.1	574	41.0	602
Good for people	1	12.5	183	11.0	162
Bad for people	2	23.0	338	24.1	354
Neither	3	22.9	336	21.4	314
(DK)	8	0.1	1	-	-
(NA)	9	2.5	37	2.5	37
Base : All			1469		1469

NB {CHIPBAD} has variable name {SPUDBAD} on the SPSS file. Since the latter was used in 1986 for a parallel question about 'potatoes' (not 'chips or roast potatoes'), the name has been changed as shown

Reasons for changing eating habits

1989   Q.A88e   {CHIPWHY1}-{CHIPWHY8};{CAKEWHY1}-{CAKEWHY8} Column Nos 960-67, 1021-28
[If recently changed amount eaten] You said that you changed the amount of chips and roast potatoes; [then] biscuits, pastries and cakes you eat. Have you changed for any of *these* reasons? (Interviewer : probe: 'any other of these reasons?' until 'No'.)

	Code	Chips or roast potatoes %	No	Biscuits, pastries and cakes %	No
{CHIPWHY1}{CAKEWHY1} Column Nos 960,1021 **To help control my weight**					
[Not asked : not recently changed amount eaten]	-1	60.4	888	59.6	876
Not given as reason	0	25.6	376	24.0	353
Given as reason	1	11.4	168	14.1	207
(DK)	8	0.1	1	0.1	1
(NA)	9	2.4	35	2.1	31
Base : All			1469		1469
{CHIPWHY2}{CAKEWHY2} Column Nos 961,1022 **I was told to for medical reasons**					
[Not asked : not recently changed amount eaten]	-1	60.4	888	59.6	876
Not given as reason	0	31.9	468	33.9	498
Given as reason	2	5.2	76	4.2	62
(DK)	8	0.1	1	0.1	1
(NA)	9	2.4	35	2.1	31
Base : All			1469		1469
{CHIPWHY3}{CAKEWHY3} Column Nos 962,1023 **It is good value for money**					
[Not asked : not recently changed amount eaten]	-1	60.4	888	59.6	876
Not given as reason	0	36.4	535	38.1	559
Given as reason	3	0.7	10	0.1	1
(DK)	8	0.1	1	0.1	1
(NA)	9	2.4	35	2.1	31
Base : All			1469		1469

DIETARY PATTERNS : CHIPS/BISCUITS (continued)

Reasons for changing eating habits (continued)

	Code	Chips or roast potatoes %	No	Biscuits, pastries and cakes %	No
{CHIPWHY4}{CAKEWHY4} Column Nos 963,1024					
It is poor value for money					
[Not asked : not recently changed amount eaten]	-1	60.4	888	59.6	876
Not given as reason	0	37.1	545	36.8	541
Given as reason	4	-	-	1.4	20
(DK)	8	0.1	1	0.1	1
(NA)	9	2.4	35	2.1	31
Base : All			1469		1469
{CHIPWHY5}{CAKEWHY5} Column Nos 964,1025					
I wanted to keep healthy					
[Not asked : not recently changed amount eaten]	-1	60.4	888	59.6	876
Not given as reason	0	20.6	303	25.4	373
Given as reason	5	16.4	241	12.8	188
(DK)	8	0.1	1	0.1	1
(NA)	9	2.4	35	2.1	31
Base : All			1469		1469
{CHIPWHY6}{CAKEWHY6} Column Nos 965,1026					
I just like it more					
[Not asked : not recently changed amount eaten]	-1	60.4	888	59.6	876
Not given as reason	0	35.0	514	34.5	507
Given as reason	6	2.0	30	3.7	54
(DK)	8	0.1	1	0.1	1
(NA)	9	2.4	35	2.1	31
Base : All			1469		1469
{CHIPWHY7}{CAKEWHY7} Column Nos 966,1027					
I just don't like it as much					
[Not asked : not recently changed amount eaten]	-1	60.4	888	59.6	876
Not given as reason	0	33.7	495	34.1	501
Given as reason	7	3.3	49	4.0	59
(DK)	8	0.1	1	0.1	1
(NA)	9	2.4	35	2.1	31
Base : All			1469		1469
{CHIPWHY8}{CAKEWHY8} Column Nos 967,1028					
[Not asked : not recently changed amount eaten]	-1	60.4	888	59.6	876
None of these reasons	0	6.5	95	5.9	87
One or more reasons given	1	30.6	450	32.3	474
(DK)	8	0.1	1	0.1	1
(NA)	9	2.4	35	2.1	31
Base : All			1469		1469

NB {CHIPWHY1} - {CHIPWHY8} have variable names {SPUDWHY1} - {SPUDWHY8} on the SPSS file. Since the latter were used in 1986 for a parallel set of questions about 'potatoes' (not 'chips or roast potatoes'), the names have been changed as shown

TAKING SUGAR IN HOT DRINKS NOWADAYS

1989   Q.A89a   {SUGNOW}   Column No 1040

Do you ever take sugar in hot drinks nowadays?

	Code	%	No
Yes	1	49.1	722
No	2	50.8	746
(NA)	9	0.1	1
Base : All			1469

NB This question replaced one asked in 1986 about how often sugar in hot drinks was taken nowadays - see {SUGFREQ} p. L-42 below

SWEET AND CHOCOLATE EATING HABITS

1989   Q.A90a,b   {CHOCNOW}{CHOCSAME}   Column Nos 1042-43

{CHOCNOW}   Column No 1042

a) Do you ever eat sweets or chocolates nowadays?

	Code	%	No
Yes	1	84.6	1243
No	2	15.3	225
(NA)	9	0.1	1
Base : All			1469

{CHOCSAME}   Column No 1043

b) [If eats sweets or chocolates nowadays] Are you eating about the *same* amount as you did two or three years ago, or *more* sweets and chocolates or *less*?

	Code	%	No
[Not asked : does not eat sweets and chocolates nowadays]	0	15.3	225
About the same amount	1	40.5	595
More	2	7.2	105
Less	3	36.5	536
(NA)	9	0.5	7
Base : All			1469

RECENT CHANGES TO HEALTHIER EATING - 2

Boiled or baked potatoes

1989   Q.A91f   {BAKEDPOT}   Column No 1049
Compared with two or three years ago, would you say you are now eating more
boiled or baked potatoes instead of chips or roast potatoes, or not?

	Code	%	No
Yes	1	56.6	831
No	2	42.6	626
(DK)	8	0.7	11
(NA)	9	0.1	1
Base : All			1469

NB This question was the sixth in a series asking about recent dietary changes (see pp. L-30 to L-31).
See also the following question, asked to elicit 'unhealthy' rather than 'healthy' changes

RECENT CHANGES TO LESS HEALTHY EATING

1989   Q.B124a-f   {BUTTER}{FRYFOOD}{REDMEAT}{FULLMILK}{WHITBRED}{CHIPS}   Column Nos 1374-79
Compared with *two or three years ago*, would you say you are now ... (read out each statement in turn):

	Yes 1		No 2		(DK) 8		(NA) 9	
Code	%	No	%	No	%	No	%	No
a) {BUTTER} Column No 1374 Using more butter *instead* of low fat spreads or soft margarine, or not	12.7	185	85.8	1253	1.0	14	0.6	8
b) {FRYFOOD} Column No 1375 Eating more fried food *instead* of grilled food, or not	8.5	124	90.5	1322	0.5	7	0.6	8
c) {REDMEAT} Column No 1376 Eating more *red meat* instead of fish and poultry, or not	15.9	232	82.2	1202	1.2	17	0.7	10
d) {FULLMILK} Column No 1377 Drinking or using more full cream milk *instead* of semi-skimmed or skimmed milk, or not	15.9	232	82.7	1209	0.8	12	0.6	8
e) {WHITBRED} Column No 1378 Eating more white bread *instead* of wholemeal bread, or not	17.6	258	81.1	1185	0.6	9	0.6	9
f) {CHIPS} Column No 1379 Eating more chips or roast potatoes *instead* of boiled or baked potatoes or not	12.7	186	85.8	1254	0.8	12	0.6	9

Base : All (n = 1461)

NB This question was introduced with 'And just a few questions on food'. See also pp. L-30 to L-31, where a similar question is asked to elicit 'healthy' rather than 'unhealthy' dietary changes

BARRIERS TO HEALTHY EATING - 1

1989   Q.A227a,d,e   *{FOODTST2}{FOODFND2}{FOODFAM2}*   Column Nos 2141, 2144-45
Please tick one box for *each* statement, to show how much you agree or disagree with it.

	Agree strongly 1		Just agree 2		Neither agree nor disagree 3		Just disagree 4		Disagree strongly 5		(DK) 8		(NA) 9	
Code	%	No	%	No	%	No	%	No	%	No	%	No	%	No
a) *{FOODTST2}* Column No 2141														
Healthy food doesn't usually taste as nice as other food	5.9	75	20.6	262	27.5	350	24.8	316	20.5	261	0.1	2	0.7	9
d) *{FOODFND2}* Column No 2144														
It is hard to find food that is good for you in supermarkets	2.7	34	13.9	177	17.8	227	43.2	550	21.7	276	0.1	1	0.7	9
e) *{FOODFAM2}* Column No 2145														
Mothers would eat healthier food if the rest of their families would let them	6.0	77	20.0	254	30.8	392	27.8	355	14.3	182	-	-	1.0	13

Base : Self-completion respondents (n = 1274)

NB   Variants of these three questions were asked in 1986; see p. L-45 below

LEVELS OF CONCERN ABOUT DIET

1989   Q.A228   *{FOODWORY}*   Column No 2152
How worried are you about the sorts of food you eat?   (Please tick one box)

	Code	%	No
Very worried	1	4.3	55
Fairly worried	2	24.1	307
Not particularly worried	3	50.4	642
Not worried at all	4	20.7	263
(NA)	9	0.5	6
Base : Self-completion respondents			1274

FEELINGS ABOUT CHANGING ONE'S DIET

1989   Q.A229   *{FOODCHNG}*   Column No 2153
Which one of these statements *best* describes how you feel about the sorts of food you eat nowadays?
(Please tick one box)

	Code	%	No
I have never felt the need to change what I eat	1	25.9	329
I have already changed as much as I am going to	2	40.7	519
I ought to change more but probably won't	3	28.3	360
I will probably be changing soon	4	4.4	56
(NA)	9	0.7	9
Base: Self-completion respondents			1274

DIETARY PATTERNS : POTATOES/SUGAR IN HOT DRINKS

1986   Q.A89a-e   {SPUDFREQ}{SPUDEVER}{SPUDSAME}{SPUDBAD}{SPUDWHY1}-{SPUWHY8};
{SUGFREQ}{SUGEVER}{SUGBAD}{SUGWHY1}-{SUGWHY8}
Column Nos 1243-45, 1326-34; 1252-53, 1353-61

Eating habits

{SPUDFREQ}{SUGFREQ}   Column Nos 1243,1252
a)   [Now, some questions on food] How often do you eat potatoes; [then] take sugar in hot drinks nowadays?

	Code	Potatoes {SPUDFREQ} %	No	Sugar in hot drinks {SUGFREQ} %	No
Every day/*15+ teaspoons per day*	1	41.3	627	4.7	72
4-6 days a week/*10-14 teaspoons per day*	2	30.9	469	9.2	140
2-3 days a week/*5-9 teaspoons per day*	3	20.0	303	16.4	249
About once a week/*1-4 teaspoons per day*	4	3.1	47	19.5	296
Less often	5	2.4	37	4.0	61
Never nowadays	6	1.8	28	45.8	695
(NA)	9	0.4	7	0.3	5
Base : All			1518		1518

{SPUDEVER}{SUGEVER}   Column Nos 1244,1253
b)   [If never eaten/*taken* nowadays] Have you *never* eaten potatoes; [then] taken sugar, or have you cut *them*/it out in the last two or three years, or longer ago?

	Code	Potatoes {SPUDEVER} %	No	Sugar in hot drinks {SUGEVER} %	No
[Not asked : eaten nowadays]	0	97.7	1483	53.9	818
Never eaten [at all]	1	-	-	7.4	112
Cut out in the last 2 or 3 years	2	0.9	13	8.1	123
Cut out longer ago	3	0.9	13	29.8	452
(NA)	9	0.6	9	0.8	12
Base : All			1518		1518

{SPUDSAME}   Column Nos 1245
c)   [If ever eaten nowadays] Are you eating about the same amount [of potatoes] as you did two or three years ago, or more, or less?

	Code	Potatoes {SPUDSAME} %	No
[Not asked : never eaten nowadays]	0	1.8	28
About the same	1	71.1	1080
More	2	6.2	94
Less	3	20.0	303
(NA)	9	0.8	12
Base : All			1518

NB For {SUGSAME}, see p. L-8 above

DIETARY PATTERNS : POTATOES/SUGAR IN HOT DRINKS (continued)

Perceived health properties

1986   Q.A89d   {SPUDBAD}{SUGBAD} Column Nos 1326,1353
[If eats/takes same amount as 2 or 3 years ago] Are potatoes; [then] is sugar in hot drinks
on the whole good for one, bad for one or neither?

	Code	Potatoes {SPUDBAD} %	No	Sugar in hot drinks {SUGBAD} %	No
[Not asked : never eats or has recently changed amount eaten]	0	28.0	425	62.9	955
Good for one	1	45.6	692	9.4	142
Bad for one	2	3.8	57	16.5	251
Neither	3	21.1	320	10.1	154
(DK)	8	0.1	1	0.1	2
(NA)	9	1.4	22	0.9	13
Base : All			1518		1518

Reasons for changing eating habits

1986   Q.A89e   {SPUDWHY1}-{SPUDWHY8};{SUGWHY1}-{SUGWHY8}
Column Nos 1327-34, 1354-61
[If recently changed amount eaten] You said that you changed the amount of potatoes; [then]
sugar in hot drinks you eat/take. Have you changed for any of *these* reasons? (Interviewer : probe:
'any other of these reasons?' until 'No')

	Code	Potatoes %	No	Sugar in hot drinks %	No
{SPUDWHY1}{SUGWHY1} Column Nos 1327,1354 **To help control my weight**					
[Not asked : not recently changed amount eaten]	-1	71.2	1080	44.0	668
Not given as reason	0	17.0	258	31.0	471
Given as reason	1	10.1	153	16.2	245
(DK)	8	0.1	2	-	-
(NA)	9	1.6	24	8.8	134
Base : All			1518		1518
{SPUDWHY2}{SUGWHY2} Column Nos 1328,1355 **I was told to for medical reasons**					
[Not asked : not recently changed amount eaten]	-1	71.2	1080	44.0	668
Not given as reason	0	25.8	391	42.9	651
Given as reason	2	1.3	20	4.3	65
(DK)	8	0.1	2	-	-
(NA)	9	1.6	24	8.8	134
Base : All			1518		1518
{SPUDWHY3}{SUGWHY3} Column Nos 1329,1356 **It is good value for money**					
[Not asked : not recently changed amount eaten]	-1	71.2	1080	44.0	668
Not given as reason	0	25.4	386	47.1	715
Given as reason	3	1.6	25	0.1	1
(DK)	8	0.1	2	-	-
(NA)	9	1.6	24	8.8	134
Base : All			1518		1518

DIETARY PATTERNS : POTATOES/SUGAR IN HOT DRINKS (continued)

Reasons for changing eating habits (continued)

			Potatoes	Sugar in hot drinks	
	Code	%	No	%	No

{SPUDWHY4}{SUGWHY4}   Column Nos 1330,1357
It is poor value for money

	Code	%	No	%	No
[Not asked : not recently changed amount eaten]	-1	71.2	1080	44.0	668
Not given as reason	0	26.9	409	46.9	712
Given as reason	4	0.1	2	0.3	4
(DK)	8	0.1	2	-	-
(NA)	9	1.6	24	8.8	134
Base : All			1518		1518

{SPUDWHY5}{SUGWHY5}   Column Nos 1331,1358
I wanted to keep healthy

	Code	%	No	%	No
[Not asked : not recently changed amount eaten]	-1	71.2	1080	44.0	668
Not given as reason	0	22.6	343	33.4	507
Given as reason	5	4.5	68	13.8	209
(DK)	8	0.1	2	-	-
(NA)	9	1.6	24	8.8	134
Base : All			1518		1518

{SPUDWHY6}{SUGWHY6}   Column Nos 1332,1359
I just like it more

	Code	%	No	%	No
[Not asked : not recently changed amount eaten]	-1	71.2	1080	44.0	668
Not given as reason	0	24.8	377	46.2	702
Given as reason	6	2.2	34	1.0	15
(DK)	8	0.1	2	-	-
(NA)	9	1.6	24	8.8	134
Base : All			1518		1518

{SPUDWHY7}{SUGWHY7}   Column Nos 1333,1360
I just don't like it as much

	Code	%	No	%	No
[Not asked : not recently changed amount eaten]	-1	71.2	1080	44.0	668
Not given as reason	0	23.6	359	35.2	535
Given as reason	7	3.4	51	11.9	181
(DK)	8	0.1	2	-	-
(NA)	9	1.6	24	8.8	134
Base : All			1518		1518

{SPUDWHY8}{SUGWHY8}   Column Nos 1334,1361
None of these reasons

	Code	%	No	%	No
[Not asked : not recently changed amount eaten]	-1	71.2	1080	44.0	668
None of these reasons	0	6.1	93	4.7	72
One or more reasons given	1	20.9	318	42.4	644
(DK)	8	0.1	2	-	-
(NA)	9	1.6	24	8.8	134
Base : All			1518		1518

BARRIERS TO HEALTHY EATING - 2

1986   Q.A222a,d,e   *{FOODTAST}{FOODFIND}{FOODFAM}*   Column Nos 1939,1942-43
Please tick one box for *each* statement to show how much you agree or disagree with it.

	Agree strongly 1		Just agree 2		Neither agree nor disagree 3		Just disagree 4		Disagree strongly 5		(DK) 8		(NA) 9	
Code	%	No	%	No	%	No	%	No	%	No	%	No	%	No
a) *{FOODTAST}* Column No 1939 Food that is good for you generally tastes nicer than other food	8.1	112	19.0	263	34.3	476	27.9	388	9.4	130	0.1	2	1.2	17
d) *{FOODFIND}* Column No 1942 It is easy to find food that is good for you in supermarkets	15.9	221	48.5	673	15.1	209	15.9	220	3.1	43	0.2	3	1.3	19
e) *{FOODFAM}* Column No 1943 Many people would eat healthier food if the rest of their families would let them	10.5	145	31.9	443	31.9	443	17.7	245	6.0	84	0.4	5	1.6	22

Base : Self-completion respondents (n = 1387)

NB Variants of these three questions were asked in 1989 (see p.L-41 above)

ADVICE ON HEALTH GIVEN TO MEN AND WOMEN

1983   Q.203a,b   *{MHINT1}{MHINT2}{WHINT1}{WHINT2}*   Column Nos 1021-24
a) Now consider a man aged 35 who smokes 20 cigarettes a day, drinks 4 pints of beer a day, is about 2 stone overweight, and takes almost no exercise. If you were advising him on the most useful action he should take to improve his health, which of the four actions below would you choose? And which next?
(Please tick one box for each)

b) Now, if we were asking about a woman of the same age, what would your answer be?
(Please tick one box for each)

	a) Man				b) Woman			
	Most useful *{MHINT1}*		Next most useful *{MHINT2}*		Most useful *{WHINT1}*		Next most useful *{WHINT2}*	
Column No	1021		1022		1023		1024	
	%	No	%	No	%	No	%	No
Reduce smoking	44.0	708	21.4	344	43.8	705	19.9	320
Reduce alcohol	12.0	193	20.2	326	12.4	200	19.6	316
Lose weight	22.4	361	26.4	425	26.9	433	29.6	477
Take more exercise	17.8	286	26.2	421	12.0	193	24.1	388
(NA)	3.8	62	5.8	93	4.9	80	6.8	109
Base : Self-completion respondents		1610		1610		1610		1610

M Morality and ethics

M1 Personal relationships

Table titles and cross references

PRE-MARITAL SEXUAL RELATIONS

{PMS}

Question: (Show card) Now I would like to ask you some questions about sexual relationships.

If a man and a woman have sexual relations before marriage, what would your general opinion be? Please choose a phrase from this card.

		1983		1984		1985		1986		1987		1989	
		%	No	%	No	%	No	%	No	%	No	%	No
Question No		89a		89a		95a				A88a		A86a	
Column No		643		635		747				741		864	
	Code												
Always wrong	1	16.5	283	14.5	239	13.7	243	-	-	13.4	187	11.6	170
Mostly wrong	2	11.3	195	12.3	203	9.3	165	-	-	11.5	160	10.7	157
Sometimes wrong	3	17.1	295	19.1	315	18.9	335	-	-	21.5	299	19.5	287
Rarely wrong	4	8.1	139	6.3	104	9.0	159	-	-	7.3	101	11.1	162
Not wrong at all	5	41.9	721	42.0	691	42.7	755	-	-	42.4	590	43.7	642
(Depends/varies)	6	4.3	74	4.4	72	4.9	87	-	-	3.3	45	2.7	39
(DK)	8	-		0.2	3	0.5	8	-	-	0.2	3	0.1	2
(NA)	9	0.8	13	1.1	18	1.0	17	-	-	0.4	5	0.7	10
Base: All			1719		1645		1769				1391		1469

1983 - No (DK)

EXTRA-MARITAL SEXUAL RELATIONS - 1

{EXMS}

Question: (Show card) **What about a *married person* having sexual relations with someone other than his or her partner?**
Please choose a phrase from this card.

			1983		1984		1985		1986		1987		1989	
			%	No	%	No	%	No	%	No	%	No	%	No
Question No			89bc		89b		95b				A88b		A86b	
Column No			644-645		636		748				742		865	
	Code													
Always wrong	1		58.8	1011	58.5	962	57.1	1010	-		63.0	876	55.1	809
Mostly wrong	2		24.9	428	26.3	433	24.9	440	-		25.3	351	28.4	418
Sometimes wrong	3		10.6	183	10.0	164	11.0	194	-		8.8	122	11.2	165
Rarely wrong	4		0.9	15	0.6	10	0.7	12	-		0.8	11	1.2	18
Not wrong at all	5		1.5	25	1.1	19	2.3	40	-		0.5	7	1.6	23
(Depends/varies)	6		2.6	44	2.2	37	2.8	49	-		1.3	18	1.7	25
(DK)	8		-		0.1	2	0.4	7	-		0.1	2	0.3	4
(NA)	9		0.9	15	1.1	18	1.0	17	-		0.2	3	0.5	7
Base: All				1719		1645		1769				1391		1469

1983 - This question was asked separately about 'a married man' {MEXMS} and 'a married woman' {WEXMS} (see p.M.1 - 17 below).
Since the distributions were virtually identifcal, responses have been combined on this table. In subsequent years,
this question was asked about 'a married person'.

HOMOSEXUAL RELATIONS

{HOMOSEX}

Question: (Show card) **What about sexual relations between two adults of the same sex? Please choose a phrase from this card.**

		1983		1984		1985		1986		1987		1989	
		%	No	%	No	%	No	%	No	%	No	%	No
Question No		89d		89c		95c				A88c		A86c	
Column No		646		637		749				743		866	
	Code												
Always wrong	1	49.6	852	53.6	882	59.1	1046	-	-	63.6	885	55.5	816
Mostly wrong	2	12.1	208	13.2	217	9.7	172	-	-	10.8	150	12.6	186
Sometimes wrong	3	8.2	141	7.2	118	7.0	125	-	-	7.8	108	9.4	137
Rarely wrong	4	3.7	63	2.4	40	3.7	66	-	-	2.2	30	3.9	57
Not wrong at all	5	17.4	299	15.7	258	12.5	220	-	-	10.7	149	13.7	201
(Depends/varies)	6	7.6	130	5.7	94	5.7	101	-	-	4.0	55	3.9	57
(DK)	8	-	-	0.9	16	0.8	14	-	-	0.6	8	0.4	6
(NA)	9	1.5	26	1.3	22	1.4	25	-	-	0.4	5	0.7	10
Base: All			1719		1645		1769				1391		1469

1983 - No (DK)

DISCRIMINATION AGAINST HOMOSEXUALS

{GAYTEASC} {GAYTEAHE} {GAYPUB}

Question: Now I would like you to tell me whether, in your opinion, it is acceptable for a homosexual person ... (read out):

		1983		1984		1985		1986		1987		1989	
		%	No	%	No	%	No	%	No	%	No	%	No
Question No		90a				96a				A89a		A87a	
Column No		647				750				744		867	

(i) {GAYTEASC}
To be a teacher in a school

	Code	%	No	%	No	%	No	%	No	%	No	%	No
Yes	1	41.0	705	-	-	36.2	641	-	-	43.2	600	45.1	662
No	2	52.7	906	-	-	53.8	951	-	-	50.2	699	46.7	686
(Depends/depends on person/as long as no proselytising)	3	-	-	-	-	5.2	91	-	-	3.6	50	5.0	74
(Depends on age/sex of pupil)	4	-	-	-	-	0.4	7	-	-	0.4	5	0.3	4
(As long as school knows)	5	-	-	-	-	0.3	5	-	-	0.2	2	0.2	3
(Other answer)	7	4.0	68	-	-	0.5	8	-	-	0.4	6	0.2	3
(DK)	8	1.5	26	-	-	2.9	51	-	-	1.7	24	2.1	30
(NA)	9	0.8	14	-	-	0.9	16	-	-	0.3	4	0.5	7
Base: All			1719				1769				1391		1469

		90a				96a				A89a		A87a	
Question No													
Column No		648				751				745		868	

(ii) {GAYTEAHE}
To be a teacher in a college or university

	Code	%	No	%	No	%	No	%	No	%	No	%	No
Yes	1	47.6	819	-	-	44.3	783	-	-	50.9	708	55.5	815
No	2	47.9	824	-	-	48.1	851	-	-	44.4	617	38.8	569
(Depends/depends on person/as long as no proselytising)	3	-	-	-	-	3.7	66	-	-	2.5	35	3.1	46
(Depends on age of students)	4	-	-	-	-	0.2	3	-	-	-	-	0.1	2
(As long as school knows)	5	-	-	-	-	0.2	4	-	-	0.1	1	0.3	4
(Other answer)	7	2.4	42	-	-	0.2	4	-	-	0.2	3	0.1	1
(DK)	8	1.2	21	-	-	2.4	42	-	-	1.5	21	1.8	26
(NA)	9	0.8	13	-	-	0.9	16	-	-	0.4	5	0.5	7
Base: All			1719				1769				1391		1469

1983 - Q reads: 'Finally in this section, I would like you...'; (Other answer) code 3.

DISCRIMINATION AGAINST HOMOSEXUALS (Continued)

		1983		1984		1985		1986		1987		1989	
		%	No	%	No	%	No	%	No	%	No	%	No
Question No		90a				96a				A89a		A87a	
Column No		649				752				746		869	
(iii) {GAYPUB} To hold a responsible position in public life	Code												
Yes	1	53.3	916	-	.	50.2	889	-	.	54.5	758	58.1	854
No	2	42.2	725	-	.	41.1	728	-	.	38.9	541	36.7	539
(Depends/depends on person/as long as no proselytising)	3	-	.	-	.	2.4	43	-	.	1.8	25	2.0	29
(Depends on position/as long as they do job)	4	0.1	2	-	.	1.4	25	-	.	1.3	18	0.8	12
(As long as not MP)	5	-	.	-	.	0.1	2	-	.	0.1	1	-	.
(As long as not working with children)	6	-	.	-	.	0.2	4	-	.	0.3	4	-	.
(Other answer)	7	2.0	35	-	.	0.9	16	-	.	0.5	7	0.2	3
(DK)	8	1.6	27	-	.	2.7	47	-	.	2.3	31	1.4	21
(NA)	9	0.8	14	-	.	0.9	16	-	.	0.3	4	0.8	11
Base: All			1719				1769				1391		1469

1983 - (Other answer), code 3

UNDERSTANDING OF THE WORD 'HOMOSEXUAL'

{HOMOMEAN}

Question: What did you understand the word 'homosexual' to mean at this question [ie about discrimination against homosexuals] ... (read out) ...

		1983		1984		1985		1986		1987		1989	
		%	No	%	No	%	No	%	No	%	No	%	No
Question No						96b				A89b		A87b	
Column No						753				747		870	
	Code												
... men only, that is, gays,	1	-	-	-	-	34.4	609	-	-	32.5	451	25.6	377
... women only, that is lesbians,	2	-	-	-	-	0.2	3	-	-	-	-	0.1	2
... or either?	3	-	-	-	-	64.1	1134	-	-	66.8	929	73.3	1076
(DK)	8	-	-	-	-	0.5	9	-	-	0.2	3	0.3	4
(NA)	9	-	-	-	-	0.8	14	-	-	0.6	8	0.7	10
Base: All							1769				1391		1469

1985 - men only, code 1; women only, code 2; either, code 3
1985, 1987 - Q reads: '... understand the phrase 'homosexual'...'

ADOPTION BY FEMALE AND MALE HOMOSEXUAL COUPLES

{FGAYADPT} {MGAYADPT}

Question: Do you think female homosexual couples - that is, lesbians - should be allowed to adopt a baby under the same conditions as other couples?

And do you think male homosexual couples - that is, gays - should be allowed to adopt a baby under the same conditions as other couples?

		1983		1984		1985		1986		1987		1989	
		%	No	%	No	%	No	%	No	%	No	%	No
Question No						96c				A89c		A87c	
Column No						754				748		871	
(i) {FGAYADPT}	Code												
[Female homosexual couples]													
Yes	1	-	-	-	-	13.2	234	-	-	10.6	148	17.9	263
No	2	-	-	-	-	81.5	1442	-	-	86.4	1202	77.8	1143
(Depends on person/couple)	3	-	-	-	-	0.8	14	-	-	0.3	4	0.8	12
(Other)	7	-	-	-	-	0.8	15	-	-	0.2	3	0.2	3
(DK)	8	-	-	-	-	2.9	51	-	-	2.4	33	2.8	41
(NA)	9	-	-	-	-	0.8	15	-	-	0.1	1	0.5	7
Base: All							1769				1391		1469

ADOPTION BY FEMALE AND MALE HOMOSEXUAL COUPLES (Continued)

		1983		1984		1985		1986		1987		1989	
		%	No	%	No	%	No	%	No	%	No	%	No
Question No						96d				A89d		A87d	
Column No	Code					755				749		872	

(ii) {MGAYADPT}
[Male homosexual couples]

	Code	1983 %	No	1984 %	No	1985 %	No	1986 %	No	1987 %	No	1989 %	No
Yes	1	-	-	-	-	5.6	99	-	-	5.4	75	9.7	143
No	2	-	-	-	-	90.7	1604	-	-	92.6	1288	86.6	1272
(Depends on person/couple)	3	-	-	-	-	0.3	5	-	-	0.2	3	0.7	10
(Other)	7	-	-	-	-	0.5	9	-	-	0.0	1	0.1	2
(DK)	8	-	-	-	-	2.1	38	-	-	1.5	20	2.3	34
(NA)	9	-	-	-	-	0.8	15	-	-	0.2	3	0.5	8
Base: All							1769				1391		1469

1983 - A similar question was asked of 'homosexual couples' (gender not specified). See {p.M.1-17} below
1985 - The phrases '... that is, lesbians ...', '... that is, gays ...' were not included in the question

CIRCUMSTANCES IN WHICH ABORTION SHOULD BE LEGAL - 1

{ABORT1} {ABORT2} {ABORT3} {ABORT4} {ABORT5} {ABORT6} {ABORT7}

Question: Here are a number of circumstances in which a woman might consider an abortion. Please say whether or not you think the law should allow an abortion in each case. (Please tick one box for each)

		1983		1984		1985		1986		1987		1989	
		%	No	%	No	%	No	%	No	%	No	%	No
Question No		204a				247a		A223a		A215a		A220a	
Column No	Code	1025				2218		1950		1571		2021	

(i) {ABORT1}
The woman decides on her own she does not wish to have the child

	Code	1983 %	No	1984 %	No	1985 %	No	1986 %	No	1987 %	No	1989 %	No
Yes	1	37.5	603	-	-	49.1	737	44.1	612	53.9	671	49.3	627
No	2	55.2	889	-	-	46.5	698	53.2	739	43.5	541	46.1	587
(DK)	8	0.3	5	-	-	0.1	1	0.6	8	0.5	6	0.3	4
(NA)	9	7.0	113	-	-	4.4	65	2.1	30	2.1	26	4.4	56
Base: Self-completion questionnaire respondents			1610				1502		1387		1243		1274

CIRCUMSTANCES IN WHICH ABORTION SHOULD BE LEGAL - 1 (Continued)

			1983		1984		1985		1986		1987		1989	
			%	No	%	No	%	No	%	No	%	No	%	No
Question No			204b				247b		A223b		A215b		A220b	
Column No			1026				2219		1951		1572		2022	

(ii) {ABORT2}   Code

The couple agree they do not wish to have the child

		1983 %	No	1984		1985 %	No	1986 %	No	1987 %	No	1989 %	No
Yes	1	46.2	743	-	-	54.8	824	56.1	779	58.7	730	59.4	756
No	2	44.8	721	-	-	39.8	598	40.0	554	37.9	471	35.4	451
(DK)	8	0.4	6	-	-	0.2	3	0.7	10	0.6	7	0.2	3
(NA)	9	8.7	140	-	-	5.2	78	3.2	44	2.9	35	5.0	64

Base: Self-completion questionnaire respondents   1610   1502   1387   1243   1274

		1983	1985	1986	1987	1989
Question No		204c	247c	A223c	A215c	A220c
Column No		1027	2220	1952	1573	2023

(iii) {ABORT3}

The woman is not married and does not wish to marry the man

		1983 %	No	1984		1985 %	No	1986 %	No	1987 %	No	1989 %	No
Yes	1	44.3	714	-	-	54.2	814	50.9	706	56.2	698	57.0	726
No	2	46.5	749	-	-	41.1	617	45.2	628	40.0	498	37.8	481
(DK)	8	0.4	6	-	-	0.1	2	0.7	10	0.5	6	0.4	5
(NA)	9	8.7	141	-	-	4.6	69	3.2	44	3.3	41	4.8	61

Base: Self-completion questionnaire respondents   1610   1502   1387   1243   1274

		1983	1985	1986	1987	1989
Question No		204d	247d	A223d	A215d	A220d
Column No		1028	2221	1953	1574	2024

(iv) {ABORT4}

The couple cannot afford any more children

		1983 %	No	1984		1985 %	No	1986 %	No	1987 %	No	1989 %	No
Yes	1	46.8	753	-	-	58.0	871	50.6	702	57.5	715	56.7	722
No	2	44.0	708	-	-	37.2	559	45.2	627	38.6	480	38.2	487
(DK)	8	0.3	5	-	-	0.1	2	0.9	13	0.6	7	0.2	3
(NA)	9	9.0	144	-	-	4.6	69	3.3	46	3.3	41	4.9	63

Base: Self-completion questionnaire respondents   1610   1502   1387   1243   1274

CIRCUMSTANCES IN WHICH ABORTION SHOULD BE LEGAL - 1 (Continued)

		1983		1984		1985		1986		1987		1989	
		%	No	%	No	%	No	%	No	%	No	%	No
Question No		204e				247e		A223e		A215e		A220e	
Column No		1029				2222		1954		1575		2025	

(v) {ABORT5}

There is a strong chance of a defect in the baby

	Code												
Yes	1	81.7	1315	-		86.5	1298	85.4	1185	89.1	1108	87.4	1113
No	2	10.7	172	-		9.6	143	11.5	159	8.5	105	9.5	121
(DK)	8	0.2	4	-		0.2	3	0.8	11	0.5	6	0.1	1
(NA)	9	7.3	118	-		3.8	57	2.3	32	2.0	24	3.0	38

Base: Self-completion questionnaire respondents: 1610, 1502, 1387, 1243, 1274

Question No		204f				247f		A223f		A215f		A220f	
Column No		1030				2223		1955		1576		2026	

(vi) {ABORT6}

The woman's health is seriously endangered by the pregnancy

	Code												
Yes	1	87.4	1407	-		91.2	1370	92.3	1281	93.6	1164	91.6	1166
No	2	6.2	100	-		5.3	79	4.9	67	3.6	45	5.4	69
(DK)	8	0.2	3	-		0.2	3	0.9	12	0.5	7	0.1	1
(NA)	9	6.2	99	-		3.3	50	1.9	27	2.3	28	2.9	37

Base: Self-completion questionnaire respondents: 1610, 1502, 1387, 1243, 1274

Question No		204g				247g		A223g		A215g		A220g	
Column No		1031				2224		1956		1577		2027	

(vii) {ABORT7}

The woman became pregnant as a result of rape

	Code												
Yes	1	85.4	1375	-		89.4	1343	90.6	1257	93.3	1161	90.8	1156
No	2	7.8	126	-		6.8	102	6.5	90	4.2	52	6.1	78
(DK)	8	0.2	4	-		0.3	4	1.0	13	0.7	8	0.1	1
(NA)	9	6.5	104	-		3.5	53	2.0	27	1.8	22	3.1	39

Base: Self-completion questionnaire respondents: 1610, 1502, 1387, 1243, 1274

1984 - In this year, the same question was asked but, experimentally, the order of the list of circumstances was changed to correspond with the proportion agreeing in 1983 that abortion should be permitted in each. The changed order generated a substantially different pattern of responses, so the 1984 data are clearly not comparable. The variable names have been changed and the data are shown on a different table (p.M.1-16 below).

ARTIFICIAL FERTILITY MEASURES

{BABYLAW1} {BABYLAW2} {BABYLAW3} {BABYLAW4} {BABYLAW5}

Question: Suppose a married couple want to have their own child, but cannot have one. Should the law allow or not allow them to use each of the methods below? Please assume in each case that it is the only method open to them on medical advice. (Please tick one box for each)

		1983		1984		1985		1986		1987		1989	
		%	No	%	No	%	No	%	No	%	No	%	No
Question No						248a				A216a		A221a	
Column No						2225				1608		2028	

(i) {BABYLAW1}

They try to have a child by _artificial insemination_, using the _husband_ as donor

	Code												
It should be allowed by law	1	-	.	-	.	90.4	1358	-	.	89.0	1107	90.8	1156
It should not be allowed by law	2	-	.	-	.	6.9	104	-	.	8.5	106	6.6	84
(DK)	8	-	.	-	.	0.4	6	-	.	0.6	7	0.1	1
(NA)	9	-	.	-	.	2.3	34	-	.	1.8	23	2.6	33
							1502				1243		1274

Base: Self-completion questionnaire respondents

Question No						248b				A216b		A221b	
Column No						2226				1609		2029	

(ii) {BABYLAW2}

They try to have a child by _artificial insemination_, using an anonymous donor

	Code												
It should be allowed by law	1	-	.	-	.	52.7	791	-	.	49.6	616	53.7	684
It should not be allowed by law	2	-	.	-	.	42.2	634	-	.	46.7	581	42.5	541
(DK)	8	-	.	-	.	0.3	5	-	.	0.5	7	0.2	2
(NA)	9	-	.	-	.	4.8	72	-	.	3.2	39	3.7	47
							1502				1243		1274

Base: Self-completion questionnaire respondents

ARTIFICIAL FERTILITY MEASURES (Continued)

	Code	1983 %	1983 No	1984 %	1984 No	1985 %	1985 No	1986 %	1986 No	1987 %	1987 No	1989 %	1989 No
Question No						248c				A216c		A221c	
Column No						2227				1610		2030	

(iii) {BABYLAW3}

They try to have a child by having their own 'test-tube' embryo implanted

	Code	1983 %	1983 No	1984 %	1984 No	1985 %	1985 No	1986 %	1986 No	1987 %	1987 No	1989 %	1989 No
It should be allowed by law	1	-	-	-	-	83.3	1252	-	-	85.3	1060	86.6	1102
It should not be allowed by law	2	-	-	-	-	12.2	183	-	-	11.6	145	9.8	124
(DK)	8	-	-	-	-	0.5	8	-	-	0.6	7	0.3	4
(NA)	9	-	-	-	-	3.9	59	-	-	2.5	31	3.4	43

Base: Self-completion questionnaire respondents

	1985	1987	1989
	1502	1243	1274

	1985	1987	1989
Question No	248d	A216d	A221d
Column No	2228	1611	2031

(iv) {BABYLAW4}

They find a 'surrogate' mother who agrees, without payment, to bear a child for them (by artificial insemination, using the husband as donor)

	Code	1983 %	1983 No	1984 %	1984 No	1985 %	1985 No	1986 %	1986 No	1987 %	1987 No	1989 %	1989 No
It should be allowed by law	1	-	-	-	-	46.3	695	-	-	35.7	443	30.6	390
It should not be allowed by law	2	-	-	-	-	49.3	740	-	-	60.8	756	65.2	831
(DK)	8	-	-	-	-	0.4	6	-	-	0.5	6	0.2	3
(NA)	9	-	-	-	-	4.1	61	-	-	3.1	38	3.9	50

Base: Self-completion questionnaire respondents

	1985	1987	1989
	1502	1243	1274

	1985	1987	1989
Question No	248e	A216e	A221e
Column No	2229	1612	2032

(v) {BABYLAW5}

They find a 'surrogate' mother who is paid to bear a child for them (by artificial insemination, using the husband as donor)

	Code	1983 %	1983 No	1984 %	1984 No	1985 %	1985 No	1986 %	1986 No	1987 %	1987 No	1989 %	1989 No
It should be allowed by law	1	-	-	-	-	27.0	406	-	-	22.5	280	18.0	229
It should not be allowed by law	2	-	-	-	-	68.9	1035	-	-	74.2	922	77.9	992
(DK)	8	-	-	-	-	0.4	6	-	-	0.5	7	0.4	5
(NA)	9	-	-	-	-	3.6	55	-	-	2.7	34	3.7	48

Base: Self-completion questionnaire respondents

	1985	1987	1989
	1502	1243	1274

AVAILABILITY OF PORNOGRAPHY

{PORNO}

Question: **Which of these statements comes *closest* to your views on the availability of pornographic magazines and films?**
(Please tick one box)

		1983		1984		1985		1986		1987		1989	
		%	No	%	No	%	No	%	No	%	No	%	No
Question No		211								A217		A222	
Column No		1063								1613		2033	
	Code												
They should be banned altogether	1	32.7	527	-	-	-	-	-	-	38.0	473	39.1	497
They should be available in special adult shops but not displayed to the public	2	51.6	831	-	-	-	-	-	-	42.4	528	42.2	537
They should be available in special adult shops with public display permitted	3	6.8	109	-	-	-	-	-	-	8.1	101	9.8	125
They should be available in any shop for sale to adults only	4	6.7	107	-	-	-	-	-	-	8.2	102	7.3	93
They should be available in any shop for sale to anyone	5	0.7	12	-	-	-	-	-	-	1.1	14	0.2	3
(DK)	8	-	.	-	-	-	-	-	-	0.1	1	-	.
(NA)	9	1.5	24	-	-	-	-	-	-	2.1	26	1.5	18
Base: Self-completion questionnaire respondents			1610								1243		1274

1983 - No (DK)

CIRCUMSTANCES IN WHICH EUTHANASIA SHOULD BE LEGAL

{EXIT1} {EXIT2}

Question: Suppose a person has a painful incurable disease. Do you think that doctors should be allowed by law to end the patient's life if the patient requests it? (Please tick one box)

And if a person is not incurably sick but simply tired of living, should doctors be allowed by law to end that person's life if he or she requests it? (Please tick one box)

			1983		1984		1985		1986		1987		1989	
			%	No	%	No	%	No	%	No	%	No	%	No
	Question No		205a		205a								A223a	
	Column No		1032		1544								2034	
(i) *{EXIT1}*		Code												
	Yes	1	76.9	1238	75.1	1143	-	.	-	.	-	.	78.7	1002
	No	2	22.5	362	23.7	361	-	.	-	.	-	.	20.0	254
	(DK)	8	0.2	4	0.6	9	-	.	-	.	-	.	0.2	3
	(NA)	9	0.4	7	0.6	9	-	.	-	.	-	.	1.1	14
Base: Self-completion questionnaire respondents				1610		1522								1274
	Question No		205b		205b								A223b	
	Column No		1033		1545								2035	
(ii) *{EXIT2}*														
	Yes	1	13.2	213	11.4	174	-	.	-	.	-	.	14.0	179
	No	2	86.2	1387	87.3	1329	-	.	-	.	-	.	83.9	1068
	(DK)	8	0.2	4	0.6	9	-	.	-	.	-	.	0.3	3
	(NA)	9	0.4	6	0.7	11	-	.	-	.	-	.	1.8	23
Base: Self-completion questionnaire respondents				1610		1522								1274

AVAILABILITY OF CONTRACEPTION FOR YOUNG PEOPLE

{SEXADV16}

Question: Please tick one box to show how much you agree or disagree with [this statement].

Doctors should be allowed to give contraceptive advice and supplies to young people under 16 without having to inform parents

		1983		1984		1985		1986		1987		1989	
		%	No	%	No	%	No	%	No	%	No	%	No
Question No						234f				A207f		A230f	
Column No						2151				1551		2159	
	Code												
Agree strongly	1	-	-	-	-	11.9	179	-	-	6.8	84	6.8	86
Agree	2	-	-	-	-	23.3	350	-	-	24.0	299	25.7	327
Neither agree nor disagree	3	-	-	-	-	12.7	190	-	-	8.6	107	11.5	146
Disagree	4	-	-	-	-	33.2	498	-	-	33.7	419	35.9	457
Disagree strongly	5	-	-	-	-	17.2	259	-	-	26.1	325	19.5	249
(DK)	8	-	-	-	-	0.1	2	-	-	0.2	2	-	-
(NA)	9	-	-	-	-	1.6	24	-	-	0.6	7	0.7	9
							1502				1243		1274

Base: Self-completion questionnaire respondents

1985, 1987, 1989 - This question was the last in a battery of six, the first five of which asked about attitudes towards the welfare state

ADVICE TO YOUNG UNMARRIED PEOPLE

1989   Q.A204a,b   *{YWOMLIVE}{YMANLIVE}* Column Nos 1827-28

{YWOMLIVE} Column No 1827
a) If you were advising a *young woman*, which of the following ways of life would you recommend ...
(please tick one box only) ...

{YMANLIVE} Column No 1828
b) If you were advising a young *man*, which of the following ways of life would you recommend ...
(please tick one box only) ...

	Code	a) Young woman {YWOMLIVE} %	No	b) Young man {YMANLIVE} %	No
... to live alone, without a steady partner,	1	4.1	53	4.7	60
to live with a steady partner, without marrying,	2	4.0	50	5.2	67
to live with a steady partner for a while, and then marry,	3	42.8	545	42.2	537
[or,] to marry without living together first?	4	36.8	469	35.8	456
Can't choose	8	11.2	142	10.6	136
(NA)	9	1.1	14	1.4	18
Base : Self-completion respondents			1274		1274

CIRCUMSTANCES IN WHICH ABORTION SHOULD BE LEGAL - 2

1984   Q.204a-g   {ABORT841} - {ABORT847} Column Nos 1537-43

Here are a number of circumstances in which a woman might consider an abortion. Please say whether or not you think the law should allow an abortion in each case.

	Code	Yes 1		No 2		(DK) 8		(NA) 9	
		%	No	%	No	%	No	%	No
a) {ABORT841} Column No 1537 The woman's health is seriously endangered by the pregnancy		92.1	1402	5.5	84	0.6	9	1.9	28
b) {ABORT842} Column No 1538 The woman became pregnant as a result of rape		89.2	1358	7.5	114	0.4	5	2.9	45
c) {ABORT843} Column No 1539 There is a strong chance of a defect in the baby		81.9	1247	13.4	205	0.7	11	3.9	60
d) {ABORT844} Column No 1540 The couple cannot afford any more children		37.2	567	57.5	876	0.8	12	4.4	67
e) {ABORT845} Column No 1541 The woman is not married and does not wish to marry the man		31.8	483	63.6	968	0.9	14	3.7	57
f) {ABORT846} Column No 1542 The couple agree that they do not wish to have the child		32.3	491	62.8	957	0.7	11	4.2	64
g) {ABORT847} Column No 1543 The woman decides on her own she does not wish to have the child		28.8	439	66.4	1011	0.8	12	4.0	61

Base : Self-completion respondents (n = 1522)

NB This question was also asked in 1983, 1985-87 and 1989 with the list of circumstances in a different order (see note on p. M.1-9 above). The variable names have been changed from {ABORT1}-{ABORT7}

EXTRA-MARITAL SEXUAL RELATIONS - 2

1983   Q.89b,c   {MEXMS}{WEXMS} Column Nos 644-45
(Show card) Now I would like to ask you some questions about sexual relationships.

	Code	Always wrong 1		Mostly wrong 2		Sometimes wrong 3		Rarely wrong 4		Not at all wrong 5		(Depends/ varies) 6		(NA) 9	
		%	No	%	No	%	No	%	No	%	No	%	No	%	No
b) {MEXMS} Column No 644 What about a married *man* having sexual relations with a woman other than his wife		58.1	999	25.0	430	10.8	185	1.0	17	1.6	27	2.7	46	0.9	15
c) {WEXMS} Column No 645 What about a married *woman* having sexual relations with a man other than her husband		59.4	1022	24.7	425	10.4	180	0.7	13	1.3	23	2.4	42	0.9	15

Base : All (n = 1719)

NB In 1984 and subsequently, these two questions were replaced by a single question: 'What about a married person ...' (see p. M.1-2 above).

ADOPTION BY HOMOSEXUAL COUPLES

1983   Q.90b   {GAYADOPT} Column No 650
And do you think homosexual couples should be allowed to adopt a baby under the same conditions as other couples?

	Code	%	No
Yes	1	8.5	145
No	2	87.3	1501
(Other answer)	3	1.1	19
(Not *male* couples)	4	0.5	9
(DK)	8	2.0	34
(NA)	9	0.7	11
Base : All			1719

NB In 1985 and subsequently, this single question was replaced by two questions asking separately about female and male homosexual couples (see pp. M.1-6 and M.1-7 above)

M Morality and ethics

M2 Social behaviour

Table titles and cross references

TAX AVOIDANCE

{TAXAVOID} {TAXSNEAK}

Question: It is said that many people manage to avoid paying their full income tax. Do you think that they should *not* be allowed to get away with it - or do you think good luck to them if they can get away with it?

		1983		1984		1985		1986		1987		1989	
		%	No	**%**	No	**%**	No	**%**	No	**%**	No	**%**	No
Question No		24a								17a		17a	
Column No		279								246		257	
(i) *{TAXAVOID}*	Code												
Should not be allowed	1	73.6	1265	-	.	-	.	-	.	74.7	2066	75.7	2217
Good luck if they can get away with it	2	26.0	447	-	.	-	.	-	.	24.5	678	23.8	696
(DK)	8	0.3	6	-	.	-	.	-	.	0.6	16	0.5	14
(NA)	9	0.1	1	-	.	-	.	-	.	0.2	6	0.1	3
Base: All			1719								2766		2930

		1983		1984		1985		1986		1987		1989	
Question No		24b								17b		17b	
Column No		280								247		258	
(ii) *{TAXSNEAK}*													
[If tax avoidance not tolerated] If you knew of somebody who wasn't paying their full income tax, would you be inclined to report him or her?													
[Not asked: tax avoidance tolerated]	0	26.0	447	-	.	-	.	-	.	24.5	678	23.8	696
Yes	1	9.8	168	-	.	-	.	-	.	9.5	264	10.6	312
No	2	61.7	1060	-	.	-	.	-	.	60.9	1684	60.8	1780
Other answer	7	1.6	28	-	.	-	.	-	.	2.0	55	1.6	47
(DK)	8	-	.	-	.	-	.	-	.	2.0	55	2.3	69
(NA)	9	0.9	16	-	.	-	.	-	.	1.1	29	0.9	26
Base: All			1719								2766		2930

1983 - No (DK); Other answer, code 3

JUDGEMENTS OF WRONGDOING - 1

{*CLAIM50*}

Question:　(Show card)　**Please say which of the phrases on this card comes closest to what you think of [this] situation.**

	Code	1983 %	No	1984 %	No	1985 %	No	1986 %	No	1987 %	No	1989 %	No
Question No				90i						A90a			
Column No				638						756			

A company employee exaggerates his
claims for travel expenses over a
period and makes £50

	Code	1983 %	No	1984 %	No	1985 %	No	1986 %	No	1987 %	No	1989 %	No
Nothing wrong	1	-	.	3.8	63	-	.	-	.	5.2	73	-	-
Bit wrong	2	-	.	17.3	285	-	.	-	.	20.3	282	-	.
Wrong	3	-	.	54.0	889	-	.	-	.	51.7	719	-	.
Seriously wrong	4	-	.	23.4	385	-	.	-	.	14.7	205	-	.
Very seriously wrong	5	-	.	-	.	-	.	-	.	7.8	108	-	.
(DK)	8	-	.	0.6	9	-	.	-	.	0.2	2	-	.
(NA)	9	-	.	0.8	14	-	.	-	.	0.0	1	-	.
Base: All					1645						1391		

1984 - No 'very seriously wrong', code 5

1984, 1987 - This question was one of a long series of situations for which respondents were asked to give their judgements on how wrong each one was

JUDGEMENTS OF WRONG AND LIKELY ACTION - 1

{VATCHEAT} {VATDO}

Question: (Show card) Still using this card to say what comes closest to what you think about the situation:

		1983		1984		1985		1986		1987		1989	
		%	No	%	No	%	No	%	No	%	No	%	No
Question No				92a						A91a			
Column No				655						765			

(i) {VATCHEAT}

A householder is having a repair job done by a local plumber. He is told that if he pays cash he will not be charged VAT. So he pays cash.

Code

		1983		1984		1985		1986		1987		1989	
Nothing wrong	1	-	-	31.0	509	-	-	-	-	26.1	362	-	-
Bit wrong	2	-	-	31.3	514	-	-	-	-	29.3	407	-	-
Wrong	3	-	-	31.8	524	-	-	-	-	35.7	496	-	-
Seriously wrong	4	-	-	3.5	57	-	-	-	-	6.3	87	-	-
Very seriously wrong	5	-	-	-	-	-	-	-	-	1.9	26	-	-
(DK)	8	-	-	1.6	26	-	-	-	-	0.8	11	-	-
(NA)	9	-	-	0.9	15	-	-	-	-	-	-	-	-

Base: All

1645   1391

Question No	92b	A91b
Column No	656	766

(ii) {VATDO}

Might you do this if the situation came up?

		1983		1984		1985		1986		1987		1989	
Yes	1	-	-	66.4	1093	-	-	-	-	67.2	935	-	-
No	2	-	-	26.9	443	-	-	-	-	26.8	373	-	-
(DK)	8	-	-	5.3	87	-	-	-	-	5.0	70	-	-
(NA)	9	-	-	1.3	22	-	-	-	-	1.0	14	-	-

Base: All

1645   1391

1984 - {VATCHEAT} No 'very seriously wrong', code 5

JUDGEMENTS OF WRONG AND LIKELY ACTION - 2

{CHNGKP10} {CHNGDO10}

Question: (Show card) **A man gives a £5 note for goods he is buying in a big store. By mistake, he is given change for a £10 note. He notices but keeps the change.**

		1983		1984		1985		1986		1987		1989	
		%	No	%	No	%	No	%	No	%	No	%	No
Question No				93a						A92a			
Column No				656						766			
(i) {CHNGKP10}	Code												
Nothing wrong	1	-	-	6.0	99	-	-	-	-	7.6	106	-	-
Bit wrong	2	-	-	15.1	249	-	-	-	-	20.0	278	-	-
Wrong	3	-	-	61.4	1011	-	-	-	-	58.1	808	-	-
Seriously wrong	4	-	-	16.4	269	-	-	-	-	9.6	133	-	-
Very seriously wrong	5	-	-	-	-	-	-	-	-	4.7	65	-	-
(DK)	8	-	-	0.3	5	-	-	-	-	-		-	-
(NA)	9	-	-	0.8	13	-	-	-	-	-		-	-
Base: All					1645						1391		

		1983		1984		1985		1986		1987		1989	
Question No				93b						A92b			
Column No				658						768			
(ii) {CHNGDO10}													
Might you do this if the situation came up?													
Yes	1	-	-	17.9	295	-	-	-	-	23.6	328	-	-
No	2	-	-	77.1	1268	-	-	-	-	73.2	1018	-	-
(DK)	8	-	-	3.7	60	-	-	-	-	2.6	36	-	-
(NA)	9	-	-	1.3	21	-	-	-	-	0.6	9	-	-
Base: All					1645						1391		

1984 - {CHNGKP10} No 'very seriously wrong', code 5

1984, 1987 - {CHNGKP10} appears on the SPSS file as {STORCHKP}. {CHNGDO10} appears on the SPSS file as {STORCHDO}

JUDGEMENTS OF WRONGDOING - 2

1987   Q.A90b-i   {CLAIM200}{TAX500}{CHARG200}{TILL200}{WDWORM50}{FIRMCAR}{INSUR500}{MANCAR}
Column Nos 757-64

(Show card) I am now going to read out some situations that might come up. As I read out each one,
please say which of the phrases on this card comes closest to what you think of the situation. (Read out)

	Nothing wrong 1		Bit wrong 2		Wrong 3		Seriously wrong 4		Very Seriously wrong 5		(DK) 8		(NA) 9	
Code	%	No	%	No	%	No	%	No	%	No	%	No	%	No
b) {CLAIM200} Column No 757 A company employee exaggerates his claims for travel expenses over a period and makes £200	1.6	22	6.7	94	38.0	529	35.9	499	17.3	241	0.2	3	0.3	4
c) {TAX500} Column No 758 A local plumber does some of his business for cash and does not declare it for tax. Over a period he avoids paying £500 to the Inland Revenue	5.0	70	16.6	231	46.2	643	21.7	302	9.9	138	0.4	6	0.1	1
d) {CHARG200} Column No 759 A milkman slightly overcharges customers over a period and makes £200	0.2	3	3.9	54	38.5	535	36.7	510	20.5	285	0.1	2	0.1	2
e) {TILL200} Column No 760 A shop assistant sometimes rings up less on the till than the customer pays. He keeps the difference and over a period makes £200	0.6	8	3.1	44	36.5	508	38.7	538	20.7	288	0.1	2	0.3	4
f) {WDWORM50} Column No 761 A man selling a piece of old furniture conceals the fact that it has woodworm. The price he can get increases by about £50	3.5	48	11.1	154	49.2	684	26.2	365	9.8	136	0.2	3	0.1	1
g) {FIRMCAR} Column No 762 A large firm of car dealers conceals the fact that a used car was in a serious accident. The price they can get increases by about £500	0.4	5	1.4	19	14.1	196	29.9	416	54.1	752	0.1	2	0.0	1
h) {INSUR500} Column No 763 In making an insurance claim, a man whose home has been flooded exaggerates the value of what was damaged by £500	4.8	66	14.7	204	45.4	632	24.9	346	10.0	139	0.2	3	0.0	1
i) {MANCAR} Column No 764 A man selling his car conceals the fact that it was in a serious accident. The price he can get increases by about £500	1.7	24	2.2	30	19.4	270	30.0	418	46.5	647	0.1	2	0.0	1

Base : All (n = 1391)

JUDGEMENTS OF WRONG AND LIKELY ACTION - 3

1987   Q.A93a,b   *{SHOPCHKP}{SHOPCHDO}* Column Nos 769-70

{SHOPCHKP} Column No 769

a) A man gives a £5 note for goods he is buying in a *corner shop*. By mistake, he is given change for a £10 note. He notices but keeps the change.

	Code	%	No
Nothing wrong	1	4.0	56
Bit wrong	2	11.8	164
Wrong	3	63.3	880
Seriously wrong	4	14.7	205
Very seriously wrong	5	5.9	82
(NA)	9	0.3	4
Base : All			1391

{SHOPCHDO} Column No 770

b) Might you do this if the situation came up?

	Code	%	No
Yes	1	10.2	142
No	2	87.5	1216
(DK)	8	1.0	14
(NA)	9	1.3	18
Base : All			1391

JUDGEMENTS OF WRONG AND LIKELY ACTION - 4

1987   Q.A94a,b   *{INSUR100}{INSDO100}* Column Nos 771-72

{INSUR100} Column No 771

a) (Show card) In making an insurance claim, a man whose home has been burgled exaggerates the value of what was stolen by £100.

	Code	%	No
Nothing wrong	1	9.1	126
Bit wrong	2	24.3	337
Wrong	3	52.6	731
Seriously wrong	4	10.4	145
Very seriously wrong	5	3.3	45
(DK)	8	0.2	3
(NA)	9	0.1	2
Base : All			1391

{INSDO100} Column No 772

b) Might you do this if the situation came up?

	Code	%	No
Yes	1	26.5	368
No	2	68.7	955
(DK)	8	4.2	59
(NA)	9	0.6	9
Base : All			1391

NB {INSUR100} appears on the SPSS file as {INSUREUP}. {INSDO100} appears on the SPSS file as {INSUREDO}

LIKELY COURSE OF ACTION ON FINDING VARIOUS SUMS OF MONEY

1987   Q.A95a-c   {FIND5}{FIND20}{FIND100} Column Nos 773-75

{FIND5} Column No 773
a) Now, suppose you are alone in an empty street, no-one is likely to come by and see you. There is a £5 note lying on the pavement. Would you ... (read out) ...

{FIND20} Column No 774
b) Suppose it was a £20 note lying there. What would you do ... (read out) ...

{FIND100} Column No 775
c) Suppose it was £100 in notes lying there. What would you do ... (read out) ...

	Code	a) £5 note {FIND5} Column No 773 %	No	b) £20 note {FIND20} Column No 774 %	No	c) £100 in notes {FIND100} Column No 775 %	No
... leave it there,	1	1.4	19	0.7	10	0.7	9
pick it up and hand it in at the police station,	2	26.7	372	47.6	662	75.2	1046
or - pick it up and pocket it?	3	68.6	954	48.1	669	21.3	296
(Can't say)	8	2.6	37	2.9	40	2.4	33
(NA)	9	0.7	10	0.6	9	0.5	7
Base : All			1391		1391		1391

JUDGEMENTS OF WRONGDOING IN PUBLIC LIFE

1984   Q.90ii-xv   {MANGFT50}{MANASKS}{MANLUNCH}{OFFGIFT}{OFFASKS}{OFFLUNCH}{OFFJOB}
{OFFCLAIM}{HOUSHELP}{HOUSGIFT}{TENTOFFR}{PCASKS}{DRIVOFFR}{PCFORGET}   Column Nos 639-52
(Show card) I am now going to read out some situations that might come up. As I read out each one, please
say which of the phrases on this card comes closest to what you think of the situation. (Read out)

	Code	Nothing wrong 1 % No	Bit wrong 2 % No	Wrong 3 % No	Seriously wrong 4 % No	(DK) 8 % No	(NA) 9 % No
ii) {MANGFT50} Column No 639 A company manager accepts a Christmas present worth £50 from a firm from which he buys products		38.7 636	22.6 372	29.3 483	7.1 117	1.4 23	0.9 15
iii) {MANASKS} Column No 640 A manager *asks* a firm from which he buys products for a £50 gift for himself		2.2 37	6.3 104	45.7 752	44.1 725	0.7 11	1.0 17
iv) {MANLUNCH} Column No 641 A firm selling products to another company regularly takes a manager in that company to expensive lunches		39.2 645	26.7 440	26.0 428	6.0 99	1.2 19	0.9 15
v) {OFFGIFT} Column No 642 A council official accepts a Christmas present worth £50 from a private firm that supplies services to the council		12.9 212	13.6 224	43.0 707	28.2 463	1.5 25	0.8 14
vi) {OFFASKS} Column No 643 A council official *asks* a firm that supplies services to the council for a £50 gift for himself		0.9 14	3.8 62	37.8 622	56.1 924	0.5 8	0.9 15
vii) {OFFLUNCH} Column No 644 A firm supplying services to the council regularly takes a council official to expensive lunches		22.0 361	21.9 360	40.8 671	13.4 221	1.0 17	0.9 15
viii) {OFFJOB} Column No 645 A council official uses his influence to get a relative a job with the council		11.2 184	19.4 319	45.1 742	22.8 375	0.7 12	0.8 14
ix) {OFFCLAIM} Column No 646 A council official exaggerates his claims for travel expenses over a period and makes £50		2.0 32	11.6 191	52.0 856	32.8 540	0.7 12	0.8 14

Base : All (n = 1645)

NB {MANGFT50} appears as {MANGIFT} on the SPSS file

JUDGEMENTS OF WRONGDOING IN PUBLIC LIFE (continued)

		Nothing wrong		A bit wrong		Wrong		Seriously wrong		(DK)		(NA)	
Code		1		2		3		4		8		9	
		%	No	%	No	%	No	%	No	%	No	%	No

x) *{HOUSHELP}*   Column No 647
A council tenant applies for a transfer to a better house. An official in the housing department notices that the application is from an old friend. He *decides* to put the application near the front of the queue

		2.0	32	11.3	186	52.4	862	33.0	542	0.5	9	0.8	14

xi) *{HOUSGIFT}*   Column No 648
A council tenant applies for a transfer to a better house. An official in the housing department *asks* for £50 to put the application near the front of the queue

		0.3	5	1.3	21	25.7	423	71.6	1178	0.3	5	0.8	14

xii) *{TENTOFFR}*   Column No 649
A council tenant applies for a transfer to a better house. He *offers* an official in the housing department £50 to put the application near the front of the queue

		0.9	15	4.2	69	40.7	670	53.0	872	0.3	5	0.8	14

xiii) *{PCASKS}*   Column No 650
A policeman stops a driver for speeding. The policeman *asks* for £50 to forget the incident

		0.2	3	0.7	12	17.2	283	80.8	1330	0.2	3	0.9	15

xiv) *{DRIVOFFR}*   Column No 651
A policeman stops a driver for speeding. The driver *offers* £50 to forget the incident

		0.6	10	3.7	61	36.1	594	58.6	964	0.2	4	0.8	14

xv) *{PCFORGET}*   Column No 652
A policeman stops a driver for speeding. The driver is an old friend. The policeman *decides* simply to forget the incident

		2.9	48	13.6	223	50.8	836	31.4	517	0.4	7	0.8	14

Base : All (n = 1645)

NB {PCFORGET} is {PCHELP} on the SPSS file; but since {PCHELP} relates to a different question (Q.74b asked in 1983 - see p. B-14), the variable name in 1984 has been changed to {PCFORGET}

JUDGEMENTS OF WRONG AND LIKELY ACTION - 5

1984   Q.91a,b   *{DUSTBRIB}{DUSTDO}*   Column Nos 653-54
(Show card) **Still using the card to say what comes closest to what you think about [this] situation :**

{DUSTBRIB}   Column No 653
a) **A man offers the dustmen £5 to take away rubbish they are not supposed to pick up.**

	Code	%	No
Nothing wrong	1	31.6	520
A bit wrong	2	35.0	576
Wrong	3	29.3	482
Seriously wrong	4	2.6	42
(DK)	8	0.7	12
(NA)	9	0.8	13
Base : All			1645

{DUSTDO}   Column No 654
b) **Might you do this if the situation came up?**

	Code	%	No
Yes	1	57.6	948
No	2	38.0	626
(DK)	8	2.9	48
(NA)	9	1.4	23
Base : All			1645

N Family relationships and gender issues

N1 Family relationships

Table titles and cross references

EASE OF OBTAINING A DIVORCE

{DIVORCE}

Question: (Interviewer: if interviewing in England or Wales, ask about 'Britain'; if interviewing in Scotland, ask about 'Scotland') **Do you think that divorce in *(Britain/Scotland)* should be** ... (read out) ...

		1983 %	1983 No	1984 %	1984 No	1985 %	1985 No	1986 %	1986 No	1987 %	1987 No	1989 %	1989 No
Question No		85		80						A81		A85	
Column No		630		564						711		863	
	Code												
... easier to obtain than it is now,	1	10.7	183	12.9	212	-	-	-	-	9.8	136	12.9	190
... more difficult,	2	30.8	529	30.0	494	-	-	-	-	37.6	522	29.7	437
... or should things remain as they are?	3	55.1	948	54.1	890	-	-	-	-	50.1	697	53.1	781
(DK)	8	3.1	53	2.5	42	-	-	-	-	2.4	34	4.2	61
(NA)	9	0.3	6	0.5	8	-	-	-	-	0.1	1	-	-
Base: All			1719		1645						1391		1469

1983 - Q reads: 'Do you think that divorce in Britain should be ...'; (DK), code 4
1986 - The variable {DIVORCE} relates to a different question (see p.N.1 - 37 below) and has been renamed {DIVMRDIF}

HOUSEHOLD TYPE

{HHTYPE}

Variable derived from details collected about household members

		1983 %	1983 No	1984 %	1984 No	1985 %	1985 No	1986 %	1986 No	1987 %	1987 No	1989 %	1989 No
Column No		962		1655		1058		2330		2228		2345	
	Code												
Single adult, aged 60 or over	1	7.9	135	7.4	122	7.2	128	6.9	210	6.3	173	7.2	212
Two adults, one or both aged 60 or over	2	16.5	284	18.5	304	15.2	269	15.4	471	16.0	441	16.3	477
Single adult, aged 18-59	3	4.4	76	4.4	72	5.1	91	3.6	112	4.5	123	4.2	124
Two adults, both aged 18-59	4	14.8	255	14.0	230	14.0	247	14.5	444	14.4	399	14.6	429
Youngest person aged 0-4	5	13.7	235	13.6	224	15.2	268	14.3	437	12.9	357	14.5	426
Youngest person aged 5-17	6	23.6	406	25.5	420	25.0	443	26.5	812	27.0	746	23.2	681
Three or more adults	7	17.8	306	15.1	248	17.6	311	18.3	560	18.3	505	19.4	568
Insufficient information	9	1.3	22	1.5	25	0.7	12	0.6	19	0.7	20	0.5	14
Base: All			1719		1645		1769		3066		2766		2930

MARITAL STATUS

{MARSTAT}

Question: Can I just check your own marital status? At present are you ... (read out) ...

		1983		1984		1985		1986		1987		1989	
		%	No	%	No	%	No	%	No	%	No	%	No
Question No		87a		82		97b		A105b/B113b		A83a/B102		900a	
Column No		633		566		758		1510		713		1408	
	Code												
... married,	1	68.5	1177	68.5	1126	65.1	1152	66.8	2049	66.9	1849	65.2	1912
... living as married,	2	-	-	-	-	2.4	42	2.8	87	3.3	91	4.6	136
... separated or divorced,	3	5.3	92	5.5	90	4.7	83	4.8	146	4.7	130	5.1	150
... widowed,	4	10.2	176	9.5	157	8.7	154	8.7	268	7.2	199	8.7	255
... or not married?	5	15.7	271	16.3	268	18.6	329	16.5	505	17.9	495	16.3	477
(DK)	8	-	-	-	-	-	-	-	-	-	-	-	-
(NA)	9	0.2	4	0.2	4	0.5	9	0.3	11	0.0	1	0.0	1
Base: All			1719		1645		1769		3066		2766		2930

1983 - Q reads: 'Can I just check your own marital status ...?'; Married (legally) and living with husband/wife, code 1; Separated/divorced, code 2; Widowed, code 3; Never married, code 4; No (DK). Then the interviewer was instructed to 'probe to find out if living as married' (see p.N.1 - 39 below)

1984 - Married or living as married, code 1

HOUSEHOLD SIZE

{HOUSEHLD}

Question: [And a few questions about you and your household.]
Including yourself, how many people live here regularly as members of this household?

	Code	1983 %	1983 No	1984 %	1984 No	1985 %	1985 No	1986 %	1986 No	1987 %	1987 No	1989 %	1989 No
Question No		91		94		97a		A105a/B113a		900		900b	
Column No						756-57		1908-09		1208-09		1409-10	
One	1	12.3	212	12.1	199	12.4	219	10.5	323	10.7	297	11.5	338
Two	2	32.3	555	33.8	556	30.3	535	31.0	951	31.8	879	32.2	945
Three	3	19.2	330	19.3	318	20.9	369	20.6	630	21.7	599	22.6	663
Four	4	23.3	400	22.6	371	22.3	395	23.0	706	23.2	642	21.3	624
Five	5	9.0	155	7.5	123	10.0	177	10.5	322	8.7	242	9.0	264
Six	6	2.3	39	3.6	59	2.2	38	2.8	84	2.8	78	2.3	68
Seven	7	1.3	22	0.8	13	1.1	20	0.9	29	0.6	15	0.7	20
Eight	8	0.1	2	0.1	2	0.5	9	0.4	11	0.1	4	0.2	7
Nine	9	0.2	3	0.1	2	0.1	2	0.1	3	0.2	5	-	-
Ten	10	-	-	0.1	2	0.1	1	0.2	6	0.1	3	0.0	1
Eleven	11	-	-	-	-	0.1	2	-	-	-	-	0.0	1
Twelve	12	-	-	-	-	-	-	-	-	-	-	0.0	1
Sixteen	16	-	-	-	-	0.1	1	-	-	-	-	-	-
(DK)	98	-	-	-	-	-	-	-	-	-	-	-	-
(NA)	99	-	-	-	-	-	-	-	-	0.0	1	-	-
Base: All			1719		1645		1769		3066		2766		2930

1983, 1984 - Variable not on SPSS file, so the figures presented here have been derived from information coded on the 'household grid'

CHILDREN FORMERLY IN HOUSEHOLD

{OTHCHILD}

Question: *Apart* from people [you've just mentioned] who live in your household, have you had any *(other)* children, including stepchildren, who grew up in your household?   (Interviewer: includes children no longer living)

		1983		1984		1985		1986		1987		1989	
		%	No	%	No	%	No	%	No	%	No	%	No
Question No										902		902	
Column No										1260		1470	
	Code												
Yes	1	-	-	-	-	-	-	-	-	37.3	1031	37.0	1084
No	2	-	-	-	-	-	-	-	-	62.5	1727	62.8	1841
(DK)	8	-	-	-	-	-	-	-	-	-	-	-	-
(NA)	9	-	-	-	-	-	-	-	-	0.3	8	0.2	6
Base: All											2766		2930

CHILDREN AGED UNDER 16 IN HOUSEHOLD

{KIDSU16}

Question: And are there any children under 16 years old in this household?

		1983		1984		1985		1986		1987		1989	
		%	No	%	No	%	No	%	No	%	No	%	No
Question No				83						A83b			
Column No				567						714			
	Code												
[Not asked: not currently married/ living as married]	0	-	-	31.3	515	-	-	-	-	-	-	-	-
Yes	1	-	-	29.5	485	-	-	-	-	35.9	499	-	-
No	2	-	-	38.9	640	-	-	-	-	63.8	887	-	-
(DK)	8	-	-	-	-	-	-	-	-	-	-	-	-
(NA)	9	-	-	0.3	5	-	-	-	-	0.4	5	-	-
Base: All					1645						1391		

1984 -   Asked only of those who were married or living as married, so data for the two years are not comparable without further analysis

ATTITUDES TOWARDS MARRIAGE AND PARENTHOOD

1989   Q.A205a-j   *{MARVIEW1}-{MARVIEW0}* Column Nos 1829-38
Do you agree or disagree [with the following statements]? (Please tick one box for each)

	Code	Strongly agree 1		Agree 2		Neither agree nor disagree 3		Disagree 4		Strongly disagree 5		Can't choose 8		(NA) 9	
		%	No	%	No	%	No	%	No	%	No	%	No	%	No
a) *{MARVIEW1}* Column No 1829 Married people are generally happier than unmarried people		7.6	97	25.4	324	39.5	503	19.4	247	3.8	49	3.8	49	0.4	5
b) *{MARVIEW2}* Column No 1830 Personal freedom is more important than the companionship of marriage		2.6	33	9.4	119	25.3	322	52.5	668	6.2	79	3.3	42	0.8	10
c) *{MARVIEW3}* Column No 1831 The main advantage of marriage is that it gives financial security		2.9	37	14.7	187	16.9	215	51.1	651	12.2	155	1.6	21	0.6	8
d) *{MARVIEW4}* Column No 1832 The main purpose of marriage these days is to have children		3.0	38	16.8	214	15.5	198	54.2	690	8.2	104	1.6	20	0.7	9
e) *{MARVIEW5}* Column No 1833 It is better to have a bad marriage than no marriage at all		0.9	11	1.6	20	3.3	42	46.9	598	45.4	578	1.2	15	0.8	10
f) *{MARVIEW6}* Column No 1834 People who want children ought to get married		24.6	314	45.5	580	10.2	130	14.4	184	3.0	38	1.1	14	1.1	14
g) *{MARVIEW7}* Column No 1835 A single mother can bring up her child as well as a married couple		4.5	57	25.9	329	16.9	215	41.6	530	9.0	115	1.4	17	0.8	10
h) *{MARVIEW8}* Column No 1836 A single father can bring up his children as well as a married couple		2.9	37	21.1	268	17.5	223	44.4	566	12.4	158	1.1	14	0.6	8
i) *{MARVIEW9}* Column 1837 Couples don't take marriage seriously enough when divorce is easily available		14.8	188	46.0	586	14.0	179	20.1	256	2.7	34	1.7	22	0.6	8
j) *{MARVIEW0}* Column 1838 Homosexual couples should have the right to marry one another		2.5	32	10.7	136	15.1	192	28.4	361	37.8	481	4.8	61	0.8	10

Base : Self-completion respondents (n = 1274)

IDEAL FAMILY SIZE - 1

1989   Q.A206   *{IDLNCHLD-Banded}* Column Nos 1839-40

All in all, what do you think is the ideal number of children for a family to have? (Please write the number in the box)

	Code	%	No
None	0	0.5	6
One	1	0.7	9
Two	2	60.2	767
Three	3	17.8	226
Four	4	8.9	114
Five or more		0.7	9
(DK)	98	1.2	16
(NA)	99	9.9	126
Base : Self-completion respondents			1274

NB Numbers above four have been banded. A similar question was asked in 1986 on the interview questionnaire - see p. N.1 - 10

FAMILY SIZE

1989   Q.A207a-e   *{FAMSIZE0}-{FAMSIZE4}* Column Nos 1841-45

In general, what do you feel about each of these family sizes? (Please tick one box for each)

	Code	Very desirable 1		Desirable 2		Neither desirable nor undesirable 3		Un- desirable 4		Very un- desirable 5		Can't choose 8		(NA) 9	
		%	No	%	No	%	No	%	No	%	No	%	No	%	No
a) *{FAMSIZE0}* Column No 1841 No children		1.8	23	4.9	62	39.7	505	31.9	406	9.8	125	6.4	82	5.5	70
b) *{FAMSIZE1}* Column No 1842 One child		2.6	33	32.9	419	26.4	336	23.8	303	3.1	39	4.0	51	7.3	92
c) *{FAMSIZE2}* Column No 1843 Two children		28.7	366	52.0	663	11.6	148	1.6	20	0.3	3	2.5	32	3.3	42
d) *{FAMSIZE3}* Column No 1844 Three children		10.3	131	36.3	462	27.2	347	13.5	172	3.2	41	5.2	66	4.4	56
e) *{FAMSIZE4}* Column No 1845 Four children or more		4.9	62	16.2	206	23.2	296	29.1	370	16.1	205	6.4	81	4.2	54

Base : Self-completion respondents (n = 1274)

IMPORTANCE OF CHILDREN IN PEOPLE'S LIVES

1989   Q.A208a-f   {CHDVIEW1}-{CHDVIEW6} Column Nos 1846-51
Do you agree or disagree [with the following statements]? (Please tick one box for each)

	Code	Strongly agree 1		Agree 2		Neither agree nor disagree 3		Disagree 4		Strongly disagree 5		Can't choose 8		(NA) 9	
		%	No	%	No	%	No	%	No	%	No	%	No	%	No
a) {CHDVIEW1} Column No 1846 Children are more trouble than they are worth		1.7	22	1.9	25	9.3	118	50.7	646	35.0	446	0.8	11	0.6	7
b) {CHDVIEW2} Column No 1847 Watching children grow up is life's greatest joy		29.2	372	52.3	666	12.8	163	3.6	46	0.5	6	1.3	16	0.4	6
c) {CHDVIEW3} Column No 1848 Having children interferes too much with the freedom of parents		1.7	21	7.8	99	16.8	214	56.7	722	15.3	195	0.9	11	0.9	11
d) {CHDVIEW4} Column No 1849 A marriage without children is not fully complete		10.2	129	35.0	446	20.2	257	26.3	335	6.0	76	1.7	22	0.6	8
e) {CHDVIEW5} Column No 1850 It is better *not* to have children as they are such a heavy burden		1.2	16	1.4	18	8.1	104	58.3	743	29.2	371	1.0	12	0.8	10
f) {CHDVIEW6} Column No 1851 People who have never had children lead empty lives		6.7	85	16.7	213	21.2	270	38.6	491	13.0	165	3.1	39	0.8	10

Base : Self-completion respondents (n = 1274)

RELAXING THE DIVORCE LAWS

1989   Q.A209-211   {EASYDIV1}-{EASYDIV3}   Column Nos 1852-54

Q.A209   {EASYDIV1}   Column No 1852
[And,] In general, would you say that the law now makes it easy or difficult for people who want to get divorced? (Please tick one box only)

Q.A210   {EASYDIV2}   Column No 1853
How easy or difficult do you think the law should make it for *couples without young children* to get a divorce? (Please tick one box only)

Q.A211   {EASYDIV3}   Column No 1854
[And] what about *couples with young children*? How easy or difficult *should* the law make it for *couples with young children* to get a divorce? (Please tick one box only)

	Code	Q.A209 People in general {EASYDIV1} %	No	Q.A210 Without young children {EASYDIV2} %	No	Q.A211 With young children {EASYDIV3} %	No
Very easy	1	27.1	346	13.0	165	2.4	31
Fairly easy	2	48.2	614	31.5	402	14.3	182
Neither easy nor difficult	3	14.4	184	28.8	367	30.9	394
Fairly difficult	4	5.5	70	16.8	214	29.9	381
Very difficult	5	1.3	16	5.5	70	15.8	201
Impossible	6	-	-	0.5	6	2.2	28
Can't choose	8	3.1	40	3.6	46	4.2	54
(NA)	9	0.3	4	0.3	3	0.3	3
Base : Self-completion respondents			1274		1274		1274

BEST COURSE OF ACTION IN AN UNHAPPY MARRIAGE

1989   Q.A212-214   {BETRDIV1}-{BETRDIV3}   Column Nos 1855-57

Q.A212   {BETRDIV1}   Column No 1855
When a marriage is troubled and unhappy, do you think it is generally better for the *children* if the couple stays together or gets divorced? (Please tick one box only)

Q.A213   {BETRDIV2}   Column No 1856
And when a marriage is troubled and unhappy, is it generally better for the *wife* if the couple stays together or gets divorced? (Please tick one box only)

Q.A214   {BETRDIV3}   Column No 1857
And when a marriage is troubled and unhappy, is it generally better for the *husband* if the couple stays together or gets divorced? (Please tick one box only)

	Code	Q.A212 For the children {BETRDIV1} %	No	Q.A213 For the wife {BETRDIV2} %	No	Q.A214 For the husband {BETRDIV3} %	No
Much better to divorce	1	14.4	183	14.6	186	13.6	174
Better to divorce	2	45.1	575	51.2	653	51.9	661
Worse to divorce	3	16.6	211	9.0	115	8.7	110
Much worse to divorce	4	3.0	38	1.6	20	1.8	23
Can't choose	8	20.3	259	22.9	292	23.5	299
(NA)	9	0.6	7	0.6	8	0.5	7
Base : Self-completion respondents	1274		1274		1274		

RESPONDENT: WHETHER EVER BEEN DIVORCED

1989   Q.A216   {DIVORCED} Column No 1860
Have you ever been divorced?   (Please tick one box only)

	Code	%	No
Yes	1	13.0	165
No	2	71.3	908
Never married	3	14.8	189
(NA)	9	0.9	11
Base : Self-completion respondents			1274

SPOUSE/PARTNER: WHETHER EVER BEEN DIVORCED

1989   Q.A218a   {SDIVORCD} Column No 1862
[If married/cohabiting] Has your husband or wife or partner ever been divorced?
(Please tick one box only)

	Code	%	No
[Not asked: not married/cohabiting]	-1	31.3	399
Yes	1	8.0	102
No	2	59.6	759
(NA)	9	1.1	14
Base : Self-completion respondents			127

WHETHER LIVED TOGETHER BEFORE MARRIAGE

1989   Q.A218b   {COHABITD} Column No 1863
[If married/cohabiting] Did you live with your husband or wife or partner before you got married?
(Please tick one box)

	Code	%	No
[Not asked: not married/cohabiting]	-1	31.3	399
Yes	1	14.1	179
No	2	51.0	649
Not married [ie still cohabiting]	3	1.9	24
(NA)	9	1.7	22
Base : Self-completion respondents			1274

WHICH PARTNER EARNS MORE MONEY?

1989   Q.A219a,b   *{BOTHWORK}{EARNMOST}*   Column Nos 1864-65

1989   Q.A219a   *{BOTHWORK}*   Column No 1864
[If married/cohabiting] **Do you and your husband or wife or partner *both* have paid work at the moment?**
(Please tick one box)

	Code	%	No
[Not asked : not married/cohabiting]	-1	31.3	399
Yes	1	31.6	402
No	2	36.7	468
(NA)	9	0.4	5
Base : Self-completion respondents			1274

1989   Q.A219b   *{EARNMOST}*   Column No 1865
[If married/cohabiting and both in paid work] **Who earns more money? (Please tick one box only)**

	Code	%	No
[Not asked : not married/cohabiting; one or other not in paid work]	-1	68.4	871
Husband earns *much* more	1	21.4	272
Husband earns a *bit* more	2	6.0	76
We earn about the *same* amount	3	1.8	23
Wife earns a *bit* more	4	1.4	18
Wife earns *much* more	5	0.8	10
(NA)	9	0.3	4
Base : Self-completion respondents			1274

IDEAL FAMILY SIZE - 2

1986   Q.A71a   *{IDEALCHN-Banded}*   Column Nos 1008-09
What would you say is the ideal number of children for a couple to have these days?
(Interviewer : do not prompt; write in [exact number] or code 'There is no ideal/depends on couple')

	Code	%	No
None	0	0.6	9
One	1	2.0	31
Two	2	71.1	1078
Three	3	12.8	195
Four	4	2.8	43
Five or more		0.3	5
There is no ideal/ depends on couple	97	8.5	129
(DK)	98	1.6	24
(NA)	99	0.1	4
Base : All			1518

NB As the first question in this series, it was introduced by: 'Now I'd like to ask you a few questions about families
and children'. Numbers above four have been banded. A similar question was asked in 1989 on the self-completion questionnaire
(see p.N.1 - 6). However, this mode of administering the question produced a rather different distribution of responses;
furthermore no 'depends' code was offered in 1989. So responses to the two questions are shown on two different tables.

FAMILY SIZE AND PARENTAL CHOICE

1986   Q.A71b   {DECIDCHN} Column No 1010

Who do you think *should* decide how many children to have? Should it be ... (read out) ...

	Code	%	No
... the father,	1	0.7	11
the mother,	2	4.4	66
a joint decision,	3	89.7	1361
or - left to nature?	4	4.1	62
(DK)	8	0.6	10
(NA)	9	0.5	8
Base : All			1518

PARENTS' DUTY TO THEIR CHILDREN

1986   Q.A72   {PNTSDUTY} Column No 1011

(Show card) Which of the statements on this card best describes your views?

	Code	%	No
Parents' duty is to do the best for their children, even at the expense of their own well-being	1	83.8	1272
Parents have a life of their own and should not be asked to sacrifice their own well-being for the sake of their children	2	10.8	163
(Neither/both)	3	4.4	67
(Depends/depends on age of children)	4	0.2	3
(Other answer)	7	0.6	9
(DK)	8	0.2	3
(NA)	9	0.0	1
Base : All			1518

RESPONSIBILITY FOR CHILD REARING

1986   Q.A73a   {CHLDBRNG} Column No 1012

Have you had, or do you have, any responsibility for bringing up a child? (Interviewer: probe for correct precode)

	Code	%	No
Yes, used to	1	36.6	556
Yes, now	2	38.6	585
No	3	24.8	376
(NA)	9	-	1
Base : All			1518

DECISION-MAKING IN THE FAMILY

1986   Q.A73c   {DECISION} Column No 1014
[If has or had responsibility for bringing up a child] Suppose there *(is)/(was)* a big decision being made, say, over going on holiday, or having someone come to live in your household for a while. Please look at this card and tell me what you think *(should happen)/(used to happen)/(usually happens)* in your household?

	Code	%	No
The parent(s) decide and tell the child(ren) afterwards	1	25.4	290
The parent(s) decide after discussing it with the child(ren)	2	27.6	315
Everyone discusses it and the family decides together	3	43.9	501
The children have the final say	4	0.6	7
(It depends on the age of the children)	5	0.9	11
(Other answer)	7	0.3	3
(DK)	8	0.5	6
(NA)	9	0.8	9
Base : Respondents with responsibility for bringing up children			1142

CHANGES IN PARENT-CHILD RELATIONSHIPS

1986   Q.A74a-g   {CHLDPRIV}{CHLDDECN}{CHLDAFFC}{CHLDBHVR}{CHLDINT}{CHLDEXPR}{CHLDFRND}
Column Nos 1015-21
[If ever responsible for bringing up a child] (Show card) Compare the way you *(brought)/(bring)* up your own children with the way your parents brought you up. Who would be more likely to ... (read out each in turn):

	Code	I with my children 1 %	No	My parents with me 2 %	No	No difference 3 %	No	(DK) 8 %	No	(NA) 9 %	No
a) {CHLDPRIV} Column No 1015 Allow the child privacy, or is there no difference		43.6	497	2.5	28	51.7	590	1.4	16	0.9	10
b) {CHLDDECN} Column No 1016 Let the child have a say in decisions		66.4	757	1.4	16	30.2	345	1.2	14	0.8	9
c) {CHLDAFFC} Column No 1017 Show affection towards the child		39.2	447	1.6	18	57.7	658	0.7	9	0.8	9
d) {CHLDBHVR} Column No 1018 Take a strong line on behaviour		24.0	274	31.0	354	43.5	496	0.6	7	0.9	11
e) {CHLDINT} Column No 1019 Show an interest in the child's activities		54.9	627	1.8	21	42.1	480	0.4	5	0.8	9
f) {CHLDEXPR} Column No 1020 Allow the child to express him- or herself freely		64.7	738	0.9	11	33.1	377	0.4	5	0.9	10
g) {CHLDFRND} Column No 1021 Treat the child as a friend		55.6	634	1.8	21	40.7	465	0.9	10	0.9	11

Base : All ever responsible for bringing up a child (n = 1142)

PARENTAL INFLUENCE ON CHILDREN'S VIEWS - 1

1986   Q.A75a   *{PTSRELGN}{PTSSEX}{PTSMORAL}{PTSPLTCS}* Column Nos 1022-25
(Show card) **Thinking back to how you were brought up, do you remember how hard your parents tried to get you to share their own ...** (read out):

	Code	Very hard 1		Quite hard 2		Not very hard 3		Not at all hard 4		(Never talked about) 5		(Don't remember) 8		(NA) 9	
		%	No	%	No	%	No	%	No	%	No	%	No	%	No
{PTSRELGN} Column No 1022															
i) Religious beliefs		11.8	178	15.7	238	34.1	517	36.2	549	1.0	16	0.8	13	0.5	8
{PTSSEX} Column No 1023															
ii) Views about sexual behaviour		6.9	105	10.3	157	16.9	257	29.8	453	34.5	524	0.9	14	0.6	9
{PTSMORAL} Column No 1024															
iii) Attitudes to right and wrong		47.7	723	39.3	596	8.1	123	2.7	41	0.8	13	1.0	15	0.5	7
{PTSPLTCS} Column No 1025															
iv) Political point of view		3.3	50	7.1	107	25.6	389	52.4	796	9.6	146	1.4	22	0.5	8

Base : All respondents (n = 1518)

PARENTAL INFLUENCE ON CHILDREN'S VIEWS - 2

1986   Q.A75b   *{OWNRELGN}{OWNSEX}{OWNMORAL}{OWNPLTCS}* Column Nos 1026-29
[If ever responsible for bringing up a child] (Continue showing card) **And how hard** *(did)/(do)/(will)* **you try to get** *your* **children to share your own ...** (read out):

	Code	[Not asked: not responsible for child-rearing] 0		Very hard 1		Quite hard 2		Not very hard 3		Not at all hard 4		(Never talked about) 5		(Don't remember) 8		(NA) 9	
		%	No	%	No	%	No	%	No	%	No	%	No	%	No	%	No
{OWNRELGN} Column No 1026																	
i) Religious beliefs		24.8	376	3.6	54	10.8	164	28.6	434	31.2	473	0.7	10	0.1	1	0.5	7
{OWNSEX} Column No 1027																	
ii) Views about sexual behaviour		24.8	376	9.0	137	26.2	397	19.8	301	12.5	189	7.0	106	0.3	5	0.5	8
{OWNMORAL} Column No 1028																	
iii) Attitudes to right and wrong		24.8	376	38.6	586	30.2	458	4.2	63	1.4	22	0.3	4	0.1	2	0.5	7
{OWNPLTCS} Column No 1029																	
iv) Political point of view		24.8	376	1.8	27	4.6	70	19.3	293	46.1	700	3.0	45	0.1	1	0.5	7

Base : All respondents (n = 1518)

IMPORTANT FACTORS FOR A SUCCESSFUL MARRIAGE

1986   Q.A77a-m   *{FAITHFUL}{ADQTINCM}{SAMEBKGD}{RESPECT}{SAMERLGN}{GDHOUSG}{SAMPLTCS}*
{TOLERNCE}{NOINLAWS}{HAPPYSEX}{SHAREJBS}{HAVCHLDN}{CMNTASTE}   Column Nos 1034-46
(Show card) As I read from this list, please look at the card and tell me how important you think each one
is to a successful marriage ... (read out) :

	Code	Very important 1 % No	Quite important 2 % No	Not very important 3 % No	Not at all important 4 % No	(DK) 8 % No	(NA) 9 % No
a) *{FAITHFUL}* Column No 1034 **Faithfulness**		86.3 1310	12.4 188	0.9 14	0.1 1	0.1 2	0.2 3
b) *{ADQTINCM}* Column No 1035 **An adequate income**		34.0 516	57.0 865	8.3 126	0.4 6	0.1 2	0.2 3
c) *{SAMEBKGD}* Column No 1036 **Coming from the same social background**		11.4 173	36.7 557	42.9 651	7.7 117	1.0 16	0.2 3
d) *{RESPECT}* Column No 1037 **Mutual respect and appreciation**		76.6 1163	21.5 326	1.1 17	0.1 2	0.4 6	0.2 4
e) *{SAMERLGN}* Column No 1038 **Shared religious beliefs**		9.2 140	26.9 409	42.9 651	19.6 298	1.1 16	0.3 4
f) *{GDHOUSG}* Column No 1039 **Good housing**		33.1 502	57.6 875	8.4 127	0.4 6	0.2 3	0.3 5
g) *{SAMPLTCS}* Column No 1040 **Agreement on politics**		2.5 39	12.4 188	55.5 842	28.3 429	1.1 17	0.2 3
h) *{TOLERNCE}* Column No 1041 **Understanding and tolerance**		68.8 1044	28.9 439	1.5 23	- -	0.5 8	0.3 5
i) *{NOINLAWS}* Column No 1042 **Living apart from in-laws**		55.1 836	30.1 457	11.5 174	2.2 33	1.0 15	0.2 3
j) *{HAPPYSEX}* Column No 1043 **A happy sexual relationship**		50.3 764	44.2 671	4.2 64	0.1 2	0.7 11	0.4 5
k) *{SHAREJBS}* Column No 1044 **Sharing household chores**		25.3 384	51.7 784	19.2 291	2.9 43	0.8 12	0.3 4
l) *{HAVCHLDN}* Column No 1045 **Having children**		31.1 472	40.7 618	22.3 339	4.6 70	0.9 13	0.3 5
m) *{CMNTASTE}* Column No 1046 **Tastes and interests in common**		20.7 314	58.6 889	18.5 281	1.8 28	0.2 3	0.2 3

Base : All (n = 1518)

SUFFICIENT GROUNDS FOR DIVORCE

1986   Q.A79a-j   *{DIVILL}{DIVBROKE}{DIVDRINK}{DIVVIOLT}{DIVUNFTH}{DIVNOSEX}{DIVNOLOV}*
{DIVRLTVS}{DIVNOCHN}{DIVPERST}   Column Nos 1051-60
Please tell me which of these you think are sufficient reasons for divorce ... (read out each in turn):

	Code	Yes 1		No 2		(DK) 8		(NA) 9	
		%	No	%	No	%	No	%	No
a) *{DIVILL}* Column No 1051 When either partner is ill for a long time		3.3	50	95.3	1446	1.1	17	0.3	5
b) *{DIVBROKE}* Column No 1052 When they are financially broke		3.6	55	94.9	1440	1.1	16	0.4	6
c) *{DIVDRINK}* Column No 1053 When either partner consistently drinks too much		59.2	899	35.9	544	4.5	69	0.4	6
d) *{DIVVIOLT}* Column No 1054 When either partner is violent		92.4	1402	5.7	87	1.4	22	0.4	7
e) *{DIVUNFTH}* Column No 1055 When either partner is consistently unfaithful		93.7	1422	4.8	72	1.1	17	0.4	7
f) *{DIVNOSEX}* Column No 1056 When the sexual relationship is not satisfactory		27.5	417	64.9	986	6.9	105	0.6	9
g) *{DIVNOLOV}* Column No 1057 When either partner has ceased to love the other		74.9	1137	20.6	313	4.0	61	0.5	7
h) *{DIVRLTVS}* Column No 1058 When they can't get along with each other's relatives		4.0	61	94.9	1440	0.7	11	0.4	6
i) *{DIVNOCHN}* Column No 1059 When they can't have children		7.0	106	88.8	1347	3.8	57	0.4	7
j) *{DIVPERST}* Column No 1060 When their personalities don't match		42.0	637	52.0	790	5.5	84	0.4	7

Base : All (n = 1518)

KINSHIP : KEEPING IN TOUCH WITH ONE'S MOTHER

1986   Q.A201a-d   {MUMALIVE}{MUMVISIT}{MUMJURNY}{MUMCNTCT}   Column Nos 1809-12

{MUMALIVE} Column No 1809

a) First, *your mother*. Is she still alive?

	Code	%	No
Yes	1	56.3	781
No	2	42.8	594
(NA)	9	0.9	13
Base : Self-completion respondents			1387

{MUMVISIT} Column No 1810

b) [If mother still alive] How often do you see or visit your mother? (Please tick one box)

	Code	%	No
[Not asked : mother not alive]	-1	42.8	594
She lives in the same household	1	11.5	160
Daily	2	3.5	49
At least several times a week	3	6.8	95
At least once a week	4	15.2	211
At least once a month	5	6.5	91
Several times a year	6	7.5	105
Less often	7	4.9	68
(NA)	9	1.1	15
Base : Self-completion respondents			1387

{MUMJURNY} Column No 1811

c) [If mother still alive and not in same household] About how long would it take you to get to where your mother lives? Think of the time it *usually* takes door to door. (Please tick one box)

	Code	%	No
[Not asked : mother in same household]	-2	11.5	160
[Not asked : mother not alive]	-1	42.8	594
Less than 15 minutes	1	14.1	196
Between 15 and 30 minutes	2	11.1	154
Between 30 minutes and an hour	3	6.8	94
Between 1 and 2 hours	4	3.9	55
Between 2 and 3 hours	5	1.7	23
Between 3 and 5 hours	6	2.7	37
Between 5 and 12 hours	7	2.5	34
Over 12 hours	8	1.7	23
(NA)	9	1.1	16
Base : Self-completion respondents			1387

KINSHIP : KEEPING IN TOUCH WITH ONE'S MOTHER (continued)

{MUMCNTCT} Column No 1812

d) [If mother still alive and not living in same household] **And how often do you have any other contact with your mother, besides visiting, either by telephone or letter?** (Please tick one box)

	Code	%	No
[Not asked : mother in same household]	-2	11.5	160
[Not asked : mother not alive]	-1	42.8	594
Daily	1	3.2	44
At least several times a week	2	7.9	110
At least once a week	3	17.5	242
At least once a month	4	5.9	82
Several times a year	5	3.1	42
Less often	6	6.4	89
(NA)	9	1.7	24
Base : Self-completion respondents			1387

NB   As the first question in the ISSP module on family networks and support systems, it was preceded by the words :
'In the first part of this questionnaire, we would like to ask you about your family and friends. For example, about how often you see and visit them, and when you turn to them for help and advice'.

KINSHIP : KEEPING IN TOUCH WITH ONE'S FATHER

1986   Q.A202a-d   *{DADALIVE}{DADVISIT}{DADJURNY}{DADCNTCT}*   Column Nos 1813-16

{DADALIVE} Column No 1813

a) **Is your father still alive?**

	Code	%	No
Yes	1	41.8	580
No	2	57.4	796
(NA)	9	0.8	11
Base : Self-completion respondents			1387

{DADVISIT} Column No 1814

b) [If father still alive] **How often do you see or visit your father?** (Please tick one box)

	Code	%	No
[Not asked : father not alive]	-1	57.4	796
He lives in the same household	1	9.1	127
Daily	2	2.0	27
At least several times a week	3	4.1	58
At least once a week	4	10.4	144
At least once a month	5	5.4	75
Several times a year	6	6.1	85
Less often	7	4.5	62
(NA)	9	1.0	14
Base : Self-completion respondents			1387

KINSHIP : KEEPING IN TOUCH WITH ONE'S FATHER (continued)

{DADJURNY} Column No 1815

c) [If father still alive and not in same household] About how long would it take you to get to where your father lives? Think of the time it *usually* takes door to door. (Please tick one box)

	Code	%	No
[Not asked : father in same household]	-2	9.1	127
[Not asked : father not alive]	-1	57.4	796
Less than 15 minutes	1	9.4	130
Between 15 and 30 minutes	2	7.6	105
Between 30 minutes and an hour	3	5.4	75
Between 1 and 2 hours	4	3.1	43
Between 2 and 3 hours	5	1.3	19
Between 3 and 5 hours	6	2.2	31
Between 5 and 12 hours	7	1.9	27
Over 12 hours	8	1.3	18
(NA)	9	1.2	17
Base : Self-completion respondents			1387

{DADCNTCT} Column No 1816

d) [If father still alive and not living in same household] And how often do you have any other contact with your father, besides visiting, either by telephone or letter? (Please tick one box)

	Code	%	No
[Not asked : father in same household]	-2	9.1	127
[Not asked : father not alive]	-1	57.4	796
Daily	1	1.4	19
At least several times a week	2	4.6	64
At least once a week	3	11.3	157
At least once a month	4	4.8	67
Several times a year	5	3.4	47
Less often	6	6.8	94
(NA)	9	1.2	16
Base : Self-completion respondents			1387

KINSHIP : KEEPING IN TOUCH WITH ONE'S SISTER

1986   Q.A203a-d   {SISTERS}{SISVISIT}{SISJURNY}{SISCNTCT} Column Nos 1817-20

{SISTERS} Column No 1817

a) How many sisters aged 18 or older do you have? (We mean sisters who are still alive; please include step-sisters, half-sisters and adopted sisters) (Please tick one box)

	Code	%	No
None	0	36.2	502
One	1	32.2	447
Two	2	17.1	237
Three	3	7.9	109
Four	4	3.4	48
Five or more	5	2.5	35
(NA)	9	0.7	10
Base : Self-completion respondents			1387

KINSHIP : KEEPING IN TOUCH WITH ONE'S SISTER (continued)

The [next three] questions are about your sister. If you have more than one adult sister, please think about the sister you have *most contact* with.

{SISVISIT} Column No 1818
b) [If adult sister] How often do you see or visit your sister? (Please tick one box)

	Code	%	No
[Not asked : no adult sister]	-1	36.2	502
She lives in the same household	1	2.5	34
Daily	2	1.7	24
At least several times a week	3	5.5	76
At least once a week	4	12.0	167
At least once a month	5	10.3	143
Several times a year	6	14.9	206
Less often	7	15.3	212
(NA)	9	1.6	23
Base : Self-completion respondents			1387

{SISJURNY} Column No 1819
c) [If adult sister and not living in same household] About how long would it take you to get to where your sister lives? Think of the time it *usually* takes door to door. (Please tick one box)

	Code	%	No
[Not asked : sister in same household]	-2	2.5	34
[Not asked : no adult sister]	-1	36.2	502
Less than 15 minutes	1	12.6	174
Between 15 and 30 minutes	2	13.1	182
Between 30 minutes and an hour	3	10.3	143
Between 1 and 2 hours	4	7.4	103
Between 2 and 3 hours	5	3.7	51
Between 3 and 5 hours	6	4.9	67
Between 5 and 12 hours	7	4.6	64
Over 12 hours	8	2.6	37
(NA)	9	2.2	31
Base : Self-completion respondents			1387

{SISCNTCT} Column No 1820
d) [If adult sister and not living in same household] And how often do you have any other contact with your sister, besides visiting, either by telephone or letter? (Please tick one box)

	Code	%	No
[Not asked : sister in same household]	-2	2.5	34
[Not asked : no adult sister]	-1	36.2	502
Daily	1	1.2	17
At least several times a week	2	5.3	74
At least once a week	3	16.6	230
At least once a month	4	12.2	170
Several times a year	5	10.5	146
Less often	6	12.9	180
(NA)	9	2.5	35
Base : Self-completion respondents			1387

KINSHIP : KEEPING IN TOUCH WITH ONE'S BROTHER

1986   Q.A204a-d   {BROTHERS}{BROVISIT}{BROJURNY}{BROCNTCT}   Column Nos 1821-24

{BROTHERS} Column No 1821

a) How many brothers aged 18 or older do you have? (We mean brothers who are still alive; please include step-brothers, half-brothers and adopted brothers) (Please tick one box)

	Code	%	No
None	0	37.8	524
One	1	30.8	427
Two	2	16.8	233
Three	3	8.7	121
Four	4	3.1	42
Five or more	5	2.3	32
(NA)	9	0.6	8
Base : Self-completion respondents			1387

The [next three] questions are about your brother. If you have more than one adult brother, please think about the brother you have *most contact* with.

{BROVISIT} Column No 1822

b) [If adult brother] How often do you see or visit your brother? (Please tick one box)

	Code	%	No
[Not asked : no adult brother]	-1	37.8	524
He lives in the same household	1	4.1	56
Daily	2	1.6	23
At least several times a week	3	2.8	39
At least once a week	4	7.2	100
At least once a month	5	10.4	145
Several times a year	6	16.3	226
Less often	7	18.8	260
(NA)	9	1.1	15
Base : Self-completion respondents			1387

{BROJURNY} Column No 1823

c) [If adult brother and not living in same household] About how long would it take you to get to where your brother lives? Think of the time it *usually* takes door to door. (Please tick one box)

	Code	%	No
[Not asked : brother in same household]	-2	4.1	56
[Not asked : no adult brother]	-1	37.8	524
Less than 15 minutes	1	10.0	139
Between 15 and 30 minutes	2	12.5	174
Between 30 minutes and an hour	3	10.4	145
Between 1 and 2 hours	4	6.5	91
Between 2 and 3 hours	5	3.5	48
Between 3 and 5 hours	6	4.5	62
Between 5 and 12 hours	7	5.3	73
Over 12 hours	8	3.7	51
(NA)	9	1.7	24
Base : Self-completion respondents			1387

KINSHIP : KEEPING IN TOUCH WITH ONE'S BROTHER (continued)

{BROCNTCT} Column No 1824

d) [If adult brother and not living in same household] And how often do you have any other contact with your brother, besides visiting, either by telephone or letter? (Please tick one box)

	Code	%	No
[Not asked : brother in same household]	-2	4.1	56
[Not asked : no adult brother]	-1	37.8	524
Daily	1	1.1	15
At least several times a week	2	2.3	32
At least once a week	3	8.1	113
At least once a month	4	11.7	162
Several times a year	5	14.6	203
Less often	6	18.0	249
(NA)	9	2.4	34
Base : Self-completion respondents			1387

KINSHIP : KEEPING IN TOUCH WITH ONE'S DAUGHTER

1986   Q.A205a-d   *{DAUGHTRS}{DAUVISIT}{DAUJURNY}{DAUCNTCT}* Column Nos 1825-28

{DAUGHTRS} Column No 1825

a) How many daughters aged 18 or older do you have? (We mean daughters who are still alive; please include step-daughters, and adopted daughters.) (Please tick one box)

	Code	%	No
None	0	64.9	900
One	1	19.7	273
Two	2	9.0	125
Three	3	3.5	48
Four	4	0.8	10
Five or more	5	0.5	6
(NA)	9	1.7	24
Base : Self-completion respondents			1387

The [next three] questions are about your daughter. If you have more than one adult daughter, please think about the daughter you have *most contact* with.

{DAUVISIT} Column No 1826

b) [If adult daughter] How often do you see or visit your daughter? (Please tick one box)

	Code	%	No
[Not asked : no adult daughter]	-1	64.9	900
She lives in the same household	1	9.6	133
Daily	2	3.3	45
At least several times a week	3	5.6	77
At least once a week	4	6.5	90
At least once a month	5	2.8	39
Several times a year	6	3.5	48
Less often	7	2.0	28
(NA)	9	1.9	26
Base : Self-completion respondents			1387

KINSHIP : KEEPING IN TOUCH WITH ONE'S DAUGHTER (continued)

{DAUJURNY} Column No 1827

c) [If adult daughter and not living in same household] About how long would it take you to get to where your daughter lives? Think of the time it *usually* takes door to door. (Please tick one box)

	Code	%	No
[Not asked : daughter in same household]	-2	9.6	133
[Not asked : no adult daughter]	-1	64.9	900
Less than 15 minutes	1	7.0	97
Between 15 and 30 minutes	2	5.5	76
Between 30 minutes and an hour	3	3.4	48
Between 1 and 2 hours	4	2.4	34
Between 2 and 3 hours	5	1.2	17
Between 3 and 5 hours	6	1.6	22
Between 5 and 12 hours	7	0.9	13
Over 12 hours	8	1.1	15
(NA)	9	2.3	32
Base : Self-completion respondents			1387

{DAUCNTCT} Column No 1828

d) [If adult daughter and not living in same household] And how often do you have any other contact with your daughter, besides visiting, either by telephone or letter? (Please tick one box)

	Code	%	No
[Not asked : daughter in same household]	-2	9.6	133
[Not asked : no adult daughter]	-1	64.9	900
Daily	1	2.8	39
At least several times a week	2	7.0	97
At least once a week	3	7.2	100
At least once a month	4	2.2	31
Several times a year	5	1.1	15
Less often	6	2.4	34
(NA)	9	2.7	37
Base : Self-completion respondents			1387

KINSHIP : KEEPING IN TOUCH WITH ONE'S SON

1986   Q.A206a-d   {SONS}{SONVISIT}{SONJURNY}{SONCNTCT} Column Nos 1829-32

{SONS} Column No 1829

a) How many sons aged 18 or older do you have? (We mean sons who are still alive; please include step-sons, and adopted sons) (Please tick one box)

	Code	%	No
None	0	61.9	859
One	1	19.7	273
Two	2	12.1	167
Three	3	2.6	36
Four	4	1.2	17
Five or more	5	0.4	5
(NA)	9	2.2	30
Base : Self-completion respondents			1387

KINSHIP : KEEPING IN TOUCH WITH ONE'S SON (continued)

The [next three] questions are about your son. If you have more than one adult son, please think about the son you have *most contact* with.

{*SONVISIT*} Column No 1830
b) [If adult son] How often do you see or visit your son? (Please tick one box)

	Code	%	No
[Not asked : no adult son]	-1	61.9	859
He lives in the same household	1	11.2	155
Daily	2	1.5	20
At least several times a week	3	3.4	48
At least once a week	4	7.6	105
At least once a month	5	4.6	64
Several times a year	6	4.5	62
Less often	7	2.6	36
(NA)	9	2.8	39
Base : Self-completion respondents			1387

{*SONJURNY*} Column No 1831
c) [If adult son and not living in same household] About how long would it take you to get to where your son lives? Think of the time it *usually* takes door to door. (Please tick one box)

	Code	%	No
[Not asked : son in same household]	-2	11.2	155
[Not asked : no adult son]	-1	61.9	859
Less than 15 minutes	1	4.7	65
Between 15 and 30 minutes	2	6.0	84
Between 30 minutes and an hour	3	4.1	57
Between 1 and 2 hours	4	2.3	32
Between 2 and 3 hours	5	1.7	24
Between 3 and 5 hours	6	2.5	35
Between 5 and 12 hours	7	1.5	21
Over 12 hours	8	0.9	13
(NA)	9	3.1	42
Base : Self-completion respondents			1387

{*SONCNTCT*} Column No 1832
d) [If adult son and not living in same household] And how often do you have any other contact with your son, besides visiting, either by telephone or letter? (Please tick one box)

	Code	%	No
[Not asked : son in same household]	-2	11.2	155
[Not asked : no adult son]	-1	61.9	859
Daily	1	1.0	14
At least several times a week	2	4.2	58
At least once a week	3	10.0	138
At least once a month	4	4.2	58
Several times a year	5	1.6	23
Less often	6	2.2	31
(NA)	9	3.7	52
Base : Self-completion respondents			1387

LIVING ARRANGEMENTS WITH PARTNER

1986   Q.A207   *{PARTNER}* Column No 1833
Which of these statements applies to you? (Please tick one box)

	Code	%	No
I am married and living in the same household as my husband or wife	1	67.2	932
I am living as married and my partner and I live together in the same household	2	3.8	52
I have a husband or wife or steady partner but we don't live in the same household	3	5.8	81
I don't have a steady partner	4	20.9	290
(NA)	9	2.3	32
			1387

Base : Self-completion respondents

KINSHIP : OTHER LIVING ADULT RELATIVES

1986   Q.A208a   *{GRANDPTS}{GRANDCHN}{AUNTUNCS}{INLAWS}{COUSINS}* Column Nos 1834-42
Now thinking of all your other adult relatives - those still living and aged 18 or older. How many of each do you have? (Begin with your grandparents. Please write in a number to show how many grandparents you have. If you have none, tick 'none', and then go on to the next relative)

		Grandmother, grandfather *{GRANDPTS}*		Adult grandchidren *{GRANDCHN}*		Aunts, uncles *{AUNTUNCS}*		Parents-in-law, etc *{INLAWS}*		Adult nieces, etc *{COUSINS}*	
Column No		1834		1835-36		1837-38		1839-40		1841-42	
	Code	%	No	%	No	%	No	%	No	%	No
None	0	74.2	1029	77.5	1076	22.7	315	16.5	230	8.7	121
One	1	10.4	144	1.6	22	7.7	107	9.9	138	2.2	31
Two	2	5.4	74	2.5	35	7.9	110	12.4	172	4.5	63
Three	3	2.7	37	1.1	15	6.4	88	9.9	138	4.4	61
Four	4	0.7	10	1.4	19	8.0	111	9.8	137	5.1	71
Five	5			0.5	7	5.5	76	8.7	120	4.1	57
Six	6			0.3	4	5.5	76	5.8	80	6.6	92
Seven	7			0.1	1	3.0	41	4.3	59	3.4	47
Eight	8			0.2	3	4.1	57	4.6	64	5.4	75
Nine	9			-	-	2.1	30	1.9	27	2.2	31
Ten	10			0.1	2	4.4	61	2.2	31	7.6	105
Eleven	11			0.1	1	1.6	22	0.7	9	1.1	15
Twelve	12			0.1	1	2.9	41	1.4	20	4.4	62
Thirteen	13			0.1	2	1.0	14	0.3	4	0.8	11
Fourteen	14			0.1	1	1.3	18	0.5	7	1.5	21
Fifteen	15			0.1	1	0.8	12	0.4	6	3.5	49
Sixteen to twenty				-	-	3.7	52	1.1	16	11.7	162
Twenty-one or more				0.1	2	1.0	14	0.3	4	13.1	182
(DK)	98					0.1	1			0.7	10
(NA)	99	6.6	92	14.2	198	10.2	141	9.2	128	8.9	123
Base : Self-completion respondents			1387		1387		1387		1387		1387

NB On the questionnaire {INLAWS} : 'parents-in-law and adult brothers-in-law and sisters-in-law'; {COUSINS} : 'adult nieces, nephews, cousins and other relatives (an approximate number will do)'. Numbers from sixteen upwards are banded on this table

KINSHIP : CONTACT WITH OTHER ADULT RELATIVES

1986   Q.A208b   {*MOSTCNTC*} Column No 1843-44

Thinking of all these adult relatives, which *one* do you have *most contact* with?
(Please tick one box)

	Code	%	No
Grandmother	1	6.5	91
Grandfather	2	0.8	11
Granddaughter	3	3.3	46
Grandson	4	2.2	30
Aunt	5	8.3	116
Uncle	6	2.4	33
Mother-in-law	7	20.2	280
Father-in-law	8	4.6	64
Sister-in-law	9	14.2	197
Brother-in-law	10	11.8	163
Other adult female relative	11	7.5	104
Other adult male relative	12	3.0	42
None of these	13	10.6	147
(No adult relative)	90	2.0	28
(NA)	99	2.6	35
Base : Self-completion respondents			1387

The [next three] questions on this page are about the adult relative you have just ticked, that is the *one* you have *most contact* with.

KINSHIP : KEEPING IN TOUCH WITH NEAREST OTHER ADULT RELATIVE

1986   Q.A208c-e   {*RTVVISIT*}{*RTVJURNY*}{*RTVCNTCT*} Column Nos 1845-47

{*RTVVISIT*} Column No 1845

c) How often do you see or visit this relative? (Please tick one box)

	Code	%	No
[Not asked : no close relative]	-3	10.6	147
[Not asked : no adult relative]	-1	2.0	28
He/she lives in the same household	1	1.4	19
Daily	2	3.5	49
At least several times a week	3	10.2	142
At least once a week	4	24.3	337
At least once a month	5	18.3	254
Several times a year	6	18.1	251
Less often	7	8.4	117
(NA)	9	3.1	43
Base : Self-completion respondents			1387

KINSHIP : KEEPING IN TOUCH WITH NEAREST OTHER ADULT RELATIVE (continued)

{*RTVJURNY*} Column No 1846

d) About how long would it take you to get to where this relative lives? Think of the time it *usually* takes door to door. (Please tick one box)

	Code	%	No
[Not asked : no close relative]	-3	10.6	147
[Not asked : all relatives in same household]	-2	1.4	19
[Not asked : no adult relative]	-1	2.0	28
Less than 15 minutes	1	24.0	333
Between 15 and 30 minutes	2	20.9	289
Between 30 minutes and an hour	3	14.6	203
Between 1 and 2 hours	4	7.8	108
Between 2 and 3 hours	5	3.9	54
Between 3 and 5 hours	6	5.8	80
Between 5 and 12 hours	7	4.3	60
Over 12 hours	8	1.5	20
(NA)	9	3.4	46
Base : Self-completion respondents			1387

{*RTVCNTCT*} Column No 1847

e) And how often do you have any other contact with this relative, besides visiting, either by telephone or letter? (Please tick one box)

	Code	%	No
[Not asked : no close relative]	-3	10.6	147
[Not asked : all relatives in same household]	-2	1.4	19
[Not asked : no adult relative]	-1	2.0	28
Daily	1	2.7	38
At least several times a week	2	9.7	135
At least once a week	3	22.5	312
At least once a month	4	18.4	255
Several times a year	5	12.9	179
Less often	6	16.1	223
(NA)	9	3.8	52
Base : Self-completion respondents			1387

PATTERNS OF FRIENDSHIP

1986   Q.A209a-c   {PALS}{WRKPALS}{NBRPALS}   Column Nos 1848-50
Thinking now of *close friends* - *not* your husband, or wife, or partner, or family members - but people you feel fairly close to.

a) How many close friends would you say you have? (Please write in number or tick box if 'None')

b) How many of these friends are people you work with now? (Please write in number or tick box if 'None')

c) How many of these friends are your close neighbours? (Please write in number or tick box if 'None')

		a) Close friends {PALS} Column No 1848		b) Workmates/colleagues as friends {WRKPALS} Column No 1849		c) Neighbours as friends {NBRPALS} Column No 1850	
	Code	%	No	%	No	%	No
[Not asked : no close friends]	-1			13.6	189	13.6	189
None	0	13.6	189	53.4	740	42.1	584
One	1	8.0	111	10.7	148	13.3	185
Two	2	12.2	169	7.2	100	12.7	176
Three	3	9.5	132	2.1	29	2.7	37
Four	4	13.0	181	2.4	34	2.2	31
Five	5	6.0	83	1.0	14	0.5	7
Six	6	11.2	155	1.0	14	1.5	21
Seven	7	1.5	21	0.1	1	0.1	1
Eight or more	8	21.4	296	1.6	22	1.2	17
(NA)	9	3.6	50	6.9	96	10.1	140
Base : Self-completion respondents			1387		1387		1387

1986   Q.A209d   {SEXPAL}   Column No 1851
Now thinking of your best friend or the friend you feel closest to. Is this friend a man or a woman?
(Please tick one box)

	Code	%	No
[Not asked : no close friends]	-1	13.6	189
Man	1	34.1	473
Woman	2	46.4	643
(NA)	9	5.9	82
Base : Self-completion respondents			1387

PATTERNS OF FRIENDSHIP (continued)

1986   Q.A209e-g   {PALVISIT}{PALJURNY}{PALCNTCT} Column Nos 1852-54

1986   Q.A209e   {PALVISIT} Column No 1852
How often do you see or visit this friend? (Please tick one box)

	Code	%	No
[Not asked : no close friend]	-1	13.6	189
He/she lives in the same household	1	0.4	5
Daily	2	10.6	147
At least several times a week	3	19.8	275
At least once a week	4	22.8	317
At least once a month	5	14.4	200
Several times a year	6	9.8	135
Less often	7	4.1	57
(NA)	9	4.4	62
Base : Self-completion respondents			1387

1986   Q.A209f   {PALJURNY} Column No 1853
About how long would it take you to get to where this friend lives? Think of the time it *usually* takes door to door. (Please tick one box)

	Code	%	No
[Not asked : friend in same household]	-2	0.4	5
[Not asked : no close friend]	-1	13.6	189
Less than 15 minutes	1	39.7	550
Between 15 and 30 minutes	2	20.0	278
Between 30 minutes and an hour	3	11.1	155
Between 1 and 2 hours	4	3.3	46
Between 2 and 3 hours	5	2.0	28
Between 3 and 5 hours	6	2.0	28
Between 5 and 12 hours	7	1.9	26
Over 12 hours	8	1.1	16
(NA)	9	4.9	68
Base : Self-completion respondents			1387

1986   Q.A209g   {PALCNTCT} Column No 1854
And how often do you have any other contact with this friend, besides visiting, either by telephone or letter? (Please tick one box)

	Code	%	No
[Not asked : friend in same household]	-2	0.4	5
[Not asked : no close friend]	-1	13.6	189
Daily	1	5.9	83
At least several times a week	2	12.3	171
At least once a week	3	25.4	352
At least once a month	4	14.5	201
Several times a year	5	9.2	127
Less often	6	13.1	181
(NA)	9	5.7	79
Base : Self-completion respondents			1387

SEEKING HELP : HOUSEHOLD AND GARDEN JOBS

1986   Q.A210a,b   {HELPJOB1}{HELPJOB2} Column Nos 1855-58

Now we'd like to ask you about some problems that can happen to anyone. First, there are some household and garden jobs you really can't do alone - for example, you may need someone to hold a ladder, or to help you move furniture.

a) Who would you turn to first for help?

b) And who would you turn to second?

(Please tick only one as your first choice and one as your second choice)

| | | a) Turn to first for help {HELPJOB1} | | b) Turn to second for help {HELPJOB2} | |
| | | 1855-56 | | 1857-58 | |
Column Nos	Code	%	No	%	No
No-one	0	0.5	6	1.6	23
Husband/wife/partner	1	62.0	860	3.3	45
Mother	2	2.7	38	5.4	74
Father	3	6.0	83	6.9	95
Daughter	4	3.9	54	8.3	116
Son	5	10.0	138	18.8	261
Sister	6	0.7	10	3.1	43
Brother	7	3.1	43	5.1	71
Other relative, including in-laws	8	2.3	31	8.7	120
Closest friend	9	2.6	37	11.1	153
Other friend	10	0.9	13	5.5	77
Neighbour	11	2.9	41	15.8	219
Someone you work with	12	0.4	5	0.8	12
Social services, or home help	13	0.3	4	0.6	8
Someone you *pay* to help	14	0.8	12	1.7	24
Other	97	0.1	2	0.1	1
(DK)	98	0.1	1	0.2	3
(NA)	99	0.8	11	3.1	42
Base : Self-completion respondents			1387		1387

Before going on to the next question, please check to see that you have only one first choice and one second choice.

SEEKING HELP : IN CASE OF ILLNESS

1986   Q.A211a,b   *{HELPILL1}{HELPILL2}* Column Nos 1859-62
Suppose you had the 'flu and you had to stay in bed for a few days, and needed help around the home, with shopping and so on.

a) Who would you turn to first for help?

b) And who would you turn to second?
(Please tick only one as your first choice and one as your second choice)

Column Nos	Code	a) Turn to first for help *{HELPILL1}* 1859-60		b) Turn to second for help *{HELPILL2}* 1861-62	
		%	No	%	No
No-one	0	0.8	12	3.4	48
Husband/wife/partner	1	64.1	890	3.7	51
Mother	2	12.2	170	10.6	147
Father	3	0.8	12	4.6	64
Daughter	4	8.0	111	19.2	266
Son	5	3.1	42	9.7	134
Sister	6	1.9	27	6.8	94
Brother	7	0.6	9	2.2	30
Other relative, including in-laws	8	0.9	13	8.8	122
Closest friend	9	2.7	38	10.5	145
Other friend	10	0.5	8	4.0	55
Neighbour	11	2.5	34	11.7	162
Someone you work with	12	0.1	2	0.5	7
Social services, or home help	13	0.1	2	0.1	1
Church, clergy or priest	14	-	-	0.2	3
Someone you *pay* to help	15	-	-	0.8	11
Other	97	0.6	9	0.4	6
(DK)	98	-	-	-	-
(NA)	99	0.7	10	3.0	42
Base : Self-completion respondents			1387		1387

Before going on to the next question, please check to see that you have only one first choice and one second choice

SEEKING HELP : BORROWING MONEY

1986   Q.A212a,b   {HELPMNY1}{HELPMNY2} Column Nos 1863-66
Suppose you needed to borrow a large sum of money.

a) Who would you turn to first for help?

b) And who would you turn to second?
(Please tick only one as your first choice and one as your second choice)

		a) Turn to first for help {HELPMNY1}		b) Turn to second for help {HELPMNY2}	
Column Nos		1863-64		1865-66	
	Code	%	No	%	No
No-one	0	6.3	88	16.3	226
Husband/wife/partner	1	21.8	302	3.0	41
Mother	2	8.8	122	8.4	117
Father	3	8.0	110	8.7	121
Daughter	4	2.3	32	3.8	52
Son	5	3.6	50	4.4	62
Sister	6	1.9	27	3.0	42
Brother	7	2.0	28	5.3	74
Other relative, including in-laws	8	2.7	38	10.3	142
Closest friend	9	1.4	19	4.8	66
Other friend	10	0.1	1	0.8	12
Neighbour	11	0.1	1	-	-
Someone you work with	12	0.1	2	0.2	3
Bank, building society or other financial institution	13	37.6	521	18.9	262
Employer	14	0.6	8	4.4	61
Government or social services	15	1.6	23	3.0	42
Other	97	0.1	2	0.1	1
(DK)	98	0.1	1	0.1	2
(NA)	99	1.0	14	4.4	61
Base: Self-completion respondents			1387		1387

Before going on to the next question, please check to see that you have only one first choice and one second choice

SEEKING HELP : MARITAL PROBLEMS

1986   Q.A213a,b   {HELPPRB1}{HELPPRB2} Column Nos 1867-70
Suppose you were very upset about a problem with your husband, wife or partner, and haven't been able to sort it out with them. Even if you are not married or have no partner, what would you do if you were?

a) Who would you turn to first for help?

b) And who would you turn to second?
(Please tick only one as your first choice and one as your second choice)

Column Nos	Code	a) Turn to first for help {HELPPRB1} 1867-68 %	No	b) Turn to second for help {HELPPRB2} 1869-70 %	No
No-one	0	7.5	104	13.2	183
Husband/wife/partner	1	12.7	176	0.7	10
Mother	2	15.1	210	7.4	103
Father	3	2.9	40	4.0	56
Daughter	4	10.1	140	6.3	88
Son	5	7.2	100	7.3	101
Sister	6	9.1	126	6.4	89
Brother	7	2.1	29	5.2	72
Other relative, including in-laws	8	4.0	56	8.5	118
Closest friend	9	18.5	257	14.8	205
Other friend	10	1.2	16	6.3	88
Neighbour	11	0.5	7	1.0	14
Someone you work with	12	0.6	8	1.8	26
Church, clergy or priest	13	1.9	26	2.7	38
Family doctor (GP)	14	2.7	38	5.7	79
Psychologist, psychiatrist, marriage guidance or other professional counsellor	15	1.7	23	4.4	61
Other	97	0.1	2	0.1	2
(DK)	98	0.4	5	0.5	7
(NA)	99	1.6	23	3.4	47
Base : Self-completion respondents			1387		1387

Before going on to the next question, please check to see that you have only one first choice and one second choice

SEEKING HELP : WHEN FEELING DEPRESSED

1986   Q.A214a,b   *{HELPDPRI}{HELPDPR2}* Column Nos 1871-74
Now suppose you felt just a bit down or depressed, and you wanted to talk about it.

a) Who would you turn to first for help?

b) And who would you turn to second?
(Please tick only one as your first choice and one as your second choice)

		a) Turn to first for help {HELPDPRI}		b) Turn to second for help {HELPDPR2}	
Column Nos		1871-72		1873-74	
	Code	%	No	%	No
No-one	0	2.6	36	8.5	118
Husband/wife/partner	1	52.6	729	3.8	53
Mother	2	6.8	95	10.1	140
Father	3	0.6	8	2.9	40
Daughter	4	6.5	91	9.8	136
Son	5	2.5	34	6.9	95
Sister	6	5.3	74	7.2	100
Brother	7	1.0	13	3.2	45
Other relative, including in-laws	8	0.9	12	4.9	67
Closest friend	9	14.1	196	21.0	292
Other friend	10	1.2	16	5.9	82
Neighbour	11	0.5	7	1.6	22
Someone you work with	12	0.4	6	3.2	44
Church, clergy or priest	13	0.6	8	1.0	14
Family doctor (GP)	14	3.1	43	6.2	86
Psychologist, psychiatrist, marriage guidance or other professional counsellor	15	0.4	5	1.1	16
Other	97	0.1	2	0.2	3
(DK)	98	0.1	1	0.2	2
(NA)	99	0.8	12	2.3	32
Base : Self-completion respondents			1387		1387

Before going on to the next question, please check to see that you have only one first choice and one second choice

SEEKING HELP : ABOUT A BIG CHANGE IN ONE'S LIFE

1986   Q.A215a,b   *{HELPADVI}{HELPADV2}* Column Nos 1875-78

And suppose you needed advice about an important change in your life - for example about a job, or moving to another part of the country.

a) Who would you turn to first for help?

b) And who would you turn to second?

(Please tick only one as your first choice and one as your second choice)

		a) Turn to first for help *{HELPADVI}*		b) Turn to second for help *{HELPADV2}*	
Column Nos		1875-76		1877-78	
	Code	%	No	%	No
No-one	0	4.8	66	10.8	150
Husband/wife/partner	1	61.9	858	2.1	29
Mother	2	7.1	99	11.9	165
Father	3	4.6	64	8.4	116
Daughter	4	4.5	62	9.6	133
Son	5	4.2	59	11.5	159
Sister	6	2.2	30	5.8	81
Brother	7	1.2	17	5.1	70
Other relative, including in-laws	8	1.0	14	6.1	85
Closest friend	9	3.9	54	16.2	225
Other friend	10	0.5	7	2.5	35
Neighbour	11	-	1	0.4	6
Someone you work with	12	0.3	4	2.9	40
Church, clergy or priest	13	0.4	6	0.6	9
Family doctor (GP)	14	0.2	3	0.7	10
Psychologist, psychiatrist, marriage guidance or other professional counsellor	15	0.4	5	0.7	9
Solicitor/lawyer	16	1.3	19	1.4	19
Other	97	0.1	2	0.3	4
(DK)	98	-	-	0.1	1
(NA)	99	1.2	17	2.9	40
Base: Self-completion respondents			1387		1387

Before going on to the next question, please check to see that you have only one first choice and one second choice

IMPORTANT QUALITIES PARENTS CAN TRY TO TEACH THEIR CHILDREN

1986   Q.A216   *{TEACHQ1}-{TEACHQ19}* Column Nos 1908-09

Here are some qualities which parents can try to teach their children. Please choose *up to five* that you consider to be especially important. (Please tick only up to five boxes)

	Code	%	No
{TEACHQ1} Good manners			
(Box not ticked : not especially important)	0	26.6	368
Especially important	1	72.4	1005
(DK)	98	0.1	1
(NA)	99	0.9	13
Base : All			1387
{TEACHQ2} Cleanness and neatness			
(Box not ticked : not especially important)	0	56.9	790
Especially important	1	42.1	584
(DK)	98	0.1	1
(NA)	99	0.9	13
Base : All			1387
{TEACHQ3} Independence			
(Box not ticked : not especially important)	0	75.2	1044
Especially important	1	23.8	330
(DK)	98	0.1	1
(NA)	99	0.9	13
Base : All			1387
{TEACHQ4} Hard work			
(Box not ticked : not especially important)	0	75.1	1042
Especially important	1	23.9	331
(DK)	98	0.1	1
(NA)	99	0.9	13
Base : All			1387
{TEACHQ5} Honesty			
(Box not ticked: not especially important)	0	13.5	187
Especially important	1	85.5	1186
(DK)	98	0.1	1
(NA)	99	0.9	13
Base : All			1387
{TEACHQ6} To act responsibly			
(Box not ticked : not especially important)	0	63.6	883
Especially important	1	35.4	491
(DK)	98	0.1	1
(NA)	99	0.9	13
Base : All			1387
{TEACHQ7} Patience			
(Box not ticked : not especially important)	0	91.0	1263
Especially important	1	8.0	111
(DK)	98	0.1	1
(NA)	99	0.9	13
Base : All			1387

IMPORTANT QUALITIES THAT PARENTS CAN TRY TO TEACH THEIR CHILDREN (continued)

	Code	%	No
{TEACHQ8} Imagination			
(Box not ticked : not especially important)	0	93.2	1293
Especially important	1	5.8	81
(DK)	98	0.1	1
(NA)	99	0.9	13
Base : All			1387
{TEACHQ9} Respect for other people			
(Box not ticked : not especially important)	0	32.3	448
Especially important	1	66.7	925
(DK)	98	0.1	1
(NA)	99	0.9	13
Base : All			1387
{TEACHQ10} Leadership			
(Box not ticked : not especially important)	0	97.0	1345
Especially important	1	2.0	28
(DK)	98	0.1	1
(NA)	99	0.9	13
Base : All			1387
{TEACHQ11} Self-control			
(Box not ticked : not especially important)	0	79.7	1106
Especially important	1	19.3	267
(DK)	98	0.1	1
(NA)	99	0.9	13
Base : All			1387
{TEACHQ12} Being careful with money			
(Box not ticked : not especially important)	0	77.5	1075
Especially important	1	21.5	298
(DK)	98	0.1	1
(NA)	99	0.9	13
Base : All			1387
{TEACHQ13} Determination and perseverance			
(Box not ticked : not especially important)	0	78.9	1094
Especially important	3	20.1	279
(DK)	98	0.1	1
(NA)	99	0.9	13
Base : All			1387
{TEACHQ14} Religious faith			
(Box not ticked : not especially important)	0	89.6	1243
Especially important	4	9.4	130
(DK)	98	0.1	1
(NA)	99	0.9	13
Base : All			1387
{TEACHQ15} Unselfishness			
(Box not ticked : not especially important)	0	76.4	1060
Especially important	5	22.6	313
(DK)	98	0.1	1
(NA)	99	0.9	13
Base : All			1387

IMPORTANT QUALITIES THAT PARENTS CAN TRY TO TEACH THEIR CHILDREN (continued)

	Code	%	No
{TEACHQ16} Obedience			
(Box not ticked : not especially important)	0	86.7	1202
Especially important	6	12.3	171
(DK)	98	0.1	1
(NA)	99	0.9	13
Base : All			1387
{TEACHQ17} Loyalty			
(Box not ticked : not especially important)	0	77.0	1069
Especially important	7	22.0	305
(DK)	98	0.1	1
(NA)	99	0.9	13
Base : All			1387

NB The SPSS file lists variable {TEACHQ18} Column No. 1909, (DK) = Code 8 (n = 1);
   and {TEACHQ19} Column No. 1909, (NA) = Code 9 (n = 13)

MARRIAGE AS AN INSTITUTION

1986   Q.A217a-e   *{DIVORCE2}{YNGCOUPS}{SAVEMARR}{NEEDPNTS}{MARLIGHT}* Column Nos 1910-14
Please tick one box for each statement to show how much you agree or disagree with it.

	Agree strongly		Just Agree		Neither agree nor disagree		Just Disagree		Disagree strongly		(DK)		(NA)	
Code	1		2		3		4		5		8		9	
	%	No	%	No	%	No	%	No	%	No	%	No	%	No
a) *{DIVORCE2}* Column No 1910 Divorce in Britain should be made more difficult to obtain than it is now	16.7	232	22.4	311	33.0	457	16.2	224	10.8	149	0.4	6	0.6	8
b) *{YNGCOUPS}* Column No 1911 Most young couples start their married life well prepared for its ups and downs	6.1	84	23.4	325	17.1	237	36.3	504	16.2	224	0.2	3	0.7	10
c) *{SAVEMARR}* Column No 1912 As a society, we ought to do more to safeguard the institution of marriage	36.9	512	34.2	475	21.4	297	5.0	69	1.3	18	0.3	4	1.0	13
d) *{NEEDPNTS}* Column No 1913 To grow up happily, children need a home with both their own father and mother	61.3	850	17.1	238	8.6	120	8.2	114	4.1	56	0.1	2	0.6	8
e) *{MARLIGHT}* Column No 1914 Most people nowadays take marriage too lightly	37.7	524	36.6	508	15.4	214	7.6	105	1.7	24	-	1	0.9	12

Base : Self-completion respondents (n = 1387)

NB {DIVORCE2} is {DIVORCE} on the SPSS file. Since this variable name had been used for a different question (see p.N.1 - 1 above), this question has been given another variable name

GOVERNMENT INTERVENTION TO PROTECT THE WELFARE OF CHILDREN

1985   Q.218a-h   *{CHLDCRE1} - {CHLDCRE8}* Column Nos 2056-2063

Sometimes public authorities intervene with parents in raising their children. Please show in each of the following cases how far you think public authorities should go in dealing with a *10 year old* child and his or her parents. (Please tick one box for each)

	Take no action		Give warnings or counselling		Take the child from his or her parents		Can't choose		(NA)	
Code	1		2		3		8		9	
	%	No	%	No	%	No	%	No	%	No
a) *{CHLDCRE1}* Column No 2056										
The child uses drugs and the parents don't do anything about it	0.8	12	59.8	897	36.4	546	1.2	19	1.8	27
b) *{CHLDCRE2}* Column No 2057										
The child frequently skips school and the parents don't do anything about it	1.2	19	91.9	1380	4.6	69	0.7	11	1.5	23
c) *{CHLDCRE3}* Column No 2058										
The parents regularly let the child stay out late at night without knowing where the child is	6.6	100	77.9	1170	12.1	182	1.6	24	1.8	27
d) *{CHLDCRE4}* Column No 2059										
The parents fail to provide the child with proper food and clothing	1.9	28	40.2	603	53.7	806	2.8	43	1.5	22
e) *{CHLDCRE5}* Column No 2060										
The parents regularly beat the child	0.6	9	11.8	177	84.6	1270	1.5	23	1.5	23
f) *{CHLDCRE6}* Column No 2061										
The parents refuse essential medical treatment for the child because of their religious beliefs	4.7	71	43.2	648	42.2	634	8.2	124	1.7	25
g) *{CHLDCRE7}* Column No 2062										
The parents refuse to send their child to school because they wish to educate the child at home	25.3	380	59.7	896	4.3	65	9.0	136	1.7	26
h) *{CHLDCRE8}* Column No 2063										
The parents allow the child to watch violent or pornographic films	8.2	124	74.0	1111	11.3	170	5.1	76	1.4	21

Base : Self-completion respondents (n = 1502)

RESPONSIBILITY FOR DISABLED, SICK OR ELDERLY PEOPLE

1984   Q.98c   *{OLDRESP}*   Column No 853
Some people have responsibilities for looking after a disabled, sick or elderly friend or relative.
Is there anyone like this who depends on you to provide some regular care for them?

	Code	%	No
Yes	1	12.9	211
No	2	84.8	1395
(NA)	9	2.4	39
Base : All			1645

WHETHER LIVING TOGETHER AS MARRIED

1983   Q.87b   *{COHABIT}*   Column No 634
[If separated, divorced, widowed or never married]   (Interviewer : probe to find out if living as married)

	Code	%	No
[Not asked : married]	0	68.7	1181
Yes	1	1.8	32
No	2	26.4	453
(NA)	9	3.1	53
Base : All			1719

NB   In 1984-87 and 1989, 'living as married' was incorporated into the question on marital status (see p. N.1-2 above)

N Family relationships and gender issues

N2 Gender issues

Table titles and cross references

WOMEN, WORK AND THE FAMILY - 1

{FEMJOB} {MWEXTRAS} {SEXROLE} {FEMHOME} {WWHAPPIR} {WANTHOME}

Question: Please tick one box for *each* statement below to show how much you agree or disagree with it.

		1983		1984		1985		1986		1987		1989	
		%	No	%	No	%	No	%	No	%	No	%	No
Question No				220i						A223j		A201g	
Column No				1641						1642		1814	

(i) {FEMJOB}

Having a job is the best way for a woman to be an independent person

	Code	%	No	%	No	%	No	%	No	%	No	%	No
Agree strongly	1	-	.	30.3	462	-	.	-	.	26.5	330	9.2	118
Agree	2	-	.	35.7	544	-	.	-	.	33.1	412	52.9	674
Neither agree nor disagree	3	-	.	22.1	337	-	.	-	.	24.5	305	16.0	204
Disagree	4	-	.	6.5	99	-	.	-	.	9.4	117	18.6	237
Disagree strongly	5	-	.	3.8	58	-	.	-	.	5.7	70	1.4	18
(DK)	8	-	.	0.1	1	-	.	-	.	0.1	1	1.3	17
(NA)	9	-	.	1.4	22	-	.	-	.	0.6	7	0.5	6
Base: Self-completion questionnaire respondents					1522						1243		1274

		1983		1984		1985		1986		1987		1989	
Question No				220ii						A223g			
Column No				1642						1639			

(ii) {MWEXTRAS}

Most married women work only to earn money for extras, rather than because they need the money

	Code	%	No	%	No	%	No	%	No	%	No	%	No
Agree strongly	1	-	.	16.0	244	-	.	-	.	13.9	172	-	.
Agree	2	-	.	30.0	457	-	.	-	.	30.8	383	-	.
Neither agree nor disagree	3	-	.	13.2	201	-	.	-	.	15.7	196	-	.
Disagree	4	-	.	21.7	331	-	.	-	.	23.0	286	-	.
Disagree strongly	5	-	.	17.7	270	-	.	-	.	15.9	198	-	.
(DK)	8	-	.	0.1	1	-	.	-	.	0.1	2	-	.
(NA)	9	-	.	1.2	19	-	.	-	.	0.5	7	-	.
Base: Self-completion questionnaire respondents					1522						1243		

1984 - Agree strongly, code 5; just agree, code 4; just disagree, code 2; disagree strongly, code 1

1987 - Agree slightly, code 2; disagree slightly, code 4

1989 - {FEMJOB} SPSS file lists variable name as {JOBBEST}, even though the question was identical to that asked in earlier years. Consequently the variable name has been changed to {FEMJOB}

WOMEN, WORK AND THE FAMILY - 1 (Continued)

		1983		1984		1985		1986		1987		1989	
		%	No	%	No	%	No	%	No	%	No	%	No
Question No				220v						A223a		A201i	
Column No				1645						1633		1816	

(iii) {SEXROLE}

A husband's job is to earn the money;
a wife's job is to look after the
home and family

	Code												
Agree strongly	1	-	-	23.2	353	-	-	-	-	23.5	292	6.7	85
Agree	2	-	-	19.6	299	-	-	-	-	24.1	300	21.7	276
Neither agree nor disagree	3	-	-	18.7	284	-	-	-	-	19.1	238	18.0	230
Disagree	4	-	-	15.5	237	-	-	-	-	13.0	161	35.0	446
Disagree strongly	5	-	-	21.9	334	-	-	-	-	19.8	246	17.6	224
(DK)	8	-	-	0.1	1	-	-	-	-	0.1	1	0.8	10
(NA)	9	-	-	1.0	16	-	-	-	-	0.4	5	0.2	2

Base: Self-completion
questionnaire respondents

| | | | | | 1522 | | | | | | 1243 | | 1274 |

		220xi						A223d		
Question No		220xi						A223d		
Column No		1651						1636		

(iv) {FEMHOME}

In times of high unemployment married
women should stay at home

	Code										
Agree strongly	1	-	-	18.1	275	-	-	-	-	14.1	176	-	-
Agree	2	-	-	17.1	260	-	-	-	-	17.9	223	-	-
Neither agree nor disagree	3	-	-	17.4	266	-	-	-	-	19.5	242	-	-
Disagree	4	-	-	20.6	314	-	-	-	-	24.5	305	-	-
Disagree strongly	5	-	-	25.6	390	-	-	-	-	23.3	289	-	-
(DK)	8	-	-	0.1	1	-	-	-	-	0.1	1	-	-
(NA)	9	-	-	1.1	16	-	-	-	-	0.6	8	-	-

Base: Self-completion
questionnaire respondents

| | | | | | 1522 | | | | | | 1243 |

1984 - Agree strongly, code 5; just agree, code 4; just disagree, code 2; disagree strongly, code 1.

1987 - Agree slightly, code 2; disagree slightly, code 4

1989 - {SEXROLE} SPSS file lists variable name as {HJOBEARN}, even though the question was identical to that asked in earlier years. Consequently the variable name has been changed to {SEXROLE}

WOMEN, WORK AND THE FAMILY - 1 (Continued)

			1983		1984		1985		1986		1987		1989	
			%	No	%	No	%	No	%	No	%	No	%	No
Question No											A223b		A201d	
Column No											1634		1811	

(v) *{WWHAPPIR}*

A woman and her family will all be happier if she goes out to work

	Code	1983 %	1983 No	1984 %	1984 No	1985 %	1985 No	1986 %	1986 No	1987 %	1987 No	1989 %	1989 No
Agree strongly	1	-	.	-	.	-	.	-	.	2.8	35	1.3	16
Agree	2	-	.	-	.	-	.	-	.	10.8	135	17.2	219
Neither agree nor disagree	3	-	.	-	.	-	.	-	.	39.7	494	38.3	488
Disagree	4	-	.	-	.	-	.	-	.	27.4	340	35.4	450
Disagree strongly	5	-	.	-	.	-	.	-	.	18.8	233	3.9	49
(DK)	8	-	.	-	.	-	.	-	.	0.1	1	3.7	48
(NA)	9	-	.	-	.	-	.	-	.	0.4	5	0.2	3
Base: Self-completion questionnaire respondents											1243		1274	

Question No											A223e		A201e	
Column No											1637		1812	

(vi) *{WANTHOME}*

A job is all right but what most women really want is a home and children

	Code	1983 %	1983 No	1984 %	1984 No	1985 %	1985 No	1986 %	1986 No	1987 %	1987 No	1989 %	1989 No
Agree strongly	1	-	.	-	.	-	.	-	.	13.6	169	5.5	70
Agree	2	-	.	-	.	-	.	-	.	22.7	282	25.9	330
Neither agree nor disagree	3	-	.	-	.	-	.	-	.	21.5	268	18.9	241
Disagree	4	-	.	-	.	-	.	-	.	21.2	264	35.2	449
Disagree strongly	5	-	.	-	.	-	.	-	.	20.5	255	11.1	141
(DK)	8	-	.	-	.	-	.	-	.	0.1	1	2.5	32
(NA)	9	-	.	-	.	-	.	-	.	0.5	6	0.8	11
Base: Self-completion questionnaire respondents											1243		1274	

1987 - Agree slightly, code 2; disagree slightly, code 4

1989 - {WWHAPPIR}: SPSS file lists variable as {WOMWKHAP}; {WANTHOME}: SPSS file lists variable name as {WOMNWANT} even though these two questions were identical to those asked in 1987. Consequently the variable names have been changed to {WWHAPPIR} and {WANTHOME}.

RESPONSIBLITY FOR GENERAL DOMESTIC DUTIES - 1

{DUTYRESP} {ELSEDUTY} {SHREDUTY}

Question: [If more than one person in household] **Who is the person *mainly* responsible for general domestic duties in this household?** (Interviewer: if 'someone else mainly' or 'duties shared equally', specify relationship to respondent)

		1983		1984		1985		1986		1987		1989	
		%	No	%	No	%	No	%	No	%	No	%	No
Question No				98a		103		A110a/B118a		906a		905b	
Column No				847-49		907-09		1626-28		1326-28		1518-20	
{DUTYRESP}	Code												
[Not asked: single person household]	0	-	-	12.1	199	12.4	219	10.5	323	10.7	297	11.5	338
Respondent mainly	1	-	-	37.2	612	36.3	642	37.5	1150	37.8	1045	37.3	1093
Someone else mainly	2	-	-	36.3	598	38.4	680	39.1	1198	37.4	1034	36.5	1068
Duties shared equally	3	-	-	12.2	201	11.2	199	11.6	355	13.1	363	13.7	400
(NA)	9	-	-	2.2	35	1.6	28	1.3	40	0.9	26	1.1	32
Base: All					1645		1769		3066		2766		2930
{ELSEDUTY}													
[Not asked: single person household or respondent mainly responsible for domestic duties]	0	-	-	63.7	1047	61.6	1089	60.9	1868	62.6	1731	63.5	1862
Domestic duties responsibility of:													
wife/female partner	1	-	-	25.3	417	25.7	454	27.1	831	26.3	726	25.3	741
mother/mother-in-law	2	-	-	8.0	131	9.3	165	9.3	286	8.4	232	7.9	231
husband/male partner	3	-	-	0.5	8	0.4	7	0.6	20	0.6	15	1.0	28
other female	4	-	-	1.5	25	1.6	28	1.3	40	1.1	32	1.7	50
other male	5	-	-	0.4	7	0.5	8	0.3	10	0.5	13	0.3	8
Other answer	7	-	-	0.1	2	0.3	6	0.2	7	0.4	11	0.2	6
(NA)	9	-	-	0.5	9	0.6	11	0.1	4	0.2	6	0.1	4
Base: All					1645		1769		3066		2766		2930
{SHREDUTY}													
[Not asked: single person household or duties not shared]	0	-	-	87.8	1444	88.8	1570	88.4	2711	86.9	2402	86.3	2530
Domestic duties responsibility of:													
respondent *and* spouse/partner	1	-	-	7.4	122	5.9	105	7.6	234	8.5	234	9.0	263
whole family	2	-	-	1.2	20	1.2	21	0.8	25	0.6	16	1.3	39
Other answer	7	-	-	2.9	47	2.3	41	2.3	72	3.0	82	2.2	64
(NA)	9	-	-	0.7	11	1.9	33	0.8	24	1.1	31	1.1	34
Base: All					1645		1769		3066		2766		2930

RESPONSIBILITY FOR CHILDCARE

{CHLDRESP} {ELSECHLD} {SHRECHLD}

Question: [If child aged under 16 in household] **Who is the person *mainly* responsible for the general care of the child(ren) here?** (Interviewer: if 'someone else mainly' or 'duties shared equally', specify relationship to respondent)

		1983		1984		1985		1986		1987		1989	
		%	No	%	No	%	No	%	No	%	No	%	No
Question No				98b				A110b/B118b		906b		905d	
Column No				850-52				1629-31		1629-31		1522-24	
(i) *{CHLDRESP}*	Code												
[Not asked: no child aged under 16 in household]	0	-	-	65.3	1074	-	-	64.2	1969	64.7	1789	66.6	1950
Respondent mainly	1	-	-	14.0	230	-	-	16.2	495	15.0	414	14.9	435
Someone else mainly	2	-	-	13.2	216	-	-	12.6	388	13.4	371	12.5	366
Duties shared equally	3	-	-	6.5	106	-	-	5.9	181	5.9	162	5.5	161
(NA)	9	-	-	1.1	18	-	-	1.1	33	1.1	30	0.6	17
Base: All					1645				3066		2766		2930
(ii) *{ELSECHLD}*													
[Not asked: no child aged under 16 in household or respondent mainly responsible for childcare]	0	-	-	86.8	1429	-	-	87.4	2678	86.6	2395	87.5	2565
Childcare main responsibility of:													
wife/female partner	1	-	-	10.5	172	-	-	10.4	318	10.8	298	10.0	294
mother/mother-in-law	2	-	-	1.8	29	-	-	1.5	47	1.7	46	1.3	37
husband/male partner	3	-	-	0.6	10	-	-	0.1	2	0.1	4	0.2	5
other female	4	-	-	0.1	2	-	-	0.6	18	0.7	21	0.9	27
other male	5	-	-	0.1	1	-	-	0.0	1	0.0	1	0.0	1
Other answer	7	-	-	-	-	-	-	-	-	-	-	0.0	1
(NA)	9	-	-	0.2	3	-	-	0.0	2	0.1	2	0.0	1
Base: All					1645				3066		2766		2930
(iii) *{SHRECHLD}*													
[Not asked no child aged under 16 or duties not shared]	0	-	-	93.5	1539	-	-	94.1	2885	94.1	2603	94.5	2769
Childcare main responsibility of:													
respondent *and* spouse/partner	1	-	-	5.2	86	-	-	4.8	148	5.1	140	4.6	134
whole family	2	-	-	-	-	-	-	0.8	1	-	-	0.0	1
Other answer	7	-	-	0.5	8	-	-	0.8	23	0.4	11	0.3	9
(NA)	9	-	-	0.8	13	-	-	0.3	8	0.4	12	0.6	17
Base: All					1645				3066		2766		2930

SEX DISCRIMINATION LAW

{SEXLAW}

Question: There is a law in Britain against sex discrimination, that is against giving unfair preference to men - or to women - in employment, pay and so on. Do you generally support or oppose the idea of a law for this purpose?

		1983		1984		1985		1986		1987		1989	
		%	No	%	No	%	No	%	No	%	No	%	No
Question No		86		81						A82			
Column No		632		565						712			
	Code												
Support	1	75.8	1304	79.9	1315	-	-	-	-	75.4	1049	-	-
Oppose	2	21.6	371	17.4	286	-	-	-	-	22.2	308	-	-
(DK)	8	1.9	32	2.2	36	-	-	-	-	2.3	32	-	-
(NA)	9	0.7	12	0.5	8	-	-	-	-	0.1	1	-	-
Base: All			1719		1645						1391		

1983 - Q reads: '... unfair preference to men - or to women - in jobs, housing and so on ...'

MARRIED/LIVING AS MARRIED: DOMESTIC DIVISION OF LABOUR

{DOCHORE1} {DOCHORE2} {DOCHORE3} {DOCHORE4} {DOCHORE5} {DOCHORE6} {DOCHORE7} {DOCHILD1} {DOCHILD2}

Question: [If married or living as married] I would like to ask about how you and your *(husband/wife/partner)* generally share some family jobs. Who *does* the household shopping: mainly the man, mainly the woman or is the task shared equally?

			1983		1984		1985		1986		1987		1989	
			%	No	%	No	%	No	%	No	%	No	%	No
Question No			88		84						A84			
Column No			635		568						715			
(i) {DOCHORE1}		Code												
Who does the household shopping														
Mainly man	1		4.8	58	5.8	65	-	-	-	-	7.0	69	-	-
Mainly woman	2		51.3	620	53.7	605	-	-	-	-	50.0	492	-	-
Shared equally	3		43.8	530	38.9	438	-	-	-	-	42.5	418	-	-
(Other answer)	7		-	-	0.2	2	-	-	-	-	0.1	1	-	-
(DK)	8		-	-	-	-	-	-	-	-	-	-	-	-
(NA)	9		0.2	2	1.4	16	-	-	-	-	0.3	3	-	-
Base: All married/living as married				1209		1126						984		

			1983		1984		1985		1986		1987		1989	
Question No			88		84						A84			
Column No			636		569						716			
(ii) {DOCHORE2}														
Who makes the evening meal														
Mainly man	1		5.0	60	5.2	59	-	-	-	-	5.6	55	-	-
Mainly woman	2		77.3	934	76.6	862	-	-	-	-	76.8	756	-	-
Shared equally	3		17.4	210	16.3	183	-	-	-	-	17.1	168	-	-
(Other answer)	7		0.2	2	0.5	6	-	-	-	-	0.1	1	-	-
(DK)	8		-	-	-	-	-	-	-	-	-	-	-	-
(NA)	9		0.2	2	1.4	16	-	-	-	-	0.3	3	-	-
Base: All married/living as married				1209		1126						984		

1983 - SPSS file lists variable names as {CHORE1} - {CHORE7}. However, variables {DOCHORE1} - {DOCHORE7} were created to separate out respondents who were married or living as married. An eighth item {CHORE8}, renamed {DOCHORE8}, was omitted in subsequent years, (see pp N.2 - 31 and N.2 - 32 below). {DOCHILD1}, {DOCHILD2} were not asked in 1983; (Other answer), code 4, on all seven variables

MARRIED/LIVING AS MARRIED: DOMESTIC DIVISION OF LABOUR (Continued)

		1983		1984		1985		1986		1987		1989	
		%	No	%	No	%	No	%	No	%	No	%	No
Question No		88		84						A84			
Column No		637		570						717			

(iii) {DOCHORE3}
Who does the evening dishes

	Code	1983 %	No	1984 %	No	1985 %	No	1986 %	No	1987 %	No	1989 %	No
Mainly man	1	17.2	208	17.8	200	-	-	-	-	22.0	216	-	-
Mainly woman	2	40.4	489	37.5	422	-	-	-	-	38.8	382	-	-
Shared equally	3	40.3	487	40.7	458	-	-	-	-	36.1	355	-	-
(Other answer)	7	0.3	4	2.6	29	-	-	-	-	1.9	19	-	-
(DK)	8	-	.	-	.	-	-	-	-	-	-	-	-
(NA)	9	1.8	22	1.5	17	-	-	-	-	1.0	10	-	-

Base: All married/living as married   1209   1126   984

Question No		88		84						A84			
Column No		638		571						718			

(iv) {DOCHORE4}
Who does the household cleaning

	Code	1983 %	No	1984 %	No	1985 %	No	1986 %	No	1987 %	No	1989 %	No
Mainly man	1	3.5	42	3.1	35	-	-	-	-	3.6	35	-	-
Mainly woman	2	71.6	866	71.7	807	-	-	-	-	71.8	707	-	-
Shared equally	3	24.2	293	23.2	261	-	-	-	-	23.1	227	-	-
(Other answer)	7	0.1	1	0.6	7	-	.	-	-	0.6	6	-	-
(DK)	8	-	.	-	.	-	-	-	-	-	.	-	-
(NA)	9	0.6	7	1.5	17	-	-	-	-	0.7	7	-	-

Base: All married/living as married   1209   1126   984

Question No		88		84						A84			
Column No		639		572						719			

(v) {DOCHORE5}
Who does the washing and ironing

	Code	1983 %	No	1984 %	No	1985 %	No	1986 %	No	1987 %	No	1989 %	No
Mainly man	1	1.0	12	1.0	11	-	-	-	-	1.7	17	-	-
Mainly woman	2	89.1	1077	88.3	994	-	-	-	-	87.9	865	-	-
Shared equally	3	9.6	116	8.9	100	-	-	-	-	9.3	92	-	-
(Other answer)	7	-	.	0.4	5	-	-	-	-	0.3	3	-	-
(DK)	8	-	.	-	.	-	-	-	-	-	.	-	-
(NA)	9	0.4	5	1.4	16	-	-	-	-	0.6	6	-	-

Base: All married/living as married   1209   1126   984

MARRIED/LIVING AS MARRIED: DOMESTIC DIVISION OF LABOUR (Continued)

		1983		1984		1985		1986		1987		1989	
		%	No	%	No	%	No	%	No	%	No	%	No
Question No		88		84						A84			
Column No		640		573						720			

(vi) {DOCHORE6}
Who repairs the household equipment

	Code	%	No	%	No	%	No	%	No	%	No	%	No
Mainly man	1	82.4	996	82.8	932	-		-		82.2	809	-	-
Mainly woman	2	6.5	78	6.4	72	-		-		6.1	60	-	
Shared equally	3	9.8	119	8.3	93	-		-		8.4	83	-	
(Other answer)	7	-		0.6	7	-		-		0.8	8	-	
(DK)	8	-		-		-		-		-			
(NA)	9	1.2	15	2.0	22	-		-		2.3	23	-	

Base: All married/living as married   1209   1126   984

Question No		88		84						A84			
Column No		641		574						721			

(vii) {DOCHORE7}
Who organises the household money and payment of bills

	Code	%	No	%	No	%	No	%	No	%	No	%	No
Mainly man	1	29.2	353	32.1	361	-		-		32.0	315	-	
Mainly woman	2	38.9	470	38.3	431	-		-		37.7	371	-	
Shared equally	3	31.6	382	28.2	317	-		-		29.9	294	-	
(Other answer)	7	-		-		-		-		-		-	
(DK)	8	-		-		-		-		-		-	
(NA)	9	0.2	3	1.5	17	-		-		0.3	3	-	

Base: All married/living as married   1209   1126   984

MARRIED/LIVING AS MARRIED: DOMESTIC DIVISION OF LABOUR (Continued)

		1983		1984		1985		1986		1987		1989	
		%	No	%	No	%	No	%	No	%	No	%	No
Question No				84						A84			
Column No				575						722			
(viii) {DOCHILD1}	Code												
Who looks after the child(ren) when they are sick													
[Not asked: no children aged under 16 in household]	0	-	-	56.9	641	-	-	-	-	56.9	560	-	-
Mainly man	1	-	-	0.4	5	-	-	-	-	0.8	8	-	-
Mainly woman	2	-	-	27.1	305	-	-	-	-	28.7	282	-	-
Shared equally	3	-	-	15.2	171	-	-	-	-	12.7	125	-	-
(Other answer)	7	-	-	0.2	2	-	-	-	-	-	-	-	-
(DK)	8	-	-	-	-	-	-	-	-	-	-	-	-
(NA)	9	-	-	0.3	3	-	-	-	-	0.9	9	-	-

Base: All married/living as married   1126   984

		1983		1984		1985		1986		1987		1989	
Question No				84						A84			
Column No				576						723			
(ix) {DOCHILD2}													
Who teaches the child(ren) discipline													
[Not asked: no children aged under 16 in household]	0	-	-	56.9	641	-	-	-	-	56.9	560	-	-
Mainly man	1	-	-	4.5	51	-	-	-	-	5.4	53	-	-
Mainly woman	2	-	-	5.1	57	-	-	-	-	7.9	78	-	-
Shared equally	3	-	-	33.1	373	-	-	-	-	28.8	283	-	-
(Other answer)	7	-	-	-	-	-	-	-	-	-	-	-	-
(DK)	8	-	-	-	-	-	-	-	-	-	-	-	-
(NA)	9	-	-	0.4	4	-	-	-	-	0.9	9	-	-

Base: All married/living as married   1126   984

PRESCRIPTIVE DOMESTIC DIVISION OF LABOUR - 1

{SHCHORE1} {SHCHORE2} {SHCHORE3} {SHCHORE4} {SHCHORE5} {SHCHORE6} {SHCHORE7}
{SHCHILD1} {SHCHILD2}

Question: (Now) I would like to ask about how you think family jobs *should generally* be shared between men and women. For example, who do you think *should* do the household shopping: mainly the man, mainly the woman or should the task be shared equally?

			1983		1984		1985		1986		1987		1989	
			%	No	%	No	%	No	%	No	%	No	%	No
	Question No				85i						A85i			
	Column No				607						724			
(i) *{SHCHORE1}*		Code												
Who should do the household shopping														
Mainly man	1		-	-	0.3	5	-	-	-	-	0.8	11	-	-
Mainly woman	2		-	-	34.4	566	-	-	-	-	30.1	418	-	-
Shared equally	3		-	-	62.6	1030	-	-	-	-	67.8	943	-	-
(Other answer)	7		-	-	1.1	17	-	-	-	-	-	-	-	-
(DK)	8		-	-	0.2	3	-	-	-	-	0.1	2	-	-
(NA)	9		-	-	1.4	24	-	-	-	-	1.2	16	-	-
Base: All						1645						1391		
	Question No				85ii						A85ii			
	Column No				608						725			
(ii) *{SHCHORE2}*														
Who should make the evening meal														
Mainly man	1		-	-	0.7	12	-	-	-	-	0.4	5	-	-
Mainly woman	2		-	-	57.4	944	-	-	-	-	52.1	724	-	-
Shared equally	3		-	-	38.5	633	-	-	-	-	44.5	619	-	-
(Other answer)	7		-	-	1.8	30	-	-	-	-	-	-	-	-
(DK)	8		-	-	0.1	2	-	-	-	-	0.5	8	-	-
(NA)	9		-	-	1.5	24	-	-	-	-	2.5	35	-	-
Base: All						1645						1391		

1983 - {SHCHORE1} - {SHCHORE7} This question was asked on the first survey, but only of those not currently married or living as married; the same variable names were used (with an extra item {SHCHORE8} not subsequently repeated). These have been changed to {SHCHR831} - {SHCHR838} (see p.N.2 - 32 below). {SHCHILD1} and {SHCHILD2} were not asked in 1983

PRESCRIPTIVE DOMESTIC DIVISION OF LABOUR - 1 (Continued)

		1983		1984		1985		1986		1987		1989	
		%	No	%	No	%	No	%	No	%	No	%	No
Question No				85iii						A85iii			
Column No				609						726			

(iii) {SHCHORE3}
Who should do the evening dishes

	Code	1983 %	No	1984 %	No	1985 %	No	1986 %	No	1987 %	No	1989 %	No
Mainly man	1	-	-	11.5	189	-	-	-	-	10.8	150	-	-
Mainly woman	2	-	-	19.9	328	-	-	-	-	16.8	234	-	-
Shared equally	3	-	-	65.6	1080	-	-	-	-	70.3	977	-	-
(Other answer)	7	-	-	1.3	21	-	-	-	-	-	-	-	-
(DK)	8	-	-	0.2	3	-	-	-	-	0.2	3	-	-
(NA)	9	-	-	1.5	24	-	-	-	-	1.9	26	-	-
Base: All					1645						1391		

| Question No | | | | 85iv | | | | | | A85iv | | | |
| Column No | | | | 610 | | | | | | 727 | | | |

(iv) {SHCHORE4}
Who should do the household cleaning

	Code	1983 %	No	1984 %	No	1985 %	No	1986 %	No	1987 %	No	1989 %	No
Mainly man	1	-	-	0.4	6	-	-	-	-	0.6	8	-	-
Mainly woman	2	-	-	49.2	810	-	-	-	-	44.2	614	-	-
Shared equally	3	-	-	47.6	783	-	-	-	-	53.6	745	-	-
(Other answer)	7	-	-	1.3	21	-	-	-	-	-	-	-	-
(DK)	8	-	-	0.2	4	-	-	-	-	0.1	2	-	-
(NA)	9	-	-	1.3	22	-	-	-	-	1.5	21	-	-
Base: All					1645						1391		

| Question No | | | | 85v | | | | | | A85v | | | |
| Column No | | | | 611 | | | | | | 728 | | | |

(v) {SHCHORE5}
Who should do the washing and ironing

	Code	1983 %	No	1984 %	No	1985 %	No	1986 %	No	1987 %	No	1989 %	No
Mainly man	1	-	-	0.2	3	-	-	-	-	0.1	1	-	-
Mainly woman	2	-	-	75.4	1240	-	-	-	-	69.0	959	-	-
Shared equally	3	-	-	21.9	361	-	-	-	-	29.7	413	-	-
(Other answer)	7	-	-	1.1	18	-	-	-	-	-	-	-	-
(DK)	8	-	-	0.1	1	-	-	-	-	0.2	3	-	-
(NA)	9	-	-	1.4	23	-	-	-	-	1.1	15	-	-
Base: All					1645						1391		

PRESCRIPTIVE DOMESTIC DIVISION OF LABOUR - 1 (Continued)

			1983		1984		1985		1986		1987		1989	
			%	No	%	No	%	No	%	No	%	No	%	No
	Question No				85vi						A85vi			
	Column No				612						729			
(vi) {SHCHORE6}	Code													
Who should repair the household equipment														
Mainly man	1		-	-	77.5	1276	-	-	-	-	72.5	1008	-	-
Mainly woman	2		-	-	1.6	26	-	-	-	-	1.3	18	-	-
Shared equally	3		-	-	18.5	305	-	-	-	-	24.4	339	-	-
(Other answer)	7		-	-	0.9	14	-	-	-	-	-	-	-	-
(DK)	8		-	-	0.2	4	-	-	-	-	0.4	6	-	-
(NA)	9		-	-	1.3	21	-	-	-	-	1.4	20	-	-
Base: All						1645						1391		

			1983		1984		1985		1986		1987		1989	
	Question No				85vii						A85vii			
	Column No				613						730			
(vii) {SHCHORE7}														
Who should organise the household money and payment of bills														
Mainly man	1		-	-	21.0	345	-	-	-	-	21.7	302	-	-
Mainly woman	2		-	-	16.3	269	-	-	-	-	14.9	207	-	-
Shared equally	3		-	-	58.9	970	-	-	-	-	61.2	851	-	-
(Other answer)	7		-	-	1.9	32	-	-	-	-	-	-	-	-
(DK)	8		-	-	0.2	4	-	-	-	-	0.4	6	-	-
(NA)	9		-	-	1.6	26	-	-	-	-	1.8	25	-	-
Base: All						1645						1391		

			1983		1984		1985		1986		1987		1989	
	Question No				85viii						A85viii			
	Column No				614						731			
(viii) {SHCHILD1}														
Who should look after the children when they are sick														
Mainly man	1		-	-	0.1	1	-	-	-	-	0.4	6	-	-
Mainly woman	2		-	-	50.0	822	-	-	-	-	46.5	646	-	-
Shared equally	3		-	-	46.5	765	-	-	-	-	51.4	715	-	-
(Other answer)	7		-	-	0.7	11	-	-	-	-	-	-	-	-
(DK)	8		-	-	0.2	4	-	-	-	-	0.1	2	-	-
(NA)	9		-	-	2.5	41	-	-	-	-	1.6	22	-	-
Base: All						1645						1391		

PRESCRIPTIVE DOMESTIC DIVISION OF LABOUR - 1 (Continued)

		1983		1984		1985		1986		1987		1989	
		%	No	%	No	%	No	%	No	%	No	%	No
Question No				85ix						A85ix			
Column No				615						732			
(ix) {SHCHILD2}	Code												
Who should teach the children discipline													
Mainly man	1	-	-	12.4	204	-	-	-	-	12.1	168	-	-
Mainly woman	2	-	-	5.7	94	-	-	-	-	4.6	64	-	-
Shared equally	3	-	-	78.7	1295	-	-	-	-	82.2	1143	-	-
(Other answer)	7	-	-	0.5	8	-	-	-	-	-	-	-	-
(DK)	8	-	-	0.1	2	-	-	-	-	0.2	3	-	-
(NA)	9	-	-	2.6	42	-	-	-	-	0.9	13	-	-
Base: All					1645						1391		

GENDER DISCRIMINATION AT WORK

{PROMOTE}

Question: Some people think that women are generally less likely than men to be promoted at work, even when their qualifications and experience are the same. Do you think this happens ... (read out) ...

		1983		1984		1985		1986		1987		1989	
		%	No	%	No	%	No	%	No	%	No	%	No
Question No				87						A86			
Column No				621						733			
	Code												
... a lot,	1	-	-	40.2	661	-	-	-	-	44.4	617	-	-
... a little,	2	-	-	42.0	691	-	-	-	-	37.0	514	-	-
... or hardly at all?	3	-	-	10.1	166	-	-	-	-	12.1	168	-	-
(DK)	8	-	-	7.2	119	-	-	-	-	6.5	90	-	-
(NA)	9	-	-	0.5	8	-	-	-	-	0.1	1	-	-
Base: All					1645						1391		

FAMILY FINANCE ARRANGEMENTS

{ORGMONEY}

Question: [If currently married/living as married] (Show card) How do you and your partner organise the money that comes into your household? Please choose the phrase on this card that comes closest.

	1983		1984		1985		1986		1987		1989	
	%	No	%	No	%	No	%	No	%	No	%	No
Question No							A78b		A87a			
Column No							1048-49		734-35			
	Code											
[Not asked: not currently married/ living as married]	0	-	-	-	-	-	-	28.5	432	29.3	407	-	-
I manage all the money and give my partner his/her share	1	-	-	-	-	-	-	12.5	190	8.3	116	-	-
My partner manages all the money and gives me my share	2	-	-	-	-	-	-	11.1	169	9.6	133	-	-
We pool all the money and each take out what we need	3	-	-	-	-	-	-	36.2	550	40.0	556	-	-
We pool some of the money and keep the rest separate	4	-	-	-	-	-	-	6.9	105	8.3	116	-	-
We each keep our own money separate	5	-	-	-	-	-	-	3.8	58	4.4	61	-	-
(Other answer)	97	-	-	-	-	-	-	0.4	6	0.1	1	-	-
(DK)	98	-	-	-	-	-	-	0.1	2	-	-		
(NA)	99	-	-	-	-	-	-	0.4	6	0.1	1	-	-

Base: All

							1518		1391				

WOMEN'S OPPORTUNITIES FOR UNIVERSITY EDUCATION

{FEMEDOP}

Question: Would you say that opportunities for university education are, in general, better or worse for women than for men?

		1983		1984		1985		1986		1987		1989	
		%	No	%	No	%	No	%	No	%	No	%	No
Question No						211				A218			
Column No						2037				1614			
	Code												
Much better for women	1	-	-	-	-	1.2	19	-	-	1.1	13	-	
Better for women	2	-	-	-	-	2.1	32	-	-	1.1	14	-	
No difference	3	-	-	-	-	68.4	1028	-	-	75.5	939	-	
Worse for women	4	-	-	-	-	14.9	224	-	-	10.2	127	-	
Much worse for women	5	-	-	-	-	1.5	22	-	-	0.8	9	-	
Can't choose	8	-	-	-	-	11.1	167	-	-	11.1	138	-	
(NA)	9	-	-	-	-	0.7	10	-	-	0.2	3	-	
Base:							1502				1243		

Base: Self-completion questionnaire respondents

JOB OPPORTUNITIES FOR WOMEN

{FEMJOBOP}

Question: How about job opportunities for women: do you think they are, in general, better or worse than job opportunities for men with similar education and experience?

		1983		1984		1985		1986		1987		1989	
		%	No	%	No	%	No	%	No	%	No	%	No
Question No						212				A219			
Column No						2038				1615			
	Code												
Much better for women	1	-	-	-	-	1.8	27	-	-	1.4	17	-	
Better for women	2	-	-	-	-	4.8	72	-	-	4.1	51	-	
No difference	3	-	-	-	-	37.1	557	-	-	33.7	419	-	
Worse for women	4	-	-	-	-	46.9	704	-	-	49.2	612	-	
Much worse for women	5	-	-	-	-	4.6	69	-	-	4.6	57	-	
Can't choose	8	-	-	-	-	4.2	64	-	-	6.7	84	-	
(NA)	9	-	-	-	-	0.6	9	-	-	0.3	4	-	
Base:							1502				1243		

Base: Self-completion questionnaire respondents

PAY LEVELS FOR WOMEN COMPARED WITH MEN

{FEMINC}

Question: And how about income and wages: compared with men who have similar education and jobs - are women, in general, paid better or worse than men?

		1983		1984		1985		1986		1987		1989	
		%	No	%	No	%	No	%	No	%	No	%	No
Question No						213				A220			
Column No						2039				1616			
	Code												
Women are paid much better	1	-	-	-	-	0.5	8	-	-	0.1	1	-	-
Women are paid better	2	-	-	-	-	1.6	25	-	-	0.9	12	-	-
No difference	3	-	-	-	-	30.5	458	-	-	27.0	335	-	-
Women are paid worse	4	-	-	-	-	55.7	836	-	-	60.2	748	-	-
Women are paid much worse	5	-	-	-	-	4.8	72	-	-	5.5	68	-	-
Can't choose	8	-	-	-	-	6.4	96	-	-	6.2	78	-	-
(NA)	9	-	-	-	-	0.5	7	-	-	0.1	2	-	-
							1502				1243		

Base: Self-completion questionnaire respondents

GENDER STEREOTYPING OF JOBS

{JOBMF1} {JOBMF2} {JOBMF3} {JOBMF4} {JOBMF5} {JOBMF6} {JOBMF7} {JOBMF8} {JOBMF9} {JOBMF10} {JOBMF11}

Question: For each of the jobs below, please tick a box to show whether you think the job is particularly suitable for men only, particularly suitable for women only, or suitable for both men and women equally?

		1983		1984		1985		1986		1987		1989	
		%	No	%	No	%	No	%	No	%	No	%	No
Question No					219					A221			
Column No					1630					1617			

(i) *{JOBMF1}*
Social worker

	Code	1983 %	No	1984 %	No	1985 %	No	1986 %	No	1987 %	No	1989 %	No
Particularly suitable for men	1	-	-	0.7	10	-	-	-	-	1.0	13	-	-
Particularly suitable for women	2	-	-	10.7	163	-	-	-	-	15.0	186	-	-
Suitable for both equally	3	-	-	86.9	1322	-	-	-	-	83.1	1033	-	-
(DK)	8	-	-	0.1	1	-	-	-	-	-	-	-	-
(NA)	9	-	-	1.7	26	-	-	-	-	0.9	11	-	-
					1522						1243		

Base: Self-completion questionnaire respondents

GENDER STEREOTYPING OF JOBS (Continued)

		1983		1984		1985		1986		1987		1989	
		%	No	%	No	%	No	%	No	%	No	%	No
Question No				219						A221			
Column No				1631						1618			
(ii) {JOBMF2}	Code												
Police officer													
Particularly suitable for men	1	-	-	49.1	748	-	-	-	-	36.5	454	-	-
Particularly suitable for women	2	-	-	0.3	5	-	-	-	-	0.5	6	-	-
Suitable for both equally	3	-	-	48.9	745	-	-	-	-	62.4	775	-	-
(DK)	8	-	-	0.1	1	-	-	-	-	-	-	-	-
(NA)	9	-	-	1.6	25	-	-	-	-	0.6	8	-	-
Base: Self-completion questionnaire respondents					1522						1243		

		1983		1984		1985		1986		1987		1989	
Question No				219						A221			
Column No				1632						1619			
(iii) {JOBMF3}													
Secretary													
Particularly suitable for men	1	-	-	0.7	11	-	-	-	-	0.6	8	-	-
Particularly suitable for women	2	-	-	59.8	911	-	-	-	-	54.1	673	-	-
Suitable for both equally	3	-	-	37.5	572	-	-	-	-	44.3	550	-	-
(DK)	8	-	-	0.1	2	-	-	-	-	-	-	-	-
(NA)	9	-	-	1.8	27	-	-	-	-	1.0	13	-	-
Base: Self-completion questionnaire respondents					1522						1243		

		1983		1984		1985		1986		1987		1989	
Question No				219						A221			
Column No				1633						1620			
(iv) {JOBMF4}													
Car mechanic													
Particularly suitable for men	1	-	-	72.4	1103	-	-	-	-	67.3	837	-	-
Particularly suitable for women	2	-	-	0.8	12	-	-	-	-	0.6	8	-	-
Suitable for both equally	3	-	-	24.8	378	-	-	-	-	31.0	386	-	-
(DK)	8	-	-	0.1	1	-	-	-	-	-	-	-	-
(NA)	9	-	-	1.9	29	-	-	-	-	1.1	13	-	-
Base: Self-completion questionnaire respondents					1522						1243		

GENDER STEREOTYPING OF JOBS (Continued)

			1983		1984		1985		1986		1987		1989	
			%	No	%	No	%	No	%	No	%	No	%	No
	Question No				219						A221			
	Column No	Code			1639						1621			
(v) {JOBMF5}														
Nurse														
Particularly suitable for men	1		-	-	0.3	4	-	-	-	-	0.4	5	-	-
Particularly suitable for women	2		-	-	41.0	625	-	-	-	-	31.4	390	-	-
Suitable for both equally	3		-	-	56.6	861	-	-	-	-	67.3	837	-	-
(DK)	8		-	-	0.2	3	-	-	-	-	-	-	-	-
(NA)	9		-	-	1.9	29	-	-	-	-	0.9	11	-	-
Base: Self-completion questionnaire respondents						1522						1243		

			1983		1984		1985		1986		1987		1989	
	Question No				219						A221			
	Column No				1635						1622			
(vi) {JOBMF6}														
Computer programmer														
Particularly suitable for men	1		-	-	5.6	85	-	-	-	-	3.9	48	-	-
Particularly suitable for women	2		-	-	2.7	42	-	-	-	-	1.9	24	-	-
Suitable for both equally	3		-	-	89.0	1355	-	-	-	-	93.0	1156	-	-
(DK)	8		-	-	0.4	7	-	-	-	-	-	-	-	-
(NA)	9		-	-	2.2	34	-	-	-	-	1.2	15	-	-
Base: Self-completion questionnaire respondents						1522						1243		

			1983		1984		1985		1986		1987		1989	
	Question No				219						A221			
	Column No				1636						1623			
(vii) {JOBMF7}														
Bus driver														
Particularly suitable for men	1		-	-	48.8	742	-	-	-	-	40.0	497	-	-
Particularly suitable for women	2		-	-	0.6	9	-	-	-	-	0.5	7	-	-
Suitable for both equally	3		-	-	48.7	741	-	-	-	-	58.5	728	-	-
(DK)	8		-	-	0.1	2	-	-	-	-	-	-	-	-
(NA)	9		-	-	1.9	28	-	-	-	-	1.0	12	-	-
Base: Self-completion questionnaire respondents						1522						1243		

GENDER STEREOTYPING OF JOBS (Continued)

			1983		1984		1985		1986		1987		1989	
			%	No	%	No	%	No	%	No	%	No	%	No
Question No					219						A221			
Column No					1637						1624			
(viii) {JOBMF8}		Code												
Bank manager														
Particularly suitable for men	1		-	-	39.1	595	-	-	-	-	28.2	351	-	-
Particularly suitable for women	2		-	-	0.7	11	-	-	-	-	0.6	7	-	-
Suitable for both equally	3		-	-	57.9	882	-	-	-	-	70.2	873	-	-
(DK)	8		-	-	0.2	3	-	-	-	-	-	-	-	-
(NA)	9		-	-	2.1	32	-	-	-	-	1.0	12	-	-
Base: Self-completion questionnaire respondents						1522						1243		
Question No					219						A221			
Column No					1638						1625			
(ix) {JOBMF9}														
Family doctor/GP														
Particularly suitable for men	1		-	-	10.3	156	-	-	-	-	5.7	71	-	-
Particularly suitable for women	2		-	-	1.4	22	-	-	-	-	0.8	10	-	-
Suitable for both equally	3		-	-	86.6	1318	-	-	-	-	92.5	1151	-	-
(DK)	8		-	-	0.1	1	-	-	-	-	-	-	-	-
(NA)	9		-	-	1.7	25	-	-	-	-	0.9	12	-	-
Base: Self-completion questionnaire respondents						1522						1243		
Question No					219						A221			
Column No					1639						1626			
(x) {JOBMF10}														
Local councillor														
Particularly suitable for men	1		-	-	12.3	187	-	-	-	-	7.2	89	-	-
Particularly suitable for women	2		-	-	0.7	11	-	-	-	-	0.9	11	-	-
Suitable for both equally	3		-	-	84.8	1290	-	-	-	-	91.0	1132	-	-
(DK)	8		-	-	0.2	3	-	-	-	-	0.1	1	-	-
(NA)	9		-	-	2.0	31	-	-	-	-	0.8	10	-	-
Base: Self-completion questionnaire respondents						1522						1243		

GENDER STEREOTYPING OF JOBS (Continued)

			1983		1984		1985		1986		1987		1989	
			%	No	%	No	%	No	%	No	%	No	%	No
	Question No				219						A221			
	Column No				1640						1627			
(xi) *{JOBMF11}*		Code												
Member of Parliament														
Particularly suitable for men	1	-	.	**15.8**	241	-	.	-	.	**9.6**	119	-	.
Particularly suitable for women	2	-	.	**0.5**	7	-	.	-	.	**0.5**	6	-	.
Suitable for both equally	3	-	.	**81.5**	1241	-	.	-	.	**89.2**	1109	-	.
(DK)	8	-	.	**0.1**	2	-	.	-	.	**0.1**	1	-	.
(NA)	9	-	.	**2.1**	32	-	.	-	.	**0.6**	8	-	.
					—						—			
Base: self-completion						1522						1243		
questionnaire respondents														

WOMEN, WORK AND THE FAMILY - 2

1989   Q.A201a-c,f,h,j   {WWRELCHD}{WWCHDSUF}{WWFAMSUF}{HWIFEFFL}{BOTHEARN}{ENJOYJOB}
Column Nos 1808-10,1813,1815,1817

[To begin,] we have some questions about women. Do you agree or disagree [with the following statements]?
(Please tick one box for each)

	Agree strongly 1		Agree 2		Neither agree nor disagree 3		Disagree 4		Disagree strongly 5		(DK) 8		(NA) 9	
Code	%	No	%	No	%	No	%	No	%	No	%	No	%	No
a) {WWRELCHD} Column No 1808 A working mother can establish just as warm a relationship with her children as a mother who does not work	15.1	192	42.6	543	11.6	147	23.3	297	5.1	65	1.7	21	0.7	9
b) {WWCHDSUF} Column No 1809 A pre-school child is likely to suffer if his or her mother works	10.0	127	36.5	465	16.6	211	28.7	365	6.1	78	1.8	23	0.4	5
c) {WWFAMSUF} Column No 1810 All in all, family life suffers when the woman has a full-time job	8.0	101	33.6	428	16.8	213	31.5	401	8.7	111	0.9	12	0.5	6
f) {HWIFEFFL} Column No 1813 Being a housewife is just as fulfilling as working for pay	6.6	84	34.8	443	20.7	264	28.8	366	5.7	72	2.8	35	0.7	9
h) {BOTHEARN} Column No 1815 Both the husband and wife should contribute to the household income	12.8	163	40.3	513	24.1	306	18.6	237	1.7	21	2.1	27	0.4	6
j) {ENJOYJOB} Column No 1817 I would enjoy having a job even if I didn't need the money	8.2	105	54.0	688	9.4	120	21.3	271	3.5	44	2.8	36	0.8	10

Base : Self-completion respondents (n = 1274)

MOTHERS IN PAID WORK

1989   Q.A202a-d   {WWCHLD1}-{WWCHLD4} Column Nos 1818-21

Do you think that women should work outside the home *full-time, part-time* or *not at all* under these circumstances?
(Please tick one box for each)

	Work full-time 1		Work part-time 2		Stay at home 3		Can't choose 8		(NA) 9	
Code	%	No	%	No	%	No	%	No	%	No
a) {WWCHLD1} Column No 1818 After marrying and before there are children	76.9	979	13.6	173	2.3	30	6.2	79	1.1	14
b) {WWCHLD2} Column No 1819 When there is a child under school age	2.3	30	26.2	333	63.7	811	6.3	81	1.5	19
c) {WWCHLD3} Column No 1820 After the youngest child starts school	12.7	162	67.7	862	11.3	144	6.7	85	1.6	21
d) {WWCHLD4} Column No 1821 After the children leave home	56.9	725	28.4	362	2.6	33	10.5	134	1.6	20

Base : Self-completion respondents (n = 1274)

PREFERRED CHILDCARE ARRANGEMENTS FOR WORKING PARENTS

1989   Q.A203a-e   *{CHDCARE1}-{CHDCARE5}* Column Nos 1822-26
Think of a child under 3 years old whose parents *both have full-time jobs*.
How suitable do you think each of these childcare arrangements would be for the child?

		Very suitable		Somewhat suitable		Not very suitable		Not at all suitable		Can't choose		(NA)	
	Code	1		2		3		4		8		9	
		%	No	%	No	%	No	%	No	%	No	%	No
a) *{CHDCARE1}* Column No 1822 A state or local authority nursery		28.8	367	37.5	477	16.9	215	7.7	98	4.9	63	4.1	52
b) *{CHDCARE2}* Column No 1823 A private creche or nursery		29.7	379	41.6	530	12.0	152	6.4	81	4.7	60	5.6	71
c) *{CHDCARE3}* Column No 1824 A childminder or baby-sitter		16.4	208	38.1	485	26.8	342	10.2	130	3.3	42	5.2	66
d) *{CHDCARE4}* Column No 1825 A neighbour or friend		9.6	122	31.9	406	35.5	452	14.3	183	3.2	41	5.5	70
e) *{CHDCARE5}* Column No 1826 A relative		39.3	501	37.1	472	12.3	156	5.8	74	2.1	27	3.3	43

Base : Self-completion respondents (n = 1274)

WHETHER OWN MOTHER HAD PAID JOB

1989   Q.A215   *{MTHRWRKD}* Column No 1858
Did your mother ever work for pay for as long as one year after you were born and before you were 14?
(Please tick one box only)

	Code	%	No
Yes, she worked	1	49.1	625
No	2	47.7	608
Did not live with mother	3	2.0	26
(DK)	8	0.3	4
(NA)	9	0.8	10
Base : Self-completion respondents			1274

RESPONSIBILITY FOR GENERAL DOMESTIC DUTIES - 2

1989   Q.B203   *{CHORRESP}* Column No 1917
Are you the person responsible for doing the general domestic duties - like cleaning, cooking, washing
and so on - in your household? (Please tick one box only)

	Code	%	No
Yes, I am *mainly* responsible	1	46.5	584
Yes, I am *equally* responsible with someone else	2	18.1	227
No, *someone else* is *mainly* responsible	3	34.1	428
(NA)	9	1.3	16
Base : Self-completion respondents			1255

WORKING EXPERIENCE OF MOTHERS

1989   Q.A903a-d   {MARWOWK1}-{MARWOWK4}   Column Nos 1474-77
[If married woman with child(ren)] (Show card) Please use this card to say whether you worked *full-time, part-time* or *not at all*:

	Worked full-time 1		Worked part-time 2		Stayed at home 3		Does not apply 8		(NA) 9		[Not asked: not married woman with child(ren)] 0	
Code	%	No	%	No	%	No	%	No	%	No	%	No
a) {MARWOWK1} Column No 1474 *After* marrying and *before* you had children	20.5	301	2.7	40	5.1	74	0.4	6	0.3	4	71.0	1044
b) {MARWOWK2} Column No 1475 And what about when a child was *under school age*	2.5	37	8.1	120	17.8	261	0.3	4	0.3	4	71.0	1044
c) {MARWOWK3} Column No 1476 After the *youngest* child started school	4.1	60	12.3	181	6.9	102	5.4	79	0.3	4	71.0	1044
d) {MARWOWK4} Column No 1477 And how about *after* the children left home	4.1	60	5.2	76	3.3	48	16.0	235	0.4	6	71.0	1044

Base : All (n = 1469)

MARRIED/LIVING AS MARRIED : DOMESTIC DIVISION OF MONEY

1987   Q.A87b,c   {PGETMONY}{RGETMONY}   Column Nos 736-37

{PGETMONY} Column No 736
a) [If married/living as married and manages all the household money] Does your partner ask for *his/her* share of the household money whenever *he/she* needs it, or does *he/she* get a regular allowance?
(Interviewer: probe for best description before accepting code 3)

{RGETMONY} Column No 737
b) [If married/living as married and *partner* manages all the household money] Do you ask for your share of the household money whenever you need it, or do you get a regular allowance? (Interviewer: probe for best description before accepting code 3)

	Code	b) Partner {PGETMONY} %	No	c) Self {RGETMONY} %	No
Asks for when needed	1	4.1	40	3.5	34
Gets regular allowance	2	5.8	57	8.7	86
(Mixture of both)	3	1.7	17	1.0	10
[Not asked : respondent/partner does not manage all the money]	6	88.1	867	86.3	849
(NA)	9	0.2	2	0.5	5
Base : All married/living as married			984		984

DUTY OF WOMEN TO GO OUT TO WORK

1987   Q.A222a-e   {WOMWORK1}-{WOMWORK5} Column Nos 1628-32

People's views about whether a woman ought to work or not often change according to her circumstances. Please tick one box on each line to show which is closest to *your* view about a woman in the following circumstances

{WOMWORK1} Column No 1628

a) A married woman whose children have all left school

	Code	%	No
She ought to go out to work if she's fit	1	8.0	100
It's up to her whether to go out to work or not	2	81.7	1016
She should only go out to work if she really needs the money	3	8.6	107
She ought to stay at home	4	1.2	15
(NA)	9	0.5	7
Base : Self-completion respondents			1243

{WOMWORK2} Column No 1629

b) A married woman whose children are at school

	Code	%	No
She ought to go out to work if she's fit	1	2.3	28
It's up to her whether to go out to work or not	2	50.0	622
She should only go out to work if she really needs the money	3	31.5	392
She ought to stay at home	4	15.1	187
(NA)	9	1.1	14
Base : Self-completion respondents			1243

{WOMWORK3} Column No 1630

c) A married woman with children under school age

	Code	%	No
She ought to go out to work if she's fit	1	0.7	9
It's up to her whether to go out to work or not	2	19.5	242
She should only go out to work if she really needs the money	3	22.2	277
She ought to stay at home	4	56.7	705
(NA)	9	0.9	12
Base : Self-completion respondents			1243

{WOMWORK4} Column No 1631

d) A married woman with no children

	Code	%	No
She ought to go out to work if she's fit	1	23.2	289
It's up to her whether to go out to work or not	2	70.0	870
She should only go out to work if she needs the money	3	5.5	69
She ought to stay at home	4	0.5	6
(NA)	9	0.8	10
Base : Self-completion respondents			1243

DUTY OF WOMEN TO GO OUT TO WORK (continued)

{WOMWORK5} Column No 1632

e) **A single woman with no family responsibilities**

	Code	%	No
She ought to go out to work if she's fit	1	69.8	867
It's up to her whether to go out to work or not	2	27.5	342
She should only go out to work if she really needs the money	3	1.9	23
She ought to stay at home	4	0.1	1
(NA)	9	0.8	10
			1243

Base : Self-completion respondents

WOMEN, FAMILY AND CAREER

1987   Q.A223c,f,h,i   *{WOMWKKID}{WOMWKGD}{WOMSUFFR}{WOMRIGHT}*
Column Nos 1635,1638,1640-41

Please tick one box for each statement below to show how much you agree or disagree with it.

	Code	Agree strongly 1 % No	Agree slightly 2 % No	Neither agree nor disagree 3 % No	Disagree slightly 4 % No	Disagree strongly 5 % No	(DK) 8 % No	(NA) 9 % No
{WOMWKKID} Column No 1635 c) Women shouldn't try to combine a career with children		13.0 161	19.0 237	22.2 276	27.2 339	18.0 224	0.1 1	0.5 6
{WOMWKGD} Column No 1638 f) If the children are well looked after, it's good for a woman to work		16.9 210	39.3 489	27.9 347	10.6 132	4.9 61	0.1 1	0.4 5
{WOMSUFFR} Column No 1640 h) If a woman takes several years off to look after her children, it's only fair her career should suffer		6.2 76	23.2 288	25.3 314	23.9 297	20.2 251	0.2 3	1.1 14
{WOMRIGHT} Column No 1641 i) Married women have a right to work if they want to, whatever their family situation		31.4 390	31.1 387	15.3 190	13.0 162	8.5 106	0.1 1	0.6 7

Base : Self-completion respondents (n = 1243)

PREFERRED WORKING ARRANGEMENT FOR PARENTS

1986   Q.A76a,b   {CHNUNDR5}{TEENAGRS} Column Nos 1030-31, 1032-33

a)   {CHNUNDR5} Column Nos 1030-31
(Show card) For a family with children *under five years old*, which one of the arrangements on this card do you think is best?

b)   {TEENAGRS} Column Nos 1032-33
(Continue showing card) And for a family with children *in their early teens*, which one of these arrangements is best?

	Code	a) Under five {CHNUNDR5} %	No	b) Early teens {TEENAGRS} %	No
Both parents working full-time	1	1.0	16	14.7	223
Father working full-time and mother at home	2	76.3	1158	18.9	287
Mother working full-time and father at home	3	0.2	4	0.4	7
Both parents working part-time	4	2.3	35	2.8	42
Father working full-time and mother part-time	5	16.9	257	60.0	911
Mother working full-time and father part-time	6	0.1	2	0.3	4
Other answer	97	2.2	33	2.0	30
(DK)	98	0.6	10	0.8	12
(NA)	99	0.3	4	0.2	3
Base : All			1518		1518

MARRIED/LIVING AS MARRIED : PARENTS' HOUSEHOLD FINANCIAL ARRANGEMENTS

1986 Q.A78c   {PTSMONEY} Column No 1050
[If married/living as married] Do you remember how your *parents* organised the money that came into their household? Was it ... (read out) ...

	Code	%	No
... in the same way,	1	33.4	363
or - differently?	2	51.8	562
(Does not apply)	6	1.9	21
(Other answer)	7	0.2	2
(Don't remember)	8	11.7	127
(NA)	9	1.0	11
Base : All married/living as married			1086

NB Two respondents who did not (in answer to the preceding question {ORGMONEY}) describe their own household finance arrangements were not asked this question

INCREASED OPPORTUNITIES FOR WOMEN

1985   Q.214a-c   {FEMGOV1}-{FEMGOV3}   Column Nos 2041-43

Here are three things the government might do. Some people are in favour of them while other people are against them. Please tick one box for each statement to show how you feel.

	Strongly in favour 1		In favour 2		Neither in favour nor against 3		Against 4		Strongly against 5		(DK) 8		(NA) 9	
Code	%	No	%	No	%	No	%	No	%	No	%	No	%	No
a) {FEMGOV1} Column No 2041 The government should increase opportunities for women in business and industry	16.2	243	39.4	592	32.8	493	8.8	132	1.5	22	0.1	1	1.3	20
b) {FEMGOV2} Column No 2042 The government should increase opportunities for women to go to university	11.2	168	32.9	494	45.0	675	7.8	117	1.2	18	0.0	-	1.9	28
c) {FEMGOV3} Column No 2043 Women should be given preferential treatment when applying for jobs or promotion	2.9	43	4.4	66	27.1	407	45.5	684	18.2	273	0.1	1	1.9	28

Base : Self-completion respondents (n = 1502)

SUPPORT FOR LAWS GIVING WOMEN GREATER EQUALITY

1984   Q.86a-e   {SEXWORK1} - {SEXWORK5}   Column Nos 616-20

There are a number of laws which aim at giving women greater equality with men, particularly at work. I am going to read out some of them, and I would like you to tell me for each one, whether you support or oppose it.

	Support 1		Oppose 2		(DK) 8		(NA) 9	
Code	%	No	%	No	%	No	%	No
a) {SEXWORK1} Column No 616 Laws giving men and women equal pay for equal work	93.5	1538	4.9	81	1.1	18	0.5	9
b) {SEXWORK2} Column No 617 The right to six weeks maternity pay if a woman has been in her job for two years	88.3	1454	7.6	125	3.6	59	0.5	8
c) {SEXWORK3} Column No 618 The opportunity for boys and girls to study the same subjects at school	96.3	1585	2.2	36	1.0	16	0.5	9
d) {SEXWORK4} Column No 619 The right for a woman to return to her job within six months of having a baby	77.4	1273	17.5	288	4.6	75	0.5	9
e) {SEXWORK5} Column No 620 Laws making it illegal to treat men and women differently at work	81.0	1333	13.9	229	4.6	75	0.5	9

Base : All (n = 1645)

REASONS FOR MARRIED WOMEN WORKING

1984   Q.88a   {MWWORK1}-{MWWORK10}   Column Nos 622-31

a) (Show card) I'd like you to look at the statements on this card. In general, which ones do you think best describe the reasons why many *married women* work? Any others? (Interviewer: code all that apply)

		Code	%	No
{MWWORK1}	Column No 622			
Working is the normal thing to do				
	Given as reason	1	6.4	106
	(DK)	8	0.7	11
	(NA)	9	0.5	9
	[Not given as reason]	0	92.4	1520
Base : All				1645
{MWWORK2}	Column No 623			
Need money for basic essentials such as food, rent or mortgage				
	Given as reason	2	63.8	1050
	(DK)	8	0.7	11
	(NA)	9	0.5	9
	[Not given as reason]	0	35.0	575
Base : All				1645
{MWWORK3}	Column No 624			
To earn money to buy extras				
	Given as reason	3	71.3	1174
	(DK)	8	0.7	11
	(NA)	9	0.5	9
	[Not given as reason]	0	27.5	452
Base : All				1645
{MWWORK4}	Column No 625			
To earn money of their own				
	Given as reason	4	45.6	750
	(DK)	8	0.7	11
	(NA)	9	0.5	9
	[Not given as reason]	0	53.2	876
Base : All				1645
{MWWORK5}	Column No 626			
For the company of other people				
	Given as reason	5	38.0	625
	(DK)	8	0.7	11
	(NA)	9	0.5	9
	[Not given as reason]	0	60.8	1001
Base : All				1645
{MWWORK6}	Column No 627			
Because they enjoy working				
	Given as reason	6	27.9	459
	(DK)	8	0.7	11
	(NA)	9	0.5	9
	[Not given as reason]	0	70.9	1167
Base : All				1645

REASONS FOR MARRIED WOMEN WORKING (continued)

		Code	%	No
{MWWORK8}	Column No 628			
To follow a career				
Given as reason		2	40.7	670
(DK)		8	0.7	11
(NA)		9	0.5	9
[Not given as reason]		0	58.1	956
Base : All				1645

		Code	%	No
{MWWORK9}	Column No 629			
For a change from children or housework				
Given as reason		7	0.5	8
(DK)		8	0.7	11
(NA)		9	0.5	9
[Not given as reason]		0	98.3	1618
Base : All				1645

		Code	%	No
{MWWORK7}	Column No 630			
Other reason(s)				
Given as reason(s)		1	29.7	489
(DK)		8	0.7	11
(NA)		9	0.5	9
[Not given as reason]		0	69.1	1137
Base : All				1645

		Code	%	No
{MWWORK10}	Column No 631			
[Derived variable]				
One or more reason given		0	98.8	1626
(DK)		8	0.7	11
(NA)		9	0.5	9
Base : All				1645

MAIN REASON FOR MARRIED WOMEN WORKING

1984   Q.88b   {MWWKMAIN} Column Nos 632-33

[If more than one reason given] And which one of these would you say is generally the *main* reason why married women work?

	Code	%	No
Working is the normal thing to do	1	0.6	10
Need money for basic essentials such as food, rent or mortgage	2	44.9	739
To earn money to buy extras	3	35.4	582
To earn money of their own	4	8.0	132
For the company of other people	5	2.0	33
Because they enjoy working	6	1.7	28
To follow a career	7	1.8	29
For a change from children or housework	8	3.4	56
Other reason(s)	97	0.2	4
(DK)	98	1.2	20
(NA)	99	0.7	12
Base : All			1645

EQUAL PAY FOR WOMEN AND MEN

1984   Q.220(vi)   {*EQUALPAY*} Column No 1646
[Finally,] please tick one box ... to show how much you agree or disagree with [this statement].

Women should be paid the same as men for doing the same work.

	Code	%	No
Disagree strongly	1	1.6	24
Just disagree	2	2.3	35
Neither agree nor disagree	3	4.3	65
Just agree	4	23.1	351
Agree strongly	5	67.6	1029
(DK)	8	0.1	1
(NA)	9	1.1	17
Base : Self-completion respondents			1522

NB This item was part of a longer battery of questions all of which except this one and {BRITPOWR} were repeated between 1985 and 1989. The original question wording invited respondents to 'tick one box for each statement below'

DIVISION OF HOUSEHOLD TASKS

1983   Q.88(A)   {*DOCHORE8*} Column No 642
Variable derived from {CHORE8}
[If married/living as married] I would like to ask about how you and your *husband/wife/partner* generally share some family jobs. Who *does* decide what colour to decorate the living room? ... (read out) ...

	Code	%	No
[Not asked : not married/ living as married]	0	29.7	510
... mainly the man,	1	3.4	59
... mainly the woman,	2	34.1	585
or is the task shared equally?	3	32.5	558
(Other)	4	0.0	1
(NA)	9	0.3	6
Base : All			1719

NB   This was the last in a list of eight tasks, and was not included in subsequent years (see pp. N.2-7 to N.2-10 above). The responses of those married/living as married and those not married/living as married are combined in the source variable {CHORE8}, as both versions were coded on the same column. Responses are separated out in the derived variables {DOCHORE8} and {SHCHR838}, which also appear on the SPSS file. (See p. N.2-32 for the latter)

PRESCRIPTIVE DOMESTIC DIVISION OF LABOUR - 2

1983   Q.88(B) i)-viii)   *{SHCHR831}-{SHCHR838} - Variables derived from {CHORE1}-{CHORE8}*   Column No 635-42

[If not married/living as married] I would like your opinion on how you think some of the family jobs should generally be shared. For example, who *should do* the household shopping - mainly the man, mainly the woman or should the task be shared equally?

		i) Should do the household shopping {SHCHR831}		ii) Should make the evening meal {SHCHR832}	
Column No		635		636	
[Not asked : not married/	Code	%	No	%	No
living as married]	0	70.3	1209	70.3	1209
Mainly man	1	0.5	8	-	-
Mainly woman	2	10.3	176	15.5	266
Shared equally	3	18.2	314	13.4	230
(Other)	4	-	-	-	-
(NA)	9	0.7	12	0.8	14
Base : All			1719		1719

		iii) Should do the evening dishes {SHCHR833}		iv) Should do the household cleaning {SHCHR834}	
Column No		637		638	
[Not asked : not married/	Code	%	No	%	No
living as married]	0	70.3	1209	70.3	1209
Mainly man	1	2.8	48	0.1	2
Mainly woman	2	5.7	99	13.4	230
Shared equally	3	20.5	352	15.5	267
(Other answer)	4	-	-	-	-
(NA)	9	0.6	11	0.6	11
Base : All			1719		1719

		v) Should do the washing and ironing {SHCHR835}		vi) Should repair the household equipment {SHCHR836}	
Column No		639		640	
[Not asked : not married/	Code	%	No	%	No
living as married]	0	70.3	1209	70.3	1209
Mainly man	1	-	-	22.5	388
Mainly woman	2	21.7	373	0.4	7
Shared equally	3	7.3	125	6.2	106
(Other)	4	-	-	-	-
(NA)	9	0.7	12	0.6	10
Base : All			1719		1719

		vii) Should organise the household money and payment of bills {SHCHR837}		viii) Should decide what colour to decorate the living room {SHCHR838}	
Column No		641		642	
{No asked : not married/	Code	%	No	%	No
living as married]	0	70.3	1209	70.3	1209
Mainly man	1	7.0	120	0.7	12
Mainly woman	2	5.1	87	9.0	155
Shared equally	3	16.9	291	19.5	334
(Other)	4	-	-	-	-
(NA)	9	0.7	12	0.5	9
Base : All			1719		1719

NB The responses of those married/living as married and those <u>not</u> married/living as married are combined in the source variables {CHORE1}-{CHORE8}, as both versions were coded on the same column. Responses are separated out in the derived variables {SHCHORE1}-{SHCHORE8}, renamed as above since in subsequent years these questions were asked of all respondents

O Race

Table titles and cross references

ETHNIC ORIGIN (INTERVIEWER-CODED)

{ETHNICGP}

Interviewer: code from observation for all respondents.

		1983		1984		1985		1986		1987		1989	
		%	No	%	No	%	No	%	No	%	No	%	No
Question No		94		78a		102		69		78		83	
Column No		820		555		875		570		668		815	
	Code												
White/European	1	94.8	1630	97.5	1604	96.0	1699	95.6	2930	96.6	2671	97.1	2846
Indian/East African Asian/Pakistani Bangladeshi/Sri Lankan	2	1.3	23	1.2	19	1.6	28	2.1	64	1.5	43	1.4	40
Black/African/West Indian	3	1.3	22	0.5	9	0.9	16	1.6	50	1.1	30	1.2	35
Other (inc. Chinese)	4	2.5	42	0.1	2	0.1	2	0.5	14	0.6	17	0.3	8
(NA)	9	0.1	2	0.7	11	1.4	24	0.3	8	0.2	6	0.0	1
		—		—		—		—		—		—	
Base: All			1719		1645		1769		3066		2766		2930

1983 - Indian (inc. E African), code 1; Black, African, W Indian, code 2; White/European, code 3; Other non-white, code 4

EXTENT OF RACIAL PREJUDICE AGAINST ASIANS

{PREJAS}

Question: Now I would like to ask you some questions about racial prejudice.

First, thinking of *Asians* - that is, people whose families were originally from India and Pakistan - who now live in Britain. Do you think there is a lot of prejudice against them in Britain nowadays, a little, or hardly any?

		1983		1984		1985		1986		1987		1989	
		%	No	%	No	%	No	%	No	%	No	%	No
Question No		80a		76a		94a		70a		79a		84a	
Column No		607		543		736		571		669		816	
	Code												
A lot	1	53.7	922	55.8	919	57.1	1011	61.3	1879	62.0	1716	61.1	1790
A little	2	37.2	640	35.3	580	32.4	574	30.2	927	29.5	816	30.6	898
Hardly any	3	6.3	108	5.8	95	7.1	126	5.6	170	6.2	173	5.9	172
(DK)	8	2.6	45	2.5	42	2.9	52	2.7	83	2.1	58	2.2	65
(NA)	9	0.2	4	0.6	9	0.4	7	0.2	6	0.1	4	0.2	6
		—		—		—		—		—		—	
Base: All			1719		1645		1769		3066		2766		2930

1983, 1984 - Q reads: 'Asians - that is people originally from India and Pakistan'
1983 - (DK), code 4

EXTENT OF RACIAL PREJUDICE AGAINST BLACKS

{PREJBLK}

Question: And *black* people - that is people whose families were originally from the West Indies or Africa - who now live in Britain. Do you think there is a lot of prejudice against them in Britain nowadays, a little, or hardly any?

		1983		1984		1985		1986		1987		1989	
		%	No	%	No	%	No	%	No	%	No	%	No
Question No		80b		76b		94b		70b		79b		84b	
Column No		608		544		737		572		670		817	
	Code												
A lot	1	50.5	867	51.0	840	49.7	880	55.4	1697	57.0	1576	52.2	1529
A little	2	39.7	682	38.6	635	37.7	667	34.7	1063	33.3	921	37.1	1086
Hardly any	3	6.8	117	7.2	118	7.7	137	6.6	202	7.3	203	7.8	230
(DK)	8	2.5	43	2.3	38	4.3	77	3.0	91	2.0	56	2.3	67
(NA)	9	0.6	10	0.9	15	0.5	9	0.4	12	0.4	10	0.6	18
Base: All			1719		1645		1769		3066		2766		2930

1983, 1984 - Q reads: ' ... black people - that is West Indians and Africans - who now live ...'
1983 - (DK), code 4

PERCEPTION OF LEVEL OF RACIAL PREJUDICE IN PAST

{PREJNOW}

Question: Do you think there is generally *more* racial prejudice in Britain now than there was 5 years ago, *less*, or about the *same* amount?

		1983		1984		1985		1986		1987		1989	
		%	No	%	No	%	No	%	No	%	No	%	No
Question No		80c		76c		94c		70c		79c		84c	
Column No		609		545		738		573		671		818	
	Code												
More now	1	45.2	777	39.7	652	37.5	664	48.6	1490	50.0	1383	31.4	919
Less now	2	16.0	275	20.3	334	20.2	358	12.4	382	12.6	348	21.4	628
About the same	3	36.4	625	37.4	616	39.4	698	35.9	1102	35.1	971	44.3	1298
(Other answer)	7	1.6	28	0.3	5	0.7	12	0.5	14	0.1	4	0.2	6
(DK)	8	-	-	1.6	27	2.0	36	2.2	69	1.9	51	2.1	60
(NA)	9	0.8	14	0.7	11	0.2	3	0.3	10	0.3	9	0.6	19
Base: All			1719		1645		1769		3066		2766		2930

1983 - Other answer, code 4; No (DK)

PREDICTIONS FOR LEVEL OF RACIAL PREJUDICE IN FUTURE

{PREJFUT}

Question: Do you think there will be *more, less* or about the *same* amount of racial prejudice in Britain in 5 years time compared with now?

	Code	1983 %	No	1984 %	No	1985 %	No	1986 %	No	1987 %	No	1989 %	No
Question No		80d		76d		94d		70d		79d		84d	
Column No		610		546		739		574		672		819	
More in 5 years	1	42.1	724	40.4	665	41.7	737	46.3	1419	46.4	1283	32.3	945
Less	2	17.3	297	17.8	293	18.0	318	13.1	402	12.4	343	18.6	545
About the same	3	36.4	625	37.6	619	35.1	621	35.6	1090	37.0	1022	45.0	1318
(Other answer)	7	3.1	53	1.6	26	2.4	42	1.2	36	1.1	29	0.7	20
(DK)	8	-	-	2.1	34	2.7	49	3.7	115	2.9	82	3.2	94
(NA)	9	1.1	20	0.5	9	0.1	2	0.1	4	0.2	7	0.3	8
Base: All			1719		1645		1769		3066		2766		2930

1983 · Other answer, code 4; No (DK)

SELF-RATED RACIAL PREJUDICE

{SRPREJ}

Question: How would you describe yourself ... (read out) ...

	Code	1983 %	No	1984 %	No	1985 %	No	1986 %	No	1987 %	No	1989 %	No
Question No		80e		76e		94e		70e		79e		84e	
Column No		611		547		740		575		673		820	
... as very prejudiced against people of other races,	1	4.4	76	2.9	48	5.2	92	3.7	113	4.5	123	4.2	124
... a little prejudiced,	2	31.2	537	33.6	552	28.7	508	31.9	978	34.1	943	32.0	938
... or not prejudiced at all?	3	63.7	1095	62.1	1022	65.1	1152	63.4	1943	60.2	1664	63.0	1846
(Other answer)	7	0.3	5	0.9	14	0.5	9	0.6	19	0.7	19	0.2	7
(DK)	8	-	-	0.1	1	0.2	4	0.1	3	0.3	9	0.3	8
(NA)	9	0.4	6	0.5	9	0.2	4	0.3	9	0.3	9	0.3	8
Base: All			1719		1645		1769		3066		2766		2930

1983 · Other, code 4

ETHNIC GROUPS AGAINST WHICH RESPONDENT IS PREJUDICED - 1

{PREJWHO1} + {PREJWHO2} + {PREJWHO3}

Question: [If 'very' or 'a little' prejudiced against people of other races]

Against any race in particular?
(Interviewer: probe for races and record. If 'black' or 'coloured' mentioned, probe for whether West Indian, Asian, general etc. Record verbatim everything mentioned)

	Code	1983 %	1983 No	1984 %	1984 No	1985 %	1985 No	1986 %	1986 No	1987 %	1987 No	1989 %	1989 No
Question No		80f		76f		94f		70f		79f		84f	
Column No		612-17		548-53		741-46		608-13		674-79		821-26	
[Not asked: not prejudiced against people of other races]	0	64.0	1100	63.0	1036	66.1	1169	64.1	1963	60.1	1682	63.0	1846
Asians	1	5.2	90	6.0	98	6.6	116	5.7	176	5.9	163	7.1	208
'Blacks'	2	2.0	35	2.1	35	2.0	36	2.6	79	3.6	100	2.8	82
'Coloureds'	3	2.4	41	1.0	17	0.8	14	1.7	52	1.2	34	1.3	37
Pakistanis	4	3.0	52	4.7	77	4.6	81	4.1	127	4.0	110	3.4	99
Indians	5	1.5	26	2.7	45	2.8	49	1.7	52	1.9	53	1.4	42
Sikhs	6	0.1	2	0.1	1	0.2	3	0.1	4	0.2	6	0.1	4
West Indians	7	3.3	57	3.0	50	1.9	34	3.1	96	3.7	101	2.5	74
Africans	8	0.6	10	0.5	8	0.7	12	0.8	26	1.3	37	0.8	24
Other specified races/nationalities/ countries	9	2.3	40	1.5	24	2.1	37	1.4	42	1.6	43	1.9	57
Against all races (other than whites)/no race in particular	10	-	-	18.9	311	15.7	278	18.1	555	19.6	541	17.6	516
Other answer	97	20.2	347	3.6	59	2.3	40	2.2	67	2.6	71	2.1	61
(DK)	98	0.2	3	0.1	2	0.1	1	0.1	2	0.0	1	0.1	3
(NA)	99	1.2	20	0.8	13	0.2	4	0.6	19	1.0	28	1.7	49
Base: All			1719		1645		1769		3066		2766		2930

1983 - No interviewer instruction to 'Record verbatim everything mentioned'; No code 10, which in large part accounts for the high proportion of other answers. For a summary of responses to this question, see p. O - 13 below

1983 - 1987, 1989 - {PREJWHO2}, {PREJWHO3}: No other race mentioned, code 96

RACIAL PREJUDICE IN EMPLOYMENT AGAINST ASIANS

{*ASJOB*}

Question: On the whole, do you think people of Asian origin in Britain are *not* given jobs these days *because* of their race ... (read out) ...

		1983		1984		1985		1986		1987		1989	
		%	No	%	No	%	No	%	No	%	No	%	No
Question No		81a						B71a				B85a	
Column No		618						614				831	
	Code												
... a lot,	1	20.4	350	-	-	-	-	23.6	365	-	-	17.8	260
... a little,	2	40.3	692	-	-	-	-	38.2	591	-	-	38.3	559
... or hardly at all?	3	30.6	525	-	-	-	-	28.1	434	-	-	33.7	492
(DK)	8	8.3	142	-	-	-	-	9.4	146	-	-	10.1	147
(NA)	9	0.5	9	-	-	-	-	0.8	12	-	-	0.2	4
Base: All			1719						1548				1461

1983 - DK, code 4

RACIAL PREJUDICE IN EMPLOYMENT AGAINST BLACKS

{*WIJOB*}

Question: And on the whole, do you think people of West Indian origin in Britain are *not* given jobs these days *because* of their race ... (read out) ...

		1983		1984		1985		1986		1987		1989	
		%	No	%	No	%	No	%	No	%	No	%	No
Question No		81b						B71b				B85b	
Column No		619						615				832	
	Code												
... a lot,	1	24.6	423	-	-	-	-	28.7	444	-	-	24.4	356
... a little,	2	39.5	679	-	-	-	-	37.7	584	-	-	37.5	548
... or hardly at all?	3	27.4	470	-	-	-	-	23.4	363	-	-	28.5	416
(DK)	8	8.1	139	-	-	-	-	9.4	145	-	-	9.4	138
(NA)	9	0.5	8	-	-	-	-	0.8	13	-	-	0.2	4
Base: All			1719						1548				1461

1983 - (DK), code 4

LEGISLATION AGAINST RACIAL DISCRIMINATION

{RACELAW}

Question: There is a law in Britain *against* racial discrimination, that is against giving unfair preference to a particular race in housing, jobs and so on. Do you generally *support* or *oppose* the idea of a law for this purpose?

		1983		1984		1985		1986		1987		1989	
		%	No	%	No	%	No	%	No	%	No	%	No
Question No		82a		77				B72a				B86a	
Column No		620		554				616				833	
	Code												
Support	1	69.0	1186	69.6	1145	-	-	64.6	1000	-	-	68.4	1000
Oppose	2	28.3	487	25.5	419	-	-	31.8	492	-	-	27.7	405
(DK)	8	2.0	35	3.2	53	-	-	3.1	48	-	-	2.9	43
(NA)	9	0.7	11	1.7	28	-	-	0.6	9	-	-	1.0	14
Base: All			1719		1645				1548				1461

HELP FOR ASIAN AND WEST INDIAN IMMIGRANTS

{IMMHELP}

Question: Do you think, on the whole, that Britain gives *too little* or *too much* help to Asians and West Indians who have settled in this country, or are present arrangements about right?

		1983		1984		1985		1986		1987		1989	
		%	No	%	No	%	No	%	No	%	No	%	No
Question No		82b						B72b				B86b	
Column No		621						617				834	
	Code												
Too little	1	7.4	128	-	-	-	-	10.2	158	-	-	10.1	147
Present arrangements right	2	54.6	939	-	-	-	-	50.2	777	-	-	45.8	669
Too much	3	32.4	557	-	-	-	-	32.6	505	-	-	36.6	534
(Other answer)	7	0.5	8	-	-	-	-	0.5	8	-	-	0.7	11
(DK)	8	4.1	71	-	-	-	-	6.1	95	-	-	6.1	89
(NA)	9	1.0	17	-	-	-	-	0.3	5	-	-	0.8	12
Base: All			1719						1548				1461

1983 - Other answer, code 4

ACCEPTABILITY OF ASIAN BOSS

{OBOSSAS} {SBOSSAS}

Variables derived from {OTHBOSS} and {SELFBOSS}

Question: [If white/European] Do you think *most* white people in Britain would mind or not mind if a suitably qualified person of *Asian* origin were appointed as their boss? [If would mind] A lot or a little?

			1983		1984		1985		1986		1987		1989	
			%	No	%	No	%	No	%	No	%	No	%	No
	Question No		83a(A)		78c(A)				B74a(A)				B88a(A)	
	Column No		623		557				620				837	
(i) {OBOSSAS}		Code												
Mind a lot	1		23.4	209	25.7	197	-	-	27.3	196	-	-	22.4	159
Mind a little	2		30.2	269	28.2	217	-	-	28.8	207	-	-	34.2	243
Not mind	3		43.0	384	42.9	330	-	-	38.8	279	-	-	38.9	276
(Other answer)	7		2.2	19	1.2	9	-	-	1.6	11	-	-	0.9	7
(DK)	8		-	-	2.0	16	-	-	3.3	24	-	-	2.9	20
(NA)	9		1.2	10	-	-	-	-	0.1	1	-	-	0.6	4
Base: Random half-sample of white/European respondents				892		769				719				709

			1983		1984		1985		1986		1987		1989	
	Question No		83b(A)		78d(A)				B74b(A)				B88b(A)	
	Column No		624		558				621				838	
(ii) {SBOSSAS}														
And you personally? Would you mind or not mind? [If would mind] A lot or a little?														
Mind a lot	1		10.9	97	11.0	85	-	-	6.9	50	-	-	8.7	62
Mind a little	2		8.3	74	11.0	85	-	-	9.8	71	-	-	11.2	80
Not mind	3		79.5	709	75.8	583	-	-	81.9	588	-	-	78.3	555
(Other answer)	7		1.0	9	1.1	8	-	-	0.4	3	-	-	0.5	4
(DK)	8		-	-	0.9	7	-	-	0.6	4	-	-	0.6	5
(NA)	9		0.3	3	0.3	2	-	-	0.4	3	-	-	0.6	4
Base: Random half-sample of white/European respondents				892		769				719				709

1983 - Other answer, code 4; no (DK); both questions asked of everyone, not just white/European respondents

1984, 1986, 1989 - Respondents were asked about either Asians or West Indians, according to whether the serial number of the address was odd or even

1983 - Interviewers were instructed to 'ask version B for alternate respondents', a less rigorous method which resulted in an inbalance in the numbers of respondents asked each version

1983, 1984, 1986 - Derived variables {OBOSSAS} and {SBOSSAS} were created only in 1989, but have now been added to the SPSS files for earlier years

1983,1984,1986,1989 - Source variables for this question are {OTHBOSS} and {SELFBOSS}, where attitudes towards Asians and West Indians are combined

1989 - Derived variables {OBOSSAS} and {SBOSSAS} created

ACCEPTABILITY OF WEST INDIAN BOSS

{OBOSSWI} {SBOSSWI}

Variables derived from {OTHBOSS} and {SELFBOSS}

Question: [If white/European]   Do you think *most* white people in Britain would mind or not mind if a suitably qualified person of *West Indian* origin were appointed as their boss? [If would mind] **A lot or a little?**

			1983 %	1983 No	1984 %	1984 No	1985 %	1985 No	1986 %	1986 No	1987 %	1987 No	1989 %	1989 No
Question No			83a(B)		78c(B)				B74a(B)				B88a(B)	
Column No			623		557				620				837	
(i) {OBOSSWI}		Code												
Mind a lot	1		25.1	200	25.9	204	-	-	23.5	176	-	-	19.4	138
Mind a little	2		29.1	232	32.0	253	-	-	30.9	231	-	-	34.1	243
Not mind	3		42.3	337	38.3	302	-	-	41.8	314	-	-	42.7	304
(Other answer)	7		2.4	19	1.1	8	-	-	1.5	12	-	-	0.9	6
(DK)	8		-	-	2.6	20	-	-	2.0	15	-	-	2.5	18
(NA)	9		1.2	9	0.1	1	-	-	0.3	2	-	-	0.6	4
Base: Random half-sample of white/European respondents				798		789				750				713

			1983 %	1983 No	1984 %	1984 No	1985 %	1985 No	1986 %	1986 No	1987 %	1987 No	1989 %	1989 No
Question No			83b(B)		78d(B)				B74b(B)				B88b(B)	
Column No			624		558				621				838	
(ii) {SBOSSWI}														

And you personally? Would you mind or not mind? [If would mind] A lot or a little?

			1983 %	1983 No	1984 %	1984 No	1985 %	1985 No	1986 %	1986 No	1987 %	1987 No	1989 %	1989 No
Mind a lot	1		8.5	68	8.4	66	-	-	8.9	67	-	-	8.7	62
Mind a little	2		11.7	94	12.0	94	-	-	9.0	68	-	-	11.8	84
Not mind	3		79.1	631	78.9	622	-	-	80.6	604	-	-	77.6	553
(Other answer)	7		0.5	4	0.3	3	-	-	0.5	4	-	-	0.6	5
(DK)	8		-	-	0.3	2	-	-	0.5	4	-	-	0.6	4
(NA)	9		0.1	1	0.1	1	-	-	0.4	3	-	-	0.7	5
Base: Random half-sample of white/European respondents				798		789				750				713

1983 - Other answer, code 4; no (DK); both questions asked of everyone, not just white/European respondents

1984, 1986, 1989 - Respondents were asked about either Asians or West Indians, according to whether the serial number of the address was odd or even

1983 - Interviewers were instructed to 'ask version B for alternate respondents', a less rigorous method which resulted in an inbalance in the numbers of respondents asked each version

1983, 1984, 1986, - Derived variables {OBOSSWI} and {SBOSSWI} were created only in 1989, but have now been added to the SPSS files for earlier years

1983,1984,1986,1989 - Source variables for this question are {OTHBOSS} and {SELFBOSS}, where attitudes towards Asians and West Indians are combined

1989 - Derived variables {OBOSSWI} and {SBOSSWI} created

ACCEPTABILITY OF ASIAN MARRIAGE PARTNER

{OMARAS} {SMARAS}

Variables derived from {OTHMAR} and {SELFMAR}

Question: [If white/European] Do you think *most* white people in Britain would mind or not mind if one of their close relatives were to marry a person of *Asian* origin? [If would mind] A lot or a little?

			1983		1984		1985		1986		1987		1989	
			%	No	%	No	%	No	%	No	%	No	%	No
	Question No		83c(A)		78e(A)				B74c(A)				B88c(A)	
	Column No		625		559				622				839	
(i) {OMARAS}		Code												
Mind a lot	1		41.9	374	41.0	316	-	-	45.5	327	-	-	45.4	322
Mind a little	2		34.7	310	35.1	270	-	-	33.5	241	-	-	34.8	247
Not mind	3		19.6	175	20.2	155	-	-	15.5	111	-	-	15.3	108
(Other answer)	7		2.5	23	0.7	6	-	-	1.3	10	-	-	0.6	4
(DK)	8		-	-	2.8	21	-	-	4.0	29	-	-	3.5	25
(NA)	9		1.2	11	0.1	1	-	-	0.1	1	-	-	0.4	3
Base: Random half-sample of white/European respondents				892		769				719				709

			1983		1984		1985		1986		1987		1989	
	Question No		83d(A)		78f(A)				B74d(A)				B88d(A)	
	Column No		626		560				623				840	
(ii) {SMARAS}														

And you personally? Would you mind or not mind? [If would mind] A lot or a little?

			1983		1984		1985		1986		1987		1989	
Mind a lot	1		31.2	278	29.9	230	-	-	27.2	196	-	-	27.9	198
Mind a little	2		19.9	177	22.9	176	-	-	22.9	165	-	-	21.5	152
Not mind	3		47.3	422	45.9	353	-	-	46.4	333	-	-	47.9	339
(Other answer)	7		1.1	10	0.4	3	-	-	2.1	15	-	-	1.1	8
(DK)	8		-	-	0.8	6	-	-	1.1	8	-	-	1.1	18
(NA)	9		0.6	5	0.1	1	-	-	0.3	2	-	-	0.6	4
Base: Random half-sample of white/European respondents				892		769				719				709

1983 - Other answer, code 4; no (DK); both questions asked of everyone, not just white/European respondents

1984, 1986, 1989 - Respondents were asked about either Asians or West Indians, according to whether the serial number of the address was odd or even

1983 - Interviewers were instructed to 'ask version B for alternate respondents', a less rigorous method which resulted in an inbalance in the numbers of respondents asked each version

1983,1984,1986,1989 - Source variables for this question are {OTHMAR} AND {SELFMAR}, where attitudes towards Asians and West Indians are combined

1983, 1984, 1986 - Derived variables {OMARAS} and {SMARAS} were created only in 1989, but have now been added to the SPSS files for earlier years

1989 - Derived variables {OMARAS} and {SMARAS} created

ACCEPTABILITY OF WEST INDIAN MARRIAGE PARTNER

{OMARWI} {SMARWI}

Variables derived from *{OTHMAR}* and *{SELFMAR}*

Question: [If white/European] Do you think *most* white people in Britain would mind or not mind if one of their close relatives were to marry a person of *West Indian* origin? [If would mind] **A lot or a little?**

		1983		1984		1985		1986		1987		1989	
		%	No	%	No	%	No	%	No	%	No	%	No
Question No		83c(B)		78e(B)				B74c(B)				B88c(B)	
Column No		625		559				622				839	
(i) {OMARWI}	Code												
Mind a lot	1	48.6	387	46.8	369	-	-	44.9	337	-	-	37.2	265
Mind a little	2	30.2	241	34.6	273	-	-	31.2	234	-	-	40.3	288
Not mind	3	18.0	144	15.0	118	-	-	18.5	139	-	-	18.0	129
(Other answer)	7	2.4	19	0.6	5	-	-	1.0	8	-	-	0.7	5
(DK)	8	-	-	2.9	23	-	-	4.2	32	-	-	3.0	22
(NA)	9	0.9	7	0.1	1	-	-	0.1	1	-	-	0.7	5
Base: Random half-sample of white/European respondents			798		789				750				713

		1983		1984		1985		1986		1987		1989	
Question No		83d(B)		78f(B)				B74d(B)				B88d(B)	
Column No		626		560				623				840	
(ii) {SMARWI}													
And you personally? Would you mind or not mind? [If would mind] **A lot or a little?**													
Mind a lot	1	33.0	263	29.0	229	-	-	26.8	201	-	-	27.7	197
Mind a little	2	24.3	194	22.4	177	-	-	19.5	147	-	-	23.9	171
Not mind	3	40.8	326	46.6	367	-	-	51.1	384	-	-	46.0	328
(Other answer)	7	1.9	15	1.4	11	-	-	1.8	14	-	-	0.6	4
(DK)	8	-	-	0.6	5	-	-	0.6	5	-	-	1.1	8
(NA)	9	-	-	-	-	-	-	0.1	1	-	-	0.7	5
Base: Random half-sample of white/European respondents			798		789				750				713

1983 - Other answer, code 4; no (DK); both questions asked of everyone, not just white/European respondents

1984, 1986, 1989 - Respondents were asked about either Asians or West Indians, according to whether the serial number of the address was odd or even

1983 - Interviewers were instructed to 'ask version B for alternate respondents', a less rigorous method which resulted in an inbalance in the numbers of respondents asked each version

1983,1984,1986,1989 - Source variables for this question are {OTHMAR} and {SELFMAR}, where attitudes towards Asians and West Indians are combined

1983, 1984, 1986 - Derived variables {OMARWI} and {SMARWI} were created only in 1989, but have now been added to the SPSS files for earlier years

1989 - Derived variables {OMARWI} and {SMARWI} created

CONTROLS ON IMMIGRATION

{AUSIEIMM} {ASIANIMM} {EECIMM} {WIIMM}

Question: Britain controls the numbers of people from abroad that are allowed to settle in this country. Please say, for *each* of the groups below, whether you think Britain should allow more settlement, less settlement, or about the same amount as now. (Please tick one box for each)

		1983		1984		1985		1986		1987		1989	
		%	No	%	No	%	No	%	No	%	No	%	No
Question No		215a		218				B229a				B222a	
Column No		1074		1626				2151				2058	
(i) {AUSIEIMM}	Code												
Australians and New Zealanders													
More settlement	1	15.7	254	11.5	176	-	-	8.6	113	-	-	9.0	112
Less settlement	2	27.7	446	35.0	532	-	-	33.9	446	-	-	31.8	399
About the same as now	3	55.1	887	51.2	779	-	-	55.8	734	-	-	56.7	711
(DK)	8	-	.	0.6	9	-	-	0.1	2	-	-	0.3	4
(NA)	9	1.5	23	1.8	27	-	-	1.5	20	-	-	2.3	29
Base: Self-completion questionnaire respondents			1610		1522				1315				1255

		1983		1984				1986				1989	
Question No		215a		218				B229a				B222a	
Column No		1075		1627				2152				2059	
(ii) {ASIANIMM}													
Indians and Pakistanis													
More settlement	1	1.9	30	2.0	30	-	-	2.0	26	-	-	1.2	15
Less settlement	2	71.2	1146	73.5	1119	-	-	67.6	890	-	-	66.9	839
About the same as now	3	25.6	412	22.4	341	-	-	29.1	383	-	-	29.5	370
(DK)	8	-	.	0.6	9	-	-	0.1	2	-	-	0.3	4
(NA)	9	1.3	21	1.6	24	-	-	1.2	16	-	-	2.1	27
Base: Self-completion questionnaire respondents			1610		1522				1315				1255

		1983		1984				1986				1989	
Question No		215a		218				B229a				B222a	
Column No		1076		1628				2153				2060	
(iii) {EECIMM}													
People from common market countries													
More settlement	1	6.9	111	5.4	83	-	-	5.7	74	-	-	8.0	100
Less settlement	2	44.4	714	49.2	749	-	-	45.8	603	-	-	40.5	508
About the same as now	3	46.8	754	42.6	649	-	-	47.0	618	-	-	48.8	612
(DK)	8	-	.	0.7	11	-	-	0.1	2	-	-	0.3	4
(NA)	9	1.9	30	2.0	31	-	-	1.4	18	-	-	2.4	30
Base: Self-completion questionnaire respondents			1610		1522				1315				1255

CONTROLS ON IMMIGRATION (Continued)

	Code	1983 %	1983 No	1984 %	1984 No	1985 %	1985 No	1986 %	1986 No	1987 %	1987 No	1989 %	1989 No
Question No		215a		218				B229a				B222a	
Column No		1077		1629				2154				2061	
(iv) {WIIMM} **West Indians**													
More settlement	1	1.9	31	2.2	33	-	-	2.2	29	-	-	1.7	22
Less settlement	2	66.7	1074	68.9	1049	-	-	64.3	846	-	-	61.5	772
About the same as now	3	28.4	458	26.0	395	-	-	32.0	421	-	-	34.1	428
(DK)	8	-	-	0.7	11	-	-	0.1	2	-	-	0.3	4
(NA)	9	3.0	48	2.3	34	-	-	1.3	18	-	-	2.4	30
Base: Self-completion questionnaire respondents			1610		1522				1315				1255

1983 - No (DK)

CONTROLS ON SETTLEMENT OF DEPENDENTS

{RELCONTL}

Question: Now thinking about the families (husbands, wives, children, parents) of people who have *already* settled in Britain, would you say in general that Britain should ... (please tick one box) ...

	Code	1983 %	1983 No	1984 %	1984 No	1985 %	1985 No	1986 %	1986 No	1987 %	1987 No	1989 %	1989 No
Question No		215b						B229b				B222b	
Column No		1078						2155				2062	
...be *stricter* in controlling the settlement of close relatives,	1	56.8	914	-	-	-	-	58.1	764	-	-	58.1	730
...or be *less strict* in controlling the settlement of close relatives,	2	8.4	135	-	-	-	-	9.8	129	-	-	9.2	116
...or keep the controls about the *same* as now?	3	34.0	547	-	-	-	-	30.5	401	-	-	30.3	380
(DK)	8	-	-	-	-	-	-	0.1	2	-	-	0.6	7
(NA)	9	0.9	14	-	-	-	-	1.5	20	-	-	1.8	22
Base: Self-completion questionnaire respondents			1610						1315				1255

1983 - No DK

ETHNIC ORIGIN (SELF-RATED)

1989   Q.A106/B125   {RACEORIG}   Column No 1380
[And now a few questions about yourself] (Show card) **To which of these groups do you
consider you belong?**

	Code	%	No
(Refused/NA)	0	0.2	7
Black : of *African* or *Carribean* or *other* origin	1	1.5	44
Asian : of *Indian* origin	2	0.8	25
Asian : of *Pakistani* origin	3	0.4	12
Asian : of *Bangladeshi* origin	4	-	-
Asian : of *Chinese* origin	5	0.1	2
Asian : of *other* origin	6	0.1	4
White : of *British* origin	7	92.1	2700
White : of *Irish* origin	8	2.8	82
White : of *other* origin	9	1.9	56
Base : All			2930

NB For interviewer-coded ethnic origin, see p. 0-1 above

ETHNIC GROUPS AGAINST WHICH RESPONDENT IS PREJUDICED - 2

1983   Q.80f   {RPREJBLK}{RPREJASN}{RPREJOTH}{RPREJNO} Column Nos 965-68 (variables derived
from Column Nos 612-17)
[If very or a little prejudiced against people of other races] **Against any race in particular?** (Interviewer :
probe and record. If 'black' or 'coloured' mentioned, probe for whether West Indian, Asian, general, etc)

	Code	%	No
{RPREJBLK} Column No 965			
Prejudiced against black people	1	5.4	93
(All other records)	0	94.6	1626
Base : All			1719
{RPREJASN} Column No 966			
Prejudiced against Asians	1	7.9	137
(All other records)	0	92.1	1582
Base : All			1719
{RPREJOTH} Column No 967			
Prejudiced against other ethnic group(s)	1	3.7	64
(All other records)	0	96.3	1655
Base : All			1719
{RPREJNO} Column No 968			
Prejudiced, but no information about which ethnic group	1	21.5	370
(All other records)	0	78.5	1349
Base : All			1719

NB More than one response was allowed at this question. For 1984-87 and 1989, see p. 0-4 above

P Social class

Table titles and cross references

EFFECT OF SOCIAL CLASS ON OPPORTUNITIES

{SCOPPORT}

Question: Now moving on to the subject of social class in Britain.

To what extent do you think a person's social class affects his or her opportunities in Britain today ... (read out) ...

		1983		1984		1985		1986		1987		1989	
		%	No	%	No	%	No	%	No	%	No	%	No
Question No		76b		73a		91a		66a		75a		80a	
Column No		567		534		728		561		659		772	
	Code												
... a great deal,	1	25.1	432	25.2	415	29.4	521	24.0	735	28.1	778	26.8	786
... quite a lot,	2	44.7	769	38.0	625	37.1	655	39.5	1211	38.6	1067	41.8	1226
... not very much,	3	24.6	422	28.0	461	26.7	472	28.3	869	26.5	734	24.9	728
... or not at all?	4	3.0	52	5.7	93	4.1	72	5.5	168	4.7	131	4.0	118
(Other answer)	7	0.2	4	0.8	13	1.0	18	0.4	12	0.4	11	0.1	2
(DK)	8	2.0	34	2.0	33	1.6	28	2.3	69	1.4	39	2.2	63
(NA)	9	0.3	6	0.4	6	0.1	2	0.1	3	0.2	5	0.3	8
Base: All			1719		1645		1769		3066		2766		2930

1983 - Other answer (5)

IMPORTANCE OF SOCIAL CLASS COMPARED WITH THE RECENT PAST

{SCIMPAGO}

Question: Do you think social class is *more* or *less* important now in affecting a person's opportunities than it was 10 years ago, or has there been no real change?

		1983		1984		1985		1986		1987		1989	
		%	No	%	No	%	No	%	No	%	No	%	No
Question No		76c		73b		91b		66b		75b		80b	
Column No		568		535		729		562		660		773	
	Code												
More important now	1	21.7	373	22.4	369	24.9	440	24.2	741	25.6	707	25.3	742
Less important now	2	30.3	520	29.7	489	27.8	492	29.5	905	28.5	788	30.0	879
No change	3	45.9	789	45.4	748	44.9	795	43.7	1341	43.4	1201	42.1	1233
(DK)	8	0.5	8	1.9	31	2.3	40	2.5	76	2.4	66	2.4	69
(NA)	9	1.6	28	0.5	8	0.1	2	0.1	3	0.1	3	0.2	7
Base: All			1719		1645		1769		3066		2766		2930

IMPORTANCE OF SOCIAL CLASS IN THE NEAR FUTURE

{SCIMPFUT}

Question: Do you think that in 10 years' time social class will be *more* or *less* important than it is now in affecting a person's opportunities, or will there be no real change?

		1983		1984		1985		1986		1987		1989	
		%	No	%	No	%	No	%	No	%	No	%	No
Question No		76d		73c		91c		66c		75c		80c	
Column No		569		536		730		563		661		774	
	Code												
More important in 10 years' time	1	16.0	275	18.9	310	22.3	395	20.7	635	23.7	656	23.6	693
Less important in 10 years' time	2	31.8	546	27.2	447	26.5	469	26.4	809	24.6	680	25.9	759
No change	3	49.3	847	50.0	823	47.9	847	48.4	1483	48.0	1327	46.4	1359
(Other)	7	-	.	-	.	0.1	2	-	.	-	.	-	.
(DK)	8	2.4	42	3.1	51	3.1	54	4.3	133	3.5	96	3.6	106
(NA)	9	0.5	9	0.9	14	0.2	3	0.2	6	0.2	6	0.4	12
Base: All			1719		1645		1769		3066		2766		2930

SOCIAL CLASS OF PARENTS

{PRSOCCL}

Question: (Show card) And which social class would you say your *parents* belonged to when you started at primary school?

		1983		1984		1985		1986		1987		1989	
		%	No	%	No	%	No	%	No	%	No	%	No
Question No		77b		74b				67b		76b		81b	
Column No		571		538				565		663		776	
	Code												
Upper middle	1	2.4	41	2.1	35	-	.	1.8	56	2.3	64	2.3	66
Middle	2	15.8	272	18.5	304	-	.	16.6	509	17.7	490	17.0	499
Upper working	3	12.4	213	10.5	172	-	.	12.2	374	12.1	336	11.2	330
Working	4	57.5	989	58.9	969	-	.	58.9	1805	59.1	1635	59.4	1742
Poor	5	9.1	157	8.0	132	-	.	8.2	252	6.8	188	8.5	248
(DK)	8	2.2	38	1.2	20	-	.	1.9	58	1.2	34	1.0	31
(NA)	9	0.5	8	0.8	13	-	.	0.4	11	0.7	19	0.5	14
Base: All			1719		1645				3066		2766		2930

1983, 1984, 1986, 1987 - Show card reads: Upper middle class, Middle class, Upper working class, Working class, Poor
1983 - (DK), Code 6

SOCIAL AND COMMUNITY SOLIDARITY

1989   Q.B233a-f   {CLSEBORN}{CLSECLAS}{CLSERELG}{CLSERACE}{CLSELIVE}{CLSEPOL} Column Nos 2252-57

People feel closer to some groups than to others. For *you personally*, how close would you say you feel towards ...
(please tick one box for each):

	Very close 1		Fairly close 2		A little close 3		Not very close 4		Not at all close 5		(DK) 8		(NA) 9	
Code	%	No	%	No	%	No	%	No	%	No	%	No	%	No
a) {CLSEBORN} Column No 2252														
People born in the same area as you	9.8	123	39.5	495	26.3	330	14.0	175	8.8	111	-	-	1.6	20
b) {CLSECLAS} Column No 2253														
People who have the same social background as yours	10.2	128	48.6	610	27.4	344	9.1	114	3.1	39	0.1	1	1.6	20
c) {CLSERELG} Column No 2254														
People who have the same religious background as yours	8.8	111	26.8	337	26.2	328	20.4	256	15.0	188	-	-	2.7	34
d) {CLSERACE} Column No 2255														
People of the same race as you	13.8	173	42.2	530	25.9	325	10.5	132	5.4	67	-	-	2.2	28
e) {CLSELIVE} Column No 2256														
People who live in the same area as you do now	8.9	112	37.2	467	32.2	404	14.8	186	5.3	66	-	-	1.6	20
f) {CLSEPOL} Column No 2257														
People who have the same political beliefs as you	7.0	87	27.1	340	30.8	387	20.9	263	11.5	145	0.2	2	2.5	31

Base : Self-completion respondents (n = 1255)

PRESENT JOB : RESPONDENT-CLASSIFIED - 1

Type of work

1987   Q.A226a-c   *{RSORTJOB}{REMPA}{RSVISOR}* Column Nos 1650-53

{RSORTJOB} Column Nos 1650-51
a) Please tick one box to show which *best* describes the sort of work you do. (If you are not working now, please tick a box to show what you did in your *last* job)

	Code	%	No
Farmer or farm manager	1	**1.1**	14
Farm worker	2	**1.1**	13
Skilled manual work (for example: plumber, electrician, fitter, train driver, cook, hairdresser	3	**14.4**	178
Semi-skilled or unskilled manual work (for example: machine operator, assembler, postman, waitress, cleaner, labourer)	4	**26.1**	324
Professional or technical work (for example: doctor, accountant, school teacher, social worker, computer programmer)	5	**18.5**	230
Manager or administrator (for example: company director, manager, executive officer, local authority officer)	6	**9.0**	111
Clerical (for example: clerk, secretary)	7	**15.2**	189
Sales (for example: commercial traveller, shop assistant)	8	**8.2**	101
(Never had a job)	9	**2.9**	36
(NA)	99	**3.6**	45
Base : Self-completion respondents			1243

Employment status

{REMPA} Column No 1652
b) Are you self-employed or do you work for someone else as an employee? (Please tick one box).
(If you are not working now, please answer about your *last* job)

	Code	%	No
Self-employed	1	**10.1**	126
Employee	2	**80.2**	997
Never had a job	3	**2.9**	36
(DK)	9	**6.7**	84
Base : Self-completion respondents			1243

Whether or not supervisor

{RSVISOR} Column No 1653
c) As your position at work, are you (or were you) ...(please tick one box) ...

	Code	%	No
... a supervisor or foreman of manual workers	1	**13.5**	168
a supervisor of non-manual workers	2	**15.3**	191
or - not a supervisor or foreman?	3	**61.4**	763
(Never had job)	4	**2.9**	36
(NA)	9	**6.9**	86
Base : Self-completion respondents			1243

NB   A slightly different version of Q.A226a-c was asked on the B version of the 1987 self-completion questionnaire (see p. P-10 below)

FACTORS HELPING A PERSON TO GET AHEAD IN LIFE

1987   Q.B201a-m   {AHEAD1} - {AHEAD13} Column Nos 1709-21

[To begin,] we have some questions about opportunities for getting ahead.
(Please tick one box for each of these to show *how important you think it is for getting ahead in life*.)

		Essential		Very important		Fairly important		Not very important		Not important at all		Can't choose		(NA)	
	Code	1		2		3		4		5		8		9	
		%	No	%	No	%	No	%	No	%	No	%	No	%	No
a) {AHEAD1} Column No 1709 First, how important is coming from a wealthy family		4.1	49	16.4	194	33.3	394	30.0	355	13.9	164	1.6	19	0.6	7
b) {AHEAD2} Column No 1710 Having well educated parents		3.3	39	23.5	278	45.1	533	19.5	230	7.3	86	0.9	10	0.4	5
c) {AHEAD3} Column No 1711 Having a good education yourself		23.4	276	48.4	572	23.8	281	2.8	33	0.7	8	0.5	6	0.5	6
d) {AHEAD4} Column No 1712 Ambition		37.6	444	41.8	494	16.7	198	2.1	25	0.7	8	0.5	6	0.5	6
e) {AHEAD5} Column No 1713 Natural ability - how important is that for getting ahead in life		14.4	170	42.6	503	37.3	441	4.0	48	0.7	8	0.8	9	0.2	2
f) {AHEAD6} Column No 1714 Hard work - how important is that		35.7	422	47.8	564	13.7	162	1.4	17	0.7	9	0.3	4	0.3	3
g) {AHEAD7} Column No 1715 Knowing the right people		13.0	153	26.4	312	40.7	480	16.8	199	2.7	32	0.2	2	0.2	3
h) {AHEAD8} Column No 1716 Having political connections		2.1	25	4.8	57	13.7	161	47.7	563	28.3	334	3.3	39	0.1	2
i) {AHEAD9} Column No 1717 A person's race - how important is that for getting ahead in life		2.6	30	13.6	161	30.8	364	31.3	369	18.2	215	3.4	41	0.1	1
j) {AHEAD10} Column No 1718 A person's religion		1.9	22	3.4	41	8.5	101	39.7	469	45.3	535	0.9	11	0.1	2
k) {AHEAD11} Column No 1719 The part of the country a person comes from		1.0	12	6.3	74	20.6	244	40.7	481	30.1	356	1.2	14	0.1	1
l) {AHEAD12} Column No 1720 Being born a man or a woman - how important is that		1.8	21	9.5	113	21.5	254	32.3	382	30.2	357	4.2	50	0.4	5
m) {AHEAD13} Column No 1721 A person's political beliefs, how important are they for getting ahead in life		0.9	10	4.0	47	18.4	217	47.6	562	26.3	310	2.5	29	0.5	6

Base : Self-completion respondents (n = 1181)

EXTENT OF CONTACT BETWEEN SOCIAL GROUPS

1987   Q.B210a-f   {CONFLIC1} - {CONFLIC6}   Column Nos 1945-50

In all countries there are differences or even conflicts between different social groups. In your opinion, in Britain how much conflict is there between ... (please tick one box on each line):

	Very strong conflicts		Strong conflicts		Not very strong conflicts		There are no conflicts		Can't choose		(NA)	
Code	1		2		3		4		8		9	
	%	No	%	No	%	No	%	No	%	No	%	No
a) {CONFLIC1} Column No 1945 Poor people and rich people	13.2	155	37.6	444	39.2	462	5.0	60	3.6	42	1.4	16
b) {CONFLIC2} Column No 1946 The working class and the middle class	3.5	42	15.6	184	62.3	736	13.2	155	3.2	38	2.3	27
c) {CONFLIC3} Column No 1947 The unemployed and people with jobs	8.2	97	29.4	347	43.2	510	12.2	144	4.0	48	2.9	34
d) {CONFLIC4} Column No 1948 Management and workers	9.2	109	43.5	514	37.5	443	3.9	46	3.4	41	2.4	28
e) {CONFLIC5} Column No 1949 Farmers and city people	4.3	51	21.2	250	45.1	533	21.2	250	5.9	70	2.2	26
f) {CONFLIC6} Column No 1950 Young people and older people	7.0	83	28.9	341	43.4	513	14.3	169	4.5	54	1.8	22

Base : Self-completion respondents (n = 1181)

SELF-RATED POSITION IN THE SOCIAL STRUCTURE

1987   Q.B211   {SOCSCALE} Column Nos 1951-52

In our society there are groups which tend to be towards the top and groups which tend to be towards the bottom. Below is a scale that runs from top to bottom. Where would you put yourself on this scale? (Please tick one box)

	Code	%	No
Top	1	0.8	10
	2	1.6	19
	3	4.9	58
	4	11.4	135
	5	29.3	346
	6	18.5	218
	7	12.7	149
	8	9.7	114
	9	3.2	38
Bottom	10	3.5	41
(Refused)	97	0.1	1
(DK)	98	0.5	6
(NA)	99	3.8	45
Base : Self-completion respondents			1181

NB Points 2-9 of this scale were not labelled.

STATUS OF OWN JOB COMPARED WITH FATHER'S

1987   Q.B212   *{RJOBFJOB}* Column No 1953
Please think of your present job (or the last one if you don't have one now).
If you compare this job with the job your father had when you were 16, would you say that the level or
status of *your* job is (*or was*) ... (please tick one box) ...

	Code	%	No
... much higher than your father's,	1	16.4	194
higher,	2	29.7	350
about equal,	3	25.9	306
lower,	4	16.6	197
much lower than your father's?	5	4.2	50
(I never had a job)	6	2.4	28
(Never knew father/father never had a job)	7	1.9	22
(DK)	8	0.6	7
(NA)	9	2.4	28
Base : Self-completion respondents			1181

FATHER'S JOB : RESPONDENT-CLASSIFIED

Occupation

1987   Q.B213a,b   *{FTYPEJOB}{FEMP}* Column Nos 1954-55, 1956

{FTYPEJOB} Column Nos 1954-55
a) Here is a list of different types of jobs. Which type did your *father* have when you were 16?
(If your father did not have a job then, please give the job he used to have) (Please tick one box)

	Code	%	No
Professional and technical (for example: doctor, teacher, engineer, artist, accountant)	1	9.0	106
Higher administrator (for example: banker, executive in big business, high government official, union official)	2	4.4	52
Clerical (for example: secretary, clerk, office manager, bookkeeper)	3	7.3	86
Sales (for example: sales manager, shop owner, shop assistant, insurance agent)	4	7.8	92
Service (for example: restaurant owner, police officer, waiter, barber, caretaker)	5	4.7	56
Skilled worker (for example: foreman, motor mechanic, printer, tool and die maker, electrician	6	22.1	261
Semi-skilled worker (for example: bricklayer, bus driver, cannery worker, carpenter, sheet metal worker, baker)	7	19.4	229
Unskilled worker (for example: labourer, porter, unskilled factory worker)	8	12.3	145
Farm (for example: farmer, farm labourer, tractor driver)	9	5.8	69
(Never knew father/father never had a job)	10	2.7	32
(DK)	98	0.1	1
(NA)	99	4.5	53
Base : Self-completion respondents			1181

Employment status

{FEMP} Column No 1956
b) Was your father self-employed, or did he work for someone else? (Please tick one box)

	Code	%	No
Self-employed, had own business or farm	1	17.4	205
Worked for someone else	2	74.3	878
(Never knew father/father never had a job)	3	2.6	31
(DK)	8	0.1	1
(NA)	9	5.6	66
Base : Self-completion respondents			1181

FIRST JOB : RESPONDENT-CLASSIFIED

Type of work

1987   Q.B214a,b   {RITYPEJB}{RIEMP} Column Nos 1958-59, 1960

{RITYPEJB} Column Nos 1958-59
a) [And] how about your *first* job - the first job you had after you finished full-time education?
(Even if it was many years ago, we would still like to know about it). (Please tick one box)

	Code	%	No
Professional and technical (for example: doctor, teacher, engineer, artist, accountant)	1	12.4	146
Higher administrator (for example: banker, executive in big business, high government official, union official)	2	0.5	6
Clerical (for example: secretary, clerk, office manager, bookkeeper)	3	22.3	264
Sales (for example: sales manager, shop owner, shop assistant, insurance agent)	4	12.6	148
Service (for example: restaurant owner, police officer, barber, waitress, caretaker)	5	6.0	71
Skilled worker (for example: foreman, motor mechanic, printer, seamstress, electrician	6	12.4	147
Semi-skilled worker (for example: bricklayer, bus driver, cannery worker, carpenter, sheet metal worker, baker)	7	8.9	105
Unskilled worker (for example: labourer, porter, unskilled factory worker)	8	17.1	202
Farm (for example: farmer, farm labourer, tractor driver)	9	3.2	38
(Never had a job)	10	2.8	33
(NA)	99	1.8	21
Base : All			1181

Employment status

{RIEMP} Column No 1960
Were you self-employed, or did you work for someone else? (Please tick one box)

	Code	%	No
Self-employed, had own business or farm	1	1.9	23
Worked for someone else	2	88.8	1049
(Never had a job)	3	2.7	32
(NA)	9	6.5	77
Base : All			1181

PRESENT JOB : RESPONDENT-CLASSIFIED - 2

1987   Q.B215a,b   *{RTYPEJOB}{REMPB}*   Column No 1963-64, 1965

Occupation

{RTYPEJOB} Column Nos 1963-4
a) [And] how about your job *now*? (Please tick one box) (If you are not working now, please tell us about your *last* job)

	Code	%	No
Professional and technical (for example: doctor, teacher, engineer, artist, accountant)	1	18.0	212
Higher administrator (for example: banker, executive in big business, high government official, union official)	2	2.9	34
Clerical (for example: secretary, clerk, office manager, bookkeeper)	3	17.4	206
Sales (for example: sales manager, shop owner, shop assistant, insurance agent)	4	11.7	138
Service (for example: restaurant owner, police officer, waitress, barber, caretaker)	5	8.5	100
Skilled worker (for example: foreman, motor mechanic, printer, seamstress, electrician)	6	13.7	162
Semi-skilled worker (for example: bricklayer, bus driver, cannery worker, carpenter, sheet metal worker, baker)	7	9.7	115
Unskilled worker (for example: labourer, porter, unskilled factory worker)	8	10.5	124
Farm (for example: farmer, farm labourer, tractor driver)	9	1.7	21
(Never knew father/father never had a job)	10	2.9	35
(NA)	99	3.0	35
Base : Self-completion respondents			1181

Employment status

{REMPB} Column No 1965
b) Are you self-employed, or do you work for someone else? (Please tick one box)

	Code	%	No
Self-employed, have own business or farm	1	10.4	122
Work for someone else	2	78.5	927
(Never had a job)	3	2.9	34
(NA)	9	8.3	98
Base : Self-completion respondents			1181

AWARENESS OF CLASS DIFFERENCES

1983   Q.76a   *{SCAWARE}*   Column No 566
To what extent do you think people are aware of social class differences in Britain today ... (read out) ...

	Code	%	No
... very aware,	1	29.3	503
quite aware,	2	43.0	740
not very aware,	3	20.4	351
or not at all aware?	4	3.2	56
(DK)	5	3.8	65
(NA)	9	0.3	5
Base : All			1719

RESPONDENT: REGISTRAR GENERAL'S SOCIAL CLASS

{RRGCLASS}

Variable derived from occupational details collected

		1983		1984		1985		1986		1987		1989	
		%	No	%	No	%	No	%	No	%	No	%	No
Column No				1667		939		2347		2245		2363	
	Code												
Never had a job	0	-	.	9.4	154	7.4	131	7.8	238	4.8	132	4.1	122
Social class I	1	2.5	43	2.6	44	3.4	61	3.4	105	3.8	105	4.1	119
Social class II	2	16.9	291	18.1	298	18.9	335	19.9	609	22.4	619	21.0	615
Social class III (non-manual)	3	15.6	268	23.0	378	22.2	393	23.5	722	22.9	634	23.7	695
Social class III (manual)	4	21.2	365	22.4	369	20.7	366	20.5	628	20.6	570	21.7	637
Social class IV	5	12.7	218	17.1	281	18.3	324	17.7	542	17.7	491	18.4	540
Social class V	6	4.7	81	6.0	99	6.8	120	5.2	161	5.7	159	5.1	149
[Not coded: outside labour market]	7	20.1	346	-	.	-	.	-	.	-	.	-	.
Insufficient information to classify	9	6.2	106	1.4	23	2.2	39	2.0	62	2.0	55	1.8	54
Base: All			1719		1645		1769		3066		2766		2930

1983 - 1987, 1989 - Based on current or last job held

1983 - Respondents coded as 'in full-time education', 'permanently sick or disabled', 'looking after the home' or 'doing something else' were not asked for
their occupational details; and code 9 included those who had never had a job (separate code 0 in subsequent years). So data for 1983 are not
comparable with those for 1984 onwards

RESPONDENT: REGISTRAR GENERAL'S SOCIO-ECONOMIC GROUP

{RSEG}

Variable derived from occupational details collected

	Code	1983 %	1983 No	1984 %	1984 No	1985 %	1985 No	1986 %	1986 No	1987 %	1987 No	1989 %	1989 No
Column No		828-29		861-62		932-33		1639-40		1339-40		1573-74	
Never had a job	0	4.5	77	9.4	154	7.4	131	7.8	238	4.8	132	4.1	122
Employers and managers in central and local government, industry, commerce, etc - large establishments	1	4.1	71	3.0	49	4.4	79	5.5	169	5.5	152	5.3	155
Employers and managers in industry, commerce, etc - small establishments	2	5.9	101	7.2	119	6.6	116	6.3	193	6.4	177	6.4	187
Professional workers - self-employed	3	0.6	10	0.3	5	0.7	12	0.8	25	0.4	10	0.7	21
Professional workers - employees	4	1.9	34	2.3	39	2.7	48	2.6	81	3.5	96	3.4	98
Intermediate non-manual workers	5	10.8	186	13.4	220	10.9	193	11.9	365	12.0	331	12.3	360
Junior non-manual workers	6	11.5	199	17.8	294	19.9	353	20.0	614	20.6	570	20.9	613
Professional service workers	7	3.4	58	6.3	104	5.9	104	6.5	200	5.8	161	6.8	199
Foremen and supervisors - manual	8	5.8	99	7.0	115	2.9	51	3.8	115	2.6	71	3.6	106
Skilled manual workers	9	11.7	201	11.0	181	13.2	233	12.0	368	13.2	366	12.7	371
Semi-skilled manual workers	10	9.2	159	11.3	185	11.4	201	11.7	359	11.9	328	11.5	337
Unskilled manual workers	11	4.6	79	5.9	97	6.5	115	5.1	156	5.6	154	4.7	137
Self-employed workers (other than professional)	12	2.9	50	2.1	34	4.0	72	2.8	86	4.1	113	4.7	137
Farmers (employers and managers)	13	0.4	8	0.3	5	0.2	3	0.2	7	0.4	11	0.2	6
Farmers - own account	14	0.1	2	0.3	5	0.3	5	0.2	6	0.3	8	0.1	3
Agricultural workers	15	0.6	11	0.9	14	0.7	12	0.7	20	1.0	29	0.7	21
Members of armed forces	16	0.2	3	0.1	2	0.3	5	0.3	9	0.6	16	0.5	14
Insufficient information to classify	17	1.6	28	1.4	23	2.1	37	1.8	55	1.5	42	1.5	43
[Not coded: outside labour market]	18	20.1	346	-	-	-	-	-	-	-	-	-	-
Base: All			1719		1645		1769		3066		2766		2930

1983 - 1987, 1989 -   Based on current or last job held

1983 -   Respondents coded as 'in full-time education', 'permanently sick or disabled', 'looking after the home' or 'doing something else' were not asked for their occupational details, so data for this year are not comparable with those for subsequent years

RESPONDENT: REGISTRAR GENERAL'S SOCIO-ECONOMIC GROUP (COMPRESSED)

{RSEGGRP}

Variable derived from occupational details collected

		1983		1984		1985		1986		1987		1989	
		%	No	%	No	%	No	%	No	%	No	%	No
Column No				1660		938		2343		2241		2361	
	Code												
Never had a job	0	-	-	9.4	154	7.4	131	7.8	238	4.8	132	4.1	122
Professional workers	1	-	-	2.6	44	3.4	60	3.4	105	3.8	105	4.1	119
Employees and managers	2	-	-	10.5	173	11.2	198	12.1	370	12.3	339	11.9	349
Intermediate (non-manual)	3	-	-	13.4	220	10.9	193	11.9	365	12.0	331	12.3	360
Junior (non-manual)	4	-	-	17.8	294	19.9	353	20.0	614	20.6	570	20.9	613
Skilled (manual)	5	-	-	20.4	336	20.4	361	18.8	576	20.2	557	21.0	617
Semi-skilled (manual)	6	-	-	18.5	304	17.9	317	18.9	579	18.7	518	18.3	536
Unskilled (manual)	7	-	-	5.9	97	6.5	115	5.1	156	5.6	154	5.4	159
Other occupation	8	-	-	0.1	2	0.3	5	0.3	9	0.6	16	0.5	14
Insufficient information to classify	9	-	-	1.4	23	2.1	37	1.8	55	1.5	42	1.5	43
Base: All					1645		1769		3066		2766		2930

1984 - 1987, 1989 - Based on current or last job held

RESPONDENT: GOLDTHORPE CLASS SCHEMA

{RGHCLASS}

Variable derived from occupational details collected.

		1983		1984		1985		1986		1987		1989	
		%	No	%	No	%	No	%	No	%	No	%	No
Column No								1645-46		1345-46		1579-80	
	Code												
Never had a job	0	-	-	-	-	-	-	7.8	238	4.8	132	4.1	122
SALARIAT:													
- professional and managerial (higher grade)	1	-	-	-	-	-	-	8.5	260	9.3	258	9.1	266
- professional and managerial (lower grade)	2	-	-	-	-	-	-	13.7	420	14.3	395	14.4	423
ROUTINE NON-MANUAL WORKERS:													
- routine office workers	3	-	-	-	-	-	-	15.4	472	16.7	463	17.1	503
- sales and personal service workers	4	-	-	-	-	-	-	6.4	196	5.1	141	5.4	159
PETTY BOURGEOISIE:													
- small proprietors with employees	5	-	-	-	-	-	-	3.1	95	2.8	77	2.8	82
- small proprietors with no employees	6	-	-	-	-	-	-	2.7	83	3.8	106	4.6	134
- farmers and smallholders	7	-	-	-	-	-	-	0.5	14	0.8	22	0.3	10
LOWER TECHNICIANS AND FOREMEN/ SUPERVISORS	8	-	-	-	-	-	-	6.0	183	4.6	127	6.0	176
WORKING CLASS:													
- skilled manual workers	9	-	-	-	-	-	-	10.4	318	11.5	319	10.9	321
- semi-skilled/unskilled manual workers	10	-	-	-	-	-	-	23.3	714	23.8	657	23.0	674
- agricultural workers (employees)	11	-	-	-	-	-	-	0.6	19	0.9	25	0.7	21
Insufficient information to classify	99	-	-	-	-	-	-	1.7	54	1.5	42	1.5	43
Base: All									3066		2766		2930

1986, 1987, 1989 - Based on current or last job held

SELF-RATED SOCIAL CLASS

{SRSOCCL}

Question: (Show card) Most people see themselves as belonging to a particular social class. Please look at this card and tell me which social class you would say *you* belong to?

		1983		1984		1985		1986		1987		1989	
		%	No	%	No	%	No	%	No	%	No	%	No
Question No		77a		74a		92		67a		76a		81a	
Column No		537		731		564		564		662		775	
	Code												
Upper middle	1	1.4	25	1.7	28	1.5	26	1.2	38	1.5	41	1.4	40
Middle	2	24.2	416	25.0	411	26.4	467	24.4	749	26.0	719	28.0	821
Upper working	3	23.2	400	19.4	319	18.5	327	20.8	637	21.3	589	21.4	628
Working	4	45.6	783	47.9	789	47.4	838	47.8	1464	46.0	1272	44.1	1291
Poor	5	2.5	43	2.8	47	3.5	62	3.2	98	2.9	80	2.6	77
(DK)	8	2.7	47	2.2	36	2.3	41	2.0	62	1.4	38	1.8	52
(NA)	9	0.4	7	1.0	17	0.4	8	0.6	17	0.9	26	0.7	21
			—		—		—		—		—		—
Base: All			1719		1645		1769		3066		2766		2930

1983 - 1987 - Show card reads: Upper middle class, Middle class, Upper working class, Working class, Poor

1983 - (DK), Code 6

SPOUSE/PARTNER: REGISTRAR GENERAL'S SOCIAL CLASS

{SRGCLASS}

Variable derived from occupational details collected

	Code	1983 %	No	1984 %	No	1985 %	No	1986 %	No	1987 %	No	1989 %	No
Column No						1021		2349		2247		2364	
[Not coded: not married/living as married; spouse/partner never had a job or last job more than 20 years ago]	0	-	-	-	-	39.9	706	35.9	1100	35.5	981	31.4	921
Social class I	1	-	-	2.5	41	2.8	49	3.3	101	2.7	74	3.1	91
Social class II	2	-	-	14.0	230	12.3	218	14.0	429	15.9	441	15.9	467
Social class III (non-manual)	3	-	-	14.8	244	14.7	261	15.3	470	14.7	408	17.0	499
Social class III (manual)	4	-	-	15.8	259	15.3	271	15.3	470	15.4	427	15.3	448
Social class IV	5	-	-	11.1	183	10.9	193	11.6	357	11.7	324	11.7	344
Social class V	6	-	-	3.8	62	3.1	54	3.3	101	3.2	87	3.5	103
Insufficient information to classify	9	-	-	38.0	626	1.0	17	1.3	39	0.9	24	2.0	58
Base: All					1645		1769		3066		2766		2930

1984 - Respondents whose spouse/partner was not economically active were not asked for information about their spouse's/partner's present (or last) job. So there was no information by which to code the social class of spouses/partners outside the labour market

1984 - 1987, 1989 - Based on current or last job held

1985 - 1987, 1989 - Respondents were not asked for information about their spouse's/partner's job, if they left their last one more than twenty years ago

SPOUSE/PARTNER: REGISTRAR GENERAL'S SOCIO-ECONOMIC GROUP

{SSEG}

Variable derived from occupational details collected

		1983		1984		1985		1986		1987		1989	
		%	No	%	No	%	No	%	No	%	No	%	No
Column No				934-35		1014-15		1715-16		1415-16		1642-43	
	Code												
[Not coded: not married/living as married; spouse/partner never had a job or last job more than 20 years ago]	0	-	-	36.4	598	39.9	706	35.9	1102	35.5	981	31.4	921
Employers and managers in central and local government, industry, commerce etc. - large establishments	1	-	-	3.2	52	3.4	61	4.0	122	4.2	117	4.0	118
Employers and managers in industry, commerce etc - small establishments	2	-	-	4.6	76	3.8	67	3.8	115	5.4	151	5.3	154
Professional workers - self-employed	3	-	-	0.3	5	0.5	9	0.8	23	0.5	13	0.6	17
Professional workers - employees	4	-	-	2.2	36	2.2	39	2.5	77	2.2	61	2.5	74
Intermediate non-manual workers	5	-	-	7.7	127	6.8	121	8.0	245	7.6	211	8.0	234
Junior non-manual workers	6	-	-	12.4	204	12.6	223	13.1	401	13.1	361	15.1	443
Personal service workers	7	-	-	3.6	58	3.4	60	4.0	124	3.7	103	4.3	126
Foremen and supervisors - manual	8	-	-	4.0	65	2.7	48	3.1	95	2.2	60	1.7	51
Skilled manual workers	9	-	-	8.2	135	9.8	174	8.3	256	9.6	265	9.4	276
Semi-skilled manual workers	10	-	-	7.7	127	7.6	135	7.7	237	7.5	208	7.7	224
Unskilled manual workers	11	-	-	3.6	60	2.9	51	3.1	95	3.0	84	3.4	99
Self-employed workers (other than professional)	12	-	-	2.3	38	2.5	44	3.0	92	3.3	90	3.7	108
Farmers (employers and managers)	13	-	-	0.6	10	0.1	2	0.3	8	0.2	7	0.2	5
Farmers - own account	14	-	-	0.4	7	0.3	5	0.3	8	0.2	5	0.1	3
Agricultural workers	15	-	-	0.7	11	0.3	5	0.4	13	0.5	14	0.3	9
Members of armed forces	16	-	-	0.3	5	0.2	4	0.4	11	0.2	6	0.4	13
Insufficient information to classify	17	-	-	1.8	29	0.9	15	1.3	41	1.0	28	1.8	53
Base: All					1645		1769		3066		2766		2930

1984-1987, 1989 - Based on current or last job held

1985 - 1987, 1989 - Respondents were not asked for information about their spouse's/partner's job, if they left their last one more than twenty years ago

SPOUSE/PARTNER: REGISTRAR GENERAL'S SOCIO-ECONOMIC GROUP (COMPRESSED)

{SSEGGRP}

Variable derived from occupational details collected

		1983		1984		1985		1986		1987		1989	
		%	No	%	No	%	No	%	No	%	No	%	No
Column No							1020		2345		2243		2362	
	Code												
[Not coded: not married/living as married; spouse/partner never had a job or last job more than 20 years ago]	0	-	-	-	-	39.9	706	35.9	1100	35.5	981	31.4	921
Professional workers	1	-	-	2.5	41	2.8	49	3.3	101	2.7	74	3.1	91
Employers and managers	2	-	-	8.4	138	7.3	129	8.1	247	9.9	275	9.5	277
Intermediate (non-manual)	3	-	-	7.7	127	6.8	121	8.0	245	7.6	211	8.0	234
Junior (non-manual)	4	-	-	12.4	204	12.6	223	13.1	401	13.1	361	15.1	443
Skilled (manual)	5	-	-	14.9	246	15.3	271	14.7	452	15.2	421	15.0	439
Semi-skilled (manual)	6	-	-	11.9	196	11.3	200	12.2	374	11.7	325	12.0	350
Unskilled (manual)	7	-	-	3.6	60	2.9	51	3.1	95	3.0	84	3.7	108
Other occupation	8	-	-	2.1	34	0.2	4	0.4	11	0.2	6	0.4	13
Insufficient information to classify	9	-	-	36.4	598	0.9	15	1.3	41	1.0	28	1.8	53
Base: All					1645		1769		3066		2766		2930

1984 - Respondents whose spouse/partner was not economically active were not asked for information about their spouse's/partner's present (or last) job. So there was no information by which to code the social class of spouses/partners outside the labour market. Those cases for which no information was collected (no spouse/partner, spouse/partner never had a job) were coded as 9, not separately as 0 as in subsequent years

1984 - 1987, 1989 - Based on current or last job held

SPOUSE/PARTNER: GOLDTHORPE CLASS SCHEMA

{SGHCLASS}

Variable derived from occupational details collected.

		1983		1984		1985		1986		1987		1989	
		%	No	%	No	%	No	%	No	%	No	%	No
Question No								1721-22		1421-22		1648-49	
Column No													
	Code												
[Not coded: not married/living as married; spouse/partner never had a job or last job more than 20 years ago]	0	-	.	-	.	-	.	35.9	1100	35.5	981	31.4	921
SALARIAT:		-	.	-	.	-	.						
- professional and managerial (higher grade)	1	-	.	-	.	-	.	7.2	222	6.9	190	7.5	220
- professional and managerial (lower grade)	2	-	.	-	.	-	.	9.1	279	9.0	248	9.7	286
ROUTINE NON-MANUAL WORKERS:													
- routine office workers	3	-	.	-	.	-	.	9.8	302	9.7	269	12.0	352
- sales and personal service workers	4	-	.	-	.	-	.	3.9	121	4.2	117	4.0	118
PETTY BOURGEOISIE:													
- small proprietors with employees	5	-	.	-	.	-	.	2.0	62	3.2	88	2.4	70
- small proprietors with no employees	6	-	.	-	.	-	.	2.9	90	3.2	88	3.6	105
- farmers and smallholders	7	-	.	-	.	-	.	0.6	17	0.5	13	0.4	11
LOWER TECHNICIANS AND FOREMEN/ SUPERVISORS	8	-	.	-	.	-	.	4.7	144	3.4	94	3.5	102
WORKING CLASS:													
- skilled manual workers	9	-	.	-	.	-	.	6.7	206	7.8	216	7.6	224
- semi-skilled/unskilled manual workers	10	-	.	-	.	-	.	15.5	474	15.2	421	15.9	466
- agricultural workers (employees)	11	-	.	-	.	-	.	0.4	11	0.5	14	0.2	7
Insufficient information to classify	99	-	.	-	.	-	.	1.2	37	0.9	26	1.7	49
Base: All									3066		2766		2930

1986, 1987, 1989 - Based on current or last job held. Respondents were not asked for information about their spouse's/partner's job, if they left their last one more than twenty years ago

Q Religion

Table titles and cross references

RELIGIOUS AFFILIATION

{RELIGION}

Question: Do you regard yourself as belonging to any particular religion? [If yes] Which?

		1983		1984		1985		1986		1987		1989	
		%	No	%	No	%	No	%	No	%	No	%	No
Question No		79a		75a		93a		68a		77a		82a	
Column No		574-75		539-40		732-33		566-67		664-65		808-09	
(i) *{RELIGION}* **Self**	Code												
No religion	1	31.3	538	32.2	530	34.3	607	33.9	1041	34.3	949	34.4	1009
Christian - no denomination	2	3.1	54	1.7	29	2.8	49	2.8	87	3.4	93	3.2	93
Roman Catholic	3	9.6	164	12.1	199	10.6	187	10.2	314	10.3	284	11.1	326
Church of England/Anglican	4	39.8	684	39.4	649	35.8	633	37.1	1139	36.6	1013	36.7	1074
Baptist	5	1.3	23	1.5	25	1.8	31	1.7	52	1.7	47	1.3	39
Methodist	6	4.4	75	2.9	48	4.1	72	3.3	101	4.2	115	4.0	117
Presbyterian/Church of Scotland	7	4.9	85	5.2	85	5.3	93	4.4	136	4.5	125	4.5	133
Free Presbyterian	21	-	.	-	.	-	.	-	.	-	.	0.1	4
Brethren	22	-	.	-	.	-	.	-	.	-	.	0.1	2
United Reform Church (URC)/ Congregational	23	1.2	21	1.0	17	0.9	15	1.4	43	0.9	24	1.0	31
Other Protestant	27	-	.	-	.	-	.	-	.	-	.	0.9	27
Other Christian	8	2.1	35	1.6	27	2.1	37	2.2	67	1.6	44	0.7	22
Hindu	9	0.4	8	0.5	9	0.7	12	0.8	24	0.4	12	0.2	6
Jewish	10	0.6	11	0.4	7	0.4	7	0.4	13	0.8	21	0.4	12
Islam/Muslim	11	0.6	10	0.3	5	0.6	11	1.0	30	0.8	23	0.4	13
Sikh	12	0.2	3	0.2	3	0.2	3	0.2	6	0.1	1	0.2	7
Buddhist	13	-	.	-	.	0.1	1	0.2	6	0.1	2	0.1	4
Other non-Christian	14	0.2	3	0.3	5	0.3	5	0.2	6	0.3	9	0.3	8
Refused/unwilling to say	97	-	.	-	.	-	.	-	.	-	.	0.1	2
(DK)	98	-	.	-	.	0.0	1	0.0	1	-	.	-	.
(NA)	99	0.3	6	0.4	7	0.3	5	-	.	0.1	3	0.1	3
Base: All			1719		1645		1769		3066		2766		2930

1983 - United Reform Church (URC)/Congregational, code 5; Baptist, code 6; Methodist, code 7; Presbyterian/Church of Scotland, code 8; Other Christian, code 9; Hindu, code 13; Jew, code 14; Muslim, code 15; Sikh, code 16; Buddhist, code 17; Other non-Christian, code 18. Free Presbyterian, Brethren, Other Protestant, Refused/unwilling to say, (DK) - all not included

1984-1987 inclusive - Hindu, code 10; Jew, code 11; Islam/Muslim, code 12; Sikh, code 13; Buddhist, code 14; Other non-Christian, code 15; Free Presbyterian, Brethren, Other Protestant, Refused/unwilling to say - all not included

RELIGIOUS ATTENDANCE - 1

{ATTENDCH}

Question: [If belongs to any religion] Apart from such special occasions as weddings, funerals and baptisms, how often nowadays do you attend services or meetings connected with your religion? (Probe as necessary)

		1983		1984		1985		1986		1987		1989	
		%	No	%	No	%	No	%	No	%	No	%	No
Question No		79c		75b		93b		68b		77b			
Column No		578		541-42		734-35		568-69		666-67			
	Code												
[Not asked: does not belong to any religion]	0	31.3	538	32.2	530	34.3	607	33.9	1041	34.3	949	-	-
Once a week or more	1	13.0	224	12.2	201	11.1	197	12.5	385	11.9	330	-	-
Less often but at least once in two weeks	2	2.6	44	2.5	42	2.2	39	2.5	76	2.4	66	-	-
Less often but at least once a month	3	5.6	96	5.4	89	6.1	107	5.4	165	5.8	162	-	-
Less often but at least twice a year	4	10.1	174	11.9	196	10.8	190	10.2	314	11.7	323	-	-
Less often but at least once a year	5	5.8	100	6.6	108	5.7	100	5.2	159	4.9	136	-	-
Less often	6	6.1	105	4.9	80	5.8	103	4.5	137	3.8	105	-	-
Never or practically never	7	24.2	416	23.3	384	23.4	413	24.8	760	24.4	675	-	-
Varies too much to say	8	0.5	9	0.5	9	0.2	4	0.5	17	0.4	11	-	-
Refused/unwilling to answer	97	-	-	-	-	-	-	-	-	-	-	-	-
(DK)	98	-	-	-	-	-	-	-	-	-	-	-	-
(NA)	99	0.7	13	0.4	7	0.5	8	0.4	13	0.4	10	-	-
Base: All			1719		1645		1769		3066		2766		

1983 - No (DK); (NA), code 9

1983-1987 inclusive - Varies, code 8; No Refused/unwilling to answer, code 97

1989 - This question was also asked of those who said that they were brought up in a religion: see p.Q - 3 below, where the variable name has been changed to {CHATTEND}

RELIGION IN CHILDHOOD

1989   Q.82b   {*RELIGFAM*} Column Nos 810-11
[If does not belong to any particular religion] In what religion were you brought up? (Interviewer: probe if necessary)
What was your family's religion? (Interviewer: do not prompt)

	Code	%	No
[Not asked : belongs to a religion]	0	65.6	1922
No religion	1	5.3	156
Christian - no denomination	2	0.9	27
Roman Catholic	3	2.8	82
Church of England/Anglican	4	19.4	569
Baptist	5	0.6	17
Methodist	6	1.9	57
Presbyterian/Church of Scotland	7	2.0	59
Other Christian	8	0.1	4
Hindu	9	0.1	2
Jewish	10	0.1	3
Islam/Muslim	11	-	-
Sikh	12	-	-
Buddhist	13	-	-
Other non-Christian	14	-	-
Free Presbyterian	21	0.1	2
Brethren	22	-	-
United Reform Church (URC)/ Congregational	23	0.3	10
Other Protestant	27	0.4	13
Refused/unwilling to say	97	0.2	6
(NA)	99	0.2	5
Base : All			2930

RELIGIOUS ATTENDANCE - 2

1989   Q.82c   {*CHATTEND*} Column Nos 812-13

[If belongs to, or brought up in, any religion] Apart from such special occasions as weddings, funerals and baptisms, how
often nowadays do you attend services or meetings connected with your religion? (Probe as necessary)

	Code	%	No
[Not asked : does not belong to, or was not brought up in, any religion]	0	5.3	156
Once a week or more	1	13.0	382
Less often but at least once in two weeks	2	2.7	78
Less often but at least once a month	3	5.3	154
Less often but at least twice a year	4	12.0	351
Less often but at least once a year	5	6.1	180
Less often	6	5.8	169
Never or pratically never	7	47.6	1396
Varies too much to say	8	0.6	18
Refused/unwilling to answer	97	0.1	4
(DK)	98	-	-
(NA)	99	1.4	42
Base : All			2930

NB Between 1983 and 1987 this question was asked only of those who said that they did not belong to any religion (see p. Q-2 above). Since the 1989
figures are not comparable with the earlier ones, the variable name for 1989 has been changed from {ATTENDCH} to {CHATTEND}

SELF-RATED RELIGIOUS PREJUDICE

1989   Q.B103   {*SRRLPREJ*} Column No 1214
How would you describe yourself ... (read out) ...

	Code	%	No
... as very prejudiced against			
people of other religions,	1	0.8	12
a little prejudiced,	2	7.3	106
or - not prejudiced at all?	3	90.6	1324
(Other answer)	7	0.7	10
(DK)	8	0.1	1
(NA)	9	0.6	9
Base : All			1461

PARENTS' RELIGION

1989   Q.B105   {*PARLGSAM*} Column No 1225
Were both your parents of the same religion? (Interviewer: if necessary, add - say, **Protestant or Catholic**
or **Muslim or Hindu or Jewish** and so on)

	Code	%	No
Yes	1	82.1	1199
No	2	15.1	221
Refused	6	0.1	1
(DK)	8	2.0	30
(NA)	9	0.8	11
Base : All			1461

OWN-RELIGION *VERSUS* MIXED-RELIGION SCHOOLING

1989   Q.B106   {*OWNMXSCH*} Column No 1238
If you were deciding where to send your children to school, would you prefer a school with children of
only your own religion, or a *mixed-religion* school? (Interviewer: probe if necessary)
Say if you *did* have school-age children ...

	Code	%	No
Own religion only	1	14.9	218
Mixed-religion school	2	65.6	959
(No preference)	3	17.6	257
(DK)	8	1.2	17
(NA)	9	0.7	10
Base : All			1461

RELIGION OF SPOUSE/PARTNER

1989   Q.912   {*RELIGSAM*} Column No 1663
[If married/living as married] What about your *spouse/partner*? Is *he/she* the same religion as you?
(Interviewer : probe as necessary - 'that is, Protestant or Catholic or Muslim or Hindu and so on')

	Code	%	No
[Not asked : not married/living as married]	0	30.1	883
Yes	1	54.9	1609
No	2	14.4	423
(DK)/(NA)	8	0.3	8
Refused	9	0.3	8
Base : All			2930

RELIGIOUS AFFILIATION AT AGE OF SIXTEEN

1983   Q.79b   {*RELIG16*} Column Nos 576-77
Thinking back to the period when you were about 16, would you have described yourself as belonging
to a particular religion then? Which? (Interviewer: code one only)

	Code	%	No
No religion	1	24.6	422
Christian - no denomination	2	2.1	37
Roman Catholic	3	10.9	187
Church of England/Anglican	4	42.5	731
United Reform Church (URC)/			
Congregational	5	1.8	31
Baptist	6	1.9	33
Methodist	7	5.5	95
Presbyterian	8	5.7	97
Other Christian	9	1.7	29
Hindu	13	0.4	8
Jew	14	0.5	9
Muslim	15	0.6	10
Sikh	16	0.2	3
Buddhist	17	-	-
Other non-Christian	18	0.1	2
(NA)	99	1.5	26
Base : All			1719

NB In 1989 (Q. 82b), respondents were asked 'In what religion were you brought up?' (see p. Q-3 below)

R Housing

Table titles and cross references

SATISFACTION WITH OWN ACCOMMODATION

{HOUSESAT}

Question: (Show card) Now, a few questions on housing. First, in general how satisfied or dissatisfied are you with your own *house/flat*? Choose a phrase from the card.

		1983		1984		1985		1986		1987		1989	
		%	No	%	No	%	No	%	No	%	No	%	No
Question No		61				74		A92		A96		A98/B110	
Column No		526				649		1446		808		1311	
	Code												
Very satisfied	1	43.8	752	-	-	40.4	715	41.8	634	38.2	531	41.6	1220
Quite satisfied	2	42.3	727	-	-	42.6	753	45.9	697	46.9	653	45.5	1334
Neither satisfied nor dissatisfied	3	4.4	76	-	-	8.1	143	4.4	66	5.8	80	5.1	150
Quite dissatisfied	4	4.6	80	-	-	4.5	80	4.5	68	4.8	67	4.8	140
Very dissatisfied	5	4.8	82	-	-	4.4	77	3.3	51	4.2	58	2.5	75
(DK)	8	-	-	-	-	-	-	-	-	-	-	-	-
(NA)	9	0.1	2	-	-	0.1	1	0.1	2	0.1	1	0.4	12
Base: All			1719				1769		1518		1391		2930

1983 - Very dissatisfied, code 1; Quite dissatisfied, code 2; Quite satisfied, code 4; Very satisfied, code 5; NA, code 9
1986 - Q introduced by: 'In general how satisfied ...'

CHANGES IN LOCAL AREA IN RECENT PAST

{AREAPAST}

Question: How about the area you live in? Taking everything into account, would you say this area has got better, worse or remained about the same as a place to live during the *last two* years?

		1983		1984		1985		1986		1987		1989	
		%	No	%	No	%	No	%	No	%	No	%	No
Question No		62a								A97a		A99a/B111a	
Column No		527								809		1312	
	Code												
Better	1	10.5	180	-		-		-		9.8	136	14.1	413
Worse	2	19.9	342	-		-		-		22.4	311	19.9	584
About the same	3	66.1	1137	-		-		-		64.2	893	62.2	1824
(DK)	8	3.4	58	-		-		-		3.5	49	3.3	97
(NA)	9	0.1	2	-		-		-		0.1	1	0.4	13
Base: All			1719								1391		2930

1987, 1989 - SPSS file lists variable name as {AREACHNG}, although the question was identical. Consequently, the variable name has been changed to {AREAPAST}, as in 1983

PREDICTIONS ABOUT FUTURE OF LOCAL AREA

{AREANEXT}

Question: And what do you think will happen during the *next two* years: will this area get better, worse or remain about the same as a place to live?

		1983		1984		1985		1986		1987		1989	
		%	No	%	No	%	No	%	No	%	No	%	No
Question No		62b								A97b		A99b/B111b	
Column No		528								810		1313	
	Code												
Better	1	10.5	181	-		-		-		12.1	168	14.6	429
Worse	2	16.2	278	-		-		-		18.0	250	16.9	494
About the same	3	70.3	1208	-		-		-		67.9	944	65.3	1914
(DK)	8	2.5	43	-		-		-		2.0	27	2.4	70
(NA)	9	0.5	9	-		-		-		0.1	1	0.8	23
Base: All			1719								1391		2930

1987, 1989 - SPSS file lists variable name as {AREAFUT}, although the question was identical. Consequently, the variable name has been changed to {AREANEXT}, as in 1983

TENURE OF PRESENT ACCOMMODATION

{TENURE1}

Question: **Does your household own or rent this accommodation?** [If owns] **Outright or on a mortgage?** [If rents] **From whom?** (Interviewer: local authority includes GLC and London Residuary Body)

		Code	1983 %	1983 No	1984 %	1984 No	1985 %	1985 No	1986 %	1986 No	1987 %	1987 No	1989 %	1989 No
	Question No		63		97		75		A93/B109		A98/B103		A100/B112	
	Column No		529-30		845-46		650-51		1447-8		811-12		1314-15	
Owns:	Own (leasehold/freehold) outright	1	65.3	1123	65.7	1081	23.8	422	28.6	878	28.2	781	26.3	771
	Buying (leasehold/freehold) on mortgage	2	-	-	-	-	37.4	661	39.1	1199	40.0	1106	43.9	1285
Rents:	Local authority	3	25.1	432	24.7	407	29.3	518	24.0	736	22.5	622	21.1	618
	New Town Development Corporation	4	0.6	10	0.8	13	0.5	8	0.2	5	0.2	6	0.2	7
	Housing Association	5	1.7	30	0.9	15	2.0	35	1.6	50	1.1	29	1.7	50
	Property company	6	0.6	10	0.9	14	0.8	14	0.7	21	0.6	16	0.6	18
	Employer	7	0.9	16	1.9	32	1.2	21	0.8	26	2.0	56	0.9	25
	Other organisation	8	1.5	26	0.7	11	0.7	12	1.3	39	0.9	26	0.5	13
	Relative	9	0.9	15	0.2	3	0.3	5	0.4	12	0.3	9	0.2	7
	Other individual	10	3.1	53	3.7	61	4.1	72	3.0	91	3.9	107	3.4	101
Rent free:	Rent free, squatting etc	11	-	-	-	-	-	-	-	-	-	-	0.8	22
	(DK)	98	-	-	0.1	1	-	-	-	-	0.1	2	0.0	1
	(NA)	99	0.3	6	0.4	6	0.1	2	0.2	6	0.1	4	0.4	13
Base: All				1719		1645		1769		3066		2766		2930

1983 - Owned/being bought leasehold or freehold, code 1; Rented from <u>organisation</u>: Local authority (inc. GLC), code 2; New Town Development Corporation, code 3; Housing Association, code 4; Property company, code 5; Other organisation, code 6; Rented from <u>individual</u>: Relative, code 7; Employer, code 8; Other individual, code 9; (NA), code 99

1984 - Owned/being bought leasehold or freehold, code 1; <u>rented from</u>: Local authority (incl. GLC), code 2; New Town Development Corporation, code 3; Housing Association, code 4; Property Company, code 5; Employer, code 6; Other organisation, code 7; Relative, code 8; Other individual, code 9; (DK), code 98; (NA), code 99

1985, 1986, 1987, 1989 - <u>Own</u>: Own leasehold or freehold outright, code 1; Buying leasehold or freehold on mortgage, code 2; <u>rented from</u>: Local authority (incl. GLC), code 3; New Town Development Corporation, code 4; Housing Association, code 5; Property company, code 6; Employer, code 7; Other organisation, code 8; Relative, code 9; Other individual, code 10; (DK), code 98; (NA), code 99

1989 - 'London Residuary Body' added to interviewer instruction

LA TENANTS: LIKELIHOOD OF BUYING PRESENT HOME

{*CNCLBUY*}

Question: [If local authority or New Town Development Corporation tenant] **Is it *likely* or *unlikely* that you - or the person responsible for paying the rent - will buy this accommodation at some time in the future?**
[If likely or unlikely] **Very or quite?**

		1983		1984		1985		1986		1987		1989	
		%	No	%	No	%	No	%	No	%	No	%	No
Question No		64a				76a		A94/B110		A99/B104		B113	
Column No		531				652		1449		813		1316	
	Code												
Very likely	1	4.6	20	-	-	5.5	29	6.4	48	7.7	49	6.3	21
Quite likely	2	7.1	31	-	-	7.0	37	10.5	79	8.4	53	10.7	36
Quite unlikely	3	3.7	16	-	-	6.6	35	10.5	79	7.4	47	5.9	20
Very unlikely	4	76.3	334	-	-	75.8	400	65.9	495	70.8	448	67.0	227
Not allowed to buy	5	5.9	26	-	-	3.2	17	3.3	25	2.5	16	3.8	13
(DK)	8	1.1	5	-	-	1.3	7	2.1	16	2.2	14	3.3	11
(NA)	9	1.4	6	-	-	0.6	3	1.2	9	0.9	6	2.8	10
Base: All LA or NTDC tenants			438				528		751		633		338

1983 - Asked of local authority tenants only, not of NTDC tenants also; (DK), code 6

TENANTS: RENT LEVEL OF PRESENT ACCOMMODATION

{*RENTLEVL*}

Question: [If tenant] **How would you describe the *rent* - not including rates - for this accommodation? Would you say it was ... (read out) ...**

		1983		1984		1985		1986		1987		1989	
		%	No	%	No	%	No	%	No	%	No	%	No
Question No								A95		A100a		B114	
Column No								1450		814		1317	
	Code												
... on the high side,	1	-	-	-	-	-	-	46.2	223	50.2	227	42.6	177
... reasonable	2	-	-	-	-	-	-	49.3	238	42.0	190	52.8	219
... or on the low side?	3	-	-	-	-	-	-	2.5	12	5.3	24	3.6	15
(DK)	8	-	-	-	-	-	-	-		-		0.6	3
(NA)	9	-	-	-	-	-	-	2.5	12	2.7	12	0.4	2
Base: All tenants									483		454		415

1983, 1985 - Q asked of local authority tenants only: see p.R - 27 below
1987 - [If accommodation currently rented from any landlord]; No (DK)
1989 - [If lives in rented accommodation]

OWNERS: WHETHER EXERCISED 'RIGHT TO BUY'

{BUYFRMLA}

Question: [If owner] **Did you, or the person responsible for the mortgage, buy your present home from the local authority as a tenant?** (Interviewer: 'local authority' includes GLC, London Residuary Body and New Town Development Corporation)

	Code	1983 %	No	1984 %	No	1985 %	No	1986 %	No	1987 %	No	1989 %	No
Question No Column No								A96a/B111 1451		A102/B105 818		B115a 1318	
Yes	1	-		-		-		10.8	112	11.4	215	11.6	120
No	2	-		-		-		88.9	922	87.7	1661	87.5	903
(DK)	8	-		-		-		-		-		-	
(NA)	9	-		-		-		0.3	3	0.9	17	0.9	10
Base: All owners									1037		1894		1033

1985 - This question (Q.77 on Column 654) was asked only of those buying on a mortgage, and excludes those who owned their present accommodation outright. The variable name was {BUYMORTG} and the distributions were: Yes (Code 1) 12.7% (n=84); No (Code 2) 87.0% (n=575); (NA) (Code 9) 0.3% (n=2). Base: All buying on a mortgage (n=661)

1985-1987 - Interviewer instruction did not include 'London Residuary Body'

1986 - Data from B version of the questionnaire are missing from the SPSS file

OWNERS: WHETHER EVER LIVED IN RENTED ACCOMMODATION

{EVERRENT}

Question: [If owner but did not buy present home from LA/NTDC] **Have you *ever* lived in rented accommodation?**

	Code	1983 %	No	1984 %	No	1985 %	No	1986 %	No	1987 %	No	1989 %	No
Question No Column No								A96b 1452				B115b 1319	
Yes	1	-		-		-		54.5	565	-		49.3	509
No	2	-		-		-		34.4	357	-		38.1	393
[Not asked: bought present home from LA/NTDC]	7	-		-		-		10.8	112	-		11.6	120
(NA)	9	-		-		-		0.3	3	-		1.0	11
Base: All owners									1037				1033

OWNERS: HOW LONG AGO LIVED IN RENTED ACCOMMODATION

{WHENRENT - Banded}

Question: [If owner and ever lived in rented accommodation] **How long ago was it that you *last* lived in rented accommodation?** (Interviewer: includes present house/flat; write in number of years)

	Code	1983 %	No	1984 %	No	1985 %	No	1986 %	No	1987 %	No	1989 %	No
Question No								A96c				B115c	
Column No								1453-54				1320-21	
[Not asked: never lived in rented accommodation]	0	-	.	-	.	-	.	34.5	357	-	.	38.1	393
One year ago or less	1	-	.	-	.	-	.	2.9	30	-	.	4.7	49
2 up to 5 years ago		-	.	-	.	-	.	14.3	148	-	.	10.5	109
6 up to 10 years ago		-	.	-	.	-	.	10.5	109	-	.	11.4	117
11 up to 20 years ago		-	.	-	.	-	.	17.5	182	-	.	15.8	163
More than 20 years ago		-	.	-	.	-	.	19.5	203	-	.	18.5	191
(DK)	98	-	.	-	.	-	.	0.4	4	-	.	0.0	1
(NA)	99	-	.	-	.	-	.	0.5	5	-	.	1.0	11

Base: All owners   1037   1033

OWNERS: LANDLORD OF LAST ACCOMMODATION RENTED

{WHOMRENT}

Question: [If owner and ever lived in rented accommodation] **Were you renting then from a local authority or from someone else?** (Local Authority includes GLC, London Residuary Body and New Town Development Corporation)

		1983		1984		1985		1986		1987		1989	
		%	No	%	No	%	No	%	No	%	No	%	No
Question No								A96d				B115d	
Column No								1455				1322	
	Code												
[Not asked: never rented]	0	-		-		-		34.4	357	-		38.0	393
Local authority	1	-		-		-		27.9	289	-		28.6	291
(Private landlord/private company)	2	-		-		-		32.4	336	-		29.6	306
(Rent free/came with job/tied accommodation)	3	-		-		-		3.5	36	-		2.0	21
Someone else	7	-		-		-		0.4	4	-		0.7	7
(DK)	8	-		-		-		0.2	2	-		0.3	3
(NA)	9	-		-		-		1.2	12	-		1.3	13
Base: All owners									1037				1033

1986 - Interviewer instruction did not include 'London Residuary Body'

DESIRE TO MOVE FROM PRESENT HOME

{HOMEMOVE}

Question: If you had a free *choice*, would you choose to stay in your present home, or would you choose to move out?

		1983		1984		1985		1986		1987		1989	
		%	No	%	No	%	No	%	No	%	No	%	No
Question No						79a		A97a				B116a	
Column No						657		1456				1323	
	Code												
Would choose to stay	1	-		-		56.0	990	62.1	943	-		62.3	910
Would choose to move out	2	-		-		42.2	746	35.8	543	-		35.6	521
(DK)	8	-		-		1.8	31	1.8	27	-		1.5	22
(NA)	9	-		-		0.1	1	0.3	4	-		0.6	9
Base: All							1769		1518				1461

KEENNESS TO MOVE FROM PRESENT HOME

{HOMEKEEN}

Question: [If would choose to move out] How keen are you to move out? Are you ... (read out) ...

	Code	1983 %	No	1984 %	No	1985 %	No	1986 %	No	1987 %	No	1989 %	No
Question No						79b		97b				B116b	
Column No						658		1457				1324	
[Not asked: would choose to stay]	0	-	.	-	.	57.7	1022	63.9	970	-	.	62.3	910
... very keen	1	-	.	-	.	15.5	275	12.0	182	-	.	13.1	192
... fairly keen,	2	-	.	-	.	15.5	275	13.8	210	-	.	14.1	206
... or not that keen?	3	-	.	-	.	10.3	183	9.7	147	-	.	8.2	120
(DK)	8	-	.	-	.	0.1	1	-	.	-	.	-	.
(NA)	9	-	.	-	.	0.8	14	0.6	9	-	.	2.3	33
Base: All						1769		1518				1461	

EXPECTATIONS FOR MOVING IN NEAR FUTURE

{HOMEEXPT}

Question: [And] apart from what you would *like*, where do you *expect* to be living in *two* years time - do you expect
to ... (read out) ...

	Code	1983 %	No	1984 %	No	1985 %	No	1986 %	No	1987 %	No	1989 %	No
Question No						80a		A98a				B117a	
Column No						659		1458				1325	
... stay in this house/flat,	1	-	.	-	.	72.6	1284	76.4	1159	-	.	74.0	1081
... or move elsewhere?	2	-	.	-	.	23.1	409	20.5	312	-	.	22.0	321
(DK)	8	-	.	-	.	4.2	74	2.9	43	-	.	3.5	51
(NA)	9	-	.	-	.	0.1	2	0.2	3	-	.	0.6	9
Base: All						1769		1518				1461	

EXPECTED TENURE OF NEXT HOME

{TENREXPT}

Question: [If expects to move] **Which do you think is most likely - that you will *buy* or *rent* your next home?**
(Interviewer: if rent, probe for local authority/council or other landlord)

		1983		1984		1985		1986		1987		1989	
		%	No	%	No	%	No	%	No	%	No	%	No
Question No						80b		A98b				B117b	
Column No						660		1459				1326	
	Code												
[Not asked: expects to stay in same house/flat]	0	-	-	-	-	76.8	1358	79.2	1202	-	-	74.0	1081
Buy	1	-	-	-	-	13.7	242	14.1	214	-	-	15.3	223
Rent from local authority/council	2	-	-	-	-	5.3	94	3.7	56	-	-	3.0	44
Rent from other landlord	3	-	-	-	-	2.5	44	1.8	27	-	-	2.5	37
(Other answer)	7	-	-	-	-	0.1	1	-	-	-	-	-	-
(DK)	8	-	-	-	-	1.0	17	0.8	12	-	-	1.0	14
(NA)	9	-	-	-	-	0.7	12	0.4	5	-	-	4.3	63
Base: All							1769		1518				1461

TENANTS: PREFERRED TENURE

{RENTPREF}

Question: [If tenant] **If you had a free *choice* would you choose to rent accommodation, or would you choose to buy?**

		1983		1984		1985		1986		1987		1989	
		%	No	%	No	%	No	%	No	%	No	%	No
Question No						82a		A99a		A100b		B118b	
Column No						674		1460		815		1328	
	Code												
Would choose to rent	1	-	-	-	-	31.7	218	31.3	151	25.3	115	29.5	122
Would choose to buy	2	-	-	-	-	62.6	430	65.2	315	70.9	322	68.2	283
(DK)	8	-	-	-	-	3.3	23	1.4	7	3.1	14	2.0	8
(NA)	9	-	-	-	-	2.3	16	2.1	10	0.7	3	0.4	2
Base: All tenants							686		483		454		415

1985, 1986 - [If currently renting from any landlord]
1987 - [If accommodation currently rented from any landlord]
1989 - [If lives in rented accommodation]

TENANTS: EXPECTATIONS FOR BUYING THEIR HOME

{RENTEXPT}

Question: [If tenant] And apart from what you would *like*, do you *expect* to buy a house or a flat in the next *two* years, or not?

		1983		1984		1985		1986		1987		1989	
		%	No	%	No	%	No	%	No	%	No	%	No
Question No						82b		A99b		A100c		B118c	
Column No						675		1461		816		1329	
	Code												
Yes - expect to buy	1	-	-	-	-	12.0	82	18.2	88	17.5	79	15.4	64
No - do not expect to buy	2	-	-	-	-	82.5	566	76.2	368	79.0	357	79.2	328
(DK)	8	-	-	-	-	3.1	21	3.1	15	2.9	13	3.9	16
(NA)	9	-	-	-	-	2.5	17	2.5	12	0.7	3	1.5	6
Base: All tenants							686		483		454		415

1985, 1986 - [If currently renting from any landlord]
1987 - [If accommodation currently rented from any landlord]
1989 - [If lives in rented accommodation]

TENANTS: WHETHER EVER OWNED ACCOMMODATION

{EVEROWND}

Question: [If tenant] Have you *ever* owned your own accommodation? That is, lived in a house or flat, which was in your sole or joint name?

		1983		1984		1985		1986		1987		1989	
		%	No	%	No	%	No	%	No	%	No	%	No
Question No								A100a				B119a	
Column No								1462				1330	
	Code												
Yes	1	-	-	-	-	-	-	13.2	64	-	-	14.7	61
No	2	-	-	-	-	-	-	84.9	411	-	-	85.1	353
(DK)	8	-	-	-	-	-	-	-		-	-	-	
(NA)	9	-	-	-	-	-	-	1.7	8	-	-	0.2	1
Base: All tenants									483				415

1986 - [If currently renting from any landlord]
1989 - [If lives in rented accommodation]; No DK

TENANTS: HOW LONG AGO OWNED ACCOMMODATION

{OWNEDYRS - Banded}

Question: [If tenant] How long ago was it that you last owned your own accommodation?

		1983		1984		1985		1986		1987		1989	
		%	No	%	No	%	No	%	No	%	No	%	No
Question No								A100b				B119b	
Column No								1463-64				1331-32	
	Code												
[Not asked: never owned own accommodation]	0	-	.	-	.	-	.	85.1	411	-	.	85.1	353
One year ago or less	1	-	.	-	.	-	.	1.0	5	-	.	1.2	5
2 up to 5 years ago		-	.	-	.	-	.	1.9	9	-	.	3.4	14
6 up to 10 years ago		-	.	-	.	-	.	3.6	17	-	.	2.7	11
11 up to 20 years ago		-	.	-	.	-	.	4.1	20	-	.	4.1	17
More than 20 years ago		-	.	-	.	-	.	2.3	11	-	.	3.1	13
(DK)	98	-	.	-	.	-	.	-	.	-	.	-	.
(NA)	99	-	.	-	.	-	.	2.3	11	-	.	0.4	2
Base: All tenants									483				415

1986 - [If currently renting from any landlord]
1989 - [If lives in rented accommodation]

TENANTS: FACTORS INHIBITING HOME PURCHASE

{NOTBUY1} {NOTBUY2} {NOTBUY3} {NOTBUY4} {NOTBUY5} {NOTBUY6} {NOTBUY7} {NOTBUY8} {NOTBUY9} {NOTBUY10}

Question: [If tenant] Here are some reasons people might give for *not* wanting to buy a home. As I read out each one, please tell me whether or not it applies to you, *at present* ... (read out):

		1983		1984		1985		1986		1987		1989	
		%	No	%	No	%	No	%	No	%	No	%	No
Question No								A101a				B120a	
Column No								1465				1333	
(i) *{NOTBUY1}*	Code												
I could not afford the deposit													
Applies	1	-	.	-	.	-	.	71.4	345	-	.	70.3	298
Does not apply	2	-	.	-	.	-	.	26.3	127	-	.	25.3	107
(DK)	8	-	.	-	.	-	.	0.4	2	-	.	1.2	5
(NA)	9	-	.	-	.	-	.	1.9	9	-	.	3.2	14
Base: All tenants									483				423

TENANTS: FACTORS INHIBITING HOME PURCHASE (Continued)

			1983		1984		1985		1986		1987		1989	
			%	No	%	No	%	No	%	No	%	No	%	No
Question No									A101b				B120b	
Column No									1466				1334	

(ii) {NOTBUY2}

I would not be able to get a mortgage

	Code	1983 %	No	1984 %	No	1985 %	No	1986 %	No	1987 %	No	1989 %	No
Applies	1	-	.	-	.	-	.	61.1	295	-	.	65.6	278
Does not apply	2	-	.	-	.	-	.	32.9	159	-	.	28.4	120
(DK)	8	-	.	-	.	-	.	4.1	20	-	.	3.0	13
(NA)	9	-	.	-	.	-	.	1.9	9	-	.	3.0	13

Base: All tenants   483   423

Question No									A101c				B120c	
Column No									1467				1335	

(iii) {NOTBUY3}

It might be difficult to keep up the repayments

	Code	1983 %	No	1984 %	No	1985 %	No	1986 %	No	1987 %	No	1989 %	No
Applies	1	-	.	-	.	-	.	69.8	337	-	.	72.4	306
Does not apply	2	-	.	-	.	-	.	26.3	127	-	.	22.1	94
(DK)	8	-	.	-	.	-	.	2.1	10	-	.	2.3	10
(NA)	9	-	.	-	.	-	.	1.9	9	-	.	3.2	14

Base: All tenants   483   423

Question No									A101d				B120d	
Column No									1468				1336	

(iv) {NOTBUY4}

I can't afford any of the properties I'd want to buy

	Code	1983 %	No	1984 %	No	1985 %	No	1986 %	No	1987 %	No	1989 %	No
Applies	1	-	.	-	.	-	.	69.2	334	-	.	76.7	325
Does not apply	2	-	.	-	.	-	.	27.5	133	-	.	18.7	79
(DK)	8	-	.	-	.	-	.	1.7	8	-	.	1.4	6
(NA)	9	-	.	-	.	-	.	1.9	9	-	.	3.2	14

Base: All tenants   483   423

TENANTS: FACTORS INHIBITING HOME PURCHASE (Continued)

			1983		1984		1985		1986		1987		1989	
			%	No	%	No	%	No	%	No	%	No	%	No
	Question No								A101e				B120e	
	Column No								1469				1337	
(v) {NOTBUY5}		Code												
I do not have a secure enough job														
Applies	1		-	.	-	.	-	.	57.1	276	-	.	55.0	233
Does not apply	2		-	.	-	.	-	.	40.2	194	-	.	38.5	163
(DK)	8		-	.	-	.	-	.	0.6	3	-	.	3.3	14
(NA)	9		-	.	-	.	-	.	2.1	10	-	.	3.2	14
Base: All tenants										483				423

			1983		1984		1985		1986		1987		1989	
	Question No								A101f				B120f	
	Column No								1470				1338	
(vi) {NOTBUY6}														
I would not want to be in debt														
Applies	1		-	.	-	.	-	.	69.8	337	-	.	70.9	300
Does not apply	2		-	.	-	.	-	.	28.0	135	-	.	24.7	105
(DK)	8		-	.	-	.	-	.	0.2	1	-	.	1.2	5
(NA)	9		-	.	-	.	-	.	2.1	10	-	.	3.2	14
Base: All tenants										483				423

			1983		1984		1985		1986		1987		1989	
	Question No								A101g				B120g	
	Column No								1471				1339	
(vii) {NOTBUY7}														
It would cost too much to repair and maintain														
Applies	1		-	.	-	.	-	.	62.1	300	-	.	59.1	250
Does not apply	2		-	.	-	.	-	.	34.0	164	-	.	35.9	152
(DK)	8		-	.	-	.	-	.	2.1	10	-	.	2.1	9
(NA)	9		-	.	-	.	-	.	1.9	9	-	.	3.0	13
Base: All tenants										483				423

TENANTS: FACTORS INHIBITING HOME PURCHASE (Continued)

		1983		1984		1985		1986		1987		1989	
		%	No	%	No	%	No	%	No	%	No	%	No
Question No Column No								A101h 1472				B120h 1340	
(viii) {NOTBUY8} **I might not be able to resell the property when I wanted to**	Code												
Applies	1	-	.	-	.	-	.	38.3	185	-	.	38.3	162
Does not apply	2	-	.	-	.	-	.	56.1	271	-	.	52.3	221
(DK)	8	-	.	-	.	-	.	3.7	18	-	.	6.2	26
(NA)	9	-	.	-	.	-	.	1.9	9	-	.	3.2	14
Base: All tenants									483				423
Question No Column No								A101i 1473				B120i 1341	
(ix) {NOTBUY9} **It is just too much of a responsibility**								53.2	257			55.0	233
Applies	1	-	.	-	.	-	.	44.3	214	-	.	40.0	169
Does not apply	2	-	.	-	.	-	.	0.8	4	-	.	1.8	8
(DK)	8	-	.	-	.	-	.	1.9	9	-	.	3.2	14
(NA)	9	-	.	-	.	-	.						
Base: All tenants									483				423
Question No Column No								A101j 1474				B120j 1342	
(x) {NOTBUY10} **At my age, I would not want to change**													
Applies	1	-	.	-	.	-	.	47.6	230	-	.	50.1	212
Does not apply	2	-	.	-	.	-	.	49.9	241	-	.	45.6	193
(DK)	8	-	.	-	.	-	.	0.6	3	-	.	1.3	6
(NA)	9	-	.	-	.	-	.	1.9	9	-	.	3.0	13
Base: All tenants									483				423

TENURE OF PARENTS' ACCOMMODATION

{PTENURE}

Question: When you were a child, did your parents own their home, rent it from a local authority, or rent it from someone else? (Interviewer: if different types of tenure, probe for longest)

		1983		1984		1985		1986		1987		1989	
		%	No	%	No	%	No	%	No	%	No	%	No
Question No								A102				B121	
Column No								1475				1344	
	Code												
Owned it	1	-	-	-	-	-	-	36.1	548	-	-	37.4	547
Rented from local authority	2	-	-	-	-	-	-	35.3	536	-	-	33.5	489
Rented from someone else	3	-	-	-	-	-	-	25.1	381	-	-	26.0	380
(Rent free/came with job/tied house or cottage)	4	-	-	-	-	-	-	1.9	29	-	-	-	-
(Other)	7	-	-	-	-	-	-	0.5	8	-	-	2.1	31
(DK)	8	-	-	-	-	-	-	0.5	8	-	-	0.3	4
(NA)	9	-	-	-	-	-	-	0.5	8	-	-	0.7	11
Base: All								1518				1461	

1989 -   No 'Rent free/came with job/tied house or cottage', code 4

TYPE OF PRESENT ACCOMMODATION

{HOMETYPE}

Question: (Interviewer: code from observation and check with respondent) **Would I be right in describing this accommodation as a...............?**

	Code	1983 %	No	1984 %	No	1985 %	No	1986 %	No	1987 %	No	1989 %	No
Question No						78a		A103/B112		A103/B106		A101/B122	
Column No						655		1476		819		1345	
Detached house or bungalow	1	-	.	-	.	20.0	354	21.5	660	21.9	605	22.4	655
Semi-detached house or bungalow	2	-	.	-	.	33.0	584	37.2	1142	37.4	1034	37.7	1105
Terraced house	3	-	.	-	.	28.3	501	25.0	768	26.0	718	23.9	700
Self-contained, purpose-built flat/ maisonette (including in tenement block)	4	-	.	-	.	12.5	221	12.0	367	10.4	289	11.8	346
Self-contained converted flat/ maisonette	5	-	.	-	.	4.2	75	2.6	79	2.8	76	3.3	97
Room(s) - not self-contained	6	-	.	-	.	1.4	25	0.6	17	0.5	15	0.3	7
Other answer	7	-	.	-	.	0.4	8	0.8	24	0.7	18	0.2	7
(DK)	8	-	.	-	.	-	.	-	.	-	.	-	.
(NA)	9	-	.	-	.	0.1	2	0.3	8	0.4	11	0.4	13
Base: All							1769		3066		2766		2930

LENGTH OF TIME IN PRESENT ACCOMMODATION

{HOMELGTH}

Question: [And] how long have you lived in your present home?

		1983		1984		1985		1986		1987		1989	
		%	No	%	No	%	No	%	No	%	No	%	No
Question No						78b		A104ab		A104/B107		A102/B123	
Column No						656		1477-79		820		1346	
	Code												
Less than 1 year	1	-	.	-	.	8.2	144	7.0	107	9.4	259	8.3	244
1 year, less than 2 years	2	-	.	-	.	9.2	162	4.3	65	6.8	189	7.1	207
2 years, less than 5 years	3	-	.	-	.	19.8	351	20.8	316	19.4	538	21.4	627
5 years, less than 10 years	4	-	.	-	.	19.9	353	18.9	287	18.6	514	17.9	525
10 years, less than 20 years	5	-	.	-	.	22.2	392	26.7	405	22.8	631	22.7	665
20 years or more	6	-	.	-	.	19.9	352	22.1	336	22.8	632	22.3	653
(DK)	8	-	.	-	.	-		-		-		-	
(NA)	9	-	.	-	.	0.9	15	0.2	3	0.1	4	0.3	10
Base: All							1769		1518		2766		2930

1986 - Variable called {LIVEHOME - Banded} (see p. R - 31 below). Q reads: 'How long have you lived in your present home ... (read out) ...less than a year (code 1), or - one year or more? (code 2)'; [If one year or more] 'How many years?' (Interviewer: probe for best estimate and write in number).   To aid comparison across the last four survey years, collapsed data for 1986 are included in this table

LEGAL RESPONSIBILITY FOR ACCOMMODATION - 1

{RRESP}

On questionnaire: Record whether respondent has legal responsibility for accommodation (including joint and shared)

		1983		1984		1985		1986		1987		1989	
		%	No	%	No	%	No	%	No	%	No	%	No
Question No		91d		94d		98d		A106/B114d		901d		901d	
Column No		655		666		763		1514		1214		1414	
	Code												
Respondent has:													
no legal responsibility	0	26.6	458	23.4	385	22.0	389	20.0	614	19.3	535	17.2	503
legal responsibility (sole or shared)	1	73.3	1260	75.8	1247	74.2	1313	77.1	2365	78.6	2174	81.1	2378
No-one in household has legal responsibility	2	-		-		-		-		-		0.3	7
(NA)	9	0.1	1	0.8	13	3.8	67	2.8	87	2.1	57	1.4	42
Base: All			1719		1645		1769		3066		2766		2930

LEGAL RESPONSIBILITY FOR ACCOMMODATION - 2

{LEGALRES} {LEGLRESP}

Variable derived from details collected about household members

		1983		1984		1985		1986		1987		1989	
		%	No	%	No	%	No	%	No	%	No	%	No
Column No				1664		1070		2369		2267		2375	
	Code												
Sole	1	-	-	29.5	485	28.5	505	25.6	786	25.5	707	23.4	684
Shared	2	-	-	46.3	762	45.7	808	51.5	1579	53.1	1467	57.8	1694
None	3	-	-	23.4	385	22.0	389	20.0	614	19.3	535	17.4	511
No information	9	-	-	0.8	13	3.8	67	2.8	87	2.1	57	1.4	42
Base: All					1645		1769		3066		2766		2930

1983 - Although the variable name on the SPSS file, {LEGALRES}, was the same, the data were coded differently (at Q.91d): 'Respondent has sole responsibility', (code 0), 31.9% (n = 548); 'Other household member has sole responsibility', (code 1), 26.6% (n = 458); 'Shared responsibility', (code 2), 41.5% (n = 713). The information was coded on Column No 963. The 1983 variable name has been changed to {LEGLRESP}

INCOME GROUP BENEFITING MOST FROM GOVERNMENT SPENDING ON HOUSING

{HSEVALUE}

Question: Central government provides financial support to housing in two main ways. First, by means of allowances to low income tenants. Second, by means of tax relief to people with mortgages. On the whole, which of these three types of family would you say benefits *most* from central government support for housing? (Please tick one box)

		1983		1984		1985		1986		1987		1989	
		%	No	%	No	%	No	%	No	%	No	%	No
Question No		213a		217		235a		A218a		A208a		B224a	
Column No		1066		1625		2152		1915		1552		2069	
	Code												
Families with *high* incomes	1	31.8	511	37.0	563	33.2	499	33.1	459	40.2	500	41.5	521
Families with *middle* incomes	2	26.9	432	20.5	312	20.1	302	22.0	305	20.2	251	19.5	245
Families with *low* incomes	3	38.6	622	38.3	584	41.6	624	40.3	560	36.2	450	35.4	444
(Makes no difference)	4	-	.	-	.	-	.	-	.	0.1	1	-	.
(DK)	8	-	.	2.4	37	1.0	16	1.8	24	1.2	15	1.2	16
(NA)	9	2.8	44	1.8	28	4.1	61	2.9	40	2.1	26	2.3	29
Base: Self-completion questionnaire respondents			1610		1522		1502		1387		1243		1255

1983 - No (Makes no difference); No (DK)

SUPPORT FOR 'RIGHT TO BUY'

{*CNCLSALE*}

Question: **Which of these three views comes closest to your own on the sale of council houses and flats to tenants?**
(Please tick one box)

	Code	1983		1984		1985		1986		1987		1989	
		%	No	%	No	%	No	%	No	%	No	%	No
Question No		213b				235b		A218b		A208b		B224b	
Column No		1067				2153		1916		1553		2070	
Council tenants *should not* be allowed to buy their houses or flats	1	11.0	177	-	-	9.1	137	7.9	109	9.5	118	10.5	132
Council tenants *should* be allowed to buy but *only* in areas with no housing shortage	2	30.8	496	-	-	28.6	429	27.6	383	27.8	346	32.5	408
Council tenants *should generally* be allowed to buy their houses or flats	3	57.2	921	-	-	60.1	903	62.9	873	61.1	760	55.8	700
(DK)	8	-	-	-	-	0.4	6	0.5	7	0.5	7	0.1	1
(NA)	9	1.0	16	-	-	1.9	28	1.1	15	1.0	13	1.1	13
Base: Self-completion questionnaire respondents			1610				1502		1387		1243		1255

1983 - No (DK)

PERCEPTIONS OF LOCAL AUTHORITY HOUSING

{COUNCIL1} {COUNCIL2} {COUNCIL3}

Question: Which of the following statements do you think are generally true and which false?
(Please tick one box for each)

			1983		1984		1985		1986		1987		1989	
			%	No	%	No	%	No	%	No	%	No	%	No
Question No			213c				236		A219		A209		B225	
Column No			1068				2154		1917		1554		2071	

(i) {COUNCIL1}
Council tenants pay low rents

	Code	1983 %	No	1984 %	No	1985 %	No	1986 %	No	1987 %	No	1989 %	No
True	1	24.2	389	-	-	26.1	392	25.6	355	28.4	353	33.0	415
False	2	69.3	1115	-	-	65.8	989	64.5	894	66.3	824	60.1	754
(DK)	8	-	.	-	-	1.3	19	1.6	22	1.4	18	1.2	15
(NA)	9	6.6	106	-	-	6.8	102	8.4	116	3.9	48	5.7	71

Base: Self-completion
questionnaire respondents

	1983	1985	1986	1987	1989
	1610	1502	1387	1243	1255

	1983	1985	1986	1987	1989
Question No	213c	236	A219	A209	B225
Column No	1069	2155	1918	1555	2072

(ii) {COUNCIL2}
Councils give a poor standard of repairs and maintenance

	Code	1983 %	No	1984 %	No	1985 %	No	1986 %	No	1987 %	No	1989 %	No
True	1	59.7	961	-	-	60.9	914	65.5	909	65.0	808	57.3	719
False	2	35.4	570	-	-	32.5	489	27.8	386	30.7	382	36.7	461
(DK)	8	-	.	-	-	1.1	17	1.6	22	1.6	20	2.0	25
(NA)	9	4.9	78	-	-	5.4	82	5.1	71	2.7	33	4.0	50

Base: Self-completion
questionnaire respondents

	1983	1985	1986	1987	1989
	1610	1502	1387	1243	1255

	1983	1985	1986	1987	1989
Question No	213c	236	A219	A209	B225
Column No	1070	2156	1919	1556	2073

(iii) {COUNCIL3}
Council estates are generally pleasant places to live

	Code	1983 %	No	1984 %	No	1985 %	No	1986 %	No	1987 %	No	1989 %	No
True	1	38.9	627	-	-	35.7	536	37.3	517	33.9	422	36.0	452
False	2	55.2	889	-	-	56.8	853	54.7	759	60.9	758	58.4	733
(DK)	8	-	.	-	-	1.0	16	1.5	21	1.5	18	1.4	17
(NA)	9	5.9	94	-	-	6.4	97	6.5	90	3.7	46	4.2	53

Base: Self-completion
questionnaire respondents

	1983	1985	1986	1987	1989
	1610	1502	1387	1243	1255

1983 - No (DK)

ADVICE TO A YOUNG COUPLE ABOUT BUYING A HOME

{RENTBUY}

Question: Suppose a newly-married young couple, both with steady jobs, asked your advice about whether to buy or rent a home. If they had the choice, what would you advise them to do? (Please tick one box)

		1983		1984		1985		1986		1987		1989	
		%	No	%	No	%	No	%	No	%	No	%	No
Question No								A220a				B226a	
Column No								1920				2074	
	Code												
To buy a home as soon as possible	1	-	.	-	.	-	.	74.3	1031	-	.	77.9	978
To wait a bit, then try to buy a home	2	-	.	-	.	-	.	19.7	274	-	.	16.9	212
Not to plan to buy a home at all	3	-	.	-	.	-	.	0.9	13	-	.	1.4	17
Can't choose	8	-	.	-	.	-	.	4.2	58	-	.	3.5	44
(NA)	9	-	.	-	.	-	.	0.8	11	-	.	0.3	4

Base: Self-completion
questionnaire respondents   1387   1255

ADVANTAGES AND DISADVANTAGES OF HOME PURCHASE

{HOMERISK} {BUYCHEAP} {MOVEHOME} {MONEYTIE} {FREEDOM} {FINBURDN} {LEAVEFAM} {HOMERESP} {RISKJOB} {WAITFAM}

Question: Still thinking of what you might say to this young couple, please tick one box for *each* statement below to show how much you agree or disagree with it

		1983		1984		1985		1986		1987		1989	
		%	No	%	No	%	No	%	No	%	No	%	No
Question No								A220b				B226b	
Column No								1921				2075	

(i) {HOMERISK}

Owning your home can be a risky investment

	Code	%	No	%	No	%	No	%	No	%	No	%	No
Agree strongly	1	-	.	-	.	-	.	5.4	74	-	.	6.2	77
Just agree	2	-	.	-	.	-	.	19.6	272	-	.	19.7	247
Neither agree nor disagree	3	-	.	-	.	-	.	15.6	216	-	.	17.2	216
Just disagree	4	-	.	-	.	-	.	23.5	326	-	.	27.4	344
Disagree strongly	5	-	.	-	.	-	.	33.5	465	-	.	27.2	341
(DK)	8	-	.	-	.	-	.	0.2	3	-	.	0.2	2
(NA)	9	-	.	-	.	-	.	2.3	32	-	.	2.2	28

Base: Self-completion
questionnaire respondents   1387   1255

ADVANTAGES AND DISADVANTAGES OF HOME PURCHASE (Continued)

		1983		1984		1985		1986		1987		1989	
		%	No	%	No	%	No	%	No	%	No	%	No
Question No								A220b				B226b	
Column No								1922				2076	
(ii) {BUYCHEAP}	Code												
Over time, buying a home works out less expensive than paying rent													
Agree strongly	1	-	.	-	.	-	.	44.1	612	-	.	40.8	513
Just agree	2	-	.	-	.	-	.	38.6	535	-	.	39.9	501
Neither agree nor disagree	3	-	.	-	.	-	.	8.3	115	-	.	10.8	136
Just disagree	4	-	.	-	.	-	.	4.9	68	-	.	4.9	62
Disagree strongly	5	-	.	-	.	-	.	2.0	27	-	.	2.1	26
(DK)	8	-	.	-	.	-	.	0.2	3	-	.	0.2	2
(NA)	9	-	.	-	.	-	.	1.9	27	-	.	1.3	16
Base: Self-completion questionnaire respondents									1387				1255

								1986				1989	
Question No								A220b				B226b	
Column No								1923				2077	
(iii) {MOVEHOME}													
Owning your home makes it easier to move when you want to													
Agree strongly	1	-	.	-	.	-	.	27.4	380	-	.	28.0	351
Just agree	2	-	.	-	.	-	.	36.2	502	-	.	37.4	470
Neither agree nor disagree	3	-	.	-	.	-	.	18.9	262	-	.	21.1	265
Just disagree	4	-	.	-	.	-	.	11.8	163	-	.	9.6	120
Disagree strongly	5	-	.	-	.	-	.	3.6	49	-	.	2.5	31
(DK)	8	-	.	-	.	-	.	0.2	3	-	.	0.1	1
(NA)	9	-	.	-	.	-	.	2.0	28	-	.	1.4	17
Base: Self-completion questionnaire respondents									1387				1255

ADVANTAGES AND DISADVANTAGES OF HOME PURCHASE (Continued)

		1983		1984		1985		1986		1987		1989	
		%	No	%	No	%	No	%	No	%	No	%	No
Question No								A220b				B226b	
Column No								1924				2078	
(iv) {MONEYTIE}	Code												
Owning a home ties up money you may need urgently for other things													
Agree strongly	1	-	.	-	.	-	.	7.3	102	-	.	9.4	117
Just agree	2	-	.	-	.	-	.	27.4	380	-	.	25.9	325
Neither agree nor disagree	3	-	.	-	.	-	.	22.5	312	-	.	28.5	358
Just disagree	4	-	.	-	.	-	.	26.4	367	-	.	26.0	327
Disagree strongly	5	-	.	-	.	-	.	13.6	188	-	.	8.5	106
(DK)	8	-	.	-	.	-	.	0.2	3	-	.	0.2	2
(NA)	9	-	.	-	.	-	.	2.6	36	-	.	1.5	19
Base: Self-completion questionnaire respondents									1387				1255

		1983		1984		1985		1986		1987		1989	
		%	No	%	No	%	No	%	No	%	No	%	No
Question No								A220b				B226b	
Column No								1925				2079	
(v) {FREEDOM}													
Owning a home gives you the freedom to do what you want to it													
Agree strongly	1	-	.	-	.	-	.	40.1	557	-	.	35.8	450
Just agree	2	-	.	-	.	-	.	42.1	585	-	.	44.9	563
Neither agree nor disagree	3	-	.	-	.	-	.	8.4	117	-	.	10.2	129
Just disagree	4	-	.	-	.	-	.	5.9	82	-	.	5.6	71
Disagree strongly	5	-	.	-	.	-	.	1.4	19	-	.	2.3	28
(DK)	8	-	.	-	.	-	.	0.1	2	-	.	0.1	1
(NA)	9	-	.	-	.	-	.	1.9	26	-	.	1.1	14
Base: Self-completion questionnaire respondents									1387				1255

ADVANTAGES AND DISADVANTAGES OF HOME PURCHASE (Continued)

		1983		1984		1985		1986		1987		1989	
		%	No	%	No	%	No	%	No	%	No	%	No
Question No								A220b				B226b	
Column No								1926				2080	
(vi) {FINBURDN}	Code												

Owning a home is a big financial burden to repair and maintain

	Code	1983 %	No	1984 %	No	1985 %	No	1986 %	No	1987 %	No	1989 %	No
Agree strongly	1	-	.	-	.	-	.	15.7	218	-	.	14.3	180
Just agree	2	-	.	-	.	-	.	34.0	471	-	.	39.5	496
Neither agree nor disagree	3	-	.	-	.	-	.	22.1	307	-	.	24.4	306
Just disagree	4	-	.	-	.	-	.	20.7	287	-	.	16.1	202
Disagree strongly	5	-	.	-	.	-	.	5.3	73	-	.	4.3	55
(DK)	8	-	.	-	.	-	.	0.3	4	-	.	0.1	1
(NA)	9	-	.	-	.	-	.	1.9	26	-	.	1.2	15

Base: Self-completion questionnaire respondents — 1387 — 1255

Question No								A220b				B226b	
Column No								1927				2108	

(vii) {LEAVEFAM}

Your own home will be something to leave your family

	Code	1983 %	No	1984 %	No	1985 %	No	1986 %	No	1987 %	No	1989 %	No
Agree strongly	1	-	.	-	.	-	.	39.2	544	-	.	40.5	508
Just agree	2	-	.	-	.	-	.	41.1	571	-	.	44.4	557
Neither agree nor disagree	3	-	.	-	.	-	.	12.4	172	-	.	10.4	130
Just disagree	4	-	.	-	.	-	.	2.7	37	-	.	2.2	28
Disagree strongly	5	-	.	-	.	-	.	2.1	29	-	.	1.0	13
(DK)	8	-	.	-	.	-	.	0.1	2	-	.	0.1	1
(NA)	9	-	.	-	.	-	.	2.3	33	-	.	1.4	17

Base: Self-completion questionnaire respondents — 1387 — 1255

ADVANTAGES AND DISADVANTAGES OF HOME PURCHASE (Continued)

		1983		1984		1985		1986		1987		1989	
		%	No	%	No	%	No	%	No	%	No	%	No
Question No								A220b				B226b	
Column No								1928				2109	
(viii) {HOMERESP}	Code												
Owning a home is just too much of a responsibility													
Agree strongly	1	-	.	-	.	-	.	4.2	58	-	.	3.9	49
Just agree	2	-	.	-	.	-	.	7.8	108	-	.	6.9	87
Neither agree nor disagree	3	-	.	-	.	-	.	15.6	217	-	.	20.0	250
Just disagree	4	-	.	-	.	-	.	34.3	475	-	.	34.4	431
Disagree strongly	5	-	.	-	.	-	.	35.9	498	-	.	33.2	417
(DK)	8	-	.	-	.	-	.	0.1	2	-	.	0.1	1
(NA)	9	-	.	-	.	-	.	2.1	30	-	.	1.5	19
Base: Self-completion questionnaire respondents									1387				1255

		1983		1984		1985		1986		1987		1989	
Question No								A220b				B226b	
Column No								1929				2110	
(ix) {RISKJOB}													
Owning a home is too much of a risk for couples without secure jobs													
Agree strongly	1	-	.	-	.	-	.	24.2	336	-	.	23.8	299
Just agree	2	-	.	-	.	-	.	35.2	489	-	.	34.2	429
Neither agree nor disagree	3	-	.	-	.	-	.	14.1	196	-	.	17.9	225
Just disagree	4	-	.	-	.	-	.	19.0	264	-	.	17.5	219
Disagree strongly	5	-	.	-	.	-	.	5.1	71	-	.	5.3	67
(DK)	8	-	.	-	.	-	.	0.2	3	-	.	0.1	1
(NA)	9	-	.	-	.	-	.	2.1	29	-	.	1.2	15
Base: Self-completion questionnaire respondents									1387				1255

ADVANTAGES AND DISADVANTAGES OF HOME PURCHASE (Continued)

		1983		1984		1985		1986		1987		1989	
		%	No	%	No	%	No	%	No	%	No	%	No
Question No								A220b				B226b	
Column No								1930				2111	
(x) {WAITFAM}	Code												
Couples who buy their own homes would be wise to wait before starting a family													
Agree strongly	1	-	.	-	.	-	.	23.1	320	-	.	24.6	309
Just agree	2	-	.	-	.	-	.	36.0	499	-	.	35.7	448
Neither agree nor disagree	3	-	.	-	.	-	.	22.8	317	-	.	24.2	303
Just disagree	4	-	.	-	.	-	.	11.6	161	-	.	10.1	127
Disagree strongly	5	-	.	-	.	-	.	4.4	61	-	.	3.8	48
(DK)	8	-	.	-	.	-	.	0.1	2	-	.	0.1	1
(NA)	9	-	.	-	.	-	.	2.0	27	-	.	1.6	20
Base: Self-completion questionnaire respondents									1387				1255

LA TENANTS: RENT LEVEL OF PRESENT ACCOMMODATION

{CNCLRNT}

Question: [If local authority tenant] **How would you describe the *rent* - not including rates - for this accommodation?**
Would you say it was ... (read out) ...

		1983		1984		1985		1986		1987		1989	
		%	No	%	No	%	No	%	No	%	No	%	No
Question No		64b				76b							
Column No		532				652							
	Code												
... on the high side,	1	50.9	223	-	.	48.6	257	-		-		-	
... reasonable,	2	39.7	174	-	.	46.0	243	-		-		-	
... or on the low side?	3	1.1	5	-	.	2.1	11	-		-		-	
(DK)	8	-	.	-	.	2.5	13	-		-		-	
(NA)	9	8.4	37	-	.	0.8	4	-		-		-	
Base: All LA or NTDC tenants			438				528						

1983 - Asked of local authority tenants only, not of NTDC tenants also
1986, 1987, 1989 - Asked of all tenants: (see p. R - 4 above)

TENANTS : SATISFACTION WITH LANDLORD

1987   Q.A101   {PRENTREP} Column No 817

[If currently rents accommodation] (Show card) In general, how satisfied are you with the standard of repairs
and maintenance your landlord provides? Please choose a phrase from this card.

	Code	%	No
Very satisfied	1	12.6	57
Quite satisfied	2	33.6	152
Neither satisfied nor dissatisfied	3	10.2	46
Quite dissatisfied	4	21.4	97
Very dissatisfied	5	20.8	94
(DK)	8	0.2	1
(NA)	9	1.5	7
Base : All tenants			454

NB The SPSS file contains a category 'Not asked : not renting' (code 0) which elsewhere is taken to be a missing value. To maintain
comparability with other questions, code 0 (n = 938) is also treated as a missing value.

WHETHER LIVES ON A HOUSING ESTATE

1987   Q.A105   {HOMEEST} Column No 821

May I check, is your home part of a housing estate? *(Scotland: or scheme?)*
(Interviewer: may be public or private, but it is the respondent's view we want)

	Code	%	No
Yes, part of estate	1	47.9	666
No	2	51.1	710
(DK)	8	0.1	1
(NA)	9	1.0	14
Base : All			1391

GOOD FEATURES OF COUNCIL ESTATES

1987   Q.A106a   {ESTGOOD1}+{ESTGOOD2}+{ESTGOOD3}+{ESTGOOD4} Column Nos 822-23, 824-25, 826-27, 828-29

Thinking now just of *council estates (Scotland : or housing schemes.)* What do you think are the *good things* about living on a council estate? *(Scotland : or housing scheme?)* (Interviewer: probe fully and record verbatim.)

	Code	%	No
GOOD FEATURES:			
Provide housing for people who need it	1	9.6	133
Good/quick/free repairs and maintenance service	2	12.8	178
Cheap(ish) rents	3	7.8	109
Have [good] facilities/amenities	4	8.3	115
Friendly/neighbourly	5	26.0	361
Attractive	6	3.3	46
Quiet/peaceful	7	1.4	20
Council estates have got worse	8	0.8	11
Nothing/none (no other response)	9	29.3	408
Other answers (no other response)	97	6.5	90
(DK)	98	15.5	215
(NA)	99	1.1	15
Base : All			1391

NB Up to 4 responses were coded for each respondent, so percentages add up to more than 100%

BAD FEATURES OF COUNCIL ESTATES

1987   Q.A106b   {ESTBAD1}+{ESTBAD2}+{ESTBAD3}+{ESTBAD4} Column Nos 834-35, 836-37, 838-39, 840-41

[And] what do you think are the *bad things* about living on a council estate? *(Scotland : or housing scheme?)* (Interviewer : probe fully and record verbatim)

	Code	%	No
BAD FEATURES:			
Are neglected by *tenants*	1	16.5	230
Are neglected by *council/caretakers*	2	7.8	108
Are neglected (unspecified by whom)	3	8.6	120
Get a [bad] name/reputation [as ghettos]	4	9.3	129
Attacks on *people*	5	3.6	50
Attacks on *property*	6	6.0	84
Vandalism, lack of respect for *other people's* property	7	19.6	272
Crime (unspecified)	8	2.9	40
Rowdiness, hooliganism, noisy neighbours/motor vehicles/children	9	28.6	393
Racial tension/violence	10	0.1	1
Poorly designed/unattractive housing/estates badly planned	11	6.4	168
Impersonal/unfriendly/tenants feel isolated	12	2.3	32
No choice of [type of] property	13	2.4	33
Overcrowding	14	7.3	101
Lack of privacy	15	5.5	76
Lacking specific facilities/amenities	16	5.6	80
Council estates have got worse	17	0.6	9
Nothing/none (no other response)	18	11.3	157
Other answer (no other response)	97	3.2	104
(DK)	98	9.3	130
(NA)	99	1.0	14
Base : All			1391

NB Up to 4 responses were coded for each respondent, so percentages add up to more than 100%

LENGTH OF TIME LIVED IN PRESENT NEIGHBOURHOOD

1986   Q.A91a,b   {NGHBRHD - Banded} Column Nos 1444-45

a) How long have you lived in your present neighbourhood ... (read out) ... **less than a year, or one year or more?**

b) [If one year or more] How many years? (Interviewer : probe for best estimate and write in)

	Code	%	No
Less than a year	0	4.6	69
One year	1	2.5	38
Two years	2	5.5	84
Three years	3	6.2	94
Four years	4	4.0	61
Five years	5	4.4	66
Six years	6	2.8	42
Seven years	7	2.6	40
Eight years	8	3.4	51
Nine years	9	3.0	46
Ten years	10	4.7	72
Eleven to fifteen years		12.1	184
Sixteen to twenty years		13.9	210
Twenty-one to twenty-five years		8.0	122
Twenty-six to thirty years		6.5	98
Thirty-one to forty years		7.7	117
Forty-one to fifty years		4.2	64
More than fifty years		3.5	54
(NA)	99	0.3	4
Base : All			1518

NB   Responses to these two questions were combined at the coding stage; column no 1443 was not used. Eleven years and upwards are banded

LENGTH OF TIME LIVED IN PRESENT HOME

1986   Q.A104a,b   *{LIVEHOME - Banded}* Column Nos 1478-79

a) How long have you lived in your present home ... (read out) ... less than a year, or one year or more?

b) [If one year or more] How many years? (Interviewer : probe for best estimate and write in)

	Code	%	No
Less than a year	0	7.0	107
One year	1	4.3	65
Two years	2	8.0	121
Three years	3	7.7	116
Four years	4	5.2	79
Five years	5	4.9	74
Six years	6	4.0	60
Seven years	7	3.3	50
Eight years	8	3.7	57
Nine years	9	3.0	46
Ten years	10	4.3	65
Eleven to fifteen years		12.8	194
Sixteen to twenty years		12.1	184
Twenty-one to twenty-five years		7.3	111
More than twenty-five years		12.1	183
(NA)	99	0.2	3
Base : All			1518

NB   Responses to these two questions were combined at the coding stage; column no 1477 was not used. Eleven years and upwards are banded. A similar question, with bands of years precoded, was asked in 1985 and subsequent years (see p. R-17 above)

REASONS FOR NOT EXPECTING TO MOVE IN NEAR FUTURE

1985   Q.81b   {NOMOVE1} - {NOMOVE3}   Column Nos 662-63, 664-65, 666-67
[If would choose to move but does not expect to] You said that you would *like* to move, but
that you don't *expect* to in the next two years. Why do you think you will not move? (Interviewer:
probe fully and record verbatim)

	Code	%	No
[Not asked: would not choose to move/ would choose to move out and expects to]	0	77.9	1378
Money - can't afford mortgage/increased mortgage	1	5.1	91
Money - legal expenses, transaction/ *moving* costs	2	1.4	24
Money - shortage of finance (unspecified)	3	6.2	110
Shortage/inflexibility of council provision	4	2.5	45
Preference for council *house* (rather than flat)	5	0.2	4
Owns former council house/restrictions on moving	6	0.7	12
Housing shortage (unspecified)	7	0.6	10
Can't afford *area* would like to move to	8	0.3	6
Difficulty in finding work in area would like to move to	9	0.7	13
Accommodation tied to job	10	0.6	10
Differences between household members about moving	11	1.1	19
Family obligations (eg older family members) keep respondent in home area	12	1.6	29
Too old to move	13	1.5	27
Present home/area preferred in some (but not necessarily *all*) ways	14	3.6	63
Other answers (no other response)	95	0.7	13
(DK)	97	-	-
(NA)	99	0.2	4
Base : All			1769

NB Up to 3 responses were coded for each respondent, so percentages add up to more than 100%. Variables
{NOMOVE4} and {NOMOVE5} (for more than 3 answers per respondent) were not used

REASONS FOR NOT EXPECTING TO BUY IN NEAR FUTURE

1985   Q.83b   *{NOBUY1} - {NOBUY3}*   Column Nos 677-78, 679-80, 707-08
[If would choose to buy but does not expect to] You said that you would *like* to buy, but that
you don't *expect* to in the next two years. Why do you think you will not buy? (Interviewer: probe
fully and record verbatim)

	Code	%	No
[Not asked: would not choose to buy/ would choose to buy and expects to]	0	**81.0**	1433
Money: can't afford mortgage repayments/not enough capital	1	**2.0**	35
Money: shortage of finance/low income (unspecified)	2	**12.0**	213
Too old to buy	3	**4.1**	73
Accommodation tied to/convenient for job	4	**0.3**	5
Can't buy/chooses not to buy present council accommodation	5	**0.6**	10
Differences between household members about buying	6	**0.1**	1
Economic position/employment too uncertain to buy	7	**2.5**	44
Other fears/uncertainty about buying	8	**0.2**	3
Prefer to stay in present home	9	**0.2**	4
Other answers (no other response)	97	**0.4**	7
(DK)	98	**0.1**	1
(NA)	99	**0.1**	2
Base : All			1769

NB Up to 3 responses were coded for each respondent, so percentages add up to more than 100%. Variables
{NOBUY4} and {NOBUY5} (for more than 3 answers per respondent) were not used

S Countryside and environment

Table titles and cross references

SERIOUSNESS OF VARIOUS ENVIRONMENTAL THREATS - 1

{ENVIR1} {ENVIR2} {ENVIR3} {ENVIR4} {ENVIR5} {ENVIR6} {ENVIR7}

Question: How serious an effect on our environment do you think each of these things has? (Please tick one box for each)

			1983		1984		1985		1986		1987		1989	
			%	No	%	No	%	No	%	No	%	No	%	No
	Question No		208a		208a		237a		B218a		B228a		B234a	
	Column No		1049		1560		2157		2108		2068		2267	
(i) *{ENVIR1}*		Code												
Noise from aircraft														
	Very serious	4	7.9	126	6.5	99	5.7	85	9.2	121	7.2	85	9.4	117
	Quite serious	3	22.1	355	24.2	369	24.0	361	33.1	435	26.5	313	32.7	411
	Not very serious	2	51.1	823	50.1	763	53.9	810	46.4	610	55.6	656	46.4	582
	Not at all serious	1	17.0	274	17.4	265	14.4	216	9.8	128	8.4	99	9.4	118
	(DK)	8	-	.	0.2	3	0.1	1	0.2	2	0.2	2	-	.
	(NA)	9	1.9	31	1.5	23	1.9	28	1.4	19	2.2	26	2.1	26
Base: Self-completion questionnaire respondents				1610		1522		1502		1315		1181		1255

			1983		1984		1985		1986		1987		1989	
	Question No		208b		208b		237b		B218b		B228b		B234b	
	Column No		1050		1561		2158		2109		2069		2268	
(ii) *{ENVIR2}*		Code												
Lead from petrol														
	Very serious	4	48.0	772	45.1	687	38.6	580	42.2	554	33.8	399	45.1	566
	Quite serious	3	36.2	583	39.2	597	41.6	625	42.5	559	51.3	605	42.9	538
	Not very serious	2	11.8	190	11.2	171	15.5	233	12.8	169	12.0	142	9.3	117
	Not at all serious	1	2.2	36	1.9	29	2.6	39	1.1	15	1.0	12	1.0	13
	(DK)	8	-	.	0.4	6	0.1	2	0.2	2	0.1	2	0.0	1
	(NA)	9	1.8	29	2.1	32	1.5	22	1.3	17	1.8	21	1.7	21
Base: Self-completion questionnaire respondents				1610		1522		1502		1315		1181		1255

SERIOUSNESS OF VARIOUS ENVIRONMENTAL THREATS - 1 (Continued)

		1983		1984		1985		1986		1987		1989	
		%	No	%	No	%	No	%	No	%	No	%	No
Question No		208c		208c		237c		B218c		B228c		B234c	
Column No		1051		1562		2159		2110		2070		2269	

(iii) {ENVIR3} — Code
Industrial waste in the rivers and sea

	Code	%	No	%	No	%	No	%	No	%	No	%	No
Very serious	4	62.0	999	66.7	1015	55.5	833	65.4	860	60.4	713	75.0	941
Quite serious	3	29.2	470	25.0	381	34.0	511	28.5	375	35.0	413	19.8	248
Not very serious	2	5.6	90	5.9	90	6.9	104	4.4	58	2.9	34	2.1	27
Not at all serious	1	1.6	25	1.0	16	1.4	20	0.5	6	0.2	2	1.5	19
(DK)	8	-	.	0.4	7	0.3	5	0.1	1	0.1	1	0.0	1
(NA)	9	1.6	26	1.0	15	1.9	28	1.1	15	1.5	18	1.6	20

Base: Self-completion questionnaire respondents — 1610, 1522, 1502, 1315, 1181, 1255

Question No		208d		208d		237d		B218d		B228d		B234d	
Column No		1052		1563		2160		2111		2071		2270	

(iv) {ENVIR4}
Waste from nuclear electricity stations

	Code	%	No	%	No	%	No	%	No	%	No	%	No
Very serious	4	62.7	1009	69.0	1051	58.2	874	72.3	951	59.6	703	67.1	842
Quite serious	3	19.8	319	17.6	267	24.3	365	18.0	237	23.4	277	22.0	277
Not very serious	2	11.0	178	8.6	130	11.7	175	6.8	89	12.9	153	6.9	86
Not at all serious	1	3.8	61	2.4	36	3.3	49	1.5	20	2.1	24	2.2	27
(DK)	8	-	.	0.5	8	0.4	6	0.2	2	0.2	2	0.0	1
(NA)	9	2.7	43	1.9	29	2.1	32	1.2	16	1.8	22	1.8	23

Base: Self-completion questionnaire respondents — 1610, 1522, 1502, 1315, 1181, 1255

Question No		208e		208e		237e		B218e		B228e		B234e	
Column No		1053		1564		2161		2112		2072		2271	

(v) {ENVIR5}
Industrial fumes in the air

	Code	%	No	%	No	%	No	%	No	%	No	%	No
Very serious	4	41.0	661	45.6	695	43.2	649	45.8	602	43.7	517	60.0	753
Quite serious	3	42.3	681	39.8	606	40.5	608	43.1	566	43.8	517	30.3	381
Not very serious	2	12.5	202	10.7	163	12.2	183	8.6	113	9.9	116	6.7	84
Not at all serious	1	2.1	33	1.7	25	1.9	29	1.0	14	0.6	7	1.4	17
(DK)	8	-	.	0.4	6	0.2	3	0.1	1	0.1	1	0.0	1
(NA)	9	2.1	33	1.8	27	2.0	31	1.5	19	2.0	23	1.6	21

Base: Self-completion questionnaire respondents — 1610, 1522, 1502, 1315, 1181, 1255

SERIOUSNESS OF VARIOUS ENVIRONMENTAL THREATS - 1 (Continued)

		1983		1984		1985		1986		1987		1989	
		%	No	%	No	%	No	%	No	%	No	%	No
Question No		208f		208f		237f		B218f		B228f		B234f	
Column No		1054		1565		2162		2113		2073		2272	

(vi) {ENVIR6}
Noise and dirt from traffic — Code

	Code	%	No	%	No	%	No	%	No	%	No	%	No
Very serious	4	22.8	367	20.1	307	21.2	319	24.6	324	24.8	292	30.6	384
Quite serious	3	42.8	689	45.1	686	46.2	694	48.5	638	48.3	571	50.1	629
Not very serious	2	28.5	458	29.0	442	27.6	415	23.6	311	23.6	279	15.2	190
Not at all serious	1	4.4	72	4.0	60	3.1	47	2.1	27	1.7	20	2.1	27
(DK)	8	-		0.1	2	0.1	1	0.1	1	0.1	1	0.0	1
(NA)	9	1.5	24	1.6	25	1.8	27	1.2	15	1.6	19	2.0	25
Base: Self-completion questionnaire respondents			1610		1522		1502		1315		1181		1255

Question No								B218g		B228g		B234g	
Column No								2114		2074		2273	

(vii) {ENVIR7}
Acid rain

	Code	%	No	%	No	%	No	%	No	%	No	%	No
Very serious	4	-		-		-		53.6	705	50.0	590	57.5	721
Quite serious	3	-		-		-		32.6	429	35.6	420	30.9	388
Not very serious	2	-		-		-		10.3	135	10.6	125	8.2	103
Not at all serious	1	-		-		-		2.0	26	1.5	17	1.4	18
(DK)	8	-		-		-		0.3	4	0.3	4	0.1	2
(NA)	9	-		-		-		1.2	16	2.0	24	1.9	24
Base: Self-completion questionnaire respondents									1315		1181		1255

1989 - Two further items were added to this question in 1989 (see p.S - 19 below)

POSSIBLE SOLUTIONS TO BRITAIN'S ELECTRICITY NEEDS

{POWER}

Question: Which one of these three possible solutions to Britain's electricity needs would you favour most?
(Please tick one box)

	Code	1983 %	1983 No	1984 %	1984 No	1985 %	1985 No	1986 %	1986 No	1987 %	1987 No	1989 %	1989 No
Question No		209a		209a		238a		B219a		B229a		B235a	
Column No		1055		1566		2163		2115		2075		2276	
We should make do with the power stations we have already	1	32.0	515	37.7	574	33.5	503	34.1	448	24.9	294	44.2	555
We should build more coal-fuelled power stations	2	46.6	749	43.6	663	40.8	613	52.2	687	48.3	570	36.6	460
We should build more nuclear power stations	3	18.6	300	15.5	236	22.5	337	10.7	141	22.2	263	16.1	201
(DK)	8	-	-	1.1	17	0.7	11	0.6	8	0.6	8	0.6	8
(NA)	9	2.8	46	2.2	33	2.4	37	2.4	32	3.9	46	2.5	32
Base: Self-completion questionnaire respondents			1610		1522		1502		1315		1181		1255

RISKS POSED BY NUCLEAR POWER STATIONS

{NUCPOWER}

Question: As far as *nuclear* power stations are concerned, which of these statements comes closest to your own feelings?
(Please tick one box)

	Code	1983 %	1983 No	1984 %	1984 No	1985 %	1985 No	1986 %	1986 No	1987 %	1987 No	1989 %	1989 No
Question No		209b		209b		238b		B219b		B229b		B235b	
Column No		1056		1567		2164		2116		2076		2277	
They create very serious risks for the future	1	35.2	567	37.4	569	30.3	455	48.5	638	36.9	435	39.7	498
They create quite serious risks for the future	2	27.8	447	30.0	457	31.4	472	29.3	386	26.8	317	33.0	414
They create only slight risks for the future	3	26.2	421	22.8	348	26.0	391	16.6	219	24.4	288	19.3	242
They create hardly any risks for the future	4	8.6	139	7.7	118	9.1	137	3.8	50	8.2	97	5.8	72
(DK)	8	-	-	1.0	15	1.0	15	0.4	6	0.5	6	0.4	5
(NA)	9	2.2	35	1.0	15	2.2	33	1.3	17	3.3	39	1.9	24
Base: Self-completion questionnaire respondents			1610		1522		1502		1315		1181		1255

DAMAGE TO THE COUNTRYSIDE *VERSUS* HIGHER PRICES

{*DAMAGE*}

Question: Which one of these two statements comes *closest* to your own views? (Please tick one box)

		1983		1984		1985		1986		1987		1989	
		%	No	%	No	%	No	%	No	%	No	%	No
Question No				210		239		B220		B230a		B236a	
Column No				1568		2165		2117		2077		2278	
	Code												
Industry should be prevented from causing damage to the countryside, even if this sometimes leads to higher prices,	1	-	-	76.8	1169	78.4	1178	82.3	1083	83.1	981	88.1	1105
... or industry should keep prices down, even if this sometimes causes damage to the countryside	2	-	-	22.0	335	19.3	290	16.3	214	12.8	151	9.6	120
(DK)	8	-	-	0.5	8	0.4	6	0.3	4	0.4	5	0.2	2
(NA)	9	-	-	0.7	11	1.8	27	1.1	14	3.7	44	2.2	28
Base: Self-completion questionnaire respondents					1522		1502		1315		1181		1255

PROTECTION OF THE COUNTRYSIDE *VERSUS* NEW JOBS

{*CTRYJOBS*}

Question: [And] which of these two statements comes *closest* to your own views? (Please tick one box)

		1983		1984		1985		1986		1987		1989	
		%	No	%	No	%	No	%	No	%	No	%	No
Question No										B230b		B236b	
Column No										2078		2279	
	Code												
The countryside should be protected from development, even if this sometimes leads to fewer new jobs,	1	-	-	-	-	-	-	-	-	60.0	708	72.1	905
.. or - new jobs should be created, even if this sometimes causes damage to the countryside	2	-	-	-	-	-	-	-	-	34.5	407	23.3	292
(DK)	8	-	-	-	-	-	-	-	-	0.7	9	0.2	3
(NA)	9	-	-	-	-	-	-	-	-	4.8	57	4.3	55
Base: Self-completion questionnaire respondents											1181		1255

ROLE OF FARMERS IN THE COUNTRYSIDE

{COUNTRY1} {COUNTRY2} {COUNTRY3} {COUNTRY4}

Question: Here are some statements about the countryside. Please tick one box for *each* to show whether you agree or disagree with it.

		1983		1984		1985		1986		1987		1989	
		%	No	%	No	%	No	%	No	%	No	%	No
Question No						240a		B221a		B231a		B237a	
Column No						2166		2118		2108		2308	

(i) *{COUNTRY1}*

Modern methods of farming have caused damage to the countryside

		Code	1983		1984		1985		1986		1987		1989	
Agree strongly		1	-	-	-	-	17.6	265	18.5	243	17.4	205	21.1	265
Agree		2	-	-	-	-	45.5	684	44.6	587	50.3	594	51.2	642
Disagree		3	-	-	-	-	33.2	498	33.3	438	26.8	316	24.4	306
Disagree strongly		4	-	-	-	-	0.7	10	1.6	21	1.5	18	1.0	13
(DK)		8	-	-	-	-	0.5	8	0.3	4	0.3	4	0.4	5
(NA)		9	-	-	-	-	2.5	37	1.6	22	3.7	43	2.0	25

Base: Self-completion questionnaire respondents

	1985	1986	1987	1989
	1502	1315	1181	1255

		1985	1986	1987	1989
Question No		240b	B221b	B231b	B237b
Column No		2167	2119	2109	2309

(ii) *{COUNTRY2}*

If farmers have to choose between producing more food and looking after the countryside, they should produce more food

		Code	1983		1984		1985		1986		1987		1989	
Agree strongly		1	-	-	-	-	6.9	104	7.9	103	4.8	56	5.2	65
Agree		2	-	-	-	-	45.6	684	36.9	485	30.8	363	31.0	389
Disagree		3	-	-	-	-	40.6	610	47.6	626	54.2	640	52.6	660
Disagree strongly		4	-	-	-	-	3.1	47	5.3	70	6.2	74	8.7	109
(DK)		8	-	-	-	-	0.2	3	0.2	3	0.6	8	0.2	3
(NA)		9	-	-	-	-	3.6	54	2.1	28	3.4	40	2.3	29

Base: Self-completion questionnaire respondents

	1985	1986	1987	1989
	1502	1315	1181	1255

ROLE OF FARMERS IN THE COUNTRYSIDE (Continued)

		1983		1984		1985		1986		1987		1989	
		%	No	%	No	%	No	%	No	%	No	%	No
Question No						240c		B221c		B231c		B237c	
Column No						2168		2120		2110		2310	

(iii) {COUNTRY3}

All things considered, farmers do a good job in looking after the countryside

	Code	1983 %	No	1984 %	No	1985 %	No	1986 %	No	1987 %	No	1989 %	No
Agree strongly	1	-	-	-	-	8.6	128	11.8	155	8.9	105	7.6	96
Agree	2	-	-	-	-	66.7	1002	66.5	875	65.0	767	64.4	808
Disagree	3	-	-	-	-	20.2	304	17.7	233	20.0	236	23.0	289
Disagree strongly	4	-	-	-	-	1.9	29	1.7	22	2.5	29	2.4	30
(DK)	8	-	-	-	-	0.2	4	0.3	5	0.4	5	0.5	6
(NA)	9	-	-	-	-	2.3	35	1.9	26	3.3	39	2.1	26

Base: Self-completion questionnaire respondents — 1985: 1502, 1986: 1315, 1987: 1181, 1989: 1255

		1985	1986	1987	1989
Question No		240d	B221d	B231d	B237d
Column No		2169	2121	2111	2311

(iv) {COUNTRY4}

Government should withhold some subsidies from farmers and use them to protect the countryside, even if this leads to higher prices

	Code	1983 %	No	1984 %	No	1985 %	No	1986 %	No	1987 %	No	1989 %	No
Agree strongly	1	-	-	-	-	7.3	109	8.7	114	6.9	82	9.7	122
Agree	2	-	-	-	-	39.3	591	40.5	532	44.4	525	50.5	634
Disagree	3	-	-	-	-	45.3	681	44.1	580	41.7	492	33.4	420
Disagree strongly	4	-	-	-	-	4.3	64	4.0	52	2.5	30	3.1	39
(DK)	8	-	-	-	-	0.5	8	0.3	5	0.8	10	0.6	7
(NA)	9	-	-	-	-	3.2	48	2.4	32	3.6	43	2.7	34

Base: Self-completion questionnaire respondents — 1985: 1502, 1986: 1315, 1987: 1181, 1989: 1255

LOOKING AFTER THE COUNTRYSIDE

{FARMERS}

Question: Which of these two statements comes *closest* to your own views? (Please tick one box)

		1983		1984		1985		1986		1987		1989	
		%	No	%	No	%	No	%	No	%	No	%	No
Question No						241		B222		B232		B238	
Column No						2170		2122		2112		2312	
	Code												
Looking after the countryside is too important to be left to farmers - government authorities should have more control over what's done and built on farms,	1	-	-	-	-	34.0	511	33.6	442	37.9	448	46.3	581
... or farmers know how important it is to look after the countryside - there are enough controls and farmers should be left to decide what's done on farms	2	-	-	-	-	50.6	759	47.0	619	43.7	516	36.7	461
Can't choose	8	-	-	-	-	13.5	203	18.2	240	14.8	175	15.6	195
(NA)	9	-	-	-	-	1.9	28	1.2	16	3.5	42	1.4	18
Base: Self-completion questionnaire respondents							1502		1315		1181		1255

1987 -   Can't choose, code 3 on questionnaire but not on SPSS file

RECENT PARTICIPATION IN COUNTRYSIDE ACTIVITIES

{LEISURE} {LEISURE6}

Question: Now I'd like to ask you a few questions about the countryside.
(Show card) **On this card are some activities people do in their leisure time. Have you taken part in any of these leisure activities** *in the last four weeks?*

		1983		1984		1985		1986		1987		1989	
		%	No	%	No	%	No	%	No	%	No	%	No
(i) {LEISURE}	Question No							B100a		B95a			
	Column No							808		1008			
		Code											
Yes	1	-	-	-	-	-	-	63.9	990	58.6	806	-	-
No	2	-	-	-	-	-	-	35.7	552	41.1	565	-	-
(DK)	8	-	-	-	-	-	-	-	-	-	-	-	-
(NA)	9	-	-	-	-	-	-	0.4	7	0.3	4	-	-
Base: All									1548		1375		

		1983		1984		1985		1986		1987		1989	
(ii) {LEISURE6}	Question No					64b		B100b		B95b			
	Column No					569		809		1009			

Can you remember when you *last* **did any of these activities in the countryside?** [If yes] **How long ago was that?**

		1983		1984		1985		1986		1987		1989	
[Not asked: one or more countryside activity done in last four weeks]	0	-	-	-	-	60.4	1068	63.9	990	58.6	806	-	-
Within past month	1	-	-	-	-	0.2	3	0.8	13	0.9	12	-	-
1-3 months ago	2	-	-	-	-	3.8	67	5.7	88	5.6	77	-	-
4-6 months ago	3	-	-	-	-	3.3	59	5.0	77	10.0	137	-	-
7-12 months ago	4	-	-	-	-	16.5	291	11.7	181	14.8	203	-	-
More than one year ago	5	-	-	-	-	11.4	202	8.7	135	6.4	89	-	-
No, can't remember/(DK)	8	-	-	-	-	2.7	47	3.7	57	2.9	40	-	-
(NA)	9	-	-	-	-	1.8	31	0.5	8	0.7	10	-	-
Base: All						1769		1548		1375			

1985 - {LEISURE}: see p. S - 29 below, for a question at which each of five activities was asked about separately. Q reads: 'I'm going to mention a number of activities people do in their leisure time. Could you tell me whether or not you have taken part in any of these activities in the <u>last four weeks</u>?'

1986, 1987 - {LEISURE} Card reads: In the last four weeks, have you ...
    ... been for a drive, outing or picnic <u>in the countryside</u>
    ... been for a long walk, ramble or hike (of more than 2 miles) <u>in the countryside</u>
    ... visited any historic or stately homes, gardens, zoos or wildlife parks <u>in the countryside</u>
    ... gone fishing, horse riding, shooting or hunting <u>in the countryside</u>
    ... visited the seacoast or cliffs

1985 - {LEISURE6} Interviewer instruction: if necessary remind respondent of activities. Although the question was administered in a different way in this year, data users may have confidence that the data are comparable with those for subsequent years

PERCEPTIONS OF CHANGE IN THE COUNTRYSIDE

{CTRYSAME} {CTRYBETR}

Question: Do you think the countryside *generally* is much the same as it was twenty years ago, or do you think it has changed? [If changed] Has it changed a bit or a lot?

		1983		1984		1985		1986		1987		1989	
		%	No	%	No	%	No	%	No	%	No	%	No
Question No						65a		B101a		B96a			
Column No						570		810		1010			
(i) {CTRYSAME}	Code												
Much the same	1	-	-	-	-	20.4	360	21.8	337	20.3	279	-	-
Changed a bit	2	-	-	-	-	23.3	412	24.8	385	21.4	294	-	-
Changed a lot	3	-	-	-	-	49.3	872	47.9	742	55.2	759	-	-
(DK)	8	-	-	-	-	7.1	125	5.1	80	2.7	37	-	-
(NA)	9	-	-	-	-	-	-	0.4	6	0.4	6	-	-
Base: All							1769		1548		1375		

		1983		1984		1985		1986		1987		1989	
Question No						65c		B101b		B96b			
Column No						607		811		1011			

(ii) {CTRYBETR}

[If changed a bit or a lot] **Do you think the *countryside generally* has changed for the better or worse?**

		1983		1984		1985		1986		1987		1989	
[Not asked: thinks countryside much the same as twenty years ago]	0	-	-	-	-	27.4	485	21.8	337	20.3	279	-	-
Better	1	-	-	-	-	11.1	197	13.1	203	12.2	168	-	-
Worse	2	-	-	-	-	49.4	874	50.9	789	56.2	773	-	-
(Better in some ways/worse in others)	3	-	-	-	-	11.0	195	7.9	122	7.9	109	-	-
(DK)	8	-	-	-	-	0.3	6	0.3	5	0.2	3	-	-
(NA)	9	-	-	-	-	0.7	12	6.0	93	3.1	43	-	-
Base: All							1769		1548		1375		

1985 - Those answering 'Don't know' to Q.65a were not asked Q.65c. Nor were they asked Q.65b, an open question about ways in which the countryside was thought to have changed (see p. S - 30 below)

CONCERN ABOUT THE COUNTRYSIDE

{CTRYCONC}

Question: Are you personally concerned about things that may happen to the countryside, or does it not concern you particularly? [If concerned] Are you very concerned, or just a bit concerned?

		1983		1984		1985		1986		1987		1989	
		%	No	%	No	%	No	%	No	%	No	%	No
Question No						66		B102		B97			
Column No						608		812		1012			
	Code												
Very concerned	1	-	.	-	.	30.9	547	39.9	618	44.2	608	-	.
A bit concerned	2	-	.	-	.	36.7	649	34.5	534	32.7	450	-	.
Does not concern me particularly	3	-	.	-	.	32.2	570	25.2	391	22.3	307	-	.
(DK)	8	-	.	-	.	-	.	-	.	0.1	1	-	.
(NA)	9	-	.	-	.	0.2	3	0.4	6	0.6	9	-	.
Base: All							1769		1548		1375		

THREATS TO THE COUNTRYSIDE

{CTHREAT1} {CTHREAT2}

Question: (Show card) Which, if any, of the things on this card to you think is the *greatest threat* to the countryside; if you think none of them is a threat, please say so.

		1983		1984		1985		1986		1987		1989	
		%	No	%	No	%	No	%	No	%	No	%	No
Question No						68a				B98a			
Column No						635-36				1013-14			
(i) {CTHREAT1}	Code												
Motorways and road building	1	-	.	-	.	11.6	205	-	.	11.1	152	-	.
Industrial pollution	2	-	.	-	.	29.5	522	-	.	32.4	445	-	.
Removal by farmers of traditional landscape, such as hedgerows, woodlands	3	-	.	-	.	12.0	212	-	.	10.6	146	-	.
Tourism and visitors	4	-	.	-	.	1.3	22	-	.	1.0	14	-	.
Litter	5	-	.	-	.	11.3	199	-	.	8.8	121	-	.
Urban growth and housing development	6	-	.	-	.	12.3	218	-	.	15.5	213	-	.
Use of chemicals and pesticides in farming	7	-	.	-	.	17.4	308	-	.	17.9	246	-	.
None of these	97	-	.	-	.	1.6	28	-	.	1.1	15	-	.
(DK)	98	-	.	-	.	2.9	52	-	.	1.1	15	-	.
(NA)	99	-	.	-	.	0.1	2	-	.	0.6	8	-	.
Base: All							1769				1375		

THREATS TO THE COUNTRYSIDE (Continued)

			1983		1984		1985		1986		1987		1989	
			%	No	%	No	%	No	%	No	%	No	%	No
	Question No						68b				B98b			
	Column No						637-38				1015-16			
(ii) {CTHREAT2} And which do you think is the *next greatest* threat?	Code													
Motorways and road building	1		-	.	-	.	9.4	166	-	.	11.0	151	-	.
Industrial pollution	2		-	.	-	.	17.5	309	-	.	21.0	289	-	.
Removal by farmers of traditional landscape, such as hedgerows, woodlands	3		-	.	-	.	12.6	223	-	.	12.0	165	-	.
Tourism and visitors	4		-	.	-	.	1.8	31	-	.	1.9	26	-	.
Litter	5		-	.	-	.	14.4	255	-	.	11.8	162	-	.
Urban growth and housing development	6		-	.	-	.	12.8	227	-	.	12.4	171	-	.
Use of chemicals and pesticides in farming	7		-	.	-	.	25.3	447	-	.	26.0	357	-	.
None of these	97		-	.	-	.	2.3	40	-	.	1.6	22	-	.
(DK)	98		-	.	-	.	2.9	51	-	.	1.6	22	-	.
(NA)	99		-	.	-	.	1.1	20	-	.	0.8	11	-	.
Base: All								1769				1375		

ENDORSEMENT OF PARTY ENVIRONMENT POLICIES

{ENVIRPTY}

Question: Which political party's views on the environment would you say come closest to your own views?
(Interviewer: do not prompt. Code one only)

		1983		1984		1985		1986		1987		1989	
		%	No	%	No	%	No	%	No	%	No	%	No
Question No								B107a		B100a			
Column No								852		1023			
	Code												
Conservative	1	-	-	-	-	-	-	12.8	198	15.5	213	-	-
Labour	2	-	-	-	-	-	-	13.6	211	11.8	162	-	-
Liberal	3	-	-	-	-	-	-	3.6	56	4.0	55	-	-
SDP/Social Democrat	4	-	-	-	-	-	-	3.2	49	3.2	44	-	-
Alliance	5	-	-	-	-	-	-	2.0	32	2.6	35	-	-
Green Party/Ecology Party	6	-	-	-	-	-	-	4.3	67	6.0	82	-	-
Other	7	-	-	-	-	-	-	0.9	13	0.3	4	-	-
DK	8	-	-	-	-	-	-	54.2	839	53.3	733	-	-
None	0	-	-	-	-	-	-	4.8	75	2.7	37	-	-
(NA)	9	-	-	-	-	-	-	0.7	10	0.8	11	-	-
Base: All								1548		1375			

MEMBERSHIP OF 'COUNTRYSIDE' ORGANISATIONS

{CLUB1} {CLUB2} {CLUB3} {CLUB4} {CLUB5}

Question: (Show card) Are you or anyone in your household, a member of any of the groups, clubs or organisations listed
on this card? (If yes) Which ones?

		1983		1984		1985		1986		1987		1989	
		%	No	%	No	%	No	%	No	%	No	%	No
Question No						104		B107b		B100b			
Column No						910		853		1024			
(i) *{CLUB1}* National Trust	Code												
Not given as answer	0	-	-	-	-	94.2	1667	92.2	1427	90.7	1248	-	-
Given as answer	1	-	-	-	-	5.8	102	7.8	121	8.7	120	-	-
(NA)	9	-	-	-	-	-		-		0.6	8	-	-
Base: All						1769		1548		1375			

MEMBERSHIP OF 'COUNTRYSIDE' ORGANISATIONS (Continued)

		1983		1984		1985		1986		1987		1989	
		%	No	%	No	%	No	%	No	%	No	%	No
Question No						104		B107b		B100b			
Column No						911		854		1025			

(ii) {CLUB2}
Royal Society for the Protection of Birds — Code

	Code	%	No	%	No	%	No	%	No	%	No	%	No
Not given as answer	0	-	-	-	-	96.4	1706	94.6	1464	94.9	1306	-	-
Given as answer	2	-	-	-	-	3.6	63	5.4	84	4.5	62	-	-
(NA)	9	-	-	-	-	-	-	-	-	0.6	8	-	-
Base: All							1769		1548		1375		

		%	No	%	No	%	No	%	No	%	No	%	No
Question No						104		B107b		B100b			
Column No						912		855		1026			

(iii) {CLUB3}
Other wildlife or countryside protection group

	Code	%	No	%	No	%	No	%	No	%	No	%	No
Not given as answer	0	-	-	-	-	95.7	1694	95.5	1479	95.5	1314	-	-
Given as answer	3	-	-	-	-	4.3	75	4.5	70	3.9	53	-	-
(NA)	9	-	-	-	-	-	-	-	-	0.6	8	-	-
Base: All							1769		1548		1375		

		%	No	%	No	%	No	%	No	%	No	%	No
Question No						104		B107b		B100b			
Column No						913		856		1027			

(iv) {CLUB4}
Countryside sports/leisure organisation

	Code	%	No	%	No	%	No	%	No	%	No	%	No
Not given as answer	0	-	-	-	-	91.7	1622	93.4	1447	92.7	1275	-	-
Given as answer	4	-	-	-	-	8.3	147	6.6	102	6.7	92	-	-
(NA)	9	-	-	-	-	-	-	-	-	0.6	8	-	-
Base: All							1769		1548		1375		

		%	No	%	No	%	No	%	No	%	No	%	No
Question No						104		B107b		B100b			
Column No						914		857		1028			

(v) {CLUB5}
Summary

	Code	%	No	%	No	%	No	%	No	%	No	%	No
Member of 1 or more	0	-	-	-	-	17.1	302	19.3	299	19.5	269	-	-
None of these	1	-	-	-	-	82.7	1463	80.3	1243	79.9	1098	-	-
(NA)	9	-	-	-	-	0.2	4	0.4	7	0.6	8	-	-
Base: All							1769		1548		1375		

HOW RESPONDENT DESCRIBES HIS/HER LOCALITY

{AREALIVE}

Question: (Interviewer: code from observation and check with respondent) **Can I just check, would you describe the place where you live as being ... (read out) ...**

		1983		1984		1985		1986		1987		1989	
		%	No	%	No	%	No	%	No	%	No	%	No
Question No						62a		B108a		B101a			
Column No						561		866		1029			
	Code												
... in a big city,	1	-	-	-	-	8.3	146	10.5	162	9.2	126	-	-
...in the suburbs or outskirts of a city	2	-	-	-	-	29.8	528	33.6	521	29.1	400	-	-
... in a small city or town,	3	-	-	-	-	36.9	653	33.4	517	36.3	499	-	-
... in a *country* village or town,	4	-	-	-	-	21.2	375	18.9	292	20.4	280	-	-
... or in the countryside?	5	-	-	-	-	3.7	66	3.6	56	4.4	60	-	-
(DK)	8	-	-	-	-	-	-	-	-	0.1	1	-	-
(NA)	9	-	-	-	-	0.1	1	-	-	0.6	8	-	-
Base: All							1769		1548		1375		

WHETHER EVER LIVED IN THE COUNTRY

{CNTRYLIV}

Question: [If lives in city, suburbs or small city/town] **Have you *ever* lived in the countryside, or in a country village or town - for instance, when you were a child or at some time before now?**

		1983		1984		1985		1986		1987		1989	
		%	No	%	No	%	No	%	No	%	No	%	No
Question No						62b		B108b		B101b			
Column No						562		867		1030			
	Code												
[Not asked: lives in country village or town, or in the countryside]	0	-	-	-	-	25.0	442	22.5	348	24.8	340	-	-
Yes	1	-	-	-	-	28.1	498	31.7	490	30.6	421	-	-
No	2	-	-	-	-	45.4	804	45.3	701	43.7	601	-	-
(DK)	8	-	-	-	-	-	-	-	-	-	-	-	-
(NA)	9	-	-	-	-	1.5	26	0.5	9	0.9	13	-	-
Base: All							1769		1548		1375		

1987 · No (DK)

DISTANCE FROM NEAREST OPEN COUNTRYSIDE

{CNTRYDIS}

Question: [If respondent lives in city, suburbs, or any village/town] **About how far do you live from the nearest** *open countryside* **that you can visit or walk in? Please do not include city parks.** (Interviewer: if not sure, probe for estimate)

		1983		1984		1985		1986		1987		1989	
		%	No	%	No	%	No	%	No	%	No	%	No
Question No						63		B108c		B101c			
Column No						563		868		1031			
	Code												
[Not asked: lives in the countryside]	0	-	-	-	-	3.7	66	3.6	56	4.4	60	-	-
Less than 1/2 mile (15 mins. walk)	1	-	-	-	-	31.6	559	29.7	460	34.9	480	-	-
1/2, up to 1 mile (15-30 mins. walk)	2	-	-	-	-	13.7	242	12.8	197	15.3	210	-	-
Over 1 mile, up to 3 miles	3	-	-	-	-	20.0	353	22.7	352	18.3	251	-	-
Over 3 miles, up to 10 miles	4	-	-	-	-	20.4	362	22.3	345	18.2	250	-	-
Over 10 miles	5	-	-	-	-	6.4	114	5.9	91	6.9	95	-	-
(DK)	8	-	-	-	-	3.0	54	1.9	29	1.3	19	-	-
(NA)	9	-	-	-	-	1.1	20	1.2	18	0.7	9	-	-
Base: All							1769		1548		1375		

POLICY PREFERENCES FOR THE COUNTRYSIDE

{CTRYFARM} {CTRYHSNG} {WILDLIFE} {CTRYROAD} {PICNIC}

Question: Please tick one box on each line to show how you feel about:

		1983		1984		1985		1986		1987		1989	
		%	No	%	No	%	No	%	No	%	No	%	No
Question No								B223a		B233a			
Column No								2123		2113			
(i) {CTRYFARM}	Code												
Increasing the amount of country-side being farmed													
It should be stopped altogether	1	-	-	-	-	-	-	7.7	102	8.9	106	-	-
It should be discouraged	2	-	-	-	-	-	-	44.8	590	45.8	541	-	-
Don't mind one way or the other	3	-	-	-	-	-	-	34.9	460	31.3	369	-	-
It should be encouraged	4	-	-	-	-	-	-	10.3	135	9.2	109	-	-
(DK)	8	-	-	-	-	-	-	0.3	4	-	-	-	-
(NA)	9	-	-	-	-	-	-	1.9	25	4.7	56	-	-
Base: Self-completion questionnaire respondents									1315		1181		

POLICY PREFERENCES FOR THE COUNTRYSIDE (Continued)

			1983		1984		1985		1986		1987		1989	
			%	No	%	No	%	No	%	No	%	No	%	No
Question No									B223b		B233b			
Column No									2124		2114			
(ii) {CTRYHSNG}		Code												
Building new housing in country areas														
It should be stopped altogether	1		-		-		-		13.9	182	15.3	180	-	-
It should be discouraged	2		-		-		-		50.2	660	48.6	573	-	-
Don't mind one way or the other	3		-		-		-		22.3	293	21.7	256	-	-
It should be encouraged	4		-		-		-		11.8	155	10.9	129	-	-
(DK)	8		-		-		-		0.2	3	-		-	-
(NA)	9		-		-		-		1.7	23	3.6	42	-	-
Base: Self-completion questionnaire respondents									1315		1181			

			1983		1984		1985		1986		1987		1989	
Question No									B223c		B233c			
Column No									2125		2115			
(iii) {WILDLIFE}														
Putting the needs of farmers before protection of wildlife														
It should be stopped altogether	1		-		-		-		15.3	202	15.4	182	-	-
It should be discouraged	2		-		-		-		53.8	707	56.8	671	-	-
Don't mind one way or the other	3		-		-		-		19.9	261	16.2	191	-	-
It should be encouraged	4		-		-		-		9.4	124	7.6	90	-	-
(DK)	8		-		-		-		0.2	3	-		-	-
(NA)	9		-		-		-		1.4	19	4.0	47	-	-
Base: Self-completion questionnaire respondents									1315		1181			

POLICY PREFERENCES FOR THE COUNTRYSIDE (Continued)

		1983		1984		1985		1986		1987		1989	
		%	No	%	No	%	No	%	No	%	No	%	No
Question No								B223d		B233d			
Column No	Code							2126		2116			

(iv) {CTRYROAD}
Providing more roads in country areas

	Code	1983 %	No	1984 %	No	1985 %	No	1986 %	No	1987 %	No	1989 %	No
It should be stopped altogether	1	-	-	-	-	-	-	9.8	129	9.9	117	-	-
It should be discouraged	2	-	-	-	-	-	-	40.3	530	45.6	538	-	-
Don't mind one way or the other	3	-	-	-	-	-	-	28.5	375	27.3	322	-	-
It should be encouraged	4	-	-	-	-	-	-	19.7	259	13.2	156	-	-
(DK)	8	-	-	-	-	-	-	0.2	2	-	-	-	-
(NA)	9	-	-	-	-	-	-	1.5	20	4.0	48	-	-

Base: Self-completion questionnaire respondents — 1986: 1315, 1987: 1181

								B223e		B233e			
Question No / Column No								2127		2117			

(v) {PICNIC}
Increasing the number of picnic areas and camping sites in the countryside

	Code	1983 %	No	1984 %	No	1985 %	No	1986 %	No	1987 %	No	1989 %	No
It should be stopped altogether	1	-	-	-	-	-	-	2.8	36	3.9	47	-	-
It should be discouraged	2	-	-	-	-	-	-	13.8	182	16.2	192	-	-
Don't mind one way or the other	3	-	-	-	-	-	-	28.4	373	27.9	329	-	-
It should be encouraged	4	-	-	-	-	-	-	53.8	708	48.6	574	-	-
(DK)	8	-	-	-	-	-	-	0.1	1	-	-	-	-
(NA)	9	-	-	-	-	-	-	1.2	15	3.3	39	-	-

Base: Self-completion questionnaire respondents — 1986: 1315, 1987: 1181

SERIOUSNESS OF VARIOUS ENVIRONMENTAL THREATS - 2

1989   Q.B234h,i   {ENVIR8}{ENVIR9} Column Nos 2274-75
How serious an effect on the environment do you think each of these things has?

{ENVIR8}   Column No 2274
h) Certain aerosol chemicals in the atmosphere

{ENVIR9}   Column No 2275
i) Cutting down tropical rainforests

	Code	h) Aerosol chemicals {ENVIR8} %	No	i) Cutting down rainforests {ENVIR9} %	No
Very serious	4	67.3	845	68.2	856
Quite serious	3	24.4	307	21.9	275
Not very serious	2	5.6	70	6.6	82
Not at all serious	1	1.0	13	1.7	21
(DK)	8	0.1	2	0.1	2
(NA)	9	1.6	20	1.5	19
Base : Self-completion respondents			1255		1255

NB These two items were added in 1989 to an existing list of seven environmental hazards (see pp. S-1 to S-3 above)

ALTERNATIVE USES OF FARMLAND

1987   Q.B99a-c   {LANDUSE1}-{LANDUSE3} Column Nos 1017-22

a) (Show card) Modern farming methods have meant it now takes less land to produce the same amount of food. On this card are some ways that land no longer needed for farming might be used. Which do *you* think would be the *best* use?

b) ... and which *next best?*

c) And which do you think would be the *worst* way to use this land?

	Code	a) Best {LANDUSE1} 1017-18 %	No	b) Next best {LANDUSE2} 1019-20 %	No	c) Worst {LANDUSE3} 1021-22 %	No
Pay farmers to return to methods of farming which need more land	1	9.6	131	7.0	96	15.5	214
Plant forests of pine and conifers for timber and woodlands	2	10.5	144	11.2	154	4.3	59
Plant forests of oak and beech for timber and woodlands	3	20.2	278	24.3	334	0.6	8
Provide places for countryside recreation, such as riding and golf	4	6.6	91	11.9	164	7.5	103
Create national parks and wildlife reserves	5	37.6	517	25.9	356	1.1	15
Develop new housing areas	6	6.8	93	5.0	69	37.5	515
Develop new areas for rural industries	7	5.1	70	10.1	139	24.9	343
None of these	90	0.6	9	0.8	11	2.4	33
(DK)	98	2.3	32	2.9	41	5.2	71
(NA)	99	0.7	10	0.9	13	1.0	14
Base : All			1375		1375		1375

ENCROACHMENTS ON THE COUNTRYSIDE

1987   Q.B234a-e   {HOUSBUIL}{KEEPBELT}{PLANLAWS}{FARMRSAY}{LESSVIST}   Column Nos 2120-24

Please tick one box on each line to show whether you agree or disagree with each of the following statements.

	Agree Strongly 1		Agree 2		Neither agree nor disagree 3		Disagree 4		Disagree Strongly 5		(DK) 8		(NA) 9	
Code	%	No	%	No	%	No	%	No	%	No	%	No	%	No
a) {HOUSBUIL} Column No 2120 New housing should be built in cities, towns and villages rather than in the countryside	25.6	302	56.5	667	11.3	133	4.1	48	0.3	3	0.1	1	2.2	26
b) {KEEPBELT} Column No 2121 It is more important to keep green-belt areas than to build new homes there	28.2	333	49.4	583	12.3	145	7.2	85	0.6	7	0.0	-	2.4	28
c) {PLANLAWS} Column No 2122 Planning laws should be relaxed so that people who want to live in the countryside may do so	5.0	59	28.9	341	22.8	269	35.1	414	5.6	66	0.3	3	2.4	29
d) {FARMRSAY} Column No 2123 Compared with other users of the countryside, farmers have too much say	5.3	63	24.5	289	39.2	463	26.2	310	2.1	24	0.1	2	2.7	31
e) {LESSVIST} Column No 2124 The beauty of the countryside depends on stopping too many people from visiting it	2.5	29	11.3	134	20.5	243	54.4	642	8.5	101	0.1	1	2.6	31

Base : All self-completion respondents (n = 1181)

LIKELY ACTIVISM OVER COUNTRYSIDE ISSUES - 1

1986   Q.B103a,b   {CONDEVT} {DEVTDO1}-{DEVTDO9} Column Nos 813-22

a) Suppose you heard that a housing development was being planned in a part of the countryside you knew and liked. Would you be concerned by this, or not?

{CONDEVT}		Code	%	No
	Column No 813			
	Yes, concerned	1	71.4	1105
	No, not concerned	2	22.1	342
	(DK/depends)	8	6.2	96
	(NA)	9	0.4	6
Base : All				1548

b) [If would be concerned] (Show card) Would you personally be likely to do any of these things about it? Any others? (Interviewer : code all that apply)

		Code	%	No
{DEVTDO1}	Column No 814			
Would take no action				
	Wouldn't do	0	78.9	1221
	Would do	1	14.3	221
	(DK)	8	0.3	4
	(NA)	9	6.6	101
Base : All				1548
{DEVTDO2}	Column No 815			
Contact MP or councillor				
	Wouldn't do	0	70.0	1084
	Would do	2	23.2	359
	(DK)	8	0.3	4
	(NA)	9	6.6	101
Base : All				1548
{DEVTDO3}	Column No 816			
Contact a government or planning department				
	Wouldn't do	0	82.3	1275
	Would do	3	10.8	168
	(DK)	8	0.3	4
	(NA)	9	6.6	101
Base : All				1548
{DEVTDO4}	Column No 817			
Contact radio, TV or a newspaper				
	Wouldn't do	0	86.3	1336
	Would do	4	6.9	106
	(DK)	8	0.3	4
	(NA)	9	6.6	101
Base : All				1548
{DEVTDO5}	Column No 818			
Sign a petition				
	Wouldn't do	0	48.6	752
	Would do	5	44.6	690
	(DK)	8	0.3	4
	(NA)	9	6.6	101
Base : All				1548

LIKELY ACTIVISM OVER COUNTRYSIDE ISSUES - 1 (continued)

	Code	%	No

{DEVTDO6}   Column No 819
Join a conservation group

	Code	%	No
Wouldn't do	0	85.1	1317
Would do	6	8.1	125
(DK)	8	0.3	4
(NA)	9	6.6	101
Base : All			1548

{DEVTDO7}   Column No 820
Give money to a campaign

	Code	%	No
Wouldn't do	0	82.8	1282
Would do	7	10.3	160
(DK)	8	0.3	4
(NA)	9	6.6	101
Base : All			1548

{DEVTDO8}   Column No 821
Volunteer to work for a campaign

	Code	%	No
Wouldn't do	0	85.7	1326
Would do	1	7.5	116
(DK)	8	0.3	4
(NA)	9	6.6	101
Base : All			1548

{DEVTDO9}   Column No 822
Go on a protest march or demonstration

	Code	%	No
Wouldn't do	0	87.5	1355
Would do	2	5.7	88
(DK)	8	0.3	4
(NA)	9	6.6	101
Base : All			1548

LIKELY ACTIVISM OVER COUNTRYSIDE ISSUES - 2

1986   Q.B104a,b   {CONFLWR} {FLWRDO1}-{FLWRDO9} Column Nos 823-32

a) [Now] suppose you heard that a protected site where wildflowers grew was going to be ploughed for farmland. Would you be concerned by this, or not?

		Code	%	No
{CONFLWR}	Column No 823			
	Yes, concerned	1	54.7	848
	No, not concerned	2	39.6	613
	(DK/depends)	8	5.3	83
	(NA)	9	0.4	6
Base : All				1548

b) [If would be concerned] (Show card) Would you personally be likely to do any of these things about it? Any others? (Interviewer : code all that apply)

		Code	%	No
{FLWRDO1}	Column No 824			
Would take no action				
	Wouldn't do	0	82.1	1272
	Would do	1	12.0	186
	(DK)	8	0.1	1
	(NA)	9	5.8	89
Base : All				1548
{FLWRDO2}	Column No 825			
Contact MP or councillor				
	Wouldn't do	0	78.7	1218
	Would do	2	15.5	240
	(DK)	8	0.1	1
	(NA)	9	5.8	89
Base : All				1548
{FLWRDO3}	Column No 826			
Contact a government or planning department				
	Wouldn't do	0	87.4	1353
	Would do	3	6.7	104
	(DK)	8	0.1	1
	(NA)	9	5.8	89
Base : All				1548
{FLWRDO4}	Column No 827			
Contact radio, TV or a newspaper				
	Wouldn't do	0	89.4	1384
	Would do	4	4.8	74
	(DK)	8	0.1	1
	(NA)	9	5.8	89
Base : All				1548
{FLWRDO5}	Column No 828			
Sign a petition				
	Wouldn't do	0	61.0	945
	Would do	5	33.1	513
	(DK)	8	0.1	1
	(NA)	9	5.8	89
Base : All				1548

LIKELY ACTIVISM OVER COUNTRYSIDE ISSUES - 2 (continued)

		Code	%	No
{FLWRDO6}	Column No 829			
Join a conservation group				
	Wouldn't do	0	86.2	1335
	Would do	6	7.9	123
	(DK)	8	0.1	1
	(NA)	9	5.8	89
Base : All				1548
{FLWRDO7}	Column No 830			
Give money to a campaign				
	Wouldn't do	0	86.7	1342
	Would do	7	7.5	115
	(DK)	8	0.1	1
	(NA)	9	5.8	89
Base : All				1548
{FLWRDO8}	Column No 831			
Volunteer to work for a campaign				
	Wouldn't do	0	89.4	1384
	Would do	1	4.7	73
	(DK)	8	0.1	1
	(NA)	9	5.8	89
Base : All				1548
{FLWRDO9}	Column No 832			
Go on a protest march or demonstration				
	Wouldn't do	0	90.7	1405
	Would do	2	3.4	53
	(DK)	8	0.1	1
	(NA)	9	5.8	89
Base : All				1548

LIKELY ACTIVISM OVER COUNTRYSIDE ISSUES - 3

1986   Q.B105a,b   {CONACID} {ACIDDO1}-{ACIDDO9}   Column Nos 833-42

a) [And] suppose you read a report that forests in Britain were in danger of being damaged by acid rain. Would you be concerned by this, or not?

		Code	%	No
{CONACID}	Column No 833			
	Yes, concerned	1	83.5	1293
	No, not concerned	2	12.3	191
	(DK/depends)	8	3.9	60
	(NA)	9	0.4	6
Base : All				1548

b) [If would be concerned] (Show card) Would you personally be likely to do any of these things about it? Any others? (Interviewer : code all that apply)

		Code	%	No
{ACIDDO1}	Column No 834			
Would take no action				
	Wouldn't do	0	77.4	1199
	Would do	1	18.1	281
	(DK)	8	0.1	2
	(NA)	9	4.3	67
Base : All				1548
{ACIDDO2}	Column No 835			
Contact MP or councillor				
	Wouldn't do	0	74.0	1146
	Would do	2	21.5	333
	(DK)	8	0.1	2
	(NA)	9	4.3	67
Base : All				1548
{ACIDDO3}	Column No 836			
Contact a government or planning department				
	Wouldn't do	0	86.3	1335
	Would do	3	9.3	144
	(DK)	8	0.1	2
	(NA)	9	4.3	67
Base : All				1548
{ACIDDO4}	Column No 837			
Contact radio, TV or a newspaper				
	Wouldn't do	0	88.0	1362
	Would do	4	7.5	117
	(DK)	8	0.1	2
	(NA)	9	4.3	67
Base : All				1548
{ACIDDO5}	Column No 838			
Sign a petition				
	Wouldn't do	0	45.0	696
	Would do	5	50.6	783
	(DK)	8	0.1	2
	(NA)	9	4.3	67
Base : All				1548

LIKELY ACTIVISM OVER COUNTRYSIDE ISSUES - 3 (continued)

	Code	%	No
{ACIDDO6}	Column No 839		
Join a conservation group			
Wouldn't do	0	86.0	1332
Would do	6	9.5	148
(DK)	8	0.1	2
(NA)	9	4.3	67
Base : All			1548
{ACIDDO7}	Column No 840		
Give money to a campaign			
Wouldn't do	0	82.3	1274
Would do	7	13.2	205
(DK)	8	0.1	2
(NA)	9	4.3	67
Base : All			1548
{ACIDDO8}	Column No 841		
Volunteer to work for a campaign			
Wouldn't do	0	87.8	1360
Would do	1	7.7	119
(DK)	8	0.1	2
(NA)	9	4.3	67
Base : All			1548
{ACIDDO9}	Column No 842		
Go on a protest march or demonstration			
Wouldn't do	0	90.7	1405
Would do	2	4.8	74
(DK)	8	0.1	2
(NA)	9	4.3	67
Base : All			1548

PAST ACTIVISM OVER COUNTRYSIDE ISSUES

1986   Q.B106a,b   {CTRYDONE}{CTRYDONI}-{CTRYDON8} Column Nos 843-51

{CTRYDONE} Column No 843

a) (Show card) Have you ever done any of the things on the card *about a countryside issue?*

		Code	%	No
	Yes	1	24.7	382
	No	2	74.9	1160
	(DK)	8	0.1	1
	(NA)	9	0.4	6
Base : All				1548

{CTRYDONI}-{CTRYDON8} Column Nos 844-51

b) [If has done anything] (Continue showing card) Which ones have you ever done about a countryside issue?
Any others? (Interviewer: code all that apply)

		Code	%	No

{CTRYDONI}   Column No 844
Contacted MP or councillor

		Code	%	No
	(Not done)	0	95.3	1476
	Done	1	4.2	65
	(NA)	9	0.4	7
Base : All				1548

{CTRYDON2}   Column No 845
Contacted a government or
    planning department

		Code	%	No
	(Not done)	0	95.8	1483
	Done	2	3.8	59
	(NA)	9	0.4	7
Base : All				1548

{CTRYDON3}   Column No 846
Contacted radio, TV or a newspaper

		Code	%	No
	(Not done)	0	98.7	1529
	Done	3	0.9	13
	(NA)	9	0.4	7
Base : All				1548

{CTRYDON4}   Column No 847
Signed a petition

		Code	%	No
	(Not done)	0	81.5	1261
	Done	4	18.1	281
	(NA)	9	0.4	7
Base : All				1548

ACTIVISM OVER COUNTRYSIDE ISSUES (continued)

	Code	%	No

{CTRYDON5} Column No 848
Joined a conservation group

	Code	%	No
(Not done)	0	96.1	1488
Done	5	3.5	54
(NA)	9	0.4	7
Base : All			1548

{CTRYDON6} Column No 849
Given money to a campaign

	Code	%	No
(Not done)	0	92.4	1431
Done	6	7.2	111
(NA)	9	0.4	7
Base : All			1548

{CTRYDON7} Column No 850
Volunteered to work for a campaign

	Code	%	No
(Not done)	0	97.3	1507
Done	7	2.3	35
(NA)	9	0.4	7
Base : All			1548

{CTRYDON8} Column No 851
Gone on a protest march or demonstration

	Code	%	No
(Not done)	0	98.5	1526
Done	8	1.0	16
(NA)	9	0.4	7
Base : All			1548

CARE ABOUT THE COUNTRYSIDE

1986   Q.B224   **{CTRYCARE}** Column No 2128
Which of these statements comes *closest* to your own views? (Please tick one box)

	Code	%	No
I care about what happens to the countryside and I get a lot of *personal* enjoyment from it	1	72.1	948
I care about what happens to the countryside, but I don't get a lot of *personal* enjoyment from it	2	23.7	311
I don't care much what happens to the countryside - I'm just not that bothered	3	3.0	39
(NA)	9	1.3	17
Base : Self-completion respondents			1315

RECENT PARTICIPATION IN VARIOUS COUNTRYSIDE LEISURE ACTIVITIES

1985   Q.64a   {LEISURE1}-{LEISURE5} Column Nos 564-68

I'm going to mention a number of activities people do in their leisure time. Could you tell me whether or not you have taken part in any of these activities in the *last four weeks*?   In the last four weeks have you ...
(read out):

	Code	Yes 1		No 2		(NA) 9	
		%	No	%	No	%	No
i) {LEISURE1} Column No 564 Been for a drive, outing or picnic *in the countryside*		44.0	779	56.0	990	-	-
ii) {LEISURE2} Column No 565 Been for a long walk, ramble or hike (of more than 2 miles) *in the countryside*		28.5	504	71.5	1265	-	-
iii){LEISURE3} Column No 566 Visited any historic or stately homes, gardens, zoos or wildlife parks *in the countryside*		15.4	273	84.5	1495	0.1	1
iv) {LEISURE4} Column No 567 Gone fishing, horse riding, shooting or hunting *in the countryside*		4.5	79	95.4	1688	0.1	2
v) {LEISURE5} Column No 568 Visited seacoast or cliffs		25.2	445	74.5	1318	0.3	6

Base : All (n = 1769)

NB In 1986 and 1987, respondents were asked about these activities in a slightly different way (see p. S-9 above).
First they were shown a card listing the five activities, and asked which they had taken part in within the previous four weeks; and for each mentioned, they were asked how long ago they did it

WAYS IN WHICH THE COUNTRYSIDE IS THOUGHT TO HAVE CHANGED

1985   Q.65b   *{CNTRYSD1} - {CNTRYSD5}* Column Nos 571-72, 573-74, 575-76, 577-78, 579-80

[If thinks that countryside has changed a bit or a lot in last 20 years] **In what ways do you think the countryside is different now? Any other ways?** (Interviewer: probe fully and record verbatim)

	Code	%	No
[Not asked : countryside not thought to have changed/ or DK whether it has changed]	0	27.4	485
Changes for the worse			
Fewer trees/hedgerows/wild flowers	1	24.3	429
Less wildlife	2	8.3	147
Disappearance of other traditional features of countryside	3	1.3	23
Access to countryside more restricted/contained/fenced in	4	6.7	119
Countryside disappearing because more built-up areas	5	39.6	700
Countryside disappearing because more roads/motorways	6	20.0	353
Less countryside/countryside disappearing/less wild country	7	3.3	58
More litter/dirt/vandalism	8	13.3	236
More industrial waste/pollution/traffic pollution	9	4.1	73
More farm waste/pollution	10	4.8	85
Farmers reclaiming wild land/more cultivated land /bigger farms, fields	11	6.3	112
Factory farming	12	1.0	17
Countryside commercialised/developed for tourists	13	3.0	53
More people in countryside	14	4.5	80
More noise/less quiet in countryside	15	1.6	29
Changes in country living	16	1.9	33
Countryside not like it used to be/nostalgia for old ways	17	1.7	30
Other changes for worse	18	1.4	24
Less safe	19	1.2	21
Changes for the better			
Countryside cleaner/neater - less litter/dirt	20	2.2	39
Countryside cleaner - less pollution	21	0.5	9
Countryside more accessible - better roads/footpaths, etc	22	2.3	41
More/better rural facilities (affecting country living)	23	0.5	8
More/better amenities for those visiting countryside	24	3.4	61
More care/preservation of wildlife/countryside/ traditional features	25	1.1	20
Mechanisation of farm work	26	2.1	38
Countryside still nice, but different from past	27	0.2	3
Other changes for better	28	0.6	10
Other answer (no other response)	97	0.7	13
(DK)	98	0.5	8
Base : All			1769

NB Up to 5 responses were coded for each respondent, so percentages will add up to more than 100%

PERCEIVED CHANGES IN THE COUNTRYSIDE

1985   Q.67a,b   *{CNTRYCH1}-{CNTRYCH9}*   Column Nos 609-26, 627-34

a) (Show card) Here are some ways people have said the countryside generally has changed over the last twenty years. Which of them do *you* think has changed? If you think none of them has changed, please say so.

b) (Interviewer: for each item mentioned as changed, ask) You said that the countryside has changed in the _____ (read out each change). Do you think this is a change for the better or worse?

	Changed for the better		Changed for the worse		Changed (depends)		Changed (NA)		Not changed		(DK whether changed)	
Code	1		2		3		4		5		8	
	%	No	%	No	%	No	%	No	%	No	%	No
i) *{CNTRYCH1}* Column Nos 609-10,627 Provision of roads and motorways	31.3	555	23.8	421	9.6	169	0.1	1	31.7	561	3.5	62
ii) *{CNTRYCH2}* Column Nos 611-12,628 Access via footpaths	11.3	200	17.7	314	1.5	26	0.1	1	65.9	1166	3.5	62
iii) *{CNTRYCH3}* Column Nos 613-14,629 Number of hedgerows	2.0	36	38.5	680	1.0	18	-	-	55.0	972	3.5	62
iv) *{CNTRYCH4}* Column Nos 615-16,630 Number of picnic areas and camping sites	31.8	562	9.5	167	2.6	45	-	-	52.7	932	3.5	62
v) *{CNTRYCH5}* Column Nos 617-18,631 Number of people visiting and tourists	21.6	381	13.2	233	6.7	119	0.3	6	54.7	968	3.5	62
vi) *{CNTRYCH6}* Column Nos 619-20,632 Amount of cultivated farmland	8.0	142	21.8	385	4.3	76	0.1	2	62.3	1102	3.5	62
vii) *{CNTRYCH7}* Column Nos 621-22,633 Level of pollution	4.2	74	52.4	927	0.7	12	-	-	39.2	694	3.5	62
viii) *{CNTRYCH8}* Column Nos 623-24,634 Amount of wildlife	2.6	45	43.6	772	1.3	24	-	-	48.9	866	3.5	62

Base : All (n = 1769)

NB A derived variable {CNTRYCH9} Column Nos 625-26 produced:

	Code	%	No
More than one change mentioned	0	92.4	1635
None of these changes mentioned	96	4.0	71
(DK)	98	3.5	62
Base : All			1769

T Attitude scales and classificatory information

T1 Attitude scales

Table titles and cross references

LEFT - RIGHT SCALE

{REDISTRB} {BIGBUSNN} {WEALTH} {RICHLAW} {INDUST4}

Question: Please tick *one* box for *each* statement below to show how much you agree or disagree with it.

		1983		1984		1985		1986		1987		1989	
		%	No	%	No	%	No	%	No	%	No	%	No
Question No								B231ix		A227a/B238a		A231a/B231a	
Column No								2169		1654		2161	
i) *{REDISTRB}*	Code												
Government should redistribute income from the better-off to those who are less well off													
Agree strongly	1	-	.	-	.	-		11.2	147	14.9	361	18.6	470
Agree	2	-	.	-	.	-	.	32.1	423	30.0	726	31.5	797
Neither agree nor disagree	3	-	.	-	.	-		25.4	334	20.1	488	20.0	506
Disagree	4	-	.	-	.	-	.	24.7	326	26.2	635	22.0	557
Disagree strongly	5	-	.	-	.	-		5.1	68	7.2	174	6.6	167
(DK)	8	-	.	-	.	-		0.3	4	0.1	2	0.1	3
(NA)	9	-	.	-	.	-		1.1	15	1.6	38	1.1	27
Base: Self-completion questionnaire respondents									1315		2424		2529

		1983		1984		1985		1986		1987		1989	
Question No								B231v		A227b/B238b		A231b/B231b	
Column No								2165		1655		2162	
ii) *{BIGBUSNN}*													
Big business benefits owners at the expense of workers													
Agree strongly	1	-	.	-	.	-		14.8	195	12.3	298	14.2	358
Agree	2	-	.	-	.	-	.	39.1	514	38.8	940	38.6	977
Neither agree nor disagree	3	-	.	-	.	-		25.6	337	24.7	600	24.2	611
Disagree	4	-	.	-	.	-	.	17.2	226	18.9	459	18.9	478
Disagree strongly	5	-	.	-	.	-		1.8	24	3.2	78	2.6	66
(DK)	8	-	.	-	.	-		0.2	2	0.3	7	0.1	3
(NA)	9	-	.	-	.	-		1.3	17	1.8	43	1.4	37
Base: Self-completion questionnaire respondents									1315		2424		2529

LEFT - RIGHT SCALE (Continued)

		1983		1984		1985		1986		1987		1989	
		%	No	%	No	%	No	%	No	%	No	%	No
Question No								B231vi		A227c/B238c		A231c/B231c	
Column No								2166		1656		2163	
iii) {WEALTH}	Code												

Ordinary working people do not get their fair share of the nation's wealth

	Code	1983 %	No	1984 %	No	1985 %	No	1986 %	No	1987 %	No	1989 %	No
Agree strongly	1	-	.	-	.	-	.	20.2	266	17.5	423	19.9	504
Agree	2	-	.	-	.	-	.	45.3	595	46.8	1134	45.3	1145
Neither agree nor disagree	3	-	.	-	.	-	.	19.1	251	17.3	419	17.7	448
Disagree	4	-	.	-	.	-	.	13.2	173	14.8	359	14.4	364
Disagree strongly	5	-	.	-	.	-	.	1.2	16	2.0	49	1.6	42
(DK)	8	-	.	-	.	-	.	0.2	2	0.2	4	0.1	4
(NA)	9	-	.	-	.	-	.	0.8	11	1.5	36	0.9	22

Base: Self-completion questionnaire respondents — 1315, 2424, 2529

		1986		1987		1989	
Question No		B231iv		A227d/B238d		A231d/B231d	
Column No		2164		1657		2164	

iv) {RICHLAW}

There is one law for the rich and one for the poor

	Code	1983 %	No	1984 %	No	1985 %	No	1986 %	No	1987 %	No	1989 %	No
Agree strongly	1	-	.	-	.	-	.	24.3	320	25.5	619	29.9	757
Agree	2	-	.	-	.	-	.	35.1	462	40.4	979	38.7	978
Neither agree nor disagree	3	-	.	-	.	-	.	17.2	226	14.1	343	14.1	356
Disagree	4	-	.	-	.	-	.	18.2	240	16.1	391	13.2	333
Disagree strongly	5	-	.	-	.	-	.	4.1	53	2.6	64	3.2	81
(DK)	8	-	.	-	.	-	.	0.1	1	0.1	2	0.0	1
(NA)	9	-	.	-	.	-	.	1.0	14	1.1	26	0.9	22

Base: Self-completion questionnaire respondents — 1315, 2424, 2529

LEFT - RIGHT SCALE (Continued)

		1983		1984		1985		1986		1987		1989	
		%	No	%	No	%	No	%	No	%	No	%	No
Question No						243d		B230d		A227e/B238e		A231e/B231e	
Column No						2210		2159		1658		2165	

v) *{INDUST4}*

Management will always try to get the better of employees if it gets the chance

	Code	1983 %	No	1984 %	No	1985 %	No	1986 %	No	1987 %	No	1989 %	No
Agree strongly	1	-	.	-	.	10.9	164	12.9	170	18.7	454	18.4	464
Agree	2	-	.	-	.	40.6	610	38.7	508	42.2	1022	39.7	1003
Neither agree nor disagree	3	-	.	-	.	21.2	318	19.8	261	17.8	431	21.4	541
Disagree	4	-	.	-	.	22.9	344	24.1	318	17.6	428	17.5	443
Disagree strongly	5	-	.	-	.	1.7	26	3.2	42	2.2	53	1.9	49
(DK)	8	-	.	-	.	0.1	2	0.1	1	0.1	2	-	
(NA)	9	-	.	-	.	2.5	37	1.1	15	1.4	35	1.1	27

| Base: Self-completion questionnaire respondents | | | | | | 1502 | | 1315 | | 2424 | | 2529 | |

1985-87, 1989 - {INDUST4} This item is one of a battery of five questions on attitudes to management and industry and so also appears on p.G.1 -12 above

LIBERAL - AUTHORITARIAN SCALE

{TRADVALS} {STIFSENT} {PROTMEET} {DEATHAPP} {PROTLEAF} (OBEY) {PROTDEMO} {WRONGLAW} {CENSOR}

Question: Please tick *one* box for *each* statement below to show how much you agree or disagree with it.

		1983		1984		1985		1986		1987		1989	
		%	No	%	No	%	No	%	No	%	No	%	No
Question No								B232i		A227f		A231f/B231f	
Column No								2208		1659		2166	

(i) {TRADVALS}

Young people today don't have enough respect for traditional British values

		1983		1984		1985		1986		1987		1989	
Agree strongly	1	-	.	-	.	-	.	24.5	322	18.6	231	18.4	464
Agree	2	-	.	-	.	-	.	41.5	546	47.9	595	43.2	1093
Neither agree nor disagree	3	-	.	-	.	-	.	20.3	266	20.5	255	22.5	568
Disagree	4	-	.	-	.	-	.	11.4	149	10.3	128	13.1	332
Disagree strongly	5	-	.	-	.	-	.	1.7	22	1.9	23	1.9	47
(DK)	8	-	.	-	.	-	.	0.1	1	0.0	1	0.1	2
(NA)	9	-	.	-	.	-	.	0.6	8	0.8	10	0.9	22

Base: Self-completion questionnaire respondents — 1315, 1243, 2529

		1983		1984		1985		1986		1987		1989	
Question No								B232x		A227g		A231g/B231g	
Column No								2217		1660		2167	

(ii) {STIFSENT}

People who break the law should be given stiffer sentences

		1983		1984		1985		1986		1987		1989	
Agree strongly	1	-	.	-	.	-	.	31.3	412	36.7	456	33.1	836
Agree	2	-	.	-	.	-	.	41.0	539	42.9	533	44.3	1120
Neither agree nor disagree	3	-	.	-	.	-	.	19.9	262	15.1	187	15.4	390
Disagree	4	-	.	-	.	-	.	5.9	77	4.0	50	5.6	143
Disagree strongly	5	-	.	-	.	-	.	0.9	12	0.9	11	0.7	19
(DK)	8	-	.	-	.	-	.	0.2	3	0.0	1	-	
(NA)	9	-	.	-	.	-	.	0.8	10	0.5	6	0.9	21

Base: Self-completion questionnaire respondents — 1315, 1243, 2529

LIBERAL - AUTHORITARIAN SCALE (Continued)

			1983		1984		1985		1986		1987		1989	
			%	No	%	No	%	No	%	No	%	No	%	No
Question No											A227h		A231h/B231h	
Column No											1661		2168	

iii) {PROTMEET}

People should be allowed to organise public meetings to protest against the government

	Code	1983 %	1983 No	1984 %	1984 No	1985 %	1985 No	1986 %	1986 No	1987 %	1987 No	1989 %	1989 No
Agree strongly	1	-	.	-	.	-	.	-	.	15.0	187	16.7	422
Agree	2	-	.	-	.	-	.	-	.	45.8	569	48.1	1217
Neither agree nor disagree	3	-	.	-	.	-	.	-	.	26.3	327	25.0	632
Disagree	4	-	.	-	.	-	.	-	.	9.7	120	7.9	200
Disagree strongly	5	-	.	-	.	-	.	-	.	2.4	30	1.3	34
(DK)	8	-	.	-	.	-	.	-	.	0.2	2	-	.
(NA)	9	-	.	-	.	-	.	-	.	0.6	8	0.9	24
Base: Self-completion questionnaire respondents											1243		2529

			1983		1984		1985		1986		1987		1989	
			%	No	%	No	%	No	%	No	%	No	%	No
Question No										B232iii		A227i		A231i/B231i	
Column No										2210		1662		2169	

iv) {DEATHAPP}

For some crimes, the death penalty is the most appropriate sentence

	Code	1983 %	1983 No	1984 %	1984 No	1985 %	1985 No	1986 %	1986 No	1987 %	1987 No	1989 %	1989 No
Agree strongly	1	-	.	-	.	-	.	41.0	539	42.6	529	40.1	1014
Agree	2	-	.	-	.	-	.	33.0	434	31.1	387	34.1	862
Neither agree nor disagree	3	-	.	-	.	-	.	6.4	84	8.8	109	7.1	181
Disagree	4	-	.	-	.	-	.	9.5	125	9.8	121	9.9	251
Disagree strongly	5	-	.	-	.	-	.	9.3	123	7.0	88	7.9	201
(DK)	8	-	.	-	.	-	.	0.2	2	-	.	-	.
(NA)	9	-	.	-	.	-	.	0.6	8	0.7	9	0.8	20
Base: Self-completion questionnaire respondents									1315		1243		2529

LIBERAL - AUTHORITARIAN SCALE (Continued)

		1983		1984		1985		1986		1987		1989	
		%	No	%	No	%	No	%	No	%	No	%	No
Question No										A227j		A231j/B231j	
Column No										1663		2170	

v) {PROTLEAF}

People should be allowed to publish leaflets to protest against the government

Agree strongly	1	-	.	-	.	-	.	-	.	14.7	183	17.3	437
Agree	2	-	.	-	.	-	.	-	.	43.3	539	45.9	1161
Neither agree nor disagree	3	-	.	-	.	-	.	-	.	28.4	354	26.0	658
Disagree	4	-	.	-	.	-	.	-	.	10.4	129	8.3	210
Disagree strongly	5	-	.	-	.	-	.	-	.	2.2	28	1.5	39
(DK)	8	-	.	-	.	-	.	-	.	0.2	2	0.0	1
(NA)	9	-	.	-	.	-	.	-	.	0.7	9	0.9	23
											1243		2529

Base: Self-completion questionnaire respondents

		1983		1984		1985		1986		1987		1989	
Question No								B232iv		A227k		A231k/B231k	
Column No								2211		1664		2171	

vi) {OBEY}

Schools should teach children to obey authority

Agree strongly	1	-	.	-	.	-	.	31.7	417	31.8	396	32.5	822
Agree	2	-	.	-	.	-	.	50.9	670	51.5	641	51.3	1296
Neither agree nor disagree	3	-	.	-	.	-	.	9.5	124	10.5	131	10.5	266
Disagree	4	-	.	-	.	-	.	5.9	78	5.2	65	4.4	110
Disagree strongly	5	-	.	-	.	-	.	1.1	14	0.4	5	0.3	9
(DK)	8	-	.	-	.	-	.	0.2	2	-	-	-	-
(NA)	9	-	.	-	.	-	.	0.7	10	0.5	6	1.0	25
									1315		1243		2529

Base: Self-completion questionnaire respondents

LIBERAL - AUTHORITARIAN SCALE (Continued)

		1983		1984		1985		1986		1987		1989	
		%	No	%	No	%	No	%	No	%	No	%	No
Question No										A227l		A231l/B231l	
Column No	Code									1665		2172	

vii) {PROTDEMO}

People should be allowed to organise protest marches and demonstrations

	Code	1983 %	No	1984 %	No	1985 %	No	1986 %	No	1987 %	No	1989 %	No
Agree strongly	1	-	.	-	.	-	.	-	.	9.0	112	9.9	251
Agree	2	-	.	-	.	-	.	-	.	44.5	554	46.4	1173
Neither agree nor disagree	3	-	.	-	.	-	.	-	.	29.1	361	28.4	718
Disagree	4	-	.	-	.	-	.	-	.	13.3	166	11.8	300
Disagree strongly	5	-	.	-	.	-	.	-	.	3.0	38	2.4	60
(DK)	8	-	.	-	.	-	.	-	.	0.1	1	0.0	1
(NA)	9	-	.	-	.	-	.	-	.	1.0	12	1.0	25

Base: Self-completion questionnaire respondents — 1987: 1243, 1989: 2529

		1983		1984		1985		1986		1987		1989	
		%	No	%	No	%	No	%	No	%	No	%	No
Question No								B232v		A227m		A231m/B231m	
Column No	Code							2212		1666		2173	

viii) {WRONGLAW}

The law should always be obeyed, even if a particular law is wrong

	Code	1983 %	No	1984 %	No	1985 %	No	1986 %	No	1987 %	No	1989 %	No
Agree strongly	1	-	.	-	.	-	.	12.4	163	9.1	113	7.9	199
Agree	2	-	.	-	.	-	.	32.8	432	36.5	453	36.4	920
Neither agree nor disagree	3	-	.	-	.	-	.	22.2	292	23.5	292	25.6	647
Disagree	4	-	.	-	.	-	.	27.3	359	25.8	321	25.8	651
Disagree strongly	5	-	.	-	.	-	.	4.2	55	3.7	46	3.3	85
(DK)	8	-	.	-	.	-	.	0.2	3	-	.	-	.
(NA)	9	-	.	-	.	-	.	0.9	11	1.5	18	1.1	27

Base: Self-completion questionnaire respondents — 1986: 1315, 1987: 1243, 1989: 2529

LIBERAL - AUTHORITARIAN SCALE (Continued)

			1983		1984		1985		1986		1987		1989	
			%	No	%	No	%	No	%	No	%	No	%	No
Question No									B232ix		A227n		A231n/B231n	
Column No	Code								2216		1667		2174	

ix) {CENSOR}
Censorship of films and magazines is necessary to uphold moral standards

	Code	1983 %	No	1984 %	No	1985 %	No	1986 %	No	1987 %	No	1989 %	No
Agree strongly	1	-	.	-	.	-	.	23.6	311	19.9	248	19.4	490
Agree	2	-	.	-	.	-	.	42.2	555	51.2	637	49.2	1244
Neither agree nor disagree	3	-	.	-	.	-	.	15.2	200	13.9	173	15.2	385
Disagree	4	-	.	-	.	-	.	13.8	181	11.6	144	12.4	314
Disagree strongly	5	-	.	-	.	-	.	4.0	53	2.6	32	2.8	72
(DK)	8	-	.	-	.	-	.	0.2	3	-	-	0.0	1
(NA)	9	-	.	-	.	-	.	1.0	13	0.8	10	0.9	23

Base: Self-completion questionnaire respondents — 1315, 1243, 2529

WELFARIST SCALE

{MOREWELF} {UNEMPJOB} {SOCHELP} {DOLEFIDL} {WELFFEET}

Question: Please tick *one* box for *each* statement below to show how much you agree or disagree with it.

			1983		1984		1985		1986		1987		1989	
			%	No	%	No	%	No	%	No	%	No	%	No
Question No											A227o		A231o/B231o	
Column No	Code										1668		2175	

i) {MOREWELF}
The government should spend more money on welfare benefits for the poor, even if it leads to higher taxes

	Code	1983 %	No	1984 %	No	1985 %	No	1986 %	No	1987 %	No	1989 %	No
Agree strongly	1	-	.	-	.	-	.	-	.	16.3	203	18.3	463
Agree	2	-	.	-	.	-	.	-	.	38.3	476	42.3	1069
Neither agree nor disagree	3	-	.	-	.	-	.	-	.	22.8	283	23.0	581
Disagree	4	-	.	-	.	-	.	-	.	19.3	239	13.8	350
Disagree strongly	5	-	.	-	.	-	.	-	.	2.6	33	1.5	38
(DK)	8	-	.	-	.	-	.	-	.	-	-	0.1	2
(NA)	9	-	.	-	.	-	.	-	.	0.7	9	1.0	26

Base: Self-completion questionnaire respondents — 1243, 2529

WELFARIST SCALE (Continued)

		1983		1984		1985		1986		1987		1989	
		%	No	%	No	%	No	%	No	%	No	%	No
Question No										A227p		A231p/B231p	
Column No										1669		2176	
ii) {UNEMPJOB}	Code												

Around here, most unemployed people could find a job if they really wanted one

	Code	1983 %	No	1984 %	No	1985 %	No	1986 %	No	1987 %	No	1989 %	No
Agree strongly	1	-	-	-	-	-	-	-	-	7.8	97	11.9	301
Agree	2	-	-	-	-	-	-	-	-	33.2	413	40.2	1016
Neither agree nor disagree	3	-	-	-	-	-	-	-	-	16.3	203	18.8	476
Disagree	4	-	-	-	-	-	-	-	-	31.4	390	22.0	557
Disagree strongly	5	-	-	-	-	-	-	-	-	10.2	127	6.1	154
(DK)	8	-	-	-	-	-	-	-	-	0.2	2	-	-
(NA)	9	-	-	-	-	-	-	-	-	0.9	11	1.0	25
											1243		2529

Base: Self-completion questionnaire respondents

Question No										A227q		A231q/B231q	
Column No										1670		2177	

iii) {SOCHELP}

Many people who get social security don't really deserve any help

	Code	1983 %	No	1984 %	No	1985 %	No	1986 %	No	1987 %	No	1989 %	No
Agree strongly	1	-	-	-	-	-	-	-	-	6.9	86	6.1	154
Agree	2	-	-	-	-	-	-	-	-	24.2	300	21.6	546
Neither agree nor disagree	3	-	-	-	-	-	-	-	-	23.7	295	26.6	673
Disagree	4	-	-	-	-	-	-	-	-	33.7	420	34.2	864
Disagree strongly	5	-	-	-	-	-	-	-	-	10.9	136	10.4	263
(DK)	8	-	-	-	-	-	-	-	-	0.0	1	0.1	2
(NA)	9	-	-	-	-	-	-	-	-	0.6	7	1.1	28
											1243		2529

Base: Self-completion questionnaire respondents

WELFARIST SCALE (Continued)

		1983		1984		1985		1986		1987		1989	
		%	No	%	No	%	No	%	No	%	No	%	No
Question No										A227r		A231r/B231r	
Column No										1671		2178	
iv) {DOLEFIDL}	Code												
Most people on the dole are fiddling in one way or another													
Agree strongly	1	-	.	-	.	-	.	-	.	6.6	82	7.2	182
Agree	2	-	.	-	.	-	.	-	.	25.4	315	23.9	604
Neither agree nor disagree	3	-	.	-	.	-	.	-	.	28.1	349	30.8	780
Disagree	4	-	.	-	.	-	.	-	.	31.4	390	29.1	735
Disagree strongly	5	-	.	-	.	-	.	-	.	8.0	99	7.9	199
(DK)	8	-	.	-	.	-	.	-	.	0.1	2	0.2	5
(NA)	9	-	.	-	.	-	.	-	.	0.5	7	1.0	25
Base: Self-completion questionnaire respondents										1243		2529	

										1987		1989	
Question No										A227s		A231s/B231s	
Column No										1672		2179	
v) {WELFFEET}	Code												
If welfare benefits weren't so generous people would learn to stand on their own two feet													
Agree strongly	1	-	.	-	.	-	.	-	.	7.8	97	7.6	192
Agree	2	-	.	-	.	-	.	-	.	25.1	312	22.6	572
Neither agree nor disagree	3	-	.	-	.	-	.	-	.	21.3	265	23.1	585
Disagree	4	-	.	-	.	-	.	-	.	31.6	393	33.4	845
Disagree strongly	5	-	.	-	.	-	.	-	.	13.7	171	12.3	312
(DK)	8	-	.	-	.	-	.	-	.	-	.	0.0	1
(NA)	9	-	.	-	.	-	.	-	.	0.5	6	0.8	21
Base: Self-completion questionnaire respondents										1243		2529	

MISCELLANEOUS ATTITUDE QUESTIONS - 1

1986   Q.B231a,b,c,g,h,j,k
{UNEFAULT}{CREATEJB}{PRIVENT}{HANDOUTS}{SOCPLAN}{POLPOWER}{DEATHPEN}
Column Nos 2161,2162,2163,2167,2168,2170,2171
Please tick one box for each statement to show how much you agree or disagree with it.

	Agree strongly 1		Agree 2		Neither agree nor disagree 3		Disagree 4		Disagree strongly 5		(DK) 8		(NA) 9	
Code	%	No	%	No	%	No	%	No	%	No	%	No	%	No
a) *{UNEFAULT}* Column No 2161 When somebody is unemployed, it's usually his or her own fault	0.8	11	6.2	82	20.2	265	49.9	656	21.9	288	0.2	2	0.9	12
b) *{CREATEJB}* Column No 2162 The government should spend more money to create jobs	28.1	370	51.3	675	11.4	150	6.8	89	1.3	17	0.1	1	1.0	14
c) *{PRIVENT}* Column No 2163 Private enterprise is the best way to solve Britain's economic problems	10.7	140	33.8	445	35.3	464	15.0	198	3.5	46	0.2	3	1.5	20
g) *{HANDOUTS}* Column No 2167 Too many people these days like to rely on government handouts	16.0	210	40.7	535	16.5	217	19.8	260	5.6	74	0.2	2	1.3	17
h) *{SOCPLAN}* Column No 2168 More socialist planning is the best way to solve Britain's economic problems	6.9	91	18.5	243	36.2	477	28.3	373	7.9	104	0.6	7	1.6	21
j) *{POLPOWER}* Column No 2170 The police should be given more power	14.2	187	28.3	372	21.6	284	27.9	367	7.0	92	0.2	3	0.8	11
k) *{DEATHPEN}* Column No 2171 Britain should bring back the death penalty	38.2	503	28.0	369	10.5	138	10.2	134	11.8	155	0.4	5	1.0	13

Base : Self-completion respondents (n = 1315)

MISCELLANEOUS ATTITUDE QUESTIONS - 2

1986   Q.B232b,h,k   {PHONETAP}{WELFCARE}{BANORGS}   Column Nos 2209,2215,2218
Please tick one box for each statement to show how much you agree or disagree with it.

	Code	Agree strongly 1		Agree 2		Neither agree nor disagree 3		Disagree 4		Disagree strongly 5		(DK) 8		(NA) 9	
		%	No	%	No	%	No	%	No	%	No	%	No	%	No
b) {PHONETAP} Column No 2209 Government should be allowed to tap telephone conversations of people who are politically active		4.5	60	20.3	267	17.9	235	36.5	481	19.8	261	0.1	1	0.8	10
h) {WELFCARE} Column No 2215 The welfare state makes for a more caring society		6.4	84	36.5	481	29.9	394	22.9	301	3.0	39	0.2	2	1.2	15
k) {BANORGS} Column No 2218 The government should be allowed to ban organisations which do not believe in democracy		14.0	184	24.7	325	29.4	387	25.1	330	5.5	72	0.4	5	1.0	13

Base : Self-completion respondents (n = 1315)

MISCELLANEOUS ATTITUDE QUESTIONS - 3

1983   Q.217a-o, u-w   *{WOMPOL}{SAKECH}{MOTHSMCH}{WOMRSP}{WIFEEARN}{CHLDDISC}{AGEDPAR}*
{NUMCHILD}{CHILDHAP}{BABYHOSP}{CONADYNG}{LEGCAN}{COSMTEST}{MEDITEST}{FOXHUNT}
{DOCRELY}{EARLYRET}{OLDJOBOP} Column Nos 1113-27,1133-35
[Finally], please tick one box for each statement below to show how much you agree or disagree with it.

	Disgree strongly 1		Just Disagree 2		Neither agree nor disagree 3		Just Agree 4		Agree strongly 5		(NA) 9	
Code	%	No	%	No	%	No	%	No	%	No	%	No
a) *{WOMPOL}* Column No 1113 More women should enter politics	4.1	66	4.1	67	35.4	570	28.6	461	26.9	434	0.8	13
b) *{SAKECH}* Column No 1114 Parents with unhappy marriages should stay together for the sake of their children	27.9	449	24.5	394	19.6	315	16.9	273	10.4	167	0.8	13
c) *{MOTHSMCH}* Column No 1115 It is wrong for mothers of small children to go out to work	14.2	228	19.5	314	20.7	333	17.8	287	27.1	437	0.7	11
d) *{WOMRSP}* Column No 1116 Women generally handle positions of responsibility better than men do	9.7	156	17.1	275	48.4	779	14.7	237	9.2	148	0.9	15
e) *{WIFEEARN}* Column No 1117 A wife should avoid earning more than her husband does	37.7	607	23.4	377	22.9	369	8.2	132	6.6	107	1.1	18
f) *{CHLDDISC}* Column No 1118 Children nowadays get too little discipline from their parents	3.2	52	7.1	114	9.6	155	25.0	402	54.2	873	0.9	14
g) *{AGEDPAR}* Column No 1119 Children have an obligation to look after their parents when they are old	16.0	258	18.9	305	22.2	358	22.8	367	19.2	309	0.8	13
h) *{NUMCHILD}* Column No 1120 It should be the woman who decides how many children a couple has	25.1	403	20.2	325	25.1	404	13.9	224	15.1	244	0.6	10
i) *{CHILDHAP}* Column No 1121 Children are essential for a happy marriage	24.7	397	19.6	316	24.2	389	12.2	196	18.4	296	1.0	16
j) *{BABYHOSP}* Column No 1122 Women should always have their babies in a hospital or nursing home	7.6	122	17.5	281	23.2	373	22.4	361	28.4	457	1.0	15
k) *{CONADYNG}* Column No 1123 Contraceptive advice and supplies should be available to all young people whatever their age	22.2	358	17.6	284	12.4	200	25.4	408	21.1	340	1.2	20

Base : Self-completion respondents (n = 1610)

MISCELLANEOUS ATTITUDE QUESTIONS - 3 (continued)

	Code	Disagree strongly 1		Just disagree 2		Neither agree nor disagree 3		Just agree 4		Agree strongly 5		(NA) 9	
		%	No	%	No	%	No	%	No	%	No	%	No
l) {LEGCAN} Column No 1124 Smoking cannabis (marijuana) should be legalised		62.1	999	14.7	236	10.0	160	6.1	98	6.2	100	1.0	16
m) {COSMTEST} Column No 1125 It is acceptable to use animals for testing and improving cosmetics		59.1	951	17.7	286	10.2	164	8.5	138	3.0	48	1.4	23
n) {MEDITEST} Column No 1126 It is acceptable to use animals for testing medicines if it could save human lives		8.2	132	8.1	131	9.6	155	41.5	668	31.1	501	1.5	23
o) {FOXHUNT} Column No 1127 Fox hunting should be banned by law		12.3	197	14.2	229	27.0	435	12.7	204	32.8	527	1.1	18
u) {DOCRELY} Column No 1133 People rely too much on doctors instead of taking more responsibility for their own health		7.0	113	17.7	285	18.9	304	35.5	571	19.8	318	1.1	19
v) {EARLYRET} Column No 1134 Older people should be encouraged to retire earlier to reduce unemployment		5.5	88	10.4	168	13.3	215	33.9	546	35.9	577	1.0	16
w) {OLDJOBOP} Column No 1135 Employers give too few opportunities to older people when recruiting staff		2.7	43	9.9	159	23.8	383	35.4	569	27.0	435	1.2	20

Base : Self-completion respondents (n = 1610)

T Attitude scales and classificatory information

T2 Classificatory information

Table titles and cross references

DAILY NEWSPAPER READERSHIP

{READPAP}

Question: Do you normally read any daily *morning* newspaper at least three times a week?

			1983		1984		1985		1986		1987		1989	
			%	No	%	No	%	No	%	No	%	No	%	No
Question No			1a		1a		1a		1a		1a		1a	
Column No			132		148		207		209		209		216	
		Code												
Yes	1		77.1	1324	72.3	1189	73.0	1291	72.6	2225	70.7	1955	69.7	2043
No	2		22.9	393	27.7	455	27.0	478	27.4	840	29.3	810	30.3	887
(DK)	8		-	-	-	-	-	-	-	-	-	-	-	-
(NA)	9		0.1	1	0.1	1	-	-	0.0	1	-	-	0.0	1
Base: All				1719		1645		1769		3066		2766		2930

_____

1983 - No (DK)

DAILY MORNING NEWSPAPER NORMALLY READ

{WHPAPER}

Question: [If reads daily morning paper at least three times a week] **Which one do you normally read?**
[If more than one] **Which one do you read *most* frequently?**

	Code	1983 %	1983 No	1984 %	1984 No	1985 %	1985 No	1986 %	1986 No	1987 %	1987 No	1989 %	1989 No
Question No		1b		1b		1b		1b		1b		1b	
Column No		133-34		149-50		208-09		210-11		210-11		217-18	
[Not asked: no paper read]	0	22.9	393	27.7	455	27.0	478	27.4	840	29.3	810	30.3	887
(Scottish) Daily Express	1	7.7	133	8.9	146	7.3	130	7.6	233	7.7	213	6.5	189
Daily Mail	2	10.2	175	7.5	123	8.2	145	8.4	257	7.5	207	7.8	229
Daily Mirror/Record	3	17.6	302	18.0	297	18.7	330	15.8	483	15.5	428	17.2	505
Daily Star	4	4.2	73	4.3	70	4.1	73	3.9	120	3.7	103	2.5	74
The Sun	5	16.8	288	16.2	266	17.4	308	17.1	524	15.7	434	14.9	437
Today	6	-	.	-	.	-	.	1.1	34	0.9	26	1.8	54
Daily Telegraph	7	5.8	100	5.3	88	4.0	71	5.1	157	4.9	137	5.1	151
Financial Times	8	0.3	5	0.3	5	0.6	10	0.5	15	0.4	10	0.4	12
The Guardian	9	3.0	51	1.8	30	2.7	48	3.2	97	3.2	87	2.4	72
The Independent	10	-	.	-	.	-	.	-	.	1.4	38	2.3	67
The Times	11	1.4	24	1.9	30	1.5	27	1.8	56	1.8	49	1.4	42
Morning Star	12	-	.	0.4	7	0.1	2	0.2	6	0.1	4	0.0	1
Other Irish/Northern Irish/ Scottish/Welsh/regional or local *daily morning* paper	94	6.4	111	5.4	89	4.3	75	5.9	180	5.4	150	4.7	138
Other answer	95	0.5	8	0.3	6	0.3	5	0.1	2	0.3	7	0.1	2
(More than one paper read with equal frequency)	96	3.1	53	2.0	32	3.3	59	1.9	58	2.2	62	2.2	64
(DK)	98	-	.	-	.	-	.	-	.	-	.	-	.
(NA)	99	0.2	4	0.1	2	0.4	6	0.1	3	0.0	1	0.2	7
Base: All			1719		1645		1769		3066		2766		2930

Papers added since 1983 necessitating code changes:

1983, 1984, 1985 - Daily Telegraph, code 6; Financial Times, code 7; The Guardian, code 8; The Times, code 9; Morning Star, code 10; Other Scottish/Welsh/regional or local <u>daily</u> morning paper, code 11; Other answer, code 12; More than one, code 13; (DK), code 98; (not 1983).

1986 - Today, code 10; Morning Star, code 11; Other Scottish/Welsh/regional or local <u>daily</u> morning paper, code 12; Other answer, code 13; More than one, code 14; (DK), code 98.

1987 - Other Scottish/Welsh/regional or local <u>daily morning</u> paper, code 94

SEX

{RSEX}

On questionnaire: [Record respondent's] sex

		1983		1984		1985		1986		1987		1989	
		%	No	%	No	%	No	%	No	%	No	%	No
Question No		91a		94a		98a		A106a/B114a		901a		901a	
Column No		651		662		759		1511		1211		1411	
	Code												
Male	1	46.1	793	47.1	775	46.5	822	46.9	1439	47.0	1299	46.3	1356
Female	2	53.9	926	52.9	871	53.5	947	53.1	1627	53.0	1467	53.7	1575
Base: All			1719		1645		1769		3066		2766		2930

AGE

{RAGEGRP} - New variable derived from {RAGE}: exact age

Respondent's age categorised

		1983		1984		1985		1986		1987		1989	
		%	No	%	No	%	No	%	No	%	No	%	No
Source question No		91b		94b		98b		A106b/B114b		901b		901b	
Source column No		652-53		663-64		760-61		1512-13		1212-13		1412-13	
	Code												
18-24	1	12.9	222	13.0	214	15.7	278	14.8	454	13.4	371	12.6	370
25-29	2	8.7	149	9.5	157	10.2	180	8.8	270	8.9	247	10.0	294
30-34	3	9.4	161	9.4	154	9.1	161	9.8	300	10.3	285	9.1	266
35-39	4	10.8	186	11.0	180	11.2	198	10.2	314	9.6	266	9.3	273
40-44	5	8.3	143	6.8	113	8.8	156	9.7	297	10.5	290	10.0	294
45-49	6	7.0	120	6.9	114	7.1	125	8.3	256	7.9	220	9.3	272
50-54	7	8.4	144	6.7	110	6.6	117	7.4	228	7.4	205	7.2	212
55-59	8	7.7	132	7.9	130	6.7	119	7.6	232	7.5	207	6.5	191
60-64	9	6.8	117	8.9	146	7.7	137	6.7	204	7.9	218	6.2	180
65+	10	19.6	337	19.1	314	16.5	293	16.6	509	16.4	454	19.5	571
(NA)	99	0.3	6	0.8	14	0.3	5	0.1	3	0.2	5	0.2	6
Base: All			1719		1645		1769		3066		2766		2930

1983-1987, 1989 - This new variable, with age up to 65 in five-year bands, is shown instead of {RAGECAT} (already in the dataset) where ages 25-54 are in ten year bands

AGE WITHIN SEX

{RSEXAGE}

Variable derived from *{RSEX}* and *{RAGE}*

	Code	1983 %	1983 No	1984 %	1984 No	1985 %	1985 No	1986 %	1986 No	1987 %	1987 No	1989 %	1989 No
Column No				1652-53		1055-56		2318-19		2216-17		2339-40	
Male:													
18-24	1	6.2	106	6.6	108	7.5	133	7.7	237	7.2	198	6.2	180
25-34	2	8.8	152	8.9	146	8.7	154	8.6	264	8.7	241	9.3	272
35-44	3	9.7	166	8.7	143	9.7	171	9.0	277	9.6	266	8.2	240
45-54	4	6.9	118	6.4	105	6.6	117	7.6	232	7.0	194	7.7	226
55-59	5	3.5	61	3.7	62	3.5	61	3.5	109	3.5	97	3.4	100
60-64	6	3.0	51	3.9	65	3.6	64	3.2	98	3.4	94	3.0	88
65+	7	8.0	138	8.7	144	6.8	120	7.3	222	7.5	208	8.5	249
(Refusal/NA)	8	-	-	0.2	3	0.1	2	-	-	-	-	0.0	1
Female:													
18-24	9	6.7	116	6.4	105	8.2	146	7.1	218	6.3	173	6.5	190
25-34	10	9.2	159	10.1	165	10.6	187	10.0	305	10.5	291	9.8	289
35-44	11	9.5	163	9.2	151	10.4	183	10.9	334	10.5	289	11.1	326
45-54	12	8.5	146	7.2	118	7.1	125	8.2	252	8.3	231	8.8	259
55-59	13	4.1	71	4.1	68	3.2	57	4.0	123	4.0	110	3.1	92
60-64	14	3.9	67	4.9	81	4.1	73	3.4	106	4.5	124	3.2	93
65+	15	11.6	199	10.4	171	9.8	173	9.3	286	8.9	245	11.0	321
(Refusal/NA)	16	0.3	6	0.6	11	0.2	3	0.1	3	0.2	5	0.2	5
Base: All			1719		1645		1769		3066		2766		2930

CAR OWNERSHIP OR USE

{CAROWN}

Question: Do you, or does anyone else in your household, own or have the regular use of a car or a van?

	Code	1983		1984		1985		1986		1987		1989	
		%	No	%	No	%	No	%	No	%	No	%	No
Question No						105a		A116/B124		912		913	
Column No						915		1738		1438		1664	
Yes	1	-	.	-	.	69.6	1230	68.3	2095	74.0	2047	76.2	2232
No	2	-	.	-	.	30.4	539	30.5	936	25.6	707	23.7	695
(DK)	8	-	.	-	.	-	.	-		-		-	.
(NA)	9	-	.	-	.	-	.	1.2	36	0.4	12	0.1	4
							—		—		—		—
Base: All							1769		3066		2766		2930

GROSS ANNUAL HOUSEHOLD INCOME

{HHINCOME}

Question: (Show card) **Which of the letters on this card represents the total income of your household from** *all* **sources** *before* **tax? Please just tell me the letter.** (Includes income from benefits, savings etc)

		1983		1984		1985		1986		1987		1989	
		%	No	%	No	%	No	%	No	%	No	%	No
Question No		99a		103a		111a		A118a/B126a		914a		918a	
Column No		869-70		949-50		1031-32		1753-54		1453-54		1725-26	
	Code												
Less than £2,000 pa	1	5.8	100	6.1	100	4.4	77	2.3	72	1.9	52	1.2	36
£2,000 - £2,999 pa	2	8.6	148	7.9	129	7.5	132	6.8	209	6.3	175	5.5	161
£3,000 - £3,999 pa	3	9.7	167	9.0	148	8.5	150	6.9	212	7.4	206	5.3	155
£4,000 - £4,999 pa	4	7.5	129	7.1	116	7.0	123	6.7	206	5.5	153	5.9	173
£5,000 - £5,999 pa	5	8.4	145	7.5	124	4.7	84	5.6	170	5.2	143	5.0	146
£6,000 - £6,999 pa	6	7.7	132	7.8	129	5.4	95	5.3	162	5.8	161	4.2	124
£7,000 - £7,999 pa	7	5.5	94	7.6	125	5.4	96	5.4	165	4.5	124	3.4	99
£8,000 - £9,999 pa	8	9.7	166	9.2	151	9.7	172	9.7	298	7.9	219	6.1	178
£10,000 - £11,999 pa	9	8.2	140	8.6	142	9.0	159	9.1	280	8.1	223	8.3	244
£12,000 - £14,999 pa	10	7.7	133	8.0	132	9.3	165	9.6	296	10.5	290	9.6	283
£15,000 - £17,999 pa (1983-85: £15,000+ pa)	11	9.6	165	9.1	149	14.3	253	6.9	212	7.5	206	7.8	229
£18,000 - £19,999 pa	12	-		-		-		4.2	128	4.4	122	5.6	164
£20,000 - £22,999 pa (1986, 1987: £20,000+ pa)	13	-		-		-		9.1	280	12.1	335	5.2	153
£23,000+ pa	14	-		-		-		-		-		14.0	410
(DK)	98	6.6	114	7.4	121	8.3	147	8.3	255	9.5	262	8.4	246
(NA)	99	5.0	85	4.9	80	6.4	114	3.9	120	3.4	95	4.4	130
Base: All			1719		1645		1769		3066		2766		2930

1983 - Q reads: 'Which of the letters on this card represents the gross income from all sources of your household?'

1984, 1985, 1986 - Q reads: 'Which of the letters on this card represents the total income from all sources of your household?'

1987 - Q reads: 'Which of the letters on this card represents the total income of your household from all sources, before tax?'

GROSS ANNUAL INDIVIDUAL EARNINGS

{REARN}

Question: [If in paid work] (Show card) **Which of the letters on this card represents your *own* gross or total *earnings*, *before* deduction of income tax and national insurance?**

	Code	1983 %	1983 No	1984 %	1984 No	1985 %	1985 No	1986 %	1986 No	1987 %	1987 No	1989 %	1989 No
Question No		99b		103b		111b		A118b/B126b		914b		918b	
Column No		871-72		951-52		1033-34		1755-56		1455-56		1727-28	
[Not asked: not in paid work]	0	47.2	812	48.4	797	46.6	824	44.5	1364	44.7	1235	43.6	1278
Less than £2,000 pa	1	5.0	86	4.8	78	3.9	68	4.3	130	3.7	103	2.8	82
£2,000 - £2,999 pa	2	5.1	88	3.3	55	4.5	79	4.9	150	3.9	109	2.8	83
£3,000 - £3,999 pa	3	5.5	94	4.3	70	4.6	81	3.7	113	3.3	91	3.2	92
£4,000 - £4,999 pa	4	5.6	96	5.5	91	4.9	86	4.6	142	4.7	129	3.2	92
£5,000 - £5,999 pa	5	6.2	107	6.8	112	5.7	100	5.5	168	4.9	135	3.9	114
£6,000 - £6,999 pa	6	4.7	81	4.7	78	4.7	84	4.3	131	5.6	154	3.7	109
£7,000 - £7,999 pa	7	5.1	87	4.3	71	4.7	84	4.1	125	4.2	116	4.1	121
£8,000 -£9,999 pa	8	5.1	87	4.9	81	5.7	100	6.5	200	5.4	148	6.1	177
£10,000 - £11,999 pa	9	3.0	52	4.1	67	4.5	79	5.5	170	5.6	154	5.8	170
£12,000 - £14,999 pa	10	1.5	26	2.3	39	2.3	41	4.1	125	5.3	147	6.7	198
£15,000 - £17,999 pa (1983-85: £15,000+ pa)	11	2.0	34	1.7	27	3.6	63	1.7	52	2.5	70	3.8	110
£18,000 - £19,999 pa	12	-	.	-	.	-	.	0.7	22	1.1	31	2.0	58
£20,000 - £22,999 pa (1986, 1987: £20,000+ pa)	13	-	.	-	.	-	.	2.2	67	2.1	57	0.9	26
£23,000+ pa	14	-	.	-	.	-	.	-	.	-	.	3.5	103
(DK)	98	-	.	0.9	14	0.2	3	0.3	8	0.5	13	0.5	15
(NA)	99	3.9	68	4.0	66	4.4	78	3.2	99	2.7	74	3.5	102
Base: All			1719		1645		1769		3066		2766		2930

1983 - Q reads: 'Which of the letters on this card represents your <u>own</u> gross <u>earnings</u>, before deduction of income tax and national insurance?'

REGISTRAR GENERAL'S STANDARD REGION

{STREGION}

Variable derived from {AREA} (Parliamentary constituency code)

	Code	1983 %	1983 No	1984 %	1984 No	1985 %	1985 No	1986 %	1986 No	1987 %	1987 No	1989 %	1989 No
Column No				109-11		163-64		2325-26		2223-24		2342-43	
Scotland	1	10.6	183	10.7	177	9.8	174	10.2	312	9.6	266	9.7	283
Northern	2	5.5	95	5.0	82	6.6	117	5.8	177	6.4	178	6.3	183
North West	3	11.4	196	11.2	184	11.7	207	11.3	345	11.5	319	9.9	291
Yorkshire and Humberside	4	9.6	165	10.6	174	8.3	147	9.3	285	10.3	284	9.4	276
West Midlands	5	9.1	157	9.9	162	10.5	186	9.7	296	9.0	248	9.3	271
East Midlands	6	7.6	130	7.3	120	7.1	126	6.7	204	6.7	186	7.6	224
East Anglia	7	4.2	73	3.7	61	3.1	69	4.4	136	4.1	113	3.3	96
South West	8	8.7	149	7.6	125	8.1	143	8.4	259	8.8	242	8.7	255
South East	9	17.2	295	18.8	309	18.0	318	18.2	557	17.5	484	18.8	550
Greater London (excluding South East)	10	11.1	191	9.5	157	10.3	183	10.6	325	10.3	286	11.4	335
Wales	11	5.0	87	5.7	94	5.6	99	5.5	169	5.8	160	5.6	166
Base: All			1719		1645		1769		3066		2766		2930

1983 - 1987, 1989 - South East and Greater London, although strictly one Standard Region, are (as customarily) shown separately

WHETHER METROPOLITAN OR NON-METROPOLITAN AREA

{AREATYPE}

Variable derived from {AREA} (Parliamentary constituency code)

	Code	1983 %	1983 No	1984 %	1984 No	1985 %	1985 No	1986 %	1986 No	1987 %	1987 No	1989 %	1989 No
Column No		969		1654		162		2323		2221			
Metropolitan	1	35.8	615	35.0	576	37.3	660	32.6	1000	31.8	880	-	-
Non-metropolitan	2	64.2	1104	65.0	1069	62.7	1110	67.4	2065	68.2	1886	-	-
Base: All			1719		1645		1769		3066		2766		

1983-1987 - Metropolitan areas comprise the metropolitan counties and Glasgow
1989 - {AREATYPE} not on SPSS file

EMIGRATION FROM BRITAIN

1989   Q.B917a,b   {*EMIGSER*}{*EMIGREAS*} Column Nos 1716-17

1989   Q.B917a   {*EMIGSER*} Column No 1716
In the last 5 years, have you thought seriously about emigrating from Britain - that is, leaving permanently?
(If yes) How seriously have you thought about it ... (read out) ...

	Code	%	No
... very seriously,	1	6.2	90
fairly seriously,	2	6.1	89
or - not very seriously?	3	7.1	104
(No, never thought about it)	4	80.1	1170
(Other)	7	-	-
(DK/can't say)	8	0.4	6
(NA)	9	0.2	3
Base : All			1461

1989   Q.B917b   {*EMIGREAS*} Column No 1717
[If thought about emigrating] (Show card) **Which of these reasons is the *main* reason why you have thought about emigrating? Please choose the closest reason on the card.**

	Code	%	No
[Not asked : not thought about emigrating]	0	80.1	1170
Family reasons	1	3.3	49
Unemployment	2	1.1	15
Fear/violence/crime	3	0.6	9
Standard of living	4	10.6	155
Health reasons	5	0.5	8
Other reason	7	2.3	34
(DK/can't say)	8	0.3	5
(NA)	9	1.1	17
Base : All			1461

COMPUTERS IN THE HOME

1985   Q.106a,b   {COMPUTR1}-{COMPUTR4} Column Nos 917-24
a) Do you have any of the following in your home ... (read out):

b) (Interviewer: for each item mentioned ask) Do you, personally, ever use _____ (read out each):

	Code	Has...								
		and uses 1		but does not use 2		Does not have 3		(Has and uses N/A) 7		(NA) 9
		%	No	%	No	%	No	%	No	%	No
i) {COMPUTR1} Column Nos 917,921 A word processor or computer printer		1.8	32	0.9	17	97.1	1718	0.1	1	0.1	2
ii) {COMPUTR2} Column Nos 918,922 A personal computer used for computer games		9.9	174	5.5	98	84.1	1489	0.4	7	0.1	1
iii) {COMPUTR3} Column Nos 919,923 A personal computer used for other purposes		5.0	89	3.7	66	90.7	1605	0.3	5	0.2	4
iv) {COMPUTR4} Column Nos 920,924 A terminal and telephone link with a computer in another place		0.2	4	0.1	2	99.5	1760	-	-	0.2	3

Base : All (n = 1769)

WHETHER EVER DRIVES HOUSEHOLD CAR

1985   Q.105b   {CARDRIVE}
[If household has regular use of a car or van] Do you ever drive the car or van yourself, that is with a full current driving licence?

	Code	%	No
[Not asked : no regular use of car or van]	0	30.4	539
Yes	1	50.8	899
No	2	18.5	327
(DK)	8	-	-
(NA)	9	0.2	4
Base : All			1769

CREDIBILITY OF MEDIA NEWS REPORTING

1984   Q.1c   {DIFFNEWS} Column No 151

Suppose you saw or heard conflicting or different reports of the same news story on radio, television and in the (daily morning paper named at Question 1b). Which of the three versions do you think you would be *most* likely to believe ... (read out) ...

	Code	%	No
[Not asked: does not read a daily morning paper 3+ times a week]	0	27.7	455
...the one on radio,	1	11.0	181
the one on television,	2	41.4	681
or - the one in the newspaper?	3	11.2	184
(DK)	8	7.2	119
(NA)	9	1.5	25
Base : All			1645

MAIN SOURCE OF NEWS

1984   Q.2   {MOSTNEWS} Column No 152

Can you tell me where you usually get *most* of your news about what's going on in Britain today: is it from newspapers, or radio, or television, or where?

	Code	%	No
Newspapers	1	19.6	322
Radio	2	14.9	245
Television	3	60.6	997
All three equally	4	1.8	29
Television and newspapers equally	5	0.8	13
Radio and television equally	6	0.9	15
(Other answer)	7	1.2	19
(DK)	8	0.3	5
Base : All			1645

Z1 Index of question numbers by year

1983					
1	T.2 - 1-2	27a	F - 9	54	F - 13
		bc	F - 36	55	K - 25
2ac	C - 1	28	G.1 - 25	56	K - 1
bde	C - 2	28,29,30	G.1 - 29	57	K - 2-4
(DV)[1]	C - 3	29	G.2 - 1	58ab	K - 5
3	C - 8	30	G.3 - 1	c	K - 27
4	C - 9-10	31	G.3 - 2-3	59	K - 27-29
5	B - 12	32	G.3 - 4-9	60	K - 8
6	C - 10	33	G.3 - 10-14	61	R - 1
7	C - 16	34	G.3 - 44	62	R - 2
8	A - 37	35	G.3 - 15-16	63	R - 3
9a	A - 1	36abc	G.3 - 16-18	64a	R - 4
b	H - 31	de	G.3 - 43-44	b	R - 27
c	H - 1	37	G.3 - 27-28	65	I - 14
10a	B - 11	38	G.3 - 28-29	66	I - 15-16
b	A - 6-7	39a	G.4 - 24	67	I - 18
b(DV)	A - 8	b	G.4 - 3	68	I - 22
c	A - 2-5	c	G.4 - 10	69	I - 21
d	A - 24	40abc	G.4 - 4-5	70a	I - 20
11a	B - 1	e	G.4 - 15	bc	I - 27
b	A - 9	41a	G.4 - 6	71	I - 19-20
12	A - 38	b	G.4 - 24	72	B - 13
13	A - 38	42	G.6 - 5-6	73	B - 13
14	D - 1	43	G.6 - 1-3	74	B - 14
15	D - 9	44ab	G.5 - 1-2	75	B - 15
16	E - 1-2	c	G.5 - 14	76a	P - 10
17	D - 2-3	d-h	G.5 - 3-7	bcd	P - 1-2
18	F - 1	45	G.5 - 8	77a	P - 15
19	F - 1	46	G.6 - 8-10	b	P - 2
20	F - 2	47ab	G.6 - 13	78	J - 19-20
21	F - 3	c	G.6 - 18	79a	Q - 1
22	F - 34-36	48	G.6 - 14-15	b	Q - 5
23	F - 3-6	49	G.6 - 18	c	Q - 2
24	M.2 - 1	50	F - 11-12	80a-f	O - 1-4
25	F - 7	51	J - 1	f(DV)	O - 13
26	F - 7-8	52	J - 2	81	O - 5
		53	J - 3	82	O - 6

---

[1]   (DV) = Derived variable

1984 cont'd					
201	F - 32	29	G.3 - 56	88	I - 20
202	D - 8	30	G.3 - 20-22	89	I - 18
203	G.1 - 21-23	31	G.3 - 23	90	I - 19-20
204	M.1 - 16	32	G.3 - 24-25	91	P - 1-2
205	M.1 - 13	33	G.3 - 56	92	P - 15
206	B - 2	34	G.3 - 56	93	Q - 1-2
207	A - 36	35	G.3 - 26-27	94	O - 1-4
208	S - 1-3	36	G.3 - 33-35	95	M.1 - 1-3
209	S - 4	37	G.3 - 35-39	96	M.1 - 4-7
210	S - 5	38	G.3 - 40-42	97a	N.1 - 3
211	B - 3-6	39	G.3 - 27	b	N.1 - 2
212	H - 29	40	G.3 - 28-29	98a	T.2 - 3
213	H - 31	41ab	G.4 - 1-3	ab(DV)	T.2 - 4
214	G.1 - 23	c	G.4 - 10	b(DV)	T.2 - 3
215	A - 23-24	42	G.4 - 3		N.1 - 1
216	F - 33	43	G.4 - 4-5	d	R - 18
217	R - 19	44	G.4 - 6-7	(DV)	R - 18
218	O - 11-12	45	G.4 - 9	99	I - 2-3
219	N.2 - 17-21	46	G.4 - 21	(DV)	I - 11
220i,ii	N.2 - 1	47	G.4 - 21	100	I - 4
iii	J - 19	48	G.4 - 11-14	101	I - 5-9
220iv	H - 19	49	G.6 - 5-6	102	O - 1
v,xi	N.2 - 2	50	G.6 - 7	103	N.2 - 4
vi	N.2 - 31	51	G.6 - 1-3	104	S - 13-14
vii	D - 9	52	G.6 - 4	105a	T.2 - 5
viii-x	J - 11-12	53	G.5 - 1-7	b	T.2 - 10
		54	G.5 - 8	106	T.2 - 10
		55	G.5 - 8-9	107(DV)	G.1 - 30,32,34,35
1985		56	G.5 - 11	(DV)	P - 11-14
		57	G.5 - 12	f	G.1 - 31
1a	T.2 - 1-2	58	G.6 - 8-10	h	G.1 - 33
2ac	C - 1	59	G.6 - 11	108	G.1 - 36-40
bde	C - 2	60	G.6 - 13	109a	G.1 - 41
(DV)	C - 3	61	G.6 - 16	b	G.1 - 43
3	A - 1-2	62	S - 15	110(DV)	G.1 - 42,45,47
4	D - 1	63	S - 16	(DV)	P - 16-18
5	D - 2	64a	S - 29	ef	G.1 - 43-44
6	D - 2-3	b	S - 9	hi	G.1 - 46-47
7	D - 3	65ac	S - 10	111	T.2 - 6-7
8	D - 4	b	S - 30	112	H - 10
9	D - 5	66	S - 11		
10	F - 1	67	S - 31	201	B - 7
11	F - 1	68	S - 11-12	202	B - 1
12	F - 2	69	F - 11-12	203	A - 20-22
13	F - 3	70	J - 1	204	B - 8
14	F - 3-6	71	J - 2	205	B - 9
15	H - 1	72	J - 3	206	B - 6
16	F - 7	73	F - 13	207	B - 10
17	F - 9	74	R - 1	208	F - 14
18	F - 10	75	R - 3	209	A - 15
19	G.1 - 25-28	76a	R - 4	210	F - 15-16
19,20,21	G.1 - 29	b	R - 27	211	N.2 - 16
20	G.2 - 1	77	R - 5	212	N.2 - 16
21	G.3 - 1	78	R - 16-17	213	N.2 - 17
22	G.3 - 2-3	79	R - 7-8	214	N.2 - 28
23	G.3 - 4-5	80	R - 8-9	215	I - 25
24	G.3 - 6-9	81b	R - 32	216	I - 26
25	G.3 - 10-13	82	R - 9-10	217	I - 26
26	G.3 - 15	83b	R - 33	218	N.1 - 38
27	G.3 - 15-16	84	I - 14	219	B - 10
28	G.3 - 19	85	I - 15-16	220	A - 33
		86	I - 17	221	F - 28
		87	I - 1	222	F - 29

1986 cont'd		B127 = A119	H - 10	B232	J - 11-12
					T.1 - 4-8
B81c	J - 10	A201	N.1 - 16-17		T.1 - 12
B82	C - 4	A202	N.1 - 17-18	B233	A - 32
B83	C - 8	A203	N.1 - 18-19		
B84	C - 10-11	A204	N.1 - 20-21		
B85	C - 11	A205	N.1 - 21-22	**1987**	
B86	A - 2-8	A206	N.1 - 22-23		
B87	A - 31	A207	N.1 - 24	1a	T.2 - 1-2
B88a	B - 1	A208	N.1 - 24-26	2a-e	C - 1-2
b	A - 9	A209	N.1 - 27-28	f	C - 4
B89	C - 5-7	A210	N.1 - 29	(DV)	C - 3
B90	C - 12-13	A211	N.1 - 30	3	A - 1-2
B91	H - 10	A212	N.1 - 31	4	D - 1
B92acd	A - 13-14	A213	N.1 - 32	5	D - 2
b	C - 16	A214	N.1 - 33	6	D - 2-3
B93	A - 14	A215	N.1 - 34	7	D - 3
B94	G.1 - 1	A216	N.1 - 35-37	8	D - 4
B95	G.1 - 2-4	A217	N.1 - 37	9	D - 5
B96	G.1 - 4-5	A218	R - 19-20	10	E - 1-2
B97	H - 1-4	A219	R - 21	11	F - 1
B98	H - 5-8	A220	R - 22-27	12	F - 1
B99	H - 9	A222ade	L - 45	13	F - 2
B100	S - 9	bc	L - 32	14	F - 3
B101	S - 10	fghijk	L - 33-35	15	F - 3-6
B102	S - 11	A223	M.1 - 7-9	16	H - 1
B103	S - 21-22			17	M.2 - 1
B104	S - 23-24			18	F - 7
B105	S - 25-26	B201	F - 26-27	19	F - 8
B106	S - 27-28	B202	A - 20-22	20	F - 9
B107	S - 13-14	B203	B - 6	21	F - 10
B108	S - 15-16	B204	F - 14	22	G.1 - 25-28
B109 = A93	R - 3	B205	A - 15	22,23,24 (DV)	G.1 - 29
B110 = A94	R - 4	B206	F - 15-16	23	G.2 - 1
B111 = A96a	R - 5	B207	F - 16	24	G.3 - 1
B112 = A103	R - 16	B208	F - 17	25	G.3 - 2-3
		B209	H - 25	26	G.3 - 4-5
B113 = A105	N.1 - 2-3	B210	H - 26	27	G.3 - 29
B114 = A106a	T.2 - 3	B211	A - 12	28a	G.3 - 30
ab(DV)	T.2 - 4	B212	H - 26-28	b-d	G.3 - 50
b(DV)	T.2 - 3	B213	H - 11-14	29	G.3 - 31
(DV)	T.2 - 3	B214	H - 15	30a	G.3 - 32
d	R - 18	B215	H - 15-19	b-d	G.3 - 51
d(DV)	R - 18	B216	H - 20-23	31	G.3 - 15-16
B115 = A107	I - 2-3	B217	A - 16-19	32	G.3 - 16-18
(DV)	1 - 11	B218	S - 1-3	33	G.3 - 26-27
B116 = A108	I - 4	B219	S - 4	34	G.3 - 33-35
B117 = A109	I - 5-9	B220	S - 5	35	G.3 - 52
B118 = A110	N.2 - 4-5	B221	S - 6-7	36	G.3 - 53
B119 = A111(DV)	G.1 - 30,32,34,35	B222	S - 8	37	G.3 - 53-54
(DV)	P - 11-13	B223	S - 16-18	38	G.3 - 35-39
f	G.1 - 31	B224	S - 28	39	G.3 - 40-42
h	G.1 - 33	B225	B - 3-6	40	G.3 - 27-28
B120 = A112	G.1 - 36-40	B226	A - 9-11	41	G.3 - 28-29
B121 = A113	G.1 - 41,43	B227	J - 19	42a-c	G.4 - 1-3
B122 = A114(DV)	G.1 - 42,45,47	B228a-d	A - 23-24	d	G.4 - 10
(DV)	P - 16-19	B228e	A - 32	43	G.4 - 4-5
ef	G.1 - 43-44	B229	O - 11-12	44	G.4 - 6-7
hi	G.1 - 46-47	B230a-e	G.1 - 11-13	45a	G.4 - 7
B123 = A115	C - 15	d	T.1 - 11	b	G.4 - 17
B124 = A116	T.2 - 5	B231a-c	T.1 - 11	46a	G.4 - 8
B125 = A117	J - 13-16	df	T.1 - 2	b-f	G.4 - 17-18
B126 = A118	T.2 - 6-7	ei	T.1 - 1	47ab	G.4 - 11-14
		ghjk	T.1 - 11		

Z2   Index of SPSS variable names

Z3 Subject index

A

Ability,
  as factor in determining pay G.1-8, G.1-15, G.2-4
  importance of in getting ahead P-5
Abortion,
  grounds for M.1-7, M.1-16
Accommodation,
  legal responsibility for R-18
  length of time in present R-17
  satisfaction with R-1
  type R-16
  also see Housing; Tenure
Acid rain,
  activism over threat posed by S-25 to S-26
  as threat to environment S-3
Activism,
  in defence of countryside S-21 to S-28
  also see Political activism; Political protest; Trade unions
Admiration,
  for other countries D-10
Adoption,
  by homosexual couples M.1-6, M.1-17
Advice,
  on cohabitation and marriage M.1-15
  on health L-45
  to couple about buying first home R-22
  also see Career advice
Aerosols,
  as threat to environment S-19
Age,
  and earning power G.1-8, G.1-15, G.2-3
  of respondents T.2-3
  of respondents, within sex T.2-4

AIDS,
  and moral attitudes K-24 to K-25
  discrimination against people with K-13 to K-14
  groups at risk from K-9 to K-12
  impact on young people of K-27
  personal experience of K-26
  predictions about spread of K-22
  resources devoted to K-15, K-23
  sympathy for people with K-14, K-23
  testing for K-26
  vaccine against K-24
Aircraft noise,
  as threat to environment S-1
Alcohol,
  and health L-45
  also see Drinking
Ambition,
  importance of in getting ahead P-5
America,
  admiration for D-10
  Britain's links with D-2
  missiles in Britain D-2
  perceived threat to world peace D-5
Animals,
  use of in tests T.1-14
  also see Fox hunting; Wildlife
Area,
  metropolitan or non-metropolitan T.2-8
  also see Neighbourhood; Region
Army, the British
  in Northern Ireland E-2
  also see Defence
Artificial fertility measures,
  acceptability of M.1-10 to M.1-11

F

G

Y